Historical Archaeology in Central Europe

NATASCHA MEHLER

Editor

SPECIAL PUBLICATION NUMBER 10,
THE SOCIETY FOR HISTORICAL ARCHAEOLOGY

SHA Journal Editor: J.W. Joseph

Library of Congress Control Number: 2013936866

Published by The PAST Foundation in the United States of America

COVER IMAGE: by Thomas Pertlwieser, Department of Prehistory and Medieval Archaeology, University of Vienna. It is a composite of elements from the following images: *Wooden gallows and breaking wheels in front of the town walls of Einbeck 1654*, by Martin Zeiller (from Zeiller 1654); and *Hoard of watches found with a metal detector at the Bad Jungbrunn site, Lavant* (Photo by H. Stadler, 2008; courtesy of the Department of Archaeology, University of Innsbruck, Austria).

BACK COVER IMAGE: *The chimneys of Krupp Steel Works in Essen, Germany* (courtesy of Stadtbildstelle Essen, ca. 1890. Exact date unknown).

Dedicated to Paul Courtney

Contents

III. TECHNOLOGY, INDUSTRY, AND MODERNIZATION

IV. LANDSCAPES AND CITIES IN CHANGE

Foreword

In *Historical Archaeology in Central Europe,* Editor Natascha Mehler presents 25 articles that provide both the historiography of historical archaeology in the region and also present archaeological analyses and interpretations on a variety of subjects from a range of nations, addressing the topics of Religion, Conflict, and Death; Technology, Industry, and Modernization; and Landscapes and Cities in Change. The result is a volume that summarizes the state of historical archaeology in the region and lays a foundation for current and future generations of central European archaeologists to build upon. It is also a volume that offers the fascinating research of the region to a broader audience.

As the historiographic review reveals, "historical archaeology" is defined and applied differently in various central European nations. Indeed, the complex interplay of cultures and landscapes throughout the region yields a landscape where the meaning of history shifts at each border crossing. The approach used in selecting and editing the articles in this volume treats historical archaeology as post-medieval archaeology or the archaeology of the modern world, as defined by 15th-century European exploration and colonization and the resulting global economy that connected various nations and cultures in a universal web of exchange.

Historical archaeology in central Europe is characterized by a wealth of subjects and methods. Authors were invited to submit articles that summarize their research and hence the articles collected for the purpose of this book offer a broad variety of topics and provide examples from urban archaeology, landscape archaeology, underwater archaeology, industrial archaeology, battlefield archaeology, aviation archaeology, Ottoman archaeology, and material culture studies. Sites and case studies presented range chronologically from the 15th to the 20th century. Furthermore, the volume presents summaries of the status and theoretical foundations of a historical archaeology in the various central European countries and offers the perspectives from each. Central European archaeological research differs markedly in approach and research tradition from that in the United States but we hope you find this to be a stimulating contrast.

The articles in this volume benefited from peer review provided by Paul Courtney and James Symonds, English translations prepared by Paul Mitchell, Sandy Hämmerle and David J. Gaul, and the copyediting of Grace Ziesing. Working with authors from various countries, in various languages, and with various scholarly customs and practices, all diligently worked to help craft a volume that is consistent in its design and presentation, and their efforts are greatly appreciated. The volume was expertly composed by Knic Pfost of the PAST Foundation.

The Society for Historical Archaeology was established in 1967 to promote archaeological research of the modern world and the dissemination of research results. As 21st century technologies provide better means to communicate and share our individual findings and analyses, the landscape of historical archaeology has expanded, from local to regional, from regional to national, and from national to global. Whether your research interests are in theory or practice, industrial sites or urban settings, material culture or cultural landscapes, we are confident that the *Historical Archaeology of Central Europe* will provide you with meaningful new perspectives on the past.

J. W. Joseph
Journal Editor, Society for Historical Archaeology
New South Associates

Natascha Mehler
Volume Editor
University of Vienna

I. Development, Current Research, and Perspectives

NATASCHA MEHLER

Breaking New Ground: Historical Archaeology in Central Europe

ABSTRACT

This article attempts to outline and conceptualize the origins, academic parameters, and practical fields of activity of historical archaeology in central Europe and its individual countries. It is obvious that such a complex variety of linguistic, geographical, historical, cultural, religious, and political features within central Europe would also have been reflected in the archaeological research traditions upon which the emerging field of historical archaeology is based. In my view, two kinds of historical archaeology exist in central Europe that hark back to these different traditions and influences. From a methodological point of view, I have provocatively chosen to differentiate between archaeology of the modern era and historical archaeology. Apart from this dichotomy, historical archaeology in central Europe is also characterized by a wealth of subjects and methods, which we should view as an opportunity rather than a burden.

Archaeological research in central Europe is currently involved in an interesting process, a sense of a new era. Traditional pre- and protohistory, the mother subject from which the archaeologies of the more recent periods derived, will only experience this process peripherally. Some time ago, however, medieval archaeology, itself still only a relatively young discipline, began to open its upper time limit, resulting in archaeologists becoming more and more interested in finds and features from the period after 1500. In many central European cities, urban archaeology is now paying as much attention to recent features as it does to the earlier remains, and the number of publications dealing with subjects dating from the period after 1500 is increasing slowly but steadily. It is a problem, however, that most archaeologists who deal with the post-medieval period are either not yet in a position to influence the future development and consolidation of the discipline to any considerable degree, do not publish their thoughts, or tend to be practitioners employed by archaeological companies who allow them to publish only extracts from their practical work.

To date, several overviews have been published on the theory, method, and practice behind pan-European or central European archaeology, which emerged before and after the fall of the Iron Curtain, including a number of works dealing with medieval archaeology (Sklenář 1983; Wienberg and Andersson 1993; Biehl et al. 2002a; Hardt et al. 2003; Schreg 2010b; Gramsch and Sommer 2011; Lozny 2011a). But hardly any research or debate has taken place on the theory and methodology of the archaeology of the period after 1500, and institutionalized links with universities are actually quite rare. Many post-medieval archaeologists have therefore turned to American and British research on historical and post-medieval archaeology for guidance and inspiration. It is mainly the proximity of the former to anthropology and the social sciences that has a particularly strong appeal. The European archaeological disciplines have traditionally shown a great affinity to historical research (Courtney 1999:3-4, 2009:180; Schuyler 1999:13; Cyngot et al. 2006; Eggert 2006:197, 230) (see Rainer Schreg and Katarina Predovnik, this volume), so that the works of our colleagues across the water now prove a welcome source of inspiration in the search for new ideas.

While the current situation is exciting, the attention is somewhat ironic. In the 19th and early 20th centuries up to World War I, archaeological research in Europe was strongly influenced by anthropology (Fetten 2002; Parzinger 2002:36-37). The *Kulturkreislehre* (culture circle school), developed at the University of Vienna, was an influential approach adopted in the early 20th century. It aimed not only to define cultural spheres from a spatial point of view but to use the material culture of a given group to examine their history (Koppers 1959; Ziegert 1964:106-112). With the emergence of National Socialism the model evolved into racial theory (Wahle 1964:125-126).[1] This also brought another change in that archaeology began to align itself with historical research (Barford 2002:79). Currently, the pendulum in parts of central Europe is swinging back toward anthropology (Tabaczyński 1993:2; Cyngot et al. 2006).

Figure 1.   Map of central Europe and its countries. (Map provided courtesy of the Department of Prehistory and Medieval Archaeology, University of Vienna).

There is also debate in central Europe—albeit to a more modest extent—as to what is meant by the terms "historical archaeology" and "post-medieval archaeology" and what the tasks and purview of such a discipline should be (Pajer 1990; Smetánka and Žegklitz 1990; Ericsson 1995; Kajzer 1996; Steuer 1997/1998; Scholkmann 2001; Laszlovszky and Rasson 2003; Frommer 2007; Krajíc 2007; Schreg 2007; Predovnik 2008; Courtney 2009; Gaimster 2009; Theune 2009; Mehler 2010:13-14, 2012). There is, however, neither national nor international agreement with regard to the definition of historical archaeology or even the archaeology of the modern era. To simplify matters, I only use the term historical archaeology for the purposes of this paper, thereby referring largely to archaeological research into the period after 1500, which also explicitly incorporates historical methodology. In this sense, historical archaeology in central Europe is currently located somewhere between a process of enthusiastic self-discovery and an already burgeoning identity crisis. Even the title of this paper contains two terms that merit further debate. What is central Europe and what does historical archaeology mean in the region?

CENTRAL EUROPE, A REGION IN CONSTANT FLUX

Central Europe is a political term, which came into use in the mid 19th century and at the time included Germany, Poland, the Dual Monarchy of Austro-Hungary, as well as Belgium and the Netherlands (Partsch 1904:177-197). After World War II, when Europe was divided into western and eastern Europe, the concept of central Europe disappeared from general linguistic usage and European understanding, only to return in the past several decades. The regional expanse of central Europe has still not been clearly defined, however, either from a geographical or from a political standpoint. Only the northern and southern borders are clearly defined by the North and Baltic Seas, and by the Apennine and Balkan Peninsulas. While the River Rhine and the Carpathian Basin are often seen as the natural borders in the west and east, the political borders do not always correspond. The concept of which countries constitute central Europe is not only based on subjective perceptions, but also greatly depends on the current political situation. This has changed several times in the history of the region, the last time when Slovenia seceded from the Socialist Federal Republic of Yugoslavia in 1991 and when Czechoslovakia split into the Czech Republic and Slovakia in 1993. Today, central Europe usually includes the countries whose historical archaeology is dealt with in this volume: Germany, Switzerland, the Principality of Liechtenstein, Austria, the Czech Republic, Slovakia, Poland, Hungary, and Slovenia (Figure 1). From a linguistic point of view, the region is largely divided into three areas, a German language group (Germany, Austria, eastern Switzerland, Liechtenstein), a Slavonic group (Czech Republic, Slovakia, Slovenia, Poland), and a Finno-Ugric language group (Hungary). There are also small enclaves of romance languages such as French, Italian, and Romansh in the western and southern parts of Switzerland. From a religious point of view central Europe is divided into a mainly Catholic region in the west, east, and south, and a Protestant area in the north (Katzenstein 1997; Ágh 1998; Wiesner-Hanks 2006). This cultural, linguistic, geographical, political, historical, and religious variety obviously manifests itself also in the development and practice of archaeological research within the individual states (Gaimster 2009:525-526).

DIVISIVE PARADIGMS?

The term historical archaeology has only recently arrived in central Europe, and has not yet taken root or been fully accepted in the individual countries. The most important reasons for this are the uncertainty regarding the chronological scope of this field of research on the one hand, and on the other the lack of methodological and theoretical discussion and exchange, both nationally and internationally, which are indispensable in the evolution of the discipline. The existing tendencies can be divided into two groups of paradigms, one being methodological and the other chronological, which can be further separated geographically into a western and eastern branch.

German-speaking researchers mainly tend to follow the approach outlined by the Swedish archaeologist Anders Andrén, who defines historical archaeology as the archaeology of all literate societies. Therefore, it not only includes archaeological research into the Middle Ages and the modern era, but also encompasses classical archaeology, for instance, or the archaeology of the Roman provinces (Andrén 1998). When Andrén published his theories, his was not a new approach. Other central European researchers before him had made similar statements, but had not elaborated further (Smetánka and Žegklitz 1990:8; Tabaczyński 1993:3). Already in 1953, Czech archaeologist Vladimír Denkstein had reflected on the contents and definition of a historical archaeology (Denkstein 1953) (see Jaromir Žegklitz, this volume). In the United States, James Deetz stated in 1977 that "Historical archaeology studies the cultural remains of literate societies that were capable of recording their own histories" and thus stands in contrast to prehistoric archaeology (Deetz 1996:5). European researchers, however, have paid more attention to Andrén's work. While he distinguishes the two options of equating the beginning of historical archaeology either with the beginning of the modern era, starting with the European expansion that brought about fundamental global changes, or else with the beginning of writing roughly 5,000 years ago, he himself chooses the latter option. Being self-critical, he admits himself, however, to be not completely happy with this choice. He also criticizes the fact that the term historical archaeology implies that non-literate societies have no history, but he still decides to use the term, rather than creating a new linguistic monstrosity such as "grapho-archaeology" (Andrén 1998:6).

Country	Terms used	Period studied	Legal background
Austria	Historical Archaeology (Historische Archäologie), or Post-Medieval Archaeology (Neuzeitarchäologie)	the literate period (ca. 1st century to today) or the period from the later Middle Ages onward (ca. 1350 to today)	no upper time limit, modern antiquities included in legislation
Czech Republic	Archaeology of the Modern Period (archeologie novověku) or Post-Medieval Archaeology (postmedievální archeologie)	late 15th century to today (Historical Archaeology) or late 15th to late 18th centuries (Post-Medieval Archaeology)	no upper time limit, modern antiquities included in legislation
Germany	Historical Archaeology (Historische Archäologie), or Post-Medieval Archaeology (Neuzeitarchäologie)	the literate period (ca. 1st century to today), the period from the later Middle Ages onward (ca. 1350 to today), or the period from ca. 1500 onwards	not consistent; most federal states have no upper time limit, but Bavaria's antiquities "as a rule date from the prehistoric and early medieval periods"
Hungary	Early Modern Archaeology (Kora újkori régészet)	1526-1711	the year 1711 is the upper time limit, older antiquities are protected by law
Poland	Historical Archaeology (archeologia historyczna), or Post-Medieval Archaeology (archeologia późnego średniowiecza i nowożytności)	10th century to today	no upper time limit, modern antiquities included in legislation
Slovakia	Historical Archaeology (archeológia stredoveku), or Post-Medieval Archaeology (archeológia novoveku)	6th century to today	no upper time limit, modern antiquities included in legislation
Slovenia	Archaeology of Later Periods (arheologija mlajših obdobij), or Post-Medieval Archaeology (arheologija novega veka)	11th century to today (Archaeology of Later Periods), ca. 1500-1900 (Post-Medieval Archaeology)	no upper time limit, modern antiquities included in legislation
Switzerland	Post-Medieval Archaeology (Neuzeitarchäologie)	ca. 1500 to today; term Historical Archaeology not used; practice of Post-Medieval Archaeology varies from canton to canton; younger archaeologists tend to regard archaeology as a discipline of methods rather then of periods	no upper time limit, modern antiquities included in legislation

Table 1.   Overview of historical archaeology in central European countries.

Proponents of the approach that defines historical archaeology as the archaeology of all literate societies feel vindicated by a perceived methodological purity and consistency (Müller 1997/1998:629; Schreg 2007:14; Theune 2009:762-763). While at first glance the approach is indeed methodological, it inevitably results in a periodization. With Andrén's approach, a unified concept of periodization of central Europe within historical archaeology is almost unobtainable, since writing began at different times in different countries. In large parts of Germany, Austria, Switzerland, and Hungary it began during the Roman period, for example in the form of votive inscriptions on buildings or altars in the years following the birth of Christ, or with the important work *Germania* written by the historian Tacitus around A.D. 98. This work, however, presents the view of an outsider (in this case a Roman citizen) and is thus not an emic, but an etic, source. In areas of former Slavic settlement, for instance in Germany, Austria, the Czech Republic, and Slovakia, written records of any kind were created much later, around the 9th and 10th centuries. Moreover, in both cases written records pertaining to the early phases are actually quite scarce.

Critics of the approach of starting historical archaeology with the introduction of writing argue that it does not take into account the history, development, and dissemination of reading and writing or the extent of the available written records. It furthermore implies that archaeologists working on an early medieval cemetery, for example, are able to make equal epistemological use of written records and archives for their interpretations as archaeologists working on an 18th-century manor house, which in practice is simply not the case (Mehler 2012:14). Moreover, Andrén's book makes no methodological suggestions as to the practical organization of such an archaeology of all literate societies, which ultimately equates to a lack of justification and reasoning for such a concept of historical archaeology. The ostensible consistency can in actual fact be viewed as a methodological weakness. In reality, written records are really not available to archaeologists in any functional manner until much later, during the so-called phases of "dense tradition." In German-speaking areas, this term is used to denote the period when written records became more abundant around the 14th and 15th centuries (Frommer 2009; Igel 2009). As Andrén had feared, the term historical archaeology experiences further rejection because it appears to be stating that non-literate societies have no history (Stephan 2012:273).

In central Europe's eastern states the debate on the term historical archaeology is held from a chronological perspective, if at all (Krajíc 2007:58-59; Smetánka and Žegklitz 1990:7) (Table 1). The beginnings of literacy only enter the discussion about the start date for historical archaeology to a limited extent. More attention is paid to important historical events, which had a lasting impact on the society concerned. In the case of Hungary and Bohemia, the battle of Mohács (1526) was such a decisive moment, when the Kingdom of Louis II (1506-1526), ruler of Hungary, Bohemia, and Croatia, was comprehensively defeated by Turkish forces. The Ottoman Empire subsequently conquered large parts of Hungary, and the territory of Bohemia also underwent changes in the wake of this event (Pálffy 2009:35-53). The upper chronological limit of historical archaeology is also not clearly defined. In England the onset of the Industrial Revolution was for a long time seen as the end of historical or post-medieval archaeology, but this line has since ceased to exist (Schuyler 1999:10; Gaimster 2009:528-529; Dixon 2011). Neither could this chronological boundary be applied to the situation in central Europe since—much like the arrival of literacy—the process of industrialization also took place at different times in different areas (in Germany for instance from ca. 1815 to 1870) (Ogilvie 1996:133; Gaimster 2009:529). In the eastern central European countries historical archaeology is mainly focused on the period from the late Middle Ages to roughly the 18th century. In the case of Hungary, the expulsion of the Turks in 1711 and the subsequent independence provide an absolute date for the end of historical archaeology. The 19th and 20th centuries are even less researched archaeologically in the eastern countries of central Europe than in the German-speaking areas.

This contradiction between methodology and chronology is currently the biggest source of friction and challenge in the formation of historical archaeology, for central Europe as a whole and for its individual countries. One must also add that archaeological research went through different processes of development in the individual countries, which led to different discussions on the scientific theory behind it and has resulted in central Europe not being unified with regard to its theoretical discourse either. The history of research and the external conditions have been outlined by others in a much more profound and eloquent manner than I could hope to achieve, as follows: Steuer (2001), Biehl et al. (2002a), Härke (2002), Parzinger (2002), Mante (2007), and Veit (2011) concerning pre- and protohistorical research; and Courtney (2009:182, 2010), and Gaimster (2009:527) for the more recent periods.[2]

ARCHAEOLOGY DURING THE COLD WAR

Traditional pre- and protohistorical research in central Europe, out of which historical archaeology evolved, was twice in danger of being abused by ideologies, first by the racial ideology of the Third Reich and then by Marxism up to the end of the Cold War (Arnold 1990; Fetten 2002:143; Neustupný 2002). At the time of the German Democratic Republic (GDR), historians in West Germany tried to distance themselves from their colleagues in East Germany and vice-versa. The Marxist-Leninist historical sciences had different foci. The aim of researchers of the modern era in the 1970s GDR was to portray revolutionary traditions. This was followed by a phase of concentrating on everyday history (*Alltagsgeschichte*) in the 1980s, the research of which was seen as an interdisciplinary task (Elkar 1990:273, 281, 301-302). Having said that, the Marxist viewpoints imposed by the state were not adopted as readily by pre- and protohistorical researchers as the authorities would have hoped. Hermann Behrens summarized the situation thus: "The value of Marxism in pre- and protohistorical research is its thought-provoking qualities and nothing more" (translation by author) (Behrens 1984:61). Most archaeologists attempted to avoid state influence in their research as much as possible or did just enough to fulfill political expectations. This applied both to the GDR and to other eastern bloc states (Biehl et al. 2002b:28; Novaković 2002:341; Parzinger 2002:44; Mante 2007:99-100). With regard to the development of historical archaeology it is important to note that archaeology of the modern era was practically non-existent in the GDR. An example of a rare exception is Ulrich Lappe's excavation in a post-medieval castle in Thuringia (Lappe 1978).

It is, however, a widely held misconception that the methods and theories of all central European archaeologies were characterized by an east-west dichotomy that resulted in the development of different schools of archaeological thought. The black-and-white thinking that led to the notion that archaeological research in western Europe was dominated by theory while archaeology in eastern Europe was caught up in Marxist thought is nowadays considered to be exaggerated and erroneous (Barford 2002:93; Novaković 2002:341). Such a dichotomy, if it existed at all, was in reality felt far less strongly by many and sometimes even described as a construct rooted in wishful thinking (Sklenář 1983; Bertemes 2002:103; Parzinger 2002:44). Moreover, some scholars outside of the central European borders

believed and continue to believe that the European archaeologies could be categorized according to three paradigms: a largely traditional cultural-historical approach to archaeological research (continental archaeology) contrasting with processual archaeology and subsequently with post-processual archaeologies (in Britain, Scandinavia, and the Netherlands). It has been repeatedly stated that this view is too simplistic and does not reflect reality (Biehl et al. 2002b:26, 28).

In actual fact, there has always been close contact and interaction between eastern and western archaeologists (Kobyliński 2005), as can be seen particularly well in the eastern areas of Austria (to name but one example) where the two parts of central Europe meet. Research and teaching at the Institute of Prehistory and Historical Archaeology in Vienna has a tradition of closely collaborating with archaeologists in neighboring eastern European countries. There was always a strong tradition of networking in prehistoric research in central Europe.

The theory and methodology discussion within archaeological, historical, and anthropological research circles in Germany would have had the biggest influence on archaeologists in other central European countries for a long time. During the period of the Cold War, in particular, the easiest way for eastern researchers to escape the political doctrine was to orient themselves toward the west (Smetánka and Žegklitz 1990:12; Härke 1991:187; Neustupný 2002; Novaković 2002:347; Parzinger 2002:44-45; Tabaczyński 2002:72; Courtney 2009:169; Lozny 2011b:212). Above that, there were (and still are) close contacts outside of central Europe. German archaeological research was linked with British archaeology from early on. From a methodological point of view, there were very close links between British and German archaeology during World War II. This was due to the highly influential work of the German prehistorian Gerhard Bersu (1889-1964), who was a close friend of the British archaeologist Vere Gordon Childe (1892-1957). Being of Jewish descent, he emigrated to England in 1937, where he spent 10 successful years. In 1947 he relocated to Ireland where he spent three years as professor at the Royal Irish Academy in Dublin (Krämer 2001:64-81; Parzinger 2002:43-44). The interaction between the different countries continued after World War II. While the French Annales School had a strong impact on Polish historians and archaeologists (Duby

1965; Tabaczyński 2002:72; Cyngot et al. 2006), researchers in the Czech Republic are nowadays increasingly influenced by English literature (Neustupný 2002:286). A particularly strong orientation toward the British research approach is perceptible in the current formative process of historical archaeology, both in the east and in the west.

Because historical archaeology is a relatively new discipline in central Europe and largely only evolved after the fall of the Iron Curtain in 1989, physical boundaries no longer exist. The preconditions for a close dialog among historical archaeologists in central Europe are therefore very good. Nowadays, the internet and freedom of mobility have made it easier for archaeologists to establish connections than would have been possible even during the period of the Cold War. Unlike America, the distances are relatively short and international conferences such as the *Forum Archaeologia Post-Medievalis*, which takes place every two years in Prague and publishes the series *Studies in Post-Medieval Archaeology*, provide great opportunities for exchange.

THEORY AND ARCHAEOLOGY

Central European researchers who follow the traditional cultural-historical approach to archaeology are often belittled for not leading any, or at least not enough, theoretical and methodological debates. As for Germany, Ulrich Veit attributes this to the suppression of questions of cultural and scientific theory on the one hand, which started not, as many assume, during the National Socialist period but as early as the beginning of the 19th century, and a generally negative perception and conveyance of the term "theory" on the other (Veit 2002:413, 415). The opinions of the supporters and opponents of this viewpoint diverge widely and cannot be outlined in detail here (Klejn 1993b; Bertemes 2002; Biehl et al. 2002b:29; Veit 2002, 2011:57, 68). German archaeologists have repeatedly published their contributions to the German theoretical discourse in English (Arnold 1990, 2002; Härke 1991, 1995, 2002; Eggert 2002; Veit 2011). Nevertheless, these seem to have very little resonance outside central Europe. Without sugar-coating the state of the central European theoretical discourse, and without intending to offend Anglo-American archaeologists and their grasp of foreign languages, I dare say that the basis of the criticism is an obvious lack of familiarity with German language publications. There are only a few exceptions where scholars took pains to gain an accurate impression of the actual theoretical debate in German-language archaeological research (Bloemers 2002; Bintliff 2001; Courtney 2009; Lucas 2012:53-61). Theoretical and methodological discussions have increased, particularly over the past 20 years. The exchange takes place, for instance, in the context of the *Theorie-AG* (working group on theory), which has been in existence since 1990; in the series *Tübinger Archäologische Taschenbücher*, which has regularly published discussions on specific topics; and in the *Forum Kritische Archäologie*, a new journal that publishes interdisciplinary critical archaeological debates.[3] Due to the institutionalized division between the various archaeologies, the theoretical and methodological discourse largely takes place within pre- and protohistoric research (Bernbeck 1997; Biehl et al. 2002a; Härke 2002; Ickerodt 2010), although it has also found its way into medieval and post-medieval archaeology in recent years (Steuer 1997/1998; Scholkmann 2003; Frommer 2007; Schreg 2007, 2010b; Müller 2009; Mehler 2010:77-81, 2012). Nevertheless, despite the fact that theory has had and continues to have its place in all types of central European archaeological research (including historical archaeology), theoretical archaeology is still not practiced nearly enough (Gramsch 2011:57).

PRACTICING HISTORICAL ARCHAEOLOGY IN CENTRAL EUROPE

How is historical archaeology actually practiced in central Europe? I have attempted to outline above the two paradigms that form the academic framework for the actual practice of such an archaeology. The attempt to conceptualize historical archaeology in central Europe reveals two distinct ways in which it is practiced, and it is important to note that both exist in each country. They differ from each other only in methodology.

Archaeology of the Modern Era

In the early days of the development of medieval archaeology as a discipline (historical archaeology would not arise for a long time to come) the German prehistorian

Herbert Jankuhn (1905-1990) defined it as a direct continuation of pre- and protohistory (Jankuhn 1973:9). His influential paper *"Umrisse einer Archäologie des Mittelalters"* (*"Outline of a Medieval Archaeology"*) had a significant impact on the subsequent development of medieval archaeology, even beyond the borders of Germany. Because Jankuhn had included methodology in his definition, he is said to this day by some to have completely omitted the use of written records from his definition of the practice of such a discipline. This does a disservice to Jankuhn, however, since his paper did, in fact, clearly demand "that medieval archaeologists must also be adept at dealing with historical sources and philological evidence, since they will not always have a settlement historian or philologist at hand" (Jankuhn 1973:12) (translation by author). It is due to this misconception, among other things, that historical archaeology is still often practiced "without written records," although it is often stated that medieval and post-medieval archaeology both work holistically, in other words with the inclusion of written and pictorial sources (Ericsson 1995; Steuer 1997/1998; Scholkmann 2003; Theune 2009). I have recently argued that this assessment is out of touch with reality (Mehler 2012:14). Most of the published work dealing with subjects dating from after 1500 in fact still manages to completely ignore written records, maps, and evidence from the oral tradition. This applies mainly to the publication of finds from the early modern period, where at best those texts are consulted that have already been interpreted and assessed by historians with regard to other research questions. There are still those who support the type of archaeological research that, in a period where written records are available, will only take into account the archaeological sources. They argue that archaeologists should not work with written records because, on the one hand, they feel it would be detrimental to both disciplines to mix archaeology and history (Klejn 1993a:347; Krause 2000:58) and, on the other, archaeologists do not have the time or training to methodologically and critically assess such sources (Igel 2009:41). Publications that omit written records, however, often degenerate into so-called *Materialschlachten*, a German term that denotes large-scale studies of vast amounts of finds, presented in thick volumes. Without the historical, cultural, and social context that written records would undoubtedly offer, these publications are nothing more than uninterpreted catalogs presenting a succession of assorted finds. These are the very publications that are characteristic of central European archaeology and are often and justifiably criticized by researchers abroad

(Gramsch 2011:52-57). With regard to its methods, such a practice of an archaeology of the modern era is indeed nothing more than a continuation of pre- and protohistory, which traditionally works with archaeological methods such as typology and chronology, but is now also using the natural sciences and technological methods such as dendrochronology or geophysics to study finds and features. In this case, the term "archaeology of the modern era" (in German, *Neuzeitarchäologie*) literally refers to an archaeology that studies the period after the Middle Ages and is thus clearly oriented chronologically rather than methodologically. In an archaeology of the modern era that ignores the written records, it does not matter whether the society being studied had written records or not, because these sources would not, in any case, be actively dealt with. Neither would it therefore comply with Andrén's notion of historical archaeology (see above).

Historical Archaeology

In contrast to central Europe, archaeologists in the United States and Great Britain have quite a clear concept, both methodologically and chronologically, of what historical archaeology is (Deetz 1996:5; Orser 2002:xvi-xvii, 2004:1-28; Wilkie 2005:340-343; Hall and Silliman 2006:1). While the many definitions set different priorities, there is basically agreement that historical archaeology begins with the modern era, or with the European global expansion to put it simply. Besides this chronological approach, it is also clear from a methodological point of view that archaeologists in practice also deal with written records, pictorial sources, and oral history (Beaudry 1988; Little 1992; Funari 1999:49; Orser 2004:1-28; Wilkie 2006). This interdisciplinarity between archaeology, the study of written and pictorial sources, oral history, and anthropology, which historical archaeology in the United States is strongly aligned to, is often stressed:

> *It is not the existence of documents that makes the field a separate discipline. The crucial factor is that a historical archaeologist, one person, must have the expertise to critically analyze and use the data from both documents and excavations, to establish the cultural context of a site. And it is anthropological theory that provides the conceptual units and tools for establishing this context from data accumulated through application of the techniques of historical and archaeological analyses [Thurman 1996:87].*

Although the term "historical archaeology" is currently being adopted from the United States or at least contemplated by central European researchers (see Table 1), many do not wish to adopt all the definitions or the contents linked to the term. The main reason for this is probably the fact that the classic American content—European colonial expansion—at first glance has very little relevance in central Europe. I will deal with this point in more detail later. Another reason may lie in the fact that the discipline in central Europe is not yet as closely associated with anthropological research as is the case in the United States. As recently as 2006, Manfred K. H. Eggert still did not detect any engagement in the areas where German is spoken of the theoretical and methodological discourse that takes place in Anglo-American historical archaeology (Eggert 2006:173). I would generally agree with this assessment. While archaeological research of remains from the period after 1500 had already been practiced for a number of years, it was actually done—bar a few exceptions (Fassbinder 2003)—without paying any heed to the theoretical and methodological discussions taking place in the United States and Great Britain.

Despite these difficulties, a number of recent works have clearly been inspired by this interdisciplinarity. Besides the theories and research questions posed by anthropologists and sociologists, economic history questions are also being increasingly studied, without, however, losing sight of the general historical questions. Moreover, not only are the topics slowly becoming more international but British and American publications are more and more absorbed. Examples that illustrate this are the studies on coarse handmade earthenware from Panama, which was used to categorize ethnic and social identities (Schreg 2010a), the study of early European colonial expansion in the North Atlantic (Mehler and Gardiner, in press), architectural surveying as a means of studying economic, social, and cultural history in Switzerland (Boschetti-Maradi 2009), historical archaeology in National Socialist concentration camps in central Europe (Theune 2010), or the works of Rainer Schreg and Michael Doneus and Thomas Kühtreiber in this volume. If such studies also actively deal with written records, they may serve to showcase an evolving central European historical archaeology.

UNTAPPED POTENTIAL FOR FUTURE RESEARCH

This new interdisciplinary approach is given an added dimension thanks to a series of scientific methods, which by now have become standard in pre- and protohistoric research and are being incorporated into the new discipline of historical archaeology by the next generation of researchers. From the domain of ceramics there are the provenience studies carried out on 15th-17th century Saxon stoneware by means of written records and neutron activation analyses (Mommsen et al. 2000) or the proveniencing of Bavarian clay pipes by means of X-ray fluorescence spectrometry (Mehler 2010:62-74). Surveying methods such as ground-penetrating radar were used on a large scale in the concentration camp of Mauthausen in Austria (Theune 2010:figure 8). Both DNA and isotope analyses were used to identify a number of skeletons from the battlefield of Lützen in Germany, which dates from the Thirty Years' War (Brandt et al. 2010; Brock and Homann 2011:70-71), euthanasia victims at a psychiatric clinic in Hall, Tyrol (Zanesco 2012), and World War II victims of the Nazi regime in Warsaw, Poland (Ławrynowicz, in press). Dendrochronology is often applied in the field of architectural analysis, for instance with regard to the architecture of houses and castles in Switzerland (Boschetti-Maradi 2009:8-9) or modern period shepherds' huts in the High Tatras in

Poland (Opała and Kaczka 2008). Archaeozoological studies, for instance, help to answer questions regarding modern era bone and ivory working (Schlenker and Wahl 1994), or the role of the camel in the Carpathian Basin during the Turkish period (Bartosiewicz 1996). In view of these and other methods, it is certainly an advantage that central European historical archaeology has its roots in pre- and protohistorical research, and perhaps it is precisely this diversity of methods that is both a strength and a general characteristic of central European historical archaeology. Moreover, other research-relevant resources are available that are still almost completely untapped. Two examples may serve to illustrate the research potential that exists in central Europe but is still largely unused.

Some central European countries have for a number of years been engaged in recording their entire territory by means of Airborne Laser Scanning. At this stage, whole tracts of land have been recorded, for instance the complete state of Lower Austria. Dedicated websites allow users to carry out targeted searches for places, areas, and landscape features. Already processed data and graphs can be purchased for a small fee from the state surveyors' offices for scientific purposes. The

Figure 2. *The deserted mission station of the* Herrnhuter Brüdergemeinde *in Hebron, Labrador, in 1978. The main building was erected between 1833 and 1837 and abandoned in 1959. The left wing contained the chapel while the right wing of the building housed the offices and living quarters of the German-Moravian missionaries (Loring and Arendt 2009:figure 1) (Courtesy of Steven Cox, Torngat Archaeological Project).*

projects have gathered an immense pool of data that could be of great value particularly for questions relating to landscape research. The area of battlefield or conflict archaeology could, for instance, use these data to study modern era fortifications, dams, or the remains from 20th-century wars in a targeted manner without having to mount excavations. The survey data of field monuments such as forgotten roads, old mining galleries, or quarries would already be available for industrial archaeologists.

From an American perspective it must be surprising that the subject of colonialism or of emigration has to date hardly been dealt with by central European archaeologists (Courtney 2009:181-182). The history and politics of colonialism in central Europe clearly differ from those in Spain, Portugal, England, France, and the Netherlands. The process began very late, was clearly less wide-ranging, and may also have had different motivations. This very contrast would, however,

lend added depth to the subject of global colonialism in archaeological research. Only the German-speaking countries, and mainly Germany itself, acquired overseas colonies. While the first small-scale expansion attempts into South America during the 16th century failed, the German colonial empire was eventually created during the German Empire (1871-1918). Compared to this the Swiss and Austrian overseas colonies in the United States and Africa were rather modest (Arlettaz 1979; Sauer 2002). German colonies were established in the South Pacific and in China, but mainly in Africa, for example in Cameroon and in German South-West Africa, present-day Namibia (Tamanini 1995; Gründer 2004; Herold 2006). To date, this inexhaustible subject has only rarely been touched on from a German perspective (Gronenborn and Magnavita 2000; Vogt 2002).

Colonialism *within* Europe would also offer an interesting field of research for historical archaeologists, since large migrations of people also took place within central

Europe. Due to cataclysmic changes in the modern era—caused by events such as war and industrialization—many colonies, enclaves, and waves of migration occurred, which in turn brought about new cultural currents, transfers of beliefs and knowledge, and zones of conflict. After the ousting of the Turks from Hungary, the Habsburgs began a program of resettlement of German immigrants, the so-called Danube Swabians in Banat, a region that comprised parts of present-day southeast Hungary, Romania, and Serbia. One of the aims was to consolidate the Roman-Catholic church in the region in the 18th and 19th centuries (Paikert 1967). In terms of archaeological research this topic remains completely unexplored. The *Herrnhuter Brüdergemeinde* (Moravian-German Mission), a community of faith that had its origins in Kunvald in the Czech Republic and in Herrnhut in Germany, would be another very interesting subject. From the 18th century onward, the community grew into the first large-scale European Protestant missionary movement, which spread across the whole world and eventually led to the rise of the Methodist church. A small number of Herrnhuter missions have been investigated by archaeological means in Labrador, Greenland, and Australia (Loring and Arendt 2009; Lydon 2009; Gulløv et al. 2011) (Figure 2).

In order for archaeologists to dare approach such subjects, structural problems within the academic and scientific world must first be overcome. Contacts must be made with leading historians of the modern era and the relevant institutions, in order to have access to the appropriate networks. Moreover, the external conditions in terms of the lack of funding necessary to pursue such research topics are rather frustrating. There is a complete absence of foundations or support institutions for such projects in central Europe. While there are large organizations at national and international levels that support archaeological research, such as the German Research Foundation (DFG) or the European Science Foundation (ESF), their decision-making bodies consist mostly of prehistorians, classical archaeologists, and archaeologists of the Roman provinces who still remain oblivious to the pleasures and significance of historical archaeology. Under these circumstances, there is no realistic chance of accessing the relevant funding. As long as these and other international subjects are or can not be dealt with, it will not be possible for central European historical archaeologists to follow Charles Orser's call to "think globally, dig locally" and to discuss such topics at a global level (Orser 1996:22; Gilchrist 2005).

CONCLUSION

Central European historical archaeology offers a wide range of topics, as well as being characterized by a diverse interdisciplinarity. In some areas it has even carried out pioneering work and has laid the foundations for further research. Battlefield archaeology, the beginnings of which date back to the 19th century (see Arne Homann, this volume), or the works of Austrian prehistorian Richard Pittioni (1906-1985) and Czech archaeologist Jiří Merta, who made considerable contributions to the formation of a European industrial archaeology, may serve as examples (Pittioni 1968; Merta 1980). Although historical archaeology is still struggling in some central European countries, we are undoubtedly faced with an ambitious young discipline that is growing in confidence. The deep rootedness in traditional pre – and protohistory, from where it originated, may act as a disadvantage for some in terms of the overriding research questions and interpretations. Others, however, will see it as an advantage because it has made available a diverse range of methods that can be used eclectically depending on the topic studied.

With regard to central Europe specifically, it is also important to note that here, as in other parts of the world, "historical archaeology means different things to different people" (Hall and Silliman 2006:1). I have tried to show that—as far as I can see—there are two approaches in central Europe. One, which I have termed historical archaeology, in my opinion has an historical orientation, i.e., it not only uses archaeological and natural scientific methods, but mainly employs the tools of historical research. The other approach, which despite the existence of written records does not use historical methods, I have deliberately separated and have provocatively applied to it the German term *Neuzeitarchäologie* (archaeology of the modern era), thereby referring to a methodologically simple continuation of prehistory. I would generally prefer to dispose of this pair of opposites, of a methodological definition (written records) versus a chronological definition (post 1500) for the archaeological study of the post-medieval periods. After all, if the discipline is defined methodologically via the existence of written records, this concept as a logical consequence will be linked with a more or less absolute date and therefore a periodization. In this respect, the allegedly methodological approach will always be mixed with the chronological approach.

In fact, we should view this complex variety, this "multiplicity of European-style archaeologies," where ideas and methods can flow freely (Courtney 2009:169, 182, 2010:326), as an opportunity, rather than letting the burden of the archaeological, historical, and anthropological research traditions in our countries weigh us down. Naturally, American historical archaeology with its different approaches is a great source of inspiration, but we may also look with confidence upon the young discipline on this side of the pond, despite the fact that many aspects of the potential are yet to be awakened. Although central Europe is now entering the international stage of historical archaeology, a global approach is still not possible (Funari 1999:57; Hicks 2005:374-375). Nevertheless, we can still work toward giving the content a more global appeal. It is up to the archaeologists on both sides of the Atlantic to lend a more international approach to their work, both with regard to content and practical aspects, and to receive each other's publications more attentively rather than constantly attempting to reinvent the wheel. As an incorrigible optimist, I am confident that the current generation, which is working in this exciting formative phase of central European historical archaeology, will be able to recognize and seize this opportunity.

NOTES

1. The German prehistorian Ernst Wahle (1889-1981) was made Professor at the University of Heidelberg in 1933. A short while later he became co-editor of the *Zeitschrift für Rassenkunde* (Journal of Race Studies) and in 1934 joined the *Kampfbund für deutsche Kultur* (Militant League for German Culture). For an overview of the archaeological research in Germany during National Socialist rule see Arnold (1990).

2. Parzinger (2002) probably gives the most analytical overview of the development and research history of prehistoric archaeology in Europe, while I would consider Courtney (2010) to be the best summary of the influences of social theory on the archaeology of the modern era.

3. The journal is bilingual (German-English) and freely accessible at http://www.kritischearchaeologie.de/fka (accessed July 2012).

REFERENCES

ÁGH, ATTILA
    1998   *The Politics of Central Europe.* Sage Publications, London, England.

ANDRÉN, ANDERS
    1998   *Between Artifacts and Texts. Historical Archaeology in Global Perspective.* Plenum Press, New York, NY.

ARLETTAZ, GERALD
    1979   Emigration et colonisation suisses en Amérique 1815-1918 [Swiss Emigration and Colonization in America 1815-1918]. *Studien und Quellen. Zeitschrift des schweizerischen Bundesarchivs* 5:91-216.

ARNOLD, BETTINA
    1990   The Past as Propaganda: Totalitarian Archaeology in Nazi Germany. *Antiquity* 64(244):464-478.

    2002   A Transatlantic Perspective on German Archaeology. In *Archaeology, Ideology and Society: The German Experience*, Heinrich Härke, editor, pp. 401-425. 2nd revised edition. Verlag Peter Lang, Frankfurt, Germany.

BARFORD, PAUL M.
    2002   East is East and West is West? Power and Paradigm in European Archaeology. In *Archäologien Europas / Archaeologies of Europe. Geschichte, Methoden und Theorien / History, Methods and Theories*, Peter F. Biehl, Alexander Gramsch, and Arkadiusz Marciniak, editors, pp. 77-99. Tübinger Archäologische Taschenbücher 3. Waxmann, Münster, Germany.

BARTOSIEWICZ, LÁSZLÓ
    1996   Camels in Antiquity: The Hungarian Connection. *Antiquity* 70(268):447-453.

BEAUDRY, MARY C. (EDITOR)
    1988   *Documentary Archaeology in the New World.* Cambridge University Press, England.

BEHRENS, HERMANN
    1984   *Die Ur- und Frühgeschichtswissenschaft in der DDR von 1945-1980 [Pre- and Protohistorical Research in the GDR from 1945 to 1980].* Arbeiten zur Urgeschichte des Menschen Vol. 9. Verlag Peter Lang, Frankfurt, Germany.

BERNBECK, REINHARD
1997   *Theorien in der Archäologie [Theories in Archaeology]*. UTB-Verlag, Stuttgart, Germany.

BERTEMES, FRANÇOIS
2002   Die mitteleuropäische Archäologie: Eine Standortbestimmung zwischen Ost und West [Central European Archaeology: The State of Play between East and West]. In *Archäologien Europas / Archaeologies of Europe. Geschichte, Methoden und Theorien / History, Methods and Theories*, Peter F. Biehl, Alexander Gramsch, and Arkadiusz Marciniak, editors, pp. 99-119. Tübinger Archäologische Taschenbücher 3. Waxmann, Münster, Germany.

BIEHL, PETER F., ALEXANDER GRAMSCH, AND ARKADIUSZ MARCINIAK
2002   Archaeologies of Europe: Histories and Identities. An Introduction. In *Archäologien Europas / Archaeologies of Europe. Geschichte, Methoden und Theorien / History, Methods and Theories*, Peter F. Biehl, Alexander Gramsch, and Arkadiusz Marciniak, editors, pp. 25-35. Tübinger Archäologische Taschenbücher 3. Waxmann, Münster, Germany.

BIEHL, PETER F., ALEXANDER GRAMSCH, AND ARKADIUSZ MARCINIAK (EDITORS)
2002   *Archäologien Europas / Archaeologies of Europe. Geschichte, Methoden und Theorien / History, Methods and Theories*. Tübinger Archäologische Taschenbücher 3. Waxmann, Münster, Germany.

BINTLIFF, JOHN
2001   Review of *Towards Translating the Past: Georg Kossack—Selected Studies in Archaeology. Ten Essays Written from the Year 1974 to 1997*, B. Hänsel and A. Harding, editors. *European Journal of Archaeology* 4(2):284-285.

BLOEMERS, TOM
2002   German Archaeology at Risk? A Neighbour's Critical View of Tradition, Structure and Serendipity. In *Archaeology, Ideology and Society: The German Experience*, Heinrich Härke, editor, pp. 375-397. 2nd revised edition. Verlag Peter Lang, Frankfurt, Germany.

BOSCHETTI-MARADI, ADRIANO
2009   Bauforschung als Wirtschafts-, Sozial – und Kulturgeschichte: Ein Wirtshaus von 1768 am Pilgerweg nach Einsiedeln [Architectural Surveying as a Means of Studying Economic, Social and Cultural History: An Inn Dating from 1768 on the Pilgrims' Way to Einsiedeln]. *Historische Archäologie* 3(2009).

BRANDT, G., C. KNIPPER, C. ROTH, A. SIEBERT, AND K. W. ALT
2010   Beprobungsstrategien für aDNA und Istopenanalysen an historischem und prähistorischem Skelettmaterial [Sampling Strategies for aDNA and Isotope Analyses on Historical and Prehistoric Skeletons]. In *Anthropologie, Isotopie, DNA*, H. Meller and K. W. Alt, editors, pp. 17-32. Landesamt für Denkmalpflege und Archäologie Sachsen-Anhalt, Halle an der Saale, Germany.

BROCK, THOMAS, AND ARNE HOMANN
2011   *Schlachtfeldarchäologie. Auf den Spuren des Krieges [Battlefield Archaeology. Following the Traces of War]*. Theiss-Verlag, Stuttgart, Germany.

COURTNEY, PAUL
1999   Different Strokes for Different Folks: The TransAtlantic Development of Historical and Post Medieval Archaeology. In *Old and New Worlds*, Geoff Egan and R. L. Michael, editors, pp. 1-10. Oxbow Books, Oxford, England.

2009   The Current State and Future Prospects of Theory in European Post-Medieval Archaeology. In *International Handbook of Historical Archaeology*, Teresita Majewski and David Gaimster, editors, pp. 169-189. Springer, New York, NY.

2010   Social Theory and Post-Medieval Archaeology: A Historical Perspective. In *Exchanging Medieval Material Culture: Studies on Archaeology and History Presented to Frans Verhaeghe*, Koen de Groote, Dries Tys, and Marnix Pieters, editors, pp. 317-346. Peeters, Leuven, Belgium.

CYNGOT, DOROTA, STANISŁAW TABACZYŃSKI, AND ANNA ZALEWSKA (EDITORS)
2006   Archaeology—Anthropology—History. Parallel Tracks and Divergences. *Archaeologia Polona* 44.

DEETZ, JAMES
1996   *In Small Things Forgotten: The Archaeology of Early American Life*. 2nd revised edition. Anchor Books, New York, NY.

DENKSTEIN, VLADIMÍR
1953   O úkolech historické archeologie [On the Tasks of Historical Archaeology]. *Časopis Národního muzea, oddíl věd společenských* CXXII:219-223.

DIXON, JAMES R.
2011   Is the Present Day Post-Medieval? *Post-Medieval Archaeology* 45(2):313-322.

DUBY, GEORGES
1965   *Villages désertés et histoire économique: XIe-XVIIIe siècle [Deserted Villages and Economic History: 11th to 18th Centuries]*. Ecole pratique des hautes études 6. S.E.V.P.E.N., Paris, France.

EGGERT, MANFRED K.H.

2002   Between Facts and Fiction: Reflections on the Archaeologist's Craft. In *Archäologien Europas / Archaeologies of Europe. Geschichte, Methoden und Theorien / History, Methods and Theories*, Peter F. Biehl, Alexander Gramsch, and Arkadiusz Marciniak, editors, pp. 119-133. Tübinger Archäologische Taschenbücher 3. Waxmann, Münster, Germany.

2006   *Archäologie: Grundzüge einer Historischen Kulturwissenschaft [Archaeology: The Main Features of an Historical Cultural Science]*. A. Francke Verlag, Tübingen, Germany.

ELKAR, RAINER S.

1990   Regionalgeschichte und Frühneuzeitforschung im Verhältnis beider deutscher Staaten. Divergenzen—Parallelen—Perspektiven [Regional History and Research on the Early Post-Medieval Period in the Context of both German States. Divergences—Parallels—Perspectives.] In *Geschichtswissenschaft in der DDR. Vol. II: Vor – und Frühgeschichte bis Neueste Geschichte*, Alexander Fischer and Günther Heydemann, editors, pp. 265-313. Duncker & Humblot, Berlin, Germany.

ERICSSON, INGOLF

1995   Archäologie der Neuzeit. Ziele und Abgrenzungen einer jungen Disziplin der archäologischen Wissenschaft [Archaeology of the Modern Era. Aims and Boundaries of a Young Discipline within Archaeological Science]. *Ausgrabungen und Funde* 40:7-13.

FASSBINDER, STEFAN

2003   *Wallfahrt, Andacht und Magie. Religiöse Anhänger und Medaillen. Beiträge zur neuzeitlichen Frömmigkeitsgeschichte Südwestdeutschlands aus archäologischer Sicht [Pilgrimage, Devotions and Magic. Religious Pendants and Medals. A Contribution to the Post-Medieval History of Devoutness in Southwestern Germany from an Archaeological Perspective]*. Zeitschrift für Archäologie des Mittelalters, Beiheft 18. Habelt-Verlag, Bonn, Germany.

FETTEN, FRANK

2002   Archaeology and Anthropology in Germany before 1945. In *Archaeology, Ideology and Society: The German Experience*, Heinrich Härke, editor, pp. 143-183. 2nd revised edition. Verlag Peter Lang, Frankfurt, Germany.

FROMMER, SÖREN

2007   *Historische Archäologie. Versuch einer methodologischen Grundlegung der Archäologie als Geschichtswissenschaft [Historical Archaeology. An Attempt at Outlining the Methods of Archaeology as an Historical Science]*. Tübinger Forschungen zur historischen Archäologie 2. Verlag Dr. Faustus, Büchenbach, Germany.

2009   Überlieferungsdichte und Interpretation im Kontext der Auswertung archäologischer Ausgrabungen [Evidence Density and Interpretation in the Context of Post Excavation Studies]. In *Zwischen Tradition und Wandel. Archäologie des 15. und 16. Jahrhunderts*, Barbara Scholkmann, Sören Frommer, Christina Vossler, and Markus Wolf, editors, pp. 25-33. Tübinger Forschungen zur historischen Archäologie 3. Dr. Faustus, Büchenbach, Germany.

FUNARI, PEDRO PAULO A.

1999   Historical Archaeology from a World Perspective. In *Historical Archaeology. Back from the Edge*, Pedro Paulo A. Funari, Martin Hall, and Siân Jones, editors, pp. 37-66. Routledge, London, England.

GAIMSTER, DAVID

2009   An Embarrassment of Riches? Post-Medieval Archaeology in Northern and Central Europe. In *International Handbook of Historical Archaeology*, Teresita Majewski and David Gaimster, editors, pp. 525-547. Springer, New York, NY.

GILCHRIST, ROBERTA

2005   Introduction: Scales and Voices in World Historical Archaeology. *World Archaeology* 37(3):329-336.

GRAMSCH, ALEXANDER

2011   Theory in Central European Archaeology: Dead or Alive? In *The Death of Archaeological Theory?* John Bintliff and Mark Pearce, editors, pp. 48-72. Oxbow Books, Oxford, England.

GRAMSCH, ALEXANDER, AND ULRIKE SOMMER (EDITORS)

2011   *A History of Central European Archaeology. Theory, Methods, and Politics*. Archaeolingua Series Minor 30. Budapest, Hungary.

GRONENBORN, DETLEF, AND CARLOS MAGNAVITA

2000   Imperial Expansion, Ethnic Change, and Ceramic Traditions in the Southern Chad Basin. A Terminal Nineteenth Century Pottery Assemblage from Dikwa, Borno State, Nigeria. *International Journal of Historical Archaeology* 4(1):35-70.

GRÜNDER, HORST

2004   *Geschichte der Deutschen Kolonien [History of the German Colonies]*. 5th edition. UTB-Verlag, Paderborn, Germany.

GULLØV, HANS CHRISTIAN, EINAR LUND JENSEN, AND KRSTINE RAAHAUGE

2011   *Cultural Encounters at Cape Farewell. East Greenland Immigrants and the German Moravian Mission in the 19th century*. Museum Tusculanum Press, Copenhagen, Denmark.

HALL, MARTIN, AND STEPHEN W. SILLIMAN

2006   Introduction: Archaeology of the Modern World.
        In *Historical Archaeology*, Martin Hall and
        Stephen W. Silliman, editors, pp. 1-23. Blackwell
        Publishing, Malden, MA.

HARDT, MATTHIAS, CHRISTIAN LÜBKE, AND DITTMAR
SCHORKOWITZ (EDITORS)

2003   *Inventing the Pasts in North Central Europe. The
        National Perception of Early Medieval History
        and Archaeology.* Gesellschaften und Staaten im
        Epochenwandel 9. Peter Lang Verlag, Frankfurt,
        Germany.

HÄRKE, HEINRICH

1991   All Quiet on the Western Front? Paradigms,
        Methods and Approaches in West German
        Archaeology. In *Archaeological Theory in Europe.
        The Last Three Decades,* Ian Hodder, editor, pp.
        187-222. Routledge, London, England.

1995   "The Hun is a Methodical Chap": Reflections on
        the German Tradition of Pre- and Proto-History.
        In *Theory in Archaeology. A World Perspective*, P.
        J. Ucko, editor, pp. 46-60. Routledge, New York,
        NY.

HÄRKE, HEINRICH (EDITOR)

2002   *Archaeology, Ideology and Society: The German
        Experience.* 2nd revised edition. Verlag Peter
        Lang, Frankfurt, Germany.

HEROLD, HEIKO

2006   *Deutsche Kolonial- und Wirtschaftspolitik
        in China 1840 bis 1914. Unter besonderer
        Berücksichtigung der Marinekolonie Kiautschou
        [German Colonial and Economic Policy in China
        from 1840 to 1914, with a Particular Emphasis on
        the Marine Colony of Kiautschou].* Ozeanverlag
        Herold, Cologne, Germany.

HICKS, DAN

2005   "Places of Thinking" from Annapolis to Bristol:
        Situations and Symmetries in "World Historical
        Archaeologies." *World Archaeology* 37(3):373-391.

ICKERODT, ULF F.

2010   *Einführung in das Grundproblem des
        archäologisch-kulturhistorischen Vergleichens
        und Deutens. Analogien-Bildung in der
        archäologischen Forschung [An Introduction to
        the Basic Problem of Archaeological and Cultural-
        Historical Comparison and Interpretation. The
        Formation of Analogies in Archaeological
        Research].* Verlag Peter Lang, Frankfurt, Germany.

IGEL, KARSTEN

2009   Historische Quelle und archäologischer Befund.
        Gedanken zur Zusammenarbeit von Archäologen
        und Historikern in einer dicht überlieferten
        Epoche [Historical Sources and Archaeological
        Features. Thoughts on the Collaboration between
        Archaeologists and Historians in a Period of
        Dense Tradition]. In *Zwischen Tradition und
        Wandel. Archäologie des 15. und 16. Jahrhunderts,*
        Barbara Scholkmann, Sören Frommer, Christina
        Vossler, and Markus Wolf, editors, pp. 33-
        43. Tübinger Forschungen zur historischen
        Archäologie 3. Verlag Dr. Faustus, Büchenbach,
        Germany.

JANKUHN, HERBERT

1973   Umrisse einer Archäologie des Mittelalters [An
        Outline of Medieval Archaeology]. *Zeitschrift für
        Archäologie des Mittelalters* 1:9-19.

KAJZER, LESZEK

1996   *Wstęp do archeologii historycznej w Polsce
        [Introduction to Historical Archaeology in
        Poland].* Publishers of the University of Łódź,
        Poland.

KATZENSTEIN, PETER (EDITOR)

1997   *Mitteleuropa. Between Europe and Germany.*
        Berghahn Books, Oxford, England.

KLEJN, LEO S.

1993a   To Separate a Centaur: On the Relationship
        between Archaeology and History in Soviet
        Tradition. *Antiquity* 67:339-348.

1993b   Is German Archaeology Atheoretical? Comments
        on Georg Kossack, Prehistoric Archaeology in
        Germany: Its History and Current Situation.
        Norwegian Archaeological Review 26:49-54.

KOBYLIŃSKI, ZBIGNIEW

2005   Neighbours: Polish-German Relations in
        Archaeology. Part 2—after 1945. *Archaeologia
        Polona* 43.

KOPPERS, WILHELM

1959   Grundsätzliches und Geschichtliches zur
        ethnologischen Kulturkreislehre [The Basic
        Principles and the History of the Ethnological
        Kulturkreislehre Approach]. In *Beiträge
        Österreichs zur Erforschung der Vergangenheit
        und Kulturgeschichte der Menschheit, mit
        besonderer Berücksichtigung Mitteleuropas,* Emil
        Breitinger, Josef Haekel, and Richard Pittioni,
        editors, pp. 110-126. Berger Verlag, Horn, Austria.

KRAJÍC, RUDOLF

2007   Archaeology of the Post-Medieval Period.
        The Current State of Research and Research
        Perspectives in Southern Bohemia. *Studies in
        Post-Medieval Archaeology* 2:57-97.

KRÄMER, WERNER
2001   Gerhard Bersu—ein deutscher Prähistoriker, 1889–1964 [Gerhard Bersu—a German Prehistorian, 1889–1964]. *Bericht der Römisch-Germanischen Kommission* 82:5-103.

KRAUSE, GÜNTER
2000   Odysseus am Niederrhein? Bemerkungen zu "historischen Analogien" und zu Versuchen, archäologische und historische Quellen aufeinander zu beziehen [Ulysses on the Lower Rhine? Remarks on "Historical Analogies" and on Attempts to Relate Archaeological to Historical Sources]. In *Vergleichen als archäologische Methode. Analogien in der Archäologie*, Alexander Gramsch, editor, pp. 57-71. BAR International Series 825, Oxford, England.

LAPPE, ULRICH
1978   Ruine Neideck in Arnstadt. Ein Beitrag zur materiellen Kultur des 17. Jahrhunderts [The Ruined Castle of Neideck in Arnstadt. A Study on 17th-Century Material Culture]. *Alt-Thüringen* 15:114-158.

LASZLOVSZKY, JÓZSEF, AND JUDITH RASSON
2003   Post-Medieval or Historical Archaeology: Terminology and Discourses in the Archaeology of the Ottoman Period. In *Archaeology of the Ottoman Period in Hungary*. Papers of the conference held at the Hungarian National Museum, Budapest, 24-26 May 2000, Ibolya Gerelyes and Gyöngyi Kovács, editors, pp. 377-382. Opuscula Hungarica 3. Magyar Nemzeti Múzeum, Budapest, Hungary.

ŁAWRYNOWICZ, OLGIERD
in press Research on the Identification of the German Nazi's Victims of Repressions from the Beginning of World War II after the Excavations on the Outskirts of Lodz and Warsaw. *Studies in Post-Medieval Archaeology* 5.

LITTLE, BARBARA J. (EDITOR)
1992   *Text-Aided Archaeology*. CRC Press, Boca Raton, FL.

LORING, STEPHEN, AND BEATRIX ARENDT
2009   "...They Gave Hebron, the City of Refuge..." (Joshua 21:13): An Archaeological Reconnaissance at Hebron, Labrador. *Journal of the North Atlantic Special Volume* 1:33-56.

LOZNY, LUDORMIR R.
2011b   Polish Archaeology in Retrospective. In *Comparative Archaeologies. A Sociological View of the Science of the Past*, Ludomir R. Lozny, editor, pp. 195-221. Springer, New York, NY.

LOZNY, LUDOMIR R. (EDITOR)
2011a   *Comparative Archaeologies. A Sociological View of the Science of the Past*. Springer, New York, NY.

LUCAS, GAVIN
2012   *Understanding the Archaeological Record*. Cambridge University Press, New York, NY.

LYDON, JANE
2009   *Fantastic Dreaming: The Archaeology of an Aboriginal Mission*. AltaMira Press, Lanham, MD.

MANTE, GABRIELE
2007   *Die deutschsprachige prähistorische Archäologie. Eine Ideengeschichte im Zeichen von Wissenschaft, Politik und europäischen Werten* [German-Language Prehistoric Archaeology. A History of Ideas in Terms of Economy, Politics and European Values]. Waxmann Verlag, Münster, Germany.

MEHLER, NATASCHA
2010   *Tonpfeifen in Bayern (ca. 1600-1745)* [Clay Tobacco Pipes in Bavaria ca. 1600-1745]. Zeitschrift für Archäologie des Mittelalters, Beiheft 22. Habelt-Verlag, Bonn, Germany.

2012   Written Sources in Post-Medieval Archaeology and the Art of Asking the Right Questions. *Studies in Post-Medieval Archaeology* 4:11-24.

MEHLER, NATASCHA, AND MARK GARDINER
in press On the Verge of Colonialism. English and Hanseatic Trade in the North Atlantic Islands. In *Exploring Atlantic Transitions: Archaeologies of Permanence and Transience in New Found Lands*, Peter Pope and Shannon Lewis-Simpson, editors. Society for Post-Medieval Archaeology Monograph no. 7. Boydell and Brewer, Woodbridge, Suffolk, England.

MERTA, JIŘÍ
1980   Průmyslová archeologie [Industrial Archaeology]. *Zkoumání výrobních objektů a technologií archeologickými metodami* 1:5-8.

MOMMSEN, H., T. BEIER, A. HEIN, E. HÄHNEL, AND A. BECKE
2000   Neue Ergebnisse zum sächsischen Steinzeug: Herkunftsbestimmung durch Neutronenaktivierungsanalyse und Auswertung von Archivalien [New Insights on Saxon Stoneware: Determining the Provenience by Means of Neutron Activation Analysis and the Study of Archival Sources]. *Keramos* 169:67-84.

MÜLLER, ULRICH
1997 /
1998   Review of *Between Artifacts and Texts. Historical Archaeology in Global Perspective*, by Anders Andrén. *Offa* 54/55:628-631.

2009   Netzwerkanalysen in der Historischen Archäologie. Begriffe und Beispiele [Network Analyses in Historical Archaeology. Terms and Examples]. In *Historia archaeologica. Festschrift für Heiko Steuer*, Sebastian Brather, Dieter Geuenich, and Christoph Huth, editors, pp. 735-754. Walter de Gruyter, Berlin, Germany.

NEUSTUPNÝ, EVŽEN

2002   Czech Archaeology at the Turn of the Millennium. In *Archäologien Europas / Archaeologies of Europe. Geschichte, Methoden und Theorien / History, Methods and Theories*, Peter F. Biehl, Alexander Gramsch, and Arkadiusz Marciniak, editors, pp. 283-289. Tübinger Archäologische Taschenbücher 3. Waxmann, Münster, Germany.

NOVAKOVIĆ, PREDRAG

2002   Archaeology in Five States—A Peculiarity or Just Another Story at the Crossroads of "Mitteleuropa" and the Balkans: A Case Study of Slovene Archaeology. In *Archäologien Europas / Archaeologies of Europe. Geschichte, Methoden und Theorien / History, Methods and Theories*, Peter F. Biehl, Alexander Gramsch, and Arkadiusz Marciniak, editors, pp. 323-353. Tübinger Archäologische Taschenbücher 3. Waxmann, Münster, Germany.

OGILVIE, SHEILAGH C.

1996   Proto-Industrialization in Germany. In *European Proto-Industrialization*, Sheilagh C. Ogilvie and Markus Cerman, editors, pp. 118-137. University Press, Cambridge, England.

OPAŁA, M., AND R. J. KACZKA

2008   Dating of Wooden Shelters in Polish High Tatras—Tree Rings Records of the Shepherding History in Carpathians. *Trace* 6:135-139.

ORSER, CHARLES E.

1996   *A Historical Archaeology of the Modern World*. Plenum Press, New York, NY.

2002   Introduction. In *Encyclopedia of Historical Archaeology*, Charles E. Orser, editor, pp. xvi-xix. Routledge, New York, NY.

2004   *Historical Archaeology*. 2nd edition. Pearson Prentice Hall, Upper Saddle River, NJ.

PAIKERT, GEZA C.

1967   *The Danube Swabians. German Populations in Hungary, Romania and Yugoslavia and Hitler's Impact on Their Patterns*. Martinus Nijhoff, The Hague, the Netherlands.

PAJER, JIŘÍ

1990   On the Development of a New Scientific Discipline—Post-Medieval Archaeology. Some Thoughts on its Current State and its Perspectives. *Studies in Post-Medieval Archaeology* 1:23-29.

PÁLFFY, GÉZA

2009   *The Kingdom of Hungary and the Habsburg Monarchy in the Sixteenth Century*. Columbia University Press, New York, NY.

PARTSCH, JOSEPH

1904   *Mitteleuropa. Die Länder und Völker von den Westalpen und dem Balkan bis an den Kanal und das Kurische Haff* [Central Europe. The Countries and Peoples between the Western Alps and the Balkan, the Channel, and the Curonian Lagoon]. Justus Perthes, Gotha, Germany.

PARZINGER, HERMANN

2002   "Archäologien" Europas und "europäische Archäologie"—Rückblick und Ausblick. ["Archaeologies" of Europe and "European Archaeology"—Review and Outlook]. In *Archäologien Europas / Archaeologies of Europe. Geschichte, Methoden und Theorien / History, Methods and Theories*, Peter F. Biehl, Alexander Gramsch, and Arkadiusz Marciniak, editors, pp. 35-53. Tübinger Archäologische Taschenbücher 3. Waxmann, Münster, Germany.

PITTIONI, RICHARD

1968   *Wesen und Methode der Industrie-Archäologie* [The Nature and Methodology of Industrial Archaeology]. Studien zur Industrie-Archäologie 1. Verlag der Österreichischen Akademie der Wissenschaften, Vienna, Austria.

PREDOVNIK, KATARINA

2008   Nova obzorja: arheologija mlajših obdobij [New Horizons: Archaeology of Later Periods]. *Arheo* 25:81-88.

SAUER, WALTER (EDITOR)

2002   *k.u.k. kolonial. Habsburgermonarchie und europäische Herrschaft in Afrika.* [k.u.k. Colonial. Habsburg Monarchy and European Rule in Africa]. Böhlau Verlag, Vienna, Austria.

SCHLENKER, BJÖRN, AND JOACHIM WAHL

1994   Neuzeitliche Knochen- und Elfenbeinverarbeitung [Post-Medieval Bone and Ivory Working]. *Archäologische Informationen aus Baden-Württemberg* 27:121-128.

SCHOLKMANN, BARBARA

2001   Archäologie des Mittelalters und der Neuzeit im Jahr 2000 [Medieval and Post-Medieval Archaeology in the Year 2000]. *Mitteilungen der Arbeitsgemeinschaft für Archäologie des Mittelalters und der Neuzeit* 12:73-81.

2003   Die Tyrannei der Schriftquellen? Überlegungen zum Verhältnis materieller und schriftlicher Überlieferung in der Mittelalterarchäologie [The Tyranny of the Written Record? Thoughts on the Relationship between Material and Written Tradition in Medieval Archaeology]. In *Zwischen Erklären und Verstehen? Beiträge zu den erkenntnistheoretischen Grundlagen archäologischer Interpretation*, M. Heinz, M.K.H. Eggert, and U. Veit, editors, pp. 239-259. Tübinger Archäologische Taschenbücher 2. Waxman Verlag, Münster, Germany.

SCHREG, RAINER

2007   Archäologie der frühen Neuzeit. Der Beitrag der Archäologie angesichts zunehmender Schriftquellen [Archaeology of the Early Modern Era. The Contribution Made by Archaeologists in View of an Increasing Number of Written Records]. *Mitteilungen der Deutschen Gesellschaft für Archäologie des Mittelalters und der Neuzeit* 18:9-21.

2010a   Panamaian Coarse Handmade Earthenware—A Melting Pot of African, American and European Traditions? *Post-Medieval Archaeology* 44(1):135-164.

2010b   Archäologie des Mittelalters und der Neuzeit: eine historische Kulturwissenschaft par excellence? [Archaeology of the Middle Ages and the Modern Era: An Historical Cultural Science Par Excellence?] In *Historische Kulturwissenschaften. Positionen, Praktiken und Perspektiven*, Jan Kusber, Mechthild Dreyer, Jörg Rogge, and Andreas Hütig, editors, pp. 335-366. transcript-Verlag, Bielefeld, Germany.

SCHUYLER, ROBERT L.

1999   The Centrality of Post-Medieval Studies to General Historical Archaeology. In *Old and New Worlds*, Geoff Egan and R. L. Michael, editors, pp. 10-17. Oxbow Books, Oxford, England.

SKLENÁŘ, KAREL

1983   *Archaeology in Central Europe: The First 500 years*. University Press, Leicester, England.

SMETÁNKA, ZDENĚK, AND JAROMIR ŽEGKLITZ

1990   Post-Medieval Archaeology in Bohemia and its Problems. *Studies in Post-Medieval Archaeology* 1:7-23.

STEPHAN, HANS-GEORG

2012   Ein Plädoyer für die Archäologie der Neuzeit: Eindrücke und Erfahrungen aus vier Jahrzehnten Arbeit in Nordrhein-Westfalen, Niedersachsen, Hessen, Thüringen, Sachsen-Anhalt und Sachsen [Making a Case for Post-Medieval Archaeology: Impressions and Experiences from Four Decades of Working in North Rhine-Westphalia, Lower Saxony, Hesse, Thuringia, Saxony-Anhalt, and Saxony]. In *Neue Zeiten. Stand und Perspektiven der Neuzeitarchäologie in Norddeutschland*, Ulrich Müller, editor, pp. 273-347. Habelt Verlag, Bonn, Germany.

STEUER, HEIKO

1997 / 1998   Entstehung und Entwicklung der Archäologie des Mittelalters und der Neuzeit in Mitteleuropa. Auf dem Weg zu einer einheitlichen Mittelalterkunde [Formation and Development of Medieval and Post-Medieval Archaeology in Central Europe. Moving Toward a Unified Field of Medieval Studies]. *Zeitschrift für Archäologie des Mittelalters* 25/26:19-38.

STEUER, HEIKO (EDITOR)

2001   *Eine hervorragend nationale Wissenschaft: deutsche Prähistoriker zwischen 1900 und 1995 [An Outstanding National Science: German Prehistorians between 1900 and 1945]*. Reallexikon der Germanischen Altertumskunde, Ergänzungsband 29, Walter de Gruyter, Berlin, Germany.

TABACZYŃSKI, STANISŁAW

1993   The Relationship between History and Archaeology: Elements of the Present Debate. *Medieval Archaeology* 37:1-14.

2002   From the History of Eastern and Western Archaeological Thought: An Introduction to Discussion. In *Archäologien Europas / Archaeologies of Europe. Geschichte, Methoden und Theorien / History, Methods and Theories*, Peter F. Biehl, Alexander Gramsch, and Arkadiusz Marciniak, editors, pp. 67-77. Tübinger Archäologische Taschenbücher 3. Waxmann, Münster, Germany.

TAMANINI, ELIZABETE

1995   História Revisitada: a imigração alemão sul do Brasil sob olhar da cultura material [History Revised: The German Immigration to Brazil in Light of Material Culture]. Unpublished typescript, University of Campinas, Brazil.

THEUNE, CLAUDIA

2009   Ganzheitliche Forschungen zum Mittelalter und zur Neuzeit [Holistic Studies on the Middle Ages and the Modern Era]. In *Historia archaeologica. Festschrift für Heiko Steuer*, Sebastian Brather, Dieter Geuenich, and Christoph Huth, editors, pp. 755-764. Walter de Gruyter, Berlin, Germany.

2010   Historical Archaeology in National Socialist Concentration Camps in Central Europe. *Historische Archäologie* 2(2010).

THURMAN, MELBURN D.

1996   Review of *A Historical Archaeology of the Modern World*, by Charles E. Orser. *Historical Archaeology* 30(3):87-90.

VEIT, ULRICH

2002   Wissenschaftsgeschichte, Theoriendebatte und Politik: Ur- und Frühgeschichtliche Archäologie in Europa am Beginn des dritten Jahrtausends [History of Science, Theoretical Debate and Politics: Pre- and Protohistorical Archaeology in Europe at the Dawn of the Third Millennium]. In *Archäologien Europas / Archaeologies of Europe. Geschichte, Methoden und Theorien / History, Methods and Theories*, Peter F. Biehl, Alexander Gramsch, and Arkadiusz Marciniak, editors, pp. 405-421. Tübinger Archäologische Taschenbücher 3. Waxmann, Münster, Germany.

2011   Toward a Historical Sociology of German Archaeology. In *Comparative Archaeologies. A Sociological View of the Science of the Past*, Ludomir R. Lozny, editor, pp. 53-79. Springer, New York, NY.

VOGT, ANDREAS

2002   *Von Tsaobis bis Namutoni: Die Wehrbauten der deutschen Schutztruppe in Deutsch-Südwestafrika (Namibia) von 1884-1915* [*From Tsaobis to Namutoni: The Fortifications of the German Protection Force in German South-West Africa (Namibia) from 1884 to 1915*]. Klaus Hess Verlag, Göttingen, Germany.

WAHLE, ERNST

1964   *Tradition im Auftrag prähistorischer Forschung* [*Tradition Commissioned by Prehistoric Research*]. Duncker & Humblot, Berlin, Germany.

WIENBERG, JENS, AND HANS ANDERSSON (EDITORS)

1993   *The Study of Medieval Archaeology. European Symposium for Teachers of Medieval Archaeology, Lund 11-15 June 1990.* Lund Studies in Medieval Archaeology 13. Almqvist & Wiksell International, Stockholm, Sweden.

WIESNER-HANKS, MERRY E.

2006   *Early Modern Europe, 1450-1789.* Cambridge University Press, Cambridge, England.

WILKIE, LAURIE A.

2005   Inessential Archaeologies: Problems of Exclusion in Americanist Archaeological Thought. *World Archaeology* 37(3):337-351.

2006   Documentary Archaeology. In *The Cambridge Companion to Historical Archaeology*, Dan Hicks and Mary C. Beaudry, editors, pp. 13-34. Cambridge University Press, Cambridge, England.

ZANESCO, ALEXANDER

2012   Anstaltsfriedhof des Psychiatrischen Krankenhauses Thurnfeldgasse 14, Gst.-Nr. 306 KG Hall in Tirol [Graveyard of the Psychiatric Hospital at Thurnfeldgasse 14, Gst.-Nr. 306 KG Hall in Tyrol]. *Kulturbericht aus Tirol 2012. 63. Denkmalbericht*:202-204.

ZIEGERT, HELMUT

1964   Archäologie und Ethnologie. Zur Zusammenarbeit zweier Wissenschaften [Archaeology and Ethnology. On the Collaboration between Two Fields of Science]. *Berliner Jahrbuch für Vor- und Frühgeschichte* 4:102-149.

Natascha Mehler
Institut für Ur- und Frühgeschichte
Universität Wien
Franz-Klein-Gasse 1
A-1190 Wien
Austria

RAINER SCHREG

Historical Archaeology, History, and Cultural Sciences in Germany: Some Reflections

ABSTRACT

Archaeology in central Europe traditionally feels part of history, but the relationship between archaeology and history is ambiguous. Conservative historians still neglect archaeological sources on the grounds that archaeology merely reiterates what we already know from texts. Remarkably, many interesting impulses for historical archaeology come from approaches labeled as "ahistorical." It may be helpful to understand historical archaeology as a field of cultural sciences rather than of history. It is the aim of this contribution to outline some aspects of past, current, and future discussions in German-speaking archaeology. The most important challenge for historical archaeology seems to come from the field of history—at least from some simplified ideas about history that are very common in archaeology.

INTRODUCTION

Archaeology in central Europe is commonly understood as a historical discipline. This is true for prehistoric archaeology, and remains unquestioned for historical archaeology. But as the number of written documents, literature, and oral traditions has increased in modern times, there has been a lively debate about the purpose of archaeological research in this field. In particular, archaeology of the 19th and 20th centuries and of the contemporary period provokes skeptical discussion about the contributions of archaeology.

Several historians take the view that archaeology is just an expensive way to learn what we already knew (Deetz 1991:1). The need for rescue excavations is often framed in terms of a need to verify written and pictorial sources or to investigate aspects of daily life and material culture. For good reasons, builders and public authorities ask for a cost-benefit analysis (Isenberg 2008).

Historical archaeology as a field of history is problematic. But by now there is little discussion about the self-concept of historical archaeology. It has been an unquestioned assumption that historical archaeology has to be a part of history.

HISTORICAL ARCHAEOLOGY AND HISTORY

The usage of the term *Historische Archäologie* in German varies from a close definition restricted to the modern period to a broader definition including medieval archaeology, or even a very general definition referring to all archaeologies dealing with literate cultures (Müller et al. 2009). In this article historical archaeology is in principle understood as the archaeology of the Middle Ages and modern period, when there is a parallel tradition of written documents. Discussion will focus, however, on the more recent period as some fundamental aspects become clearer in that context.

History on the one hand is fundamental for the way archaeology defines itself as a discipline, but on the other hand it also determines the limits of archaeological research. For a very long time the end of the pagan Merovingian cemeteries and the beginning of a written record in the 8th and 9th centuries in many parts of central Europe has been the chronological limit of archaeological research. Of course, there were some excavations on medieval sites beginning as early as the 19th century, but medieval archaeology was only established as a distinct field beginning in the 1930s and especially after World War II. A major factor in the development of medieval archaeology was an increase in building activities in the 1950s, when there were possibilities for excavations within destroyed cities. Later, towns were adapted to increasing car traffic, and churches were provided with modern sub-floor heating. For these reasons, medieval archaeology is based within cultural heritage management, and still today,

Figure 1.   Map with places mentioned in the text (in Germany, unless otherwise noted): (1) Berlin; (2) Mainz; (3) Halle; (4) Tübingen; (5) Mansfeld; (6) Eisenach; (7) Wittenberg; (8) Hohenrode; (9) Louisendorf; (10) Bamberg; (11) Nuremberg; (12) Bad Windsheim; (13) Erding; (14) Innsbruck, Austria; and (15) Vienna, Austria (Map provided courtesy of the Department of Prehistory and Medieval Archaeology, University of Vienna, Austria).

only a few universities offer a full program in medieval archaeology (Steuer 2001). Medieval archaeology can be studied in Bamberg, Halle, and Tübingen, Germany, and in Innsbruck and Vienna, Austria (Figure 1). Single classes are offered at many other universities mainly within the study of prehistoric archaeology. There is still no research institute that is truly engaged in historical archaeology. Several disciplines, such as art history, architecture, or historical geography, have been involved in the development of historical archaeology, but prehistoric archaeology became a dominant reference. This is because, in practice, academic courses in medieval

archaeology were mainly hosted in departments of prehistory. Similarly, cultural heritage management practices combined prehistoric and medieval archaeology together in one department for preservation and care of field monuments (Bodendenkmalpflege).

In recent years, archaeological engagement has extended its time span more and more to the present. Historical archaeology as the archaeology of modern times is still in an early stage in German-speaking central Europe and has not been widely accepted in the archaeological community. Some colleagues feared that responsibilities of cultural heritage management would increase while budgets stayed constant or even shrank. Others raised fundamental concerns, arguing seriously against an archaeology of modern times (*Archäologie der Neuzeit*) emphasizing that archaeology is a science of antiquity and that the term itself shows the contradiction (Behrens 1996). The drive to include more recent periods in archaeology comes rather from heritage management than from academic research, however. Until today comparatively few archaeological excavations have focused on recent centuries, and all were motivated primarily by aims of conservation. It is only in some federal states in Germany that there have been excavations at all, while in others it has not been possible even to establish medieval archaeology.[1] Fundamental discussions about the aims, theoretical self-concept, disciplinary position, and even methods of interpretation have not taken place in an adequate way. It is the aim of this contribution to outline some aspects of past, current, and future discussions.

The Burdens of History

Central European archaeologists regard archaeology and history as two separate academic disciplines, distinguished by their sources and methods. At the same time, however, archaeology (no matter if prehistoric or historical) is seen by its shared research questions as a part of history, which aims to reconstruct the past (Fehring 2000:1). Today the archaeology of the medieval and modern periods is defined as a historical discipline working with material remains, which mainly consist of the relics of daily life. Research questions focus on cultural achievements and—still to a lesser degree—on processes. There is a broad spectrum of methods used including, for example, architectural research, but at its core it is based on archaeological methods as they have been developed by prehistoric archaeology since the 19th century (Scholkmann 1997/1998:18). But when medieval archaeology was established as a distinct discipline it was more a question of the social identity of archaeologists than of scientific aims and research strategies. Most discussions of medieval archaeology as a discipline were concerned with its relationship to the well-established disciplines of medieval studies, especially medieval history (Scholkmann 1997/1998). In contrast to the Anglo American world, disciplinary identities still play an important role at German universities.

On the one hand archaeologists underline the independence of their discipline from history, on the other hand

they understand their discipline as a field of history and desire an integration. History provides orientation and is counterpart at the same time. As a consequence archaeologists emphasize that they can contribute especially to such fields where written sources are not available or rare. When Herbert Jankuhn defined three specific fields where medieval archaeology could contribute to medieval history—settlement archaeology, economic archaeology, and archaeo-technology—he emphasized that in these fields, where written sources are sparse, archaeological sources could also contribute to modern history (Jankuhn 1973). In 1995 Ingolf Ericsson sketched an archaeology of modern times (*Archäologie der Neuzeite*) as a field of historical research that aims to develop a general view of modern society in a historical perspective—in interdisciplinary cooperation. Nevertheless, he pointed out that archaeology is mainly responsible for those aspects of society that were not documented in texts, maps, or pictures (Ericsson 1995:11).

Texts and Objects

This concept of archaeology as a stopgap for history implies a hierarchy of the sources. Texts have been linked with ideas, education, and civilization, while objects refer to profane existence and represent daily life instead of sublime "culture." Given this understanding of culture, archaeology is of less relevance to cultural studies, the material sources for which come from a separate field. Only artifacts of high artistic quality are considered—an archaeological tradition that has been especially formative for research traditions in German Classical or Byzantine archaeology.

The idea of a priority of texts over material sources and the related conception of history has important effects on the synthesis of texts and artifacts in archaeological research. This is of primary importance for historical archaeology as, by definition, it employs a variety of parallel written and material sources supplemented by pictures and oral traditions.

There have been remarkably few attempts to bring material and written sources together, however. As early as 1900 the historian Ernst Bernheim presented an overview of the relationship between different sources (Bernheim 1903). Even though he focused on texts, he did at least mention archaeological artifacts. At that time, methodology and source criticism in archaeology was in its infancy, and Bernheim's arguments therefore

complementary relationship

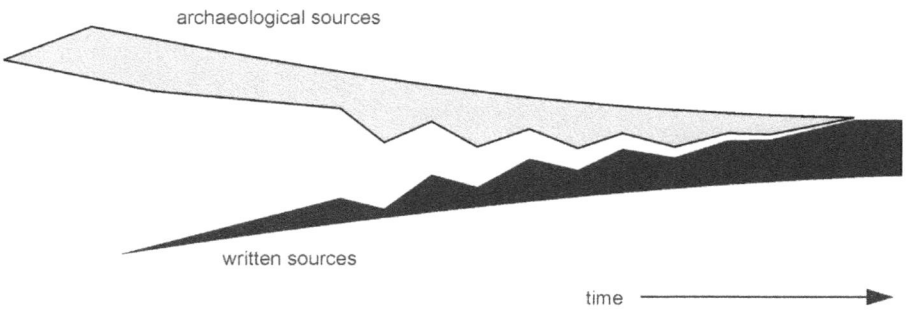

interactive relationship

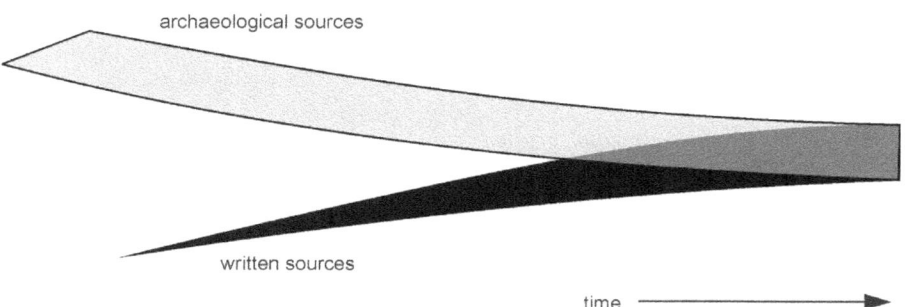

Figure 2. *Different ideas about the relationship between artifacts and texts (Graphic by author, 2010).*

Special interest has been taken in the identification of buried corpses (Last 1973). Research projects making reference to historical individuals remain of high importance today. Skeletal remains of prominent individuals, such as Friedrich Schiller or Immanuel Kant, were among the earliest research efforts to combine anthropological and archaeometric methods (Ullrich 2004; Maatsch and Schmälzle 2009). In general, however, archaeology is rarely able to identify individual prominent persons, even though recent advances in physical anthropology have enabled archaeologists to study individual lives in remarkable detail. Nevertheless, it is hard to determine the "historical role" of an individual if there are no written sources. Therefore it is a central concern of German archaeology to identify social groups—especially their leaders—and ethnic groups, as they could be understood as protagonists. This is especially true for early medieval archaeology; even today, some archaeologists fear that if archaeology relinquishes ethnic interpretation it will lose its historical identity (Bierbrauer 2004).

Swedish archaeologist Anders Andrén distinguished several modes of interaction between artifacts and texts (Andrén 1998; Schreg 2007): (1) embedding; (2) identification; (3) classification; (4) correlation, and (5) contrast. Identification and classification are interested in applying names or categories as used in texts to the archaeological record. For a very long time, these have been the main approaches to achieve a rather simple synthesis inevitably oriented toward textual information. Within this framework a synthesis of archaeological data and written sources is mainly interested in the identification of acting people, specific historical locations, and events. This kind of identification always results in a dominant role of the written texts and produces a subordination of material sources to the written ones. More complex ways of achieving a synthesis between artifacts and texts, as correlation or contrast, are seldom used. They try to compare spatial structures or processes and find correlations or contradictions.

won't satisfy modern archaeologists. In the very beginning, the main interest underlying a synthesis of artifacts and texts was in the chronology and ethnic interpretation of material remains. Nineteenth-century cultural historians in the tradition of Moriz Heyne were interested in classifying objects of daily life (Heyne 1899, 1901, 1903). They compared terms taken from written sources and oral tradition with pictures and artifacts. When Paul Grimm excavated the abandoned medieval village of Hohenrode in the 1930s, he focused on a classification of material culture according to categories taken from written sources (Grimm 1939). Narratives of archaeology were simply adopted from history, as they followed the timeline and tried to identify actors and in many cases conjecture about their intentions. This phenomenon has been described as the "tyranny of the historical record" (Champion 1990; Scholkmann 2003).

For historical archaeology (in a broader sense), it has been an important aim to identify acting people as named in texts. Major efforts have been made to name artists, architects, or noblemen and rulers responsible for the creation of material remains and buildings.

There are other possible ways to integrate texts and artifacts, however, such as through intertextuality. In many cases artifacts refer directly to texts, mainly by their iconography. There are many examples from the time of the Reformation when printing reformed communication and made texts available to a broader public. For example, the iconography of the furniture of middle-class houses referred to published texts and pictures (Pfrommer 2009). Excavations at several sites connected with the reformer Martin Luther in Mansfeld, Eisenach, and Wittenberg allowed a perspective beyond simple identification. Comparison between the archaeological records showing the daily life of Luther's family with his personal records indicated some discrepancies (Meller 2009).

In general the relationship between texts and artifacts in German archaeology can be described as a complementary one, as they concentrate on identification and classification. It is different to the approach favored in many research traditions outside central Europe and especially outside Germany (Figure 2). There, a rather interactive relationship is preferred, based on a broad variety of theoretical approaches, providing many questions beyond the traditional historical perspective. Characteristic for this interactive approach are rather abstract topics that are directly manifest neither in the written nor in the material record. They are often taken from anthropology or sociology. Colonialism or capitalism, for example, became important topics in American historical archaeology (Leone and Potter 1999; Lucas 2006a) but have had little impact in German historical archaeology.

Ideas about the Past within German Archaeology and German Historical Thinking

The dominance of identification and classification can be understood as an outcome of a rather static or normative idea of the past. Archaeologists seldom reflected on changing meanings of names and terms and understood them according to the usage by historians as static objective categories. This is true, for example, for ethnic groups or various discussions about towns and villages. Early medieval situations have been reconstructed to a very high degree by projecting modern situations into the past.

Regarding processes of cultural change, archaeological interpretation has been "historical" for a very long

time. Changes have been seen in relation to events or personal action, and innovations have been seen as technical invention rather than in the context of economic, social, and environmental changes. Rather abstract concepts of cultural contact and adaptation have been subordinated under migrations and political and personal relationships.

German historical thinking (Iggers 2007; Courtney 2009) with its strong traditions forms an important background for the performance and acceptance of historical archaeology. Its roots go back to the 19th century, when after the French Revolution and the Napoleonic Wars there was a process of reorientation in Germany. The desire for a reestablishment of a united German national state strengthened nationalism and provoked the ideal of a strong state. Both aspects became fundamental for archaeological narratives.

Georg Wilhelm Friedrich Hegel (1770-1831) has to be mentioned because his lectures on the philosophy of history (Hegel 2002) mark changing ideas about history during this period. The belief of the Age of Enlightenment in universal ethical and political values was destroyed after the revolutionary wars. Instead, the conviction was developed that ethical values and juridical norms have their origin in history and nationality. For Hegel, history was driven by reason as it developed from imperfect to the perfect. It is the historical task of nations to solve the dialectics, but in general, heroic individuals fulfill the will of the world spirit (*Weltgeist*).

Leopold von Ranke (1795-1886) transformed history from rather philosophical reconsiderations to a field of critical scientific research. In the course of the 19th century, a tradition of German historiography that is called "historicism" developed. Several points were characteristic for this approach: (1) the individuality of every historical situation; (2) the high weight of the state, understood as the aim of history; (3) the high weight of the nation, understood as a community determining history; (4) the relativity of values; (5) a specific methodology that aims to understand actors rather than to explain historical situations; and (6) a chronological narrative of events (Ranke 1971).

Certainly, since the 19th century there have been many changes in historical research, but the offshoots of these ideas are still an important factor affecting the difficult acceptance of historical archaeology today. In consequence, nearly all approaches within history that emphasized daily life, lower classes, or economic or environmental aspects and that attempted to understand processes of cultural changes were not widely accepted and in many cases are still today not integrated within history (Iggers 2007).

Social and economic history in most universities form separate departments. Traditional cultural history is often part of European ethnology; environmental history is based on very different disciplines such as physical anthropology, technical history, or ecology. Also, approaches of the French historical Annales School with their ideas of *histoire totale* and *longue durée* had remarkably little resonance in German historiography (Schöttler 1994; Oexle 1997). Today there is a broad variety of different approaches in German historiography. Many of them are interesting for historical archaeology, such as environmental history or social history. But these developments in historical research and theory based on written sources have been little reflected within archaeology. Archaeological historical thinking is still influenced by the tradition of historicism that was the main theoretical concept of historians when prehistoric archaeology developed as an academic discipline in the late 19th century and beginning of the 20th century. Even if historicism is not a closed theory, the importance of single individuals and the importance of politics and law and the individuality of each historical situation "next to god" (Ranke 1971:59-60) had wide-ranging consequences for the idea of history within archaeology.

The influence of 19th-century ideas is deeply rooted in German history even to the present day. German archaeologists concentrated on an antiquarian approach as well, collecting and editing archaeological data with little interpretation. Though archaeologists always felt themselves to be part of the discipline of history, historians did not really accept them. When archaeology formed as a subject in the mid-19th century it was mainly practiced by private individuals such as pharmacists, teachers, priests (mainly Protestant), and officers interested in creating a long-term continuous national history. The founding of the Römisch-Germanisches Zentralmuseum (Romano-Germanic Museum) at Mainz and the Germanisches Nationalmuseum at Nuremberg in 1852 was realized in close cooperation with the association of local historical societies, in which few professional historians were involved. At that time history was already an established academic discipline that looked down on the amateurs. When

historians—such as Johann Gustav Droysen (1808-1884) and Ernst Bernheim (1850-1942)—established a general historiology (*Historik*) reflecting on the different sources for learning about the past, archaeological remains were mentioned only in passing (Bernheim 1903; Droysen 2009). Even today, historical heuristics often do not include archaeological sources.

Interdisciplinary cooperation between archaeology and history was problematic from the very beginning. After historical arguments had been misused for nationalistic and National Socialist propaganda, it was a common reaction after World War II to strictly separate history and archaeology. It was common sense for archaeology and history of that time to follow the device of Prussian general Helmuth von Moltke to march apart and strike together (*getrennt marschieren—vereint schlagen*) (Wenskus 1979:637). Many categories of former archaeological interpretation were disqualified by their National Socialist past, as for example the concepts of space (*Raum*), race, and ethnic identification, which were misused for propaganda (Arnold 2006). Prehistoric as well as medieval archaeology after World War II avoided sensitive topics—a well known phenomenon of post-war German society (Longerich 2006)—and therefore made little effort to transcend the old categories (Härke 1991). For this reason, many paradigms remained unexamined, unconsciously preventing the acceptance of various modern concepts.

In recent years, a younger generation started to work on archaeological research history and to challenge many paradigms (Eggert 2005). At least partially, the increased standing of historical archaeology seems to be due to a changing understanding of history. In recent years several articles have reviewed the state of the discipline, and there seems to be a certain consensus that historical archaeology needs a holistic approach integrating archaeology and history (Steuer 1997/1998; Theune 2009).

Dealing with a Difficult Past

But there is another burden of history: German contemporary history is still suffering from 20th-century dictatorships in National Socialist Germany and in the German Democratic Republic. Topics in German historical archaeology dealing with the more recent past are closely related to the material relics of these periods. As cultural heritage management has in most cases taken the initiative for archaeological monuments, work has concentrated on monuments with obvious "public interest." The aim was their preservation or documentation rather than a higher historical research interest. This is why there are many observations on industrial complexes, on military remains of World War I, National Socialist monuments such as concentration camps or bunkers, or even on the Berlin Wall and the German-German borderline from the Cold War period (Kernd'l 2002; Cramer 2005). Quite early on, this was understood as part of the public memorial and as a medium of historical didactics, primarily concerning the dark past of 20th-century Germany (Linse 1988).

Research interests in historical archaeology therefore remained within a rather traditional historical framework. Although there are quite different approaches coming from political, technical, or cultural history, nearly all are closely related to specific sites and follow an inductive research strategy. Studies integrating material culture, written and pictorial evidence, and oral history into a dense description are lacking.

HISTORICAL ARCHAEOLOGY AND CULTURAL HISTORY

German prehistoric archaeology has been divided since its beginnings in the 19th century. On the one hand there have been close ties to the natural sciences, especially geology. For a long time this tradition took an evolutionary approach that had little understanding of specific historical dimensions and of the role of human action and ideas. Major foci of this research were the Paleolithic period and prehistoric pile dwellings. On the other hand, archaeologists dealing with early history instead oriented themselves toward the historical paradigm emphasizing, for example, migrations. But clearly, in the 19th century there were some approaches that represent a more cultural view of history rather than an evolutionary or event-oriented one.

In 1866 when Ludwig Lindenschmit (1809-1893) sketched the field of archaeology, he emphasized an aim of looking for levels of cultivation and education (*Bildungszustände*) (Lindenschmit 1866:44). At that time—it was the period when romanticism and nationalism evolved in German countries, unified within the Wilhelminian Empire only in 1871—the creation of a national identity brought increased interest not only in archaeology, but also in more recent material culture. Collections of the material culture of daily life and of arts and crafts (*Gewerbemuseen*) were founded, mostly taken from middle-class and noble households focusing on medieval and Renaissance culture, as for example at Nuremberg.[2] An important work of this research tradition was written by Moriz Heyne (1837-1906). In his five books on German civil antiquities (*Fünf Bücher deutscher Hausaltertümer*) (Heyne 1899, 1901, 1903), he focused on dwelling, nutrition, and hygiene and integrated written, pictorial, and material sources. Archaeological studies on medieval and later material culture often refer directly to this research

tradition of the 19th century (Felgenhauer-Schmiedt 1995:43; Fehring 2000:193-194).

In the 1980s some bewailed a crisis in traditional cultural history (*Kulturgeschichte*) (Gambrich 1983), but since then the "cultural turn" of the humanities has broadened the research fields of historical cultural studies (Hardtwig and Wehler 1996; Lutter et al. 2004; Landwehr 2005). Modern cultural history includes a broad spectrum of methods, perspectives, and research topics. This cultural turn had little effect on historical archaeology in central Europe, though many publications since the 1980s have referred to cultural history in their titles.[3] When in 1995 Walter Janssen published archaeological finds from an early modern hospital at Bad Windsheim, Bavaria, he presented them as an example of the possibilities of medieval archaeology within cultural history. In practice, his chapter on cultural historic aspects proved to be very traditional, as he only discussed the spatial distribution of a certain type of cooking vessel. He concluded that Bad Windsheim belonged to a common cultural space (*Kulturraum*) with Nuremberg. Like most archaeologists, Janssen treats the terms "cultural history" and "history of material culture" as synonyms (Scholkmann 1998:74-75). His idea of "culture" is rooted within an older terminology mainly used by prehistoric archaeologists, who understood culture mainly as a cluster of specific artifacts (Eggert 1978; Wotzka 2000).

Today, the common archaeological definition of culture and increased archaeological interest in material culture present some difficulties for research programs in cultural studies. Policy of Education and Research in Europe encouraged interdisciplinary research, and the "Bologna process," aimed to create a European higher education area with comparable academic degrees, forced small disciplines into closer cooperation at universities. This has provided an important impetus for the cultural sciences to form a more coherent field of research, comparable to cultural anthropology. Within the field of cultural sciences, some scholars take a historical approach. Archaeology and history in most cases were not part of this new field, however, which is dominated by linguistics, philology, philosophy, religious studies, arts, European ethnography, and sociology. Historians working in this field in most cases do not come from the center of their discipline but represent some more theoretical approaches or come from some rather specific fields such as cultural history or Byzantine or Eastern European history.

In recent years new centers of historical cultural sciences (*historische Kulturwissenschaften*) have been created at several German universities.[4] Historical cultural sciences are based on an interdisciplinary approach using a broad variety of data. Common research topics include questions of space, communication, and social behavior as well as mentality, arts, and philosophy. Although archaeologists are often involved in these centers, the profile of archaeology as historische Kulturwissenschaft is unclear, as few efforts have been made to introduce archaeological approaches into this area of cultural sciences (Ericsson 2000; Schreg 2007). Recently, Ingolf Ericsson (2000) considered medieval archaeology as a cultural science. He pointed to a dichotomy between history and cultural anthropology. Nevertheless he emphasized that medieval archaeology could integrate sociological and anthropological theories with the traditional approaches of history. Manfred K.H. Eggert (2006) characterized the various disciplines of archaeology as historische Kulturwissenschaft. As he did not focus on historical archaeology, he was referring to the methodological background. He pointed to the methodological criteria of the cultural turn, such as the close analytical connection of society and culture, critical reflection on the researcher's role, and the explicit relativism of value systems (Musner et al. 2001). Regarding specific topics Eggert was rather skeptical, as in his opinion there are only a few links to archaeology (Eggert 2006:233).

Indeed, in all research centers of cultural sciences where archaeology has been integrated, it was historical archaeology that led the way—in most cases classical or medieval archaeology—whereas prehistoric archaeology just seems to be a follower.[5]

HISTORICAL ARCHAEOLOGY AND CULTURAL ANTHROPOLOGY

In contrast to the United States, in German-speaking countries cultural anthropology is not a separate discipline. In the United States, "archaeology as anthropology" was a slogan of the new archaeology of the 1960s and 1970s. In this view, archaeology should describe general characteristics and should contribute to an explanation of social structures and cultural change. A main critique of traditional archaeology concerned the interpretation of archaeological data. According to their historical paradigm traditional archaeologists usually referred to specific historical situations and looked primarily for single events. Instead, new archaeology argued for an analysis of data based on scientific and statistical methods and an interpretation based on sociological and anthropological concepts. Historical archaeology in America received an important impetus from new archaeology in the 1960s because it was understood as an arena—besides ethnoarchaeology and experimental archaeology—in which it was possible to test archaeological interpretations and to formulate middle range theories (Binford 1983:49; South 1977). In North America archaeology and cultural anthropology were integrated into the broader field of anthropology from the very beginning and long before new archaeology. Therefore abstract subjects such as capitalism, modernity, colonialism, material culture, or identity (Johnson 1996; Burke 1999; Franklin and Fesler 1999; Leone and Potter 1999) became important topics in American historical archaeology but gained little attention in central Europe. Even more basic subjects dealing with intercultural and diachronic comparisons were not very common in central European archaeology.

There have been several debates on the role of cultural anthropology in prehistoric archaeology, especially in connection with early Iron Age polities north of the Alps (Veit 1995; Eggert 1999) where there has been some impact from Anglo American processual archaeology (Frankenstein and Rowlands 1978). Historical archaeology only recently turned to more theoretical approaches, however. Remarkably, some of the first attempts were made by prehistoric archaeologists with primarily methodological objectives. Already in 1980 a small group of prehistoric archaeologists used paintings as a test for combination statistics very common in German archaeology at that time (Eggert et al. 1980);

others tried to identify well-known modern sites by archaeological surveys to get better ideas about the interpretation of survey data (Decker and Klän 1999) or tried to use modern material for more general reconsiderations of typology (Korbel 1983).

In his 1987 introduction to medieval archaeology, however, Günter P. Fehring rejected within one short sentence the ahistorical tendencies of anthropology and new archaeology as not adequate to the historical identity of medieval archaeology (Fehring 2000:194). In general, anthropological approaches are quite sparse in central Europe. The tendency of anthropology to generalization and rather abstract research categories stands in vigorous contradiction to the historical point of view, which emphasizes the uniqueness of each specific historical situation and the major role of human individuals.

NEW RESEARCH TOPICS AND THE HISTORICAL PARADIGM

The common approaches of cultural anthropology and even modern cultural history have proven to be quite incompatible with the traditional self-conception of historical archaeology in central Europe. Some major research topics of American historical archaeology therefore had little relevance in central Europe.

Nevertheless, within the last decade there have been some more interpretive approaches that can provide new perspectives on historical archaeology beyond the historical paradigm. Modern historical cultural sciences in central Europe provide a huge variety of approaches, such as cultural history (*Kulturgeschichte*), everyday history (*Alltagsgeschichte*) and micro-history, cultural anthropology (*Kulturanthropologie*), or cultural ecology (*Kulturökologie*) (Landwehr 2005; Nünning and Nünning 2008). Archaeologists just started to use these approaches for more interpretive analyses of the archaeological record. It may be useful to sketch some of them in the light of central European research.

Material Culture and Daily Life in Micro-History

Today for most archaeologists the history of daily life is a central field of their work related to cultural sciences. "Material culture" (*materielle Kultur* or *Sachkultur*) became a key concept including every material relic of human action. In recent years there has been an increasing debate about material culture as a source for Alltagsgeschichte (Scholkmann 1993; Felgenhauer-Schmiedt 1995). German research often restricts Alltagsgeschichte to transportable objects excluding architectural remains, graves, or human impact on landscapes (Scholkmann 1998). There are many studies of material culture in early modern times, but very few on material culture from the 19th and 20th centuries. They are primarily concerned with ceramics (Keller 1999; Gross 2003; Kluttig-Altmann 2006), glass (May 1993; Scheidemantel 2002), and artifacts of daily life (Matteotti 1994) such as clay tobacco pipes (Kluttig-Altmann and Mehler 2007).

The theoretical implications of Alltagsgeschichte were neglected by archaeologists, however. Originally this approach was developed in the 1960s when the German student movement of 1968 brought Marxist ideas and anthropological approaches into history (Courtney 2009:171). When social and economic history developed, Alltagsgeschichte was thought of as an alternative approach emphasizing individual experiences (Lüdtke 1998). Most historians remained skeptical, however. As the term "material culture" was very common in Marxist archaeology, many scholars rejected it, emphasizing that archaeological relics also reflect human action and underlying value systems. In practice, only a small part of material culture is preserved. Due to various formation processes, available data are restricted and in many cases ambiguous. Consequently, a central point of discussion is how to relate material culture with human beings. Barbara Scholkmann suggested an object-based contextual analysis (*objektorientierte Umweltanalyse*), which connects objects with a specific chronological, spatial, and functional context (Scholkmann 1998:78).

Booming urban archaeology brought numerous new analyses of urban life including modern periods (Hiptmair et al. 2002). The focus on single buildings with the integration of architectural research and written sources made it possible to follow changes in daily life from the perspective of a single household over centuries and to reconstruct the circumstances of daily life in some detail (Scholkmann and Ströbele 1999; Atzbach 2005). In many cases there was quite a narrow chronological framework and it was possible to link material and textual sources by their common context.

The opportunity, however, to use these studies for a micro-historical perspective (Lüdtke 1998) was not taken in most cases. Recent debates on micro-history in historical archaeology (Lucas 2006b:37-38; Brooks and DeCorse 2008) have not yet reached German research.

The practice of excavation at prison camps and concentration camps is characterized by a close connection to individual life stories and provides an example of micro-history approaches. It is only the extreme situations of daily life under the conditions of 20th-century crimes against human dignity, however, that provoke archaeological interest. In this singular situation there are few written documents or evidence of oral history. Archaeological research on the National Socialist past has not only the goal of research, but also of remembering and teaching (Linse 1988). Objects are closely related to individuals, either victims or culprits, and therefore they open perspectives on micro-history.

Cultural Transformation as Long-Term Processes

Micro-history focuses on individuals and short time periods. This is an important strength of historical archaeology, as in well-preserved contexts chronology is often of less fundamental importance. Historical archaeology, however, is also of relevance for a long-term perspective and a global scale. In theory, historical archaeology is fundamental for historic-genetic approaches, which aim to answer the question of the development of today's cultural contexts. In the past, physical geographers focused their research on the genesis of the contemporary cultural landscape. They used quite diverse sources, but little archaeological research was realized in this context.

While earlier archaeological research concentrated mainly on continuities and correlated cultural breaks and spatial shifts of material culture with wars and migration, cultural change became an archaeological topic within processual archaeology (Renfrew 1973). In contrast to definitions of culture as a cluster of specific life habits, processual archaeologists thought of culture as the non-biological adaptation of man to his environment as part of one ecosystem (Binford 1962).

In historical archaeology, "innovation" has been a flourishing field in recent years (Müller 2002; Baeriswyl 2006), mainly focusing on the early modern period (Scholkmann et al. 2009). Effects of more recent

cultural changes in the light of material culture have been a central topic of ethnic studies (*Volkskunde*) (Wiegelmann et al. 1977). This discipline, however, retreated from material culture studies and oriented itself toward mentalities and social studies, defining its new field as European ethnography or empirical cultural studies (Brednich 1994; Hoppe 1998). Archaeologists have welcomed this development as it enables historical archaeology to integrate the study of material culture, which had previously not been part of its research agenda (Seidenspinner 1986/1987; Spindler 2003).

The perspective of cultural adaptation is of special interest in the context of colonialism. As Germany lost its colonies in 1918, archaeologists had few historical links to this field. Regarding archaeological research on the relationship between Roman and Germanic, however, German and Slavonic archaeology could provide an opportunity to challenge colonial perspectives emphasizing the supremacy of one culture over another. Case studies in historical archaeology prove that processes of cultural adaptation require a combination of a long-term perspective and approaches of micro-history (Schreg and Zeischka-Kenzler, this volume).

Identity and Social Affiliation

Questions of identity are probably the most important ones in historical archaeology. Earlier research tried to deal with rank and social stratification as they were presented in written texts. This proved to be difficult: there are many impacts of formation processes on the various sources, and social identities change over time. Changes concerned institutions and included personal social mobility. Especially in modern times, as a consequence of the political and industrial revolution, society was transformed in many ways and identities were altered. The decline of nobility and the development of a bourgeoisie and a new industrial oligarchy were just some of the transformations. Within the field of Volkskunde, the phenomenon of sinking cultural values (*sinkendes Kulturgut*) has been well known for a very long time (Wiegelmann 1972) and is also visible in the archaeological record. For example, the importation of expensive Chinese porcelain prompted multiple attempts at imitation to provide cheaper products. Archaeological material provides a broadened database that includes objects of low quality and enables a perspective from small entities such as single households. In architecture, elements of noble castles were adapted to industrial factories and the houses of the new middle

Figure 3.   *Louisendorf in northern Hesse: the barn belonging to the school was built in the early 18th century, some decades after the village's foundation by French Waldenses in 1687. In contrast to the other buildings of the village constructed in the regional timber-frame style, the barn is erected with cobblestones similar to buildings in the settlers' French homeland (Photo by author, 2010).*

striking insights into how this social group was excluded and how it kept its own identity.

Other examples, such as the Polish miners in the Ruhr basin in the late 19th century, or the French Huguenots in the late 17th century have not been the subject of archaeological research. Huguenots and Waldenses were settled in the late 17th century in the German states of Brandenburg, Hesse-Kassel, and Württemberg in old cultural landscapes. These communities were assimilated after several generations, though toponyms and personal names survived up to the present at some villages (Zögner 1966). While houses seem to follow regional indigenous traditions, at Louisendorf near Frankenau in northern Hesse a secondary building belonging to the local school was constructed with cobblestones as was common in the native country of the first settlers coming from the area of Die in southern France. This raises the question whether some other examples of cobblestone construction in the neighborhood of Louisendorf represent a cultural influence on the indigenous rural communities (Figure 3).

class. Within this concept innovations can be followed through social classes and understood as a part of social identity. The study by Ulrich Müller on medieval hand-washing-equipment (Müller 2006) provides a good example of this approach within medieval archaeology.

The importance of studies on identity in historical archaeology is twofold: on the one hand they provide important methodological experience for archaeological research in different periods and regions; on the other hand integration is an important topic in our own present. Ongoing debates on the integration of immigrants lack an understanding of integration as a long process evolving over generations. Examples taken from the past could help to get a better sense of the many dimensions of this process. Archaeology can contribute to an understanding of the material aspects of this process, such as building traditions, costumes, or religious artifacts. As immigrants usually comprise a minority, their narratives are often missing or at least underrepresented in the written record, and oral traditions may be dominated by individual fates. Artifacts of daily life could represent an important corrective. An example of failed integration is represented by research on Sinti and Roma, segregated from and discriminated against in local society. Archaeologically a burial ground excavated at Erding in Southern Bavaria (Maier 1988) provides

Compared to New World archaeology, research on identities seems to be of limited interest in central Europe. The significance of changing identities is much greater for modern American society than for central Europe. Despite migrations and refugees in the 20th century and the continuing European integration, culture is still thought to be closely connected with specific nations or ethnic identities. This is true for the popular conception of "culture," but even the archaeological definition is often a very traditional one (Schreg 2010:340-341), as indicated for example by the ongoing discussion on ethnic interpretations of the archaeological record (Bierbrauer 2004). Within this concept, cultural adaptation concerns only the migrants and not the whole society. In America, society is much more aware of different cultural backgrounds. As a result of postcolonial studies there is also an archaeology of lower classes and minorities, as for example studies of African slaves, French settlers, or indigenous populations (Walthall 1991; Haviser 1999). Nevertheless an archaeological approach in central Europe could also contribute to a better understanding of the difficult integration of immigrant workers from Italy, Turkey, and former Yugoslavia (and others) and their children and grandchildren within the present German society. Working with their material culture since the 1950s could improve our understanding of how specific groups retain some traditions and change others under specific circumstances. It proves that a specific "culture" is not a continuous or natural quality of people, but a matter of change and acceptance of interacting groups.

Research interests of historical archaeology remain within a rather historical framework. Nevertheless there are quite different approaches coming from political, technical, or cultural history, but nearly all are closely related to specific sites and follow an inductive research strategy.

One promising field of historical archaeology includes contributions to representation, prestige, communication, and literality (Steuer 1995). Increasingly, input comes from the adoption of approaches taken from different fields of cultural sciences. Recent years have seen an increasing interest in the Reformation period. Studies have been done concerning the iconographic program of tile stoves (Pfrommer 2009) or gravestones (Staecker 2003). For the more recent past, it could be an interesting topic to use material culture to explore penetration of social changes such as militarization in the period before World War I and westernization after World War II (Jarausch 2004).

Environmental History and Cultural Ecology

The interaction between humans and environment or between culture and nature is the main topic of environmental history. It explores living conditions, their configuration by humans and their transformations over time. A specific focus is on unconscious long-term effects of human actions and their feedback and consequences within natural processes (Radkau 2003). Environmental history works at three levels:

1) Natural environments of the past (understanding nature itself), 2) human modes of production (the socioeconomic realm as it interacts with the environment), and 3) perception, ideology and value (mental or intellectual, in which perceptions, ethics, laws, myths, and other structures of meaning become part of an individual's or group's dialogue with) (Worster 1988:293-307).

Environmental history is more than a reconstruction of past landscapes or the narrative of former environmental pollution, crises, or disasters. It is concerned with cultural aspects of human-environment interaction, which are seen in the context of social and economic processes and in relation to the perception of nature by past individuals and societies. The environment includes social settings and subjective perceptions. In this spirit environmental history is part of the cultural sciences, despite the importance of data coming from natural sciences.

It is one of the most important challenges within this field to deal with the different perspectives on nature and culture. Traditional ideas of history make it difficult to deal with human-environment interaction. Many important observations and categories were not accessible to people in the past; many processes are long-term processes that take several generations and were therefore hardly recognizable. Furthermore, a pre-scientific worldview did not ask about interactions but accepted nature as given by God. Therefore written texts are not an adequate basis for the reconstruction of the past. They provide much important information, but they need to be complemented by other sources. Therefore environmental history is connected with many different disciplines such as history itself, physical anthropology, technical history, and ecology (Worster 1988; Winiwarter and Knoll 2007). Traditionally, historical geography dealt with landscapes and their relics either preserved in the present or documented in maps, descriptions, and pictures. Since the 1970s historical geography has experienced a deep crisis as the discipline became oriented more towards an applied geography involved, for example, in landscape planning. Another reason probably had to do with the difficulties of dating elements of past cultural landscapes (Schenk 2000).

Today, methods taken from "extensive archaeology" and from geoarchaeology provide improved possibilities for working with cultural landscapes. As a consequence, landscape archaeology assumes more and more of the research previously done by geographers. Outstanding examples include research into the regulation of rivers, the drainage of swamps, the construction of waterways, and the exploitation of natural resources. Industrial archaeology has been involved in this research for a very long time, though focusing on technological aspects (Schreg, this volume). Promising insights come from archaeological work. Some projects, primarily on mining, succeed in connecting technological innovation to landscape history (Segers-Glocke 2000). Within a broader discussion of cultural success and collapse, the environmental history from the late medieval period of desertion to the industrialized agriculture of the 20th century poses interesting questions (Schreg 2009). Late medieval desertion and subsequent early modern population growth, plagues, famines, and changes in agriculture can probably be seen within a long-term process of human-environment interaction.

Working with past environments does not refer only to the landscape, however, but also to ecological coherencies. The term "ecology" derives from biology, and social processes have been seen as disruptive rather than integrative factors. Actually, it is necessary to understand society as a part of ecological systems and to recognize subjective perceptions as decisive elements of processes of environmental and cultural changes. Within cultural sciences cultural ecology provides different concepts

and approaches linking environmental aspects and cultural behavior. In the beginning cultural ecology aimed mainly for a better understanding of cultural adaptation. Today the perspective is much broader and "evolutionary cultural ecology" explains culture as "an ecosystemically organized product of overall evolutionary processes" (Finke 2006). The treatment of cultural energy, language, and the conception of borders are just some of the questions addressed in this approach (Bonner 1983; Finke 2003, 2006).

When human ecology was introduced into archaeology it was one aspect of processual archaeology (Butzer 1982). In central Europe it has only gained prominence in recent years, as for example in the increasing importance of geoarchaeology and in some discussions on Neolithic economy and ecology (Ebersbach 2002). Archaeology in general could play an important role in this approach. First, material sources offer important insights into environmental changes and especially their socio-economic and cultural consequences. Second, archaeology traditionally combines methods and approaches from the natural sciences with those taken from historical and cultural sciences, and therefore provides an important link within interdisciplinary research. Third, archaeology provides a long-term view as it follows cultural changes from human evolution up to the present.

CONCLUSIONS

It seems to be the most important challenge for historical archaeology to distinguish itself from history, and to develop a broader concept that integrates the needs of cultural heritage management and the possibilities of cultural anthropology as well as traditional historical approaches. Historical archaeology in central Europe today has little acceptance because it is perceived as a subdiscipline of history. There are several reasons for this.

(1) A lack of theory. Because medieval and post-medieval archaeology are dominated by rescue excavations there is no room for broader theoretical consideration. For people working in medieval and post-medieval archaeology it has been more important to legitimize their own existence and to outline their contributions.

(2) The burden of research history. After the experiences of the ideological misuse of archaeological and

historical interpretations to justify German attacks and conquest of eastern Europe, there has been a withdrawal to rather antiquarian work (Härke 1991). Overhasty synthesis and interpretation of different sources was blamed for the problematic ideological world view. As a reaction, the first decades after World War II were characterized by the motto "marching apart—striking together" (getrennt marschieren—vereint schlagen).

(3) The burden of prehistoric archaeology. In his programmatic contribution for the first volume of the "Zeitschrift für Archäologie des Mittelalters" (Journal of Medieval Archaeology) Herbert Jankuhn (1973) defined settlement archaeology, economic archaeology, and archaeo-technology as three specific fields where medieval archaeology could contribute to the history of the medieval period and modern times. Jankuhn understood the archaeology of medieval and later times merely as a continuation of prehistoric archaeology, in

terms of methods as well as in terms of research questions. As a consequence there was little reflection on how to integrate archaeological and written information.

(4) A lack of acceptance of archaeology by historians combined with insufficient theoretical reflection by archaeologists. Ideas about history held by archaeologists often still reflect 19th-century historicism.

(5) A complementary understanding of texts and artifacts. For archaeologists in Germany and in central Europe it was believed that the contribution of archaeology ended where written sources began. In theory there was no chronological border for archaeology, but only in recent years have increasing numbers of archaeologists argued for a holistic approach to texts and artifacts as interactive sources—quite common in American and British historical archaeology and theoretically favored by German historical archaeology. Instead of using the interactions of written and material sources—especially correlations, confrontations, and "intertextuality" (Schreg 2010)—as a main part of research, historical archaeology in Germany still works primarily on aspects of societies that were not documented by texts, maps, or images (Ericsson 1995:11). In some sense written texts are seen as more informative and more adequate to our interests than archaeological sources, which are perceived as just good enough to fill in some gaps. The "birth of material history," the "loss of antiquity," and the "loss of isolation" described by Dan Hicks (2003) as

a recent process in historical archaeology still has to be implemented in central Europe.

(6) Definition of history and culture. In practice different definitions of history and culture (and different ideas about humanity) represent a fundamental divide between well established disciplines and make it difficult to combine different approaches. Therefore it has been an inert process in recent decades to establish, for example, approaches of social history or environmental history within the historian community or to overcome deterministic views within geosciences.

Historical archaeology in central Europe has just begun, and there has been very little theoretical consideration. But there are many opportunities to develop stimulating perspectives based on European traditions. The cultural sciences in Germany deal with a great variety of data and sources. They follow an interdisciplinary approach and provide different alternative perspectives, criteria that historical archaeology clearly meets. Furthermore, there are many research topics and different approaches connected with cultural sciences—the reflections and remarks presented here have attempted to sketch some of the general possibilities. In order to realize its potential, however, it seems crucial to understand historical archaeology more as a subfield of the cultural sciences than as a part of traditional historical research.

NOTES

1. For example medieval archaeology is not established in Rhineland-Palatinate and Saarland, whereas in North Rhine-Westphalia (especially in Westphalia) there are several colleagues engaged in medieval and post-medieval archaeology (Schreg 2007:10).

2. Germanisches Nationalmuseum (GNM) and former Bayerisches Gewerbemuseum Nürnberg (today part of GNM).

3. For example, publication series "Lübecker Schriften zur Archäologie und Kulturgeschichte" (Lübeck Publications on Archaeology and Cultural History) (since the 1970s) and "Schweizer Beiträge zur Kulturgeschichte und Archäologie des Mittelalters" (Swiss Contributions to Cultural History and Medieval Archaeology) (since 1974) as well as many monographs such as Janssen (1995) or Friedel and Frieser (1999).

4. For example, Johannes-Gutenberg Universität Mainz <http://www.historische.kulturwissenschaften.uni-mainz.de/> (accessed 22 July 2012); Historisch-kulturwissenschaftliches Forschungszentrum Trier <http://hkfz.uni-trier.de/> (accessed 22 July 2012); and Zentrum für Kulturwissenschaft der Universität Bonn <http://www.zfkw.uni-bonn.de> (accessed 22 July 2012).

5. For example, Geisteswissenschaftliches Zentrum Geschichte und Kultur Ostmitteleuropas at Leipzig (GWZO) <http://www.uni-leipzig.de/gwzo> (accessed 22 July 2012), with an important role for medieval archaeology; and Zentrum für Europäische Geschichts-und Kulturwissenschaften Heidelberg <http://www.uni-heidelberg.de/fakultaeten/philosophie/zegk/index.html> (accessed 22 July 2012), which includes medieval archaeology only as part of art history.

REFERENCES

ANDRÉN, ANDERS

1998   *Between Artifacts and Texts: Historical Archaeology in Global Perspective.* Contributions to Global Historical Archaeology. Plenum Press, New York, NY.

ARNOLD, BETTINA

2006   "Arierdämmerung": Race and Archaeology in Nazi Germany. *World Archaeology* 38(1):8-31.

ATZBACH, RAINER

2005   *Leder und Pelz am Ende des Mittelalters und zu Beginn der Neuzeit: Die Funde aus den Gebäudehohlräumen des Mühlberg-Ensembles in Kempten (Allgäu)* [*Leather and Fur at the End of the Middle Ages and Beginning of Modern Times: Finds from Building Voids of the Mühlberg Complex in Kempten*]. Mühlbergforschungen Kempten (Allgäu), Vol. 1. Habelt, Bonn, Germany.

BAERISWYL, ARMAND

2006   Innovation und Mobilität im Spiegel der materiellen Kultur—archäologische Funde und historische Fragestellung: Ein Versuch [Innovation and Mobility in Light of Material Culture—Archaeological Finds and Historical Problems: A Test Case]. In *Europa im späten Mittelalter: Politik—Gesellschaft—Kultur,* Rainer Christoph Schwinges, editor, pp. 512-537. Oldenbourg, Munich, Germany.

BEHRENS, HERMANN

1996   Archäologie der Neuzeit. Eine Frage der Nomenklatur oder der Terminologik? [Archaeology of Modern Times. A Question of Nomenclature or Terminology?]. *Archäologisches Nachrichtenblatt* 1:228-229.

BERNHEIM, ERNST

1903   *Lehrbuch der Historischen Methode und der Geschichtsphilosophie* [*Textbook of Historical Methodology and Philosophy of History*]. Duncker, Leipzig, Germany.

BIERBRAUER, VOLKER

2004   Zur ethnischen Interpretation in der frühgeschichtlichen Archäologie [On Ethnic Interpretation in Protohistorical Archaeology]. In *Die Suche nach den Ursprüngen: Von der Bedeutung des frühen Mittelalters,* Walter Pohl, editor, pp. 45-84. Verlag der Österreichischen Akademie der Wissenschaften, Vienna, Austria.

BINFORD, LEWIS R.

1962   Archaeology as Anthropology. *American Antiquity* 28:217-225.

BINFORD, LEWIS R. (EDITOR)

1983   *Working at Archaeology. Studies in Archaeology.* Academic Press, London, England.

BONNER, JOHN TYLER

1983   *Kultur-Evolution bei Tieren* [*The Evolution of Culture in Animals*]. Paul Parey, Berlin, Germany.

BREDNICH, ROLF W. (EDITOR)

1994   *Grundriß der Volkskunde. Einführung in die Forschungsfelder der Europäischen Ethnologie* [*Outline of Ethnic Studies. Introduction to the Research Fields of European Ethnology*]. Reimer, Dietrich, Berlin, Germany.

BROOKS, JAMES F., AND CHRISTOPHER R. DeCORSE (EDITORS)

2008   *Small Worlds: Method, Meaning, & Narrative in Microhistory.* School of American Research Press, Santa Fe, NM.

BURKE, HEATHER

1999   *Meaning and Ideology in Historical Archaeology. Style, Social Identity, and Capitalism in an Australian Town.* Kluwer Academic/Plenum Press, New York, NY.

BUTZER, KARL W.

1982   *Archaeology as Human Ecology.* Cambridge University Press, Cambridge, England.

CHAMPION, TIMOTHY C.

1990   Medieval Archaeology and the Tyranny of the Historical Record. In *From the Baltic to the Black Sea: Studies in Medieval Archaeology,* David Austin and Leslie Alcock, editors, pp. 79-95. Unwin Hyman, London, England.

COURTNEY, PAUL

2009   The Current State and Future Prospects of Theory in European Post-Medieval Archaeology. In *International Handbook of Historical Archaeology,* David R. M. Gaimster and Teresita Majewski, editors, pp. 169-189. Springer, New York, NY.

CRAMER, JOHANNES

2005   Der Gartenzaun um Berlin—Was blieb von der Berliner Mauer? [The Fence around Berlin—What is Left from the Berlin Wall?]. In *Der unbestechliche Blick: Festschrift zu Ehren von Wolfgang Wolters zu seinem siebzigsten Geburtstag = Lo sguardo incorruttibile,* Martin Gaier, editor, pp. 235-241. Porta-Alba-Verlag, Trier, Germany.

DECKER, RAYMOND, AND NICOLE KLÄN

1999   Hätten wir ihn erkannt? Feldbegehungen auf einem neuzeitlichen Hof in Veeze [Recognizable? Field Walking at a Modern Farmstead in Veeze]. *Archäologie im Rheinland* 186-188.

DEETZ, JAMES
1991   Archaeological Evidence of Sixteenth – and
        Seventeenth-Century Encounters. In *Historical
        Archaeology in Global Perspective*, Lisa Falk,
        editor, pp. 1-10. Smithsonian Institution Press,
        Washington, DC.

DROYSEN, JOHANN GUSTAV
2009   *Outline of the Principles of History (Grundriss der
        Historik)*. BiblioLife, LLC.

EBERSBACH, RENATE
2002   *Von Bauern und Rindern. Eine Ökosystemanalyse
        zur Bedeutung der Rinderhaltung in bäuerlichen
        Gesellschaften als Grundlage zur Modellbildung
        im Neolithikum [On Peasants and Cattle. An
        Ecosystem Analysis on the Meaning of Cattle
        Breeding in Rural Societies as a Basis for
        Modeling Neolithic Economy]*. Basler Beiträge zur
        Archäologie, Vol. 15. Basel, Switzerland.

EGGERT, MANFRED K. H.
1978   Zum Kulturkonzept in der prähistorischen
        Archäologie [The Conception of Culture in
        Prehistoric Archaeology]. *Bonner Jahrbuch* 178:1-
        20.

1999   Der Tote von Hochdorf. Bemerkungen zum
        Modus archäologischer Interpretation [The
        Dead Man of Hochdorf. Remarks on the Ways of
        Archaeological Interpretation]. *Archäologisches
        Korrespondenzblatt* 29:211-222.

2005   Archäologie im Umbruch: Einführung in die
        Thematik [Archaeology in Transition. An
        Introduction]. *Archäologisches Nachrichtenblatt*
        10(2):111-124.

2006   *Archäologie. Grundzüge einer historischen
        Kulturwissenschaft [Archaeology. Outline of
        a Historical Cultural Science]*. UTB, Vol. 2728.
        Francke, Tübingen, Germany.

EGGERT, MANFRED K. H., SIEGFRIED KURZ, AND HANS-PETER
VATHA
1980   Historische Realität und archäologische
        Datierung. Zur Aussagekraft der
        Kombinationsstatistik [Historical Reality and
        Archaeological Chronology. On the Value of
        Seriation]. *Praehistorische Zeitschrift* 55:110-145.

ERICSSON, INGOLF
1995   Archäologie der Neuzeit [Archaeology of Modern
        Times]. *Ausgrabungen und Funde* 40:7-13.

2000   Archäologie des Mittelalters—eine
        Kulturwissenschaft? [Medieval Archaeology—A
        Cultural Science?]. *Das Mittelalter* 5:141-148.

FEHRING, GÜNTER P.
2000   *Die Archäologie des Mittelalters: Eine Einführung
        [Medieval Archaeology: An Introduction]*. 3rd
        edition. Theiss, Stuttgart, Germany.

FELGENHAUER-SCHMIEDT, SABINE
1995   *Die Sachkultur des Mittelalters im Lichte der
        archäologischen Funde [Medieval Material
        Culture in the Light of Archaeology]*. 2nd edition.
        Europäische Hochschulschriften, Reihe 38,
        Archäologie, Vol. 42. Lang Europ. Verl. der Wiss.,
        Frankfurt am Main, Germany.

FINKE, PETER
2003   Kulturökologie [Cultural Ecology]. In *Konzepte
        der Kulturwissenschaften: Theoretische
        Grundlagen—Ansätze—Perspektiven*, Ansgar
        Nünning and Vera Nünning, editors, pp. 248-277.
        Metzler, Stuttgart, Germany.

2006   Die Evolutionäre Kulturökologie: Hintergründe,
        Prinzipien und Perspektiven einer neuen Theorie
        der Kultur [Evolutionary Cultural Ecology:
        Background, Principles, and Perspective of a
        New Cultural Theory]. *Anglia—Zeitschrift für
        englische Philologie* 124(1):175-217.

FRANKENSTEIN, S., AND MICHAEL J. ROWLANDS
1978   The Internal Structure and Regional Context
        of Early Iron Age Society in South-Western
        Germany. *Bulletin of the Institute for Archaeology
        (London)* 15:73-112.

FRANKLIN, MARIA, AND GARRETT FESLER (EDITORS)
1999   *Historical Archaeology, Identity Formation,
        and the Interpretation of Ethnicity*. Colonial
        Williamsburg Research Publications, Richmond,
        VA.

FRIEDEL, BIRGIT, AND CLAUDIA FRIESER (EDITORS)
1999   *Nürnberg: Archäologie und Kulturgeschichte: "...
        nicht eine einzige Stadt, sondern eine ganze Welt
        ...." 1050-2000, 950 Jahre Nürnberg [Nuremberg:
        Archaeology and Cultural History: "...Not a
        Single Town, but a Whole World..." 1050-2000,
        Nuremberg's 950th Anniversary]*. Dr. Faustus,
        Büchenbach, Germany.

GAMBRICH, E.H.
1983   *Die Krise der Kulturgeschichte. Gedanken zum
        Wertproblem in den Geisteswissenschaften
        [The Crisis of Cultural History: Remarks on the
        Problem of Values in the Humanities]*. Deutscher
        Taschenbuchverlag, Munich, Germany.

GRIMM, PAUL
1939   *Hohenrode, eine mittelalterliche Siedlung
        im Südharz [Hohenrode, a Medieval
        Settlement in the Southern Harz Mountains]*.
        Veröffentlichungen der Landesanstalt für
        Volksheitskunde Halle, Vol. 11. Halle, Germany.

GROSS, UWE
2003   *Neuzeitliche Keramik im nördlichen Baden (16.-19.
        Jh.): Ein Überblicksversuch anhand ausgewählter
        Fundkomplexe [Modern Potters in Northern
        Badenia (16th-19th Centuries): An Outline
        based on Selected Find Complexes]*. Heidelberg,
        Germany.

HARDTWIG, WOLFGANG, AND HANS-ULRICH WEHLER (EDITORS)

1996   *Kulturgeschichte Heute* [*Cultural History Today*]. Vandenhoeck & Rupprecht, Göttingen, Germany.

HÄRKE, HEINRICH H.

1991   All Quiet on the Western Front? Paradigms, Methods and Approaches in West German Archaeology. In *Archaeological Theory in Europe. The Last Three Decades*, Ian Hodder, editor, pp. 187-222. Routledge, London, England.

HAVISER, JAY B. (EDITOR)

1999   *African Sites Archaeology in the Caribbean*. Ian Randle Publishers, Kingston, Jamaica.

HEGEL, GEORG WILHELM FRIEDRICH

2002   *Vorlesungen über die Philosophie der Geschichte* [*The Philosophy of History*]. Critical edition by F. Brunstäd, originally published 1840. Reclam, Stuttgart, Germany.

HEYNE, MORIZ

1899   *Das deutsche Wohnungswesen von den ältesten geschichtlichen Zeiten bis zum 16. Jahrhundert* [*German Dwelling from the Earliest Historical Period to the 16th Century*]. Fünf Bücher deutscher Hausaltertümer, Vol. 1. Hirzel, Leipzig, Germany.

1901   *Das deutsche Nahrungswesen von den ältesten geschichtlichen Zeiten bis zum 16. Jahrhundert* [*German Diet from the Earliest Historical Period to the 16th Century*]. Fünf Bücher deutscher Hausaltertümer, Vol. 2. Hirzel, Leipzig, Germany.

1903   *Körperpflege und Kleidung bei den Deutschen von den ältesten geschichtlichen Zeiten bis zum 16. Jahrhundert* [*Personal Hygiene and Clothing among the Germans from the Earliest Historical Period to the 16th Century*]. Fünf Bücher deutscher Hausaltertümer, Vol. 3. Hirzel, Leipzig, Germany.

HICKS, DAN

2003   Archaeology Unfolding: Diversity and the Loss of Isolation. *Oxford Journal of Archaeology* 22:315-329.

HIPTMAIR, PETER, MARTIN KROKER, AND HARTMUT OLBRICH

2002   *Zwischen Wallstrasse und Altmarkt—Archäologie eines Altstadtquartiers in Dresden* [*Between Wallstrasse and Altmarkt—Archaeology of an Urban Quarter in Dresden*]. Veröffentlichungen des Landesamtes für Archäologie mit Landesmuseum für Vorgeschichte Dresden, Vol. 34. Dresden, Germany.

HOPPE, JENS (EDITOR)

1998   *Die Volkskunde auf dem Weg ins nächste Jahrtausend. Ergebnisse einer Bestandsaufnahme* [*Ethnic Studies en Route to the Next Millenium. Results of a Review*]. Münsteraner Schriften zur Volkskunde, europäischen Ethnologie, Vol. 1. Waxmann, Münster, Germany.

IGGERS, GEORG G.

2007   *Geschichtswissenschaft im 20. Jahrhundert* [*History in the 20th Century*]. Ein kritischer Überblick im internationalen Zusammenhang. Vandenhoeck & Rupprecht, Göttingen, Germany.

ISENBERG, GABRIELE

2008   "Man weiß doch eigentlich schon alles." Die Bedeutung der Mittelalter – und Neuzeitarchäologie ["In Principle We Already Know Everything." The Meaning of Medieval and Modern Archaeoogy]. In Stratigraphie und Gefüge: Beiträge zur Archäologie des Mittelalters und der Neuzeit und zur historischen Bauforschung; Festschrift für Hartmut Schäfer zum 65. Geburtstag, pp. 31-36. Forschungen und Berichte zur Archäologie des Mittelalters in Baden-Württemberg 28. Theiss, Stuttgart, Germany.

JANKUHN, HERBERT

1973   Umrisse einer Archäologie des Mittelalters [An Outline of Medieval Archaeology]. *Zeitschrift für Archäologie des Mittelalters* 1:9-19.

JANSSEN, WALTER

1995   *Der Windsheimer Spitalfund aus der Zeit um 1500: Ein Dokument reichsstädtischer Kulturgeschichte des Reformationszeitalters* [*Archaeological Finds from the Windsheim Hospital around 1500: A Document of Urban Cultural History during the Reformation*]. Wissenschaftliche Beibände zum Anzeiger des Germanischen Nationalmuseums, Vol. 11. Verlag des Germanischen Nationalmuseums, Nuremburg, Germany.

JARAUSCH, KONRAD H.

2004   *Die Umkehr: Deutsche Wandlungen 1945-1995* [*After Hitler: Recivilizing Germans, 1945-1995* (English edition, Oxford University Press, 2006)]. Schriftenreihe der Bundeszentrale für politische Bildung, Vol. 469. Bundeszentrale für Politische Bildung, Bonn, Germany.

JOHNSON, MATTHEW

1996   *An Archaeology of Capitalism: Social Archaeology*. Blackwell Publishers, Malden, MA.

KELLER, CHRISTINE

1999 *Gefässkeramik aus Basel: Untersuchungen zur spätmittelalterlichen und frühneuzeitlichen Gefässkeramik aus Basel; Typologie, Technologie, Funktion, Handwerk* [*Pottery from Basel: Research on Late Medieval and Early Modern Pottery from Basel: Typology, Technology, Function, Handicraft*]. Materialhefte zur Archäologie in Basel, Vol. 15. Archäologische Bodenforschung des Kantons Basel-Stadt, Basel, Switzerland.

KERND'L, ALFRED

2002 Archäologie des 20. Jahrhunderts. Das Beispiel Berlin [Archaeology of the 20th Century: Berlin for Example]. In *Menschen, Zeiten, Räume. Archäologie in Deutschland: Archäologie in Deutschland,* Wilfried Menghin and Dieter Planck, editors, pp. 389-391. Theiss, Stuttgart, Germany.

KLUTTIG-ALTMANN, RALF

2006 *Von der Drehscheibe bis zum Scherbenhaufen: Leipziger Keramik des 14. bis 18. Jahrhunderts im Spannungsfeld von Herstellung, Gebrauch und Entsorgung* [*From the Turn Table to a Pile of Sherds: Leipzig Pottery of the 14th-18th Centuries between Production, Usage and Disposal*]. Veröffentlichungen des Landesamtes für Archäologie mit Landesmuseum für Vorgeschichte Dresden, Vol. 47. Landesamt für Archäologie Sachsen, Dresden, Germany.

KLUTTIG-ALTMANN, RALF, AND NATASCHA MEHLER

2007 Die Emanzipation der deutschen Tonpfeifenforschung. Frühe deutsche Tonpfeifenproduktion im 17. Jahrhundert [Emancipation of German Research on Tobacco Pipes]. *Mitteilungen der Deutschen Gesellschaft für Archäologie des Mittelalters und der Neuzeit* 18:71-80.

KORBEL, GÜNTHER

1983 Eine Typologie der Portweinflaschen mit Hilfe eines Dreieckdiagramms: Der methodische Aspekt [A Typology of Port Wine Bottles based on a Triangle Diagram: Methodological Aspects]. *Zeitschrift für Archäologie des Mittelalters* 11:109-114.

LANDWEHR, ACHIM

2005 Kulturwissenschaft und Geschichtswissenschaft [Cultural Studies and History]. In *Kulturwissenschaft interdisziplinär,* Klaus Stierstorfer and Laurenz Volkmann, editors, pp. 39-57. Narr, Tübingen, Germany.

LAST, MARTIN

1973 Arnegunde-Grab [The Burial of Arnegunde]. In *Reallexikon der germanischen Altertumskunde* Vol. 1, Johannes Hoops, Heinrich Beck, Herbert Jankuhn, Kurt Ranke, Reinhard Wenskus, Dieter Geuenich, and Heiko Steuer, editors, (1973), pp. 426-432. 2nd edition. de Gruyter, Berlin, Germany.

LEONE, MARK P., AND PARKER B. POTTER

1999 *Historical Archaeologies of Capitalism.* Contributions to Global Historical Archaeology. Kluwer Academic Publishers, New York, NY.

LINDENSCHMIT, LUDWIG

1866 Die deutsche Alterthumsforschung [German Antiquarian Studies]. *Archiv für Anthropologie* 1:43-60.

LINSE, ULRICH

1988 Die wiedergefundene Erinnerung. Zur Archäologie der Zeitgeschichte [Recalled Memories: Archaeology of Contemporary History]. *Geschichte in Wissenschaft und Unterricht* 53, pp. 427-430.

LONGERICH, PETER

2006 *"Davon haben wir nichts gewusst!": Die Deutschen und die Judenverfolgung 1933-1945* [*"We Didn't Know!" Germans and the Persecution and Murder of Jews 1933-1945*]. Lizenzausg. Schriftenreihe der Bundeszentrale für politische Bildung, Vol. 557. Bundeszentrale für Politische Bildung, Bonn, Germany.

LUCAS, GAVIN

2006a *An Archaeology of Colonial Identity: Power and Material Culture in the Dwars Valley, South Africa.* Contributions to Global Historical Archaeology. Kluwer Academic Publishers Group, New York, NY.

2006b Historical Archaeology and Time. In *The Cambridge Companion to Historical Archaeology,* Dan Hicks and Mary C. Beaudry, editors, pp. 34-37. Cambridge University Press, Cambridge, England.

LÜDTKE, ALF

1998 Alltagsgeschichte, Mikro-Historie, historische Anthropologie [Everyday History, Micro-History, and Historical Anthropolgy]. In *Geschichte. Ein Grundkurs,* Hans-Jürgen Goertz, editor, pp. 557-578. rororo, Reinbek, Germany.

LUTTER, CHRISTINA, MARGIT SZÖLLŐSI-JANZE, AND HEIDEMARIE UHL (EDITORS)

2004 *Kulturgeschichte: Fragestellungen, Konzepte, Annäherungen* [*Cultural History: Problems, Conceptions, Approaches*]. Querschnitte, Vol. 15. Studien Verlag, Innsbruck, Austria.

MAATSCH, JONAS, AND CHRISTOPH SCHMÄLZLE (EDITORS)

2009 *Schillers Schädel: Physiognomie einer fixen Idee* [*Schiller's Skull: Physiognomy of a Craze*]. Wallstein, Göttingen, Germany.

MAIER, RUDOLF ALBERT

1988   Nochmals zum nichtchristlichen
        Totenbrauchtum auf einem neuzeitlichen
        Bestattungsplatz bei der Stadt Erding, Landkreis
        Erding, Oberbayern [Pagan Burial Customs
        at a Modern Burial Place near Erding]. *Das
        Archäologische Jahr in Bayern* 1998:168-171.

MATTEOTTI, RENÉ

1994   *Die Alte Landvogtei in Riehen. Ein
        archäologischer Beitrag zum Alltagsgerät der
        Neuzeit [The Alte Landvogtei Complex at Riehen:
        An Archaeological Contribution on Modern
        Everyday Material Culture]*. Materialhefte zur
        Archäologie in Basel, Vol. 9. Basel, Switzerland.

MAY, D.

1993   Zur Entwicklung der Weinflasche im 19.
        Jahrhundert am Beispiel des südwestdeutschen
        Raums [The Evolution of 19th-Century Wine
        Bottles in Southwest Germany]. In *Annales
        du 12e Congrès de l'Association internationale
        pour l'histoire du Verre, Wien 1991*, pp. 529-540.
        Amsterdam, the Netherlands.

MELLER, HARALD (EDITOR)

2009   *Fundsache Luther: Archäologen auf den Spuren
        des Reformators [Luther Lost and Found:
        Archaeologists Searching for the Reformer]*.
        Theiss, Stuttgart, Germany.

MÜLLER, ULRICH

2002   Innovation und Technologietransfer im
        Handwerk. Einführende Bemerkungen
        [Innovation and Technology Transfer in
        Handicraft: Introductory Remarks]. *Mitteilungen
        der Deutschen Gesellschaft für Archäologie des
        Mittelalters und der Neuzeit* 13:11-22.

2006   *Zwischen Gebrauch und Bedeutung. Studien
        zur Funktion von Sachkultur am Beispiel
        mittelalterlichen Handwaschgeschirrs (5./6. bis
        15./16. Jahrhundert) [Between Usage and Meaning:
        Studies on the Function of Material Culture
        based on the Example of Hand Washing Dishes]*.
        Zeitschrift für Archäologie des Mittelalters,
        Beiheft, Vol. 20. Habelt, Bonn, Germany.

MÜLLER, ULRICH, JÖRN STAECKER, CLAUDIA THEUNE, AND
NATASCHA MEHLER

2009   Die Onlinezeitschrift "Historische Archäologie"
        [The Online Journal "Historical Archaeology"].
        Historische Archäologie, Editorial <http://www.
        histarch.uni-kiel.de/histarch_dt.pdf>. Accessed
        22 July 2012.

MUSNER, LUTZ, GOTTHART WUNEBERG, AND CHRISTINA
LUTTER (EDITORS)

2001   *Cultural Turn: Zur Geschichte der
        Kulturwissenschaften [The Cultural Turn: The
        History of Cultural Studies]*. Kultur.wissenschaft,
        Vol. 3. Internationales Forschungszentrum
        Kulturwissenschaften, Turia + Kant, Vienna,
        Austria.

NÜNNING, ANSGAR, AND VERA NÜNNING (EDITORS)

2008   *Einführung in die Kulturwissenschaften:
        Theoretische Grundlagen—Ansätze—
        Perspektiven [Introduction to Cultural Sciences:
        Theoretical Basis—Approaches—Perspectives]*.
        Metzler, Stuttgart, Germany.

OEXLE, OTTO GERHARD

1997   Jacques Le Goff in Germany. In *The Work of
        Jacques Le Goff and the Challenges of Medieval
        History: Proceedings of a Conference Held in 1994*,
        Marek Rubin, editor, pp. 79-84. Boydell Press,
        Woodbridge, England.

PFROMMER, JOCHEM

2009   Zwischen Identifikation und Distinktion. Die
        Interaktion von Habitus und materieller Kultur
        am Beispiel der Reformationszeit [Between
        Identification and Distinction. The Interaction of
        Habits and Material Culture in the Reformation
        Period]. In *Zwischen Tradition und Wandel.
        Archäologie des 15. und 16. Jahrhunderts*, Barbara
        Scholkmann, Sören Frommer, Christina Vossler,
        and Markus Wolf, editors, pp. 343-351. Dr.
        Faustus, Büchenbach, Germany.

RADKAU, JOACHIM

2003   Nachdenken über Umweltgeschichte
        [Reconsiderations on Environmental History].
        In *Umweltgeschichte. Themen und Perspektiven*,
        Wolfram Siemann, editor, pp. 165-186. C.H. Beck,
        Munich, Germany.

RANKE, LEOPOLD VON

1971   *Über die Epochen der neueren Geschichte
        [On the Epochs of Modern History]*. With the
        collaboration of Theodor Schieder and Helmut
        Berding. Oldenbourg, Munich, Germany.

RENFREW, COLIN (EDITOR)

1973   *The Explanation of Culture Change*. Duckworth,
        London, England.

SCHEIDEMANTEL, DIRK

2002   *Frühneuzeitliche Hohlglasfunde aus Leipzig,
        Petersstraße 28 [Early Modern Glass from
        Leipzig, Poststrasse 28]*. Veröffentlichungen
        des Landesamtes für Archäologie mit
        Landesmuseum für Vorgeschichte Dresden, Vol.
        36. Dresden, Germany.

SCHENK, WINFRIED

2000   Aufgaben der genetischen Siedlungsforschung
        in Mitteleuropa aus der Sicht der Geographie
        [The Tasks of Genetic Settlement Research in
        Central Europe in a Geographical Perspective].
        *Siedlungsforschung. Archäologie—Geschichte—
        Geographie* 18:29-50.

SCHOLKMANN, BARBARA

1993   The Archaeology of Medieval Artefacts in Central Europe. In *The Study of Medieval Archaeology. European Symposium for Teachers of Medieval Archaeology, Lund 1990*, Hans Andersson and Jes Wienberg, editors, pp. 323-331. Lund, Sweden.

1997 /
1998   Archäologie des Mittelalters und der Neuzeit heute. Eine Standortbestimmung im interdisziplinären Kontext [Archaeology of the Middle Ages and Modern Periods Today: A Review in Interdisciplinary Context]. *Zeitschrift für Archäologie des Mittelalters* 25/26:7-18.

1998   Sachen und Menschen. Der Beitrag der archäologischen Mittelalter – und Neuzeitforschung [Things and Humans. The Contribution of Historical Archaeology]. In *Die Vielfalt der Dinge. Neue Wege zur Analyse mittelalterlicher Sachkultur*, Helmut Hundsbichler, Gerhard Jaritz, and Thomas Kühtreiber, editors, pp. 63-84. Verlag der Österreichischen Akademie der Wissenschaften, Vienna, Austria

2003   Die Tyrannei der Schriftquellen? Überlegungen zum Verhältnis materieller und schriftlicher Überlieferung in der Mittelalterarchäologie [The Tyranny of the Written Record? Reconsiderations on the Relationship of Material and Written Records in Medieval Archaeology]. In *Zwischen Erklären und Verstehen? Beiträge zu den erkenntnistheoretischen Grundlagen archäologischer Interpretation*, Marlies Heinz, Manfred K. H. Eggert, and Ulrich Veit, editors, pp. 239-257. Waxmann, Münster, Germany.

SCHOLKMANN, BARBARA, SÖREN FROMMER, CHRISTINA VOSSLER, AND MARKUS WOLF (EDITORS)

2009   *Zwischen Tradition und Wandel. Archäologie des 15. und 16. Jahrhunderts [Between Tradition and Change. Archaeology of the 15th and 16th Centuries]*. Tübinger Forschungen zur historischen Archäologie, Vol. 3. Dr. Faustus, Büchenbach, Germany.

SCHOLKMANN, BARBARA, AND WERNER STRÖBELE (EDITORS)

1999   *Unter Putz und Pflasterstein: Bauforschung und Mittelalterarchäologie in Reutlingen. Zum Beispiel Pfäfflinshofstraße 4 [Underneath Plaster and Paving: Architectural and Archaeological Research in Reutlingen. Pfäfflinshofstraße 4 as Example]*. Heimatmuseum Reutlingen, Reutlingen, Germany.

SCHÖTTLER, PETER

1994   Zur Geschichte der Annales-Rezeption in Deutschland (West) [On the Reception of Annales in Germany]. In *Alles Gewordene hat Geschichte: die Schule der Annales in ihren Texten 1929-1992*, Matthias Middell, editor, pp. 40-60. Reclam, Leipzig, Germany.

SCHREG, RAINER

2007   Archäologie der frühen Neuzeit. Der Beitrag der Archäologie angesichts zunehmender Schriftquellen [Archaeology of the Early Modern Period. The Contribution of Archaeology in the Face of Increasing Written Records]. *Mitteilungen der Deutschen Gesellschaft für Archäologie des Mittelalters und der Neuzeit* 18:9-20.

2009   Nach der Wüstungsphase: Umstrukturierungen des ländlichen Raumes in der frühen Neuzeit— eine umwelthistorische Perspektive [After Desertion: Perspectives from Environmental History on the Restructuring of Rural Landscapes during Early Modern Times]. In *Zwischen Tradition und Wandel. Archäologie des 15. und 16. Jahrhunderts*, Barbara Scholkmann, Sören Frommer, Christina Vossler, and Markus Wolf, editors, pp. 451-464. Dr. Faustus, Büchenbach, Germany.

2010   Archäologie des Mittelalters und der Neuzeit: eine historische Kulturwissenschaft par excellence? [Historical Archaeology: A Cultural Science Par Excellence?]. In *Historische Kulturwissenschaften: Positionen, Praktiken und Perspektiven*, Mechthild Dreyer, Jan Kusber, Jörg Rogge, and Andreas Hütig, editors, pp. 335-366. Bielefeld, Germany.

SEGERS-GLOCKE, CHRISTIANE (EDITOR)

2000   *Auf den Spuren einer frühen Industrielandschaft. Naturraum—Mensch—Umwelt im Harz [On the Trail of an Early Industrial Landscape. Nature—Men—Environment in the Harz Mountains]*. Arbeitshefte zur Denkmalpflege in Niedersachsen, Vol. 21. Niemeyer, Hamelin, Germany.

SEIDENSPINNER, WOLFGANG

1986 /
1987   Mittelalterarchäologie und Volkskunde. Ein Beitrag zur Öffnung und Theoriebildung archäologischer Mittelalterforschung [Medieval Archaeology and Ethnic Studies. Contributions to Theory of Medieval Archaeology]. *Zeitschrift für Archäologie des Mittelalters* 14/15:9-48.

SOUTH, STANLEY

1977   *Method and Theory in Historical Archaeology*. Academic Press, New York, NY.

SPINDLER, KONRAD

2003   Mittelalter – und Neuzeitarchäologie in Forschung und Lehre an der Universität Innsbruck [The Archaeology of the Middle Ages and Modern Times at Innsbruck University]. In *Mittelalter – und Neuzeitarchäologie*, Konrad Spindler and Harald Stadler, editors, pp. 4-7. Österreichische Gesellschaft für Ur – und Frühgeschichte, Vienna, Austria.

STAECKER, JÖRN

2003 A Protestant Habitus. 16th-Century Danish
      Graveslabs as an Expression of Changes in Belief.
      In *The Archaeology of Reformation, 1480-1580*,
      David R. M. Gaimster and Roberta Gilchrist,
      editors, pp. 415-436. Maney, Leeds, England.

STEUER, HEIKO

1995 Mittelalterarchäologie und Sozialgeschichte.
      Fragestellungen, Ergebnisse und
      Zukunftsaufgaben [Medieval Archaeology
      and Social History: Problems, Results and
      Future Challenges]. In *Mittelalterarchäologie in
      Zentraleuropa. Zum Wandel der Aufgaben und
      Zielsetzungen*, Günter P. Fehring and Walter Sage,
      editors, pp. 87-104. Zeitschrift für Archäologie
      des Mittelalters, Beiheft Vol. 9. Rheinland-Verlag,
      Cologne, Germany.

1997 /
1998 Entstehung und Entwicklung der Archäologie
      des Mittelalters und der Neuzeit in Mitteleuropa
      [Origin and Development of Historical
      Archaeology in Central Europe]. *Zeitschrift für
      Archäologie des Mittelalters* 25/26:19-38.

2001 Der Weg der Mittelalterarchäologie an die
      Universitäten [Medieval Archaeology on
      the Way to University]. *Mitteilungen der
      Arbeitsgemeinschaft für Archäologie des
      Mittelalters* 12:32-42.

THEUNE, CLAUDIA

2009 Ganzheitliche Forschungen zum Mittelalter und
      zur Neuzeit [Holistic Research on Middle Ages
      and Modern Times]. In *Historia archaeologica:
      Festschrift für Heiko Steuer zum 70. Geburtstag*,
      Sebastian Brather, Dieter Geuenich, Christoph
      Huth, and Heinrich Beck, editors, pp. 755-764. de
      Gruyter, Berlin, Germany.

ULLRICH, HERBERT

2004 *Schädel-Schicksale historischer Persönlichkeiten
      [Traumatic Stories of Historical Figures]*. Pfeil,
      Munich, Germany.

VEIT, ULRICH

1995 Zwischen Geschichte und Anthropologie.
      Überlegungen zur historischen, sozialen
      und kognitiven Identität der Ur – und
      Frühgeschichtswissenschaft [Between History
      and Anthropology: Reconsiderations on the
      Historical, Social, and Cognitive Identity of
      Prehistoric Archaeology]. *Ethnographisch-
      Archäologische Zeitschrift* 36:137-143.

WALTHALL, JOHN ALLEN (EDITOR)

1991 *French Colonial Archaeology: The Illinois Country
      and the Western Great Lakes*. University of
      Illinois Press, Urbana.

WENSKUS, REINHARD

1979 Randbemerkungen zum Verhältnis von Historie
      und Archäologie, insbesondere mittelalterlicher
      Geschichte und Mittelalterarchäologie
      [Remarks on the Relationship between
      History and Archaeology, Especially Medieval
      History and Medieval Archaeology]. In
      *Geschichtswissenschaft und Archäologie:
      Untersuchungen zur Siedlungs-, Wirtschafts –
      und Kirchengeschichte*, Vol. 22, Herbert Jankuhn
      and Reinhard Wenskus, editors, pp. 637-657.
      Thorbecke, Sigmaringen, Germany.

WIEGELMANN, GÜNTER

1972 Volkskundliche Studien zum Wandel der
      Speisen und Mahlzeiten [Ethnographic
      Studies on Diet Change]. In *Der Wandel der
      Nahrungsgewohnheiten unter dem Einfluß der
      Industrialisierung*, Hans J. Teuteberg and Günter
      Wiegelmann, editors, pp. 223-368. Göttingen,
      Germany.

WIEGELMANN, GÜNTER, MATTHIAS ZENDER, AND GERHARD
HEILFURTH (EDITORS)

1977 *Volkskunde. Eine Einführung [Ethnic Studies. An
      Introduction]*. Grundlagen der Germanistik, Vol.
      12. Erich Schmidt, Berlin, Germany.

WINIWARTER, VERENA, AND MARTIN KNOLL (EDITORS)

2007 *Umweltgeschichte: Eine Einführung
      [Environmental History. An Introduction]*. UTB,
      Vol. 2521. Böhlau, Cologne, Germany.

WORSTER, DONALD

1988 Appendix: Doing Environmental History. In
      *The Ends of the Earth. Perspectives on Modern
      Environmental History*, Donald Worster, editor,
      pp. 289-307. Cambridge, England.

WOTZKA, HANS-PETER

2000 "Kultur" in der deutschsprachigen
      Urgeschichtsforschung [Conceptions of
      "Culture" in German Prehistoric Archaeology].
      In *Kultur: Ein interdisziplinäres Kolloquium zur
      Begrifflichkeit, Halle (Saale), 18. bis 21. Februar
      1999*, Siegfried Fröhlich, editor, pp. 55-80.
      Landesamt für Archäologie, Landesmuseum
      für Vorgeschichte Sachsen-Anhalt, Halle/Saale,
      Germany.

ZÖGNER, LOTHAR

1966   *Hugenottendörfer in Nordhessen* [*Huguenot Villages in Northern Hesse*]. Marburger Geographische Schriften 28. Geographisches Institut der Universität Marburg, Marburg/Lahn, Germany.

///

Rainer Schreg
Römisch-Germanisches Zentralmuseum
Forschungsinstitut für Archöologie
Ernst-Ludwig-Platz 2
D-55116 Mainz
Germany

JAROMÍR ŽEGKLITZ

Archaeology of the Modern Period in the Czech Territories: A Long Tradition and Long Beginnings

ABSTRACT

This paper deals with the development of historical archaeology in the Czech Republic. It wasn't until after World War II that interest slowly began to shift from isolated artifacts to field contexts of the modern period, even though the vast majority of these were studied as associated parts of medieval sites. A critical change came in the 1980s with the establishment of a working group for post-medieval archaeology. The excavations of early modern period contexts and more frequently of entire sites have gradually become a common part of archaeological research, even though there is still no official platform for early modern period archaeology in the Czech Republic and, unfortunately, the subject is not taught as a separate discipline at universities.

INTRODUCTION

Although the archaeology of the modern period as an independent research discipline or sub-discipline of archaeology in the Czech area does not enjoy the standing and has not developed to the level of many western democracies, the beginnings of interest in the material culture of this period can be traced back to the end of the 19th century. At that time activities in the field of post-medieval archaeology—as was the case with medieval archaeology—were mainly associated with private collectors and museums. At the time, interest in early modern period material culture was tied to a significant degree to the founding of museums, as these artifacts were far easier to obtain for collections than objects of medieval or earlier origin. Thanks to the efforts of Prague Castle architect and builder Karel Fiala (1862-1939), the foundation of the archaeological collections from excavations at Prague Castle were laid even before the establishment of Czechoslovakia (Figure 1); today these collections remain among the largest and most important assemblages of early modern finds in the Czech area. Likewise, a significant part of the archaeological collections of today's City of Prague Museum owes its existence to architect Jan Koula (1855—1919), professor at the Prague Technical University, who saved, in particular, early modern pottery during extensive earthwork projects tied mainly to the demolition of the Prague New Town walls and the expansion of the city in 1875-1885. Numerous museum collections outside of Prague share similar origins.

The predominant methodology in this early phase was naturally oriented toward art history and the applied arts. The studied artifacts were not obtained by means of proper archaeological excavations, but rather in a form of collecting that paid no attention to the relevant find context; it is hard to imagine that these early activities could have been conducted in any other way. Nevertheless, an exception in the given period were the more systematic efforts of Kliment Čermák (1852-1917), an employee of the Čáslav Museum in Eastern Bohemia, who expanded art historical research to include the study of early modern period artifacts of everyday "ordinary" life obtained by archaeological methods—even though these, naturally, were far from the standards employed today (Čermák 1896, 1897, 1906, 1914a, 1914b). The trend indicated above was also supported by the interest of several of the first Czech cultural historians, whose orientation was influenced by available written sources and the general focus on the late Middle Ages and early modern period at that time (Winter 1890-1892, 1892, 1893, 1906, 1909, 1913; Mareš 1893; Leminger 1926; Jiřík 1934a, 1934b).

The main personality who stood at the beginning of the study of early modern period archaeological material was the previously mentioned architect, Jan Koula. Although his interest in early modern pottery was almost exclusively concentrated on its value as a product of the applied arts and not primarily as an archaeological resource, many of the conclusions that he reached have retained their validity to this day and are used and

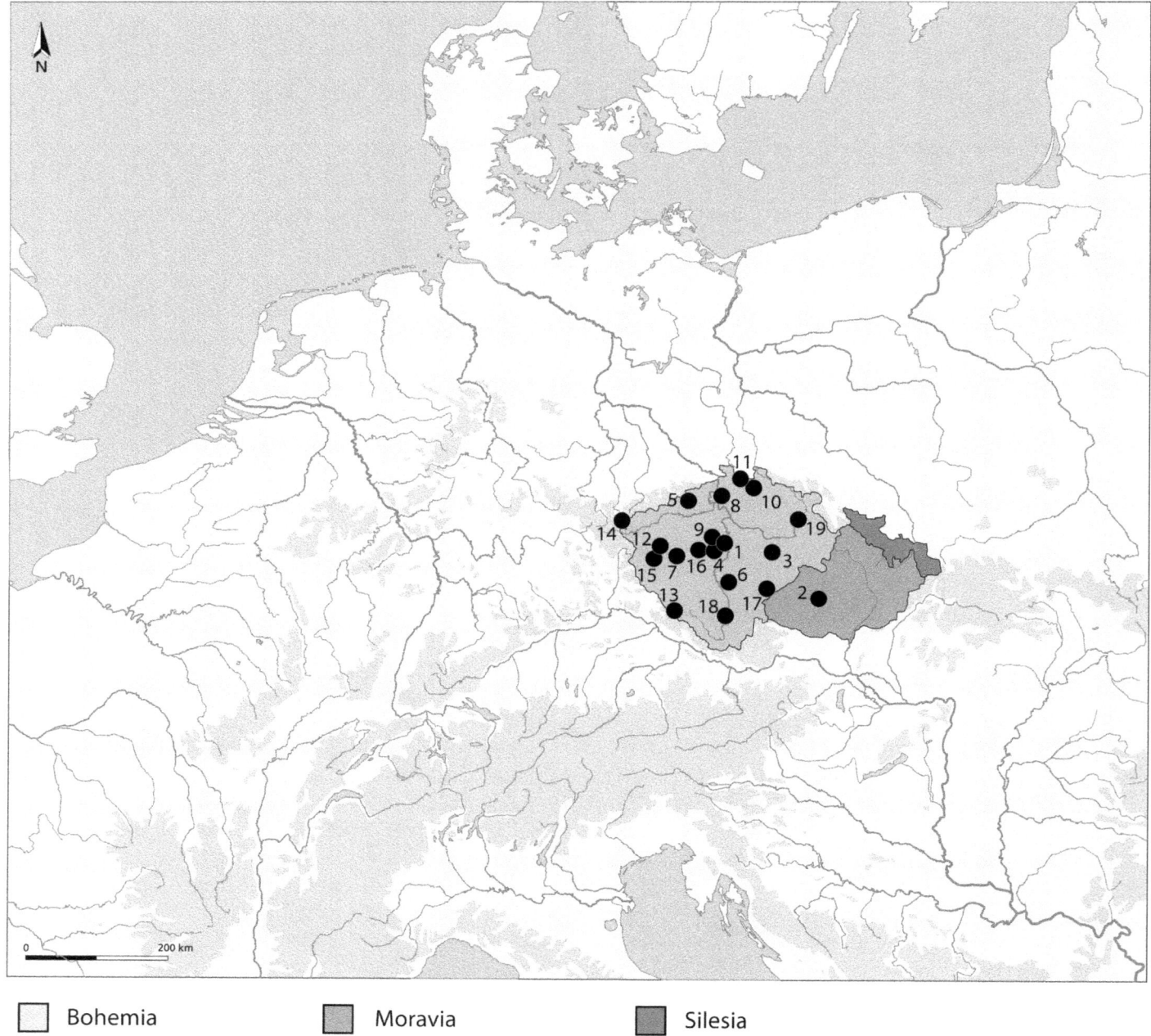

Figure 1.   *Map with places mentioned in the text (all in the Czech Republic; shaded areas are Bohemia, Moravia, and Silesia): (1) Prague; (2) Brno; (3) Čáslav; (4) Beroun; (5) Most; (6) Tábor; (7) Plzeň; (8) Levín; (9) Německá Lhota; (10) Rejdice; (11) Josefův Důl; (12) Šumava Mountains (Bohemian Forest); (13) Svahy; (14) Aš; (15) Tachov; (16) Broumy; (17) Božejov; (18) Českě Budějovice; and (19) Hradec Králové (Map provided courtesy of the Department of Prehistory and Medieval Archaeology, University of Vienna, Austria).*

cited by contemporary early modern period archae-ologists (especially the definition and dating of several production groups of early modern pottery, e.g., two groups of Beroun painted ware—red and white—then blue-etched ware, "Prague ware," and "Hostomice ware" [Koula 1888, 1917-1919, 1920]).

Interest in objects of daily use from the 16th-19th centuries, sustained mainly by art historians and experts in the applied arts, has continued in the Czech area to this day, but these objects did not attract the attention of archaeology for a long time. From the beginning archaeology had a difficult time establishing its legitimacy amongst professional historians (Novotný 1912:29), and when it finally did gain respect (Skalský 1938; Richter and Smetánka 1975), the discipline of archaeology itself remained skeptical toward its own younger branches—toward medieval archaeology for a long time and, until only recently, toward early modern archaeology. This situation was even expressed in the wording of the law: Government Regulation No. 274 from 12 June 1941 concerning archaeology as part of the system for the care of monuments defined archaeological finds as "objects made by human hands or products of nature used by man that come from the *prehistoric and early historical period*" (emphasis added). Inside the archaeological community itself the attitude toward the study of the later historical periods was reflected in the introduction to the first issue of the direct predecessor of one of today's two main Czech archaeological periodicals, the journal *Archeologické rozhledy*. The so-called *Information Service*, a periodical published by the State Institute of Archaeology, stated in its first issue of October 1946: "...in this periodical [the State Institute of Archaeology] intends to report on its own activities and those of its colleagues, on the needs for the protection of prehistoric monuments and on the main events in the field of studying prehistory and the early historical period" (Matoušek 1997:581).

An indication of a change in this attitude, albeit only on the theoretical level, appeared in 1953 in a lecture entitled "On the Tasks of Historical Archaeology" delivered to a session at the Institute of Archaeology of the Academy of Sciences of Czechoslovakia. This became an important step on the road to establishing the field of medieval archaeology in then Czechoslovakia. The author of the lecture—art historian, archaeologist, and later the director of the National Museum, Vladimír Denkstein—defined the upper time limit of "historical archaeology" (i.e., medieval archaeology) as the present day:

> The upper border is theoretically clear: as with history in general it is today, which with every passing second becomes history. Even the freshest history can be work for archaeology. But this isn't only about research methods...Even though it is not my intention to dwell on this complicated question here, I use it to illustrate that the interest of historical archaeology in monuments of modern or even the latest history is not a matter of mere theoretical principles [Denkstein 1953:220-221] [translation by David J. Gaul].

Nevertheless, a more positive attitude toward archaeological sources from the modern period gained recognition only very slowly. An important impulse in this direction was the reconstruction (and related excavation) of many buildings and sites in the historical center of Prague and the surrounding area, and especially on the grounds of Prague Castle in connection with its reconstruction to serve as the seat of the president of the newly established state. Here the previous "collecting" activities of architect Karel Fiala were followed up as early as 1925 with systematic archaeological excavations that continue to this day, albeit at reduced intensity. From the very beginning these excavations have produced extraordinarily valuable assemblages of early modern period artifacts, especially from the numerous cesspits or graves of abbesses at St. George's Convent. Unfortunately, only a small fraction of this finds inventory, one of the most important in the Czech Republic, has been published to date (Hetteš 1963; Borkovský 1975); the more systematic processing of these finds in recent years is a positive development (Blažková-Dubská 2005a, 2005b, 2005c, 2007, 2009).

In addition to Prague Castle, though on a much smaller scale, were the archaeological excavations of early modern situations in the historical center of Prague and in the surrounding areas, mostly connected with extensive building projects launched in the 1970s (Huml 1971, 1975, 1978, 1979, 1983; Hanáková et al. 1975; Havel 1980; Charvátová and Charvát 1981; Brzobohatý and Špaček 1983; Richterová 1985, 1986). These were preceded by many smaller excavations in earlier years (Frauenterka 1958; Liška 1958; Janská 1966; Mašek 1966). In this regard, development in the Czech territories was similar to the situation in western Europe, where a boom in the interest in material sources from the modern period also occurred as a result of the growth in the numbers of field excavations connected with reconstruction and redevelopment of historical cities damaged during World War II.

Noteworthy archaeological excavations outside the capital city include those in Beroun, which was one of the most prominent Czech early modern period pottery production centers (Matoušek and Scheufler 1980, 1983; Matoušek, Scheufler et al. 1985); in the north Bohemian city of Most, a medieval town relocated and destroyed as a result of the open cast mining of brown coal (Klápště et al. 1976; Velímský 1976); in Tábor (Drda 1978, 1980); Plzeň (Frýda 1979); Levín (Budinská 1976; Landsfeld 1978); or at the site of the deserted village of Německá Lhota in the Kamenné Žehrovice district (Richterová 1981, 1982).

An exception in this period were the archaeological excavations of glassworks in the Jizerské mountains, the Renaissance glassworks in Rejdice (Hejdová 1981), and baroque glassworks in the Josefův Důl municipal area (Kavan 1982). Only the non-destructive surface surveys of modern period glassworks in the territory of Šumava (Bohemian Forest) proceeded at a more intensive pace (Fröhlich 1989, 1993).

Apart from the increasing amount of field activity naturally brought about in the majority of cases by the need for excavations at imminently threatened sites, and therefore unrelated to any planned and systematic research of modern period sites and situations, the interest of archaeologists in early modern artifacts themselves was also awakened in this period. The greatest attention was logically devoted to pottery as a ubiquitous and chronologically sensitive component of archaeological assemblages, and aimed to establish the then uncertain typological and chronological development sequence of early modern pottery. The beginnings of these efforts can already be registered in the earliest synthesis devoted to Bohemian and Moravian medieval pottery (Nekuda and Reichertová 1968). Dated to this same year is B. Nechvátal's (1968) dissertation on pottery production and the pottery of the 16th century in Bohemia. Published in practically the same period and remaining inspirational to this day are the analytical texts by Z. Smetánka on medieval and early modern period Bohemian stove-tiles (Smetánka 1968, 1969).

At the same time, archaeological artifacts—and more recently, in some cases, even archaeological methods—remained a subject of interest for related historical disciplines. These trends are particularly apparent in the works of ethnographer V. Scheufler on folk pottery (Scheufler 1972, 1979), as well as in art-history works on medieval and early modern period glass (Braunová 1979; Drahotová 1985).

The beginnings of interest in Moravia in the early modern period are connected with the amateur study of Anabaptist sites conducted as early as the 1930s by ceramist Heřman Landsfeld (1950, 1953, 1956, 1971a, 1971b, 1976) and with the research efforts of ethnographer and archaeologist Karel Černohorský (1931, 1941). These were continued in a modern vein at the end of the 1970s by Jiří Pajer, who was the first in the country to begin the systematic study of the early modern period; he expanded the specifically Moravian subject of Anabaptist faience to include the study of ordinary utilitarian earthenware based on modern archaeological research methods (Pajer 1982, 1983). As was the case in Bohemia, early modern period sites in Moravia and Silesia at this time were mainly studied as part of the extensive excavations of the medieval centers of towns (Měřínský 1979); excavations of purely early modern period sites or the processing and publication of early modern contexts were also rather rare and unsystematic in Moravia up until the end of the 1980s (Fialová 1957; Novotný 1959; Michna 1977; Bláha 1983; Šebela and Vaněk 1985).

It is clear from the cited literature that the initial phase focused nearly exclusively on artifacts of the "applied arts." The attention of archaeologists began in the 1950s to turn slowly toward modern period field situations and to the material culture of everyday life in the late medieval and early modern periods. Excavations of sites dated exclusively to the modern period were, however, rare; in the majority of cases modern situations were studied mainly in urban environments as unavoidable parts of sites where the medieval period was the primary interest of researchers.

This shift on the theoretical level and in fieldwork was also reflected in the new law "On State Care of Monuments" from 1987. Section 23, Paragraph 1 characterized an archaeological find as "an object (or assemblage of objects) that is evidence or a remnant of human life and human activities *from the start of human existence up to the modern period* and has typically been preserved under the ground" (emphasis added; translation by David J. Gaul).

The necessity of solving the problem of processing the ever growing amount of modern material and the need for exchanging experiences in the excavation of modern sites naturally led to the establishment of a working group five years earlier, in 1982, for post-medieval archaeology. This group was initially affiliated with the working group for medieval archaeology operating at the Czechoslovak Archaeological Society of the Czechoslovak Academy of Sciences, but the working group for post-medieval archaeology became an independent entity in 1987. The fact that the vast majority of individuals involved in the activities of this group were medieval archaeologists for whom the modern period was a side interest to their main focus limited the group's activities at the beginning to irregular meetings to swap experiences and new information. Lacking a specialized periodical, the results of excavations, often part of the analysis of sites with continual development from medieval times to the modern period, were mainly published in journals and anthologies primarily focused on medieval archaeology (Hazlbauer and Špaček 1986; Kundera and Měřínský 1987; Žegklitz 1987, 1988; Boháčová, Frolík, Tomková et al. 1988; Frolík and Žegklitz 1988; Frolík, Žegklitz et al. 1988; Fröhlich and Scheufler 1988a, 1988b; Hazlbauer 1988; Kubů and Zavřel 1988; Boháčová, Frolík, Žegklitz 1989; Hejdová and Drahotová 1989; Huml 1989; Reichertová 1989; Boháčová, Frolík, Petříčková et. al 1990; Brych et al. 1990; Frolík, Klápště, Smetánka et al. 1992).

The most significant accomplishment of the group was the seminar organized by Beroun District Museum in 1986 entitled "The tasks of the archaeological study of modern history in Bohemia," which was focused exclusively on modern period archaeology and open to all individuals interested in the subject. Several of the papers presented at the seminar later served as the foundation of the anthology *Studies in Postmediaeval Archaeology 1* prepared during the last years of communist régime and published by the Institute of Archaeology of the Czechoslovak Academy of Sciences in 1990 (Smetánka and Žegklitz 1990b). In the introductory text of this anthology the editors presented the first outline of the development of research in the field of modern period archaeology in Bohemia and Moravia and attempted to define the content, chronological framework, problems, and prospects of this new discipline in the given territory (Smetánka and Žegklitz 1990a:7-21); this text was followed up by Žegklitz and Smetánka (1989). The considerable content and qualitative variety of the entire anthology is a faithful reflection of the status of modern period archaeology in Bohemia and Moravia at the time.

In 1979 the Technical Museum at Brno had established a tradition of regular seminars in Brno entitled "Studying Production Sites and Technologies using Archaeological Methods." In the first volume of an anthology of the same title the editor attempted to define the term "industrial archaeology." He rejected the minority opinion that found the mission of industrial archaeology to be the study of all industries from the beginning of human development and instead leaned toward the generally accepted chronological definition that saw the aim of this discipline as studying the beginnings of modern industry arising from the Industrial Revolution (Merta 1980). Although these seminars continue and the anthology—since 1992 under the title *Archeologia technica*—is still being published, the words of the editor from the first volume remain valid in the Czech environment: "There are no preconditions in establishing industrial archaeology as an independent field of study" (Merta 1980:7). Thus, despite the aforementioned "program text" from the first volume, the anthology publishes articles on production sites and technologies not only from the modern period, but also from medieval and prehistoric times.

The willingness of the Institute of Archaeology in Prague to become the sponsor of the newly emerging branch of archaeological research was manifested not only in the publication of the first anthology devoted exclusively to the modern period (Smetánka and Žegklitz 1990b), but also in its patronage of the archaeological excavations of the field fortifications from the Thirty Years' War in the municipal district of Svahy in western Bohemia, the first phase of which was conducted in 1988-89 (Matoušek 2006). These excavations, a continuation of the previous broadly conceived excavations of the field fortifications from the Seven Years' War in Nebesa outside the town of Aš (Matoušek, Hájek et al. 1990; Hájek et al. 1992), were to be part of an extensive project focused on modern period military camps and fortifications and were also—beside the nascent study of the beginnings of early modern pottery—apparently the only project for which at least limited personnel and material resources existed in the second half of the 1980s.

Sweeping social changes came about at the end of 1989. The fall of the criminal communist régime and opening of the country to democracy also had an effect on the field of archaeological research. On the one hand, the unstable anchoring of the archaeology of the modern period in existing institutions became evident (e.g., the absence of specialized workplaces or at least a more solid network of specialized professionals due to, among other things, the absence of instruction in this field at universities). On the other hand, the social changes led to more considerable competition in the sciences. Together with the unprecedented and practically continuous growth of building activities, these social changes have also shown themselves in the rapid growth not only of archaeologically examined, but also published, modern period sites and situations. Hopefully, the times when early modern layers were overlooked for various reasons or even frankly removed in an effort to reach medieval horizons as quickly as possible are irretrievably over. Instead, the past twenty years have shown a growth in the number of excavations of exclusively early modern sites.

It would be unnecessary to list here all the individual cases, especially when we can refer to a well-arranged overview with abundant literature published recently in English, that is, in a language accessible to readers of this book (Krajíc 2007). It is worth explicitly mentioning the long-term comprehensive excavation of a battlefield at Tachov in West Bohemia, dating from the Thirty Year's War, the results of which (including a skillful illustration of landscape transformation of the given site from the perspective of a range of historical and natural sciences) were recently published in an extensive monograph (Matoušek 2006). At the same time, a range of other sites of a similar type was being researched from the early 1990s onwards; results of these excavations were analyzed in many separate studies (Grabolle et al. 2009).

In comparison to the previous period, research of early modern villages following from the tradition of excavations of deserted medieval settlements developed substantially in the 1990s, taking place on two levels. Deserted early modern villages, or their individual parts, are identified and archaeologically examined (by non-destructive methods) as part of studies in settlement history and in the transformation of historical landscapes (Fröhlich 1990; Vařeka et al. 2008). At the same time, excavations take place in existing villages (Škabrada 1992; Nováček and Vařeka 1996, 1997; Dohnal and Vařeka 1997; Dohnal et al. 2001; Meduna et al. 2001).

Substantial attention has been paid to modern period burials since the end of the 1990s. Compared to previous decades, when modern burials were mostly examined only as part of medieval burial sites and the results thereof were published merely on a sporadic basis or in brief (Janská 1966; Hrdlička and Richter 1974; Hanáková et al. 1975; Havel 1980; Hanáková and Stloukal 1988; Beranová 1989), the number of examined sites of this type rose substantially in the last decade. The processing of results improved in terms of quality (Kostka and Šmolíková 1998; Loskotová 1999; Omelka 2003; Blažková-Dubská 2005a; Kovárník et al. 2006), and more attention was paid to questions of a more general nature regarding early modern period burials and funeral rites (Unger 2000, 2002; Blažková-Dubská 2005b; Tomková 2005).

The excavations of early modern contexts as part of the long-term archaeological excavation of the most important landmark of the Czech Republic, Prague Castle (the results of which have been published from 1988 in the *Castrum Pragense* anthology, and other publications), also retain their tradition of improving the level of processing of find assemblages.

In terms of individual types of archaeological artifacts, it is worth mentioning a growth in the study of modern glass and glassmaking activities. In the Šumava (Bohemian Forest) region analysis, for the most part field surveys, of modern period glassworks continued in the 1990s (Fröhlich 1994a, 1994b, 1995a, 1995b). Also, archaeological rescue excavations took place at the sites of the Rudolphine Renaissance glassworks at Broumy (Žegklitz 2007a) and baroque glassworks at Nová Ves near Božejov (Hrubý et al. 2009). The rapidly accumulating number of finds of early modern glass coming from many archaeologically examined sites led, within the frame of a professional group on glass history of the Czech Archaeological Society, to the establishment of a working group aimed at the study of Renaissance glass. The result of their work is the first comprehensive overview of Renaissance glass from archaeological excavations in the Czech Republic (Krajíc et al. 2005). The aforesaid synthesis was naturally preceded by a range of separate studies that, compared to the preceding period during which medieval glass and museum exhibits were more the focus, tended—from the mid 1990s—to concentrate on Renaissance glass that was obtained using archaeological methods (Drobný and Sedláčková 1997; Teryngerová 1997; Sedláčková 1997, 1998, 2000, 2001, 2003; Drahotová and Žegklitzová-Veselá 2003; Krajíc 2003; Podliska 2003; Jordánková and Sedláčková 2004).

Finally, significant progress can also be seen in the field of early modern ceramic studies, primarily of stove-tiles. During the course of the past decade, a strong trend has become evident that, in publishing find assemblages or museum collections, looks beyond the limits of medieval material toward later periods (Brych 2004; Pavlík and Vitanovský 2004; Krasnokutská 2005; Orna 2005; Menoušková and Měřínský 2008). The range of separate studies on this topic exceeds the prevailing narrow focus on typology or iconography and attempts to lay emphasis on and seek answers to more general cultural-historical issues (Žegklitz 2006, 2011, 2012a; Jordánková and Loskotová 2007; Holub et al. 2009; Žegklitz et al. 2009).

The absence of a deeper tradition of modern archaeological examination of the modern period is, however, still perceptible. The shift that took place in the past 20 years means, for the most part, only growth of a quantitative nature. The non-existent organizational base, or at least the absence of a network of specialized workplaces or workplaces with professionals focusing on modern period archaeology, does not permit even regular exchange of know-how, and even less so the staking out of potential thematic circles for further research and formulation of more general strategic principles and aims for such research. As in the previous period, even today the majority of archaeologists examining sites with early modern contexts and publishing the results of such excavations specialize in the archaeology of the Middle Ages, and topics lapping over into later periods are seen by many of them merely as a supplement to their primary interests, despite them often being a natural and necessary part thereof. The majority of archaeologists has been fully occupied for a number of years with rescue work, that is, excavations brought on by construction activities, which very often involve modern contexts. Both human resources and material capacity are still lacking and therefore stand in the way of focused and thematic excavations. This gap has unfortunately not been filled even by that workplace, which on the basis of its standing in the Czech archaeological system and its own self-view (Jiráň 1999:239-240) should be leading such activities—that is, the Institute of Archaeology of the Academy of Sciences of the Czech Republic.

The causes of this state of affairs are, however, deeper and their roots can be found in the way archaeology is taught at universities. Of seven universities offering archaeology as an independent field of study (Prague, Plzeň, České Budějovice, Hradec Králové, Brno, Olomouc, and Opava), only two declare an intention—alongside the general subjects of prehistoric and medieval archaeology—to study also the archaeology of the modern period (České Budějovice and Plzeň). Nevertheless, the state of affairs in terms of studying

programs, lectures, and topics of bachelor or dissertation studies can hardly be recognized as satisfactory.

Over and above all the problems mentioned facing Czech modern period archaeology, some success was recently achieved with the idea of having gatherings of parties interested in this young field of archaeology. Twenty years after the first seminar in Beroun, the first conference, entitled "Forum Archaeologiae Post-Mediaevalis: Material Culture from the End of the 15th Century and its Reflection in Archaeological, Written and Iconographic Sources," took place in Prague in 2006 upon the initiative of the non-profit organization Archaia Praha o.p.s. A year later, 19 papers presented there were included in the second volume of the *Studies in Post-Medieval Archaeology* anthology (Žegklitz 2007b). Since then, two further conferences have taken place ("Post-Medieval Ceramics. Production, Assortment, Usage" in 2008 and "Written and Iconographic Sources in Post-Medieval Archaeology" in 2010). An anthology of the former was published in 2009 (Žegklitz 2009) and an anthology of the latter in 2012 (Žegklitz 2012b). It is clear from the content in the volumes published to date that precedence in Czech modern archaeology is given to the history of material culture of the 16th to 17th centuries, and less frequently to later periods. This direction in research, apparently to a large extent due to the traditional orientation of Czech archaeology toward the German archaeological environment in general, seems to offer the best rewards (on the one hand due to current state of research and personal capacities and on the other due to continuously more intensive collaboration with other fields in humanities and natural sciences) and in terms of methodology could also make a significant contribution to researchers studying earlier periods. We can but hope that in the near future Czech archaeology of the modern period will devote more effort to the resolution of theoretical issues, as has been the case recently with our neighboring and traditionally closer environment, Germany, under the influence of the Anglo-Saxon countries.

REFERENCES

BERANOVÁ, MAGDALENA
1989   Kovové vínky pražských dívek ze 17. a první poloviny 18. století. Příspěvek k lidovému šperkařství [Metal Wreaths of Prague Girls from the 17th and the First Half of the 18th Centuries. A Contribution to Folk Jewelry-Making]. *Archaeologica Pragensia* 10:269-280.

BLÁHA, JOSEF
1983   K vypovídacím možnostem olomouckého archeologického materiálu 15. až 17. století [The Informative Possibilities of Archaeological Finds from Olomouc]. *Historická Olomouc a její současné problémy* IV:307-315.

BLAŽKOVÁ-DUBSKÁ, GABRIELA

2005a   Archeologický výzkum novověkého pohřebiště u Jízdárny [The Archaeological Excavation of the Modern Period Cemetery near the Riding School]. *Castrum Pragense* 7:403-410.

2005b   Několik poznámek k archeologickému studiu novověkého pohřbívání v Čechách (Úvod ke studiu novověkých pohřebišť na Pražském hradě) [Some Comments on the Archaeological Study of Modern Period Burials in Bohemia (An Introduction to the Study of Modern Period Cemeteries at Prague Castle)]. *Castrum Pragense* 7:201-216.

2005c   Výzkum v prostoru Prašného mostu na Pražském hradě v roce 2001 [The Archaeological Excavation in the Area of Powder Bridge at Prague Castle]. *Castrum Pragense* 6:125-144.

2007   House of the Armoury Scribe at Prague Castle. *Studies in Post-Medieval Archaeology* 2:9-42.

2009   Finds of Early Modern Period Ceramics from Cesspit B at Prague Castle. *Studies in Post-Medieval Archaeology* 3:21-44.

BOHÁČOVÁ, IVANA, JAN FROLÍK, JITKA PETŘÍČKOVÁ, AND JAROMÍR ŽEGKLITZ

1990   Příspěvek k poznání života a životního prostředí na Pražském hradě a Hradčanech [A Contribution to our Knowledge of Life and the Environment at Prague Castle and in Hradčany]. *Archaeologia historica* 15:177-189.

BOHÁČOVÁ, IVANA, JAN FROLÍK, KATEŘINA TOMKOVÁ, AND JAROMÍR ŽEGKLITZ

1988   Předběžné výsledky výzkumu Pražského hradu v letech 1980-1987 [First Results from Research at Prague Castle 1980-1987]. *Archaeologia historica* 13:173-198.

BOHÁČOVÁ, IVANA, JAN FROLÍK, AND JAROMÍR ŽEGKLITZ

1989   Jiřské náměstí na Pražském hradě. Shrnutí výsledků 1. etapy výzkumu [St. George's Square at Prague Castle. Results of the First Study Phase]. *Archaeologia historica* 14:193-202.

BORKOVSKÝ, IVAN

1975   *Svatojiřská bazilika a klášter na Pražském hradě [St. George's Church and Convent at Prague Castle, Prague]*. Academia, Prague, Czech Republic.

BRAUNOVÁ, DAGMAR

1979   *Renesanční a barokní emailované sklo [Renaissance and Baroque Enameled Glass]*. Západočeské muzeum v Plzni, Plzeň, Czech Republic.

BRYCH, VLADIMÍR

2004   *Kachle doby gotické, renesanční a raně barokní [Stove-Tiles of Gothic, Renaissance and Early-Baroque Period]*. Výběrový katalog Národního muzea v Praze. National Museum, Prague, Czech Republic.

BRYCH, VLADIMÍR, DANA STEHLÍKOVÁ, AND JAROMÍR ŽEGKLITZ

1990   *Pražské kachle doby gotické a renesanční [Prague Stove-Tiles from the Gothic and Renaissance Period]*. Katalog výstavy. Pražský ústav státní památkové péče a ochrany přírody, Praque, Czech Republic.

BRZOBOHATÝ, VILIAM, AND LADISLAV ŠPAČEK

1983   Nález pozůstatků první pražské továrny na kameninu [Unearthed Remains of a Prague Creamware Factory]. *Staletá Praha* 13:219-223, 258-259.

BUDINSKÁ, JITKA

1976   *Příspěvek k dějinám hrnčířství v Levíně [A Contribution to the History of Pottery in Levín]*. Monografické studie Krajského muzea v Teplicích, sv. 10. Krajské vlastivědné muzeum, Teplice, Czech Republic.

ČERMÁK, KLIMENT

1896   Hrnčíři v Čáslavi a jejich památky [Potters in Čáslav and their Heritage]. *Památky archeologické* 17:214-223.

1897   *Hrnčířská dílna v Čáslavi [Pottery Workshop in Čáslav]*. Věstník československých museí a spolků archeologických II. Kliment Čermák, Čáslav, Czech Republic.

1906   Hrnčířské dílny v Čáslavi v době renaissanční [Pottery Workshops in Čáslav in the Renaissance Period]. *Památky archeologické* 21:567-572.

1914a   Hrnčířské památky z Čáslavska [Potter's Monuments from Čáslav]. *Jubilejní Musejník čáslavský* II:37-47.

1914b   Památky hrnčířů ledečských [Monuments of Potters from Ledeč]. *Jubilejní Musejník čáslavský* II:53-55.

ČERNOHORSKÝ, KAREL

1931   *Počátky habánských fajansí [The Beginnings of Anabaptist Faiences]*. Opava, Czech Republic.

1941   *Moravská lidová keramika [Moravian Folk Pottery]*. Nakladatelství J. Otto, s. r. o., Prague, Czech Republic.

CHARVÁTOVÁ, KATEŘINA, AND PETR CHARVÁT

1981   Keramika 16. století z Prahy—Karlova [The Sixteenth-Century Pottery from Prague—Karlov]. *Praehistorica* VIII:333-336.

DENKSTEIN, VLADIMÍR

1953   O úkolech historické archeologie [On the Tasks of Historical Archaeology]. *Časopis Národního muzea, oddíl věd společenských* CXXII:219-223.

DOHNAL, MARTIN, RASTISLAV KORENÝ, KAREL KOUCKÝ, LUBOMÍR PROCHÁZKA, AND JAN ŠAMATA

2001   Obděnice, čp. 4 (okr. Příbram). Dějiny usedlosti ve světle etnografických, archeologických, písemných a paleozoologických pramenů [No. 4, Obděnice (Příbram District). The History of a Homestead in Light of Ethnographic, Archaeological, Written, and Palaeozoological Sources]. *Archeologie ve středních Čechách* 5:721-738

DOHNAL, MARTIN, AND PAVEL VAŘEKA

1997   Výzkum novověké vesnické usedlosti v Srlíně (okr. Písek)—svědectví archeologických a písemných pramenů [Research of the Post-Medieval Homestead in Srlín (Písek District)—Archaeological and Documentary Evidence]. *Archeologické výzkumy v jižních Čechách* 10:84-106.

DRAHOTOVÁ, OLGA

1985   *Evropské sklo* [*European Glass*]. Artia, Prague, Czech Republic.

DRAHOTOVÁ, OLGA, AND JANA ŽEGKLITZOVÁ-VESELÁ

2003   Die Typen der Renaissancekelchgläser (Weingläser) in venezianischer Art aus böhmischen und mährischen Fundorten [Typology of Renaissance Goblets (Wine Glasses) from Bohemian and Moravian Find Spots]. *Beiträge zur Mittelalterarchäologie in Österreich* 19:119-126.

DRDA, MILOŠ

1978   *Archeologický výzkum Tábora 1974-1977* [*The Archaeological Excavations of the Town of Tábor in 1974-1977*]. Městský národní výbor, Tábor, Czech Republic.

1980   Archeologický výzkum Tábora [The Archaeological Excavations of the Town of Tábor]. *Archeologia historica* 5:107-113.

DROBNÝ, TOMÁŠ, AND HEDVIKA SEDLÁČKOVÁ

1997   Kachle a sklo z odpadní jímky ze 16. století v Olomouci [Stove-Tiles and Glass from a 16th-Century Rubbish Pit in Olomouc]. *Muzejní a vlastivědná práce* 35/3:129-140.

FIALOVÁ, V.

1957   Historicko-archeologický výzkum tvrze a kostela v Kralicích nad Oslavou v r. 1956 [The Archaeological and Historical Investigation of the Stronghold and Church in Kralice nad Oslavou in 1956]. *Časopis Moravského muzea—vědy společenské* XLII:67-84.

FRAUENTERKA, MIROSLAV

1958   Nález keramických forem na Malé Straně [Discovery of Ceramic Molds in the Lesser Town of Prague]. *Pražskou minulostí* II:88-97.

FRÖHLICH, JIŘÍ

1989   *Sklárny střední Šumavy. Výsledky archeologického průzkumu* [*Glassworks in the Central Part of the Bohemian Forest. Results of the Archaeological Excavations*]. Muzeum Šumavy, Sušice, Czech Republic.

1990   Vesnice zaniklé roku 1579 v oboře u Kratochvíle [Villages Deserted in 1579 in the Game Park at Kratochvíle]. *Archeologické výzkumy v jižních Čechách* 7:151-160.

1993   Archeologický výzkum šumavských skláren [Archaeological Research of the Glassworks of the Bohemian Forest]. *Archeologia technica* 8:75-83.

1994a   Renesanční sklárny na Vilémově hoře. Archeologický příspěvek k historii rožmberské a buquoyské sklárny [Renaissance Glassworks at Vilémova hora. Archaeological Contribution to the History of Rosenberg and Buquoy Glassworks]. *Jihočeský sborník historický* LXIII:3-14.

1994b   Die Glashütten des östlichen Böhmerwaldes [The Glassworks of the Eastern Part of the Bohemian Forest]. *Passauer Jahrbuch für Geschichte, Kunst und Volkskunde* 36:89-94.

1995a   Sklárny na statku Železná Ruda a v rychtách Hojsova Stráž a Hamry (výsledky archeologického průzkumu) [Glassworks at the Estate of Železná Ruda and in the Magistrate's Houses in Hojsova Stráž and Hamry (Results of Archaeological Excavations)]. *Muzejní a vlastivědná práce* 33/*Časopis společnosti přátel starožitností* 103:217-226.

1995b   Archeologický výzkum skláren v okolí Kašperských Hor [Archaeological Research at Glassworks—Sites in the Bergreichenstein Area]. *Vlastivědné zprávy Muzea Šumavy* 3:94-118.

FRÖHLICH, JIŘÍ, AND VLADIMÍR SCHEUFLER

1988a   Keramický nález z rozhraní 18. a 19. století v Písku [A Pottery Find from the Turn of the 19th Century in Písek]. *Z jihočeského národopisu* II:69-80.

1988b   Keramický nález z 2. poloviny 19. století v Písku [A Pottery Find from the Second Half of the 19th Century in Písek]. *Z jihočeského národopisu* II:81-89.

FROLÍK, JAN, JAN KLÁPŠTĚ, ZDENĚK SMETÁNKA, AND JAROMÍR ŽEGKLITZ

1992   L'archéologie et la culture spirituelle du Moyen âge. Quatre miniatures [Archaeology and Spiritual Culture of the Middle Ages. Four Miniatures]. *Památky archeologické* LXXXIII:149-173.

FROLÍK, JAN, AND JAROMÍR ŽEGKLITZ

1988   Předběžné výsledky archeologického výzkumu v areálu bývalého špitálu na Hradčanech [Preliminary Results of the Archaeological Excavations in the Area of the Former Hospital at Hradčany]. *Časopis lékařů českých* 127(4):120-123.

FROLÍK, JAN, JAROMÍR ŽEGKLITZ, AND IVANA BOHÁČOVÁ

1988   Kanovnická ulice (Canons' Street) No. 73. *Castrum Pragense* 1:43-56.

FRÝDA, FRANTIŠEK

1979   Archeologický výzkum v městě Plzni [Archaeological Research in the Town of Pilsen]. *Archaeologia historica* 4:319-322.

GRABOLLE, ROMAN, VÁCLAV MATOUŠEK, PETR MEDUNA, AND ZDENĚK SMRŽ

2009   Die Schlacht bei Třebel/Triebl im Jahr 1647 und weitere Untersuchungen zur Archäologie des Krieges in der Tschechischen Republik [The Battle at Třebel/Triebl in 1647 and Further Research into the Archaeology of War in the Czech Republic]. *Tagungen des Landesmuseums für Vorgeschichte Halle* 2:173-186.

HÁJEK, JAN, FRANTIŠEK KUBŮ, AND VÁCLAV MATOUŠEK

1992   *Srážka u Nebes. Sborník příspěvků z komplexního výzkumu vojenské epizody ze sedmileté války* [*Encounter at Nebesa. A Set of Contributions from the Comprehensive Research of a Military Episode from the Seven Years' War*]. Chebské muzeum, Cheb, Czech Republic.

HANÁKOVÁ, HANA, VLADIMÍR MARTINEC, AND LUBOŠ VYHNÁNEK

1975   Barokní pohřby od kostela sv. Jindřicha na Novém Městě pražském [Baroque-Period Burials from St. Henry's Church in the Prague New Town]. *Sborník Národního muzea* XXXI, řada B, č. 1-2:91-107.

HANÁKOVÁ, HANA, AND MILAN STLOUKAL

1988   *Pohřebiště kolem bývalého kostela svatého Benedikta v Praze* [*Burial Site at the Former Church of St. Benedict in Prague*]. Národní muzeum v Praze—Přírodovědecké museum, Prague, Czech Republic.

HAVEL, JOSEF

1980   Hromadný hrob bělohorských bojovníků [A Mass Grave of Soldiers from the White Mountain]. *Archaeologica Pragensia* 1:227-232.

HAZLBAUER, ZDENĚK

1988   Gotické a renesanční kachle z hradu Točníku [Gothic and Renaissance Stove-Tiles from Točník Castle]. *Zprávy Československé společnosti archeologické* 33.

HAZLBAUER, ZDENĚK, AND JAROSLAV ŠPAČEK

1986   Poznámky k výrobě reliéfních renesančních kachlů s přihlédnutím k nálezům ve středním Polabí [Remarks on the Production of Renaissance Stove-Tiles Based on Finds from the Central Elbe Valley]. *Časopis Národního muzea— řada historická* 155:146-166.

HEJDOVÁ, DAGMAR

1981   The Glasshouse at Rejdice in Northeastern Bohemia. Late Sixteenth-Early Seventeenth Centuries. *Journal of Glass Studies* 23:18-33.

HEJDOVÁ, DAGMAR, AND OLGA DRAHOTOVÁ

1989   *České sklo I. Sklo období středověku a renesance, 13.-1. polovina 17. století* [*Medieval Glass. 13th-15th Centuries. Renaissance Glass. 16th Century-First Half of the 17th Century*]. Uměleckoprůmyslové muzeum, Prague, Czech Republic.

HETTEŠ, KAREL

1963   Venetian Trends in Bohemian Glassmaking in the Sixteenth and Seventeenth Centuries. *Journal of Glass Studies* 5:39-53.

HOLUB, PETR, HANA JORDÁNKOVÁ, AND IRENA LOSKOTOVÁ

2009   Early Modern Period Brno Stove Tiles with a Mosaic (Tapestry) Pattern. *Studies in Post-Medieval Archaeology* 3:273-288.

HRDLIČKA, LADISLAV, AND MIROSLAV RICHTER

1974   Slovanské a středověké osídlení Oškobrhu u Poděbrad [Slavic and Medieval Settlement at Oškobrh near Poděbrady]. *Památky archeologické* 65:111-184.

HRUBÝ, PETR, PETR HEJHAL, KAREL KAŠÁK, KAREL MALÝ, AND JIŘÍ VALKONY

2009   The Deserted Baroque Glassworks in the Cadastral Territory of Nová Ves near Božejov (District of Pelhřimov). *Studies in Post-Medieval Archaeology* 3:479-500.

HUML, VÁCLAV

1971   Nález renesanční keramiky v Praze Na Slovanech [A Find of Renaissance Pottery from Prague—"Na Slovanech"]. *Archeologické rozhledy* XXIII:222-226.

1975   Vodovodní síť na Václavském náměstí v Praze v 15.-17. století [The Water Supply System at Wenceslas Square in Prague from the 15th to 17th Centuries]. *Český lid* 62:223-230.

1978 Chodovská tvrz v proměnách staletí. Archeologický výzkum zámečku v Praze 4, Chodov [The Chodov Stronghold throughout the Ages. Archaeological Research of the Manor House in Prague 4—Chodov]. *Acta Musei Pragensis* 78.

1979 Archeologické poznámky k dějinám Koňského trhu na Novém Městě pražském [Archaeological Notes on the History of the Horse Market in the New Town of Prague]. *Staletá Praha* IX:158-173, 327-328.

1983 Výsledky výzkumu v areálu býv. dvora čp. 6 v Praze 6—Bubenči [The Results of the Excavation at Farmyard No. 6 in Prague 6— Bubeneč]. *Archaeologica Pragensia* 4:185-200.

1989 Archeologický výzkum zástavby býv. Biskupského dvora u sv. Petra na Poříčí (Praha 1— Nové Město) [The Archaeological Excavation of the Buildings at the Former Bishop's Court near St. Peter's Church in Na Poříčí Street, Prague 1— New Town]. *Archaeologica Pragensia* 10:205-257.

JANSKÁ, EVA
1966 Hromadný hrob bělohorských bojovníků [The Mass Grave of Soldiers from the White Mountain]. *Staletá Praha* 2:107-110, 274.

JIRÁŇ, LUBOŠ
1999 Úvodník 2/99 [Editorial 2/99]. *Archeologické rozhledy* LI:239-242.

JIŘÍK, F. X.
1934a *České sklo* [*Czech Glass*]. Umělecko-průmyslové museum, Prague, Czech Republic.

1934b *Kniha o skle* [*The Book on Glass*]. Jan Štenc, Prague, Czech Republic.

JORDÁNKOVÁ, HANA, AND IRENA LOSKOTOVÁ
2007 A Single Type of Tile Stove in Various Late 15th Century Social Milieus. *Studies in Post-Medieval Archaeology* 2:251-260.

JORDÁNKOVÁ, HANA, AND HEDVIKA SEDLÁČKOVÁ
2004 Sklo a keramika z tabule Matouše Židlochovického v Brně [Glass and Pottery from the Household of Matouš Židlochovický in Brno]. *Brno v minulosti a dnes* 18:205-219.

KAVAN, JAROSLAV
1982 Výsledky archeologického výzkumu Karlovy hutě v Jizerských horách, která pracovala v letech 1758-75 [The Results of the Archaeological Excavation of the Karlova huť Glassworks which Operated in 1758-75]. *Ars vitraria* 7:19-72.

KLÁPŠTĚ, JAN, ANTONÍN SLAVÍČEK, AND TOMÁŠ VELÍMSKÝ
1976 *Archeologický výzkum města Mostu 1970/1975* [*Archaeological Excavations of the Town of Most 1970/1975*]. Archeologický ústav, Most, Czech Republic.

KOSTKA, MICHAL, AND MIROSLAVA ŠMOLÍKOVÁ
1998 Archeologický výzkum hřbitova u kostela sv. Klimenta v Praze—Bubnech. O pohřebním ritu 19. století [Archaeological Excavations in the Cemetery at the Church of St Clement in Prague—Bubny. On 19th-Century Burial Rites]. *Archeologické rozhledy* L:822-836.

KOULA, JAN
1888 *Příspěvky k historii hrnčířství v Čechách* [*Contributions to the History of Pottery Making in Bohemia*]. J. Otto, Prague, Czech Republic.

1917-
1919 Co nám vyprávějí pražské střepy 17. století [What Can Prague Potsherds from the 17th Century Tell Us?]. *Památky archeologické* 29/1917:12-16, 123-129, 176-184, 250-257; 30/1918:27-34, 101-108; 31/1919:25-27.

1920 Vývoj československé majoliky do 18. století [On the Development of the Czechoslovak Majolica till the 18th Century]. *Drobné umění* I:2-5, 40-42, 62-63.

KOVÁRNÍK, JAROMÍR, LADISLAVA HORÁČKOVÁ, LENKA VARGOVÁ, LADISLAV MUCHA, AND ALENA VACHUNKOVÁ
2006 Hromadné hroby vojáků na Brněnské ulici z bitvy u Znojma v roce 1809 [Mass Graves of Soldiers in Brněnská Street from the Battle of Znojmo in 1809]. *Ve službách archeologie* VII:313-328.

KRAJÍC, RUDOLF
2003 Soubor renesančního skla z táborského domu čp. 308 (předběžné sdělení) [An Assemblage of Renaissance Glass from House No. 308 in Tábor (Preliminary Report)]. *Historické sklo* 3:103-107.

2007 Archaeology of the Post-Medieval Period. The Current State of Research and Research Perspectives in Southern Bohemia. *Studies in Post-Medieval Archaeology* 2:57-96.

KRAJÍC, RUDOLF, JAROSLAV PODLISKA, HEDVIKA SEDLÁČKOVÁ, AND JANA VESELÁ
2005 Renesanční sklo v archeologických nálezech v Čechách a na Moravě [Renaissance Glass from the Archaeological Excavations in Bohemia and Moravia]. In *Historie sklářské výroby v českých zemích. I. díl. Od počátků do konce 19. století*, Olga Drahotová, editor, pp. 159-190. Academia, Prague, Czech Republic.

KRASNOKUTSKÁ, TEREZA
2005 *Středověké a novověké kachle z Opavy. Katalog nálezů z archeologických výzkumů* [*Medieval and Modern Stove-Fitting in Opava. A Catalogue of Finds from Archaeological Excavations*]. Archaeologiae Regionalis Fontes 8. Archeologické centrum Olomouc, příspěvková organizace, Olomouc, Czech Republic.

KUBŮ, FRANTIŠEK, AND PETR ZAVŘEL

1988   Pozůstatky valového opevnění rakouské armády v bitvě u Zahájí dne 25.5.1742 [The Remains of a Defensive Earthwork of the Austrian Army from the Battle near Zahájí on May 25, 1742]. *Archeologické výzkumy v jižních Čechách* 5:183-190.

KUNDERA, LUBOMÍR, AND ZDENĚK MĚŘÍNSKÝ

1987   Nález keramiky z poloviny 16. století v Dolních Věstonicích (okr. Břeclav) [Pottery Finds of the First Half of the 16th Century from Dolní Věstonice]. *Časopis Moravského muzea—vědy společenské* 72:155-161.

LANDSFELD, HEŘMAN

1950   *Lidové hrnčířství a džbánkařství* [Folk Pottery and Pitch Making]. Orbis, Prague, Czech Republic.

1953   Výroba habánské keramiky ve světle vykopávek [A Production of Anabaptist Pottery in Light of Archaeological Excavations]. *Český lid* 40:205-212.

1956   *Tisíc let keramické výroby ve Strážnici* [One Thousand Years of Pottery Making in Strážnice]. Krajské Museum, Gottwaldov, Czech Republic.

1971a Habánská hrnčina—neznámá keramika 16. a 17. století. Příspěvky k dějinám skla a keramiky 1 [Anabaptist Earthenware—Unknown Pottery of the 16th and 17th Centuries]. *Rozpravy Národního technického muzea* 45:35-59.

1971b Nález pozůstatků habánského dvora a keramických pecí ve staré Břeclavi [A Discovery of the Remains of the Anabaptist Farmstead and Pottery Kilns in Stará Břeclav]. *Malovaný kraj* 7:4-5.

1976   *Středověké a novověké kachle ze sbírek Heřmana Landsfelda* [Medieval and Postmedieval Stove-Tiles from Heřman Landasfeld´s Collection]. Ústav lidového umění, Strážnice, Czech Republic.

1978   Příspěvek k výrobě levínské keramiky v 15.-17. století [A Contribution to the Production of Levín Pottery in the 15th-17th Centuries]. *Litoměřicko—Vlastivědný sborník* XIV:85-104.

LEMINGER, EMANUEL

1926   *Umělecké řemeslo v Kutné Hoře* [Applied Arts in the Town of Kutná Hora]. Rozpravy ČAVU, tř. 1, č. 71. Česká akademie věd a umění, Prague, Czech Republic.

LIŠKA, ANTONÍN

1958   Nález středověké keramiky v ulici Politických vězňů v Praze [Finding of Medieval Pottery in Politických vězňů Street in Prague]. *Pražskou minulostí* II:36-41.

LOSKOTOVÁ, IRENA

1999   Příspěvek k hrobové výbavě 17.-18. století [A Contribution to the Furnishing of Graves in the 17th and 18th Centuries]. *Pravěk—nová řada* 9:423-430.

MAREŠ, FRANTIŠEK

1893   *České sklo. Příspěvky k dějinám jeho až do konce XVIII. století se zvláštním ohledem na jižní Čechy* [Czech Glass. Contributions to its History till the End of the 18th Century Taking Account of Southern Bohemia]. Česká akademie císaře Františka Josefa pro vědy, slovesnost a umění, Prague, Czech Republic.

MAŠEK, NORBERT

1966   Soubor keramiky a středověký zděný objekt z Jindřišské ulice v Praze [The Pottery Assemblage and the Medieval Stoned Object from Jindřišská Street in Prague]. *Archeologické rozhledy* XVIII:132, 202-203.

MATOUŠEK, VÁCLAV

1997   Redakční úvodník 4/97 [Editorial 4/97]. *Archeologické rozhledy* XLIX:581-585.

2006   *Třebel. Obraz krajiny s bitvou* [Třebel. Landscape with Battle]. Academia, Prague, Czech Republic.

MATOUŠEK, VÁCLAV, JAN HÁJEK, FRANTIŠEK KUBŮ, AND PETR MEDUNA

1990   A Complex Investigation of a Field Fortification of the Seven Years War (1756-1763) at the Site of Nebesa by Aš (Asch). *Studies in Postmediaeval Archaeology* 1:29-61.

MATOUŠEK, VÁCLAV, AND VLADIMÍR SCHEUFLER

1980   Nálezy novověké keramiky v Berouně [Finds of Modern Period Pottery in Beroun]. *Vlastivědný sborník Podbrdska* 18:53-57.

1983   Raně novověké berounské zboží ve světle archeologických výzkumů v Berouně [Early Modern Period Beroun Ware in Light of Archaeological Excavations in the Town of Beroun]. *Archaeologia historica* 8:189-196.

MATOUŠEK, VÁCLAV, VLADIMÍR SCHEUFLER, AND VÍTĚZSLAV ŠTAJNOCHR

1985   Berounské majoliky [Majolicas from the Town of Beroun]. *Časopis Národního muzea, řada historická* 154:126-139.

MEDUNA, PETR, JAN KYPTA, JAROSLAV ŠULC, AND MAREK MATĚJEK

2001   Vidim a Daminěves. Poznámky k vývoji středověké a novověké vesnice [Vidim and Daminěves. Notes on the Development of Medieval and Early Modern Villages]. *Archeologie ve středních Čechách* 5:689-718.

MENOUŠKOVÁ, DANA, AND ZDENĚK MĚŘÍNSKÝ (EDITORS)
2008   Krása, která hřeje. Výběrový katalog gotických a renesančních kachlů Moravy a Slezska [Beauty that Warms. Gothic and Renaissance Dutch Stove-Tiles of Moravia and Silesia]. Slovácké muzeum v Uherském Hradišti, Uherské Hradiště, Czech Republic.

MĚŘÍNSKÝ, ZDENĚK
1979   Záchranné archeologické výzkumy na Moravě a ve Slezsku z období 6.-16. století v letech 1970-1978 [Rescue Excavations at Moravian and Silesian Sites from the 6th to 16th Centuries, 1970-1978]. Archaeologia historica 4:55-71.

MERTA, JIŘÍ
1980   Průmyslová archeologie [Industrial Archaeology]. Zkoumání výrobních objektů a technologií archeologickými metodami 1:5-8.

MICHNA, PAVEL J.
1977   Archeologický průzkum historického jádra města Olomouce, ulice Barvířské. Předběžná zpráva o první etapě [Archaeological Research into the Historic Town Center of Olomouc, Dyers' Street. Prelimary Report from the First Phase]. Archaeologia historica 2:271-281.

NECHVÁTAL, BOŘIVOJ
1968   Studie o hrnčířství a keramice 16. století v Čechách I-III [A Study on Pottery Making and Ceramics of the 16th Century in Bohemia I-III]. Manuscript of a dissertation. Deposited in the archives of the Institute of Archaeology, Academy of Sciences of the Czech Republic.

NEKUDA, VLADIMÍR, AND KVĚTA REICHERTOVÁ
1968   Středověká keramika v Čechách a na Moravě [Medieval Ceramics in Bohemia and Moravia]. Moravské museum a Musejní spolek v Brně, Brno, Czech Republic.

NOVÁČEK, KAREL, AND PAVEL VAŘEKA
1996   Archaeological Research of Present-Day Villages of a Medieval Origin in Bohemia. Ruralia I, Památky archeologické—Supplementum 5:314-325.

1997   Archeologický výzkum žijících vesnic středověkého původu v Čechách [Archaeological Research of Present-Day Villages of a Medieval Origin in Bohemia]. Archeologie ve středních Čechách 1:429-436.

NOVOTNÝ, BORIS
1959   Hromadný nález ze 16. století v Brně [A 16th-Century Mass Find from Brno]. Fontes archaeologicae Moraviae I. Brno.

NOVOTNÝ, VÁCLAV
1912   České dějiny I/I [Czech History I/I]. Jan Laichter, Prague, Czech Republic.

OMELKA, MARTIN
2003   Archeologický výzkum ve Šporkově ulici čp. 322/III [Archaeological Excavations in Šporkova Street No. 322/III]. Výroční zpráva 2002 Státního památkového ústavu v Hlavním městě Praze. Praha, 100-106.

ORNA, JIŘÍ
2005   Gotické a renesanční kachle ve sbírkách Západočeského muzea v Plzni [Gothic and Renaissance Stove-Tiles from the Collections of the West Bohemian Museum in the Town of Plzeň]. Západočeské muzeum v Plzni, Plzeň, Czech Republic.

PAJER, JIŘÍ
1982   Hromadný nález ze začátku 17. století ve Strážnici [A Mass Find from the Beginning of the 17th Century in Strážnice]. Ústav lidového umění, Strážnice, Czech Republic.

1983   Počátky novověké keramiky ve Strážnici [The Beginnings of Modern Period Pottery in Strážnici]. Ústav lidového umění, Strážnice, Czech Republic.

PAVLÍK, ČENĚK, AND MICHAL VITANOVSKÝ
2004   Encyklopedie kachlů v Čechách, na Moravě a ve Slezsku. Ikonografický atlas reliéfů na kachlích gotiky a renesance [Encyclopedia of Stove-Tiles from Bohemia, Moravia, and Silesia. An Iconographic Atlas of Gothic and Renaissance Stove-Tile Reliefs]. Libri, Prague, Czech Republic.

PODLISKA, JAROSLAV
2003   Renesanční sklo z pražských archeologických výzkumů [Renaissance Glass from Excavations in Prague]. Historické sklo 3:21-33.

REICHERTOVÁ, KVĚTA
1989   Bývalý klášter bl. Anežky Přemyslovny v Praze 1, Na Františku. Výsledky archeologického výzkumu [The Former Monastery of Blessed Agnes of Bohemia in Prague 1, Na Františku. Results of the Archaeological Excavations]. Archaeologica Pragensia 10:133-204.

RICHTER, MIROSLAV, AND ZDENĚK SMETÁNKA
1975   Rozvoj středověké archeologie [The Development of Medieval Archaeology]. Archeologické studijní materiály AÚ ČSAV Praha 10/2:62-74, 173-174.

RICHTEROVÁ, JULIE
1981   Německá Lhota, ZSO, k. o. Kamenné Žehrovice, okr. Kladno. Historie a výzkum [Německá Lhota, a Deserted Medieval Village near Žehrovice, Kladno District. History and Research]. Archaeologia historica 6:475-479.

1982   Geodeticko-topografický průzkum na lokalitě Německá Lhota, okr. Kladno [Geodetic-Topographic Analysis at Německá Lhota, Kladno District]. Archaeologia historica 7:247-252.

1985   Výzkum na Jungmannově nám. v Praze 1 (Předběžná zpráva) [The Excavation at Jungmann Square, Prague 1 (Preliminary Report)]. *Archaeologica Pragensia* 6:173-189.

1986   Nálezový soubor z vyzděné jímky na Jungmannově náměstí v Praze 1 [A Find Assemblage from a Cesspit at Jungmann Square, Prague 1]. *Archaeologica Pragensia* 7:205-235.

SCHEUFLER, VLADIMÍR

1972   *Lidové hrnčířství v českých zemích [Folk Pottery in the Czech Lands]*. Academia, Prague, Czech Republic.

1979   Novověká keramika z lounských nálezů [Modern Period Pottery from Louny]. *Národopisné aktuality* XVI:119-124.

ŠEBELA, LUBOMÍR, AND JIŘÍ VANĚK

1985   *Hromadný nález ze studny v areálu bývalého bratrského sboru v Ivančicích. Přelom 16. a 17. století [Mass Find from the Well on the Property of the Bohemian Brothers in Ivančice. The Turn of the 17th Century]*. Okresní muzeum Brno-venkov, Ivančice, Czech Republic.

SEDLÁČKOVÁ, HEDVIKA

1997   *Renesanční sklo a další archeologické nálezy z Nymburka [Renaissance Glass and Other Archaeological Finds from Nymburk]*. Nakladatelství VEGA-L s. r. o., Libice nad Cidlinou, Czech Republic.

2000   Sklo z první poloviny 16. století na Moravě z archeologických nálezů [Moravian Glass from the First Half of the 16th Century from Archaeological Excavations]. *Pravěk—nová řada* 10:163-191.

SEDLÁČKOVÁ, HEDVIKA (EDITOR)

1998   *Renesanční Olomouc v archeologických nálezech. Sklo, slavnostní keramika a kachle. Archeologické výzkumy Památkového ústavu v Olomouci 1973-1996 [Renaissance Olomouc in Archaeological Finds. Glass, Festive Ceramics, and Tiles. Archaeological Research of the Institute of Landmark Conservation in Olomouc 1973-1996]*. Památkový ústav v Olomouci, Olomouc, Czech Republic.

2001   Soubor renesančního skla z areálu novokřtěnského dvora ve Strachotíně [Renaissance Glass from the Anabaptist Center at Strachotín]. *Jižní Morava. Vlastivědný sborník* 37:43-68.

2003   Nálezy renesančního skla z Pouzdřan, okr. Břeclav [Finds of Renaissance Glass from Pouzdřany, Břeclav District]. *Historické sklo* 3:35-46.

ŠKABRADA, JIŘÍ (EDITOR)

1992   *Vesnický dům v 16. a 17. století [Village House in the 16th and 17th Centuries]*. České vysoké učení technické, Prague, Czech Republic.

SKALSKÝ, GUSTAV

1938   Význam hmotných památek pro dějepisné bádání [The Value of Material Heritage for Historical Research]. *Časopis Národního muzea* CXII:4-14.

SMETÁNKA, ZDENĚK

1968   Technologie výroby českých kachlů od počátku 14. do počátku 16. století [The Technology of Bohemian Stove-Tile Production from the Early 14th to the Early 16th Centuries]. *Památky archeologické* LIX:543-578.

1969   K morfologii českých středověkých kachlů [The Morphology of Medieval Bohemian Stove-Tiles]. *Památky archeologické* LX:228-265.

SMETÁNKA, ZDENĚK, AND JAROMÍR ŽEGKLITZ

1990a   Post-Mediaeval Archaeology in Bohemia and its Problems. *Studies in Postmediaeval Archaeology* 1:7-21.

SMETÁNKA, ZDENĚK, AND JAROMÍR ŽEGKLITZ (EDITORS)

1990b   *Studies in Postmediaeval Archaeology* 1. Archeologický ústav ČSAV, Prague, Czech Republic.

TERYNGEROVÁ, HANA

1997   Kolekce renesančního skla z opavských archeologických nálezů [An Assemblage of Renaissance Glass from the Archaeological Excavations in Opava]. *Sborník památkového ústavu v Ostravě, 69–72*. Památkový ústav v Ostravě, Ostrava, Czech Republic.

TOMKOVÁ, KATEŘINA

2005   Pohřební ritus na Pražském hradě a jeho předpolích ve středověku a novověku—charakteristika a vývoj [Burial Rites in and around Prague Castle in the Medieval and Modern Periods]. *Castrum Pragense* 7:159-196.

UNGER, JOSEF

2000   Pohřební ritus městského obyvatelstva 13. až 18. století v archeologických pramenech Moravy a Slezska [Burial Rites of the Urban Population in the 13th to 18th Centuries in the Archaeological Sources of Moravia and Silesia]. *Archaeologia historica* 25:335-354.

2002   *Pohřební ritus a zacházení s těly zemřelých v českých zemích (s analogiemi i jinde v Evropě) v 1.-16. století [Burial Rites and the Treatment of Dead Bodies in the Czech Lands (with Analogies elsewhere in Europe) in the 1st-16th Centuries]*. Panoráma biologické a sociokulturní antropologie 9. Nadace Universitas Masarykiana, Brno, Czech Republic.

VAŘEKA, PAVEL, RADEK BALÝ, LUKÁŠ FUNK, AND LUCIE GALUSOVÁ

2008 Archeologický výzkum vesnic středověkého původu na Tachovsku zaniklých po roce 1945 [The Archaeological Excavation of Originally Medieval Villages Deserted after 1945 in the Tachov Area]. *Archaeologia historica* 33:101-117

VELÍMSKÝ, TOMÁŠ

1976 Archeologický výzkum historického jádra Mostu v roce 1974 [Town Center Excavations in Most in 1974]. *Archaeologia historica* 1:197-204.

WINTER, ZIKMUND

1890-
1892 *Kulturní obraz českých měst. Život veřejný v XV. a XVI. věku. Díl I, II* [*Cultural Outlook of the Czech Towns. Public Life in the 15th and 16th Centuries. Vol. I, II*]. Matice Česká, Prague, Czech Republic.

1892 *Kuchyně a stůl našich předků* [*Kitchen and Table of our Ancestors*]. František Bačkovský, Prague, Czech Republic.

1893 *Přepych uměleckého průmyslu v měšťanských domech XVI. věku* [*Luxury of Applied Art in Burgher Houses of the 16th Century*]. Museum království českého, Prague, Czech Republic.

1906 *Dějiny řemesel a obchodu v Čechách v XIV. a XV. věku* [*History of Crafts and Trade in Bohemia in the 14th and 15th Centuries*]. Česká akademie císaře Františka Josefa pro vědy, slovesnost a umění, Prague, Czech Republic.

1909 *Řemeslnictvo a živnosti 16. věku v Čechách* [*Crafts and Trades of the 16th Century in Bohemia*]. Česká akademie císaře Františka Josefa pro vědy, slovesnost a umění, Prague, Czech Republic.

1913 *Český průmysl a obchod v XVI. věku* [*Czech Industry and Trade in the 16th Century*]. Česká akademie císaře Františka Josefa pro vědy, slovesnost a umění, Prague, Czech Republic.

ŽEGKLITZ, JAROMÍR

1987 Pozdně gotické kachle se jmény hrnčířů [Late Gothic Stove-Tiles with Potters' Names]. *Archeologické rozhledy* XXXIX:655-671.

1988 Nález nejstarší fajánse na Pražském hradě [Earliest Faience Finds of the Prague Castle]. *Sborník kruhu přátel Muzea hlavního města Prahy* 1:207-212.

2006 Renesanční portrétní kachle z hrnčířské dílny Adama Špačka v Truhlářské ulici v Praze [Renaissance Portrait Stove-Tiles from the Pottery Workshop of Adam Špaček in Truhlářská Street, Prague]. *Archeologické rozhledy* LVIII:78-116.

2007a Renaissance Glassworks in Broumy. *Studies in Post-Medieval Archaeology* 2:145-180.

2011 Tertium "Ad lupum predicantem"—et ad Pastorem Bonum. The Reformational Struggle on Czech Gothic and Renaissance Stove Tile Reliefs. *Archeologické rozhledy* LXIII:644-665.

2012a Prints and other Artwork Models for Motifs on Stove Tiles from the Czech Lands. Renaissance Stove Tiles as a Means for Disseminating Ideas and Culture during the Age of Reformation. *Studies in Post-Medieval Archaeology* 4:25-111.

ŽEGKLITZ, JAROMÍR (EDITOR)

2007b *Studies in Post-Medieval Archaeology 2: Material Culture from the End of the 15th Century, and its Reflection in Archaeological, Written and Iconographic Sources.* Archaia Praha o. p. s., Prague, Czech Republic.

2009 *Studies in Post-Medieval Archaeology 3: Post-Medieval Ceramics—Production, Assortment, Usage.* Archaia Praha o. p. s., Prague, Czech Republic.

2012b *Studies in Post-Medieval Archaeology 4: Written and Iconographic Sources in Post-Medieval Archaeology.* Archaia Praha o. p. s., Prague, Czech Republic.

ŽEGKLITZ, JAROMÍR, AND ZDENĚK SMETÁNKA

1989 Historie a postmedieválni archeologie [History and Post-Medieval Archaeology]. *Československý časopis historický* 37:728-738.

ŽEGKLITZ, JAROMÍR, MICHAL VITANOVSKÝ, AND JAN ZAVŘEL

2009 An Assemblage of Stove Tile Moulds from the Prague Pottery Workshop of Adam Špaček and its Tile Production in the Years 1531-72. *Studies in Post-Medieval Archaeology* 3:207-272.

Jaromír Žegklitz
Archaia Praha o.p.s.
Truhlářská 20
CZ-110 00 Praha 1
Czech Republic

KATARINA PREDOVNIK

Transcending Disciplinary Boundaries: Historical Archaeology as a Problem Child—The Case of Slovenia

ABSTRACT

Historical archaeology is a vibrant field of archaeological research that rather freely transcends the boundaries between archaeology, history, and anthropology. Various definitions of historical archaeology and related concepts are discussed, among them the so-called archaeology of later periods current in Slovenia, which encompasses later medieval and post-medieval periods, as well as the archaeology of the contemporary past. The historical development of this discipline in Slovenia is outlined and evaluated in its socio-political context. Finally, the main problems are presented with which historical archaeology in central Europe and Slovenia has had to struggle as a discipline, transcending boundaries and questioning disciplinary identities.

INTRODUCTION: WHICH HISTORICAL ARCHAEOLOGY?

Speaking of the development and current state of historical archaeology in central Europe implies that such a discipline indeed exists and thrives there. How far this may be true or not depends on regionally specific theoretical and institutional developments, as well as naming preferences within individual (national) research traditions. Does the term "historical archaeology" figure at all in, say, Slovenian archaeology? If so, what does it signify? Is "historical archaeology" entirely synonymous with "post-medieval archaeology"? Is it chronologically specific or does it denote a particular archaeological approach to literate societies? The use of the same term in different countries with specific historical trajectories—or, for that matter, by different practitioners even within the same research tradition—might imply a far greater unity of understanding and usage of the term than is actually the case.

There are many definitions of historical archaeology. In the North American tradition, it is "the archaeology of the spread of European societies worldwide, beginning in the fifteenth century, and their subsequent development and impact on native peoples in all parts of the world" (Deetz 1991:1; see also Leone 1995; Paynter 2000) or else, the archaeology of those underlying currents of the modern world (Orser 1996), the global processes of capitalism (though questioned as a universally applicable historical concept by Funari [1999:43–47]) and colonialism and imperialism (Leone and Potter 1988:19; Johnson 1996). Historical archaeology is

generally understood to be an interdisciplinary field linking archaeology to both anthropology and history in its investigation of the post-prehistoric past, endeavoring to "understand the global nature of modern life" (Funari 1999:44).

Regardless of the exact wording and choice of fundamental issues stressed, such an understanding stems from a particular "colonial" perspective. Undeniably, the European expansion from around 1500 has affected the entire world and is inextricably linked to the processes of modernity. Working as a post-medieval archaeologist in central Europe, however, a region with no great colonial forces, tied up firmly into the web of feudal institutions well into the mid-19th century, one cannot help noticing the continuities and connections with the medieval world at least as much as the underlying currents of change (Funari 1999:45). For instance, the Habsburg provinces of the so-called Inner Austria (covering most of today's Slovenia) were never directly implicated in any grand imperialist and colonialist projects overseas. Understandably, imperialism and colonialism, the two constitutive themes of historical archaeology, do not figure at all as interpretative concepts in the archaeology of the early modern period in Slovenia.

Clearly such a view is not entirely justified. Even though this region was not directly involved in the overseas trade and had hardly any contact with the colonies, it did profit from the process of the "opening up" of the

Figure 1. Map with places and archaeological sites mentioned in the text (in Slovenia [shaded gray], unless otherwise noted): (1) Bled; (2) Celje; (3) Graz, Austria; (4) Ilirska Bistrica; (5) Kamnik; (6) Klagenfurt, Austria; (7) Koper; (8) Ljubljana; (9) Maribor; (10) Nomenj; (11) Nova Gorica; (12) Otok Pri Dobravi; (13) Pivka; (14) Polhov Gradec; (15) Predjama; (16) Ptuj; (17) Škofja Loka; (18) Trieste, Italy; (19) Vienna, Austria; (20) Žalec; and (21) Žiče (Map provided courtesy of the Department of Prehistory and Medieval Archaeology, University of Vienna, Austria).

world indirectly. The inflow of cheap South American silver affected even the most local currencies and monetary economies in Europe since they were based on silver (Pieper 1990; Flynn 1996). The increase in the circulation of cash stimulated the exchange of goods and services, as well as the accumulation of capital to be invested in various businesses and industries, and this holds true for Slovenian territory as well. In spite of the destabilizing effects of the Turkish incursions, the period between the late 15th and early 17th centuries was one of overall prosperity and growth, and even in

the rather conservative provinces of Inner Austria the processes of early capitalism and mercantilism were evident (Gestrin 1991). If nothing else, the foreign colonial plantation economy and imperialist trade networks brought coffee, tea (far less common in these parts than coffee, though), tobacco, and sugar to the tables of the wealthy, as well as maize, potatoes, and tomatoes to the fields of the poor (though these were fairly insignificant for local agriculture until the 19th century [Valenčič 1970:258-262]). The general intellectual development and changes in mentality in the early modern Slovenian lands were inextricably linked to the great discoveries in, and European domination over, the New World. If we are to attempt a truly complex understanding of the material world of early modern Europe, then the reverse influence of the colonies on the developments in Europe must be taken into account as our key interpretative framework (Johnson 2006).

The term "historical archaeology" is not generally accepted in (central) European archaeological traditions. In line with the general periodization schemes of European history, it is far more common to use specific terms for the archaeology of individual periods of medieval and later history, such as early-, High-, and late medieval, post-medieval or early modern, later historical archaeology, etc.

Perhaps less important, though not entirely insignificant, is the question of the absolute chronological framework of historical archaeology (Gaimster 2009:527-530). Post-medieval archaeology, as practiced in the United Kingdom and some other northern European countries, usually begins at around 1500, with the age of the great discoveries, and ends in the later 18th century, with the onset of the industrial revolution and the social upheavals resulting in the final dissolution of the feudal order. Speaking in terms of central Europe, and in particular the former Habsburg lands, it is worth noting that feudalism persisted in the Austrian empire until the abolition of serfdom in 1848 and that we can only speak of any notable process of industrialization in the later part of the 19th century. This pushes the upper chronological limit of the early modern period to a considerably later date than in the case of Britain, for instance. Of course, nowadays many archaeologists insist that the archaeological research of later periods should continue uninterruptedly to the present (Tarlow and West 1999; Buchli and Lucas 2001; McAtackney et al. 2007; Predovnik 2008; Harrison and Schofield 2010).

The conceptual differences between the Old and New World historical archaeologies are not merely the consequence of specific historical trajectories. They are linked to the very history and academic identity of archaeology. Whereas in the United States archaeologists are trained mainly in the anthropological tradition, archaeology in Europe is ranked among the humanities (for the early history of central European archaeology see Sklenář 1983) as one of the historical disciplines, producing "historical" knowledge. Some critics maintain archaeology has actually failed in developing an adequate research methodology to follow this epistemological claim (Frommer 2007) but this merely confirms the prevailing view on the nature and disciplinary status of archaeology. Thus, any archaeology is by definition historical, and the notion of a "historical archaeology" might seem to be an empty pleonasm.

This difference is reflected in the definitions and scope of North American and similar historical archaeologies, focusing on "cultural evolution, adaptation, cultural differentiation, shifting world views, and capitalism" (Hicks and Beaudry 2006a:5) on the one hand, and the more historically minded (central) European post-medieval archaeologies on the other. These have developed in the context of heritage management, the majority of their proponents working in museum and rescue archaeology, while academia was but reluctant to follow (Gaimster 2009). Such work was mostly guided by the pragmatic agenda of preservation, reconstruction, and illustration of past life-ways based on (often implicit) culture-historical premises where archaeological findings merely complete the story outlined by the written sources.

There are at least two further readings of the term "historical archaeology" current in central Europe that perhaps explain why it has not been accepted generally here. First, the adjective "historical" is understood by some as denoting the methodological and epistemological specifics of any archaeology of literate societies. In all such cases, archaeological research must take into account the existence of and knowledge based upon written documents (Andrén 1998; Moreland 2001).

Second, a literal understanding of the adjective might imply that historical archaeology is defined neither by its chronological scope (post-medieval) nor by its methodological specifics (the use of written sources alongside the material ones) but instead by its pronounced "historical" outlook on the human past as dialectical, continually changing, particular and individual, contextual and historically contingent, in opposition to the more generalizing outlook of the anthropological tradition seeking to explain the underlying general structures of human social and cultural behavior (Predovnik 2008:82).

The term historical archaeology has never gained acceptance in Slovenia. Instead, the so-called archaeology of later periods (*arheologija mlajših obdobij*) has been introduced as an archaeological study of the material remains of the more recent past, that is, the periods following the early Middle Ages or, speaking in absolute dates, from the 11th century onwards (Predovnik and Nabergoj 2010:245-247). The somewhat ambiguous term, fluid and relational, only gains substance with reference to the "older" periods, the traditional archaeological preserves of prehistory, classical antiquity, and early Middle Ages. It was conceived as an umbrella term covering the entire range of post-early medieval archaeologies, right up to the archaeology of the contemporary past, for the purposes of naming a new subject that was introduced into the archaeological curriculum at the University of Ljubljana, Faculty of Arts, in the academic year of 1990/1991. No (sub-) disciplinary distinction is made between the archaeology of the (High and late) Middle Ages and the post-medieval archaeologies. This allows a more flexible outlook on the past unhindered by the limitations of rigid periodization schemes. The individual cultural traits, social processes and structures, and other historical phenomena can be studied in continuity without the dilemmas regarding their classification in individual historical periods and assignment to specialized research fields and study courses. The basic methodological and epistemological trait of the archaeology of later periods lies in the fact that it investigates complex literate societies with abundant textual, as well as pictorial and even oral, documentation.

The term archaeology of later periods was chosen for reasons of practicality as well. The archaeological curriculum at the University of Ljubljana has a strong tradition of division in chronologically defined subjects. The name of the new course was chosen as a continuation of the traditional archaeological periods from the Paleolithic to the early Middle Ages. In fact, the term "archaeology of later periods" has never gained a general acceptance among Slovenian archaeologists. The use of other labels such as (late) medieval, early modern, or post-medieval archaeology is far more common (Štular 2008). Still, some lacunae remain; industrial archaeology, for example, is virtually non-existent. The documentation of industrial buildings and sites takes place exclusively in the heritage conservation context and is carried out by architects. A course entitled Industrial Archaeology is taught to students of architecture in Ljubljana at the B.A. level, which prepares them for practical fieldwork in conservation projects at industrial sites. Hardly any archaeological study of industrial sites has been undertaken to date in Slovenia.

I would therefore have to agree with Pedro Paolo Funari that a universal, global definition of historical archaeology is neither possible nor is it sensible. Since the practice of archaeology is in itself a form of social action, historically contingent and embedded in its contemporary academic, political, and wider socio-cultural contexts, it might after all be best simply to embrace the diversity of historical and related archaeologies and learn from it through dialog and discussion (Funari 1999:57; Johnson 1999).

ARCHAEOLOGY OF LATER PERIODS: HISTORICAL ARCHAEOLOGY IN SLOVENIA

The territory of Slovenia measures just over 20,000 km² and stretches between the northern Adriatic Sea, eastern Alps, southwestern Pannonian Plain, and the northwestern Balkans (Figure 1). With a population of around two million it is one of the smallest European countries and yet—in view of its small size—one of the most geo-ecologically diversified. Its geo-strategic position in the contact zone between the Balkan and Apennine Peninsulas and central Europe has played a significant part in the historical developments in the region. From the second half of the 6th century onwards, the territory that had once formed part of the western Roman Empire was gradually settled by the Slavs. These formed independent principalities (e.g., Carinthia and Carniola) but soon had to relinquish their autonomy to their German neighbors—first the Bavarians and then the Franks under Charlemagne. During the Middle Ages, Slovenian territory formed the southeastern frontier of the Holy Roman Empire and was divided into several provinces (Styria, Carinthia, Carniola, Goriška/Gorizia, and Istria) under Habsburg rule (Styria from A.D. 1278, Carinthia and Carniola from 1335, Goriška/Gorizia from 1500, Istria partly from 1374 and completely from 1797 until 1918). Only the parts of northern Istria with the coastal towns were under Venetian domination from the 13th century until the end of the 18th century. After the dissolution of the Austro-Hungarian Empire in 1918, the greater part of today's Slovenia was incorporated into the new Kingdom of Serbs, Croats, and Slovenes (SCS; from 1929 the Kingdom of Yugoslavia). The western part of the country belonged to Italy from 1918 until 1943; this territorial claim was based on the fact that it had once formed part of the core of the Roman Empire,

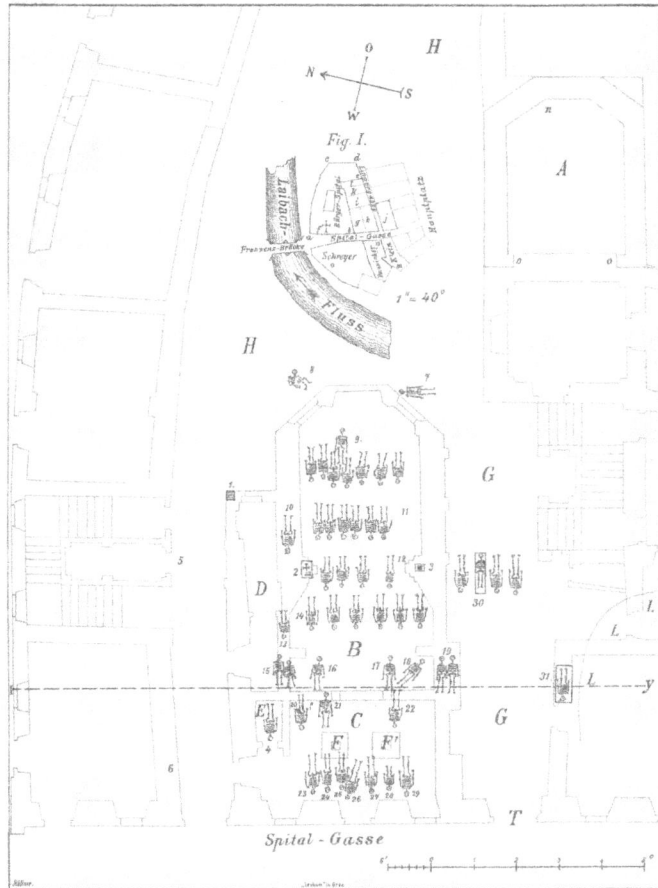

Figure 2.   Alfons Müllner's plan of his 1896-1897 excavations of the Ljubljana burghers' hospice complex with St. Elisabeth's church and burials (Müllner 1897:plate 1).

the so-called 10th Italian region Venetia et Histria. It was only after World War II that Slovenian state territory was united in its present form. In 1945 Slovenia became one of the six republics forming the socialist federation of Yugoslavia, and in 1991 it proclaimed independence (Grafenauer 1964-1974; Fischer et al. 2005; Luthar 2008).

It is important to understand these cultural and geopolitical contexts when trying to assess the development of archaeology in Slovenia. There lie the roots of our historical cultural ties with central European, German and Austrian, and, in part, Italian/Venetian worlds, as well as the actual circumstances in which the institutional and conceptual framework of the discipline took shape (Novaković 2002, 2011). In Austro-Hungarian times, until 1918, there were no major academic centers in today's Slovenia. The local intelligentsia was educated in Vienna or Graz (Austria) and to a lesser extent in Italy. The necessary institutional framework for both natural sciences and humanities was provided with the establishment of provincial museums in Graz,

Ljubljana, and Klagenfurt (Austria) in the first half of the 19th century, and somewhat later in Trieste (Italy). It was in the Carniolan Provincial Museum Rudolfinum in Ljubljana (established 1821; today the National Museum of Slovenia) that Slovenian professional archaeology was born, and this institution also played a vital role in the development of late- and post-medieval archaeology.

Trying to assess this development, it is hardly possible to draw a clear division between the medieval and post-medieval periods. Due to the continued settlement and use of many sites from the medieval—and quite often even earlier—times to this day, one inevitably encounters the remains from different periods at the same location and has to study them diachronically. The following overview, though focusing predominantly on archaeological research into the post-medieval past, will therefore necessarily address the sites, research themes, and approaches related to the medieval period as well (the following overview is based mainly on Predovnik and Nabergoj 2010).

Excavating the Middle Ages: The Early Years

As everywhere around Europe, the archaeological investigation of "historical" periods in Slovenia began in the late 19th century. In 1892 Alfons Müllner, archaeologist and curator of the Provincial Museum in Ljubljana, excavated inside the medieval castle of Predjama (Jama/Lueg) with the specific intention to "critically expose" the legend of Erasmus Lueger, a rebel knight who defied the Habsburg emperor's troops and finally met his death due to treason in his own castle in 1484 after a long siege (Müllner 1892a, 1892b, 1894). Müllner, in the true manner of a local historian, tried to trace the material evidence and check the reliability of the famous story by means of archaeological methods.

Only a few years later, in 1895, Ljubljana was devastated by an earthquake. An ambitious program to rebuild and further develop the town was started almost immediately. On the northern edge of the historic town area where a new administrative building was to be erected on the location of the medieval burghers' hospice complex, human skeletal remains were uncovered. Müllner decided to excavate the site due to its historic importance (Figure 2). In the 16th century, the hospice's church of St. Elisabeth was the spiritual center of Ljubljana's Protestant community. After the expulsion of the Protestants from the Habsburg lands, the church retained its importance as a prestigious burial location until the 18th century, and several illustrious personages are known to have been buried there. The archaeological remains turned out to be somewhat disappointing as the burials contained hardly any grave goods at all, and no grave slabs or inscriptions were found that would enable the identification of the deceased. Whatever his main motives for excavation, however, Müllner did approach the site as a whole. He duly recorded and interpreted the architectural remains of the church and other hospice buildings, and he also noted traces of skin-tanning and related activities (Stare 1991). Furthermore, Müllner excavated three house lots opposite the hospice complex trying to explain the settlement history and building development of the historic town core (Müllner 1898).

Müllner's broad, chronologically unspecific archaeological interests were defined by his professional career; he first acted as topographer-archaeologist for the Austrian state agency for the preservation of sites and monuments (*Kaiserlich-königliche Zentralkommission für Erforschung und Erhaltung der Kunst – und Historischen Denkmale*) and then from 1889 until 1903 as curator of the Provincial Museum in Ljubljana. His work on historical sites was not based on an explicit reflection regarding the specific role of archaeology in relation to documentary history. His approach was one of local historian and erudite, aiming simply at a practical application of the archaeological method (i.e., excavation) for the purpose of acquiring material evidence to answer historical questions at hand.

After World War I all of the provincial archaeological centers except Ljubljana remained outside the borders of the new Kingdom of SCS/Yugoslavia, and Slovenian archaeology was left with a very thin institutional framework consisting of one national and three municipal museums (in Celje, Ptuj, and Maribor). In 1919 the long-desired university was established in Ljubljana with an undergraduate course in archaeology first introduced in 1923/1924. Until the late 1940s though, no heritage service existed and there were only two or three archaeologists active in the country at the same time (Novaković 2002:329-330). In this, Slovenia and the other countries of former Yugoslavia stand apart from the other nation states formed after the dissolution of the Austro-Hungarian Empire, namely Hungary, Czechoslovakia, and Poland. These have tried to boost their national identity and legitimize their newly

acquired sovereignty by strengthening the historic links with the medieval kingdoms that once existed on their territories. It was in the medieval period that the roots of modern nations were sought. In this program of nation-building, archaeology clearly had a part to play as it could provide new monuments, relics of the nation's past to be revered and celebrated. The resulting early advancement of medieval (and to a limited extent, post-medieval) archaeology in these countries is undeniable (Lecziejewicz 1993:76; Smetánka 1993:92). The Kingdom of SCS/Yugoslavia was very different in this regard: it was a new multi-ethnic entity with no direct historical ancestors. No historical events, personalities, and monuments from any but the most recent past could play a part in the new national and civil identities. Archaeology was not of immediate constitutive importance to the new state.

In the case of Slovenia, another aspect is important. In the struggles for political autonomy and independence of the various ethnic groups subsumed within the Austro-Hungarian Empire in the 19th century, a process of cultural and political diversification took place in which differences between the various linguistic and ethnic groups were pronounced deliberately and new collective identities constructed through origin myths and the invention of tradition. Thus, and related to the general social upheaval aiming at the reversal of the feudal order, a myth was born of the hard-working, oppressed Slovene peasant and his oppressive German (or possibly Italian) feudal lord. This gross simplification of ethnic and linguistic identities of the various social groups and their origins was instrumentalized successfully for political mobilization. The myth survived the death of the Empire. In the context of German and Italian occupation of Slovenia during World War II and then under the communist regime it seemed to be quite irrefutable, resulting in a general lack of regard for the monuments of the feudal era (Šumi 1983:10; Štih 2001:61-62).

In spite of that, the pre-World War II period did bring some developments for the archaeology of later periods in Slovenia. Walter Schmid, Müllner's successor at the Rudolfinum until 1909 and later museum curator and professor in Graz, conducted excavations at several supposedly early medieval *Hausberge* (motte-type castles and moated sites) as well as the post-medieval ironworks near Nomenj in Bohinj. Schmid's work on late medieval and post-medieval sites was mostly led by false assumptions about their early dating (Predovnik and Nabergoj 2010:248).

Rajko Ložar's Theoretical Grounding of Medieval Archaeology

As regards the archaeology of later periods, the most interesting figure was undoubtedly Rajko Ložar, an archaeologist, art historian, ethnographer, and literary critic. Like Müllner and Schmid before him, Ložar was employed at the National Museum in Ljubljana, first as librarian and then as curator. He also taught archaeology as private professor at the university in Ljubljana for some years. His doctoral studies in Roman provincial art at the University of Vienna, Austria, have formed him in the tradition of the Vienna School of Art History. He applied stylistic and formal analysis as well as the concept of the evolution of style in his artifact studies, among which was his typo-chronology of Early Slavic and late medieval pottery (Ložar 1939; Nabergoj 1999:39-41). Ložar analyzed the early and late medieval pottery from museum collections. With few exceptions, these finds had been obtained unsystematically, which is why he adopted formal and stylistic analyses to establish their typological development and relative chronology. The absolute dating was based on published analogies from other regions, mostly Austria and Germany. Ložar's typo-chronological scheme remained the only classification and dating tool for late medieval pottery in Slovenia until the publication of Vinko Šribar's analyses of pottery from the site of Otok Pri Dobravi (Šribar 1972-1973).

Ložar was the first to form a concept of archaeology as a national discipline. He published a historical synthesis of Slovenian archaeology and discussed its key conceptual issues. His career came to a sudden end in 1945 when he migrated from Slovenia to Austria and finally to America, fearing that he would be accused of collaboration with the German occupation forces and prosecuted for his dislike of the new communist authorities (Novaković 2001, 2005). In the introduction to his paper on Early Slavic and (late) medieval pottery in Slovenia (Ložar 1939:180-183), and even more fully in an unpublished extended version of this introduction, Ložar reflected on the specific role of archaeology in studying the Middle Ages and its relationship with (medieval) history, art history, and ethnology (the manuscript is kept at the National Museum of Slovenia; for a thorough analysis see Nabergoj 2005:178-182). He pointed out continuities in the general historical

development and argued for an equal archaeological treatment of the early, High, and late Middle Ages, and even the early modern period, since an archaeological method and approach are needed to understand and interpret the material remains of the past. In this, prehistoric, medieval, and post-medieval archaeologies all share similar issues.

In Ložar's view medieval archaeology was an autonomous and self-dependent archaeological (sub-) discipline studying material remains with the aim of complementing historiography's findings. He did believe that written sources were more suitable than material ones for a comprehensive reconstruction of the past, though this was not to imply that archaeology as a discipline must be subordinate to history. He believed that each discipline was entitled, and indeed obliged, to study the past in accordance with its own research goals, epistemologies, and theoretical orientations. In Ložar's view, archaeological studies are justified whenever the specific nature of the primary sources demands the use of archaeological methods and approaches. Archaeology might thus be understood as an ancillary discipline to history but only inasmuch as history in some respects is ancillary to archaeology. Furthermore, "general historiography cannot do without archaeological work, especially in outlining the antiquities, the cultural and artistic production, and the craftsmanship of a nation, whereas it is more independent in tracing the political and other kinds of histories. Using merely written sources with regard to all of these areas would be nonsensical, and even impossible, considering that written sources from this period are generally silent on such subjects." On the other hand, archaeology should not limit itself to mere documentation and description but should provide autonomous interpretations of material culture (Nabergoj 2005:180).

Ložar's understanding of medieval archaeology *as archaeology*, discussing archaeological remains in the same way and as independently as prehistoric archaeology, was exemplified by his treatise on medieval pottery (Ložar 1939). He did not stop at the issues of typology and chronology but attempted to explain the observed changes in technology, form, and style between Early Slavic and later medieval pottery in the context of ethnic and social change accompanying the enforcement of feudalism.

With Rajko Ložar the first theoretical foundations for the archaeological study of "historic" periods in Slovenia were laid. Unfortunately, they did not have any direct consequences for the development of medieval and post-medieval archaeology in the following decades. Due to his personal fate Ložar's achievements have been "quietly overlooked" (Nabergoj 2005:182). Undoubtedly, he was an exceptional and pioneering scholar whose reflections on the epistemology of medieval archaeology and its relationship with historiography were surprisingly mature bearing in mind the rather limited scope of archaeological activity in Slovenia at the time. Even in a European context they were articulated at a very early date, since we can compare them with similar treatises published elsewhere more than three decades later (Jankuhn 1973; Dymond 1974; Schlesinger 1974).

Archaeology and History: A Troubled Relationship

In the aftermath of World War II Slovenian archaeology faced a complete rebuilding. Not only had all three active researchers fled the country, but the consequences of war (war damage, reparation claims) demanded the immediate establishment of an efficient Monument Service (Jogan 2008:54-57). The birth of a new socialist republic of Yugoslavia opened up new opportunities for institutional and conceptual renewal of the discipline. A new generation of young archaeologists took over, and soon the necessary institutional framework was created: the Department of Archaeology was established at the Faculty of Arts, University of Ljubljana, in 1946 (Novaković et al. 2004), and in 1947 the Institute of Archaeology at the Slovene Academy of Sciences and Arts (Pleterski 1997). Archaeology now claimed the role of a national discipline and saw one of its crucial tasks in rejecting Nazi and Fascist interpretations of early medieval archaeological finds on which their territorial claims had been grounded. Consequently, the previously almost non-existent Early Slavic archaeology (6th to 10th centuries A.D.) became the theme of the day, prompted by the ambiguities regarding the definition of the Yugoslav border with Italy in western Slovenia (Novaković 2002:330-331, 334-335).

In line with the official ideology of the "brotherhood and unity of the Yugoslav nations," a national archaeological organization was formed in 1950, the Yugoslav Archaeological Association. The discipline had to be advanced on a national level, preferably in accordance with historical-dialectical materialism propagated by the communist regime. Interestingly, "the official ideology and communist regime had only partial

success in rebuilding the conceptual frameworks" (Novaković 2002:341) of historical sciences. Although proclaimed at a formal level in a number of programmatic and protocol documents produced on various occasions in the 1950s and 1960s, the official Marxist ideology failed to produce "any conceptual tools applicable and operable in an archaeological context" (Novaković 2002:341). The culture-historical paradigm defined Slovenian archaeology far more than any historical materialist tendencies.

In 1950 the first meeting of Yugoslav archaeologists took place in Niška Banja in Serbia. The need to "...research the material culture of our nations starting with the period of the first Slavic kinship communities until the formation of bourgeois class society" was acknowledged as a general priority (Korošec 1950b:214), though it remains unclear whether this was supposed to mean the advent of class society with the rise of towns in the late Middle Ages or perhaps the death of the feudal order in the early industrial era. Josip Korošec, a leading figure in Slovenian and Yugoslav archaeology of the time, published his reflections on archaeology's tasks in that same year (Korošec 1950a). He expressed a very optimistic view about the potential of archaeological finds for the study of past societies, even literate ones. Regarding the relationship between archaeology and historiography, he believed that their specific methodologies made them independent of each other, yet equal and complementary. In this, Korošec was fully compliant with Ložar's opinions.

But the leading Slovenian historian of the day, Bogo Grafenauer, did not share his views. He published a polemic response to Korošec's paper the following year (Grafenauer 1951) pointing out that, while archaeological sources are indeed direct material evidence of the past, they are less reliable than "the critically assessed written sources" as they are subject to archaeologist's interpretation. Of course, the debate about the greater or lesser subjectivity of archaeological vs. documentary sources has been a common topic everywhere in Europe at some point and, for many it would seem, remains unresolved to this day (on the futility of such discussions see Tauber 1991; Moreland 1992:114). Grafenauer objected to the presumed "independence" of archaeological interpretations of material remains from "historic" periods; he believed that archaeology could only be of assistance to documentary history regarding the issues of economy, technology, and (partly) ethnogenesis. It is only in prehistoric situations that archaeology is truly independent as a discipline, out of necessity.

The polemic was not continued, and the position expressed by Grafenauer prevailed more or less implicitly. "The tyranny of the historical record" (Champion 1990) defined the limits and scope of Slovenian archaeology for a long time after that. A rather pessimistic view of archaeology's epistemological potential was expressed, for example, by Andrej Pleterski in his 1979 paper on the use of cartographic, documentary, and archaeological sources in retrograde settlement studies: "...archaeology can only function as a science in connection with other disciplines, history in particular" (Pleterski 1979:508; criticized by Slapšak 1982). The very disciplinary identity of archaeology was constituted by staking its chronological territory against historiography—the "magical" upper limit of "archaeological periods" was set to the end of the Early Slavic period around A.D. 1000 (Kastelic 1964-1965). Such an understanding has hampered the development of late and post-medieval archaeologies for decades and is still not entirely superseded, in spite of all the changes and developments that have taken place in the last twenty years. It is upheld by the division of curatorships and departments in many museums—archaeology until the end of the Early Slavic period and (cultural or art) history from the late Middle Ages onwards. The Early Slavic period is also the latest period included in the survey of the archaeology of Slovenian territory, *Zakladi tisočletij* (*Treasures of the Millennia*) (Aubelj 1999), a book published in 1999 by a team of scientists affiliated with the Institute of Archaeology at the Slovenian Academy of Sciences and Arts. This richly illustrated popular science volume might be understood as archaeology's contribution toward the construction of a new national identity after Slovenia's attainment of independence in 1991. But the image of archaeology it presents, at least as regards its chronological limits, is anachronistic both in terms of contemporary international standards and the situation in Slovenia at the time.

A Period of Pragmatism: Rescue Archaeology at Historic Sites

Until the late 1980s remains from more recent periods—if considered and documented at all—were either uncovered when excavating multi-period sites or in the context of conservation work on historic buildings, mostly churches and castles. At first, archaeologists focused on early churches where Early Slavic burials could

be expected. In the process, post-medieval burials and architectural remains would be recorded as well. The extensive excavations inside and around the Church of the Assumption on Bled Island, which took place between 1962 and 1966, represent an early example (Nabergoj 1995:9-11).

A decisive turn happened with the reorganization of the heritage protection service in the 1970s, when a network of eight regional institutes for the protection of monuments was established. In cooperation with museums an efficient public heritage service was created for the first time, trying to keep up with the increasing rate of destruction and damage to archaeological and other heritage (Slabe 1982:98-99; Jogan 2008:84-89). The number of permanently employed archaeologists on a national level rose from about 10 to 15 in the 1960s to nearly six times as many in the early 1980s (Novaković 2002:343). This increase was reflected in the number of excavations performed.

The growth in rescue excavations of historic buildings is linked to wider social changes in the 1970s and 1980s. As the damage caused to the environment by the spiraling economic growth and industrialization in the post-war decades was becoming evident, ecological awareness was raised even in Yugoslavia where "the rule of the proletariat" was biased toward industrial production and "the creation of a new reality." By the late 1970s legal measures were introduced in Slovenia to preserve and protect farmland against degradation and development for construction, resulting in a reversal of the expansion of urban settlements. From the mid-1970s, the long-neglected historic town centers experienced the renewal of infrastructure, restoration of historic buildings, and construction of new ones. Heritage services were faced with an unprecedented task of supervising these development projects in old settlement nuclei and performing the necessary rescue archaeology.

More or less unremarked upon in professional circles, yet crucial in terms of cultural politics, was the overall liberalization of Yugoslav, and in particular Slovenian, society in the late 1960s and early 1970s. The ideologically "softer" version of socialism, parting ways with the hard-line communism of the country's revolutionary beginnings, resulted (among other things) in a more positive evaluation of the past, even of the once despised monuments from the feudal era. Castles, mansions, and churches were now reinstated as highly valued national cultural heritage. Repair and conservation

Figure 3.   *Engraved and painted glazed ceramic plate with a female bust from Škofja Loka, late 16th century (Photo by Jože Štukl, 2007; courtesy of Museum of Škofja Loka).*

Soon archaeologists were faced with enormous amounts of data and artifacts from High/late medieval and later sites. There was hardly any knowledge available about the material culture from these periods and no conceptual or institutional framework for its systematic study. Archaeological evidence was recorded and collected but it played no part in the interpretation of later-period sites and monuments, which was instead left in the hands of historians and art (architectural) historians. The only exception was the systematic excavations at the castle of Celje/Cilli (1973-1984 with intermissions) where the excavation director, Tatjana Bregant from the Department of Archaeology, University of Ljubljana, attempted a full interpretation of the site based on archaeological data (Bregant 1983). Some of her interpretations have been questioned since (Kramberger and Stopar 1987; Brišnik 1999), but Bregant's research nonetheless retains its historical value as one of the few systematic research projects in the archaeology of later periods carried out prior to the 1990s.

projects boomed in a period of economic prosperity, and archaeology needed to react fast. In spite of the generally accepted notion that archaeology ends at about A.D. 1000, archaeologists could not stand idle as material evidence of the past was being uncovered and destroyed daily. Theory was overtaken by practice and, with regard to the archaeology of later periods, pragmatism set in (Predovnik and Nabergoj 2010:257-260).

This situation might also be labeled "a phase of unconceptualized practice" (Slapšak 1987:145, footnote 3). Until the late 1980s, the only systematic archaeological research on later periods was performed by the Center for Medieval Archaeology (1961-1987) at the National Museum of Slovenia under the leadership of Vinko Šribar (Stare 1993). The Center's two major research projects were the excavations on Bled Island and at Otok Pri Dobravi, the site of the deserted medieval market town of Gutenwerth. The Center was focused on the medieval period; the only work it did on post-medieval remains was at Otok Pri Dobravi where post-medieval burials and church architecture were excavated alongside medieval ones at St. Nicholas' church (Stare 2000).

This self-imposed restraint of archaeologists regarding the interpretation of their findings was questioned by a few scholars, most explicitly by Marijan Slabe who argued for a "full" archaeological approach to High/late medieval and post-medieval sites with the aim of producing relevant knowledge about the past inaccessible by other means (Slabe 1974, 1980a). Conducting rescue excavations at Mestni Trg in Škofja Loka, Slabe came upon a specific type of early modern decorated ceramic tableware that he attributed to local potteries and named *loška meščanska slikana keramika* (Loka Burghers' Painted Ware; Figure 3) (Slabe 1977; Predovnik 2009). For the first time, the issues of post-medieval pottery production and consumption and their social context were discussed based on archaeological evidence. And in 1980 Slabe published the first-ever review of archaeological research on High/late medieval and post-medieval sites in Slovenia (Slabe 1980b).

The Birth of a New Discipline

In the 1980s the Department of Archaeology at the University of Ljubljana faced a change of generations and a growth in staff. Some of the younger scholars started looking toward Anglo American archaeology for inspiration, introducing conceptual and methodological novelties foreign to the culture-historical paradigm prevalent in Slovenia. Whereas the theoretical discourse of processual (and later, post-processual) archaeology has never been widely accepted by Slovenian archaeologists, methodological innovations, introduced through joint research projects with British colleagues, have radically transformed Slovenian archaeology: for example, the "Harris" method of stratigraphic excavation and prospection techniques such as field surveys, geophysics, reconnaissance from the air, and aerial photography. These require a "neutral" approach to the archaeological record regardless of its cultural content or age, which has gradually changed the way archaeologists thought about the remains of later periods. While they had often previously been disregarded as "grandmother's

garbage," a strict application of the new fieldwork methods demanded that they be treated as relevant archaeological data in order to understand the site formation processes. The stratigraphic excavation method was first applied in rescue excavations at Kapucinski Vrt (Capuchins' Garden) in Koper in 1986-1987, at Ljubljana Castle from 1988 onwards, at the Church of St. Clara in Koper in 1989, and elsewhere (Predovnik and Nabergoj 2010:265). These were all complex multi-period sites with a significant or even predominant share of remains from later periods.

Yugoslav, and therefore Slovenian, archaeology has always been open to the western world; no restraint on travel or contact with foreign colleagues has ever been imposed by the regime. The abandonment of communism/socialism and attainment of political independence in 1991 therefore did not cause any major breaks in Slovenian archaeology in terms of conceptual development since it had never been particularly prone to Marxist approaches anyway. The new state

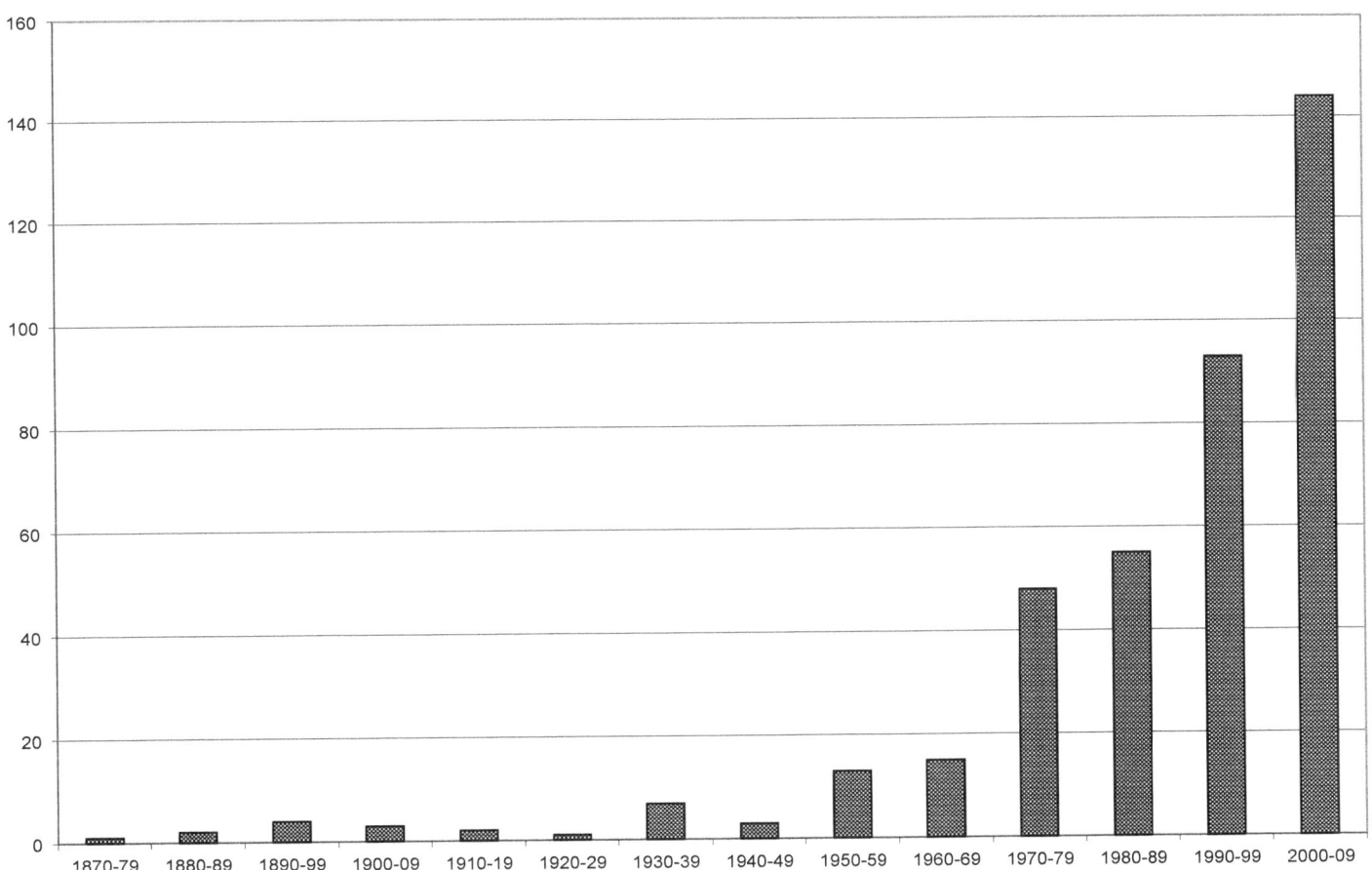

Figure 4.   *Number of archaeological interventions on sites with remains from the later periods in Slovenia by decade (based on preliminary site reports from the Varstvo Spomenikov bulletin, Nabergoj 1995, and other sources).*

did, however, bring about change in public research and heritage-management infrastructure and, perhaps most significantly, the emergence of private archaeological companies.

Regarding High/late medieval and post-medieval archaeology, the time was now ripe for another logical step forward—the introduction of these subjects to the archaeological curriculum at the University of Ljubljana, Faculty of Arts, which happened in 1990. The subject was named Archaeology of Later (Historical) Periods, and by 1995 the first students completed their studies in Ljubljana with a degree in the archaeology of later periods (Novaković et al. 2004:97-100). Until a few years ago, this was the only university in Slovenia where it was possible to study archaeology. Nowadays, the University of the Littoral (Univerza na Primorskem) in Koper and University in Nova Gorica also offer archaeological degrees at M.A. and Ph.D. levels.

In 1994 the Department of Archaeology at the Ljubljana Faculty of Arts started publishing a monograph series *Archaeologia Historica Slovenica* devoted to archaeology of later periods (to date, six volumes have been published: Guštin and Horvat 1994; Guštin and Predovnik 1997; Guštin 2001; Predovnik 2003; Podpečan 2006; Predovnik, Dacar, et al. 2008) and established a research Center for Medieval and Post-Medieval Studies (active from 1995 until 2003). The Center's research activities were focused mainly on the evaluation and analyses of documentation and finds from excavations in and around Celje. Further institutional infrastructure for the archaeology of later periods was created with the establishment of specialized curator posts at the National Museum of Slovenia and City Museum of Ljubljana. At the Institute of Archaeology at the Scientific Research Centre of the Slovenian Academy of Sciences and Arts no permanent research post for these periods exists, though the institute has been carrying out research projects on related issues for a number of years with staff employed for the duration of the project (Štular 2009; Pleterski and Šantek 2010).

Another institute active in the field of medieval and post-medieval archaeology was established in 2003, the Institute for Mediterranean Heritage at the Science and Research Centre in Koper, engaging in multi-period and interdisciplinary research. As regards the archaeology of later periods, the institute specializes in the post-medieval heritage of the eastern Adriatic coastland collaborating with partners from Italy, Croatia, Montenegro, Serbia, and Austria (Guštin 2004; Guštin, Gelichi, et al. 2006; Guštin, Bikić, et al. 2008).

Hand in hand with the institutional and curricular development went also the general growth of professional interest in medieval and post-medieval archaeology. Museum exhibitions, theme meetings and conferences, and the publication of site reports and theme studies boomed in the last 20 years, as did field research (Figure 4). This was largely due to the general advancement in fieldwork methodological standards owing to the project designed for the protection of archaeological heritage in the context of the construction of the Slovenian national motorway network. In 1994 a comprehensive methodology was prepared for preliminary and rescue archaeological fieldwork, evaluation of archaeological potential, and inclusion of archaeology into spatial planning activities from the initial stages (Djurić 2004). The prescribed methodology soon became an established norm, not just in the motorway project but in general. This resulted in a sharp increase in archaeological fieldwork performed and, with it, a rise in the number of documented and investigated sites and other remains from the later periods. In the framework of the motorway project itself, more than 20 High/late medieval and early modern settlement and production sites have been excavated (Figure 5). Quite commonly though, the medieval and post-medieval finds recorded in the course of preliminary archaeological investigations are merely the scattered traces of farming practices resulting in the "littering" of the landscape.

Last but not least, the development of underwater archaeology has contributed a fair share of sites and finds of medieval or post-medieval date. In the Adriatic Sea several World War II shipwrecks have been documented along the coastline south of Koper, such as a carrier of the type *maona,* an unidentified German warship, and the scant remains of the Italian pre-war ocean liner *Rex*, dismantled for recycling after the war (Eliseo 1992; Knific 1993; Žerjal 2001). Near the coastal town of Piran, substantial underwater deposits have been uncovered by amateur divers consisting of numerous sherds of 16th – to early 17th-century decorated ceramic vessels of the so-called *ceramica graffita* type. Among these are several half-finished products and wasters indicating local production (Guštin 2004). The Alpine lake of Bled (Gaspari 2008a), as well as the rivers Krka, Ljubljanica, and, partly, Sava, have been surveyed systematically yielding finds from the stone age to the present day, as

Figure 5. *A 16th-17th-century outbuilding of the Koper bishopric's manor farm at Valmarin near Spodnje Škofije. The building was demolished due to motorway construction in 2001. A structural survey and excavations were carried out by the Koper Regional
Museum in cooperation with the Department of Archaeology, Faculty of Arts, University of Ljubljana, as a field school for
archaeology students (Photo by Darja Grosman, 2001; courtesy of Department of Archaeology, Faculty of Arts, University of
Ljubljana).*

well as remains of bridges and settlement structures
from prehistory to the mid-20th century (PAS 1982,
1984; Gaspari and Erič 2008; Gaspari 2010). Among
these underwater contexts, the river Ljubljanica with
a barely 41-km long course deserves special mention. Several thousand objects dating from the upper
Paleolithic to the modern age are kept by the National
Museum of Slovenia (Turk et al. 2009), City Museum
of Ljubljana, and many private collectors. Though most
of these objects lack clear contextual information, and
interpretation of processes leading to their deposition
is therefore difficult, they are invaluable due to their
excellent state of preservation (Figure 6).

The development of preventive archaeology was followed by legislation, with the new Cultural Heritage
Protection Act of 2008 (Official Gazette of the Republic

of Slovenia, No. 16/2008). This law is of particular
importance to the archaeology of later periods since it
defines archaeological remains in such a way that the
time-honored upper chronological limit of archaeology
is finally abolished. In Article 3 the status of archaeological cultural heritage is granted to all material traces
of human activity that have been underground or underwater for at least one hundred years. Regarding war-
related remains, the archaeological cultural heritage
status is granted to those that have been underground
or underwater for at least 50 years.

The shorter age limit awarded to the finds, sites, and
traces of war-related activities has to do with the fact
that World War II took place only 60 years ago. This
armed conflict remains important for the Slovene national identity as a self-organized struggle for liberation

that resulted in some sort of political autonomy within socialist Yugoslavia, a first step toward the independence finally attained in 1991. On the other hand, a civil war took place in Slovenia during World War II as the partisan liberation army was taken over by the communists, and their political opponents—supported by the Church—formed separate troops, the so-called Home Guard. These made a fatal mistake when they sided with the German occupation forces against Tito's partisans who were supported by the allies. As soon as the war ended, a communist regime was established and it dealt brutally with members of the Home Guard, similar militias from other parts of Yugoslavia, and their supporters. For weeks and months in 1945 extrajudicial killings took place in utmost conspiracy (Corsellis and Ferrar 2010). This long suppressed dark chapter of Yugoslav history has only really been open to historical research upon Slovenia's independence. The mass graves in remote woodland areas and abandoned mine shafts are gradually coming to light (Ferenc 2008; Jamnik 2008), and it is in this context that the wording of the Cultural Heritage Protection Act needs to be understood as well. Though excavation of some of these mass graves has been taking place for more than a decade now, and some archaeologists have been involved, no forensic archaeology has developed in Slovenia as yet. On the other hand, archaeological research into military sites from World War I (the Isonzo front, the so-called Rupnik line of fortifications along the border with Italy) and World War II is starting to develop (Gaspari 2008b; Gaspari et al. 2010).

Though the definition of archaeological sites and finds provided by the new Heritage Act is somewhat arbitrary and not clearly grounded in terms of content (Predovnik 2008:85-86), it nonetheless institutes the archaeological study of material remains from the more recent past as a legal obligation. This has caused a lot of discontent within and outside archaeology. Some archaeologists feel, even today, that post-medieval—and even more so, "later historical"—archaeology is just not "real" archaeology. The fear is that any investment of financial, human, and spatial (in terms of museum space required for storing the finds, that is) resources in historical archaeology might simply mean less prehistoric, Roman, and early medieval archaeology. On the other hand, representatives of other disciplines involved in heritage protection also reacted with indignation, as they felt that archaeology was thus encroaching upon their territory. Archaeology was even accused of practicing disciplinary imperialism at one time; not all reactions were negative, of course. Some historians (Mihelič 2009) and anthropologists welcome the contributions archaeology can bring to their own studies, but the misconceptions about each other's disciplines persist all too often.

The debate surrounding the new Heritage Act has made two things quite obvious: first, the under-theorized, common-sensical identity of Slovenian archaeology and second, the complete lack of discussion with neighboring disciplines. Of course there will always be differences of opinion, but reflection is crucial for any kind of advancement. If anything, the new legislation and changes in archaeological practice have stirred things up a bit and this can only be healthy.

As regards the archaeology of later periods itself, some attempts at self-reflection have been made, however. As early as 1995 two theoretical texts were produced that tried to chart the territory for the new discipline. A comprehensive overview and analysis of medieval and post-medieval archaeological research in Slovenia was

Figure 6. Selection of late-medieval and post-medieval finds from the Ljubljanica riverbed (Photo by Tomaž Lauko, 2009; courtesy of National Museum of Slovenia).

Figure 7.　Remains of a fortified complex surrounding the church of St. Catherine in Dolenja Vas near Senožeče, first mentioned in 1460 (Photo by Darja Grosman, 1997; courtesy of Department of Archaeology, Faculty of Arts, University of Ljubljana).

published by Tomaž Nabergoj (1995) who pointed out the dilemmas regarding the somewhat marginal position of the discipline and its lack of self-confidence in producing relevant interpretations of material culture. I, on the other hand, traced the conceptual development of historical archaeology in Europe and the United States and discussed its epistemological possibilities using the concepts of material culture, literacy, and social theory current in contemporary post-processual archaeology (Predovnik 1995, 2000). The ambitious attempt to place theoretical reflection and introspection into the new discipline's cradle so as to link it with modern theoretic approaches and forego the pitfalls of the traditional culture-historical paradigm was not entirely successful. In a way, it is understandable that the greater part of research efforts is directed toward establishing the fundamental empirical base (through publication of site reports and artifact assemblages) and dating tools (typo-chronologies), but this should

not exclude a variety of theoretical approaches and interpretations.

Some of the theoretically more informed work in Slovenian medieval and post-medieval archaeology comes from the field of spatial studies. In my analysis of the evolution of settlement in the territory of the former Carthusian monastery of Žiče/Seitz, I explored the concept of space—landscape and architecture—as materialization of mental models, grounding my interpretations on (implicitly) phenomenological premises, the concept of habitus, and ideas about the social production of space (Predovnik 1997, 1998). The concept of landscape as a field of direct sensory perception and experience-based comprehension of space was discussed by Dimitrij Mlekuž in his case study of the soundscape around the town of Polhov Gradec in the pre-industrial era. He examined the possibilities of applying GIS tools to the type of spatial studies where space is conceptualized not as abstract and objective, but as centered on the person perceiving, experiencing, and interacting with it (Mlekuž 2002). GIS tools were also applied by Benjamin Štular in his interpretation of the dynamics of human conquest and use of the Alpine environment in the mountains around Bled (Štular 2006) and in his analysis of the logic of the spatial placement and architectural development of Mali Grad (Little Castle) in Kamnik (Štular 2009). Another study involving the use of GIS was the analysis of a landscape of conflict from the time of Ottoman incursions in the 15th and 16th centuries around Pivka and Ilirska Bistrica in southern Slovenia (Predovnik, Novaković, et al. 2010). A complex defense system consisting of signal posts, fortified churches (Figure 7), and other fortifications was modeled, and its functioning and efficiency tested. The landscape was interpreted using the theory of structuration since these fortifications had a variety of social meanings. Built by and for the peasants with their lords' consent (and sometimes without it) to protect them against the Turkish armies, they were used by the populace subversively to question the feudal authority in peasants' revolts and, in peaceful times, they served as places where the village community would be re-constituted through the exercise of power over their own individual and communal possessions (safe-keeping of goods, trade, jurisdiction).

Endeavoring to extend and transcend the discipline's limits in every aspect, Blaž Podpečan applied the approaches of the so-called archaeology of emotion, as well as principles of typology and methods from art and literary studies in his work on post-medieval tombstones in the Spodnja Savinjska Valley west of Žalec. He examined tombstones as complex sources consisting of material, pictorial, and textual elements and possessing symbolic (religious), emotional, and social meanings interlinked in a whole system of communication. Podpečan offered a convincing interpretation of the social and cultural contingency of personal emotions and seemingly individualized experience of death manifested through the material practices of mourning and commemoration (Podpečan 2006).

The described development of Slovenian archaeology of later periods can be evaluated in various ways. It might seem late and somewhat limited in scope when compared with historical archaeology as it is practiced in the United States and Britain, for example. In the context of central European research traditions, however, and taking into account the proverbial small size of Slovenian archaeology (in terms of geography, staff, and financing), the achievements might seem more satisfactory. Many weaknesses could be named, of course, such as a desperate lag in publication of field research and very limited application of the analytical tools of the natural sciences in the study of artifacts, taphonomy, demography, and environment. In contrast to historical archaeology in the New World, the big topics of giving voice to the "voiceless," examining the workings of capitalism, colonialism, and imperialism, and the issues of inequality, class, and gender have so far been almost completely neglected, which is due both to the specifics of historical developments in this part of the world and to the fact that Slovenian archaeology—like most central European archaeologies—is rather "anthropologically insensitive" (Orser 2010:113). But most importantly, Slovenian archaeology of later periods is still not entirely free from the self-imposed "tyranny of the historical record" and rarely attempts to build insightful interpretations based on material sources. This is not to imply, of course, that archaeological interpretations should be ignoring textual sources. The problem is that these are often used by archaeologists uncritically, whereas the material sources are not interpreted beyond the basic issues of practical function, use, and technology. Such a stance is undoubtedly a sign of "beginner's problems," but also of the common lack of theoretical reflection within Slovenian archaeology.

It is probably still too early for a realistic evaluation of the effects that the transcending of disciplinary boundaries by the archaeology of later periods will have on the broader understanding of the nature and subject of archaeology in Slovenia. In any case, the disciplinary transcendence should be beneficial, since it forces archaeology to reflect on the fundamental premises of its own work, its epistemological possibilities and limitations, and directs it toward a more complete and complex understanding of the past through discourse with related disciplines.

CONCLUSION: AN "ILLEGITIMATE OFFSPRING" BETWEEN DISDAIN AND ACCEPTANCE

Nowhere is the conflict about the purpose and value of archaeology more charged than in the field of medieval archaeology. Archaeological debates with historians have left the subject in a "no man's land." It is regarded as the illegitimate offspring of Prehistory and History and consequently it receives all the polite but disdainful comments that one might expect for a child of this kind [Hodges 1982:7].

Though medieval archaeology, the "illegitimate" child of this ironic statement, has matured considerably in the past thirty years, its proponents occasionally still have to struggle against the same doubts expressed by their fellow archaeologists and historians. Even more so, the legitimacy of archaeological research into early modern and later societies has been, and still is, questioned more or less openly despite the fact that historical archaeologies—and by this term I am referring to post-medieval archaeologies of all periods, however recent—have been around for decades now and have engaged actively in some of the most pressing theoretical and conceptual debates in archaeology, anthropology, and other disciplinary fields such as material culture studies (Hall and Silliman 2006; Hicks and Beaudry 2006b; Majewski and Gaimster 2009; Hicks 2010).

Much ink has been spilled about the relationship between history and archaeology. The recurring discussions about the chronological, topical, and epistemological limitations of archaeology vs. history have served hardly any other purpose than to maintain and strengthen disciplinary boundaries (Grafenauer 1951; Grierson 1959; Jankuhn 1973; Dymond 1974; Schlesinger 1974; Sawyer 1983; Driscoll 1988; Tabaczynski 1993; Ravn and Britton 1997; Scholkmann 2003). This troubled relationship is based on numerous misconceptions about one or the other discipline, their sources, methods, and epistemology. The self-imposed subordination of archaeology to history has been criticized almost as often as the implied supremacy of the written word over the object itself (Austin 1990; Champion 1990; Moreland 1998, 2001).

The differences between history and archaeology appear far less fundamental as historiography experiences a material-cultural turn. Historians have long realized the importance of material things for the personal, cultural, and social lives of people and thus for the study of any society, but have nevertheless presumed an absolute epistemological primacy of the written word over the object. Nowadays, many are focusing their research on material culture itself and the way people in the past constructed themselves through the use of words, objects, and other forms of social discourse. Thus, history is drawing closer to the objectives and approaches of archaeology and anthropology (Lubar and Kingery 1993; Auslander 2005; Harvey 2009). Archaeologists have often objected to the use of objects by historians as mere illustration, "simply to be inserted within historically determined contexts" (Riello 2009:42-43). Yet now even historians maintain that the study of material culture enriches history and helps it build more nuanced and complex narratives about the past than the exclusive use of written documents. The study of material culture is also helpful in subverting and questioning the narratives of history. "Material artefacts with their multifarious meanings, their innate opaqueness and their difficult heuristic nature remind us that history is always producing but has still a great deal more to do before covering all the corners of human experience" (Riello 2009: 43).

What is crucial to the position of archaeology with its focus on the material, is the recognition that all social relations involve things, are constituted by and lived through the material world. This conceptualization understands objects as social agents, which makes them a necessary element in the study of human present and past (Gosden 1999:120). The material setting of a given society is both the medium and tool for social reproduction and transformation, spanning various time-scales (Gosden 1994). Thus, understanding the material make-up of any society is every bit as vital as understanding it's spoken and written traditions. That is the true value of any archaeology, whether prehistoric, historical, or even of the contemporary past.

Insistence on clearly demarcated divisions between disciplines with the argument that only highly trained professionals possess the skill, knowledge, and insight to practice the trade legitimately seems logically sound. Its purpose is to ensure that relevant and verifiable knowledge claims can be produced. Disciplinary specialization certainly is a "response to the ever-growing complexity of knowledge" (Rowlands and Gledhill 1976:37). Yet modern academic disciplines and divisions between them are not "natural;" they are a product of the "condition of modernity," and therefore historically contingent (for archaeology, Thomas 2004). The fragmentation of knowledge that these academic divisions result in is not necessarily best suited to the understanding of "life-worlds," whether past or present, in a complex and holistic manner. The various historic disciplines fragment the past and thus disregard the totality of social discourse; "this does not take us very far in our attempts to understand how *people* in the past constructed themselves and their social relationships with others" (Moreland 1998:97 [emphasis in original]).

Historical archaeology has been transcending boundaries of many sorts, be they geographical (Europe, the New World, and the global cultural, social, and economic networks), temporal (medieval to post-medieval, early industrial, and lately even the contemporary past), or disciplinary (between archaeology, history, anthropology, ethnography, sociology, and others). In many parts of the world, historical archaeology has become generally accepted as "neither history nor anthropology, but a mixture of both" (Orser 2010:114), an interdisciplinary field linking diverse sources and methodologies in studying the material world of complex literate societies. Such freedom of movement between academic disciplines is not so self-evident to scholars working in central European research traditions. In spite of the vibrant development of archaeological inquiry into the "historical and contemporary past," I believe it is precisely this breaking of boundaries that generates a sense of confusion and loss of disciplinary identity for numerous archaeologists in the Old World, and particularly so in central Europe with its long tradition of clear disciplinary distinction, methodological strictness, classification, and periodization (Gaimster 2009).

In my experience—that is, Slovenian and central European—the attempts of (historical) archaeology to venture too far into the preserves of documentary history, ethnology, anthropology, or architectural and art history are more often than not dismissed by the practitioners of these disciplines as irrelevant at best, or as an attempt of encroachment upon neighboring disciplinary fields at worst. Such hegemonic discourse is partly the result of a lack of understanding and interest between the individual disciplines, but to a far greater degree it is a direct outcome of the current politics and economics of science with clear and rather rigid

divisions into separate disciplines at the academic level, and public research funding organized along the same lines. There is, of course, a very prosaic side to the protection of disciplinary boundaries—ultimately, it is about a struggle for resources and status between competing interest groups of scientists (Carver 2002:489-490). It all comes down to the question of how much public funding an individual discipline is entitled to in the fields of education and research, based on its public image and the sense of relevance for contemporary society.

This same discourse breeds also the occasional lack of acceptance of historical archaeology among archaeologists working on other periods. The interdisciplinary nature of historical archaeology following from the diversity and multiplicity of evidence it is confronted with is perceived as a fundamental Otherness by the practitioners of prehistoric, Roman, or even early medieval archaeologies: they often maintain very explicitly that historical archaeology is not "true" archaeology and that it merely inhibits the "actual" archaeological work. In Slovenia the new Cultural Heritage Protection Act of 2008, which practically instituted historical archaeology, has stimulated a lively debate among archaeologists: those active in the fields of heritage management, preservation, and in museums feel that they will be overflowed with fieldwork, data, and artifacts from historic sites to the detriment of what they should actually be doing—investigating and protecting the "actual" archaeological remains from traditional archaeological periods. Similarly, in the field of national research funding, research projects on traditional archaeological periods and issues are clearly given preference over those opening up new fields of research by introducing interdisciplinary approaches and methods. The struggle for separate disciplinary identities and privilege continues, while the inter- and sub-disciplinary boundaries continue to hold, and even abound.

Still, there is every reason to be optimistic. Historical archaeology in Slovenia has come a long way already and is growing fast. It might still be merely tolerated and not quite accepted by many archaeologists or even ignored by its sister disciplines, but attitudes are changing with the growing numbers of young archaeologists educated in medieval and post-medieval archaeologies, numerous preventive and systematic research interventions on historic sites, and the new knowledge about the past they produce. The next step historical archaeology needs to take is to enter into a debate with neighboring disciplines, clearing away misconceptions and finding common ground. But that will only be possible if historical archaeologists will produce relevant and resonant interpretations about people in the past, for this should be our ultimate goal.

REFERENCES

ANDRÉN, ANDERS
1998   *Between Artifacts and Texts: Historical Archaeology in Global Perspective.* Plenum Press, New York.

AUBELJ, BRONISLAVA (EDITOR)
1999   *Zakladi tisočletij: zgodovina Slovenije od neandertalcev do Slovanov*[*Treasures of Millenia: The History of Slovenia from the Neanderthals to the Slavs*]. Modrijan, Ljubljana, Slovenia.

AUSLANDER, LEORA
2005   Beyond Words. *The American Historical Review* 110(4):1015-1045.

AUSTIN, DAVID
1990   The "Proper Study" of Medieval Archaeology. In *From the Baltic to the Black Sea,* David Austin and Leslie Alcock, editors, pp. 9-42. One World Archaeology 18. Unwin Hyman, London, England.

BREGANT, TATJANA
1983   Prispevek arheoloških raziskav k proučevanju stavbnega razvoja Starega gradu Celje [The Contribution of Archaeological Research to the Study of the Development of the Building of the Old Castle of Celje]. *Varstvo spomenikov* 25:39-52.

BRIŠNIK, DANIJELA
1999   Stari grad nad Celjem: keramično gradivo iz sektorjev A in B [The Castle of Stari Grad above Celje: Ceramic Finds from Sectors A and B]. In *Zbornik mednarodnega simpozija Celjski grofje, stara tema—nova spoznanja, Celje, 27.-29. maj 1998,* Rolanda Fugger Germadnik, editor, pp. 261-307. Pokrajinski muzej Celje, Celje, Slovenia.

BUCHLI, VICTOR, AND GAVIN LUCAS (EDITORS)
2001   *Archaeologies of the Contemporary Past.* Routledge, London, England.

CARVER, MARTIN
2002   Marriages of True Minds: Archaeology with Texts. In *Archaeology: The Widening Debate,* Barry Cunliffe, Wendy Davies, and Colin Renfrew, editors, pp. 465-496. Oxford University Press, Oxford, England.

CHAMPION, TIMOTHY C.
1990   Medieval Archaeology and the Tyranny of the Historical Record. In *From the Baltic to the Black Sea,* David Austin and Leslie Alcock, editors, pp. 79-95. Unwin Hyman, London, England.

CORSELLIS, JOHN, AND MARCUS FERRAR
2010   *Slovenia 1945: Memories of Death and Survival after World War II.* I. B. Tauris, London, England.

DEETZ, JAMES
1991   Introduction: Archaeological Evidence of Sixteenth – and Seventeenth-Century Encounters. In *Historical Archaeology in Global Perspective,* Lisa Falk, editor, pp. 1-9. Smithsonian Institution Press, Washington, DC.

DJURIĆ, BOJAN
2004   Terra gentis humanae memoria: Archaeological Heritage Protection and the Motorway Construction Project. In *The Earth Beneath Your Feet. Archaeology on the Motorways in Slovenia. Guide to Sites,* Bojan Djurić, editor, pp. 9-28. Institute for the Protection of the Cultural Heritage of Slovenia, Ljubljana, Slovenia.

DRISCOLL, STEPHEN T.
1988   The Relationship between History and Archaeology: Artefacts, Documents and Power. In *Power and Politics in Early Medieval Britain and Ireland,* Stephen T. Driscoll and Margaret R. Nieke, editors, pp. 162-187. Edinburgh University Press, Edinburgh, Scotland.

DYMOND, DAVID P.
1974   *Archaeology and History: A Plea for Reconciliation.* Thames and Hudson, London, England.

ELISEO, MAURIZIO
1992   *REX—regis nomen, navis omen: Storia di un transatlantico—The Greyhound of the Seas.* Ermano Albertelli, Parma, Italy.

FERENC, MITJA
2008   Absent from Public Memory. Hidden Grave Sites in Slovenia 60 Years after the End of World War Two. In *1945—A Break with the Past: A History of Central European Countries at the End of World War II,* Zdenko Čepič, editor, pp. 263-274. Inštitut za novejšo zgodovino, Ljubljana, Slovenia.

FISCHER, JASNA, ŽARKO LAZAREVIĆ, ERVIN DOLENC, JURIJ PEROVŠEK, BOJAN GODEŠA, ZDENKO ČEPIČ, ALEŠ GABRIČ, NATAŠA KANDUS, AND IGOR ZEMLJIČ (EDITORS)
2005   *Slovenska novejša zgodovina: od programa Zedinjena Slovenija do mednarodnega priznanja Republike Slovenije (1848-1992)* [*Slovenian Modern History: From the Program of "United Slovenia" until the International Recognition of the Republic of Slovenia (1848-1992)*], 2 vols. Mladinska knjiga, Inštitut za novejšo zgodovino, Ljubljana, Slovenia.

FLYNN, DENNIS O. (EDITOR)
1996   *World Silver and Monetary History in the Sixteenth and Seventeenth Centuries.* Variorum, Aldershot, England.

FROMMER, SÖREN

2007   *Historische Archäologie: Ein Versuch der methodologischen Grundlegung der Archäologie als Geschichtswissenschaft [Historical Archaeology: An Attempt to Lay the Ground for Archaeology as Historical Science]*. Tübinger Forschungen zur historischen Archäologie, 2. Verlag Dr. Faustus, Büchenbach, Germany.

FUNARI, PEDRO PAULO A.

1999   Historical Archaeology from a World Perspective. In *Historical Archaeology: Back from the Edge*, Pedro Paulo A. Funari, Martin Hall, and Siân Jones, editors, pp. 37-66. Routledge, London, England.

GAIMSTER, DAVID

2009   An Embarrassment of Riches? Post-Medieval Archaeology in Northern and Central Europe. In *International Handbook of Historical Archaeology*, Teresita Majewski and David Gaimster, editors, pp. 525-547. Springer, New York, New York.

GASPARI, ANDREJ (EDITOR)

2008a   *Neznano Blejsko jezero: podvodna kulturna dediščina in rezultati arheoloških raziskav [The Unknown Lake Bled: Underwater Cultural Heritage and the Results of Archaeological Research]*. Zavod za varstvo kulturne dediščine Slovenije, Ljubljana, Slovenia.

2008b   Perspektiva arheologije bojišč in raziskav vojaških ostankov iz zadnjih dveh stoletij na Slovenskem [Battlefield Archaeology and Research of Military Remnants from the Last Two Centuries in the Territory of Modern Day Slovenia]. *Arheo* 25:101-106.

2010   Rimski in srednjeveški most čez Savo ter stolp Klauzenštajn v Zidanem Mostu [The Roman and Medieval Bridges over the Sava and Klausenstein Tower at Zidani Most]. *Varstvo spomenikov* 45:7-37.

GASPARI, ANDREJ, AND MIRAN ERIČ

2008   Arheološke raziskave struge Ljubljanice med Verdom in Vrhniko [Archaeological Research of the Ljubljanica Riverbed between Verd and Vrhnika]. *Annales, Series Historia et Sociologia* 18(2):407-430.

GASPARI, ANDREJ, JURE MILJEVIĆ, AND BRANKO MUŠIČ

2010   Raziskave razbitine lovskega letala Supermarine Spitfire F.IX MJ116 iz 73. skupine RAF ob Ižanski cesti v Ljubljani [Research on the Wreckage of Supermarine Spitfire F.IX MJ116 of RAF No. 73 Squadron near Ižanska cesta in Ljubljana]. *Arheo* 27:57-72.

GESTRIN, FERDO

1991   *Slovenske dežele in zgodnji kapitalizem [Slovenian Lands and Early Capitalism]*. Slovenska matica, Ljubljana, Slovenia.

GOSDEN, CHRISTOPHER

1994   *Social Being and Time*. Blackwell, Oxford, England.

1999   *Anthropology and Archaeology: A Changing Relationship*. Routledge, London, England.

GRAFENAUER, BOGO

1951   O arheologiji in zgodovini [On Archaeology and History]. *Zgodovinski časopis* 5:163-174. Ljubljana, Slovenia.

1964-
1964   *Zgodovina slovenskega naroda [History of the Slovenian People]*, 5 vols. Državna založba Slovenije, Ljubljana, Slovenia.

GRIERSON, PHILIP

1959   Commerce in the Dark Ages: a Critique of the Evidence. *Transactions of the Royal Historical Society* 9:123-140. London, England.

GUŠTIN, MITJA (EDITOR)

2001   *Srednjeveško Celje [Medieval Celje]*. Filozofska fakulteta, Oddelek za arheologijo, Ljubljana, Slovenia.

2004   *Srednjeveška in novoveška keramika iz Pirana in Svetega Ivana / Ceramiche medievali e postmedievali da Pirano e San Giovanni / Srednjovjekovna i novovjekovna keramika iz Pirana i Svetog Ivana [Medieval and Post-Medieval Ceramics from Piran and Sveti Ivan]*. Univerza na Primorskem, Znanstveno-raziskovalno središče, Inštitut za dediščino Sredozemlja, Koper, Slovenia, Pomorski muzej Sergej Mašera, Piran, Slovenia, Muzej grada Umaga, Umag, Croatia.

GUŠTIN, MITJA, VESNA BIKIĆ, AND ZRINKA MILEUSNIĆ (EDITORS)

2008   *Ottoman Times: The Story of Stari Bar/Osmanska vremena: priča o Starom Baru*. Univerza na Primorskem, Znanstveno-raziskovalno središče, Založba Annales, Koper, Slovenia.

GUŠTIN, MITJA, SAURO GELICHI, AND KONRAD SPINDLER (EDITORS)

2006   *The Heritage of the Serenissima: The Presentation of the Architectural and Archaeological Remains of the Venetian Republic, Proceedings of the International Conference, Izola—Venezia, 4.-9. 11. 2005*. Univerza na Primorskem, Znanstveno-raziskovalno središče, Inštitut za dediščino Sredozemlja, Založba Annales, Koper, Slovenia.

GUŠTIN, MITJA, AND MARTIN HORVAT (EDITORS)

1994   *Ljubljanski grad. Pečnice [Ljubljana Castle. Stove-Tiles]*. Filozofska fakulteta, Oddelek za arheologijo, Ljubljana, Slovenia.

GUŠTIN, MITJA, AND KATARINA PREDOVNIK (EDITORS)

1997   *Drobci nekega vsakdana [Fragments of Everyday Life]*. Filozofska fakulteta, Oddelek za arheologijo, Ljubljana, Slovenia.

HALL, MARTIN, AND STEPHEN W. SILLIMAN (EDITORS)
2006   *Historical Archaeology*. Blackwell Studies in Global Archaeology 9. Blackwell Publishing, Malden, Massachusetts.

HARRISON, RODNEY, AND JOHN SCHOFIELD
2010   *After Modernity: Archaeological Approaches to the Contemporary Past*. Oxford University Press, Oxford, England.

HARVEY, KAREN (EDITOR)
2009   *History and Material Culture: A Student's Guide to Approaching Alternative Sources*. Routledge, London, England.

HICKS, DAN
2010   The Material-Cultural Turn: Event and Effect. In *The Oxford Handbook of Material Culture Studies*, Dan Hicks and Mary C. Beaudry, editors, pp. 25-98. Oxford University Press, Oxford, England.

HICKS, DAN, AND MARY C. BEAUDRY
2006a   Introduction: The Place of Historical Archaeology. In *The Cambridge Companion to Historical Archaeology*, Dan Hicks and Mary C. Beaudry, editors, pp. 1-9. Cambridge University Press, Cambridge, England.

HICKS, DAN, AND MARY C. BEAUDRY (EDITORS)
2006b   *The Cambridge Companion to Historical Archaeology*. Cambridge University Press, Cambridge, England.

HODGES, RICHARD
1982   Method and Theory in Medieval Archaeology. *Archaeologia Medievale* 9:7-38.

JAMNIK, PAVEL
2008   Prikrita množična grobišča v Sloveniji: koliko je arheološkega dela pri izkopih grobišč in ugotavljanju njihovega obstoja? [The Secret Mass Graves of Slovenia: How Much Work is there for Archaeology in their Excavation and Detection?]. *Prispevki za novejšo zgodovino* 48(2):173-186.

JANKUHN, HERBERT
1973   Umrisse einer Archäologie des Mittelalters [Outlines of an Archaeology of the Middle Ages]. *Zeitschrift für Archäologie des Mittelalters* 1:9-19.

JOGAN, SAVIN
2008   *Pravno varstvo dediščine: ogrožanje in uničevanje kulturne in naravne dediščine ter pravni vidiki njunega varstva* [*The Legal Protection of Heritage: Endangerment and Destruction of the Cultural and the Natural Heritage and the Legal Aspects of their Protection*]. Založba Annales, Koper, Slovenia.

JOHNSON, MATTHEW H.
1996   *An Archaeology of Capitalism*. Blackwell, Oxford, England.

1999   Rethinking Historical Archaeology. In *Historical Archaeology: Back from the Edge*, Pedro Paulo A. Funari, Martin Hall, and Siân Jones, editors, pp. 23-36. Routledge, London, England.

2006   The Tide Reversed: Prospects and Potentials for a Postcolonial Archaeology of Europe. In *Historical Archaeology*, Martin Hall and Stephen W. Silliman, editors, pp. 313-331. Blackwell Studies in Global Archaeology 9. Blackwell Publishing, Malden, Massachusetts.

KASTELIC, JOŽE
1964-
1965   Nekaj problemov zgodnjesrednjeveške arheologije v Sloveniji [Some Problems Concerning Early Medieval Archaeology in Slovenia]. *Arheološki vestnik* 15-16:109-124. Ljubljana, Slovenia.

KNIFIC, TIMOTEJ
1993   Arheološki pregled morskega dna v Sloveniji [An Archaeological Survey of the Seabed in Slovenia]. In *Kultura narodnostno mešanega ozemlja slovenske Istre*, Duša Krnel-Umek, editor, pp. 13-28. Znanstveni inštitut Filozofske fakultete, Ljubljana Slovenia.

KOROŠEC, JOSIP
1950a   Arheologija in nekatere njene naloge [Archaeology and Some of its Tasks]. *Zgodovinski časopis* 4:5-22. Ljubljana, Slovenia.

1950b   Prvo posvetovanje jugoslovanskih arheologov [The First Conference of Yugoslav Archaeologists]. *Zgodovinski časopis* 4:212-218. Ljubljana, Slovenia.

KRAMBERGER, DUŠAN, AND IVAN STOPAR
1987   Program sanacije in prezentacije gradu Celje [The Program for Conservation and Presentation of the Castle of Celje]. *Celjski zbornik* 1987:85-94.

LECZIEJEWICZ, LECH
1993   Archaeology in Eastern Europe. In *The Study of Medieval Archaeology: European Symposium for Teachers of Medieval Archaeology, Lund 11-15 June 1990*, Hans Andersson and Jens Wienberg, editors, pp. 75-83. Almqvist & Wiksell, Stockholm, Sweden.

LEONE, MARK P.
1995   A Historical Archaeology of Capitalism. *American Anthropologist* 97:251-268.

LEONE, MARK P., AND PARKER B. POTTER, JR.
1988   Introduction: Issues in Historical Archaeology. In *The Recovery of Meaning: Historical Archaeology in the Eastern United States*, Mark P. Leone and Parker B. Potter, Jr., editors, pp. 1-22. Smithsonian Institution Press, Washington, DC.

LOŽAR, RAJKO

1939   Staroslovansko in srednjeveško lončarstvo v
        Sloveniji [Early Slavic and Medieval Pottery
        in Slovenia]. *Glasnik Muzejskega društva za
        Slovenijo* 20:180-225.

LUBAR, STEVEN, AND W. DAVID KINGERY (EDITORS)

1993   *History from Things: Essays on Material Culture.*
        Smithsonian Books, Washington, D.C.

LUTHAR, OTO (EDITOR)

2008   *The Land Between: A History of Slovenia.* Peter
        Lang, Frankfurt am Main, Germany.

MAJEWSKI, TERESITA, AND DAVID GAIMSTER (EDITORS)

2009   *International Handbook of Historical
        Archaeology.* Springer, New York, New York.

MCATACKNEY, LAURA, MATTHEW PALUS, AND ANGELA
PICCINI (EDITORS)

2007   *Contemporary and Historical Archaeology in
        Theory: Papers from the 2003 and 2004 CHAT
        Conferences.* BAR Int. Ser. 1677 = Studies in
        Contemporary and Historical Archaeology 4.
        Archaeopress, Oxford, England.

MIHELIČ, DARJA

2009   Das Zusammentreffen von Geschichte und
        Archäologie: methodologische Überlegungen
        zum Verhältnis Geschichte-Archäologie [The
        Encounter between History and Archaeology:
        Methodological Reflections on the Relationship
        History-Archaeology]. In *Die mittelalterliche
        Stadt erforschen: Archäologie und Geschichte
        im Dialog. Beiträge der Tagung "Geschichte und
        Archäologie: Disziplinäre Interferenzen" vom 7.
        bis 9. Februar 2008 in Zürich,* Armand Baeriswyl,
        Georges Descoeudres, Martina Stercken, and
        Dölf Wild, editors, pp. 165-172. Schweizerischer
        Burgerverein, Basel, Switzerland.

MLEKUŽ, DIMITRIJ

2002   Prisluhnimo krajinam: modeliranje preteklih
        zvočnih krajin [Listening to Landscapes:
        Modeling the Past Soundscapes]. *Arheo* 22:59-65.

MORELAND, JOHN

1992   Restoring the Dialectic: Settlement Patterns
        and Documents in Medieval Central Italy.
        In *Archaeology, Annales, and Ethnohistory,*
        Bernard A. Knapp, editor, pp. 112-129. Cambridge
        University Press, Cambridge, England.

1998   Through the Looking Glass of Possibilities:
        Understanding the Middle Ages. In *Die
        Vielfalt der Dinge: Neue Wege zur Analyse
        mittelalterlicher Sachkultur,* Helmut
        Hundsbichler, Gerhard Jaritz, and Thomas
        Kühtreiber, editors, pp. 85-116. Verlag der
        Österreichischen Akademie der Wissenschaften,
        Vienna, Austria.

2001   *Archaeology and Text.* Duckworth, London,
        England.

MÜLLNER, ALFONS

1892a   Die Felsenburg Lueg in Innerkrain [The Cave
        Castle of Lueg/Jama in the Region of Notranjska].
        Argo 1(2):14-16 and Taf. 2. Ljubljana, Slovenia.

1892b   Mittheilungen aus dem Museum
        [Communications from the Museum]. *Argo*
        1(4):78-79. Ljubljana, Slovenia.

1894   Die Felsenburg Lueg in Innerkrain [The Cave
        Castle of Lueg/Jama in the Region of Notranjska].
        Argo 3(3):57-66; 3(6):105-114. Ljubljana, Slovenia.

1897   Die Ausgrabungen in der Spitalgasse in Laibach
        1896 und 1897 [Excavations in Spital Street in
        Laibach/Ljubljana 1896 and 1987]. *Argo* 5(3):51-
        54 and Taf. 1. Ljubljana, Slovenia.

1898   Die Ausgrabungen in der Spitalgasse in Laibach
        1896 und 1897 [Excavations in Spital Street in
        Laibach/Ljubljana 1896 and 1987]. *Argo* 6(6):104-
        109. Ljubljana, Slovenia.

NABERGOJ, TOMAŽ

1995   Arheologija in gotika [Archaeology and Gothic].
        In *Gotika v Sloveniji—svet predmetov,* Maja
        Lozar Štamcar, editor, pp. 7-107. Narodni muzej,
        Ljubljana, Slovenia.

1999   Srednjeveška keramika iz Ljubljane in Ljubljanice
        iz zbirk Arheološkega oddelka Narodnega
        muzeja Slovenije [Medieval Pottery from
        Ljubljana and Ljubljanica from the Collections of
        the Archaeological Department of the National
        Museum of Slovenia]. *Argo* 42(1):39-66.

2005   Muzealec v Narodnem muzeju in začetki
        arheologije srednjega veka [Ložar as Curator at
        the National Museum and his Beginnings in the
        Archaeology of the Middle Ages]. In *Pretrgane
        korenine: sledi življenja in dela Rajka Ložarja,*
        Ingrid Slavec Gradišnik, editor, pp. 159-189.
        Založba ZRC, ZRC SAZU, Ljubljana, Slovenia.

NOVAKOVIĆ, PREDRAG

2001   Ložar, Rajko (1904-1985). In *Encyclopedia of
        Archaeology: History and Discoveries,* Tim
        Murray, editor, pp. 831-832. ABC-Clio, Santa
        Barbara, California.

2002   Archaeology in Five States—A Peculiarity
        or Just Another Story at the Crossroads of
        "Mitteleuropa" and the Balkans: A Case Study of
        Slovene Archaeology. In *Archäologien Europas:
        Geschichte, Methoden und Theorien / History,
        Methods and Theories,* Peter F. Biehl, Alexander
        Gramsch, and Arkadiusz Marciniak, editors,
        pp. 323-352. Waxmann, Münster, New York,
        New York.

2005   Ložarjev pogled na slovensko arheologijo in njegova ideja arheologije [Rajko Ložar's View on Slovenian Archaeology and his Notion of Archaeology]. In *Pretrgane korenine: sledi življenja in dela Rajka Ložarja*, Ingrid Slavec Gradišnik, editor, pp. 139-157. Založba ZRC, ZRC SAZU, Ljubljana, Slovenia.

2011   Archaeology in the New Countries of Southeastern Europe: A Historical Perspective. In *Comparative Archaeologies: A Sociological View of the Science of the Past*, Ludomir R. Lozny, editor, pp. 339-461. Springer, New York, New York.

NOVAKOVIĆ, PREDRAG, MILAN LOVENJAK, AND MIHAEL BUDJA

2004   *Osemdeset let študija arheologije na Univerzi v Ljubljani* [*Eighty Years of Archaeology Studies at the University of Ljubljana*]. Filozofska fakulteta, Oddelek za arheologijo, Ljubljana, Slovenia.

ORSER, CHARLES E., JR.

1996   *A Historical Archaeology of the Modern World.* Plenum Press, New York, New York.

2010   Twenty-First-Century Historical Archaeology. *Journal of Archaeological Research* 18:111-150.

PAS

1982   *Podvodna arheologija v Sloveniji* [*Underwater Archaeology in Slovenia*]. Narodni muzej, Ljubljana, Slovenia.

1984   *Podvodna arheologija v Sloveniji II* [*Underwater Archaeology in Slovenia II*]. Narodni muzej, Ljubljana, Slovenia.

PAYNTER, ROBERT

2000   Historical and Anthropological Archaeology: Forging Alliances. *Journal of Archaeological Research* 8(1):1-37. New York, New York.

PIEPER, RENATE

1990   The Volume of African and American Exports of Precious Metals and its Effects in Europe, 1500-1800. In *The European Discovery of the World and its Economic Effects on Pre-Industrial Society, 1500-1800: Papers of the Tenth International Economic History Congress*, Hans Pohl, editor, pp. 97-121. Franz Steiner Verlag, Stuttgart, Germany.

PLETERSKI, ANDREJ

1979   Povezovanje tvarnih in pisanih virov pri proučevanju zgodnjega srednjega veka—alpskih Slovanov [Links between Material and Written Sources in the Study of the Early Middle Ages—Alpine Slavs]. *Arheološki vestnik* 30:507-519.

1997   *Inštitut za arheologijo polstoletnik* [*Fiftieth Anniversary of the Institute of Archaeology*]. Znanstvenoraziskovalni center SAZU, Ljubljana, Slovenia.

PLETERSKI, ANDREJ, AND GORAN PAVEL ŠANTEK (EDITORS)

2010   *Mirila: kulturni fenomen* [*Mirila: A Cultural Phenomenon*]. Inštitut za arheologijo ZRC SAZU, Založba ZRC, Ljubljana, Slovenia.

PODPEČAN, BLAŽ

2006   *Nagrobnik, podoba živih* [*The Gravestone: An Image of the Living*]. Filozofska fakulteta, Oddelek za arheologijo, Ljubljana, Slovenia.

PREDOVNIK, KATARINA

1995   *O stvareh in besedah. Arheologija mlajših obdobij* [*On Things and Words: The Archaeology of Later Periods*]. Unpublished graduate thesis. Univerza v Ljubljani, Filozofska fakulteta, Oddelek za arheologijo, Ljubljana, Slovenia.

1997   Svet puščave: materializacije kartuzijanske duhovnosti [The World of Desert: Materializations of Carthusian Spirituality]. *Poligrafi* 7-8, year 2:145-174.

1998   Die Kartause Seitz: naturliche und ideologische Momente in der Genese einer Kulturlandschaft [The Charterhouse of Seitz/Žiče: Natural and Ideological Factors in the Creation of a Cultural Landscape]. In *Mensch und Natur im mittelalterlichen Europa. Archäologische, historische und naturwissenschaftliche Befunde*, Konrad Spindler, editor, pp. 261-278. Wieser, Klagenfurt, Austria.

2000   Cur archaeologia medievalis? [Why Medieval Archaeology?]. *Časopis za kritiko znanosti, domišljijo in novo antropologijo* 28(200-201):31-51.

2003   *Trdnjava Kostanjevica na Starem gradu nad Podbočjem* [*The Fortress of Kostanjevica (Veste Landestrost) at Stari Grad above the Village of Podbočje*]. Filozofska fakulteta, Oddelek za arheologijo, Znanstveni inštitut, Ljubljana, Slovenia.

2008   Nova obzorja: arheologija mlajših obdobij [New Horizons: An Archaeology of Later Periods]. *Arheo* 25:81-88.

2009   Prunk bei Tisch: Vom Beginn der Neuzeit in den slowenischen Ländern [Splendor at the Table: On the Beginnings of the Early Modern Period in Slovenian Lands]. In *Zwischen Tradition und Wandel: Archäologie des 15. und 16. Jahrhunderts*, Barbara Scholkmann, Sören Frommer, and Chistina Vossler, editors, pp. 281-290. Verlag Dr. Faustus, Erlangen, Germany.

PREDOVNIK, KATARINA, MARJANA DACAR, AND MATEVŽ LAVRINC

2008   *Cerkev sv. Jerneja v Šentjerneju: arheološka izkopavanja v letih 1985 in 1986* [*St. Bartholomew Church in Šentjernej: Archaeological Excavations in 1985 and 1986*]. Filozofska fakulteta, Znanstvena založba, Oddelek za arheologijo, Ljubljana, Slovenia.

PREDOVNIK, KATARINA, AND TOMAŽ NABERGOJ

2010   Archaeological Research into the Periods
        Following the Early Middle Ages in Slovenia.
        Arheološki vestnik 61:245-295.

PREDOVNIK, KATARINA, PREDRAG NOVAKOVIĆ, AND
MATJAŽ BIZJAK

2010   Türkenzeitliche Wehranlagen und
        Verteidigungstrategien der ländlichen
        Bevölkerung im Gebiet des heutigen Slowenien
        [Fortifications and Defense Strategies of the
        Rural Population in the Territory of Today's
        Slovenia at the Time of Turkish Incursions].
        In *"vmbringt mit starcken turnen, murn":
        Ortsbefestigungen im Mittelalter*, Olaf Wagener,
        editor, pp. 363-394. Peter Lang, Frankfurt am
        Main, Germany.

RAVN, MADS, AND RUPERT BRITTON (EDITORS)

1997   *History and Archaeology*. Special Issue of
        Archaeological Review from Cambridge 14(1).

RIELLO, GIORGIO

2009   Things that Shape History: Material Culture and
        Historical Narratives. In *History and Material
        Culture: A Student's Guide to Approaching
        Alternative Sources*, Karen Harvey, editor, pp. 24-
        46. Routledge, London, England.

ROWLANDS, MICHAEL J., AND JOHN GLEDHILL

1976   The Relation between Archaeology and
        Anthropology. *Critique of Anthropology* 2:23-37.

SAWYER, PETER

1983   English Archaeology before the Conquest:
        A Historian's View. In *25 Years of Medieval
        Archaeology*, David Hinton, editor, pp. 44-47.
        University of Sheffield, Sheffield, England   .

SCHLESINGER, WALTER

1974   Archäologie des Mittelalters in der Sicht des
        Historikers [Medieval Archaeology in the View
        of a Historian]. *Zeitschrift für Archäologie des
        Mittelalters* 2:7-31.

SCHOLKMANN, BARBARA

2003   Die Tyrannei der Schriftquellen? Überlegungen
        zum Verhältnis materieller und schriftlicher
        Überlieferung in der Mittelalterarchäologie
        [The Tyranny of Written Sources? Reflections
        on the Relationship between the Material and
        the Written Tradition in Medieval Archaeology].
        In *Zwischen Erklären und Verstehen? Beiträge
        zu den erkenntnistheoretischen Grundlagen
        archäologischer Interpretation*, Marlies Heinz,
        Manfred K. H. Eggert, and Ulrich Veit, editors,
        pp. 239-257. Waxmann, Münster, Germany.

SKLENÁŘ, KAREL

1983   *Archaeology in Central Europe: The First 500
        Years*. Leicester University Press, Leicester,
        England.

SLABE, MARIJAN

1974   Varovanje zemeljskih slojev s kulturnimi ostanki
        na področju Škofje Loke [Protection of Buried
        Cultural Remains inside the Town of Škofja Loka].
        Loški razgledi 21:73-78.

1977   Loška slikana meščanska keramika [Loka Painted
        Burghers' Ware]. *Loški razgledi* 24:55-57.

1980a   Ob otvoritvi razstave meščanske keramike [On
        Occasion of the Opening of the Exhibition on
        Burghers' Ceramics]. *Loški razgledi* 27:311-313.

1980b   Raziskovanje kulturnih ostalin mlajših dob
        [Research on Cultural Remains from the Later
        Periods]. In *Rešena arheološka dediščina Slovenije,
        1945-1980*, Peter Petru, editor, pp. 35-36. Narodni
        muzej, Ljubljana, Slovenia.

1982   Spomeniško varstvo in muzejstvo—skupne
        naloge pri celoviti skrbi za kulturno dediščino
        [Protection of Monuments and Museums—
        Common Tasks in the Comprehensive Care of
        Cultural Heritage]. *Argo* 20-21:92-99.

SLAPŠAK, BOŽIDAR

1982   O zgodovini in arheologiji [On History and
        Archaeology]. *Arheo* 2:51-54.

1987   Tabori v sistemu protiturške obrambe ["Tabors"
        in the System of Defense against the Turks].
        Kronika 35(3):143-146.

SMETÁNKA, ZDENĚK

1993   Archaeology of the Middle Ages in Bohemia:
        Its Past, Present and Future. In *The Study of
        Medieval Archaeology: European Symposium
        for Teachers of Medieval Archaeology, Lund
        11-15 June 1990*, Hans Andersson and Jens
        Wienberg, editors, pp. 91-103. Almqvist & Wiksell,
        Stockholm, Sweden.

ŠRIBAR, VINKO

1972-
1973   Razvoj srednjeveške keramike na Otoku
        pri Dobravi—freizinški trg Gutenwerth
        [Development of Medieval Pottery at the Site
        of Otok Pri Dobravi—Gutenwerth, the Market
        Town of the Bishops of Freising]. *Slovenski
        etnograf* 25-26:9-37.

STARE, VIDA

1991   Pokopališče pri sv. Elizabeti v Špitalski ulici v
        Ljubljani [The Cemetery at St. Elisabeth's in
        Spital Street in Ljubljana]. *Kronika* 39(3):17-28.

1993   Center za arheologijo srednjega veka Narodnega
        muzeja 1960-1987 [Center for Medieval
        Archaeology at the National Museum of Slovenia
        1960-1987]. *Argo* 35:27-33.

2000   Pokopališče v cerkvi sv. Miklavža na Otoku
        pri Dobravi (Gutenwert) [The Cemetery at
        St. Nicholas' at the site of Otok Pri Dobravi
        (Gutenwerth)]. *Argo* 43(2):32-47.

ŠTIH, PETER

2001   Srednjeveško plemstvo in slovensko
        zgodovinopisje [Medieval Nobility and Slovenian
        Historiography]. In *Melikov zbornik: Slovenci
        v zgodovini in njihovi srednjeevropski sosedje,*
        Vincenc Rajšp, Rajko Bratož, Janez Cvirn, Jasna
        Fischer, Walter Lukan, Branko Marušič, editors,
        pp. 61-72. Založba ZRC, ZRC SAZU, Ljubljana,
        Slovenia.

ŠTULAR, BENJAMIN

2006   Prostor blejskih planin v srednjem veku [The
        Area of the Alpine Dairy Farms of Bled in the
        Middle Ages]. In *Človek v Alpah: desetletje (1996-
        2006) raziskav o navzočnosti človeka v slovenskih
        Alpah,* Tone Cevc, editor, pp. 230-241. Založba
        ZRC, ZRC SAZU, Ljubljana, Slovenia.

2008   Kje so meje slovenske arheologije? O
        posrednjeveških arheologijah v Sloveniji [Where
        are the Limits of Slovenian Archaeology? On
        Post Medieval Archaeologies in Slovenia]. *Arheo*
        25:79-80.

2009   *Mali grad. Visokosrednjeveški grad v Kamniku
        [High Medieval Castle in Kamnik].* Inštitut za
        arheologijo ZRC SAZU, Založba ZRC, Ljubljana,
        Slovenia.

ŠUMI, NACE

1983   Mesto gradov in dvorcev v zgodovinskih
        znanostih in naši družbeni zavesti [The Place
        of Castles and Mansions in Historical Sciences
        and in our Social Consciousness]. *Varstvo
        spomenikov* 25:9-12.

TABACZYNSKI, STANISLAW

1993   The Relationship between History and
        Archaeology: Elements of the Present Debate.
        Medieval Archaeology 37:1-14.

TARLOW, SARAH, AND SUSIE WEST (EDITORS)

1999   *The Familiar Past? Archaeologies of Later
        Historical Britain.* Routledge, London, England.

TAUBER, JÜRG

1991   Aspekte zu Möglichkeiten und Grenzen einer
        Archäologie des Mittelalters [Aspects of the
        Possibilities and Limitations of an Archaeology of
        the Middle Ages]. In *Methoden und Perspektiven
        der Archäologie des Mittelalters. Tagungsberichte
        zum interdisziplinären Kolloquium vom 27.-30.
        September 1989 in Liestal (Schweiz),* Jürg Tauber,
        editor, pp. 7-30. Archäologie und Museum
        20. Amt für Museen und Archäologie, Liestal,
        Switzerland.

THOMAS, JULIAN

2004   *Archaeology and Modernity.* Routledge, London,
        England.

TURK, PETER, JANKA ISTENIČ, TIMOTEJ KNIFIC, AND TOMAŽ
NABERGOJ (EDITORS)

2009   *The Ljubljanica—a River and its Past.* Narodni
        muzej Slovenije, Ljubljana, Slovenia.

VALENČIČ, VLADO

1970   Kulturne rastline [Crops]. In *Gospodarska
        in družbena zgodovina Slovencev: Zgodovina
        agrarnih panog, Vol. I: Agrarno gospodarstvo,*
        Pavle Blaznik, Bogo Grafenauer, Milko Kos, Sergij
        Vilfan, Fran Zwitter, Josip Žontar, editors, pp.
        251-272. SAZU, Inštitut za zgodovino, Državna
        založba Slovenije, Ljubljana, Slovenia.

ŽERJAL, TINA

2001   Sidescan sonar— akustični instrument v
        podvodni arheologiji [Sidescan Sonar—The Most
        Widely used Acoustic Instrument in Underwater
        Archaeology]. *Arheo* 21:57-64.

Katarina Predovnik
Filozofska fakulteta, Oddelek za arheologijo
Univerza v Ljubljani
Aškerčeva 2
PO Box 580
SI-1001 Ljubljana
Slovenia

LESZEK KAJZER

Some Remarks about Historical Archaeology in Poland

ABSTRACT

Polish archaeology may be divided into prehistoric and historical archaeology. The former is interested in studying the oldest stages of human history. It was shaped and developed as early as the 19th century. Intensive development of historical archaeology took place after World War II. In contrast to the archaeology of Anglo-Saxon countries or the neighboring Czech Republic, however, in Poland there was interest from the beginning in both the Middle Ages (since the 14th century) and modern times. Therefore, no separation of archaeology of modern times took place. In this paper attention is paid to both epochs. The biggest achievements of contemporary historical archaeology in Poland may be connected with urban studies, not only with excavations in big centers (Gdańsk, Wrocław) but also in smaller towns (Krosno, Stargard). As far as modern times are concerned, the archaeological examination of post-war Polish exhumations of the burials of Polish officers murdered in the east by Stalin's regime during World War II can be regarded as among the most significant studies.

The Polish state lost its independence at the end of the 18th century and regained it in 1918 as a result of World War I. Therefore, in the 19th century—sometimes described as "the century of archaeology" (Abramowicz 1967, 1983, 1987)—formation and development of archaeology in Poland proceeded in accordance with the rules that were in operation in the three invader countries: the Russian Empire, the Prussian Empire, and the Austro-Hungarian Empire.

The renewed appearance of Poland as a self-dependent country on the map of Europe contributed to, among other things, the development of science and the humanities, including archaeology. The science of archaeology was taught in the universities of Warsaw, Kracow, Poznań, Lvov (now Ukraine), and Vilnius (now Lithuania) (Figure 1). Moreover, several specialized archaeological museums appeared, the most important in Warsaw and Poznań. Between World War I and World War II the main subject of interest of Polish archaeologists was prehistory. Special attention was paid to studies on so-called Lusatian culture, which had developed on Polish territory from the middle of the Bronze Age to the early Iron Age and which was identified by Polish archaeologists as associated with the early Slavs' ethnicity. In the second half of the 1930s archaeologists also began to be interested in the early Middle Ages, but, overall, these were marginal studies.

The situation generally changed after World War II. Polish archaeologists were still intensively engaged in

research of prehistory, but during this period much attention was also paid to the early Middle Ages, especially the 10th-13th centuries. This research was connected with the celebration of the Polish Millennium, the thousandth anniversary of Poland's appearance as a Christian country on the map of Europe (A.D. 966-1966). As late as the 1940s and 1950s, the conventional year 1950 was treated as the point after which archaeology "ended" and historians took over. This view changed in the middle of the 1960s when a major research program devoted to the origins of the Polish state ended (Noszczak 2002). At that time, Polish archaeologists became more intensely engaged in later periods and "historical archaeology," initially called "Old Polish archaeology," came into being. This process was parallel with a gradual decline of the influence of Marxist philosophy from Polish humanities, including archaeology (Lech 1997-1998). In present day Polish archaeology, historical archaeology is a respected component beside prehistory and the archaeology of the ancient world, often called "Mediterranean archaeology."

At the same time, here it should be noted that the term "historical archaeology" in Poland had a different meaning than in Anglo-Saxon countries, where it was reserved for post-medieval and modern archaeology. In Poland historical archaeology includes both studies on Polish later Middle Ages and modern times. Also, in numerous Polish archaeological papers the chronological limits of analyzed artifacts range between the 14th and the 18th centuries. The end of the independent Polish

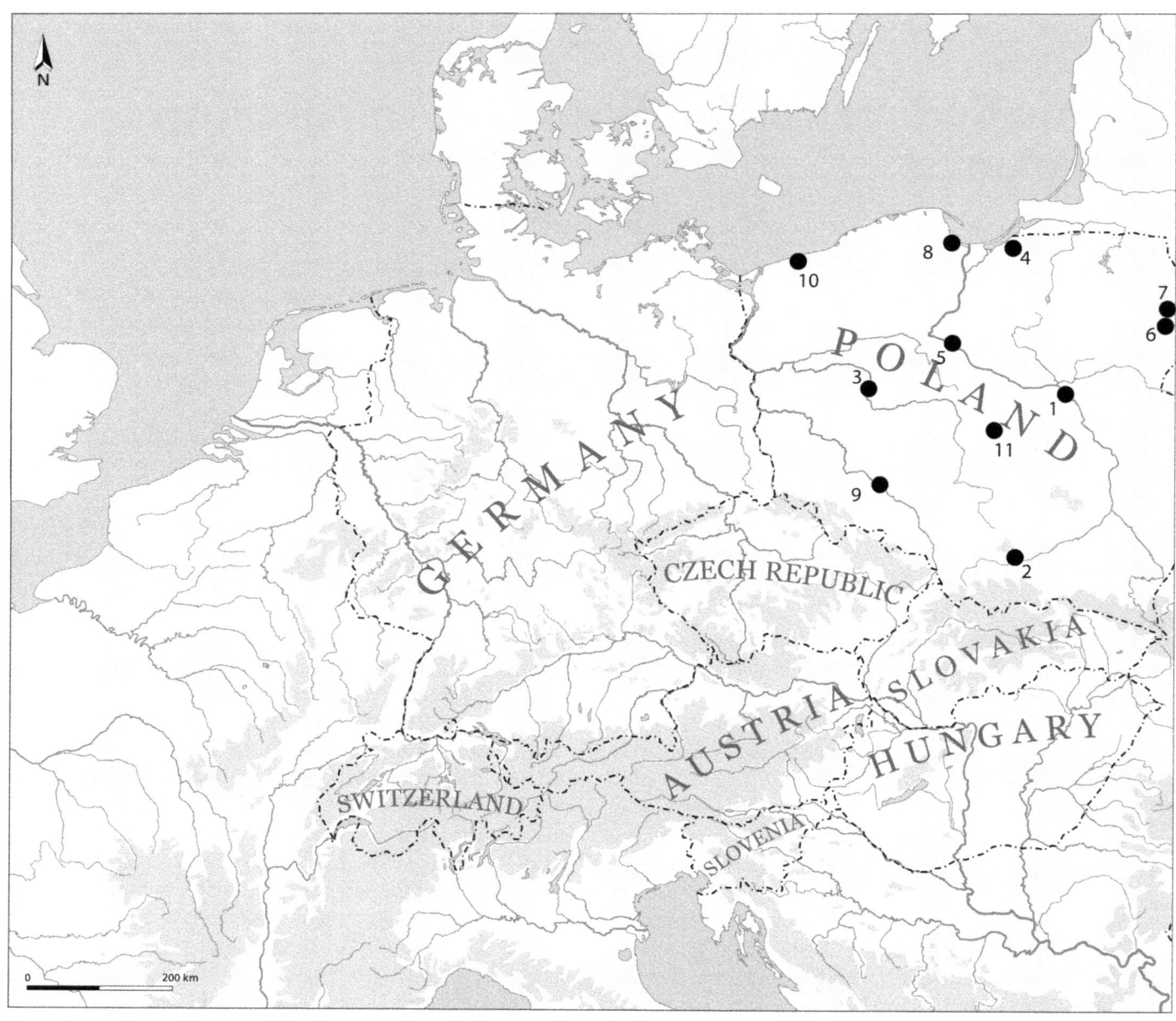

Figure 1.   Map with some of the places mentioned in the text (all in Poland): (1) Warsaw; (2) Kracow; (3) Poznań; (4) Frombork; (5) Toruń; (6) Białystok; (7) Supraśl; (8) Gdańsk; (9) Wrocław; (10) Kołobrzeg; and (11) Łódź. (Map provided courtesy of the Department of Prehistory and Medieval Archaeology, University of Vienna, Austria).

state in the late 18th century delimits the terminus of Polish archaeologists' interests. This situation explains why, in Poland, a periodical such as that published in Prague, "Studies in Post-Medieval Archaeology," has yet to be created.

Although the first excavations were conducted on historic-period sites and historical objects as early as the end of the 19th century, research intensified after World War II, especially since the middle of 1960s. It was at this time that the research emphasis of archaeologists and historians on the beginnings of Polish statehood in the 10th-13th centuries was finished and attention shifted to

sites from the late medieval period (14th-15th centuries) and then to modern sites. Preliminary characteristics of this initial period of Polish historical archaeology were summarized in 1973 by Jerzy Kruppè (1973), who characterized the contemporary state of the field and postulated future directions. Among the most interesting points he made was the disproportionate focus on the period of the late Middle Ages as compared to modern times, that is, the "Old-Polish" times. Attention was also drawn to the lack of balance between different kinds of sites and artifacts—architectonic (stone or brick relics) predominated—as well as to geographical irregularity of excavation, especially the neglect of eastern Poland. A good example of research on historic-period archaeology from this period was the publication (albeit attenuated) by J. Kruppè on Frombork. In this paper, the results of excavations conducted on the occasion of repairs to the defensive cathedral complex were described (Kruppè 1973).

The initial period of formation and development of historical archaeology in Poland was recapitulated during a symposium entitled "State and Needs of Research on the Late Medieval and Modern Times in Poland," which took place in spring 1989 in Łódź (Państwowe Wydawnictwo Naukowe 1993:36). Apart from the papers, an important product of this meeting was the publication of eight chronological maps from the late Middle Ages and modern times. These listed 1,008 excavated sites, 257 of which (over 25%) came from modern times. An observation of the eight chronological maps indicates an interesting regularity. It reveals a relatively small number of post-medieval sites in the western regions of Poland (generally to the west of the Vistula River) and also their relatively high frequency, in relation to late medieval sites, in the eastern areas. This differentiation was not only an effect of the different interests of researchers from particular regions of Poland, but also a reflection of patterns of historical development. The eastern part of Polish territory developed considerably slower economically than the western. In terms of research themes, three major area of focus emerge from the maps, consistent with other European research topics. As formulated by G.P. Fehring, the themes represented in Polish historical archaeology in 1989 were three-fold: (1) archaeology of sacred complexes and cemeteries (*Gräberfelder, Kirchen und Kirchhöfe*); (2) archaeology of defensive works (*Wehranlagen: Burgen und Pfalzen*); and (3) settlement and urban archaeology (*Ländliche und städtische Siedlungen*) (Fehring 1987:10-13).

An important event in the development of historical archaeology in Poland was the creation of the University Center of Medieval and Modern Archaeology in the spring of 1991. This center, affiliated with the University of Mikołaj Kopernik in Toruń and directed by Professor Jadwiga Chudziakowa, assembled all respected archaeologists occupied in problems of historical archaeology. Research of this group of scientists was directed toward a widely outlined cognitive program, which may be defined as "society and its culture in medieval and modern Poland." The natural focus of our science results in the fact that the term "culture" has predominately meant "material culture" because the subject of our studies are artifacts more often than ideas.

An important effect of the creation of the Center was the publication of a new periodical entitled *Archaeologia Historica Polona* (AHP), the first volume of which was published in 1995. The journal, which has now published 18 volumes, includes post-conference volumes that gather articles or lectures from symposia of the Center held and organized in different university centers, and monographs, mainly studies on many years' excavations. In my opinion, the presentation of research problems concerning the Middle Ages and the modern period is the main achievement of this publication.

Since 1989 great changes have taken place in Poland, which has gone from captivity to freedom and has experienced the change of its political system. As a result, Polish research of historical times was again reviewed in a meeting devoted to the picture of Polish historical archaeology in an anniversary of the symposium in Łódź. This symposium, jointly organized by the Institute of Archaeology of the University of Łódź, the University Center of Medieval and Modern Archaeology, and the Museum of Podlasie in Białystok, was held in spring 2009 in Supraśl near Białystok. Its title *Regions. Crafts. Categories. Archaeology of Late Middle Ages and Modern Times in Conditions of a New Political System that is 20 Years Later* needs some comment. "Regions" is a reference to the eight published maps with their lists of archaeologically researched sites, which were published among the materials of the symposium in Łódź from 1989. New contributions have shown the progress of landscape research and defined the character of a new research agenda. "Crafts" is a term enabling the discussion of the most interesting groups of products of medieval and modern craft or selected collections of artifacts obtained in the course of excavations. The last term—"categories"—is the way to arrange new research and observations in the scheme of "post-Fehring" division into the three most important categories of archaeological sites. Although the papers from the symposium held in Supraśl in 2009 are still awaiting publication, observations of lectures and discussions held there allow preliminarily insights into the contemporary state of historical archaeology in Poland. Some words should first be said about the institutional structures of historical archaeology in Poland, however.

Currently in Poland there are institutes of archaeology with full rights dealing with didactic functions in nine universities including Gdańsk, Kracow, Łódź, Poznan, Warsaw, and Wrocław, as well as small departments of archaeology in several others. Moreover, in the biggest cities (Gdańsk, Kracow, Łódź, Poznań, Warsaw, and Wrocław) there are archaeological museums. In all these institutions, although with different intensity, historical archaeology is practiced. More didactic hours are devoted to it in Institutes of Archaeology in Łódź, Toruń, Warsaw, and Wrocław, and less for instance in Kracow. In my vernacular institute in Łódź, within a lecture course, a student should attend two semesters of lectures on the late Middle Ages and modern times, which end with a common examination. The center in Kracow (together with Poznań) is traditionally the strongest center of prehistoric research.

The academic landscape is completed by the Institute of Archaeology and Ethnology of the Polish Academy of Sciences (formerly the basic research institution of Polish archaeology) located in Warsaw and having several subsidiary institutes. The Institute of Archaeology and Ethnology of the Polish Academy of Sciences continues traditions of its predecessor the Institute of Material Culture History of the Polish Academy of Sciences. The institute has published for the last 57 years a periodical *Kwartalnik Historii Kultury Materialnej,* in which papers concerning historical archaeology are regularly published.

Rescue works and other small-scale research interventions are often organized by units of conservators (also called archaeological heritage services). Unfortunately, archaeology is not the strongest component of the Polish heritage service, which is directly subordinated to the state administration. Also, directives given to archaeologists for so-called line (or large-scale) investments, which at least theoretically should concern the most specialized research units, are carried out by conservator's units.

In recent years a very important place on the map of Polish archaeology has been taken by private firms, to which conservators or other bodies entrust "archaeological cleaning of the area," that is exploration of archaeological relics within a given area in order to prepare them for future development. So, private archaeological firms work both on areas of great investments (in quarters of monumental cities, gas lines, roads, and motorways) and small projects, for instance

on the occasion of house building in an archaeologically interesting area.

The last 20 years have brought several interesting changes to Polish historical archaeology. The role, formerly a leading one, of the state-run Institute of Archaeology and Ethnology of the Polish Academy of Sciences, was diminished, as was the research activity of the national heritage service, which became administrative. At the same time, the role of regionally leading centers was taken over by big university institutions, which consolidate intellectual potential, laboratory capabilities, etc. Their primacy is not obvious, however, because in conditions of a free market they are often beaten out in bids for contracts by private firms. Unfortunately, often, but not always, it affects the quality of research when sites are treated as simple "earthen works" rather than places of archaeological value.

Conclusions about contemporary Polish historical archaeology gleaned from the symposium held in 2009 in Supraśl are hampered by the lack of data on site types. Because initiators and funders of archaeological research differ, there is no "central index of rescue and proceeding works." As a result, for the last decade no one in Poland knows on how many sites in a given year archaeological excavations were carried out. This sad conclusion concerns both prehistoric and historical archaeology. The latest year of registration was 1997 when from among almost 500 excavated sites less than 30 percent were late medieval and modern sites. It is worth noting that among the printed materials from the symposium in Supraśl there is a map of as many as 440 late medieval and modern sites excavated in the past 20 years in the Warmia and Masuria areas (annotated by Jacek Wysocki). I consider that overcoming the barrier of knowing the number and kinds of sites excavated is the most important mandate for the future success of Polish archaeology.

In Polish archaeology, as I mentioned before, the decided division into archaeology of the late Middle Ages and archaeology of modern times did not happen as it did, for instance, in the neighboring Czech Republic. An illustration of Polish archaeology's lagging focus on modern times may, for instance, be the lack of any summary study concerning modern pottery. Researchers believe that the major turning points influencing the development and decline of modern pottery were precipitated by war events that occurred in the middle of the 17th century.

The modern practice of post-medieval archaeology is increasingly marked by close contacts between Polish archaeologists and researchers from Lithuania, Belarus, and Ukraine. These are countries of common cultural and geographic roots. Within their contemporary territories lay a part of Poland in modern times, sometimes called the Republic of the Two Nations, which means belonging to the Polish and Lithuanian nations.

Overall, looking at the greatest achievements of Polish historical archaeology what is clear is that despite some gaps it is still developing within a "post-Fehring" triad of research themes in both late Middle Ages and post-medieval archaeology.

The "archaeology of sacred complexes and cemeteries" has traditionally been a major research focus. The most interesting works of recent years come from Romanesque, Gothic, and Baroque Cistercian complexes (Wyrwa et al. 1999).

"Archaeology of defensive complexes" continues to be practiced widely, with clear predominance of archaeological and architectural research. An encyclopedia of 500 Polish castle sites is a valuable publication of recent years (Kajzer et al. 2001).

"Settlement and urban archaeology" has probably been the biggest growth area over the last few decades in Poland. Archaeological studies of individual medieval and modern urban quarters are closely connected with their modernization, archaeology being an inherent element of established conservation policy. These excavations engage not only archaeologists, but also historians and historians of art (Gediga 2004). Publication series—*Archeologia Gdańska* (4 volumes to date), *Archeologia Średniowiecznego Kołobrzegu* (4 volumes), and *Vratislavia Antiqua* (10 volumes)—are devoted to Gdansk, Kołobrzeg, and Wroclaw, respectively, which are among the largest and best-researched historic cities. Urban archaeological research, closely connected with current development, is one of the "trademarks" of Polish historical archaeology.

Within the broad field "archaeology of settlement processes" I would like to bring special attention to a few key developments. The first of these is the publication of late medieval and modern sites and material culture concurrent with studies of prehistoric settlement identified during rescue works, especially resulting from linear development such as oil – or gas lines and road alignments (Bednarczyk and Kośko 2004). The second area is a particularly new development in Polish landscape research. That is, archaeological research on historical gardens, mainly of modern times (post 1500), located at great residences and palace complexes, both royal and aristocratic. The number of small publications and reports on landscapes is considerable, and the biggest list of published papers on garden archaeology is contained within the published volumes of a periodical *Monument. Studia i Materiały Krajowego Ośrodka Badań i Dokumentacji Zabytków*, produced by the National Heritage Board of Poland.

At last, the final area which I would like to cover concerns specific aspects of military archaeology, which is actively practiced in the university centers of Łódź, Toruń, and Wrocław. Here I mean not only archaeological excavations of battlefields and modern defensive camps (Głosek and Łuczak 1982; Krause 2008), but also a new field born out of the end of the Cold War and achievement of national independence in 1989.

The dissolution of the Soviet Union and renewal of political ties with our eastern neighbors, that is Russia, Belarus, and Ukraine, enabled the archaeological examination of burial sites of Polish officers and policemen imprisoned at the beginning of World War II in the Soviet Union. They were shot on the command of Stalin in spring 1940. At that time over 20,000 people died, not only those in uniform, but also reserve officers who included doctors, lawyers, and teachers among other representatives of the Polish intelligentsia. Archaeological research conducted in Katyń near Smoleńsk, in Miednoje, and in Starobielsk/Charkov (Tarczyński 1992; Głosek 2004; Kola 2005), research that may be placed on the interface between archaeology and forensic medicine, recently became the most important action of Polish post-medieval archaeology, especially in its impact on wider society (Mądro et al. 1994).

Today historical archaeology, both late medieval and post-medieval, is developing most rapidly in the university centers of Łódź, Toruń, and Wrocław. At the same time, it is generally more prevalent than prehistoric research in the heritage sector, though dependent on current conservation trends and economic circumstances. Outside influences do not always allow balanced development of our discipline, which is currently growing rapidly.

REFERENCES

ABRAMOWICZ, ANDRZEJ

1967   *Wiek archeologii* (with a summary: Un siècle d'archéologie) [*The Age of Archaeology*]. Instytut Historii Kultury Materialnej Polskiej Akademii Nauk, Warsaw, Poland.

1983   *Dzieje zainteresowań starożytniczych w Polsce. Część I. Od średniowiecza po czasy saskie i świt oświecenia* [*The History of Antiquarianism in Poland. Part I. From the Middle Ages to the Saxon Period and the Dawn of the Enlightenment Period*]. Instytut Historii Kultury Materialnej Polskiej Akademii Nauk, Wrocław, Poland.

1987   *Dzieje zainteresowań starożytniczych w Polsce. Cześć II. Czasy stanisławowskie i ich pokłosie* [*The History of Antiquarianism in Poland. Part II. The Age of Stanislaus Augustus and its Aftermath*]. Instytut Historii Kultury Materialnej Polskiej Akademii Nauk, Wrocław, Poland.

BEDNARCZYK, JÓZEF, AND ALEKSANDER KOŚKO (EDITORS)

2004   *Od długiego domu najstarszych rolników do dworu staropolskiego. Wyniki badań archeologicznych na trasach gazociągów Mogilno—Włocławek i Mogilno—Wydartowo* [*From a Long House of the Oldest Farmers to an Old Polish Mansion. Results of Archaeological Research on the Routes of Gas Pipelines Mogilno—Włocławek and Mogilno—Wydartowo*]. Instytut Prehistorii Uniwersytetu im. Adama Mickiewicza, Poznań, Poland.

FEHRING, GÜNTER

1987   *Einführung in der Archäologie des Mittelalters* [*Introduction to the Archaeology of the Middle Ages*]. Wissenschaftliche Buchgesellschaft, Darmstadt, Germany.

GEDIGA, BOGUSŁAW (EDITOR)

2004   *Dom w mieście średniowiecznym i nowożytnym* [*A House in Medieval and Modern Town*]. Wydawnictwo Uniwersytetu Wrocławskiego, Wrocław, Poland.

GŁOSEK, MARIAN (EDITOR)

2004   *Katyń w świetle badań terenowych 1994-1995* [*Katyn in Light of the Excavations of 1994 and 1995*]. Duet Publishing House, Toruń, Poland.

GŁOSEK, MARIAN, AND BOGDAN ŁUCZAK

1982   Bitwa pod Lubiszewem (17 kwietnia 1577 r.) w świetle badań archeologicznych [Battle of Lubieszewo (April 17, 1577), in Light of Archaeological Research]. *Studia i Materiały do Historii Wojskowości* 25:81-100.

KAJZER, LESZEK, STANISŁAW KOŁODZIEJSKI, AND JAN SALM (EDITORS)

2001   *Leksykon zamków w Polsce* [*Encyclopedia of Castles in Poland*]. Arkady Publishers, Warsaw.

KOLA, ANDRZEJ

2005   *Archeologia Zbrodni. Oficerowie polscy na cmentarzu ofiar NKWD w Charkowie* [*The Archaeology of the Crime. Polish Officers in the Cemetery of NKVD Victims in Charkov*]. Nicolaus Copernicus University Publishers, Toruń, Poland.

KRAUSE, EDWARD

2008   Obóz warowny z XVII – XVIII wieku w Markowicach pow. Poznań [Fortified Camp of the 17th-18th Century, Markowice, Pozań Area]. In *Wielkopolska w dziejach. Archeologia o regionie*, H. Machajewski, editor, pp. 245-249. Scientific Association of Polish Archaeologists, Poznań, Poland.

KRUPPÉ, JERZY

1973   Archeologia późnośredniowieczna i staropolska [Late Medieval Polish Archaeology]. *Kwartalnik Historii Kultury Materialnej* 21(4):633-653.

LECH, JACEK

1997-
1998   Between Captivity and Freedom: Polish Archaeology in the 20th Century. *Archeologia Polski* 35-36:25-222.

MĄDRO, ROMAN, MARIAN GŁOSEK, ALEKSANDER HERZOG, AND ANDRZEJ PRZEWOŹNIK

1994   Przebieg i wyniki ekshumacji przeprowadzonej w obrębie tak zwanej kwatery polskiej na Starym Cmentarzu Miejskim w Starobielsku [The Course and Results of Exhumations Carried within so-called Polish Section in the Old Municipal Cemetery in Starobielsk]. *Archiwum Medycyny Sądowej i Kryminologii* 44(3):293-304.

NOSZCZAK, BARTŁOMIEJ

2002   *"Sacrum" czy "profanum"—spór o istotę obchodów Millenium polskiego (1949-1966)* [*"Sacred" or "Profane"—A Dispute about the Nature of the Celebration of the Polish Millenium (1949-1966)*]. Institute of National Remembrance, Warsaw, Poland.

PAŃSTWOWE WYDAWNICTWO NAUKOWE

1993   *Materiały z ogólnopolskiej konferencji: Stan i potrzeby badań archeologicznych nad późnym średniowieczem i okresem nowożytnym w Polsce* [*Proceedings of the National Conference: The State and the Need for Archaeological Research on Late Medieval and Modern Period in Poland*]. Prace i Materiały Muzeum Archeologicznego i Etnograficznego w Łodzi. Seria Archeologiczna, Vol. 36, 1989-1990. Łódź, Poland.

TARCZYŃSKI, MAREK (EDITOR)

1992   *Zbrodnia katyńska. Droga do prawdy. Historia. Archeologia. Kryminalistyka. Polityka. Prawo* [*Katyn Massacre, the Road to Truth: History, Archaeology, Crime Detection, Politics, Law*]. Army Historical Institute, Warsaw.

WYRWA, ANDRZEJ M., STRZELCZYK JERZY, AND KACZMAREK KACZMAREK (EDITORS)

1999   *Monasticon Cisterciense Poloniae* [*Polish Cistercian Monasteries*], vol. I – II. Publishers of Poznań, Poland.

Leszek Kajzer
Instytut Archeologii Uniwersytetu
   Łódzkiego
ul. Uniwersytecka 3
PL-90-137 Łódź
Poland

MARIÁN ČURNÝ

Historical Archaeology in Slovakia

ABSTRACT

The paper discusses perspectives for historical archaeology in Slovakia. Historical archaeology in Slovakia is understood as the archaeology of the medieval and modern periods, that is, of those epochs with written sources. Post-medieval archaeology is part of historical archeology and concerns the period from the 16th century to today. The paper also discusses the teaching of historical archaeology in Slovakian universities, the publishing of monographs and periodicals on historical archaeological themes, the need for research aimed at modern-period sites, and for legislative protection for this category of sites.

INTRODUCTION

The aim of this review is to try to summarize the problems facing historical archaeology in Slovakia today. Briefly, I'm trying to show starting points for this part of archaeology, which does not yet have a long tradition in Slovakia. Modern archaeology began in Slovakia in 1939 with the archaeologist Vojtech Budinský-Krička. The first professional archaeologists started work in Slovakia in the 1950s, and in the first decades after World War II Slovakian archaeological science targeted the study of the prehistoric, proto-historic, and early historic eras. As time passed, a need to establish a framework for historical archaeology emerged, after large excavations uncovered layers from chronologically recent periods.

First, there are questions of terminology. There are different views on the periodization of the medieval period in the Slovakian area, for example from Habovštiak (1971), Hrubec (1980), and Čaplovič (1998). Generally it can be said that the Middle Ages are divided into early (500-1000), developed (1000-1400), and late (1400-1526) periods, but it is clear that this periodization scheme needs to be particularized and anchored more exactly. The change from the late Middle Ages to the modern period took place during the first half of the 16th century, corresponding to the predominant view that the beginning of the modern period in Europe dates to about 1500. Studying this historical process in Slovakia was not seen as a subject of archaeological interest, but instead of historical and ethnographical inquiry. This view has been changing slowly over the last 20-30 years. Also important is that historical archaeological study covers the period for which written sources survive. This starts at the turn of the 5th and 6th centuries A.D. after the migration period when a new population, the Slavs, arrived in the area of present-day Slovakia. After the

disintegration of the Slav state known as Great Moravia at the turn of the 9th and 10th centuries, the Slovakian area was part of the Kingdom of Hungary until 1918. Numerous written sources are available from the 12th and 13th centuries and become more voluminous from the 14th/15th centuries onwards. For the period after the year 1526 (the battle of Mohács with the Ottoman victory) we use the term modern or post-medieval period, which in today's archaeological study in Slovakia is divided into an older (16th/17th centuries) and a younger phase (18th/19th centuries). The medieval and post-medieval periods in Slovakia are the subject of historical archaeology, and post-medieval archaeology is seen as part of a wider framework.

In Slovakia there are three universities that teach archaeology: Comenius University in Bratislava, Trnava University in Trnava, and Constantine the Philosopher University in Nitra (Figure 1). Only at the Comenius University in Bratislava is the modern period part of the archaeological study program, however. In my opinion this is why Slovakian academic education produces graduates who are not ready for fully fledged work in the post-medieval period. For many years there was a good custom that archaeology was taught together with history, and students were thus able to work with historical sources to some extent and to critically evaluate these together with the results of archaeological excavations. This method has now been abandoned, and for about five years archaeology has been taught separately.

The center of archaeological studies in Slovakia is the Archaeological Institute of the Slovakian Academy of Sciences in Nitra and its detached workplaces in Bratislava, Košice, Zvolen, and Spišská Nová Ves. The best conditions for the study of the post-medieval

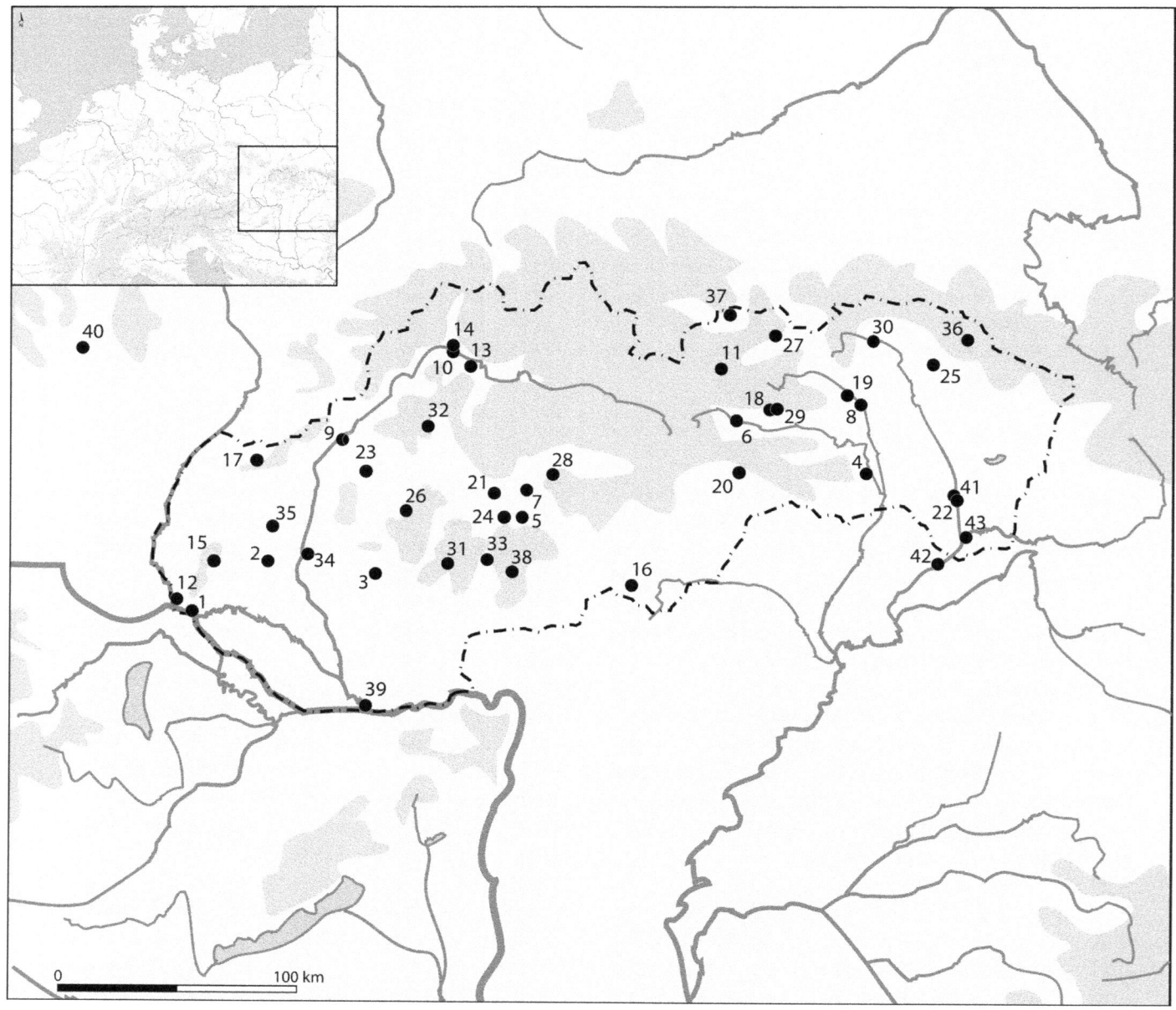

Figure 1.   Map of present-day Slovakia with places mentioned in the text: (1) Bratislava; (2) Trnava; (3) Nitra; (4) Košice; (5) Zvolen; (6) Spišská Nová Ves; (7) Banská Bystrica; (8) Prešov; (9) Trenčín; (10) Žilina; (11) Kežmarok; (12) Devín; (13) Strečno; (14) Budatín; (15) Červený Kameň; (16) Fiľakovo; (17) Branč; (18) Spišský hrad; (19) Šarišský hrad; (20) Krásna Hôrka; (21) Kremnica; (22) Parič in Trebišov; (23) Topoľčiansky hrad; (24) Pustý hrad in Zvolen; (25) Stropkov; (26) Partizánske-Šimonovany; (27) Stará Ľubovňa; (28) Slovenská Ľupča; (29) Spišská Kapitula; (30) Bardejov; (31) Hronský Beňadik; (32) Kláštor pod Znievom; (33) Banská Štiavnica; (34) Hlohovec; (35) Dechtice; (36) Krásny Brod; (37) Červený Kláštor; (38) Bzovík; (39) Komárno; (40) Brno (Czech Republic); (41) Trebišov; (42) Sárospatak (Hungary), and (43) Zemplín (Map provided courtesy of the Department of Prehistory and Medieval Archaeology, University of Vienna, Austria).

period exist in the Medieval and Early Modern Department of this institute. There were 103 museums in Slovakia in 2007 and an archaeologist was employed in 27 of them. The work of a museum archeologist has its own particularities, resulting in the possibility of research-oriented study. The fact is that in museums it is possible to combine the work of an archaeologist, historian, and ethnographer, for example in the study of the material culture of a specific region. Slovakia

has a federal administration divided into eight regions: Banská Bystrica, Bratislava, Košice, Nitra, Prešov, Trenčín, Trnava, and Žilina. Each of them has an office for cultural heritage and because of their everyday contacts with modern-period monuments the archaeologists in those offices are the most specialized in this period. Some private archaeological firms have recently started up in Slovakia, but only in a few cases are they able to combine rescue archaeological excavations with research-oriented study.

The definitive framing of historical archaeology in Slovakia will be a key question in the coming period, and the obvious reason for this is the need for adequate evaluation of archaeological excavations. In the last 30 years or so, but above all in the last 10-20 years, many archaeological excavations have taken place in historical town centers and on fortified sites or in religious buildings. Important excavations have taken place in Bratislava, Trnava, Nitra, Trenčín, Žilina, Banská Bystrica, Košice, Kežmarok, and Prešov. Most of these archaeological excavations were carried out in advance of building activities on historic plots or common open spaces. Many still unevaluated archaeological finds come from fortified sites, that is, castles. Castles in Slovakia were mostly built from the second half of the 13th century onwards, after the Kingdom of Hungary had suffered the catastrophic invasion of the Tartars (Mongols) in 1241 and 1242, and their intensive use lasted into the Renaissance and baroque eras, when many of them were abandoned in favor of incomparably more comfortable living conditions in manor houses and as part of measures against anti-Habsburg rebels. There were about 250 castles, manor houses, and other fortified structures in Slovakia, half of which are known from remains and ruins. Some of the largest collections of material culture from the modern period come from the castles at Bratislava, Devín, Nitra, Trenčín, Strečno, Budatín, Červený Kameň, Fiľakovo, Branč, Spišský hrad, Šarišský hrad, Krásna Hôrka, Kremnica, Parič in Trebišov, Topoľčiansky hrad, Pustý hrad in Zvolen, Stropkov, Partizánske-Šimonovany, Stará Ľubovňa, and Slovenská Ľupča.

Another type of excavated archaeological structure is religious buildings, that is, churches and monasteries. The most significant churches were built in the Middle Ages (e.g., St. Martin's Cathedral in Bratislava, St. Mikuláš´s Basilica in Trnava, St. Emerám´s Basilica in Nitra, St. Alžbeta´s Cathedral and St. Michal's Chapel in Košice, St. Martin's Cathedral in Spišská Kapitula, St. Mikuláš´s Cathedral in Prešov, and St. Egídius´s Basilica in Bardejov), and in most cases construction had been completed by the modern period as a result of religious fights from the 15th to the 17th and 18th centuries. Monasteries built in the modern period are a category of their own. They include the Camaldulensian monastery in Nitra from the 17th/18th centuries with its unique water supply; Benedictine monasteries in Hronský Beňadik (with the rare find of a water supply dependant upon ceramic pipes) and in Košice-Krásna nad Hornádom; a Premonstratensian monastery in Kláštor pod Znievom; Dominican monasteries in Banská Štiavnica and Košice; Francisian monasteries in Hlohovec, Slovenská Ľupča, Košice, and Dechtice; a Basilian monastery in Krásny Brod; a Carthusian, later Camaldulensian, monastery in Červený Kláštor; a Cistercian, later Premonstratensian, fortified monastery from the 16th century in Bzovík; and the Jesuit college in Komárno. The list could be extended to other sites where smaller-scale archaeological excavations have taken place.

Slovakia's main problem for historical archaeology is that insufficient results have been published from the excavations mentioned. After a critical evaluation of this important part of our work it appears there are only a few monographs from archaeological excavations: Košice-Krásna nad Hornádom, monastery (Polla 1986); Kežmarok, urban castle (Polla 1971); Bratislava, St. Martin's Cathedral (Štefanovičová 2004); Bratislava, western suburbia (Polla 1979); and Nitra, Mostná Street (Březinová and Samuel 2007). Other excavations and archaeological sites have been partially published in archaeological periodicals from Slovakia, and some of these journals deal with the needs of historical archaeological study: *Slovenská archeológia* (Nitra), *Slovenská numizmatika* (Nitra), *Štúdijné Zvesti Archeologického ústavu Slovenskej akadémie vied* (Nitra), *Monumentorum tutela* (Bratislava), *Studia Archaeologica Slovaca Mediaevala* (Bratislava), *Zborník SNM Archeológia* (Bratislava), and *Musaica* (Bratislava). Until recently the platform for publishing historical archaeological information from the late Middle Ages and modern period was the joint Czech-Moravian-Slovakian periodical *Archaeologia historica* (Brno). Recently it has been adequately replaced by the *Forum Archaeologiae Post-Mediaevalis* (Prague) from the neighboring Czech Republic in which studies in post-medieval archaeology are published regularly (see Žegklitz, this volume).

In 2004 the Department of Archaeology at the Comenius University of Bratislava organized a conference with the title "Post-Medieval Archaeological Studies in Slovakia." About 30 papers were presented, some of which were published in 2007 in the periodical *Musaica* (vol. XXV). Interesting scientific conferences about ceramic production from the High Middle Ages to the modern period (ca. 1000 to 1700) were prepared in the years 2006 and 2008 by the museum in Trebišov. Two colloquiums about pottery from the period between 1000 and 1700 took place, which are to be published as separate books. In 1996 a cooperation between museums in Trebišov and Sárospatak (Hungary) led to an exhibition called "From the Gothic to Hutterites," which dealt with medieval and post-medieval stove-tile production in the former counties of Abov, Šariš, and Zemplín, the catalog of which has been published (Feld 1996). A conference about gothic and Renaissance stoves was also organized in Trebišov in 2005, which has been published in book form (Chovanec 2005).

Since listing all the historical archaeological studies from Slovakia would be beyond the scope of a short paper (the very advanced studies about ceramic building materials or about mining in Slovakia would also need their own space), I will deal instead with Master's theses and dissertations, which imply a systematic approach to historical archaeological problems. Master's theses about pottery from the Ottoman period (16th/17th centuries) (Botoš 2003) and Renaissance stove-tiles from Devín castle (Divileková 2003) have emerged from the Department of Archaeology at the Comenius University in Bratislava. The current author presented a thesis based on the analysis of ceramic finds from the 16th-18th centuries from the manor house in Lukáčovce close to Nitra at the Department of Archaeology at Constantine the Philosopher University in Nitra in 2004 (Čurný 2004). From the Archaeological Institute of the Slovakian Academy of Sciences in Nitra there are dissertations about Renaissance stove-tiles from Parič castle in Trebišov (Chovanec 2003), pottery finds from Veľký Šariš castle and their chronology (Uličný 2004), bricks and other brick products from historical architecture (Čurný 2008), and stove-tiles from western Slovakian castles (Bielich 2009). Other theses are in the pipeline.

The need for comparative work between archaeology, history, and the auxiliary historical sciences in Slovakian archaeological literature has already been mentioned. The fact is that archaeology has not developed scientific or methodical ways of evaluating discoveries from archaeological excavations in a supra-archaeological context and this is why it is necessary to work with historians. In older works an archaeologist discussed the historical context of an excavated site on his own and within the limits of his capabilities, with not always positive results. There is, however, a very good level of historical generalization in numismatic

studies as reflected in the periodical *Slovenská numizmatika*. One of the few examples of a joint publication of archaeological, architectural, non-destructive geophysical, and historical research results is a study about Markušovce castle in the Spiš region (Bóna et al. 2008). For other Slovakian studies in which archaeologists and historians have cooperated, I refer readers to the already mentioned periodical *Archaeologia historica* (Bednár et al. 2005, for example).

From the beginning of the second half of the 20th century there was a cadre of scientists in Slovakian archaeology—"polyhistorians"—with a very good knowledge of classic languages and historical background, but later, after 40 years of communism and fundamental changes in Slovak society, we can observe an almost two-generation hiatus before the present generation of archaeologists and historians emerged. After the separation of the Czecho-Slovak federative republic in 1993 working conditions changed again. The present generation of archaeologists in Slovakia is still not fully integrated and collaborations with colleagues in the neighbor countries could be much better. In 2000 and again in 2001 Constantine the Philosopher University in Nitra organized students' archaeological and historical conferences in which students from interested departments of universities from the Czech Republic and Slovakia, but also from Hungary and Germany, took part (Koštial and Horňák 2000). An approach like this is surely helpful in improving mutual contacts and knowledge between students, some of whom have now become independent researchers.

As has been said, archaeology in Slovakia started late compared with neighboring countries and this has affected the quantity of published works. There have been few new monographs in this area since the time of Belo Polla, who wrote about historical archaeology in Slovakia in the 1960s and 1970s (Polla 1971, 1979). The trend in publishing is still to confine oneself to partial studies in the journals mentioned. This is the reason why there is still room for new work in many areas of interest in historical archaeology in Slovakia. A very big problem is that, formerly, many construction sites, often in towns, were not scrutinized, as the modern period was not seen as a legitimate subject of archaeological interest. A larger problem is methodology in fieldwork. Due to the ill-informed idea that modern-period sites are not as important as older sites, Slovakian archaeology does not have complete collections of many kinds of material culture. Thus, on the one hand emerging historical archaeological study in Slovakia is not overburdened by erroneous interpretations, but on the other hand there is no significant number of high-quality documented field situations and finds. A continuing problem today is that many archaeologists do not see modern-period finds as important and therefore systematically remove the stratigraphies in which they lie during archaeological excavations, especially in towns, because their priority is always to investigate "older and of course more important" strata and periods.

The new approach needs to begin during the educational process at universities. Slovak archaeology courses are too academic and don't prepare students for a practical life as professional archaeologists in the field. Graduates should know the basics of legislation, management, and psychology and should be able to find their feet in a field context. All of the thoughts expressed here are at least partly understood by many archaeologists, but in practice change is slow. From my point of view it is necessary to prepare a meeting of interested scientists in which the validity of post-medieval archaeology as a part of historical archaeology is affirmed, a periodization for the modern period in Slovakia suggested, and the context in which problems can be solved agreed upon. From there, the meeting participants should make suggestions about archaeology in our universities. The first meeting about problems of post-medieval archaeology in the year 2004 showed that in Slovakia there are scientists who want to work in this direction to a high professional standard. It is thanks to contemporary field research that we have acquired collections of various kinds of material culture from the modern period. Analyzing these collections to settle questions of chronology in central Europe has been seen as a priority for a long time.

There are four laws in the body of Slovakian legislation that talk about cultural heritage and archaeological finds: Law No. 27 from 1987, Law No. 49 from 2002, Law No. 208 from 2009, and Law No. 253 from 2010 (the latest version). Under these laws a cultural monument is understood as a movable or immovable object with cultural value, whatever its age, and is named a cultural monument in order to preserve it. In terms of archaeological finds, a cultural monument includes excavated movable and immovable objects discovered by the methods and techniques of archaeological excavation. The preservation of monuments is those activities and steps associated with the identification, research, evidence, conservation, renovation, restoration, recovery,

exploitation, and presentation of cultural monuments and regions. Cultural value is the only criterion against which a cultural monument is evaluated, so monuments can equally come from a chronologically younger period. The most important factor is its public meaning and value, not its age. According to Slovakian monuments legislation, monuments from the modern period are a fully valued part of the body of all protected cultural monuments in Slovakia.

The main points for historical (meaning post-medieval) archaeology in Slovakia can be summarized as follows:

- Because of the lengthy period in which the archaeological study of the modern period in Slovakia was ignored, it is necessary to argue for post-medieval archaeology as a logical part of historical archaeology. This could be achieved with the help of international cooperation, especially with neighbor countries.

- A specific platform of historical archaeological study in Slovakia is needed, which can discuss questions of its content and its study range. An international model, such as that of the Czech Republic, is very welcome.

- University teaching of the modern period in archaeology with all its particularities needs to begin at last.

- Historical archaeological problems must be reflected in the themes of Master's theses and dissertations. Within a planned research framework, we have to begin to systematically evaluate existing excavated modern-period finds from our archaeological sites.

- Detailed research based on archaeological excavation by interdisciplinary teams of scientists from fields including architecture, history, auxiliary historical sciences, and ethnography is necessary. There are still no scientific historical archaeology grant projects, which are needed for communication between universities (education) and scientific institutions (research, theory) and also between the various scientific institutions in Slovakia.

- As far as new archaeological research about the modern period is concerned, it would make sense to study chosen sites or sites of various types (town, fortified military object, church, monastery, industrial objects) in a systematic and planned fashion. The evaluation of well-documented scientific archaeological excavations will help us most in arriving at a plastic view of these problems.

REFERENCES

BEDNÁR, PETER, MAGDALÉNA KVASNICOVÁ, AND PRISKA RATIMORSKÁ

2005   Komárno—bývalá rezidencia a kolégium jezuitov. Predbežná správa o výsledkoch archeologického a umelecko-historického výskumu [Komárno–Former Jesuit Residence and College. Preliminary Report on the Results of Archaeological and Art-Historical Research]. *Archaeologia historica* 30:149-164.

BIELICH, MÁRIO

2009   Nálezy kachlíc z hradov juhozápadného Slovenska [Findings of Stove-Tiles from the Castles in Southwestern Slovakia]. Doctoral dissertation, Archaeological Institute of the Slovakian Academy of Sciences, Nitra, Slovakia.

BÓNA, MARTIN, MICHAL ŠIMKOVIC, HENRIETA ŽAŽOVÁ, MÁRIO BIELICH, MARIÁN ČURNÝ, AND JÁN TIRPÁK

2008   Výsledky doterajších výskumov šľachtického sídla v Markušovciach [The Results of Previous Research of the Patrician Residence in Markušovce]. *Dějiny staveb* 2007:23-44.

BOTOŠ, ALEXANDER

2003   Stredoveká a včasnonovoveká keramika z južnej časti stredného Slovenska [Medieval and Early Post-medieval Pottery from the Southern Part of Slovakia]. Master's thesis, Department of Archaeology, Comenius University, Bratislava, Slovakia.

BŘEZINOVÁ, GERTRÚDA, AND MARIÁN SAMUEL (EDITORS)

2007   *Tak čo, našli ste niečo? Svedectvo archeológie o minulosti Mostnej ulice v Nitre* [So What, Did You Find Something? Testimony of Archaeology of the Past of Mostná Street in Nitra]. Archeologický ústav SAV, Nitra, Slovakia.

ČAPLOVIČ, DUŠAN

1998   Poznámky k chronológii stredoveku na Slovensku [Notes on the Chronology of the Middle Ages in Slovakia]. *Studia Archaeologica Slovaca Mediaevala* I:159-176.

CHOVANEC, JÁN

2003   Gotické a renesančné kachlice. Hrad Parič a východné Slovensko [Gothic and Renaissance Stove-Tiles. Castle Parič and Eastern Slovakia]. Doctoral dissertation, Archaeological Institute of the Slovakian Academy of Sciences, Bratislava, Slovakia.

CHOVANEC, JÁN (EDITOR)

2005   *Gotické a renesančné kachlice v Karpatoch* [Gothic and Renaissance Stove-Tiles in the Carpathians]. Arx Paris, Trebišov, Slovakia.

ČURNÝ, MARIÁN

2004   Keramika zo 16.-18. stor. na juhozápadnom Slovensku na príklade nálezov z kaštieľa v Lukáčovciach [Pottery from the 16th to 18th Centuries in Southwestern Slovakia on the Example of the Mansion House in Lukáčovce]. Master's thesis, Department of Archaeology, Constantine the Philosopher University, Nitra, Slovakia.

2008   Tehla ako stavebný materiál stredovekej a novovekej architektúry na Slovensku. Pohľad archeológa [Brick as Construction Material of Medieval and Post-medieval Architecture in Slovakia. An Archaeological Perspective]. Doctoral dissertation, Archaeological Institute of the Slovakian Academy of Sciences, Nitra, Slovakia.

DIVILEKOVÁ, DENISA

2003   Stredoveké a včasnonovoveké kachlice z hradu Devín [Medieval and Early Post-medieval Stove-Tiles from Devín Castle]. Master's thesis, Department of Archaeology, Comenius University, Bratislava, Slovakia.

FELD, ISTVÁN (EDITOR)

1996   *A gótikától a habánokig. Od gotiky po Habánov. (Kályhacsempék Abaúj, Sáros és Zemplén vármegyékből. Kachlice z bývalej Abovskej, Šarišskej a Zemplínskej župy)* [From the Gothic to Hutterites. Stove-Tiles from the Former Abov, Šariš and Zemplín Counties]. Kiada a Rákoczi Múzeum Baráti Köre, Sárospatak, Hungary.

HABOVŠTIAK, ALOJZ

1971   Archeologický výskum stredovekého obdobia na Slovensku [Archaeological Research of the Medieval Period in Slovakia]. *Slovenská archeológia* 19(2):603-617.

HRUBEC, IGOR

1980   Poveľkomoravské obdobie a stredovek [After the Great Moravian Period and Middle Ages]. *Slovenská archeológia* 28(1):229-237.

Koštial, Jozef, and Milan Horňák (editors)

2000   *Patince 2000. Archeológia na prahu tretieho tisícročia očami študentov II.* [*Patince 2000. Archaeology of the Third Millennium through the Eyes of Students. Vol. II.*] Department of Archaeology, Constantine the Philosopher University, Nitra, Slovakia.

Polla, Belo

1971   *Kežmarok. Výsledky historickoarcheologického výskumu* [*Kežmarok. The Results of Historic-Archaeological Research*]. Vydavateľstvo Slovenskej akadémie vied, Bratislava, Slovakia.

1979   *Bratislava—Západné suburbium (Výsledky archeologického výskumu)* [*Bratislava–Western Suburb (The Results of Archaeological Research)*]. Východoslovenské vydavateľstvo, Košice, Slovakia.

1986   *Košice-Krásna. K stredovekým dejinám Krásnej nad Hornádom* [*Košice-Krásna. The Medieval History of Krásna nad Hornádom*]. Východoslovenské vydavateľstvo, Košice, Slovakia.

Štefanovičová, Tatiana

2004   *Dóm sv. Martina v Bratislave. Archeologický výskum 2002-2003* [*Cathedral of St. Martin in Bratislava. Archaeological Research 2002-2003*]. Vydavateľstvo Elán, Bratislava, Slovakia.

Uličný, Marián

2004   Premeny východoslovenskej keramiky v 13.-17. storočí (Na podklade analýzy keramického fondu z hradu Šariš.) [Changes in the East Slovakian Pottery from the 13th to 17th Centuries (Based on an Analysis of Ceramic Finds from the Saris Castle)]. Doctoral dissertation, Archaeological Institute of the Slovakian Academy of Sciences, Prešov, Slovakia.

Marián Čurný
Archeologický ústav SAV
Hrnčiarska 13
SK-040 01 Košice
Slovakia

GÁBOR TOMKA

Historical Archaeology in Hungary

ABSTRACT

This paper deals with the archaeology of the 16th-17th centuries within the territory of present-day Hungary. A short overview of the development and the institutional background of early modern archaeology is followed by a discussion of topics such as military and civil architecture, archaeology of settlements, cemeteries, and material culture. Archaeology of fortifications and of deserted villages is well represented due to the devastations of the Ottoman-Habsburg wars. A special emphasis is placed on potteries, stove-tiles, and Ottoman copper vessels. Scientific methods and new ways of approaching early modern archaeology are briefly summarized as well.

HISTORICAL BACKGROUND

The battle of Mohács (1526) and the fall of Buda (1541) precipitated by the expansion of the Ottoman Empire radically changed the political situation in the Kingdom of Hungary (Figure 1). From the territory of the former sovereign Catholic state, covering the whole Carpathian Basin and dominating great parts of central Europe, three new states emerged. The centers of the two largest were formed out of the Carpathian Basin. In Royal Hungary, located in the western and northern part of present-day Transdanubia and in the northern territories, the authority of the Kingdom of Hungary persisted. Hungarian kings were elected from the Habsburg dynasty beginning in 1526 and reigned from outside the country, mainly in Vienna and Prague. As part of the Habsburg Empire, but not part of the Holy Roman Empire, the independence of Royal Hungary persisted theoretically, but Hungarian nobility had practically no voice in monetary and military policy. Modern borders split the 16th-17th century Royal Hungary into parts belonging to Slovenia, Croatia, Austria, Hungary, Slovakia, Ukraine, and Romania. This article concentrates on the archaeology of present-day Hungary in spite of the fact that modern borders have little in common with those of the 16-17th centuries (Pálffy 2009).

The Eastern Hungarian Kingdom, later called the Principality of Transylvania, was located in the eastern part of the medieval country and consisted of medieval Transylvania and some eastern counties of the Kingdom of Hungary (known as *Partium Regni Hungariae*). This state was a tribute-paying vassal of the Ottoman Empire, but this dependency did not affect the survival and organic development of the medieval organization of the state. The Prince of Transylvania theoretically recognized the supremacy of the Hungarian king, but

the Habsburgs never had the power to take long-term control over Transylvania until the end of the 17th century. This part of the country will not be dealt with in the present summary since nearly all of it now belongs to modern-day Romania.

The center of the medieval Kingdom of Hungary—Ottoman Hungary—came under direct Ottoman rule. The leader of the new Ottoman province was the Pasha of Buda. The Hungarian administration was changed by the Ottomans, and the depopulated (mainly southern) territories were settled by new inhabitants arriving from the Balkan Peninsula. The bigger towns and military garrisons were mainly occupied by Muslims and some orthodox Christians. In the northern part of this territory a dual power system operated upon villages and market towns (since the Hungarian nobility fled to the Hungarian [Christian] side of the border from whence they tried to sustain their power over their old lands). Broad border zones emerged between areas of unquestioned dominance, where almost no settlement could survive long-lasting military campaigns unless it was located in the shadow of castles and military bases (Szakály 1981).

This division of the country ended with the military defeat of the Ottoman Empire by Christian armies in the last two decades of the 17th century. The medieval administrative system was not completely restored, however, as Transylvania became a separately ruled province, and in the southern territories a border zone was created under military administration.

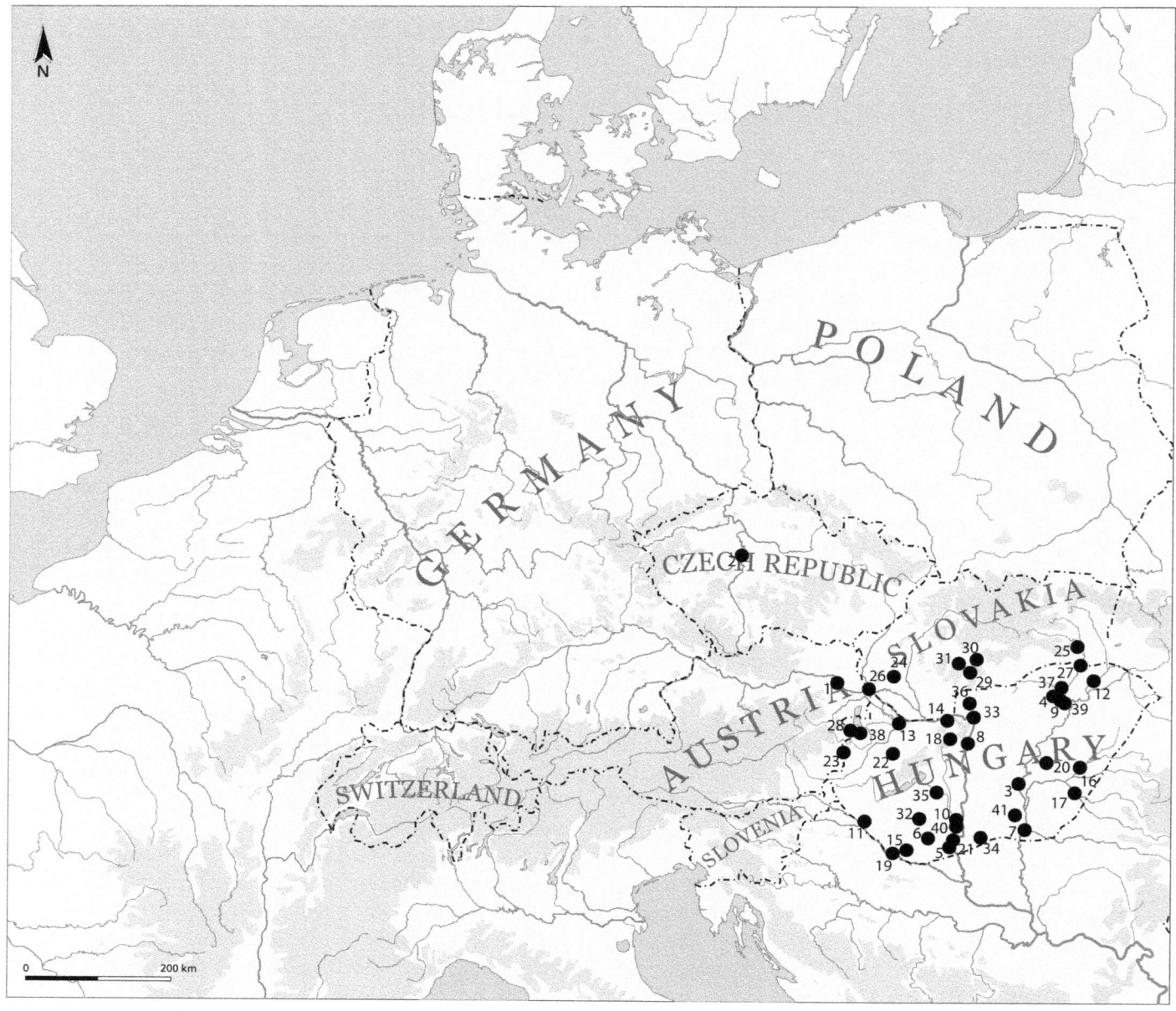

Figure 1.   Map of places mentioned in the text (in present-day Hungary, unless otherwise noted): (1) Vienna, Austria; (2) Prague, Czech Republic; (3) Szentkirály; (4) Diósgyőr; (5) Mohács; (6) Pécs; (7) Szeged; (8) Budapest; (9) Miskolc; (10) Szekszárd; (11) Bajcsavár; (12) Sárospatak; (13) Győr; (14) Esztergom; (15) Szigetvár; (16) Móric; (17) Békés-Kastélyzug; (18) Vál; (19) Barcs; (20) Törökszentmiklós; (21) Bátaszék; (22) Pápa; (23) Kőszeg; (24) Trnava, Slovakia; (25) Košice, Slovakia ; (26) Bratislava, Slovakia; (27) Kéked; (28) Sopron; (29) Banská Štiavnica, Slovakia; (30) Banská Bystrica, Slovakia; (31) Kremnica, Slovakia; (32) Dombóvár-Békató; (33) Vác; (34) Bácsalmás; (35) Ozora; (36) Nógrád ; (37) Borsod (38) Fertöd; (39) Mohi; (40) Ete; and (41) Szer (Map provided courtesy of the Department of Prehistory and Medieval Archaeology, University of Vienna, Austria).

HISTORICAL ARCHAEOLOGY IN HUNGARY

The term historical archaeology is barely used in Hungary. The generally used expression "early modern archaeology" more or less corresponds to the same subject. The terminology reflects the fact that archaeological research of the period following the 15th century is mainly restricted to the 16th-17th centuries. According to the Hungarian law for defending cultural heritage (Law 2001/LXIV) the authority of archaeology extends to the year 1711 (Laszlovszky and Rasson 2003).

Historical archaeology appeared in Hungary as an extension of medieval archaeology. It is important to stress that the term "medieval archaeology" traditionally covers a different time period in Hungary than in western Europe. Early centuries of the Middle Ages, until the end of the 10th century, fall under "archaeology of the Migration Period," which uses a slightly different method with a traditional focus on rich cemeteries. "Late Middle Ages" was the traditional term used for the last period of archaeological research (that is, until the year 1711). The main reason behind this periodization is the decisive changes in material culture brought about by political events. The Ottoman occupation of the early 16th century resulted in the destruction of most medieval buildings. This well-defined time-horizon was itself terminated by the expulsion of the Ottomans from Hungary and the following war of independence led by Ferenc Rákóczi II, a Hungarian aristocrat (1703-1711), which led to widespread destruction of Islamic architecture. Moreover, in the Marxist periodization of history that was more or less compulsory until 1989, the "Age of Feudalism" continued its hold until the revolution of 1848. So, one could easily deal with the late medieval and early modern periods as a single period. More recently, however, the term "archaeology of the early modern period" has come into fashion for the study of the 16th-17th centuries. The archaeology of the18th-20th centuries is still relatively neglected.

The discipline of Hungarian historical archaeology, and by that I mean the archaeology of the early modern period, has three main strands. The first is Ottoman-Turkish archaeology. Some elements of the culture that evolved on the territory under Ottoman rule are adaptations of Muslim cultural traditions found everywhere in the Ottoman Empire. *Camis* (mosques where Friday prayers are held), oriental baths, some elements of military architecture, and other aspects of material culture are not derived from the earlier culture of western and central Europe. It is therefore important that researchers in this area have some experience in Muslim art and culture. Outstanding orientalists and archaeologists in this field of study were Géza Fehér and Győző Gerő. Ibolya Gerelyes and Gyöngyi Kovács are both the most important leaders of Ottoman-Turkish Archaeology in Hungary today (see paper by Gerelyes, this volume). The tradition of combining Ottoman-Turkish studies with archaeology is followed by Erika Hancz and Adrienn Papp in the younger generation of archaeologists. The history of Ottoman-Turkish archaeology is summarized by the doyen of the field, Győző Gerő (2003). After the first epigraphic studies in the first half of the 19th century, descriptions of standing Ottoman buildings and building-elements followed in the second half of the century. The first Turkish artifacts found during building activities were collected in the same period. Digging up architectural remnants from the Ottoman period began in the years between World War I and World War II, focusing primarily on walls and foundations. The first interpretation of small finds is dated to 1944 (Garády 1944), and publications on this topic became more and more frequent in the 1950s and 1960s. This trend seems to persist until today. Medieval or "Christian archaeology" as it was called in the contemporary literature began around the middle of the 19th century and concentrated on walls and building elements. Some articles on small finds were published before World War II, but stratigraphic excavation was not generally practiced until the 1950s.

Not only Muslims lived in Ottoman Hungary. A large part of the newly arrived population was of Balkan origin and the eastern Orthodox Christian tradition, speaking mainly southern Slavic but eventually Neolatin languages as well. In most of this area the successors of the medieval (mainly Hungarian) population also survived, albeit in decreasing numbers. In spite of these differences the following paragraphs will not be separated into "Ottoman" and "Christian" parts.

The second strand of historical archaeology in Hungary is the restoration and research of historic monuments. Field research of historic buildings means the archaeological and architectural research of parts of the buildings as well as the research of both the inner and outer environment of the building by means of archaeological methods. For building archaeology there is no upper time limit: redevelopment in the 19th or 20th century should be as equally documented as earlier periods. Archaeological investigations of historical monuments focus primarily on medieval remnants, but research done on churches still in use, or on military objects used until the turn of the 17th and 18th centuries, has yielded information of reconstruction in the early modern and modern period as well. Methods of building archaeology developed fully in the 1960s and 1970s and match in many ways traditional vertical excavation. Trenches are substituted by research stripes, excavated ground surfaces by wall surfaces, and the stratigraphy of the soil layers by stratigraphy of building elements (such as walls, frames of wall openings, parts of vaultings, wall-plasters, wall-paints, etc.).

The third strand of historical archaeology in Hungary is ethnography (folk studies). In Hungary, due to 19th-century national romanticism and the example of German scholarship, ethnography in its Continental sense (i.e., with a focus on local peasant culture) was taken up. It is quite rare to find anything that is older than the 19th century using traditional ethnographic methods. One reason for archaeological research of late medieval and early modern villages before World War II was to investigate the origins of traditional Hungarian peasant dwelling houses (K. Szabó 1938:87). Because traditional folk culture is slowly dying out, ethnography is seeking not only new fields but also new methods of study. Now some ethnographers are trying to find the remnants of peasant or urban culture by means of archaeological excavations (Vida 1999:6). One can therefore expect that the temporal research gap between ethnography and archaeology (that is, mainly the 18th century) will gradually become the purview of archaeologists.

The leading ethnographer, the late Tibor Sabján, studied the use and variety of heating technology. His graphic reconstructions of tiled stoves, which belong to the early modern period, are based on archaeological finds from the 16th-century village of Szentkirály in the Hungarian Plain (Sabján 2002) and of a former royal, later private, border castle at Diósgyőr (Boldizsár et al. 2010). In addition to both graphic and small-scale model reconstructions of medieval dwelling houses, he presented parts of a full-scale reconstruction of the houses of Szentkirály (Sabján 2010:936-937). Gabriella Vida used archaeological finds from the 17th century for studying the origins of glazed decorated folk pottery (slip ware) (Vida 1999:15-37). She also initiated the excavation of waster-pits of 19th-century pottery workshops (Vida 1999:85).

The beginnings of battlefield archaeology can be traced back to the research carried out by László Papp at the battlefield of Mohács (L. Papp 1960) (see also Homann, this volume). The battlefield archaeology section of the Hungarian Association of Military Science was established in 2002. Since then a lot of research has been carried out mainly at World War I and World War II locations, although early modern battlefields have also been studied by Lajos Négyesi (2003).

For anybody interested in the archaeology of the early modern period in Hungary, only a handful of monographs and conference volumes are available. On Ottoman-Turkish architecture and archaeology in Hungary a monograph was published by Győző Gerő (1980), with a longer German summary. A milestone in the evolution of early modern archaeology in Hungary

was the conference book *Archaeology of the Ottoman Period in Hungary* edited by Ibolya Gerelyes and Gyöngyi Kovács, which is bilingual in both Hungarian and English (Gerelyes and Kovács 2002, 2003). It can be regarded as an unquestionable sign of the emancipation of historical archaeology that even the title of the conference held in 2006, dealing with the practice of Hungarian archaeology of the Middle Ages (which is slowly becoming a tradition in Hungary) over the last decade, treats the early modern period as equally important as the medieval period (Benkő and Kovács 2010). The latest findings of Hungarian Ottoman-Turkish archaeology have been summarized in the catalog of the exhibition "Exhibition on Ottoman Art" at Pécs (Tanman et al. 2010).

As yet, there is no independent institutional background of historical archaeology in Hungary. Hence, archaeology of the early modern period is more linked to individuals than to institutions. Students can get a Master's degree in archaeology at three universities: Janus Pannonius University at Pécs, József Attila University at Szeged, and Eötvös Loránd University in Budapest. A separate department of archaeology is available in Pécs and in Szeged. In Pécs the deputy of the head of the department (Erika Hancz) is a Turkologist and archaeologist, so archaeology of the early modern period has a special emphasis there. At the University of Szeged there is no specialist of the early modern period, so lectures are given by occasional lecturers. At the Eötvös Loránd University an archaeological institution consisting of four departments teaches archaeology. Head of the Department of Medieval and Early Modern Archaeology (István Feld) is one of the leading specialists of medieval and early modern building archaeology, so early modern archaeology is particularly stressed in the education. A great part of the research conducted at the department deals specifically with late medieval and early modern fortifications and towns.

There are four more centers of early modern archaeology in Budapest. Rescue excavations by the Budapest Történeti Múzeum (museum of the capital) have yielded plenty of early modern features and finds. The relatively great number of standing and ruined stone buildings originating in the Turkish period requires that there be a Turkish period specialist among the archaeologists of the museum. The Institute of Archaeology of the Hungarian Academy of Sciences covers the whole time-scope of archaeology. Gyöngyi Kovács is the specialist of early modern archaeology of this institute, and is one of the most important persons in Ottoman-Turkish archaeology in Hungary today. The Ottoman Collection of the Hungarian National Museum is led by Ibolya Gerelyes. The importance of both of the aforementioned scholars can be estimated by the references cited section of this paper. The writer of this paper works in the same museum, curating the late medieval collection, which incorporates some non-Turkish assemblages of the 16th-17th centuries. The team of researchers of historical monuments underwent several reorganizations in the past years. Recently the team formed a department of the Center for National Cultural Heritage (Nemzeti Örökségvédelmi Központ), which became affiliated with the Hungarian National Museum. This group conducts building archaeology and sometimes excavations in advance of renovations to historical monuments.

The role of early modern archaeology is different among territorial county museums. Excavation and collection at early modern sites are conducted in every county, but some museums are to be mentioned specifically. In the museum of Miskolc (Borsod-Abaúj-Zemplén County) several early modern find spots were researched. In Szeged (Csongrád County) an archaeologist and ethnologist tried to fill the gap between potteries of the 19th century and the early modern period. In the county of Bács-Kiskun the director of the county museum unearthed and published several early modern cemeteries with Balkanic characteristics (Wicker 2003, 2005). In the county of Tolna the county museums played an important role in the development of Ottoman-Turkish archaeology.

One can observe a marked increase in the number of surviving written and pictorial sources from the 16th-17th centuries in Hungary. This is partially due to the loss of medieval archives during the Turkish Wars. The main reason for this boom, however, is the growth of literacy in this period. New types of writing spread, and public and private administration produced more and more documents. These different forms of text—such as charters, documents of the central and urban administrations, conscriptions, inventories, legal statements, price controls, and letters—can all be used to contribute to early modern archaeology. Most of the official writings are in Latin (sometimes in German), while local conscriptions are mainly in Hungarian and in German. Some letters are in Italian, mainly in the 16th century. Here I would stress the importance of inventories (especially testamental inventories and inventories

of castles) in reconstructing ruined rooms and their onetime functions, and in recognizing elements of material culture (Domokos 1997; Simon 2002:15-66). Written sources are especially abundant in the case of Bajcsavár, whose fortification was built by the orders of the Styria state and its documents were kept meticulously in the provincial archive (Toifl 2002). Special training is essential in reading and interpreting Turkish sources (mainly tax and military salary conscriptions), which were written in Ottoman-Turkish language laced with Arabic and Persian words and written down by the means of Arabic characters. These sources can help in the interpretation of settlement and military archaeology (Dávid 2003).

Compared to western Europe, Hungarian images are relatively scarce from the 16th and 17th centuries. During the Turkish Wars, however, almost all castles and fortifications were drawn in plan and elevation. The most important fortifications (most of which were in the hands of the Christians) have several contemporary ground plans that can help reconstruct the history of construction (Domokos 2000). Images, especially engraved *vedute* (large-scale artistic images of landscapes), must be considered with caution since repeated copying made details often unreliable. In some cases, when no drawings were available, vedutes were published without any authenticity or simply by changing the text in the title of an existing picture. Authenticity is often absent in small secondary images hidden in the corners of engravings. Costumes of different social strata are more accurately depicted in costume books published from the second half of the 17th century (Oborni et al. 2010). Aristocratic costumes and weaponry are well documented on monuments or contemporary portraits and (mainly funeral) sculptures. The finding of graphic forerunners of images on stove-tiles and rare pottery vessels might help to date and interpret these items (Holl 1993:267-274).

Cooperation of historians and archaeologists is necessary in researching the early modern age. In practice, due to the limited resources available for archaeological research, the study of written sources is usually done by the archaeologists, or only published written sources are taken into consideration.

Field methods of early modern archaeology are no different from medieval or earlier archaeology. Stratigraphic excavation is now expected. Single-context recording, using separate record sheets for each stratigraphic unit, is becoming a widespread method of documentation. Pre- and post-excavation methods are somewhat different, mainly because of the many types of non-archaeological sources available. Historical archaeology in Hungary is not developed enough for real theoretical discussions at this time. Only in the last two decades has published archaeological material reached the volume necessary to allow detailed chronological and spatial typologies sufficient to form the basis for addressing further, more sophisticated questions. Discussions are mainly limited to particular questions such as the extent of cultural interactions (pottery, pipes, weapons) (Tomka 2003b), possibilities of ethnic interpretations (pottery, burial customs) (Gerelyes 1985:238-240; G. Kovács 1990-1991; Pusztai 2003:308-310; Wicker 2003:240-246), or possible origins of later phenomena (pottery, rural dwelling houses) (Vida 1999:5-50; Lajkó 2003:326-328; Sabján 2010:933-939). Theoretical approaches to terminology and processing of early modern pottery have recently been published (Vizi 2010; F. Lajkó 2010).

General changes in the circumstances of archaeological excavations have also affected early modern archaeology. Political and economic transformations of the past two decades have proven to be double-edged in their impact. Restoration works initiated by the state have become infrequent compared to the former communist era. On the other hand, ongoing building investment has caused rescue excavations to expand to a formerly unknown scale. The focus of this research was determined not by scholars but by the activities of the investors. Large-scale excavations, often linked to the construction of new motorways, have resulted in an immense expansion of knowledge of earlier ages but have affected historical archaeology to a lesser extent. Some examples of exploration of medieval settlements that were abandoned in the early modern period can be cited, however, such as Pusztai (2001).

The greatest problem of historical archaeology in Hungary is that only a small portion of the excavated material is published. The immense volume of archaeological data along with the lack of material means for publications are the main reasons for this. This could be eased by the new regulations, as excavation budgets should now also incorporate the costs of post-excavation. A special problem of historical archaeology is that being the stratigraphically uppermost level, deposits are more vulnerable to intentional or casual destruction. In addition, the great number of non-archaeological sources makes research by historical archaeologists more complicated. In former times, a lack of motivation by some archaeologists could be felt as well; shiny finds and clever original interpretations are harder to come by in historical archaeology, unlike in the research of earlier periods. Another problem is that, until the last decades, most of the archaeologists studying earlier epochs usually did not pay special attention to early modern layers.

MILITARY ARCHITECTURE

Due to the almost constant wars between the Habsburgs and the Ottomans, a number of military sites were built or rebuilt in Hungary in the 16th and 17th centuries. There is therefore a strong tendency in Hungary to study military architecture such as castles, palisades, and other fortifications. In spite of the fact that László Gerő's architectural monographs on Hungarian castles amply emphasized early modern fortifications (L. Gerő 1955:314-421, 1975:325-344), archaeological research often began as a byproduct of studies of medieval castles or monasteries. Restoration and excavation work in the 1960s and 1970s usually focused on the medieval cores of the castles. Later, restoration works included the outer, usually newer, parts of castles as well. Studies have shown that medieval castles and town fortifications were strengthened by reconstructing the gates and their defense works (such as barbicans) in the early 16th century (Feld 2008:179-182). In the 1530s an archaic keep-like tower was built in Sárospatak, apparently after Polish forerunners (Feld and Szekér 1994). A typical architectural element of this period was the double channeled loophole (the German *Hosenscharte*) built for arquebuses. Artillery towers mark the spreading application of cannons (Feld 2008:188-195). Castles (or fortresses) with a defense system supported by bastions were built from the middle of the 16th century onwards. During the modernization of smaller private castles and of strongholds of minor significance, often only one or two bastions were built to strengthen the weakest parts of the defense system (Tomka 2010:603). At crucial royal strongholds the mainly Italian architects tried to realize whole systems of bastions, leaving no dead spaces for the enemy. Even bastions with orillons ("eared" bastions) were built in the second third of the 16th century at Győr. Because of the developing artillery, new aspects were considered when positioning a

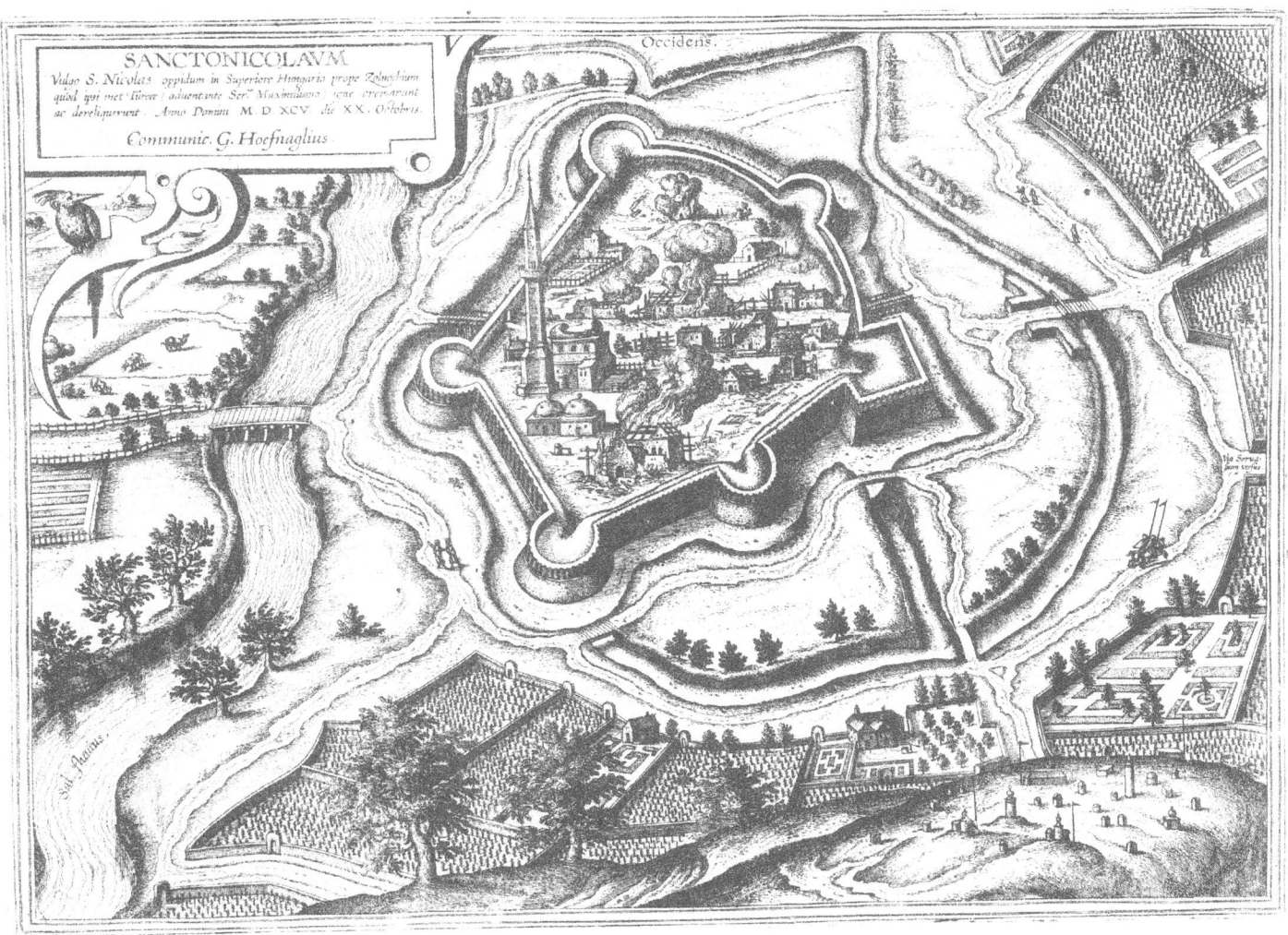

Figure 2.   *A contemporary depiction of a palanka at Törökszentmiklós (Rózsa 1955:14, table XIV).*

stronghold. Instead of hardly approachable cliffs and places dominating higher positions, fortresses were built where broad ditches or swamps made siege more difficult (L. Gerő 1975:331; Tomka 2010:602-603). Due to the revolution in strategies and tactics of warfare, a hierarchical border defense was built against the Ottomans. This hierarchy can be well documented in the archaeological record when comparing building sizes and materials or number of cannon emplacements. According to both archaeological investigations and analyses of contemporary graphics, outer defense earthworks in front of the main *enceinte* were erected mainly in the 17th century (L. Gerő 1975:338-339; Tomka 2010:602). Main fortresses or fortified towns became more and more important during the 16th-17th centuries, so resources were more and more focused on these.

On the side of the Ottomans, the most elaborate walls and defense works, often with ashlar masonry, were built at the height of Ottoman power, in the decades following the occupation of central Hungary (i.e., at Esztergom and Buda) (Tomka 2010:605-607). New strongholds made of stone or brick, such as the one at Szigetvár, were exceptions (L. Gerő 1975:268-269), but resources were concentrated on polygonal or central bulwarks at strategic points of existing fortresses. Timber-framed masonry walls were not unknown in Christian fortifications, but were typical in Ottoman strongholds (Tomka 2010:605-607). This building method assured quicker building, greater flexibility, and lesser weight of the walls without the hazard of a firestorm. Ottomans built smaller wooden fortifications, so called *palankas,* with palisade and earthen walls to fill the gaps between bigger fortifications that were usually taken over from the Christians and to secure the routes of military operations and supply (Figure 2). Although palankas differ from each other considerably, their usual archaeological traces are two parallel trenches filled with clay into which postholes are sunk at a distance of approximately 20-40 cm. The

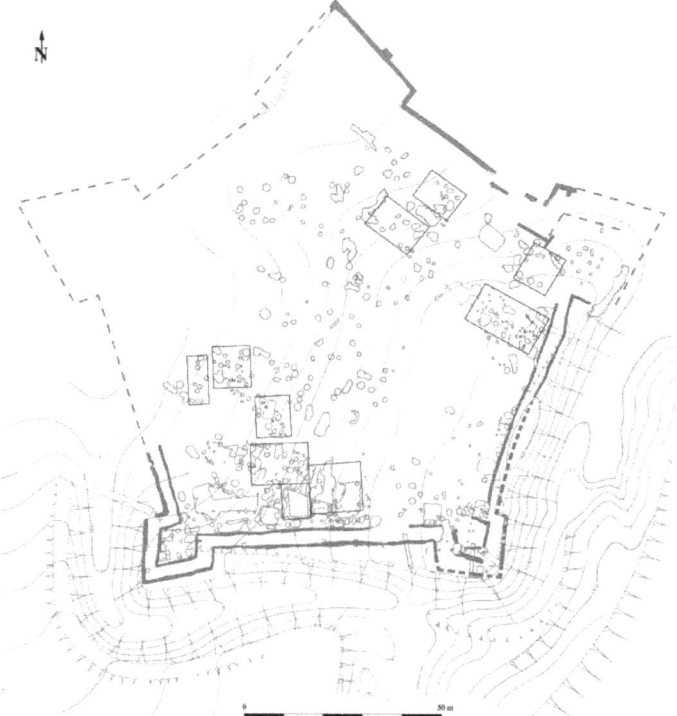

Figure 3. *Ground plan of the excavation of Bajcsavár (Vándor and Kovács 2002:51 [survey by Endre Egyed]).*

Ottoman palankas usually had a square ground plan and roundel at the corners, and similar fortifications were built by the Christians. Similar wooden structures encircled the presidial market towns and smaller towns as well. Archaeological investigations of these have been done in Pápa (Ilon 1988) and Szécsény (Mordovin and Tomka 2006:319-320), among other places. It seems that on the Christian side angular bastion-like works were preferred over roundels. The stronghold of Bajcsavár, built and supported by taxes of the Habsburg duchy of Styria, was an almost regular pentagonal wooden and earth construction with Italian-like bastions (Figure 3). Its reconstruction with brick walls was never finished (Vándor and Kovács 2002:53-54). Archaeological research covered the entirety of the intact portion of the fortification, much of which was heavily damaged by sand erosion. The extent of the research, the stronghold's short existence (1580-1600), its strong relationship to Styria, and its rich written sources make Bajcsavár of outstanding importance. Many aspects of this excavation have already been published, which unfortunately remains an exception in Hungarian historical archaeology (G. Kovács 2001b, 2002).

Specific aspects of military architecture, outposts of fortresses, and bridges used mostly by military operations have been investigated and reported in some scientific papers as well (Rózsás 2003; Tomka 2003a; Kertész et al. 2004). The remnants of two cannon foundries were unearthed in recent years. The first was run by the king in Buda from the late 15th century to the first decades of the 16th century (Belényesy 2009) while the second was built by György Rákóczi, Prince of Transylvania, at his residence in Sárospatak, in the first half of the 17th century (Ringer 2007). Both excavations yielded a surplus of information concerning bronze-working crafts and spatial organization of the cannon foundries.

gaps between posts were usually filled with wattle and daub plastered with clay to protect against combustion. This type of fortification had the advantage of quick and simple installation and the disadvantage of perishing rapidly (G. Kovács 2010:756-763). The most thoroughly excavated Ottoman palanka is Újpalánk near Szekszárd (Gaál 1985). Other palankas that were partially excavated and published include Békés-Kastélyzug (Gerelyes 1980), Vál (Hatházi and Kovács 1996, 1997), Barcs (G. Kovács and Rózsás 1996, 2010; G. Kovács 1998), Törökszentmiklós (G. Kovács 2001a), and Bátaszék (Pusztai 2003).

RELIGIOUS BUILDINGS

With the medieval predominance of the Catholic church over the Orthodox and the presence of some marginal heretic groups and Jewish communities in bigger cities, the territory of Hungary became rather fragmented religiously in the 16th century. Not only Catholic and Orthodox Christians, but different Protestant groups, Jews, and Muslims all lived together in the Carpathian Basin.

Churches built in the 16th-17th centuries within the territory of today's Hungary are very few in number. The

Catholic church was not able to restrict the spread of the Reformation in most of the territories of the medieval Kingdom of Hungary from the middle of the 16th until the second half of the 17th century. Protestants primarily used slightly altered medieval churches, but a few new edifices are known as well, such as in Kőszeg, which was once Protestant but is today the Catholic St. Emerich Church (1613-1640). Another example is the church and bell tower built in Szendrő in the middle of the 17th century of which only the tower is still standing. During the time of the Counter-Reformation larger towns usually had the power to keep their Protestant churches when Catholic friaries and Jesuit schools were being settled into the towns to recapture heretic souls. Villages followed the religion of their lord. Market towns under Ottoman occupation could keep their Protestant religions because the Ottomans encouraged (or at least tolerated) Protestants, unlike Catholics who were potentially pro-Habsburg. The typical picture of Hungarian villages today, with two or three churches of different religions, originated largely in the 19th century.

It appears that newly erected Protestant churches retained the late Gothic tradition of hall churches. Early buildings of the Counter-Reformation are mainly restricted to the western territories of the former Kingdom of Hungary; they were primarily studied by art historians. The temporary See of Esztergom in Nagyszombat (today's Trnava) as well as the Jesuit Church in Kassa (today's Košice) are both in the territory of modern Slovakia. One of the first baroque churches in Hungary is the former Jesuit, now Benedictine church in Győr. The epoch was characterized, however, by the destruction and lower quality reconstruction of former buildings, with results such as the substitution of broken vaults by wooden ceilings. In addition to military devastations, the purifying Reformation destroyed or covered the inner ornaments of medieval churches. Protestant church ornaments are usually painted floral decoration of walls and painted wooden ceilings (R. Tombor 1968).

Orthodox populations are documented in towns and castles occupied by the Ottomans. The architectural remnants of their churches are, however, yet unknown.

Islamic religious architecture is discussed in the article by Ibolya Gerelyes in this volume.

CIVIC ARCHITECTURE

Monuments of civic architecture from the 16th and 17th centuries are very scarce in Hungary. Residential royal building activity in the castle of Pozsony (today's Bratislava) was conducted within the territory of modern Slovakia. The upper and middle nobility moved from castles to more comfortable manor houses in these centuries. These manor houses were organic successors of the medieval *castella* (smaller castles), usually having a moat and a wall or palisade with a rather limited ability for defense. These castella reflect the process of the separation of military and residential architecture that was completed in the 18th century (Koppány 2006). A number of these edifices that show Renaissance architectural features are still standing (usually incorporating several later reconstructions) outside the wedge-shaped area of Ottoman occupation. One can encounter them in western Transdanubia and in Burgenland (now Austria), in the whole territory of today's Slovakia (once Lower and Upper Hungary), as well as the northeastern part of modern Hungary and in Transylvania. Enumeration of the numerous articles published on the research of different manor houses would stretch the limits of this study. Most of them can be found in different periodicals dealing with historical buildings, for example *Műemlékvédelem* and *Műemlékvédelmi Szemle*. An example is the castellum at Kéked (Cabello and Simon 1994; Feld 2000).

The most impressive and partially still standing civic buildings of the occupied towns were oriental baths. Steam baths (*hamam*) were built in many places, but they were all dysfunctional and ruined after the reconquest of the country. Thermal baths (*ilidsha*) by contrast were usually maintained. Their central parts were usually not refurbished, but their changing rooms (*apodyteria*) were often rebuilt. Their study is a traditional task of Hungarian Ottoman-Turkish archaeology, having also given rise to important recent results (G. Gerő 1980:81–116; Sudár 2004; A. Papp 2010).

URBAN ARCHAEOLOGY

The late medieval network of towns in Hungary consisted of different kinds of settlements. At the top of this hierarchy stood privileged royal towns; among these only Kőszeg, Sopron, Buda, Pest, and Szeged belong to Hungary today. The urbanized Spiš and Transylvanian Saxon region as well as mining towns such as Banská Štiavnica, Banská Bystrica, and Kremnica lie outside of the modern borders of Hungary, so their development will not be dealt with here. Market towns were settlements without all the privileges of a town, having either no defense system or a weak one, and were generally of a smaller size. They included, however, some centers of bishoprics and rich merchant towns. By contrast, the smallest market towns had only one main street, a weekly market, and few other characteristics of urbanization (Kubinyi 2004).

Stone or brick dwellings were built almost exclusively on the central main street frontages of the bigger Christian-held towns. In the territory of modern Hungary only a handful of towns such as Győr, Sopron, and Kőszeg (temporarily mortgaged to Lower Austria) contain a considerable number of newly built or rebuilt houses made of solid materials such as stone or brick. Some of them have been studied using the methods of building archaeology, but a comprehensive study has not yet been completed.

In towns such as Buda or Pécs that were occupied by the Ottomans, where the mostly German and Hungarian medieval population was changed for Balkanic people, limited maintenance of earlier buildings and newly erected wooden and wattle-and-daub construction caused a gradual alteration of the look of the settlement (G. Gerő 1980:8).

Archaeological study of smaller market towns definitively destroyed during the Turkish Wars—such as Mohi (Pusztai 2001), Ete (Miklós and Vizi 2003), and Szer (Vályi 1986)—has become more intensive over the last few years. Results of the studies show that the overwhelming majority of the houses of these smaller market towns were very similar to the houses in the villages. The difference can be seen in the density of the buildings. In the villages the distance between houses could be around 70 m (Méri 1954:140), while in market towns the houses stood only a few meters apart from each other, creating a more or less closed street view. The broad main street in Mohi was covered with gravel in the 16th century, and along this street public wells were possibly excavated (Tomka 2004a) (Figure 4). Some locations of handicraft in the market towns have also been excavated, such as a potter's workshop in Ete (Miklós and Vizi 2003:213) and a blacksmith's shop in Mohi. Around the crowded small centers of towns and market towns an external, agricultural area with gardens could be detected. It could be demonstrated

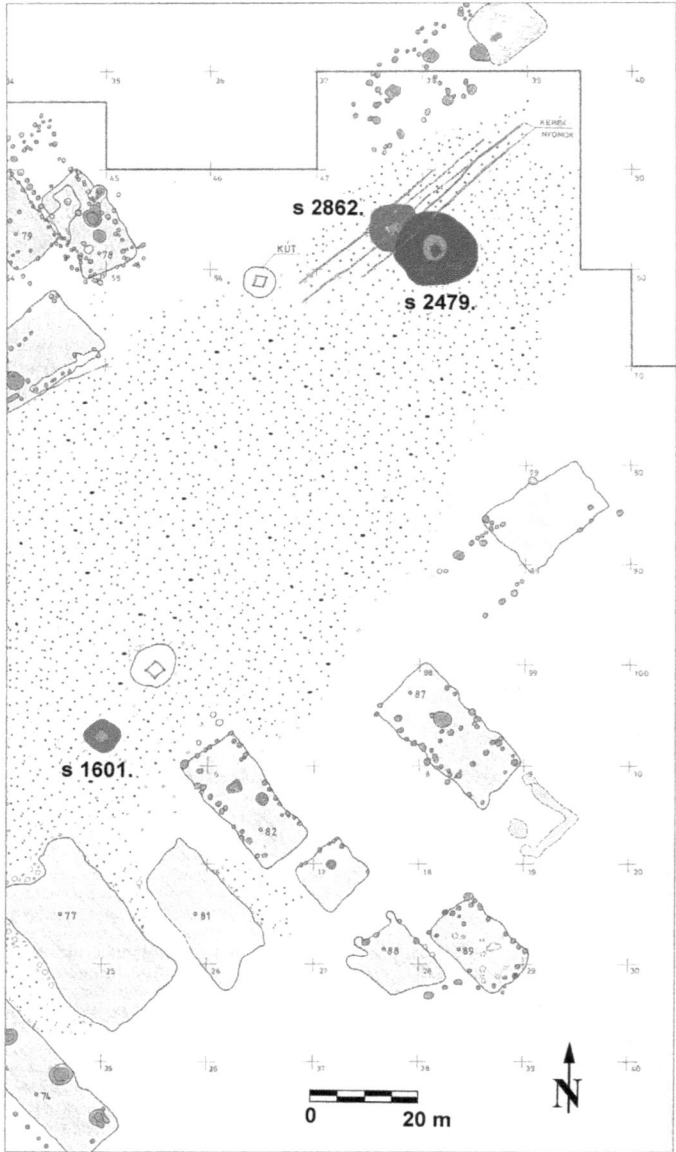

Figure 4.   Plan of the excavation of the market town Mohi. The three circular features with labels are wells that were analyzed by the author (Tomka 2004a:555).

by archaeological means that the market town with a garden outskirt did not originate in ancient Hungarian nomadic traditions of the 10th century, but rather that its development began in the early modern period (Tomka 1999).

ARCHAEOLOGY OF DESERTED VILLAGES

In the 16th and 17th centuries a great number of late medieval villages perished, especially on the Great Hungarian Plain. The pattern of settlements grew thinner and became more concentrated. The particular settlement structure of the Great Hungarian Plain is different from the neighboring lands even today. The depopulation of the villages had an economic reason hinged on the prosperity of cattle husbandry and increasing specialization within the economy of Europe, but the lengthy and great campaigns of war between the Habsburgs and the Ottomans triggered their definitive destruction. Thanks to these unlucky events there are excellent chances for the archaeological study of these villages. The archaeological study of deserted settlements was initiated by ethnographers a few decades before World War II, including László Papp and Kálmán Szabó (K. Szabó 1938). Research has shown that village destruction had three main chronological concentrations. The first was during the first half or middle of the 16th century at the time of the Ottoman invasion, producing an archaeological horizon that reflects the late medieval conditions. The second and perhaps the most crushing happened during the long war at the turn of the 16th into the 17th century (the Fifteen Years' War, 1591-1606). The third resulted from the military campaigns that caused the expulsion of the Ottomans from Hungary in the 1680s and 1690s.

At the beginning of the 1950s, István Méri studied the deserted village of Móric, which stood near Túrkeve, using stratigraphic methods borrowed from prehistoric archaeology. In spite of the fact that only a short excavation report was published, Méri's 16-page article is one of the most important sources for the archaeological study of late medieval and early modern village excavations to date (Méri 1954). Móric was destroyed in the 1590s and definitively abandoned in the first half of the 17th century, so its latest layers mirror the conditions of the early modern period (Méri 1954:140).

The professional excavation of late medieval and early modern villages is expensive work and demands much time because surface buildings usually left behind only extremely thin layers. The most thoroughly studied—but not yet so exhaustively published—village from the 15th-16th centuries in Hungary is Szentkirály. András Pálóczi Horváth carried out excavations there

between 1969 and 1990, and thanks to his results scholars were informed not only about the dwelling houses, but about the outbuildings and yards as well (Pálóczi Horváth 2003).

The houses of these villages show the persistence of the building traditions of late medieval dwellings. On the Great Hungarian Plain the most common buildings in the 16th century were single story, more than one-room (usually three-room) houses with a single entrance. These houses were built free-standing upon the ground surface. They had a wooden frame structure in which gaps were filled with blocks of dried mud or plastered wattle panels. We know from the postholes that their roofs had a ridge pole supported by posts. The roof could be covered by thatch or reed. According to parallels from the 19th century, the central room was the kitchen with an open fireplace with a hood. The fireplace was plastered on the floor at the back wall of the kitchen and an oven projected from the back wall into the yard. These protruding ovens were not used after the 16th century. From the front of the kitchen (called *pitvar*) opened the doors of the lateral rooms. In the 16th century—possibly as early as the second half of the 15th century—one of the heated rooms was smoke-free as its heating oven was made from stove-tiles and was stoked up from the kitchen side. Use of stove eyelets (a round or beaker-like stove-tile) stopped in the 17th century on the Great Hungarian Plain. The clay-made large heating ovens (*búbos kemence*), which would be noticed in great numbers in the ethnological surveys of the late 19th and early 20th centuries, are the result of a secondary regression. The function of the unheated third (and sometimes fourth) room is still uncertain. It could have been used as a living room or a storage room (K. Szabó 1938:81-87; Méri 1954:142-146; Pálóczi Horváth 2003:204).

CEMETERIES

Excavations of late medieval and early modern burials in churchyards show hardly any difference. The cemeteries around churches were used continuously until the demise of a village. Cemeteries of surviving settlements usually extend to the end of the 18th century, at which time they were moved to the settlement outskirts. In the very confined churchyards the superimposed latest graves are usually in the best condition. In most cases coffins were used, and the iron nails and sometimes even iron furnishings have been found during excavations. As a result of Christian

rituals, some elements of clothing are usually found in both late medieval and early modern graves. The late medieval fitted belts went out of fashion in the middle of the 16th century. Few finds of Renaissance metal belt-fittings have been published so far, although inventories reveal that fitted belts were in use later on. Remnants of headdresses on the skulls, made of wire and beads applied to textile strips, are noticeable from the 15th to the 16th centuries onwards. The headdresses (called *párta*) decorated unmarried young females according to the parallels from Hungarian ethnography. In the 17th and

18th centuries headdresses decorated with flower motifs and tiny sprigs were in style. Sometimes copper oxide from the headdresses has preserved part of the textile as well as the hair. Some parts of clothes are also known from the few excavated 17th – and 18th-century graves (Simonyi 2005:309-313). In high status burials jewels (clasps, rings, hair-needles, etc.) or weapons placed on the coffin can sometimes be found. In the town of Sopron a female burial was excavated recently that was excellently preserved. The woman was dressed after the style of the end of the 16th century. From the late 17th century onwards consecrated coins, the rosary, and the rood (cross) are found more often in Catholic burials. A unique opportunity presented itself for archaeologists, ethnologists, and anthropologists to bring to light a find complex from a walled-off crypt in Vác, in the Church of the White Friars (Dominicans). The 265 bodies, buried in wooden coffins, were partially preserved due to the special microclimate. The burials dated to between 1730 and 1808 and they provided unique evidence of burial rituals (black bands, painted coffins), clothes, illnesses, and nourishment of the burghers of Vác. Although presented in an exhibition at the Magyar Természettudományi Múzeum in Budapest, scientific evaluation of the finds is still in progress.

MATERIAL CULTURE STUDIES

Archaeological studies of material culture of the 16th-17th centuries were primarily inspired by the exotic and oriental nature of some types of artifacts of the Ottoman culture. At first, artifacts of the central European Christian culture were predominantly studied by art historians. An archaeological approach to these has become more and more important in the last decades.

Ceramics

Sándor Garády was the first to write an article on the ceramics of the Turkish Occupation period that came to light during excavations or were unearthed during building operations (Garády 1944:383-440). Géza Fehér processed the ceramic artifacts of the museums of Pécs and Eger from the same period, and as co-author he published the remains of the only identified Turkish pottery workshop in Esztergom (Fehér 1959, 1972; Fehér and Parádi 1960). Győző Gerő published articles mainly on the faience of Asia Minor (Iznik pottery) and Persia (G. Gerő 1989:143-148, 1990:111-118). Imre Holl presented the china and faience wares from Iznik and Persia that

Some cemeteries excavated in the southern part of Hungary can be linked to the Balkanic population. In Dombóvár-Békató burials of Vlach inhabitants were found (Gaál 1982, 2003), and at Bácsalmás skeletal remains of a Serb ethnic group were uncovered (Wicker 2003). Only eight percent of the burials of the latter example were placed in coffins. In most cases the dead were wrapped in a sheet that was put on the hollowed bottom of the grave and was covered with planks (the graves had small benches to facilitate this). The hands of the dead were often clasped in front of the body. This hand position is thought to be characteristic for Orthodox Christianity. It is supposed that the graves were covered with boughs, above which the burial mounds were piled. These signs indicate the influence of Muslim customs (Wicker 2003:19-84, 2005:325-331, 2008). An early modern cemetery excavated in Győr-Gabonavásártér was thought to be initially of a Serb provenience as well (Mithay 1985). These kinds of cemeteries can attest to the northern movement of the Balkan (in most cases Serb) population. Although found not only in graves, mention should be made of the silver jewelry of the Balkanic and Turkish population (Gerelyes 1994) and the characteristic glass bracelets (Holl 2005:166-167).

were found during the archaeological exploration of Buda Castle (Holl 2005:100-159).

Larger assemblages of pottery were published from Buda, Ozora, and Visegrád (Gerelyes 1985, 1987a, 1990; Gerelyes and Feld 1986; Holl 2005). Special attention was paid to the interpretation of sgraffito bowls (G. Kovács 1984a:20-31; Gerelyes 1986, 1987b). Gyöngyi Kovács published a reasonable amount on pottery from palankas that she investigated (G. Kovács 1984a, 1990-1991, 1998, 2001a; Hatházi and Kovács 1996:41-49).

From towns and castles that were firmly incorporated in the Ottoman Empire and inhabited mainly by Muslim and Orthodox Christian populations, characteristic types of pottery come to light. The walls of the vessels are usually quite thick and they are made of reddish clay. White slip and thick green, yellow, or brown glaze are common. Pedestaled bowls, tulip mouthed jars, and a few other types of vessels are found in these places, while these types are almost unknown in the Hungarian villages and market towns. Grey jugs with incised

Figure 5. (left) A jug from Buda, 16-17th centuries, an example of Iznik pottery (Tanman and Demirsar Arlı and Adigüzel and Sağnak 2010:178 [Cat. #54]).

Figure 6. (right) Slipware jug from Szendrő, 17th century (Photo by András Dabasi, ca. 2008).

decoration and a polished finish, fired in a reducing atmosphere, are also common finds at these sites.

On the Turkish sites, aside from the above-mentioned special wares, the typical "Hungarian pottery" can always be found (G. Kovács 1990-1991:170-171). From the southern part of the area occupied by the Ottomans, first of all from southern Transdanubia and along the Danube, archaic unglazed vessels produced on a slow wheel (mostly pots, jugs, platters, and baking lids) have been found. These are associated with Balkanic people moving to the north. Incised wavy lines, spirals, and rouletting decorate this brownish or greyish pottery (Pusztai 2003).

In 1963 Nándor Parádi published a seminal article on medieval pottery in Hungary dated by association with coin hoards. Half of the assemblage was later than 1526, so we can include it as early modern pottery

(Parádi 1963). Hungarian pottery of the 16th-17th centuries is represented mostly by finds from villages and castles. In Transdanubia, north to Lake Balaton, some early modern pottery was published from two castles (Kozák 1966). A very important and well processed and published find-spot in southwestern Transdanubia is the stronghold Bajcsa. Local and imported (Austrian and Italian) pottery was used in this fort at the end of the 16th century (G. Kovács 2001b). In excavations in the market-town Ete, mainly local pottery from the 16th century came to light (Miklós and Vizi 2003:213).

The author of the current paper presented in his doctoral dissertation the pottery from the northeastern part of modern Hungary, which was the southeastern part of the Kingdom of Hungary in the 16th-17th centuries. In this territory a special white pottery was in use, based on pure clay deposits mainly in the Gömör region (Tomka 2004b:136-138). A specially decorated earthenware characteristic of the 16th century usually had a white body as well. This ware, called Hungarian Renaissance tableware or incised glazed pottery, had geometric or, sometimes, simple floral decoration scratched into the surface of unfired jugs and bowls. Fields were filled with glazes of different colors using lead glazes or, on best pieces, white and blue tin glazes (Írásné Melis 1984; Tomka 2004b:24-37).

In the 16th century late medieval pottery was replaced by thin-walled, often glazed pottery produced on a potter's wheel operated by foot. Cooking pots were usually provided with a handle, a feature that was formerly uncommon. The technique of manufacture did not change much until the decline of local pottery production in the late 19th, early 20th centuries. Differences can be detected between the parts of the country both in forms and in decoration. There is a clear continuity of the tradition of white ceramic of the 16th century to the Gömör white ceramic well-known from ethnographic literature. These fireproof and red-painted vessels were produced in the area between Nógrád and Borsod Counties. The decorated glazed ware (slip ware) that spread across Europe beginning in the second part of the 16th century became popular in Hungary at the turn of the 16th and 17th centuries. In contrast to western Europe most of these vessels (bowls and jugs) had bright (white or ivory) slip like their southern Polish parallels. The influence of oriental ceramic was apparently minimal. The decorative motifs of folk pottery in the 19th century can be seen to be clearly derived from 17th-century predecessors, though the continuity of single potters' workshops cannot yet be shown (Vida 1999:85; Lajkó 2003:328) (Figures 5 and 6).

A special and diagnostic group of pottery is the so-called Habán faience, produced by Anabaptist communities in the 17th and early 18th centuries. The pieces survived in ecclesiastic, public, or private collections and are well-known to art historians (Katona 1974), but research on small fragments found during excavations has now begun.

Stove-Tiles

Tiled stoves first appeared in the Hungarian royal and aristocratic milieu in the second half of the 14th century (Holl 1958:215-228). Smoke-free heating by tiled stoves spread even into rural environments until the mid-16th century. The structure and design of Renaissance tiled stoves are simpler when compared to Gothic stoves.

Producing a single tile became easier, since openwork figures and tracery were replaced by simple square tiles with a bas-relief produced by pressing the clay sheet into a negative mold. The sides of the tile became shorter and the rear opening more and more square. Most of the tiles are found in areas outside the Ottoman occupation, but Hungarian market-towns presumably continued producing tiles under Ottoman rule as well (Figure 7). German and Czech influence dominates in design and composition mainly in Transdanubia and on tiles made in northwestern Hungary, now Slovakia (Holl 1993). In the northeastern parts of Hungary we can find some imported Polish stove-tiles, imitations of them, and adoptions of their ornaments (Holl 2004:352-361; Tomka 2007). In this region in the mid-16th century a particular, provincial Renaissance style developed: stove-tiles were decorated with floral and geometrical patterns (Boldizsár et al. 2010). From the 17th century, an endless motif imitating textile designs that consisted of a kind of floral pattern became popular across central Europe. Rare finds from the mid-17th century are the tin-glazed stove-tiles made by the Habán (Anabaptist) craftsmen, whose designs also gave inspiration to the stove-tile designs of the Kingdom of Hungary's northern area (Gyuricza 1992:25-34).

While inferior quality stoves in the Transdanubian area were mostly made of simple bowl-shaped tiles, on the Hungarian Great Plain different variations of the basically cup-shaped stove-tiles were in fashion in the 16th century (Sabján 2002). The stoves inside the smaller Ottoman fortresses were often made from cup-shaped eyelets without any glaze (Pusztai 2003:307-308). In wealthier towns, however, in addition to these unglazed stoves, the Balkan population could feel cozy and warm next to stoves decorated with truncated-cone-shaped stove-tiles covered with a green lead glaze. The in situ remains of such a stove in a cellar of a house in the Víziváros suburb of Buda gave a fortunate chance to reconstruct this kind of heating technology of Balkan origin (Sabján and Végh 2003).

Clay Pipes

The custom of smoking began to spread in Hungary around the year 1600. Recovered clay pipe bowls are mainly of Turkish (Balkan) nature that would have once had a wooden stem, but western European pipes with long clay stems were also used in smaller numbers in the mid-17th century, presumably foremost by western mercenaries (Figure 8). By the end of the 17th

1

2

Figure 7. **Stove-tiles depicting double-headed eagles from Szendrő, late 17th century (Tomka 2011:586).**

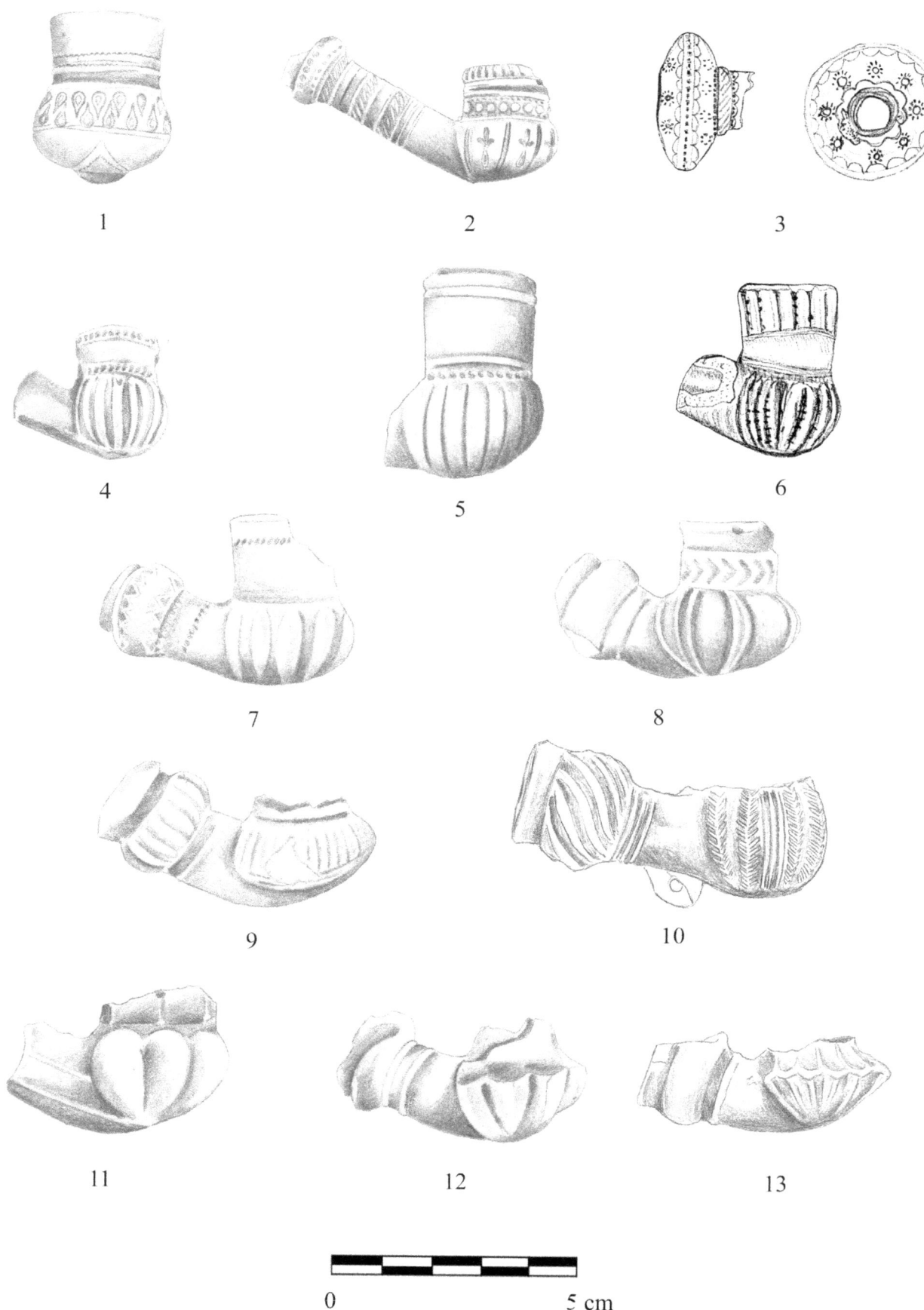

1   2   3

4   5   6

7   8

9   10

11   12   13

0   5 cm

Figure 8.   Various types of Turkish (Balkan) type clay tobacco pipes from the 17th century (Tomka 2012).

century these western pipes had disappeared and an early Hungarian pipe form developed at the beginning of the 1700s from a simple Turkish type. In the 18th century, as in the previous century, a wide variety of pipe-forms was used simultaneously. The capacity of the pipe bowls increased, but their decorative elaboration was simplified. The continuous change of type and look of this artifact can be explained with the long-term falling price of tobacco and increasing popularity of smoking. Apart from a single comprehensive early article on pipes found in the castle of Eger (B. Kovács 1963) only scattered data were published on pipes until the year 2000 (Tomka 2000). In the last decade hundreds of pipes have been processed and published, which has considerably improved our knowledge about pipes both in 17th and 18th centuries (Gaál 2004; Kondorosy 2007, 2008, 2009).

Metal Artifacts

The almost continuous warfare in the 16th-17th centuries resulted in an unusual density of hoards and deposits. Ruined and later leveled buildings often concealed assemblages of objects that would have normally been recycled and thus lost to archaeologists. Copper vessels were surely used not only by the Balkanic but also by the central European population of the Carpathian Basin, but the greater number of recovered Balkan copper vessels and their sometimes artful elaboration has made us much better informed about them. Géza Fehér published the Turkish copper vessels of the Janus Pannonius Museum in Pécs (Fehér 1959:121-122, 129) and of the Hungarian National Museum in Budapest (Fehér 1962). Several articles were published on copper vessels from Esztergom (Fehér 1968), from Buda (Bencze 2002), from the collection of the museum in Szekszárd (Gaál 1983, 1991), and from Szolnok County (G. Kovács 1984b). Ibolya Gerelyes organized an exhibition of Turkish copper vessels (Gerelyes 1997) and wrote the latest survey on this topic (Gerelyes 2010). Spouted jugs, footed bowls, cauldrons, and tulip-shaped candlesticks are the most popular forms of Turkish copper artifacts.

Everyday utensils often show little change over a long period, so it is quite difficult to separate late medieval and early modern finds when stratigraphy or lifespan of the find spot are uninformative. Basic works such as an article on products of late medieval blacksmiths (G. Szabó 1954) or a monograph on the development of agricultural tools (Müller 1982) deal with artifacts from the 15th-17th centuries. The catalog of an exhibition about the aforementioned Bajcsa fort (G. Kovács 2002) and a monograph of the metal objects found in the castle of Ozora (Gere 2003) are two outstanding publications of recent years. The artifacts presented in the former can be dated precisely to 1580-1600, while the latter contains profound descriptions and evaluations of the finds. Certain forms of knives, disc-shaped horseshoes, and boot irons are characteristic iron objects of the 16th and 17th centuries.

Weapons

A large number of 16th-17th-century weapons (including most of the elaborated items) survive in collections. This paper does not aim to enumerate the literature on them, but restricts itself to archaeologically recovered pieces. Weapons, or more frequently parts of weaponry, can be found in excavations carried out in castles. János Kalmár, author of a basic work on medieval and early modern Hungarian weaponry (Kalmár 1971) published his excavations on Fülek (Fil'akovo, Slovakia) castle in 1944. As an expert in weaponry, Kalmár identified even the smallest parts of weapons among the finds, which were later handed over to Czechoslovakia (Kalmár 1959). Apart from the above-mentioned finds from Ozora (Gere 2003) and Bajcsa (G. Kovács 2002), special mention should be made of an assemblage found during river improvements along the Danube that represented the weapons of a sunken boat used at the siege of Buda around the middle of the 16th century (T. Kovács 1994). Károly Kozák contributed to the clarification of the history of the arquebuses that were used in Hungary as late as the 17th century (Kozák 1974).

Scientific Studies

Scientific analyses are already common in prehistoric archeology. These methods have been slowly accepted and applied in historical archeology as well.

Physical anthropological tests were performed on skeletons from the mass graves of the battle of Mohács, where soldiers died in 1526 (K. Zoffmann 1982). Some data were published on Balkan cemeteries from the southern part of the country. In the cemetery of Dombóvár-Békató the population showed similar osteology to peoples from Montenegro and Albania (Éry 1982). A number of people had spinal disease and tuberculosis in the graveyard of Bácsalmás (Pálfi and Ardagna 2003).

Animal bones are often recovered from early modern layers in huge quantities (Vörös 2003). Cattle bones are quite frequent due to consumption habits, but large bones can be over-represented in archaeological finds. More evidence for poultry is found in towns than in villages, but dog bones are recovered more often at rural settlements, so it is possible that these differences are showing not different consumption habits, but rather different treatment and disposal patterns. Pig bones relate to Christian populations, while sheep and goats replace swine where larger Muslim populations lived. Species that were previously regarded as ancient Hungarian ones (such as Hungarian Grey Cattle or Hungarian sheep) were developed only in the 18th century. In the Ottoman period we can find oriental mammals such as water buffalo and camel in the Carpathian Basin. Turkey fowl occur in the 17th century, and not only in the occupied area.

Scientific material analysis verified the questioned Ottoman origin of glazed wall tiles from Sárospatak (Balla 2005). Analysis of vitrifying material of glazed earthenware confirmed an extremely high quantity of lead (up to 70%). Glazes were colored with iron and copper oxides. White and blue glaze on incised Renaissance pottery was produced by mixing tin oxide into the vitrifying complex (I. Papp et al. 1999:456-464). A project of scientific analysis of Habán pottery wares is currently running. The gradual spreading of glass products in the Middle Ages continued into the 16th and 17th centuries. From the late 15th century onwards more and more local glass workshops were founded. They were often placed in the forest region, where raw material was available nearby. This manufacture used potash for their products, as tests proved (Mester 2010:644). X-ray emission analysis was performed on a series of Turkish copper vessels (Költő 2003). The materials of the vessels have a very high content of copper (90-95%). The proportion of other metals varied according to the function of the vessel and of the function of particular parts of the vessel.

NEW TRENDS AND PERSPECTIVES

The potential of traditional archaeological studies has broadened with new methods in recent years. Because of Hungary's geographic location, Hungarian underwater archaeology can mainly focus only on river beds. Apart from some modern objects the most important discovery revealed to date consists of a sunken raft in the river Dráva from the Ottoman period (Tóth 2010). Landscape archaeology is also a new approach, but it concentrates foremost on late medieval landscape reconstructions (Zatykó 2010). To delineate the changing history of a medieval landscape, the study of the post-medieval situation is also needed. As of late, specifically post-medieval landscape studies have been published (G. Kovács 2010:633-636). Archaeological research slowly exceeds the upper time-limit of 1711 given by the heritage laws. The study of outstanding monuments such as a baroque puppet-theatre in Esterházy Castle at Fertőd (the "Hungarian Versailles") (Forgács et al. 2006) and industrial archaeology at sites such as glass workshops from the 19th century (Mester 2010:663-671) or wasters from a potter's workshop of the 19th century (Vida 1993) are examples of the archaeology of the 18th-19th centuries.

In the near future historical archaeology will become more emphatic than ever before. A good example is the fact that at the second Conference of the Young Archaeologists of the Middle-Ages in 2010, the focus of the presentations was on post-medieval topics. It is an urgent task to process and release the immense amount of unpublished finds both in conventional publication forms and with the help of the internet. Although rigid typological systems may evoke criticism, this stage of scholarly evolution cannot be bypassed in historical archaeology either. A complex archaeological study can give answers to several questions: not only to aspects of social, spatial, and ethnic fragmentation of everyday life in the past, but also to the extent of interaction between different material cultures. The extension of study into the 18th and 19th centuries can be expected because numerous questions can be answered only with archaeological methods, even in these centuries that are abundant in written records.

REFERENCES

BALLA, MÁRTA

2005 Beyond Style. A Provenance Study of Iznik Pottery by Means of Neutron Activation Analysis (NAA). In *Turkish Flowers. Studies on Ottoman Art in Hungary*, Ibolya Gerelyes, editor, pp. 63-68. Hungarian National Museum, Budapest, Hungary

BELÉNYESY, KÁROLY

2009 Ami a tűzben fogant. Kísérlet a XV-XVI. század fordulóján működő budai ágyúöntő műhely rekonstrukciójára [An Attempt at the Reconstruction of the 15th-16th-Century Cannon Foundry in Buda]. In *Régészeti dimenziók. Tanulmányok az ELTE BTK Régészettudományi Intézetének tudományos műhelyéből*, Anders Alexandra, Szabó Miklós, and Raczky Pál, editors, pp. 139-150. ELTE BTK Régészettudományi Intézet—L'Harmattan, Budapest, Hungary.

BENCZE, ZOLTÁN

2002 Török rézedények a Hadtörténeti Múzeum udvarán [Turkish Copper Dinnerware from the Court of the Museum of War History]. *Budapest Régiségei* 35/2:461-468.

BENKŐ, ELEK, AND GYÖNGYI KOVÁCS (EDITORS)

2010 *A középkor és a kora újkor régészete Magyarországon I-II [Archaeology of the Middle Ages and the Early Modern Period in Hungary I-II]*. Magyar Tudományos Akadémia Régészeti Intézete. Budapest, Hungary.

BOLDIZSÁR, PÉTER, EDIT KOCSIS, AND TIBOR SABJÁN

2010 *A diósgyőri vár 16-17. századi kályhacsempéi [Stove-Tiles of the 16th and 17th Centuries from the Diósgyőr Castle]*. Borsod-Abaúj-Zemplén megye régészeti emlékei 8, Herman Ottó Múzeum, Miskolc, Hungary.

CABELLO, JUAN, AND ZOLTÁN SIMON

1994 A Kékediek és kastélyuk [The Kékedi Family and its Castle at Kéked]. In *Gerő László 85. születésnapjára.* **Művészettörténet-Műemlékvédelem VI**, Nóra Pamer, editor, pp. 197-225. Országos Műemlékvédelmi Hivatal, Budapest, Hungary.

DÁVID, GÉZA

2003 The Connection between History and Archaeology in Researching Ottoman Rule in Hungary. In *Archaeology of the Ottoman Period in Hungary*, Ibolya Gerelyes and Gyöngyi Kovács, editors, pp. 11-16. Magyar Nemzeti Múzeum, Budapest, Hungary.

DOMOKOS, GYÖRGY

1997 A kassai királyi hadszertár fegyverzete és felszerelése a XVI-XVII. századi inventáriumok tükrében [Weapons and Equipment of the Royal Armory in Kassa in Light of Inventories from the 16th-17th Centuries]. *Hadtörténelmi közlemények* 110. 1997(4):667-747.

2000 *Ottavio Baldigara. Egy itáliai várfundáló mester Magyarországon [Ottavio Baldigara. An Italian Castle-Builder in Hungary]*. A Hadtörténeti Intézet és Múzeum milleniumi könyvtára Szerkesztő. Csákváry Ferenc, Balassi Kiadó, Budapest, Hungary.

ÉRY, KINGA

1982 Balkáni eredetű, törökkori népesség csontmaradványai Dombóvár határából [The Osteological Remains of a Turkish Period Balkan Population in the Vicinity of Dombóvár]. *Balogh Ádám Múzeum Évkönyve* 10-11:225-298.

F. LAJKÓ, ORSOLYA

2010 A kora újkori kerámia tipológiája—a néprajzi edényterminológia alkalmazásának lehetőségei a Dél-Alföldön [The Typology of Early Modern Age Ceramics—Possibilities for the Use of Ethnography's Vessel Terminology on the Great Hungarian Plain]. In *A középkor és a kora újkor régészete Magyarországon I-II*, Elek Benkő and Gyöngyi Kovács, editors, pp. 799-816. Magyar Tudományos Akadémia Régészeti Intézete, Budapest, Hungary.

FEHÉR, GÉZA

1959 A pécsi Janus Pannonius Múzeum hódoltságkori török emlékei [Monuments in the Janus Pannonius Museum in Pécs from the Period of the Turkish Repression]. *Janus Pannonius Múzeum Évkönyve* 1959:103-150.

1962 Vases de cuivre turcs dans le Musée National Hongrois [Turkish Copper Vessels in the Hungarian National Museum]. *Folia Archaeologica* 14:153-167.

1968 Esztergomi török vörösrézedények [Turkish Copper Utensils from Esztergom]. *Komárom Megyei Múzeumok Közleményei* 1:273-310.

1972 Adatok Eger török agyagművességéhez [Data on the Turkish Potters' Craft in Eger]. *Egri Múzeum Évkönyve* 10:191-214.

FEHÉR, GÉZA, AND NÁNDOR PARÁDI

1960 Esztergom-Szenttamáshegyi 1956. évi törökkori kutatások [Exploration of the Turkish Period at Esztergom-Szenttamáshegyi in 1956]. *Esztergom Évlapjai* 1:35-44.

FELD, ISTVÁN

2000   *16. századi kastélyok Északkelet-Magyarországon*
        [*Manor Houses in Northeastern Hungary in the
        16th Century*]. Minta bolt, Sárospatak,, Hungary.

2008   Ágyúvédőművek a 16. század első felének
        erődítményépítészetében [Artillery Defenses in
        Military Architecture during the First Half of the
        16th Century]. *Studia Agriensia* 27:175-196.

FELD, ISTVÁN, AND GYÖRGY SZEKÉR

1994   A sárospataki Vörös-torony építéstörténetének
        vázlata [Outline of the Building History
        of the Red Tower in Sárospatak]. In *Gerő
        László 85. születésnapjára*. Művészettörténet-
        Műemlékvédelem VI, Nóra Pamer, editor, pp.
        169-196. Országos Műemlékvédelmi Hivatal,
        Budapest, Hungary.

FORGÁCS, ZITA, ANDRÁS KOPPÁNY, AND LÁSZLÓ THÚRY

2006   Előzetes beszámoló a fertődi bábszínház és
        narancsház kutatásáról [Preliminary Report
        on the Research of the Puppet Theater and the
        Orangerie in Fertőd]. *Műemlékvédelem* 50(4):187-
        193.

GAÁL, ATTILA

1982   A dombóvár-békátói XVI-XVII. századi temető
        [The 16th-17th Century Cemetery of Dombóvár-
        Békató]. *A Szekszárdi Béri Balogh Ádám Múzeum
        Évkönyve* 10-11:133-224.

1983   A szekszárdi múzeum hódoltság kori
        rézedényei [Copper Vessels of the Szekszárd
        Museum from the Turkish Occupation Period].
        Communicationes Archaeolgicae Hungariae
        1983:163-184.

1985   Török palánkvárak a Buda-eszéki út Tolna megyei
        szakaszán [Turkish Palankas along the Sector
        in Tolna County of the Road between Buda and
        Eszék]. In *Magyar és török végvárak 1663-1684*,
        Sandor Bodó and Jola Szabó, editors, pp. 185-197.
        Dobó István Vármúzeum, Eger, Hungary.

1991   A szekszárdi múzeum hódoltság kori
        rézedényei 2 [Copper Vessels of the Szekszárd
        Museum from the Turkish Occupation Period].
        Communicationes Archaeolgicae Hungariae
        1991:191-207.

2003   The Sixteenth – to Seventeenth-Century
        Cemetery at Dombóvár-Békató. In *Archaeology
        of the Ottoman Period in Hungary*, Ibolya
        Gerelyes and Gyöngyi Kovács, editors, pp. 221-230.
        Magyar Nemzeti Múzeum, Budapest, Hungary.

2004   Hódoltságkori cseréppipák a Wosinsky Mór
        Múzeum Gyűjteményében [Clay Pipes from the
        Turkish Period in the Collection of the Wosinsky
        Mór Museum]. *A Wosinsky Mór Múzeum
        évkönyve* 27:259-296.

GARÁDY, SÁNDOR

1944   Agyagművesség [Potters' Craft]. In *Budapest
        története*, 3. kötet, Lajos Fekete, editor, pp. 382-
        401. Királyi Magyar Egyetemi Nyomda, Budapest,
        Hungary.

GERE, LÁSZLÓ

2003   *Késő középkori és kora újkori fémleletek az ozorai
        várkastélyból* [*Late Medieval and Early Modern
        Metal Finds from the Castle of Ozora*]. Opuscula
        Hungarica 4. Magyar Nemzeti Múzeum,
        Budapest, Hungary.

GERELYES, IBOLYA

1980   Előzetes jelentés a Békés-kastélyzugi törökkori
        palánkvár ásatásáról, 1975-1978 [Report on the
        Turkish Period Palisade Stronghold at Békés-
        Kastélyzug, 1975-1978]. *Archaeológiai Értesítő*
        107:102-111.

1985   Adatok a tabáni török díszkerámia keltezéséhez
        és etnikai hátteréhez [Data on the Chronology
        and Ethnic Background of Decorated Turkish
        Ceramics Found in the Tabán (Buda)]. *Folia
        Archaelogica* 36:223-247.

1986   Adatok a sgraffito-díszes török kerámia
        keltezéséhez [Data on the Age of Sgraffito-
        Ornamented Turkish Pottery]. *Keletkutatás*
        1986/3:69-84.

1987a   Török kerámia a visegrádi Alsóvárból
        [Turkish Ceramics from Alsóvár in Visegrád].
        Communicationes Archaeolgicae Hungariae
        1987:167-178.

1987b   Sgraffito-díszes török kerámia az ozorai
        várkastélyból [Turkish Sgrafitto Pottery from the
        Ozora Castle]. *Folia Archaelogica* 38:247-260.

1990   Die Balkanverbindungen der türkischen Keramik
        von der Budaer Burg [Balkan Connections of
        the Turkish Pottery Found in Buda Castle].
        *Acta Archaeologica Academiae Scientiarum
        Hungaricae* 42:269-285.

1994   *Török ékszerek* [*Turkish Jewelry*]. Évezredek,
        évszázadok kincsei 7. Magyar Nemzeti Múzeum,
        Budapest, Hungary.

1997   *Oszmán-török rézművesség, XVI-XIX. század*
        [*Ottoman-Turkish Coppersmith's Art, 16th to 19th
        Centuries*]. Magyar Nemzeti Múzeum, Budapest,
        Hungary.

2010 A Magyar Nemzeti Múzeum balkáni török fémanyagának jelentősége a régészeti kutatások tükrében. Egy gyűjtemény kialakulásának tanulságai [The Significance of the Balkanic-Turkish Metal Artifacts in the Hungarian National Museum in Light of Archaeological Research. Lessons from the Evolution of a Collection]. In *A középkor és a kora újkor régészete Magyarországon I-II*, Elek Benkő and Gyöngyi Kovács, editors, pp. 757-798. Magyar Tudományos Akadémia Régészeti Intézete, Budapest, Hungary.

GERELYES, IBOLYA, AND ISTVÁN FELD
1986 Hódoltság kori leletegyüttesek az ozorai várkastélyból [Turkish Period Find Assemblages from the Ozora Castle]. *Communicationes Archaeolgicae Hungariae* 1986:161-182.

GERELYES, IBOLYA, AND GYÖNGYI KOVÁCS (EDITORS)
2002 *A hódoltság régészeti kutatása [Archaeology of the Ottoman Period in Hungary]*. A Magyar Nemzeti Múzeumban 2000. május 24-26. között megtartott konferencia előadásai. Opuscula Hungarica 3. Magyar Nemzeti Múzeum, Budapest, Hungary.

2003 *Archaeology of the Ottoman Period in Hungary*. Papers of the conference held at the Hungarian National Museum, Budapest, 24-26 May 2000. Opuscula Hungarica 3. Magyar Nemzeti Múzeum, Budapest, Hungary.

GERŐ, GYŐZŐ
1980 *Az oszmán-török építészet Magyarországon (Dzsámik, türbék, fürdők) [Ottoman-Turkish Architecture in Hungary (Camis, Türbes, Baths)]*. Művészettörténeti füzetek 12. Akadémiai Kiadó, Budapest, Hungary.

1989 Anatolian Pottery—from Iznik and Kütahya—in Hungary in the 16th and 17th Centuries. In *First International Congress on Turkish Tiles and Ceramics*, pp. 143-148, Türk Petrol Vakfi, Istanbul, Turkey.

1990 Die Keramik von Isnik und Kütahya in Ungarn [The Pottery of Isnik and Kutahya in Hungary]. In *7th International Congress of Turkish Art Warsaw, 1983*, T. Majda, editor, pp. 111-118. Polish Scientific Publishers, Warsaw, Poland.

2003 The History of Ottoman-Turkish Archaeological Research in Hungary. In *Archaeology of the Ottoman Period in Hungary*, Ibolya Gerelyes and Gyöngyi Kovács, editors, pp. 17-22. Magyar Nemzeti Múzeum, Budapest, Hungary.

GERŐ, LÁSZLÓ
1955 *Magyarországi várépítészet (Vázlat a magyar várépítés fejezeteiről) [Castle Architecture in Hungary (Outline of the Capitals of Castle Building in Hungary)]*. "Művelt Nép" Tudományos és Ismeretterjesztő Kiadó, Budapest, Hungary.

GERŐ, LÁSZLÓ (EDITOR)
1975 *Várépítészetünk [Building History of Hungarian Castles]*. Műszaki Könyvkiadó, Budapest, Hungary.

GYURICZA, ANNA
1992 *Reneszánsz kályhacsempék Északkelet-Magyarországon [Renaissance Glazed Tiles from Northeast Hungary]*. Borsodi kismonográfiák 37. Herman Ottó Múzeum, Miskolc, Hungary.

HATHÁZI, GÁBOR, AND GYÖNGYI KOVÁCS
1996 *A váli gótikus templomtorony. Adatok Vál 14-17. századi történetéhez [The Gothic Church-Tower in Vál. Data on the History of Vál in the 14th-17th Centuries]*. Az István Király Múzeum Közleményei Series B. 45. Székesfehérvár, Hungary.

1997 A Post-Medieval Assemblage from Vál. *Acta Archaeologica Academiae Scientiarum Hungaricae* 49:195-224.

HOLL, IMRE
1958 Középkori kályhacsempék Magyarországon [Medieval Stove-Tiles in Hungary]. *Budapest Régiségei* 18:211-279.

1993 Renaissance-Öfen. Mittelalterliche Ofenkacheln in Ungarn V [Renaissance Stove-Tiles. Medieval Stove-Tiles in Hungary 5]. *Acta Archaeologica Academiae Scientiarum Hungaricae* 45:247-299.

2004 Ungarisch-polnische Beziehungen aufgrund der Ofenkacheln (Zweite Hälfte 15.-erste Hälfte 16. Jahrhundert) [Hungarian-Polish Connections Related to Stove-Tiles (Second Half 15th-Early 16th Centuries)]. *Acta Archaeologica Academiae Scientiarum Hungaricae* 55:333-375.

2005 *Fundkomplexe des 15.-17. Jahrhunderts aus dem Burgpalast von Buda [Find Assemblages from the Palace of Buda from the 15th to the 17th Centuries]*. Varia archaeologica Hungarica 17. Archäologisches Institut der UAW, Budapest, Hungary.

ILON, GÁBOR
1988 Pápa város keleti palánkjának szondázása [Trenching of the Eastern Palisade of the Town of Pápa]. *Communicationes Archaelogicae Hungariae* 1988:159–168.

ÍRÁSNÉ MELIS, KATALIN
1984 XV-XVI. századi díszedények a budai királyi palotából [Ornamental Vessels of the 15th-16th Century from the Royal Palace of Buda]. *Communicationes Archaelogicae Hungariae* 1984:205-222.

K. ZOFFMANN, ZSUZSANNA

1982   Az 1526-os Mohácsi csata 1976-ban feltárt Tömegsírjainak embertani vizsgálata [The Battle of Mohács in 1526, Anthropological Study of Mass Graves Discovered in 1976]. Biológiai Tanulmányok, 9. Budapest, Hungary.

KALMÁR, JÁNOS

1959   A füleki vár XV-XVII. századi emlékei [Monuments of the Castle of Fülek from the 15th to 17th Centuries]. Régészeti Füzetek Series II/4. Magyar Nemzeti Múzeum, Budapest, Hungary.

1971   Régi magyar fegyverek [Old Hungarian Weapons]. Natura, Budapest, Hungary.

KATONA, IMRE

1974   A habán kerámia Magyarországon [Anabaptist Pottery in Hungary]. Képzőművészeti Alap Kiadóvállalata, Budapest, Hungary.

KERTÉSZ, RÓBERT, ANDRÁS MORGÓS, DÉNES NAGY, AND ZSUZSANNA SZÁNTÓ

2004   Az első híd a Tiszán [The First Bridge above the River Tisza]. Szolnoki Tudományos Közlemények VIII. Szolnok, Hungary.

KÖLTŐ, LÁSZLÓ

2003   X-ray Emission Analysis of Turkish Copper Vessels. In Archaeology of the Ottoman Period in Hungary, Ibolya Gerelyes and Gyöngyi Kovács, editors, pp. 267-269. Magyar Nemzeti Múzeum, Budapest, Hungary.

KONDOROSY, SZABOLCS

2007   Cseréppipák az esztergomi várból I [Clay Pipes from Esztergom Castle]. Communicationes Archeologicae Hungariae 2007:305-330.

2008   A szegedi vár pipái I. A Móra Ferenc Múzeum Évkönyve. Néprajzi Tanulmányok [Pipes of the Castle of Szeged 1. The Mora Ferenc Museum Book of the Year. Ethnographic Studies]. Studia Ethnographica 6:331-364.

2009   Cseréppipák a budai felső Vízivárosból [Clay Pipes from the Upper Water Town in Buda]. Budapest Régiségei XLI:249-280.

KOPPÁNY, TIBOR

2006   A castellumtól a kastélyig [From the Castellum to the Manor House]. Históriaantik Könyvesház Kiadó, Budapest, Hungary.

KOVÁCS, BÉLA

1963   A Dobó István Vármúzeum cseréppipái [Clay Pipes in the Dobó István Castle Museum]. Egri Múzeum Évkönyve:235-262.

KOVÁCS, GYÖNGYI

1984a   Török kerámia Szolnokon [Turkish Pottery from Szolnok]. Szolnok Megyei Múzeumi Adattár 30-31. Damjanich János Múzeum, Szolnok, Hungary.

1984b   Török rézedények Szolnok megyéből [Turkish Copper Vessels from Szolnok County]. Archaeológiai Értesítő 111:78-91.

1990-
1991   16th-18th Century Hungarian Pottery Types. Antaeus 19-20:169-180.

1998   A barcsi török palánkvár kerámialeletei [The Ceramic Finds from the Turkish Palisade Fort at Barcs]. Communicationes Archaeologicae Hungariae 1998:155-180.

2001a   Törökszentmiklós a török korban. A szentmiklósi török palánk [Törökszentmikós in the Turkish Period. The Turkish Palanka of Szentmiklós]. In Fejezetek Törökszentmiklós múltjából, L. Selmeczi and A. Szabó, editors, pp. 169-221. Törökszentmiklós város Önkormányzata, Törökszentmiklós, Hungary.

2001b   Ceramic Finds from the Bajcsa Fort (1578-1600). Acta Archaeologica Academiae Scientiarum Hungaricae 52:195-221.

2010   A magyarországi oszmán-török régészet új eredményei: áttekintés a Dráva menti kutatások kapcsán [New Findings in Ottoman-Turkish Archaeology in Hungary: Topics Highlighted by Research Work along the River Drava]. In A középkor és a kora újkor régészete Magyarországon I-II, Elek Benkő and Gyöngyi Kovács, editors, pp. 757-783. Magyar Tudományos Akadémia Régészeti Intézete, Budapest, Hungary.

KOVÁCS, GYÖNGYI (EDITOR)

2002   Weitschawar. Bajcsa-vár. Egy stájer erődítmény Magyarországon a 16. század második felében [Castle Bajcsa. A Styrian Fortress in Hungary in the Second Half of the 16th Century]. Zala Megyei Múzeumok Igazgatósága, Zalaegerszeg, Hungary.

KOVÁCS, GYÖNGYI, AND MÁRTON RÓZSÁS

1996   A barcsi török palánkvár [The Turkish Hoarding Castle of Barcs]. Somogyi Múzeumok Közleményei 12:163-182.

2010   A barcsi török vár és környéke. Újabb kutatások (1999-2009) [The Ottoman-Turkish Castle at Barcs and its Surroundings. New Research (1999-2009)]. In A középkor és a kora újkor régészete Magyarországon I-II, Elek Benkő and Gyöngyi Kovács, editors, pp. 621-642. Magyar Tudományos Akadémia Régészeti Intézete, Budapest, Hungary.

KOVÁCS, TIBOR S.

1994   A kopaszi-zátonyi fegyverek [The Weapons from the Kopaszi Sand Bank]. Folia Archaeologica 43:251-278.

KOZÁK KÁROLY

1966   A sümegi és a szigligeti vár XVII. századvégi kerámiája [The Pottery from the Late 17th Century from the Castles of Sümeg and Szigliget]. Veszprém Megyei Múzeumok Közleményei 5:81-89.

1974   A magyarországi szakállas puskák fejlődéstörténetéről [The Evolution of the Arquebus in Hungary]. *Archaeológiai Értesítő* 101:290-303.

KUBINYI, ANDRÁS

2004   Városhálózat a késő középkori Kárpát—medencében [Town Network in the Late Medieval Carpathian Basin]. *Történelmi szemle* 46:1-30.

LAJKÓ, ORSOLYA

2003   Post Medieval Pottery Finds from Hódmezővásárhely-Ótemplom. In *Archaeology of the Ottoman Period in Hungary*, Ibolya Gerelyes and Gyöngyi Kovács, editors, pp. 321-328. Magyar Nemzeti Múzeum, Budapest, Hungary.

LASZLOVSZKY, JÓZSEF, AND JUDITH RASSON

2003   Post-Medieval or Historical Archaeology: Terminology and Discourses in the Archaeology of the Ottoman Period. In *Archaeology of the Ottoman Period in Hungary*, Ibolya Gerelyes and Gyöngyi Kovács, editors, pp. 377-382. Magyar Nemzeti Múzeum, Budapest, Hungary.

MÉRI, ISTVÁN

1954   Beszámoló a Tiszalök-rázompusztai és Túrkeve-mórici ásatások eredményeiről. 2 [Report on the Results of the Excavations at Tiszalök-Rázompuszta and Túrkeve-Móric 2]. *Archaeológiai Értesítő* 81:138-154.

MESTER, EDIT

2010   Üvegművesség a középkorban és a kora újkorban [Glass Art in the Middle Ages and the Early Modern Age]. In *A középkor és a kora újkor régészete Magyarországon I-II*, Elek Benkő and Gyöngyi Kovács, editors, pp. 643-675. Magyar Tudományos Akadémia Régészeti Intézete, Budapest, Hungary.

MIKLÓS, ZSUZSA, AND MÁRTA VIZI

2003   Data on the Settlement History of Ete, Medieval Market Town. In *Archaeology of the Ottoman Period in Hungary*, Ibolya Gerelyes and Gyöngyi Kovács, editors, pp. 207-220. Magyar Nemzeti Múzeum, Budapest, Hungary.

MITHAY, SÁNDOR

1985   A Győr-gabonavásártéri 16-17. századi temető [The 16th-17th-Century Cemetery at Győr-Gabonavásártér]. *Communicationes Archaelogicae Hungariae* 1985:185-198.

MORDOVIN, MAXIM, AND GÁBOR TOMKA

2006   Szécsény, belváros [Szécsény, City Center]. In *Régészeti kutatások Magyarországon 2005*, pp. 319-320. Kulturális örökségvédelmi Hivatal, Magyar Nemzeti Múzeum, Budapest, Hungary.

MÜLLER, RÓBERT

1982   *A mezőgazdasági vaseszközök fejlődése Magyarországon a késővaskortól a törökkor végéig* [The Development of Iron Agricultural Tools in Hungary from the Late Iron Age until the End of the Turkish Era]. Zalai Gyűjtemény 19. Zala Megyei Levéltár, Zalaegerszeg, Hungary.

NÉGYESI, LAJOS

2003   Csata – és hadszíntérkutatás—hadtörténelmi régészet [Battlefield Research—Archaeology of Military History]. *Hadtörténelmi Közlemények* 2003(1):198-205.

OBORNI, TERÉZ, LILLA TOMPOS, AND GÁBOR BENCSIK

2010   *A régi Erdély népeinek képeskönyve* [Picture Book of the Nations of the Old Transylvania]. Magyar Mercurius Kiadó, Budapest, Hungary.

PÁLFFY, GÉZA

2009   *The Kingdom of Hungary and the Habsburg Monarchy in the Sixteenth Century*, Thomas J. and Helen D. DeKornfeld, translators. East European Monographs No. DCCXXXV; CHSP Hungarian Studies Series No. 18. Social Science Monographs, Boulder, Colorado; Center for Hungarian Studies and Publications, Inc., Wayne, New Jersey.

PÁLFI, GYÖRGY, AND YANN ARDAGNA

2003   Spinal Diseases and Tuberculosis from the Ottoman Period. Major Palaeopathological Features of the Bácsalmás-Óalmás (Bácsalmás-Homokbánya) Sixteenth – to Seventeenth-Century Anthropological Finds. In *Archaeology of the Ottoman Period in Hungary*, Ibolya Gerelyes and Gyöngyi Kovács, editors, pp. 249-256. Magyar Nemzeti Múzeum, Budapest, Hungary.

PÁLÓCZI HORVÁTH, ANDRÁS

2003   The Survival of Szentkirály in the Ottoman Era. In *Archaeology of the Ottoman Period in Hungary*, Ibolya Gerelyes and Gyöngyi Kovács, editors, pp. 201-206. Magyar Nemzeti Múzeum, Budapest, Hungary.

PAPP, ADRIENN

2010   Oszmán-török fürdők Budán—A Rudas és a Rác fürdő régészeti kutatása (2004-2006) [Ottoman-Turkish Baths in Buda—Archaeological Research at the Rudas and Rác Baths (2004-2006)]. In *A középkor és a kora újkor régészete Magyarországon I-II*, Elek Benkő and Gyöngyi Kovács, editors, pp. 207-220. Magyar Tudományos Akadémia Régészeti Intézete, Budapest, Hungary.

PAPP, ILDIKÓ, NORBERT BABCSÁN, AND ÁRPÁD KOVÁCS
1999   Kora újkori kerámiamázak (Az ónodi és muhi feltárások kerámiamázainak anyagtudományi elemzése) [Ceramic Glazes from the Early Modern Age (Materials Science: Examination of the Excavated Ónod and Muhi Ceramic Glazes)]. *A Herman Ottó Múzeum Évkönyve* 37:447-469.

PAPP, LÁSZLÓ
1960   A mohácsi csatahely kutatása [Research of the Battlefield at Mohács]. *A Janus Pannonius Múzeum Évkönyve* 1960:198-258.

PARÁDI, NÁNDOR
1963   Magyarországi pénzleletes középkori cserépedények (XI-XVI.sz.) [Medieval Coin Hoards in Hungary (11th-17th Centuries)]. *Archaeológiai Értesítő* 90:205-251.

PUSZTAI, TAMÁS
2001   A középkori Mohi mezőváros építészeti emlékei [Architectural Relics of the Medieval Market Town of Mohi]. In *Népi építészet a Kárpát-medencében a honfoglalástól a 18. századig*, pp. 331-364. A Jász-Nagykun-Szolnok Megyei Múzeumok közleményei 58. Szolnok, Hungary.

2003   The Pottery of the Turkish Palisade at Bátaszék. In *Archaeology of the Ottoman Period in Hungary*, Ibolya Gerelyes and Gyöngyi Kovács, editors, pp. 301-310. Magyar Nemzeti Múzeum, Budapest, Hungary.

R. TOMBOR, ILONA
1968   *Magyarországi festett famennyezetek és rokon emlékek a XV-XIX. századból [Painted Wooden Ceilings and Similar Monuments from Hungary from the 15th to 19th Centuries]*. Akadémiai Kiadó, Budapest, Hungary.

RINGER, ISTVÁN
2007   *I. Rákóczi György pataki ágyúöntő műhelyének kutatása 2006-ban [Research of the Cannon Foundry of George Ráczi 1 in Patak in the Year 2006]*. <http://www.spatak.hu/spatak/index.php?option=com_content&task=view&id=6&Itemid=2>. Accessed 26 January 2011.

RÓZSA, GYÖRGY
1955   *Régi várképek [Old Pictures of Castles]*. Magyar Nemzeti Múzeum, Budapest, Hungary.

RÓZSÁS, MÁRTON
2003   A Turkish Guard Station on the Lands of Drávatamási. In *Archaeology of the Ottoman Period in Hungary*, Ibolya Gerelyes and Gyöngyi Kovács, editors, pp. 145-150. Magyar Nemzeti Múzeum, Budapest, Hungary.

SABJÁN, TIBOR
2002   Bögrés szemeskályhák az Alföldön. Gerencsérek, kályhások, tűzvigyázók. Feudáliskori kályhacsempék az Alföldről és peremvidékéről [Potters, Stove Makers, and Fire Guards—Medieval and Early Post-Medieval Stove-Tiles from the Great Hungarian Plain and Surroundings]. In *Gyulai Katalógusok 11*, P. Havassy, editor, pp. 57-72. A Békés Megyei Önkormányzat Múzeumok Igazgatósága Erkel Ferenc Múzeuma, Gyula, Hungary.

2010   Néprajz és régészet. A népi építészet kutatása két tudományág határvonalán [Ethnography and Archaeology. The Researching of Folk Architecture in the Borderlands between Two Branches of Science]. In *A középkor és a kora újkor régészete Magyarországon I-II*, Elek Benkő and Gyöngyi Kovács, editors, pp. 929-942. Magyar Tudományos Akadémia Régészeti Intézete, Budapest, Hungary.

SABJÁN, TIBOR, AND ANDRÁS VÉGH
2003   A Turkish House and Stoves from the Water-Town (Víziváros) in Buda. In *Archaeology of the Ottoman Period in Hungary*, Ibolya Gerelyes and Gyöngyi Kovács, editors, pp. 281-300. Magyar Nemzeti Múzeum, Budapest, Hungary.

SIMON, ZOLTÁN
2002   *A füzéri vár a 16-17. században. Borsod-Abaúj-Zemplén Megye Régészeti Emlékei 1 [Castle of Füzér in the 16th-17th Centuries]*. Herman Ottó Múzeum, Miskolc, Hungary.

SIMONYI, ERIKA
2005   Középkori és kora újkori temető Felsőzsolca-Nagyszilváson [Medieval and Early Modern Cemetery at Felsőzsolca-Nagyszilvás]. In *A középkori temetők kutatása*, Erika Simonyi and Ágnes Ritoók, editors, pp. 305-314. Opuscula Hungarica VI. Magyar Nemzeti Múzeum, Budapest, Hungary.

SUDÁR, BALÁZS
2004   Baths in Ottoman Hungary. *Acta Orientalia Academiae Scientiarum Hungaricae* 2004(4):391-437.

SZABÓ, GYÖRGY
1954   A falusi kovács a XV-XVI. században [The Village Smith in the 15th-16th Centuries]. *Folia Archaeologica* 6:123-145.

SZABÓ, KÁLMÁN
1938   *Az alföldi magyar népművelődéstörtréneti emlékei [Cultural Historical Monuments of the Great Hungarian Plain]*. Bibliotheca Humanitatis Historica III. Országos Magyar Történeti Múzeum, Budapest, Hungary.

SZAKÁLY, FERENC
1981   *Magyar adóztatás a török hódoltságban [Hungarian Taxation in the Territory Occupied by the Turks]*. Akadémiai Kiadó, Budapest, Hungary.

TANMAN, BAHA, BELGIN DEMIRSAR ARLI, HATICE ADIGÜZEL, AND TUFAN SAĞNAK (EDITORS)

2010   *Exhibition on Ottoman Art. 16th-17th Century Ottoman Art and Architecture in Hungary and in the Centre of the Empire.* Istanbul 2010 European Capital of Culture Agency, Istanbul, Turkey.

TOIFL, LEOPOLD

2002   Bajcsavár története stájer levéltári források alapján [History of Bajcsavár According to Styrian Archival Sources]. In *Weitschawar. Bajcsa-vár. Egy stájer erődítmény Magyarországon a 16. század második felében*, Gyöngyi Kovács, editor, pp. 27-40. Zala Megyei Múzeumok Igazgatósága, Zalaegerszeg, Hungary.

TOMKA, GÁBOR

1999   Közép és kora újkori településrészlet Mohi mezőváros belterületének peremén [Medieval and Early Post-Medieval Settlement Traces near the Center of the Market Mohi]. *A Herman Ottó Múzeum Évkönyve* 37:417-446.

2000   Excavated Pipes from the 16th to the 18th Century. In *The History of the Hungarian Pipemaker's Craft—Hungarian History through the Pipemaker's Art*, Edit Haider, Angelika Orgona, and Anna Ridovics, editors, pp. 25-32. Keszthely, Budapest, Hungary.

2003a   Andrásvár: A Guard-Tower in Royal Hungary's Border-Defence System. In *Archaeology of the Ottoman Period in Hungary*, Ibolya Gerelyes and Gyöngyi Kovács, editors, pp. 151-154. Magyar Nemzeti Múzeum, Budapest, Hungary.

2003b   Finjans, Pipes, Grey Jugs. "Turkish" Objects in the Hungarian Fortresses in Borsod County. In *Archaeology of the Ottoman Period in Hungary*, Ibolya Gerelyes and Gyöngyi Kovács, editors, pp. 311-320. Magyar Nemzeti Múzeum, Budapest, Hungary.

2004a   Három XVI-XVII. századi kút Mohiból [Three Wells from Mohi from the 16th-17th Centuries]. In *"Quasi liber et picture." Tanulmányok Kubinyi András hetvenedik születésnapjára. Studies in Honour of András Kubinyi on his Seventieth Birthday*, Miklós Szabó and Pál Raczky, editors, pp. 555-571. ELTE Régészettudományi Intézet, Budapest, Hungary.

2004b   Északkelet-Magyarország kora újkori kerámiája [Early Modern Pottery in Northeastern Hungary]. Doctoral dissertation, Budapest University, Budapest, Hungary.

2007   16. századi kályhacsempék az ónodi vár ásatásaiból [Sixteenth-Century Stove-Tiles from the Excavations at Ónod Castle]. *Archaeológiai Értesítő* 132:241-266.

2010   Kora újkori erődítések régészeti kutatása 1996-2006 között [The Archaeological Researching of Early Modern Age Fortifications 1996-2006]. In *A középkor és a kora újkor régészete Magyarországon I-II*, Elek Benkő and Gyöngyi Kovács, editors, pp. 597-620. Magyar Tudományos Akadémia Régészeti Intézete, Budapest, Hungary.

2011   Kétfejű sast ábrázoló kályhacsempék a szendrői felsővárból [Stove-Tiles from the Upper Castle in Szendrő Depicting Double-Headed Eagle]. In *Corolla Museologica Tibor Kovács Dedicata. Régészeti Füzetek Új Sorozat IV*, pp. 585-597. Szerk.: Tóth Endre-Vida István, Budapest, Hungary.

2012   Clay Pipes in Hungary from the Seventeenth Century: Ten Years On. *Journal of the Académie Internationale de la Pipe* 3(2010):[in press].

TÓTH, JÁNOS ATTILA

2010   Adatok a kora újkori Közép-Duna-medencei hajók régészetéhez [Data on the Archaeology of Early Modern Age Ships in the Middle Danube Basin Region]. In *A középkor és a kora újkor régészete Magyarországon I-II*, Elek Benkő and Gyöngyi Kovács, editors, pp. 871-883. Magyar Tudományos Akadémia Régészeti Intézete, Budapest, Hungary.

VÁLYI, KATALIN

1986   Szer középkori településtörténete a régészeti leletek tükrében [Medieval Settlement History of Szer in Light of Archaeological Finds]. In *Falvak, mezővárosok az Alföldön*, L. Novák and L. Selmeczi, editors, pp. 117-129. Az Arany János Múzeum Közleményei 4. Nagykőrös, Hungary.

VÁNDOR, LÁSZLÓ, AND GYÖNGYI KOVÁCS

2002   Bajcsavár régészeti kutatása [Archaeological Research of Bajcsavár]. In *Weitschawar. Bajcsa-vár. Egy stájer erődítmény Magyarországon a 16. század második felében*, Gyöngyi Kovács, editor, pp. 47-62. Zala Megyei Múzeumok Igazgatósága, Zalaegerszeg, Hungary.

VIDA, GABRIELLA

1993   Egy néprajzi ásatás tanulságai. Kerámiatörténeti vizsgálatok [Lessons of an Ethnographic Excavation. Research on the History of Pottery]. *A Miskolci Herman Ottó Múzeum Közleményei* 28:72-75.

1999   *A miskolci fazekasság a 16.-19. században [The 16th-19th-Century Pottery of Miskolc].* Officina Musei 8. Herman Ottó Múzeum, Miskolc, Hungary.

VIZI, MÁRTA

2010   A kora újkori kerámia feldolgozásának módszerei.
        Az ozorai várkastély leletanyagának adatbázisáról
        [Methods for the Processing of Early Modern Age
        Ceramics. On the Database for Finds from Ozora
        Castle]. In *A középkor és a kora újkor régészete
        Magyarországon I-II*, Elek Benkő and Gyöngyi
        Kovács, editors, pp. 817-838. Magyar Tudományos
        Akadémia Régészeti Intézete, Budapest, Hungary.

VÖRÖS, ISTVÁN

2003   Sixteenth – and Seventeenth-Century Animal
        Bone Finds in Hungary. In *Archaeology of the
        Ottoman Period in Hungary*, Ibolya Gerelyes and
        Gyöngyi Kovács, editors, pp. 351-364. Magyar
        Nemzeti Múzeum, Budapest, Hungary.

WICKER, ERIKA

2003   A Serb Cemetery from the Ottoman Era in
        Hungary. In *Archaeology of the Ottoman Period
        in Hungary*, Ibolya Gerelyes and Gyöngyi Kovács,
        editors, pp. 231-236. Magyar Nemzeti Múzeum,
        Budapest, Hungary.

2005   Újabb adatok a hódoltság kori délszlávok
        temetkezési szokásaihoz [Burial Rites of
        Southern Slavs at the Time of the Turkish
        Occupation]. In *A középkori temetők kutatása*,
        Erika Simonyi and Ágnes Ritoók, editors, pp. 324-
        333. Opuscula Hungarica VI. Magyar Nemzeti
        Múzeum, Budapest, Hungary.

2008   *Rácok és vlahok a hódoltság kori Észak-
        Bácskában [Rác and Vlach People in the
        Northern-Bácska Region during the Turkish Rule]*.
        A Bács-Kiskun Megyei Önkormányzat Múzeumi
        Szervezete, Kecskemét, Hungary.

ZATYKÓ, CSILLA

2010   Természeti táj—emberformálta táj: a középkori
        környezet rekonstrukciójának lehetőségei
        [Natural Landscape—Man-Made Landscape:
        Possibilities for Reconstructing the Medieval
        Environment]. In *A középkor és a kora újkor
        régészete Magyarországon I-II*, Elek Benkő and
        Gyöngyi Kovács, editors, pp. 839-852. Magyar
        Tudományos Akadémia Régészeti Intézete,
        Budapest, Hungary.

Gábor Tomka
Magyar Nemzeti Múzeum
Múzeum krt. 14-16
HU-1088 Budapest
Hungary

HISTORICAL ARCHAEOLOGY IN CENTRAL EUROPE

II. Religion, Conflict, and Death

JOST AULER

The Archaeology of Execution Sites in Early Modern Central Europe

ABSTRACT

The archaeology of the early modern period and related sciences such as anthropology have only recently begun to examine sites in central Europe where capital punishment was carried out in the early modern period. The results to date have been very impressive and are outlined in the following article. Excavated architectural features in wood and stone and findings from skeletal material, which point to methods of execution such as hanging, decapitation, and the breaking wheel, are discussed and illustrated.

INTRODUCTION

In the Middle Ages and early modern period up to about 1800, thousands of execution sites marked the landscapes of central Europe (Figure 1). Every town had punishment sites at which corporal punishment and, above all, death sentences were carried out. The scaffolds from which delinquents were hung were visible from a considerable distance. Decapitations were carried out by the executioner's sword on imposing raised platforms.

Capital punishment sites or scaffolds were mighty structures built at prominent places such as road forks, bridges and arterial roads, or upon natural or artificial mounds. Other criteria, such as the proximity to leper houses or Jewish cemeteries, often led to the choice of a site, although the full reasons for these selections are yet unknown. The execution sites were structures where the hangman and his assistants hung convicted criminals with a chain or rope as part of a public spectacle. Structures based on two or three posts with horizontal beams were common (Figure 2). They were usually wooden, but sometimes made of stone. Round or square edifices with a massive stone base and a wooden superstructure also existed. Some of the stone structures survive to this day (Auler 2008b:308-325).

Many local authorities had separate punishment places for executions by the sword or later the axe: these were raised stages (*Rabensteine* or "raven's stones") of earth, wood, or brick that could be erected for an individual execution or were permanent facilities and offered a platform on which punishment was implemented with deadly force. They were either four-sided or round (Figure 3), with external or internal steps leading upwards. The platforms were surfaced with wood or stone,

the latter often covered by grass. Only a few of these structures survive in central Europe today.

Executions were choreographed by the authorities; they were public spectacles and rituals of retribution. Thousands of spectators came from the surrounding area or from a considerable distance to be present at the killing of convicted criminals. Serious crimes and also less serious misdemeanors were expiated with punishments that today seem to us to be excessively savage. The executed were generally left hanging on the gallows. This was supposed to deter potential wrongdoers from committing crimes and must have been an unpleasant sight for citizens, vagrants, and traveling merchants (Figure 4).

Criminals who had been sentenced to death lost the right to be buried with a Christian service in normal churchyards and cemeteries. For this reason their corpses were deposited carelessly in unconsecrated earth around the punishment sites or directly under the gallows. Suicides as well as people from groups on society's margins were also buried by the executioner in these places.

In some places, if the executioner was also the knacker (in which case the actual execution work would be done exclusively by his assistants), then the carcasses of slaughtered animals could also be disposed of at the punishment site.

The young discipline of medieval and modern period archaeology disregarded these places for a long time. Central European archaeology only began to focus on execution sites about three decades ago, beginning with

Figure 1. *Map with places mentioned in the text (in Germany, unless otherwise noted): (1) Emmenbrücke, Switzerland; (2) Hundisburg; (3) Wederath-Belginum; (4) Wörth am Main; (5) Marburg; (6) Einbeck; (7) Arnsdorf/Miłków, Poland; (8) Ellwangen; (9) Löbau; and (10) Beerfelden (Map provided courtesy of the Department of Prehistory and Medieval Archaeology, University of Vienna).*

the excavation at the punishment site in Emmenbrücke (Figures 5 and 6) near Lucerne, Switzerland (Manser et al. 1992; Auler 2003:303-317, 2005:84-88, 2007:297-312).

The following paper aims to give some insight into the archaeology of early modern punishment sites, part of the larger discipline of the archaeology of the European legal system (Auler 2008a, 2010a).

OFFENSES AND THE CONSEQUENCES IN EARLY MODERN EUROPE

Offenses and crimes, violations of society's rules, were severely punished in the period under consideration. The expiation of the crimes committed and the definitive removal of the criminal from the world of the living were among the reasons for this, as was the thought of deterring potential lawbreakers.

Rehabilitation was not an objective and was not sought. The legal background to the punishment process consisted of bodies of law handed down from earlier periods, for example Emperor Charles V's "Excruciating rules of the court," *constitutio criminalis carolina*, or Karolina, from 1532 (Geus 2002). Nevertheless, similar behavior

Figure 2.   (left) Three-post gallows at Beerfelden in the Odenwald, Hesse, Germany (Photo by author, 2005).
Figure 3.   (right) Platform for execution by the sword outside the town of Marburg, Hesse, Germany (Photo by author, 2009).
Figure 4.   (below) Wooden gallows and breaking wheels in front of the town walls of Einbeck 1654, by Martin Zeiller (1589-1661) (Zeiller 1654).

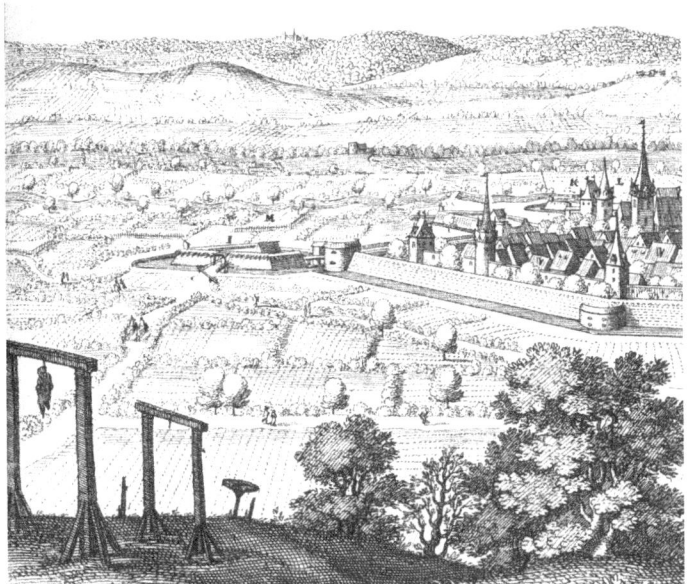

was viewed and punished differently from region to region. Generally speaking, differences in the manner of the crimes were reflected in the sentences passed: punishments were imposed, but could be reduced as an act of pardon or increased through the combination of different punishments. Sentences usually reflected the crime: an arsonist with murderous intent would be burnt underneath the gallows, for example.

Murder, that is deliberate killing for no good reason, was punishable by death. Usually the condemned person would be dragged to the place of execution as a way of increasing the punishment. Female murderers were buried or burnt alive and only rarely hanged, as hanging would allow onlookers to gaze under a woman's skirt. The murder of children for societal reasons (e.g., an "illegitimate" child) was a dreadfully common crime,

particularly in the early modern period; the body of law known as the *Schwabenspiegel*, or Swabian Mirror, demanded that the female perpetrator be drowned; the Karolina that she be buried alive or impaled. Later, punishment by the sword became the norm. In particularly grave cases of murder or in cases of multiple murders, different punishments could be combined: for example, the cutting off of a hand at the punishment site; execution by the rope, sword, or breaking wheel; and the burning of the body. Manslaughter was also regarded as a crime punishable by death: the "excruciating"—meaning painful—punishment was usually decapitation, less often the gallows. The offender was to be found innocent in cases of self-defense, however.

Deliberate arson was paid for by the executioner's sword, deadly arson—that is secret, nocturnal fire-raising—by the wheel. The Karolina from 1532 demanded the burning-alive of the criminal, a punishment mirroring the crime. Involuntary fire-raising was judged with less severity. Severe cases of theft—particularly theft of cattle or wheat, theft at night or from churches, smithies, or mills—were punishable by death. In such cases the dishonorable punishment of the gallows was often converted to decapitation, which was regarded as honorable. Female thieves were not usually hung, because women's bodies were not to be displayed publicly: instead women were buried alive or drowned. The death penalty was also applied in cases of forgery of money or deeds, fraud, robbery, rape, unnatural sexual acts, incest, bigamy, adultery, blasphemy, heresy, and witchcraft, among other things (Dülmen 1984:203-245, 1988; Hinckeldey 1989; Evans 1996, 2001; Schild 1997; Schubert 2007).

DEATH PENALTIES IN EARLY MODERN CENTRAL EUROPE

Death by hanging on the gallows was considered dishonorable and scandalous. It was the most commonly used death sentence for thieves in the early modern period. During a hanging two ladders were placed against the gallows. The executioner attached a hemp rope or a chain to a hook on the gallows. Then he and the condemned person mounted the ladders. At the top the hangman laid the noose around the delinquent's neck. Then he climbed down and pushed the ladder supporting the condemned person away. The condemned person hung in the air, and the noose contracted because of the weight, at which point either the air pipes and blood vessels were shut down or the neck was broken. To be "strung up" was a more agonizing death as it took longer to die. With this method the noose was laid around the neck of the condemned perpetrator and the rope was thrown over the joist of the gallows. Then the condemned person was pulled up by the executioner's subordinates or a by horse. Once hung, the body often remained on the gallows until it fell down of its own accord in one or several pieces as decomposition advanced, this being part of the sentence. Family members and others were forbidden to cut the body down. The body parts were casually buried as they fell by the hangman or his assistants in unconsecrated ground at the foot of the gallows. To be hung by the feet—the criminal was hung with his head down—was also considered an increased penalty; in that case death was delayed for hours or even days. Sometimes a condemned person was hung together with living dogs; this was intended to emphasize the foul character of the sentenced person and was particularly used in the execution of Jews. On other occasions a second wooden gallows was erected on top of the joists of the two or three-post gallows structure; to be thus "hung high" was an increased penalty.

Beheading was considered an honorable death penalty. A sentence of decapitation was different from other death penalties such as burning or drowning in that the actual killing was not left to natural forces (i.e., fire and water), but carried out through the executioner's sword or later the axe, fashioned and wielded by human hands. Such an execution demanded considerable skill on the part of the executioner. With his heavy sword, he had to strike a single, level blow exactly between two neck vertebrae and separate the head from the body. The criminal knelt before him on the ground or

Figure 5.   Gallows foundations and skeleton finds at Emmenbrücke, Switzerland (Photo by Kantonsarchäologie Luzern, 1988; courtesy of Denkmalpflege und Archäologie des Kantons Luzern).

Figure 6.   Human skeletons among animal remains at Emmenbrücke, Switzerland (photo by Kantonsarchäologie Luzern, 1988; courtesy of Denkmalpflege und Archäologie des Kantons Luzern).

Figure 7.   (left) Gallows foundations of stone rubble and brick at Ellwangen, Baden-Württemberg, Germany (Photo by Landesdenkmalamt Baden-Württemberg, 1991; courtesy of Landesdenkmalamt Baden-Württemberg, Archäologische Denkmalpflege).

Figure 8.   (right) Round foundations of the "well gallows" at Löbau, Saxony, Germany (Photo by Landesamt für Archäologie Sachsen, 2007; courtesy of Landesamt für Archäologie Sachsen).

on a special scaffold or headrest ("raven's stone"); his hands were tied or—as countless contemporary images show—raised in prayer. The delinquents did not have to be held down by the executioner's assistants, but had abandoned themselves to their fate. The shirt was pulled down a long way, exposing the nape of the neck. The executioner stood to the right or left of the condemned person. At first decapitations took place on the market square in front of the city hall. Later beheadings took place outside the town gates, after the punishment sites had been relocated there. After a head had been cut off it was sometimes displayed on a raised pole. Usually, however, the body was casually buried in unconsecrated earth in hastily excavated pits and without Christian rites at the punishment site. The severed head of the criminal was generally deposited between the legs or under an arm.

The feared sentence of death on the breaking wheel was overwhelmingly employed for the male condemned and was held to be a shameful and dishonorable punishment. The delinquent was laid on the ground with his arms and legs stretched out, and his hands and feet were attached to pegs. Lumber was pushed underneath his body and his extremities, so that he was completely raised above the ground. The executioner then crushed the condemned man's limbs, rib cage, and spine with a spoked wheel, the number of blows having been specified in the sentence. If the carrying out of the sentence began with the legs, then death took a long time. Delivering the first blow against the forehead or hanging or beheading the condemned man before putting him on the wheel was considered an act of mercy. The dying or dead man was broken by the spokes, meaning that his extremities were sometimes above and sometimes

underneath the wheel. Finally the wheel was attached to a pole and hoisted up.

There were other ways of executing a condemned criminal than the most commonly used death penalties of hanging, beheading, or the breaking wheel. In the case of drowning—a punishment largely used for female offenders—the delinquents were thrown into a river from a bridge with their hands and feet bound. If the execution took place at an insufficiently deep pond or dyke, then the person concerned was held down in the water with the help of long poles until dead. It was also common to sew the offender into a sack with, for example, a living dog or to carry out the drowning in a large wooden washtub. Being boiled to death in water, wine, or oil was a sentence often used for counterfeiters or heretics. Being buried alive was a punishment used above all for women in cases of infanticide, adultery, or aggravated theft. Among men, rapists, sodomites, and those guilty of incest were often executed in this way. The condemned person was laid alive and bound on their stomach in a pit at the punishment site, and covered with earth. Impalement was closely associated with this punishment—a sharpened stake was driven through the pit, the individual thus being punished after he or she had been buried alive. If in the case of this combined punishment the condemned person had been convicted of rape, then the punishment was regarded as mirroring the crime. In such cases the woman who had been the victim of the man's crime was allowed to hammer the first blows. To be walled in was a punishment pronounced instead of the death penalty for members of the higher orders. Thus the family was spared the scandal of a public execution and the criminal the touch of the dishonorable executioner. The condemned person was not allowed to leave the room into which he or she had been walled alive. The executioner or the family looked after them. Quartering was a very rare punishment, carried out on the dead body. The arms and legs of a hanged delinquent were each attached to the tail of a different horse and the horses driven apart.

Death by being burned alive meant that the criminal was almost completely removed from the world—even the ashes were disposed of in flowing water. This punishment was carried out in different ways. The delinquent was tied up and laid on a pyre, which was then ignited. The condemned person was also often tied to a stake around which a pyre was built and then set alight. Sometimes, however, the person was tied to a ladder and pushed with the ladder into the blazing pyre. To strangle or stab the criminal through the heart before the burning of the body was considered an act of mercy. In some cases the executioner tied a sack of gunpowder to the victim's carotid. If the criminal was beheaded or hung before being burned then this was equally an act of mercy, but it could also be regarded as the carrying out of several death sentences one after another if several crimes punishable by death were involved.

EXCAVATED ARCHITECTURAL FEATURES FROM THE EARLY MODERN PUNISHMENT SYSTEM

Remains of wooden gallows have been archaeologically analyzed in Hundisburg, Sachsen-Anhalt (Auler 2000:137-146), and in Wederath-Belginum, Rheinland-Pfalz, all in Germany (Haffner 2010:116-121). The features found in an excavation are postholes and/or pits in which the vertical posts of the gallows structures were wedged. Research at execution sites built of stone (Arnold 1991:335-336; Piech 2008) has revealed foundations (Figures 5, 7, and 8), which enable the architectonic reconstruction of such sites.

ARCHAEOLOGICAL SKELETAL FINDS FROM THE EARLY MODERN PUNISHMENT SYSTEM

Large numbers of human skeletons or parts of skeletons are found at former execution sites on a regular basis (Auler 2002; Busch 2002). The method of execution employed can often be uncovered if the remains are analyzed anthropologically. Examples for the dishonorable punishment of hanging, known as "execution with dry hands" because no blood was spilt, are considerably harder to prove than examples of punishment by decapitation (Auler 2001:311-315). In the latter case clear traces of deadly violence are found on the bone material, and the archaeological features are unambiguous: the skull was often deposited between the legs or feet of the executed person (Figure 9). The skeletons of criminals broken on the wheel are also easy to identify (Roth 1973), as they have very many fractured bones. Executions by burning, however, are almost impossible to prove.

ARCHAEOLOGICAL RESULTS AND HISTORICAL SOURCES

It is very occasionally possible to connect archaeological features with a particular historic event. A few such cases are known from Emmenbrücke near Lucerne in Switzerland.

Maria Remmler's head and right hand were cut off on 16 December 1638 because she had murdered her husband. Maria is probably Individual 51, as discovered during excavations at the punishment site. The relevant entry in the scientific publication of the excavation is phrased soberly:

Individual no. 51 (Finds complex 85) lay in the centre of the gallows triangle with the feet pointing north. It was particularly deep and lay beneath all other pits, with the result that it was badly and incompletely preserved. The skeleton had been severely disturbed by more recent activity. It lay on its stomach with its arms and legs for the most part extended. The skull was missing, as were the left lower leg and the entire left arm. The skeleton belonged to a woman of medium stature (161 cm), who died in her fourth decade of life [Auler 2010b:60].

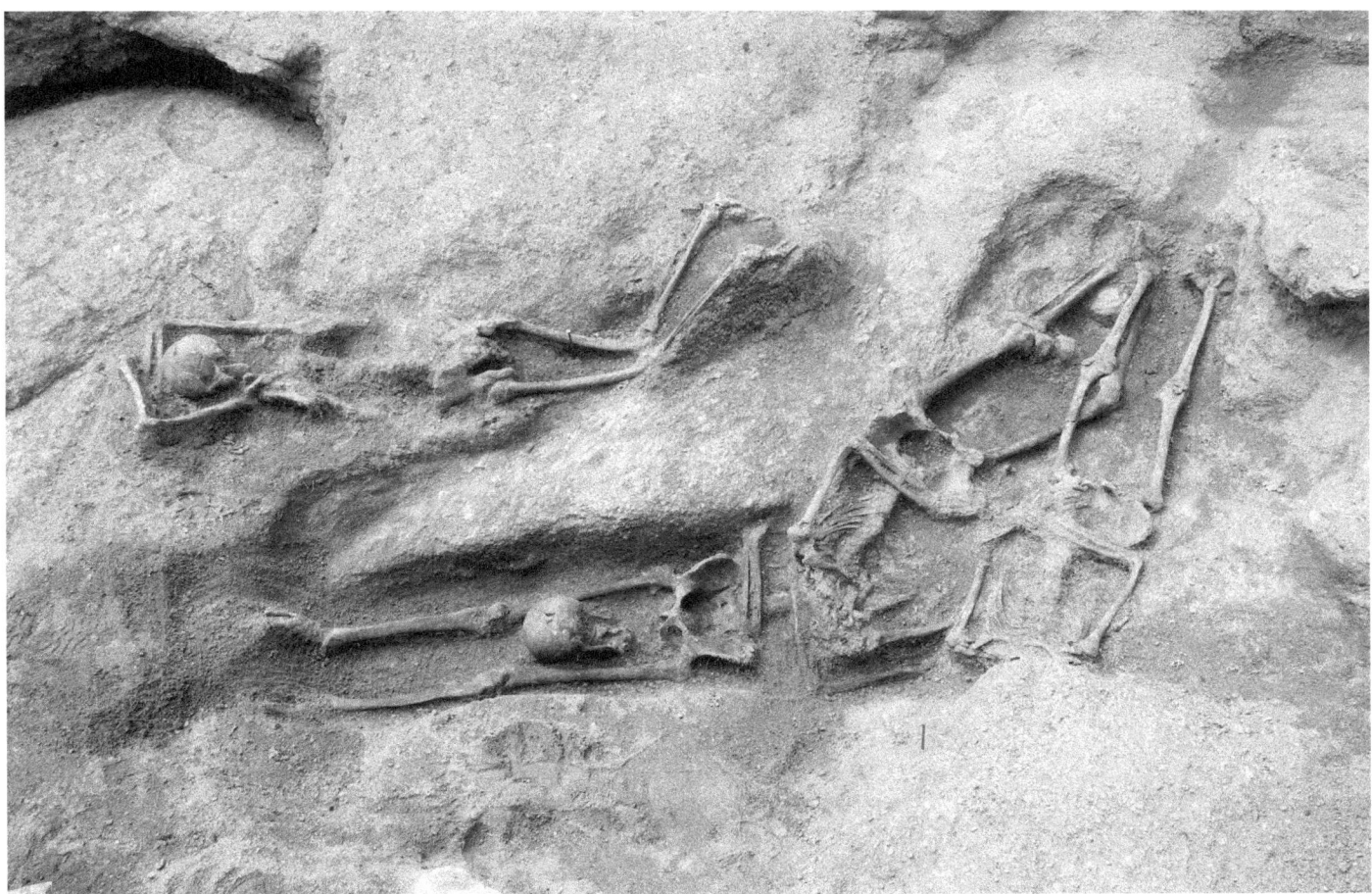

Figure 9.   A decapitated justice victim (center foreground) at Arnsdorf/Milków, Poland (photo by Daniel Wojtucki, 2008; courtesy of Dr. Mgr. Daniel Wojtucki).

Hans Waldesperg, who was not yet 20, suffered the same punishment at that place in 1630. The man was sentenced to death for "talking against the authorities." He can be connected to Individual no. 23; the right hand, together with the distal part of lower arm, was missing from this skeleton. Radius and ulna had been cut through at the same point at right angles to the line of the arm. These findings indicate a heavy blow with a sharp instrument to the middle of the lower right arm. The man had obviously had his right arm cut off (Auler 2010b:60).

SUMMARY

In the last few years the archaeology of the modern period in central Europe has turned its attention to those places at which convicted people were killed in different ways. The results show great similarities across the entire study area among the sites of gallows and decapitations and in the procedure involved in the carrying out of the death penalty.

ACKNOWLEDGMENTS

This article is dedicated to my daughters Henrike Puderbach and Neeske Auler.

REFERENCES

ARNOLD, SUSANNE

1991   Eine frühneuzeitliche Gerichtsstätte in Ellwangen, Ostalbkreis [An Early Modern Punishment Site in Ellwangen, Ostalb County]. *Archäologische Ausgrabungen in Baden-Württemberg* 1991:335-336.

AULER, JOST

2000   Archäologische Erkenntnisse zur Richtstätte bei Hundisburg (Ohrekreis) [Archaeological Findings at the Execution Site near Hundisburg, Ohre County]. *Die Kunde. Zeitschrift für Ur – und Frühgeschichte.* Neue Folge 51:137-146.

2001   Ein archäologischer Befund zur mittelalterlichen Strafjustiz bei Hessisch-Lichtenau (Werra-Meißner-Kreis) [An Archaeological Finding from the Medieval Criminal Justice System near Hessisch-Lichtenau, Werra-Meißner County]. *Archäologisches Korrespondenzblatt* 2001(2):311-315.

2002   Archäologische Erkenntnisse zur Richtstätte von Salzhausen, Ldkr. Harburg [Archaeological Findings at the Execution Site at Salzhausen, Harburg County]. *Nachrichten aus Niedersachsens Urgeschichte* 71:139-150.

2003   Richtstätten des ausklingenden Mittelalters und der frühen Neuzeit im Fokus moderner Archäologie [Execution Sites from the Late Medieval Period and the Early Modern Period Examined by Modern Archaeology]. *Düsseldorfer Jahrbuch* 74:303-317.

2005   Sühne und Abschreckung [Atonement and Deterrence]. *Abenteuer Archäologie* 3:84-88.

2007   Richtstättenarchäologie in der Schweiz—Ein Überblick [Execution Site Archaeology in Switzerland—An Overview]. *Archäologisches Korrespondenzblatt* 2007(2):297-312.

2008b   Katalog erhaltener Hochgerichte in Deutschland und einigen Nachbarländern [Catalog of Conserved Gallows Sites in Germany and Some Neighboring Countries]. In *Richtstättenarchäologie*, Jost Auler, editor, pp. 308-325. Archaeotopos-Verlag Jost Auler, Dormagen, Germany.

2010b   Hinrichtungsarten und anthropologische Nachweise [Execution Methods and Anthropological Evidence]. In *Galgen, Rad und Scheiterhaufen. Einblicke in Orte des Grauens*, Stiftung Neanderthal Museum, editors, pp. 54-77. Stiftung Neanderthal Museum, Mettmann, Germany.

AULER, JOST (EDITOR)

2008a   *Richtstättenarchäologie [Execution Site Archaeology]*. Archaeotopos-Verlag Jost Auler, Dormagen, Germany.

2010a   *Richtstättenarchäologie 2 [Execution Site Archaeology 2]*. Archaeotopos-Verlag Jost Auler, Dormagen, Germany.

BUSCH, RALF

2002   Der Galgenberg bei Salzhausen [Gallows Hill near Salzhausen]. *Hammaburg. Vor – und Frühgeschichte aus dem niederelbischen Raum*, Neue Folge 13:127-136.

DÜLMEN, RICHARD VAN

1984   Das Schauspiel des Todes. Hinrichtungsrituale in der frühen Neuzeit [Death as Performance. Rituals of Execution in the Early Modern Period]. In *Volkskultur. Zur Wiederentdeckung des vergessenen Alltags (16-20. Jahrhundert)*, Richard van Dülmen and Norbert Schindler, editors, pp. 203-245. Fischer Taschenbuch Verlag, Frankfurt am Main, Germany.

1988   Theater des Schreckens. Gerichtspraxis und Strafrituale in der frühen Neuzeit [Theater of Terror. Court Practice and Punishment Rituals in the Early Modern Period]. Verlag C. H. Beck München, Munich, Germany.

EVANS, RICHARD J.

1996   Rituals of Retribution. Capital Punishment in Germany, 1600-1987. Oxford University Press, Oxford, England.

2001   Rituale der Vergeltung. Die Todesstrafe in der deutschen Geschichte 1532-1987 [Rituals of Retribution. Capital Punishment in Germany 1532-1987]. Kindler Verlags GmbH, Berlin, Germany.

GEUS, ELMAR

2002   Mörder, Diebe, Räuber. Historische Betrachtung des deutschen Strafrechts von der Carolina bis zum Reichsstrafgesetzbuch [Murderers, Thieves, Robbers. Historical Overview of German Criminal Law from Karolina until the Imperial Penal Code]. Scrîpvaz-Verlag Krauskopf, Berlin, Germany.

HAFFNER, ALFRED

2010   Die mehrphasige hölzerne Blutsgerichtsstätte in Wederath-Belginum, Landkreis Bernkastel-Wittlich (Rheinland-Pfalz) [The Multi-Phase Wooden Execution Site in Wederath-Belginum, Bernkastel-Wittlich County (Rheinland-Pfalz)]. In *Richtstättenarchäologie 2*, Jost Auler, editor, pp. 116-121. Archaeotopos-Verlag Jost Auler, Dormagen, Germany.

HINCKELDEY, CHRISTOPH (EDITOR)

1989   *Justiz in alter Zeit [Justice in Olden Times]*. Verlag Mittelalterliches Kriminalmuseum, Rothenburg ob der Tauber, Germany.

Manser, Jürg, Kurt Diggelmann, Hansueli F. Etter, Hansjürg Häni, Michael Harrer, Doris Huggel, Johann Lang, Jürg Manser, René Pahud de Mortanges, Manuela Ros, Hans R. Stampfli, Gottlob Ueltschi, and Benedikt Zäch

1992   Richtstätte und Wasenplatz in Emmenbrücke (16.-19. Jahrhundert). Archäologische und historische Untersuchungen zur Geschichte von Strafrechtspflege und Tierhaltung in Luzern [Punishment Site and Grazing Place in Emmenbrücke (16th to 19th Centuries). Archaeological and Historical Research into the History of Criminal Law Practice and Animal Care in Lucerne]. 1-2. Schweizerischer Burgenverein, Basel, Switzerland.

Piech, Jaroslaw

2008   "mit fliegenden Fahnen" zogen sie zum Hochgericht: Der Galgen von Ellwangen an der Jagst 1701-1811 [They Went to the Place of Execution "with Flags Flying": The Gallows at Ellwangen an der Jagst 1701-1811]. In Richtstättenarchäologie, Jost Auler, editor, pp. 230-248. Archaeotopos-Verlag Jost Auler, Dormagen, Germany.

Roth, Helmut

1973   Rechtsarchäologische Beobachtungen am Skelettfund von Friedland, Kr. Göttingen [Legal System Archaeological Observations on the Skeleton Find at Friedland, Göttingen County]. Göttinger Jahrbuch 21:41-46.

Schild, Wolfgang

1997   Die Geschichte der Gerichtsbarkeit. Vom Gottesurteil bis zum Beginn der modernen Rechtsprechung. 1000 Jahre Grausamkeit. Hintergründe, Urteile, Aberglaube, Hexen, Folter, Tod [The History of Jurisdiction. From God's Judgment to the Beginnings of the Modern Legal System. 1,000 Years of Cruelty. Background, Sentences, Superstition, Witches, Torture, Death]. Nikol Verlagsgesellschaft mbH, Hamburg, Germany.

Schubert, Ernst

2007   Räuber, Henker, Arme Sünder. Verbrechen und Strafe im Mittelalter [Robbers, Hangmen, Poor Sinners. Crime and Punishment in the Middle Ages]. Wissenschaftliche Buchgesellschaft / Primus Verlag, Darmstadt, Germany.

Zeiller, Martin

1654   Topographia und Eigentliche Beschreibung Der Vornembsten Stäte, Schlösser auch anderer Plätze und Örter in denen Hertzogthümer[n] Braunschweig und Lüneburg, und denen dazu gehörende[n] Grafschaften Herrschaften und Landen [Topographia and Actual Description Vornembsten Staete...]. Frankfurt am Main, Germany.

Jost Auler
archaeotopos-Buchverlag Dormagen
Schwanenstraße 12
D-41541 Dormagen
Germany

SUSI ULRICH-BOCHSLER / CHRISTINE COOPER

Religion, Belief, and Anthropological Research in Central Europe

ABSTRACT

Burial grounds from the modern period have been the focus of archaeologists and physical anthro-pologists for only two or three decades. Ethical issues, but also questions about cultural heritage preservation and data protection and confidentiality, can arise when dealing with finds dating to the recent past. A steadily increasing number of excavated sites as well as new research methods and priorities provide insights into many aspects of life and death in a time that adds a context of abundant written and material records to anthropological studies. The anthropological evidence originates from a variety of different burial grounds including not only regular rural and urban church cemeteries but also sites with a singular background such as hospital cemeteries, mass graves, and execution places. The findings shed light on religion, beliefs and customs, and the bio-logical features of the populations under study. Today the focus often lies on clarifying the impact of environmental and social conditions on humans by means of diverse anthropological parameters. Several palaeopathological features can be considered characteristic of modern period skeletal series, for example a marked increase in cases of tertiary syphilis, generally very bad dental health, and evidence of autopsies.

INTRODUCTION

In German-speaking countries, social anthropology is generally referred to as "ethnology," whereas the term "anthropology" is used for physical anthropology and, in this paper, for osteoarchaeology in particular. During and after the excavation of historical burial grounds the physical anthropological focus lies on questions regarding burial customs, age and sex distribution, physical features, and medical conditions. Historical skeletons hold a high information potential and can be consulted on different levels, depending on the type of findings and their chronological placement. The emphasis of this article lies on Switzerland, but findings from other central European sites are addressed as well.

Written records give more precise information on a population's demographic structure for the 19th and 20th centuries than anthropological results gained by the examination of skeletons. The demographic com-position of certain skeletal samples (for example from mass graves) can be of great interest nevertheless, as can the palaeopathological findings that provide insight into the health status of a certain population group, such as hospital patients, who are rarely mentioned in written records.

Today anthropological research increasingly focuses on the reconstruction of the interaction of humans with their environment over time and the impact of living conditions on health, whereas purely descrip-tive morphological studies are taking a back seat. Archaeometrical and biomolecular methods provide new and promising prospects in the research on eco-logical interrelations. The analysis of stable C, N, and O isotopes from bone collagen and mineral allows the reconstruction of diet, subsistence strategies, and cli-matic conditions, and Sr isotopes from bone and tooth enamel can shed light on past migrations. Ancient DNA (aDNA) analysis improves the certainty of sex determination, can enlighten the degree of relatedness of individuals (family analysis) or populations (inter-population analysis), and is furthermore a diagnostic tool for diseases such as tuberculosis.

Modern period graves are a valuable resource because they originate from a cultural environment with abun-dant written, visual, and material records and can there-fore easily be integrated into ecological history. Slightly different questions arise with regard to graves from the late 19th century and especially the 20th century, and ethical guidelines are required.

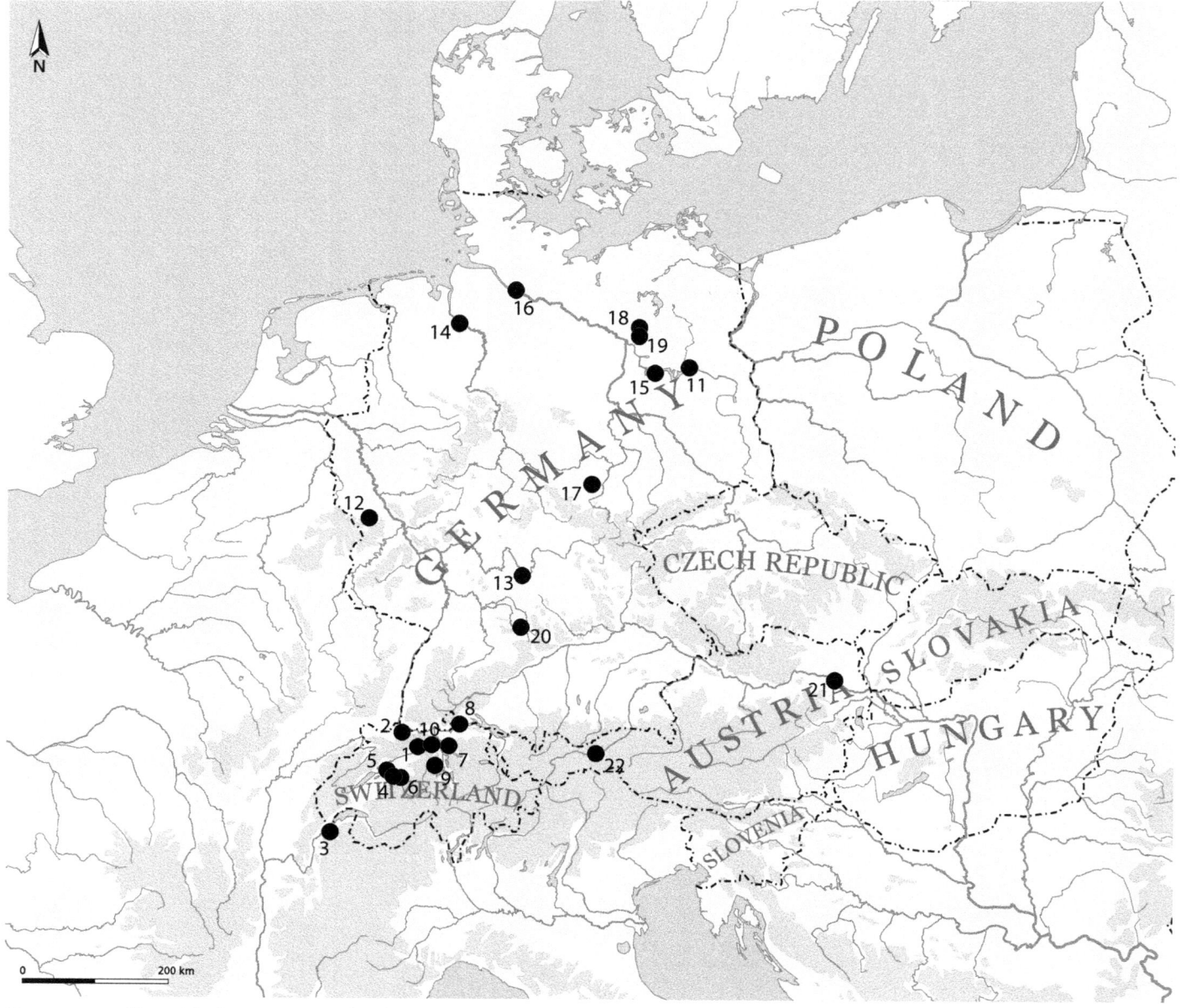

Figure 1.   Map with places mentioned in the text (in Switzerland, unless otherwise noted): (1) Olten; (2) Basel; (3) Geneva; (4) Bern; (5) Aegerten; (6) Worb; (7) Zurich; (8) Schaffhausen; (9) Emmenbrücke; (10) Lenzburg; (11) Berlin, Germany; (12) Altdorf/Düren, Germany; (13) Ochsenfurt, Germany; (14) Bremen, Germany; (15) Brandenburg/Havel, Germany; (16) Hamburg, Germany; (17) Weimar, Germany; (18) Wittstock, Germany; (19) Scharfenberg, Germany; (20) Ellwangen, Germany; (21) Vienna, Austria; and (22) Innsbruck, Austria (Map provided courtesy of the Department of Prehistory and Medieval Archaeology, University of Vienna, Austria).

EXTENT AND PROBLEMS OF POST-MEDIEVAL CEMETERY EXCAVATIONS

For only two or three decades have modern period cemeteries been considered worth excavating by archaeologists. For this reason the number of such complexes is still small, but it is increasing steadily. Graves from the 19th century that would not have been documented at all just a few decades ago now usually receive the same attention as older finds.

One example from Switzerland is an ongoing evaluation of the excavation of a 19th-century cemetery in Olten (Figure 1). The cemetery, in which 1,700 dead from Olten were buried between 1812 and 1861, is endangered by a construction project. The people buried in the cemetery can be considered to be the great-grandfathers and great-grandmothers of a number of people living in the town of Olten today.

The 19th century leads directly into our time and is personally close to us through narratives and pictures. When individual identity data are known for a skeletal series—as in the Olten case—the skeletons are an additional resource for testing the established anthropological methods or for evaluating new methods.

At the end of the 19th century and into the 1930s recently closed cemeteries were plundered, and the skeletons were integrated into collections. These questionable activities can be corrected today with a more developed sense of respect for the dead and their descendants. Knowledge about humans, including those from a not-so-distant past, is as important today as it was earlier.

ETHICAL ASPECTS, HISTORICAL HERITAGE PRESERVATION BASES, AND DATA PROTECTION AND CONFIDENTIALITY

Human remains from archaeological excavations represent a special responsibility for today's society. They are to be treated with care and respect. Clearing them with a mechanical excavator is not tolerable no matter how old the remains are. Just as contemporary cemeteries are protected against vandalism and desecration by the law, older remains are subject to a certain protection. They are counted among archaeological finds and are therefore part of our cultural heritage. Legal bases for cultural heritage preservation in Switzerland had already been established in the 19th century in the canton of Bern, for example. The most recent adjustments to present-day needs are made in the new historical heritage preservation law from the year 2000 (BELEX 2000; Erziehungsdirektion des Kantons Bern 2012).

Cultural-religious regulations such as those of the Jews can prohibit archaeological activities in a cemetery, or they allow excavations in cases of absolute necessity but not the storage of skeletons in archives. This is illustrated by the example of the 13th/14th-century medieval Jewish "ze Spalon" cemetery in Basel, Switzerland. Due to its inevitable destruction by a construction project, archaeologists were allowed to record the graves, in this case under special conditions formulated by the local Jewish community before the human remains were reburied in the Jewish cemetery of Basel. In the Jewish faith burials should not be disturbed after their deposition (Alder 2008).

When skeletons are designated for research purposes the clearing of 20th-century graves is particularly delicate. Living relatives and the institutions in charge (communal and cantonal administration) must give their consent before the exhumations can take place. Family names are made anonymous for reasons of data protection and confidentiality. One of the ten largest skeletal reference series worldwide acquired in this manner is curated in Geneva, Switzerland. The collection consists of about 500 skeletons of individuals with known identity from the first half of the 20th century. In the years 1991-1993 and 1998-2003 they were recovered from different cemeteries in the canton Vaud that are still in use today (Gemmerich 1997; Perréard Lopreno and Eades 2003).

ARCHAEOLOGICAL-ANTHROPOLOGICAL ORGANIZATION AND METHODS

Archaeological excavations are subject to authorization and are usually carried out by cantonal archaeological services in Switzerland. These services can also delegate excavation projects to designated private firms or university institutions. Basically all excavations are salvage excavations implying that only locations endangered by construction projects or erosion are examined. The finds, including human remains, stay in possession of the canton from which they originated. The cantonal service is then also responsible for the expert conservation, scientific processing, and archiving of the finds.

The cooperation between archaeology and anthropology—in the case of Bern between a cantonal service and the university—has been firmly established for the past 30 years. When human remains are found during an excavation the cooperation begins on-site and anthropologists conduct examinations of skeletons in their original position in the grave. In this manner data on funerary rites and different disturbances and a first assessment of age-at-death, sex, stature, and possible anomalies can be gained before the skeletons are removed from the site. Consequently the anthropological data are collected and the on-site findings verified in the laboratory. The field-work is of great importance because many observations linked to funerary customs and rites are only accessible when the skeletons are still lying in their original position. After the completion of all examinations the archaeological and anthropological results are combined and published together. The skeletons themselves—like all other finds—receive inventory numbers and are then packed in solid plastic containers and stored in a depot that is easily accessible to scientists.

OVERVIEW OF POST-MEDIEVAL BURIAL GROUNDS

In the Middle Ages common citizens were buried in church cemeteries or sometimes in cloistral or private burial grounds. The upper class, clerics, and notables often enjoyed special privileges and were interred inside churches or convents. Initially, little about these practices changed in areas that remained Catholic in post-medieval times. The upper class was still privileged even though the medieval "social topography" of burial grounds was less pronounced (Illi 1992). The emergence of Protestantism in the 16th century created the need to distinguish between burial practice in reformed and Catholic districts. Due to the large numbers of interments that have accumulated over centuries, it is often difficult to identify the post-medieval graves among them. Complexes spanning long time periods—from the Middle Ages to the modern period—are found in impressive numbers in Europe whereas purely modern cemeteries have not often been subject to archaeological-anthropological examinations so far.

Burning the dead as a punitive measure was still common in central Europe in the modern period. In Bern, Switzerland, for example, it was practiced until the first third of the 19th century. Cremations re-emerged only in the 19th century and at the beginning of the 20th century and because of their recent history are archaeologically insignificant. In Switzerland the introduction of cremation was facilitated by Article 53 of the 1874 federal constitution in which the control over burial grounds was withdrawn from churches and assigned to civil authorities. All confessional obstacles were thereby eliminated at once. In Berlin, Germany, the percentage of cremations was 78 percent in 2008, representing the situation in northern Germany (Wikipedia 2012). Similar values apply to Switzerland (Huber 2009).

The following outline illustrates the wide spectrum of cemeteries and other burial grounds from 1500 to the end of the 19th century and presents typical anthropological characteristics focusing on urban or

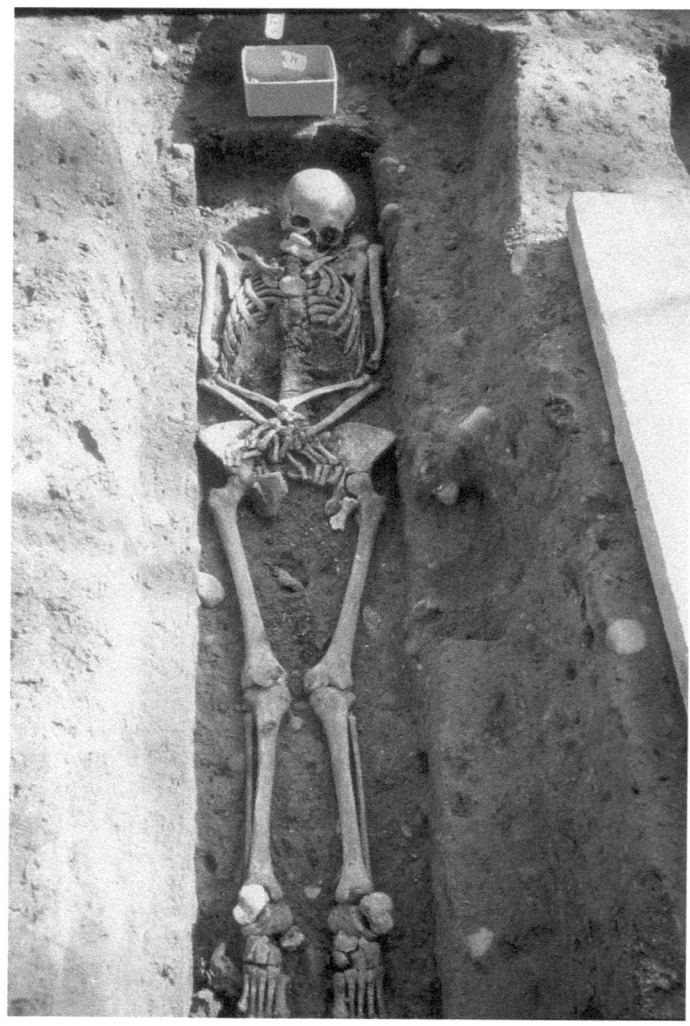

Figure 2.   Burial in Grosse Schanze, the Hintersassen cemetery in Bern (Photo by Susi Ulrich-Bochsler, 2002; courtesy of Historische Anthropologie, Universität Bern).

rural settings, confession, funerary customs, and social differentiation.

Figure 3.   *Burials in Bundesgasse, the densely occupied Burger cemetery in Bern (Photo by Susi Ulrich-Bochsler, 2003; courtesy of Historische Anthropologie, Universität Bern).*

Examples of Regular Burial Grounds

Urban Cemeteries

Two of the rare excavated modern period cemetery complexes from central Europe originate from the reformed city of Bern.

As a result of lack of space in the cemeteries that were in use since the Middle Ages, two new cemeteries were opened in the 18th century. One of them (Bundesgasse), was opened for town citizens—the Burger stand—in the old town. The other (Grosse Schanze), opened in 1769, was located outside the town boundaries and was the new burial ground for the so-called Hintersassen, a stand comprising individuals who were not citizens of the town. Members of this stand were politically and socially disadvantaged and mainly belonged to the lower social class.

Recent archaeological excavations in both cemeteries resulted in 318 unearthed skeletons from the Bundesgasse cemetery and 124 from Grosse Schanze. The main research questions concerned possible differences that could reflect the buried people's social background. The first difference was seen in the cemeteries themselves: while a strict order was observed in the Hintersassen cemetery, the situation found in the Burger cemetery was more difficult (Figures 2 and 3). The differences between "poor" and "rich" found in the skeletal remains, however, were not pronounced enough to indicate clearly different living conditions. Dental health was extremely bad in both groups, and the affliction with "stress markers" reached similarly high levels in both series. The analysis of C and N isotopes revealed no significant difference between the two groups or between males and females (McGlynn et al. 2009; McGlynn and Grupe 2009). The social distinction between the "poor" and "rich" stands did not appear to be reflected by skeletal findings indicative of a differing subsistence basis. Several skeletons and scattered finds exhibited saw marks that appeared to be associated with amputations in some cases or more often with autopsies. Autopsies were secretly performed from the 16th century onwards and systematically from the beginning of the 19th century (Ulrich-Bochsler 2002). Other palaeopathological findings included a case of tertiary syphilis (Figure 4). Even though the debate on the origins of syphilis in Europe is still ongoing (Columbian vs. pre-Columbian theories) the disease is thought to have spread rapidly throughout Europe after 1493 A.D. Most identified cases are attributable to the modern period (Dutour et al. 1994).

In cities there was a general tendency in the 19th century to relocate cemeteries to the outskirts for reasons of hygiene and lack of space for further expansion. All cemeteries in the old town of Bern were closed in 1815, but the social stratification did not cease to exist. In the Monbijou cemetery, which was used between 1815 and 1865, there were special places for foreigners, Burger, non-Burger, and suicides (Ulrich-Bochsler and Schäublin 1995). The dissociation of the Burger stand was not abandoned in terms of a real Christian confraternity until 1857 (Türler 1895).

Social stratification is noticeable in modern period cemeteries of Catholic areas as well. Some families had their own burial places in the church cemetery of the small town Schwyz, Switzerland. After 1774 there were special places for those who did not have a family grave,

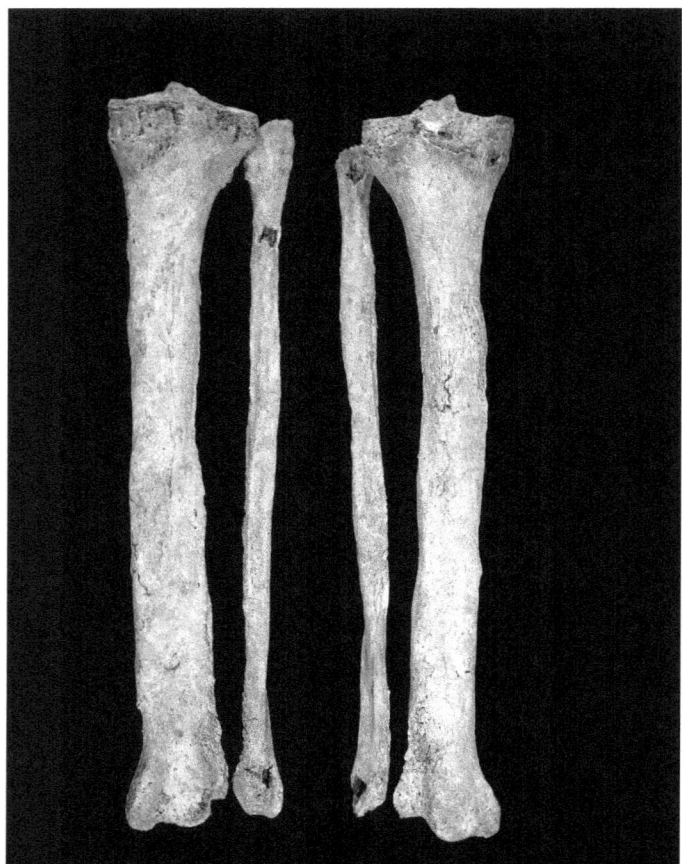

Figure 4.   A case of tertiary syphilis (grave no. 6) from Bundesgasse, the Burger cemetery in Bern (Photo by Christine Cooper, 2008; courtesy of Historische Anthropologie, Universität Bern).

namely paupers, foreigners, executioners, and the executed (Descœudres et al. 1995).

Other excavations of modern period urban cemeteries in central Europe are known from Germany for instance. These include a 19th-20th-century churchyard in Altdorf/Düren (Grigat 2008) and a 17th-18th-century site in Ochsenfurt (Global History of Health Project 2002). For these two sites the anthropological research focus lay on the poorly known health history of small town populations.

Rural Cemeteries

Church cemeteries in rural regions survive a long time, sometimes until today. Just as in urban cemeteries, the dead were interred next to each other in wooden coffins as regulated by law. The east-west orientation was no longer the only possibility in Protestant regions. Despite standardization on the one hand and renewal of funerary regulations on the other, differing treatment of certain individuals such as priests can still be observed. Even in Protestant regions with funerary

practices generally devoid of luxury and pomp, the archaeological-anthropological findings include evidence of folk beliefs that are rooted in medieval Catholic times (Scribner 2001, 2002).

According to traditional ideas, protection against uncertainties was needed in many spheres of life. Among others, this applied to pregnant women or women in childbed. They were not supposed to get frightened, should not experience a conflagration, not witness an execution, or see dead persons, etc., because this put the unborn child at risk of being born malformed or otherwise impaired. A woman in childbed was still ranked among the special dead in the modern period. When a woman died in childbed she could be sure of God's mercy. In Catholic regions it was believed that women in childbed went to heaven directly without a detour to purgatory. Some grave findings document this exceptional status and claim to protection even after death. On the one hand women who died in childbed were buried under the church eaves based on the belief that the rainwater falling from the church roof brought blessing. On the other hand they were equipped with special grave goods such as needle and thread or thimble and scissors that were thought to be needed for the care of the surviving child. The dead would also find peace this way and not haunt or harm the living (HDA 1987).

Many of these objects disintegrate in the grave and can no longer be detected during excavations. Metal objects can be preserved, though. In Aegerten, Switzerland, some 20-35 year-old women from modern period graves (second half of the 19th century) were equipped with scissors and thimbles. Apart from their age-at-death and the grave goods, their position among burials of newborns and nurslings (Figure 5) indicates that they were women who died in childbed (Bacher et al. 1990).

Unbaptized children required special protection after death as well. In the Catholic Middle Ages and modern period an unchristened person was considered a pagan and must not be buried in consecrated earth. Important innovations arrived with the Reformation: baptism was no longer a requirement for salvation and for a burial in the church cemetery. The common folk retained a certain insecurity with regard to the faith of the unchristened in the afterworld, however. Especially in rural areas unbaptized children were buried under the eaves with the assumption that the rainwater dripping off the church roof could provide a posthumous baptism. This is evidenced in the post-medieval period by both

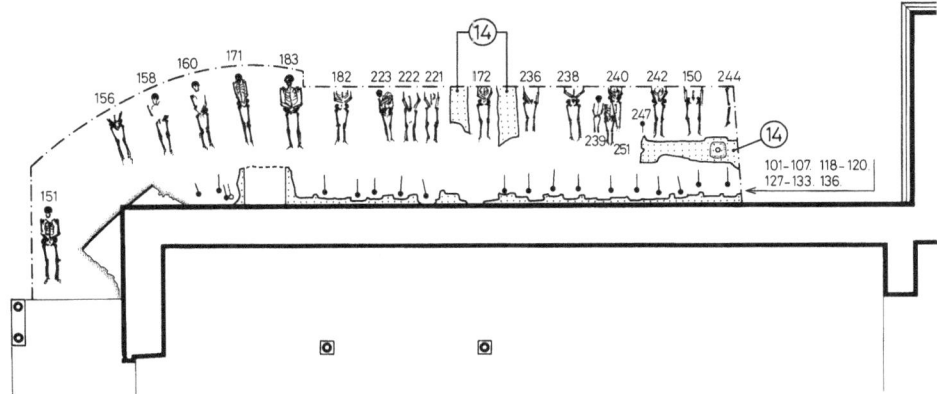

Figure 5. Burials of neonates (Traufkinder) and cemetery graves in Aegerten. Some of the women in this cemetery are equipped with scissors or thimbles and are thought to have died in childbed (among them grave nos. 172 and 222) (Illustration by Jachen Sarott, 1987; courtesy of Archäologischer Dienst des Kantons Bern).

customs. The excavations in the St. Peter's Cathedral in Bremen, Germany, in 1974-1976 and 1979 demonstrated that a dome was a burial place for an exclusive group of people. Among the 41 documented graves, only 16 can be attributed to the modern period. The medieval graves all contained men, several of whom could be identified as known archbishops. Five of the remaining 16 modern period graves belonged to women. After the Reformation, the composition of the individuals buried here changed, and privileged female citizens of Bremen also had access to a burial place in the dome as these findings demonstrated (Henke 1985).

written records (Ulrich-Bochsler 1997) and archaeological finds of Traufkinder (stillborn and neonate burials found alongside church walls) (Figure 6). Just as in the Middle Ages clusters of graves of premature infants and newborns were found inside churches and mostly at special locations such as close to the entrance or around the altars or baptismal fonts. The ages-at-death and the site contexts led to the conclusion that they were children who died unbaptized or stillborn (Ulrich-Bochsler and Meyer 1990; Ulrich-Bochsler 1997) (Figure 7). With regard to these children the Reformation did not bring a definite break. Instead old beliefs were perpetuated and stayed alive until the end of the 20th century.

Crypts such as the dome crypt in Brandenburg/Havel, Germany, the crypt under the main St. Michaelis church in Hamburg, Germany, or the Michaelergruft in Vienna, Austria, can also be noted as special burial places. The material and mental culture of the 18th and 19th centuries was reflected in coffin designs and contents as well as clothing remains from the archaeologically and anthropologically studied crypt in the parochial church in Berlin-Mitte, Germany (Wittkopp 2002). Between 1703 and 1878, 556 Protestants were entombed in this

Graves Inside Churches

Burials inside churches or convents were still commonly observed in the modern period. Today the people who receive such a burial place are without exception ministerial or church dignitaries, notables, or patricians. In Calvinistic Geneva the Saint-Hippolyte church (Grand-Saconnex) served as a burial place for Catholics. Many upper-class foreigners who died during their journey through Geneva were among the individuals buried here, and men's graves were far more numerous than women's graves (Bujard 1990; Simon 1990).

Early modern graves in churches or domes are another excellent resource for the study of funerary

Figure 6. Neonate (Traufkinder) burials alongside the church wall in Aegerten (Photo by Jachen Sarott, 1987; courtesy of Archäologischer Dienst des Kantons Bern).

walk-in crypt. Members of the town nobility, wealthy patricians, administration officials, scientists, doctors, court chaplains, and their families financed the construction and operation of the church by buying their burial places in the crypt and finally being entombed there (Vick and Ströbl 2008). Poor Protestants were also allowed burial in the crypt, with the wealthier paying a higher price than the poorer. Due to the special preservation conditions within the crypt, numerous cases of mummification were observed. Examinations were conducted on 87 mummified bodies from 110 coffins. In addition to results on age-at-death, sex, and diseases, possible connections between season of death and state of mummification were illuminated (Jungklaus 2002).

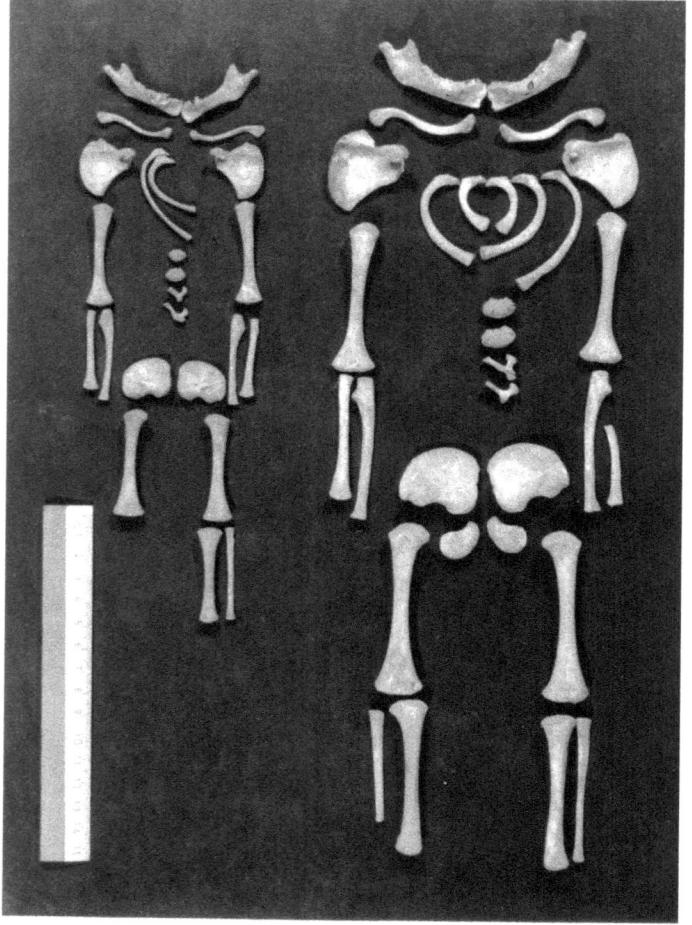

Figure 7. *Skeletons of two neonates (Traufkinder) from Aegerten. The premature individual on the left (grave no. 50) has a body length of 36 cm whereas the newborn on the right (grave no. 196) has a body length of 54 cm (Photo by Sirkka Mullis, 1988; courtesy of Historische Anthropologie, Universität Bern).*

In rural areas churches could sometimes serve as more or less private burial grounds for certain high-ranking families. One example was the church of Worb, Switzerland. Here the local patrician regime bearers (Herrschaftsinhaber) of the von Diesbach and von Graffenried families were buried under sandstone plates in the choir from the 16th century to the 18th century (Figures 8 and 9). Among them was a famous Bernese of the time, Christoph von Graffenried (1661-1743), the founder of New Bern in North Carolina in the United States. In 1710 Christoph von Graffenried sailed from England to America with one of his sons and a group of emigrants, decorated with honors by Anne, the Queen of England. Among the honors was the nomination as Landgrave of Carolina, the title "Baron of Bernbury" and "Knighthood of the Purple Band." Between the rivers Trent and News (today Neuse) Christoph von Graffenried founded the town New Bern in 1710 (Figure 10) (Todd 1920; de Graffenried and Pritchett 1958; Schär 1978; Rubli 1992; Bigler 2009). After a number of difficulties and provocations addressed to Native Americans of the Tuscarora tribe in the area of New Bern, a conflict between the Native Americans and the settlers broke out. Even though Christoph tried to be conciliatory, New Bern was nearly destroyed and many settlers were slain in an attack in 1711. When the politically difficult conditions were combined with a lack of money, Christoph was forced to return home. One of his sons stayed in North America, and up to today the family von Graffenried is represented in America. New Bern developed into a small city with 28,000 inhabitants today and celebrated its 300-year history in 2010 (Bern New Bern 2011).

In accordance with the time and his religious background, Christoph von Graffenried's grave in Worb was of a simple design. The skeleton lay in a wooden coffin and the forearms were crossed on the body (Figure 11). The head was placed on a pillow filled with chicken feathers. The coffin floor was covered with rough wood shavings. Textile remains of the clothing were not preserved.

Christoph reached the old age of 82 years. The skeleton showed several ailments he suffered in his later life (Ulrich-Bochsler and Schäublin 1987). First there were degenerative changes of joints and the spine that resulted in a partial bony bridging and stiffening in the cervical vertebrae caused by age and loading. The joints of hands and feet were pathologically deformed, probably as a result of gout. The dentition showed extensive

Figure 8. *(left) Sandstone plates over burials of members of the von Diesbach and von Graffenried families in the choir of the church in Worb (Photo by Arthur Nydegger, 1983; courtesy of Archäologischer Dienst des Kantons Bern).*

Figure 9. *(right) Sandstone plate for Christoph von Graffenried at the church of Worb, donated by his grandson Karl Emmanuel von Graffenried (Photo by Arthur Nydegger, 1983; courtesy of Archäologischer Dienst des Kantons Bern).*

carious destruction and abscesses that must have caused pain at times. Despite the skeletal evidence of afflictions Christoph von Graffenried surprisingly never mentioned his physical ailments in his notations. Were they less meaningful to him than the mental suffering caused by a lack of appreciation for his achievements in America by the old state of Bern or his lifelong financial difficulties, both of which he described at length?

The Baron de Graffenried died in 1743 of a "Fahl." This could mean a fall, possibly caused by a stroke (apoplexy). A sudden stroke is also consistent with the diagnosed gout and resulting vascular changes. Other possibilities are cardiac and circulatory troubles leading to cardio-vascular death. Naturally many questions about his personality remain unanswered by anthropologists, for example if the image of an ingenious adventurer is deserved.

World-famous central European personalities experienced very different fates after death. Mozart found his last resting-place in a paupers' grave in the central cemetery of Vienna before he became a subject of scientific study (Kritscher and Szilvassy 1991). Goethe (1749-1832) and Schiller (1759-1805), who rested next to each other in the Weimar, Germany, princes' crypt, are the controversially discussed subject matter of anthropological studies. Examinations of aDNA can contribute much to the identification of historical persons (Ullrich 2004, 2008; Wittwer-Backofen and Metzger 2008). Others could be mentioned, but since such personalities have little to do with archaeological excavations the issue shall not be addressed any further.

Special Burial Places

Special burial grounds include ones designated for a special group of people such as hospital occupants, victims of armed conflicts and epidemics, or individuals disdained by society such as the executed.

Figure 10.   Memorial plate for the town's founder in New Bern, North Carolina (Photo by Michael von Graffenried, year unknown; courtesy of Michael von Graffenried).

Post-Medieval Hospital Cemeteries

The hospital cemetery St. Johann in Basel, excavated in the 1980s and exclusively dating to the modern period, comprises 2,561 burials from the years 1845-1868. On the basis of documents and plans, most of the buried individuals could be identified (Etter et al. 1993; Etter and Lörcher 1994). The known names, provenances, occupations, ages-at-death, and causes of death allowed diverse studies of social, medical, and health history and provided a reliable image of an early industrial urban population. A high frequency of Cribra orbitalia, a so-called "stress marker" thought to be associated mainly with anemia, was found (Braun 2004). Many individuals displayed saw marks on different bones proving the performance of autopsies for scientific purposes (Etter and Lörcher 1994). Dental health was marked by very high frequencies of dental caries, calculus, periodontitis, and abscesses. Another frequent feature in dentition was rounded abrasion marks resulting from smoking clay pipes. Metal fillings of carious lesions and dental prostheses were found in individual cases (Etter and Lörcher 1994; Krummenacher 2003).

In Vienna the remains of 393 soldiers of the Austrian army who died in the military hospital nearby between 1769 and 1784 were excavated in the Marchettigasse in 2005. Multiple burials with three to six individuals as well as coffins with up to three individuals were found in some graves. Violence was not the cause of death of the 58 individuals anthropologically examined thus far. High frequencies in stress parameters, dental pathologies, and trauma pointed to high levels of pathogen exposure and poor living conditions of low status soldiers

of the Austrian army in the late 18th century (Binder 2008).

Excavation work at another modern period city and hospital cemetery at the Adolf-Pichler-Platz in Innsbruck, Austria, produced more than 400 human skeletons (McGlynn and Zanesco 2007). The campaign ended abruptly before completion of investigative documentation due to political and economic concerns, and examinations additional to those carried out in the field were not possible. The majority of burials are believed to originate from the first half of the 19th century, a period characterized by war, socio-economic turmoil, and political conflict. The skeletal remains displayed a diversity of features indicative of strenuous physical activity, infectious diseases, and trauma. Anthropological findings showed that many skeletons exhibited saw and scalpel cut marks associated with amputation and trepanation, none of which appear to have been motivated by therapeutic intention, but instead resulted from surgeons or medical students practicing operative procedures and performing autopsies. The high percentage of vertebral abnormalities and degenerative changes indicated physical

Figure 11.   The skeletal remains of Christoph von Graffenried as found on-site in the church of Worb (Photo by Urs Kindler, 1983; courtesy of Archäologischer Dienst des Kantons Bern).

overloading probably caused by arduous labor. Various forms and degrees of severity of periodontal disease indicated the introduction of greater amounts of cariogenic foods well known for this time period as well as the existence of less than optimal dental hygiene. The expectation of discovering victims of early 19th-century warfare was not fulfilled, although evidence for severe traumatic injuries of unknown cause were found.

Mass Graves From Epidemics

Even though several mass graves of the 14th-18th centuries with often hastily buried bodies are known in Europe, only few clearly date to the modern period (Kahlow 2007). They are thought to relate to plague or other epidemics, the proof of which has not yet been provided. Diagnostic tests for the detection of Yersinia pestis antigens have been successfully applied to skeletal remains of putative plague victims from the 16th-18th centuries in southeastern France (Bianucci et al. 2008).

Mass Graves From Armed Conflicts

In 1799/1800 several battles of the Second Coalition War were fought between the French and Austrian and the French and Russian armies on Swiss territory. Over the years several mass graves of soldiers have been discovered, particularly in and around Zurich, Switzerland. Many excavations at these sites took place in the first half of the 20th century. Only the more recent excavations in Zurich-Wasserwerkstrasse (1976) and Schaffhausen-Emmersbergstrasse (2002) were properly recorded by archaeologists. Even though 9,000 men are said to have fallen in the Second Battle of Zurich alone, only small numbers of skeletal remains have been excavated from all known mass graves in Zurich. It is unknown how many individuals the burial pits could have contained originally because none has been completely excavated. The skeletal positions in the documented mass graves appeared distorted and random, indicating that the bodies were carelessly thrown into the pits (Cooper 2003). The dead were not buried by other members of their own army but by the local population (Escher 1915), who were not directly involved but were adversely affected by the conflict. This could explain the careless treatment of the dead. Most of the recovered skeletons displayed signs of perimortem trauma

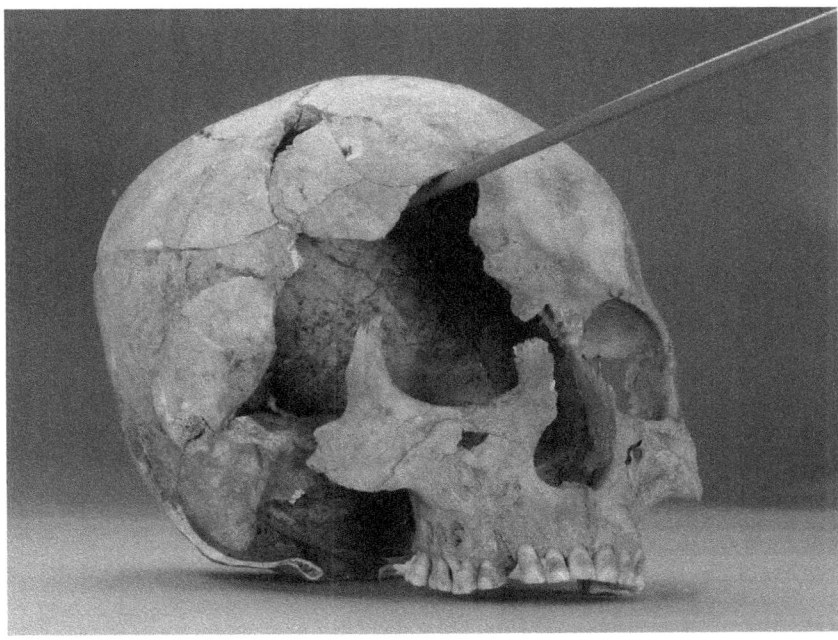

Figure 12. Gunshot injury (entry wound) in a skull from the battles of Zurich in 1799 (Zurich-Wasserwerkstrasse, skeleton no. 2) (Photo by Kriminalfotodienst, Kantonspolizei Zürich, 1998; courtesy of Christine Cooper).

(Figure 12), mainly inflicted by bayonets and firearms (Cooper 2003, 2006).

A mass grave with 70 skeletons from the Thirty Years' War (1618-1648) was excavated in 2007 in Scharfenberg near Wittstock, Germany. On the 5th of October 1636 Scharfenberg was the site of a battle between Swedish and Saxon troops. Around 40,000 soldiers were involved in the battle, and 6,000-7,000 of them fell. Anthropologically this mass grave is of special interest because a single occupational group (but presumably recruited for war from other occupations) was buried here and can answer many questions about soldiers' life almost 400 years ago. The bodies were arranged with care and buried in neat rows side-by-side, demonstrating that a mass grave does not always equal careless interment (Grothe and Jungklaus 2008).

The Excluded Places of Execution

Just as in the Middle Ages the individuals executed by means of decapitation, hanging, breaking on the wheel, burning, or drowning were buried at the place of execution. Such people were only rarely rewarded a grave in public cemeteries and then only in the peripheral areas. In the 19th century bodies of the executed—the decapitated in particular—were often placed at the disposal of anatomical institutions for research purposes.

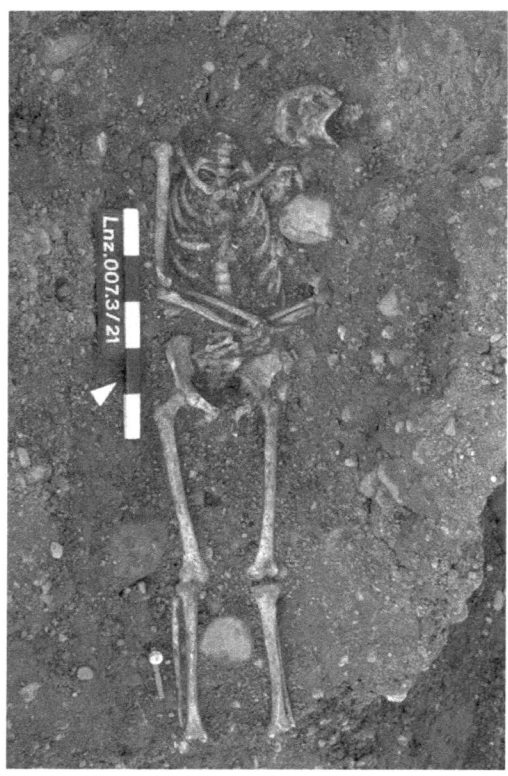

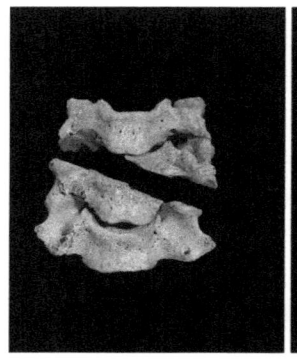 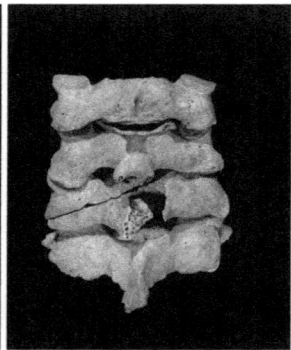 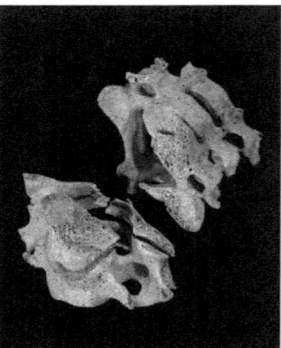

Figure 13.   *(left) The skeleton of a decapitated man (grave 3) from Lenzburg with the skull and cervical vertebrae interred next to the rest of the body (Photo by Andi Schönenberger, 2008; courtesy of Kantonsarchäologie Aargau).*

Figure 14.   *(above) Sharp force injuries in cervical vertebrae proving decapitation of a man (grave 3) from Lenzburg (Photo by Domenic Rüttimann, 2008; courtesy of Historische Anthropologie, Universität Bern).*

In recent years the interest in archaeological and anthropological study of execution places has grown. A number of sites in Switzerland, Germany, Poland, and the Czech Republic are known already (Auler, this volume), whereas skeletal remains from the sites are still rather rare (Auler 2008a, 2008b; Ulrich-Bochsler and Lanz 2008; Wojtucki 2008a, 2008b). Anthropological questions that may be addressed include assessment of the manner of death and health status prior to death, but also the samples' demographic composition.

Five complete inhumations and seven bone pits with a total of about 981 human bones were discovered in 1991 at a place of execution in Ellwangen, Germany (Piech 2009) (see also Auler, this volume). The 981 bones represented body parts that were not, or were only partly, anatomically joined at the time of interment. According to preliminary anthropological results the sample contained a minimum of 34 individuals (Piech 2009:561). Three of twelve individuals were placed in the pits in a dorsal position whereas nine were interred in a ventral position. Interment in a ventral position can indicate fear of revenants. Only one individual in the pit was found in a more or less orderly position and buried according to Christian customs (west-east orientation with the head in the west). All other grave pits appeared to be dug without much consideration for position so that the heads (or the trunks) were oriented differently. The remains of the gallows

foundations discovered in 1991 were almost certainly built in 1701. Remains of clothing such as buttons and hooks also dated to the modern period. On the basis of the bonded hands and the anthropological findings the individuals were probably hanged. Carnivore bite marks on the bones led to the conclusion that body parts were not buried immediately after falling off the gallows (Wahl 2007). So far there has been no evidence of decapitations at the Ellwangen execution site.

The place of execution in Emmenbrücke (Switzerland, 16th-18th centuries) is another archaeologically and anthropologically examined site (see also Auler, this volume). This place of execution served as a knackers yard for dead or diseased animals as well. During the excavation in 1987-1989 not only 45 human skeletons but numerous animal bones, some of which were burnt, were unearthed (Manser et al. 1992). The results of anthropological examinations and written records indicate that decapitated and hanged individuals of both sexes as well as suicides were buried here.

A smaller place of execution from the early modern period (15th/16th centuries) was discovered in Lenzburg, Switzerland, in 2008. Apparently only decapitated individuals were interred here as must be deduced from the vertebrae of men and women cut through by sharp force (Figures 13 and 14) (Schaer et al. 2009).

Prior to a large construction project one of two former gallows from the town of Bern was excavated in 2009. The site dated to the medieval and post-medieval periods, and the skeletal findings were very similar to those from Ellwangen. The bodies were interred in differently oriented single graves or in large pits with the hands bound on the back. A large pit with four complete skeletons at the bottom and numerous single bones of more than 50 individuals on top can be interpreted as a gathering place for body parts.

CONCLUSION

This paper provides an overview of anthropological research on human remains from Switzerland and some other central European sites. The scope encompasses traditional palaeopathological examinations as well as archaeometrical and biomolecular methods. In the first part, the problems associated with modern cemetery excavations are considered, followed by a discussion of archaeological-anthropological methods and a consideration of ethical issues. There then follows a series of short summaries of evidence from urban cemeteries, rural cemeteries, graves inside churches, special burial places, hospital cemeteries, mass graves from epidemics and armed conflicts, and places of execution.

This overview shows to what extent religion, folk beliefs, and culture influence burial practices and burial places.

REFERENCES

ALDER, CORNELIA

2008   Der "Judenfriedhof ze Spalon," Einblick in den mittelalterlichen jüdischen Friedhof von Basel (13. und 14. Jahrhundert). 8. Internationaler Kongress der Gesellschaft für Anthropologie (GfA), 14.-18. September 2009, München. Abstracts. [The "Jewish Cemetery ze Spalon," Insight into the Medieval Jewish Cemetery of Basel (13th and 14th Centuries). 8th International Congress of the Society for Anthropology (GfA), 14-18 September 2009, Munich. Abstracts] Bulletin der Schweizerischen Gesellschaft für Anthropologie 14(1-2):3.

AULER, JOST

2008a   Das spätmittelalterliche Grab eines enthaupteten Mannes aus Nordhessen [The Late Medieval Grave of a Decapitated Man from Northern Hesse]. In Richtstättenarchäologie, Jost Auler, editor, pp. 70-75. Archaeotopos, Dormagen, Germany.

2008b   Richtstättenarchäologie in der Schweiz— Einige Nachträge [Archaeology of Places of Execution in Switzerland—Some Postscripts]. In Richtstättenarchäologie, Jost Auler, editor, pp. 286-306. Archaeotopos, Dormagen, Germany.

BACHER RENÉ, PETER J. SUTER, PETER EGGENBERGER, SUSI ULRICH-BOCHSLER, AND LISELOTTE MEYER

1990   Aegerten: Die spätrömischen Anlagen und der Friedhof der Kirche Bürglen [Aegerten: Late Roman Structures and the Cemetery of Bürglen Church]. Staatlicher Lehrmittelverlag, Bern, Switzerland.

BELEX

2000   Verordnung über die Denkmalpflege (Denkmalpflegeverordnung, DPV) [Regulation on Conservation (Conservation Regulation, DPV)]. BELEX—Gesetzessammlungen des Kantons Berns < http://www.sta.be.ch/ belex/d/4/426_411.html>. Accessed 14 August 2012.

BERN NEW BERN

2011   New Bern, North Carolina, 300 Jahre Daughter City in America <http://www.newbern.ch/ english/300-years-new-bern-n-c/>. Accessed 14 August 2012.

BIANUCCI RAFFAELLA, LILA RAHALISON, EMMA RABINO MASSA, ALBERTO PELUSO, EZIO FERROGLIO, AND MICHEL SIGNOLI

2008   A Rapid Diagnostic Test Detects Plague in Ancient Human Remains: An Example of the Interaction Between Archaeological and Biological Approaches (Southeastern France, 16th-18th Centuries). American Journal of Physical Anthropology 136:361-367.

BIGLER, MANUEL

2009   300 Jahre New Bern [300 Years New Bern]. Berner Zeitschrift für Geschichte 71(4):1-27.

BINDER, MICHAELA

2008   Der Soldatenfriedhof in der Marchettigasse in Wien. Die Lebensbedingungen einfacher Soldaten in der theresianisch-josephinischen Armee anhand anthropologischer Untersuchungen [The Soldier Cemetery in the Marchettigasse in Vienna. Living Conditions of Simple Soldiers in the Theresian-Josephinian Army by Anthropological Examinations]. Magistrat der Stadt Wien, MA 7—Referat Stadtarchäologie, Vienna, Austria.

BRAUN, SANDRA

2004   Cribra orbitalia—Makroskopische Evaluation eines Stressors in der Skelettserie Spitalfriedhof St. Johann in Basel [Cribra Orbitalia—Macroscopic Evaluation of a Stress Marker in the Skeletal Series from the Hospital Cemetery St. Johann in Basel]. Bulletin der Schweizerischen Gesellschaft für Anthropologie 10(2):1-52.

BUJARD, JACQUES

1990   L'église Saint-Hippolyte du Grand-Saconnex [The Saint Hippolyte Church of Grand-Saconnex]. Genava 38:29-66.

COOPER, CHRISTINE

2003   Soldaten von 1799—Eine anthropologische und forensische Untersuchung der Skelette aus acht Massengräbern aus Zürich und Umgebung [An Anthropological and Forensic Examination of the Skeletons from Eight Mass Graves from Zurich and the Surrounding Area]. Master's thesis, Department of Anthropology, University of Zurich, Switzerland.

2006   Soldaten von 1799/1800: Massengräber aus Zürich und Schaffhausen [Soldiers from 1799/1800: Mass Graves from Zurich and Schaffhausen]. Bulletin der Schweizerischen Gesellschaft für Anthropologie 12:23-34.

DE GRAFFENRIED, THOMAS PRITCHETT

1958   1191-1956. Seven Hundred and Sixty-Five Years. The Graffenried Family Scrap Book. Charlottesville, VA.

DESCŒUDRES, GEORGES, ANDREAS CUENI, CHRISTIAN HESSE, AND GABRIELE KECK

1995   Sterben in Schwyz. Beharrung und Wandlung im Totenbrauchtum einer ländlichen Siedlung vom Spätmittelalter bis in die Neuzeit. Geschichte—Archäologie—Anthropologie [Dying in Schwyz. Constancy and Change in the Death Rites of a Rural Settlement from the Late Middle Ages to the Modern Period. History—Archaeology—Anthropology]. Schweizer Beiträge zur Kulturgeschichte und Archäologie des Mittelalters. Schweizerischer Burgenverein, Basel, Switzerland.

DUTOUR, OLIVIER, GYÖRGY PÁLFI, JACQUES BERATO, AND JEAN-PIERRE BRUN (EDITORS)

1994   L'origine de la syphilis en Europe. Avant ou après 1493? [The Origin of Syphilis in Europe. Before or after 1493?]. Actes du colloque internationale de Toulon, 25-28 novembre 1993. Editions Errance, Paris, France.

ERZIEHUNGSDIREKTION DES KANTONS BERN

2012   Rechtliche Grundlagen. Erziehungsdirektion des Kantons Bern [Legal Framework. Department of Education, Canton of Bern] <http://www.erz.be.ch/erz/de/index/kultur/archaeologie/rechtliche_grundlagen.html>. Accessed 14 August 2012.

ESCHER, CONRAD

1915   Chronik der Gemeinden Ober- und Unterstrass [Chronicle of the Ober- and Unterstrass Municipalities]. Verlag Orell Füssli, Zurich, Switzerland.

ETTER, HANSUELI, PETRA BOCKMÜHL, CHRISTOPH HEINRICHS, IRENE HITZ, GERHARD HOTZ, MARIANNE LÖRCHER, ERWIN RIEGERT, SABINE SCHRÖDER, AND ANNETTE UHL

1993   Armut, Krankheit, Tod im frühindustriellen Basel. Der Spitalfriedhof St. Johann in Basel. Funde und Befunde aus einer anthropologischen Ausgrabung [Poverty, Sickness, Death in Early Industrial Basel. The Hospital Cemetery St. Johann. Finds and Results from an Anthropological Excavation]. Veröffentlichungen des Naturhistorischen Museums Basel 25. Basel, Switzerland.

ETTER, HANSUELI, AND MARIANNE LÖRCHER

1994   Armut—Krankheit—Tod. Archäologie und Anthropologie am Beispiel eines frühindustriellen Spitalfriedhofs in Basel [Poverty—Sickness—Death. Archaeology and Anthropology of an Early Industrial Cemetery in Basel]. In Fabriklerleben. Industriearchäologie und Anthropologie, Hansjörg Frommelt, editor, pp. 341-364. Historischer Verein für das Fürstentum Liechtenstein Chronos Verlag, Zurich, Switzerland.

GEMMERICH, ISABELLE

1997   Collection I. Gemmerich: squelettes récents vaudois 1992-1993 (CH). Dossier documentaire [The I. Gemmerich Collection. Recent Skeletons from the Canton Vaud 1992-1993 (Switzerland). Documentation Dossier]. Bulletin der Schweizerischen Gesellschaft Für Anthropologie 3(2):1-12.

GLOBAL HISTORY OF HEALTH PROJECT

2002   Health Index. Global History of Health Project, Ohio State University <http://global.sbs.ohio-state.edu/global.php>. Accessed 16 August 2012.

GRIGAT, ANDREA

2008   The St. Pankratius Churchyard in Altdorf/Düren (North Rhine Westphalia, Germany)—Selected Pathologies from a 19th/20th Century Population. In Limping Together through the Ages. Joint Afflictions and Bone Infections, Gisela Grupe, George McGlynn, and Joris Peters, editors, pp. 61-79. Documenta Archaeobiologiae 6. Verlag Marie Leidorf, Rahden/Westfalen, Germany.

GROTHE, ANJA, AND BETTINA JUNGKLAUS

2008   Archaeological and Anthropological Examinations of a Mass Grave from the 1636 Battle at Wittstock: A Preliminary Report. In Limping Together through the Ages. Joint Afflictions and Bone Infections, Gisela Grupe, George McGlynn, and Joris Peters, editors, pp. 127-135. Documenta Archaeobiologiae 6. Verlag Marie Leidorf, Rahden/Westfalen, Germany.

HDA

1987   Artikel Wöchnerin [Article "Woman in Childbed"]. In Handbuch des deutschen Aberglaubens 9, Hanns Bächtold-Stäubli, editor, pp. 692-716. Berlin, Germany.

HENKE, WINFRIED

1985   Anthropologische Untersuchung der menschlichen Skelettreste [Examination of the Human Skeletons]. Ausgrabungen im St.-Petri-Dom zu Bremen, Band 1. E. Schweizerbart'sche Verlagsbuchhandlung, Stuttgart, Germany.

HUBER, KATHRIN

2009   Der soziale Raum des Todes. Friedhöfe in den Städten Bern und Luzern [The Social Sphere of Death. Cemeteries in the Cities Berne and Lucerne]. Neue Berner Beiträge zur Soziologie, Band 10. Bern, Switzerland.

ILLI, MARTIN

1992   Wohin die Toten gingen. Begräbnis und Kirchhof in der vorindustriellen Stadt [Where the Dead Went. Funeral and Churchyard in the Pre-Industrial Town]. Chronos Verlag, Zurich, Switzerland.

JUNGKLAUS, BETTINA

2002   Die Mumien in der Gruft der Parochialkirche—Ergebnisse der anthropologischen Untersuchung [The Mummies in the Parochial Church Crypt—Results of the Anthropological Examination]. Mitteilungen der Berliner Gesellschaft für Anthropologie, Ethnologie und Urgeschichte 23:31-39.

KAHLOW, SIMONE

2007   Die Pest als Interpretationsproblem mittelalterlicher und frühneuzeitlicher Massengräber [Pestilence as Interpretation Problem of Medieval and Post-Medieval Mass Graves]. Bulletin der Schweizerischen Gesellschaft für Anthropologie 13(1):97-104.

KRITSCHER, HERBERT, AND JOHANN SZILVASSY

1991   Zur Identifizierung des Mozartschädels [On the Identification of the Mozart Skull]. Annalen des Naturhistorischen Museums in Wien 93:1-139.

KRUMMENACHER, RENÉ

2003   Karies und Zahnsteinbefall zu Beginn des 19. Jahrhunderts [Caries and tartar at the beginning of the 19th Century]. Bulletin der Schweizerischen Gesellschaft für Anthropologie 9(1):23-58.

MANSER, JÜRG, BEITRÄGEN VON KURT DIGGELMANN, HANSUELI F. ETTER, HANSJÜRG HÄNI, MICHAEL HARRER, DORIS HUGGEL, JOHANN LANG, RENÉ PAHUD DE MORTANGES, MANUELA ROS, HANS R. STAMPFLI, GOTTLIEB UELTSCHI, AND BENEDIKT ZÄCH

1992   Richtstätte und Wasenplatz in Emmenbrücke (16.-19. Jh.). Archäologische und historische Untersuchungen zur Geschichte von Strafrechtspflege und Tierhaltung in Luzern [Execution Place and Knackers Yard in Emmenbrücke (16th-19th Centuries). Archaeological and Historical Studies on the History of Justice and Animal Husbandry in Lucerne]. Schweizerischer Burgenverein, Basel, Switzerland.

McGLYNN, GEORGE, AND ALEXANDER ZANESCO

2007   The Skeletal Series from the Innsbruck City Cemetery at Adolf Pichler Platz. In Skeletal Series and their Socio-Economic Context, Gisela Grupe and Joris Peters, editors, pp. 57-66. Documenta Archaeobiologiae 5. Verlag Marie Leidorf, Rahden/Westfalen, Germany.

McGLYNN, GEORGE, ET AL.

2009   Peasants, Elite, Paupers and City Folk: A Preliminary Analysis of Stable C and N Isotopes across Europe. In Reconstructing Health and Disease in Europe: The Early Middle Ages through the Industrial Period, Association of Physical Anthropology Meeting, April 2, 2009, Invited Poster Session, p. 4, < http://global.sbs.ohio-state.edu/AAPA_Symposium_2009.pdf >. Accessed 22 July 2012.

McGLYNN, GEORGE, AND GISELA GRUPE

2009   Stable Isotope Analysis. American Journal of Physical Anthropology Annual Meeting Issue 2009 (Supplement 48):188.

PERRÉARD LOPRENO, GENEVIÈVE, AND SUSANNE EADES

2003   Une démarche actualiste en paléoanthropologie: la collection de squelettes de référence [An Actualist Approach in Palaeoanthropology: The Reference Collection of Skeletons]. In ConstellaSion: hommage à Alain Gallay, Marie Besse, Laurence-Isaline Stahl Gretsch, and Philippe Curdy, editors, pp. 463-472. Cahiers d'archéologie romande 95. Lausanne, Switzerland.

PIECH, JAROSLAW

2009 "Mit dem Strang vom Leben zum Todt hingerichtet": Der Ellwanger Galgen und andere Galgenstandorte in Württemberg ["Executed from Life to Death with the Rope": The Gallows in Ellwangen and in Other Places in Württemberg]. Fundberichte aus Baden-Württemberg 30:521-755.

RUBLI, MARKUS F.

1992 Neuschloss Worb. Zur Geschichte eines bernischen Landsitzes [Neuschloss Worb. On the History of a Bernese Manor]. Benteli, Bern, Switzerland.

SCHAER, ANDREA, SUSI ULRICH-BOCHSLER, AND CHRISTIAN LANZ

2009 Die Richtstätte an der Aarauerstrasse. Skelettfunde bestätigen historische Quellen [The Execution Place in the Aarauerstrasse. Skeleton Finds Confirm Historical Records]. Lenzburger Neujahrsblätter 81:73-86.

SCHÄR, OSKAR

1978 New Bern. Christoph von Graffenried 1661-1743. Ein bernischer Stadtgründer [New Bern. Christoph von Graffenried 1661-1743. A Bernese City Founder]. GS-Verlag, Bern, Switzerland.

SCRIBNER, ROBERT W.

2001 Religion and Culture in Germany (1400-1800). Brill, Leiden, the Netherlands.

2002 Religion und Kultur in Deutschland 1400-1800 [Religion and Culture in Germany 1400-1800]. Vandenhoeck & Ruprecht, Göttingen, Germany.

SIMON, CHRISTIAN

1990 Les restes humains de l'église du Grand-Saconnex, Genève [The Human Remains from the Church of Grand-Saconnex, Geneva]. Genava 38:67-76.

TODD, VINCENT H.

1920 Christoph von Graffenried's Account of the Founding of New Bern. Edwards & Broughton, Raleigh, NC.

TÜRLER, HEINRICH

1895 Das Beerdigungswesen der Stadt Bern bis zur Schliessung des Monbijou-Friedhofs [Funerals in the City of Berne until the Closure of the Monbijou Cemetery]. Intelligenzblatt und Berner Stadtblatt No. 74-84 (March 28-April 9).

ULLRICH, HERBERT

2004 Schädel-Schicksale historischer Persönlichkeiten [Fates of the Skulls of Historical Personages]. Verlag Dr. Friedrich Pfeil, Munich, Germany.

2008 ...und ewig währt der Streit um Schillers Schädel [... and Forever the Dispute about Schiller's Skull Continues]. Verlag Dr. Friedrich Pfeil, Munich, Germany.

ULRICH-BOCHSLER, SUSI

1997 Anthropologische Befunde zur Stellung von Frau und Kind in Mittelalter und Neuzeit. Soziobiologische und soziokulturelle Aspekte im Lichte von Archäologie, Geschichte, Volkskunde und Medizingeschichte [Anthropological Findings on the Standing of Woman and Child in the Middle Ages and the Modern Period. Sociobiological and Sociocultural Aspects in Light of Archaeology, History, Folklore, and the History of Medicine]. Berner Lehrmittel- und Medienverlag, Bern, Switzerland.

2002 Eine Sektion aus dem Jahre 1808. Anthropologische Beobachtungen zu einem archäologischen Skelettfund aus dem Kanton Bern [An Autopsy from 1808. Anthropological Observations on an Archaeological Find of a Skeleton from the Canton Berne]. Bulletin der Schweizerischen Gesellschaft für Anthropologie 8(2):1-18.

ULRICH-BOCHSLER, SUSI, AND CHRISTIAN LANZ

2008 Mittelalterliche und neuzeitliche Skelettfunde Hingerichteter in der Schweiz. Katalog und anthropologisch-rechtsmedizinische Beurteilung [Medieval and Post-Medieval Finds of Skeletons of the Executed in Switzerland. Catalog and Anthropological-Forensical Assessment]. In Richtstättenarchäologie, Jost Auler, editor, pp. 412-433. Archaeotopos, Dormagen, Germany.

ULRICH-BOCHSLER, SUSI, AND LISELOTTE MEYER

1990 Anthropologische Untersuchungen [Anthropological Examinations]. In Aegerten: Die spätrömischen Anlagen und der Friedhof der Kirche Bürglen, René Bacher, Peter J. Suter, Peter Eggenberger, Susi Ulrich-Bochsler, Liselotte Meyer, authors, pp. 97-132. Staatlicher Lehrmittelverlag, Bern, Switzerland.

ULRICH-BOCHSLER, SUSI, AND ELISABETH SCHÄUBLIN

1987 Christoph von Graffenried (1661-1743), Gründer von New Bern: Historische Aspekte und anthropologische Befunde [Christoph von Graffenried (1661-1743), the Founder of New Bern: Historical Aspects and Anthropological Findings]. Jahrbuch des Naturhistorischen Museums Bern 9:201-215.

1995 Der Bleisarg vom Monbijou [The Lead Coffin from Monbijou]. Bulletin der Schweizerischen Gesellschaft für Anthropologie 1(1):39-45.

VICK, DANA, AND ANDREAS STRÖBL

2008 Neuzeitliche Gruftanlagen—Einzigartige Zeugnisse der Bestattungskultur [Modern Period Crypts—Unique Testimonies of Funerary Culture]. Ohlsdorf—Zeitschrift für Trauerkultur 100/101(I-II).

WAHL, JOACHIM

2007   Karies, Kampf & Schädelkult. Materialhefte
            zur Archäologie in Baden-Württemberg [Caries,
            Combat, & Skull Cult. Material Books on
            Archaeology in Baden-Württemberg]. Konrad
            Theiss Verlag, Stuttgart, Germany.

WIKIPEDIA

2012   Krematorium [Crematorium] <http://
            de.wikipedia.org/wiki/Krematorium>. Accessed
            16 August 2012.

WITTKOPP, BLANDINE

2002   Frühneuzeitliches Totenbrauchtum im Spiegel
            der Gruft der Parochialkirche in Berlin-Mitte
            [Early Modern Period Funerary Customs in
            Light of the Crypt of the Parochial Church in
            Berlin]. Mitteilungen der Berliner Gesellschaft
            für Anthropologie, Ethnologie und Urgeschichte
            23:61-74.

WITTWER-BACKOFEN, URSULA, AND MARC METZGER

2008   The Friedrich Schiller Skull and Anthropology: A
            Scientific (Re)search. 8. Internationaler Kongress
            der Gesellschaft für Anthropologie (GfA),
            14.-18. September 2009, München. Abstracts.
            Bulletin der Schweizerischen Gesellschaft für
            Anthropologie 14(1-2):70.

WOJTUCKI, DANIEL

2008a   "Richtstättenarchäologie" in Schlesien und in der
            Oberlausitz vor 1945 ["Archaeology of Execution
            Places" in Silesia and Oberlausitz before 1945].
            In Richtstättenarchäologie, Jost Auler, editor, pp.
            378-387. Archaeotopos, Dormagen, Germany.

2008b   Bestattungen von Hingerichteten und
            Selbstmördern in Schlesien und in der
            Oberlausitz vom 16. bis zum 18. Jahrhundert
            [Burials of Executed and Suicides in Silesia and
            Oberlausitz from the 16th to the 18th Century].
            In Richtstättenarchäologie, Jost Auler, editor, pp.
            532-547. Archaeotopos, Dormagen, Germany.

Susi Ulrich-Bochsler
Universität Bern
Institut für Medizingeschichte
Bühlstrasse 26
CH-3012 Bern
Switzerland

Christine Cooper
Landesarchäologie
Messinastr. 5
FL-9495 Triesen
Principality of Liechtenstein

EDGAR RING

Confessionalization in the Domestic Sphere during the 16th Century: Archaeology and Reformation

ABSTRACT

Over the course of the 16th century images and their many copies took on a greater significance. In the context of confessionalization (i.e., the process of religious identity formation) and disciplining during the Reformation process, both the "old" faith and the Protestant persuasions utilized images. Among archaeological finds, these images became more prevalent on objects of everyday use. They served in accordance with Martin Luther as objects of instruction, guidance, and persuasion. While stove-tiles are the best known and most abundant category of finds with imagery from the Reformation, images are also often found on ceramic and glass vessels bearing central motifs from the Protestant faith, Protestant Reformers, and rulers, as well as general religious content. These archaeological finds provided images for ordinary citizens in their everyday pursuit of Protestant life. It is not, however, possible to outline a detailed course of confessionalization based on the archaeological finds alone.

INTRODUCTION

Das wyr auch solche Bilder muegen an die wende malen umb gedechtnis und besser verstands willen. Syntemal sie an den wenden ia so wenig schaden, als ynn den büchern. Es ist yhe besser, man male an die wand, wie Gott die Wellt schuff wie Noe die arca bawet und was mehr guter historien sind, denn das man sonst yrgent welltlich unverschampt ding malet, Ja wollt Gott, ich kund die herrn und die reychen da hyn bereden, das sie die gantze Bibel ynnwendig und auswendig an den heusern fur ydermans augen malen liessen, das were eyn Christlich werck.

—*Martin Luther, Wider die himmlischen Propheten, von den Bilderb und Sakrament, 1525 [Luther WA 1883-2000(18):82-83].*

Although early modern period German is difficult to translate into English, Martin Luther's 1525 words show just how important he felt images were in instructing, guiding, and convincing people if used correctly. He wished to see depictions of God creating the world and Noah building the ark, he sought Christian rather than worldly pictures on the walls of houses, both inside and out—images for everyone.

The archaeological finds from the Reformation era include numerous objects with such images. The most abundant category of artifacts are stove-tiles, which show pictures and series of images that bear witness to the new Protestant faith in a central area of the house (Hallenkamp-Lumpe 2006:211-242). Glass and ceramic objects were also decorated with these images, however. Most of the depictions hark back to printed designs by Lukas Cranach, Albrecht Dürer, and Georg Pencz, among others, that were widespread in the 16th century.

In this phase of religious turmoil, particularly in places and regions where several changes in religious beliefs took place, one must raise the question as to which images in fact assisted in the process of confessionalization and disciplining. The study of archaeological finds as bearers of Protestant imagery reveals that objects can show the shared confessional identity of their owners (Ring 2007a). Protestant polemics against the Catholic Church, propagandistic depictions of Reformers and Protestant princes, and the utilization of genuinely Protestant motifs such as "law and grace" (original sin and salvation) are pictorial themes that can clearly be identified as bound to a certain denomination, even outside of a particular context of origin and usage (Hallenkamp-Lumpe 2006:224). Biblical stories, allegories, catechisms, and the depiction of virtues became popular themes over the course of the Protestant confessionalization process, but were not uniquely

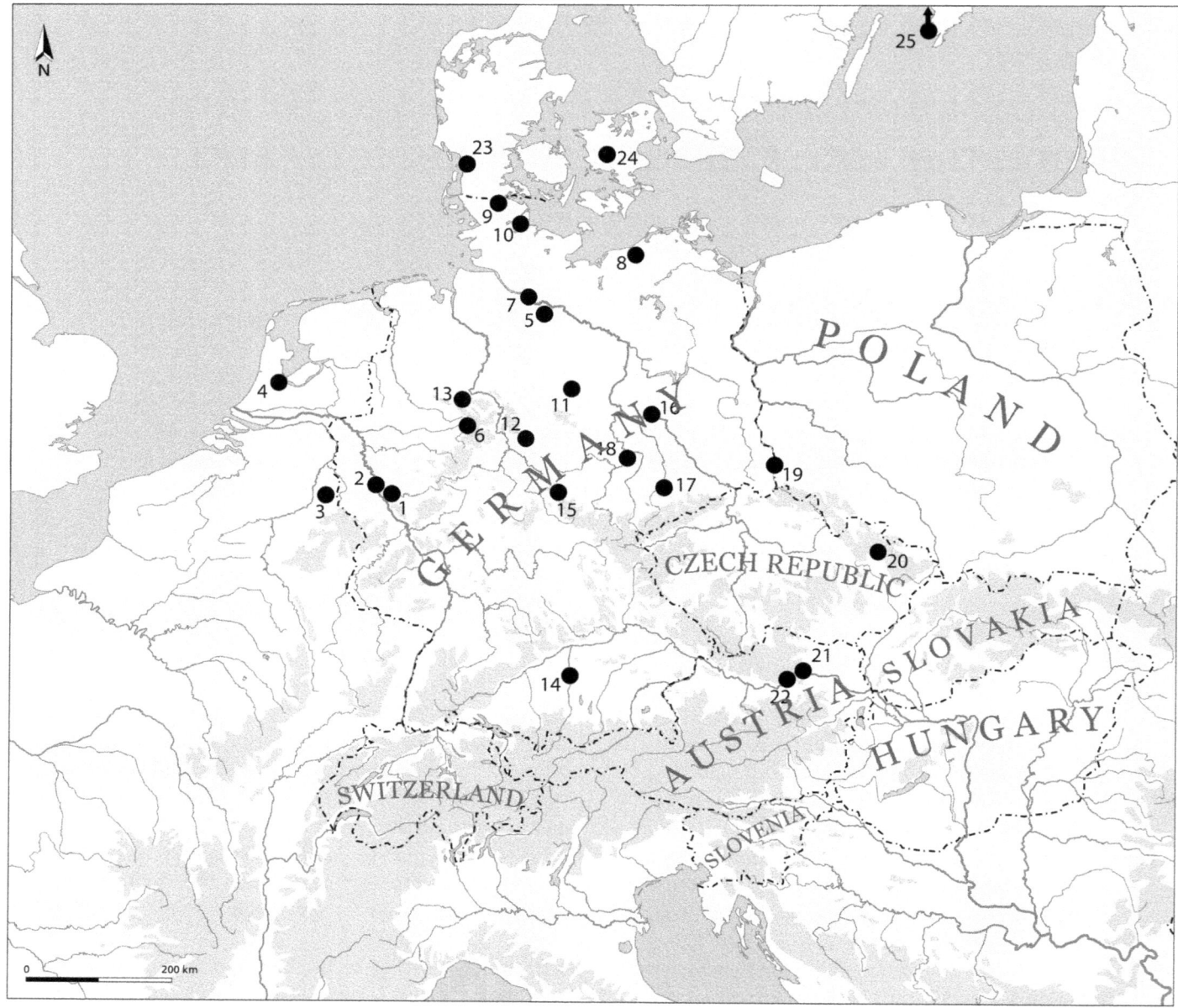

Figure 1. Map with places mentioned in the text (in Germany, unless otherwise noted): (1) Siegburg; (2) Cologne; (3) Raeren, Belgium; (4) Amsterdam, the Netherlands; (5) Lüneburg; (6) Paderborn; (7) Hamburg; (8) Rostock; (9) Flensburg; (10) Eckernförde; (11) Helmstedt; (12) Göttingen; (13) Herford; (14) Augsburg; (15) Schmalkalden; (16) Wittenberg; (17) Waldenburg; (18) Merseburg; (19) Görlitz; (20) Janovice, Czech Republic; (21) Grafenegg, Austria; (22) Weißenkirchen, Austria; (23) Ribe, Denmark; (24) Lynge, Denmark; and (25) Stockholm, Sweden (Map provided courtesy of the Department of Prehistory and Medieval Archaeology, University of Vienna, Austria).

Protestant and can therefore only be interpreted in the context of their usage and discovery.

POLEMICS AND PROPAGANDA CREATED IN SIEGBURG POTTERS' WORKSHOPS

Around the mid-16th century potters in Siegburg, a center of stoneware production near Cologne, began to manufacture drinking and serving vessels bearing round medallions and rectangular mounts with polemic and propagandistic images in relation to the battle between the religious denominations (Gaimster 1997:148) (Figure 1). The double-faced depictions showing the Pope and the devil or a cardinal and a fool (Figure 2), inspired by medals, became particularly popular (Barnard 1927; Krueger 1979:259-268;

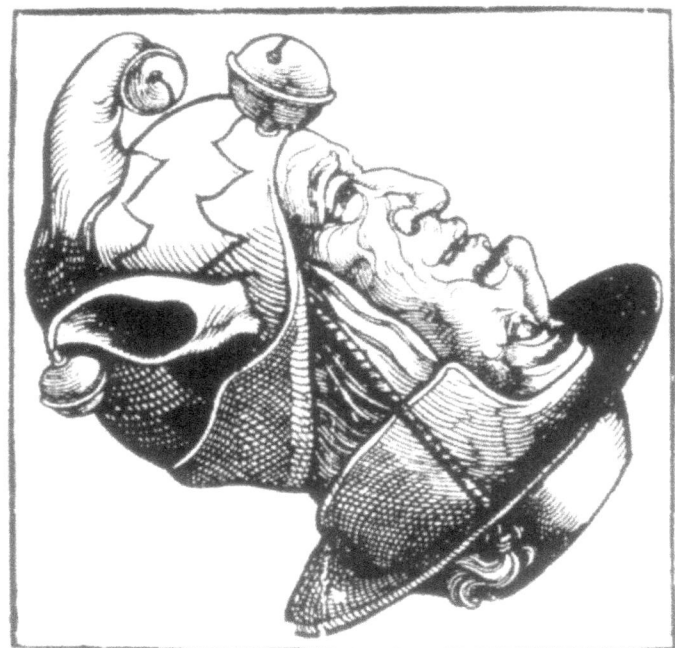

Figure 2. "Cardinal and Fool," woodcut ca. 1525 (Hallenkamp-Lumpe 2006:plate 176,5).

Kat. Bonn 2010:196). The motif had its origins in a wood engraving by an unknown German artist dating from around 1525 (Gaimster 1997:149; Hallenkamp-Lumpe 2006:pl. 176,5). Molding on jugs produced between 1550 and 1580 in Cologne, Siegburg, and Raeren polemically dealt with the Augsburg Interim, an agreement that became Imperial law in 1548, by which Charles V (1500-1558), after his victory over the Schmalkaldic League, attempted to impose his religious and political will and which in some quarters encountered strong resistance on both the Protestant and Catholic sides (Krueger 1979:268-275). In the example shown in Figure 3, the Protestant polemics are expressed in three scenes: Christ pushes the devil aside, accompanied by the inscription PACK. DICH./TEVFEL .IN/INTERIM [begone./devil .in/interim]; a three-headed monster—a Turk, the Pope, and an angel; and Christ chops down a tree with liturgical implements, accompanied by the inscription DAS VNKRVT / WILL ICH AVS / ROTEN VND / WERFEN ES / INS FEVR [the weeds / I want to eradicate and / throw them / on the fire]. The depictions were copied from printed designs.

A jug of Siegburg provenance found in Amsterdam (Figure 4) bears one of the central motifs of the Reformation: original sin and salvation—a version of the painting of the "glorious difference between the law and grace," painted in several variants by Lucas Cranach the Elder from 1529 (Weimer 1999; Krueger 2000). The central molding on the jug depicts a seated naked man praying in front of a tree whose trunk bears a plaque with the inscription HOMO. The tree is flanked by two figures that recur in the sprigs to the left and right. The lady on the left is praying to a snake hanging from a cross, the shepherd surrounded by his sheep on the right is looking up to Christ on the Cross.

An early and antagonistic confessional polemic dating from the mid-1520s depicts the theme "Sheepfold of Christ" (Figure 5) on a Siegburg jug manufactured around 1570 (Krueger 1979:284-291). The central sprig shows Christ standing in the doorway of a building, with Paul to his right. The person on the left appears to be John. Two men wearing high caps and each holding a sheep are sitting on the roof. A devil's bust can be seen between them. Two kneeling figures, a monk and a Turk identified by the inscription DER TURCK [the Turk], on either side of the sloping roof are praying to the men. Christ, the good shepherd, is threatened by thieves and robbers who are trying to steal his sheep. The robbers are identified by inscriptions as a Pharisee and a Turk.

The jugs with anti-Catholic depictions can be viewed as precious tableware used for drinking, but also flaunted as artistic and ingeniously decorated showpieces (Krueger 1979:294). It can be assumed that the buyers of such vessels with religious propaganda were not just from the Rhineland, but also from the Calvinist Netherlands and the Protestant north. Only in the case of the so-called interim jug is it possible to trace the ownership back far. The jug came from St. Catherine's Church in Hamburg and in 1876 was listed as church property "since time immemorial." It is therefore quite possible that it served as a lavabo jug or a jug for Holy Communion.

The Siegburg potters depicting anti-Catholic motifs on stoneware were not motivated solely by the chance of supplying the Calvinist or Protestant market, but also by the local denominational situation (Krueger 1979:293-294). Both the Episcopal city of Cologne and the town of Siegburg nearby saw times of religious tolerance and Counter-Reformational strictness. In Siegburg the Reformation movement had its heyday between 1568 and 1572, but after 1572 the Protestant potters were gradually forced to leave due to religious reprisals.

Figure 3.   (above) "Augsburg Interim," cylindrical tankard (Schnelle), Siegburg stoneware (Krueger 1979:figures 7, 11, 15).
Figure 4.   (below) "Law and Grace," cylindrical tankard (Schnelle), Siegburg stoneware (Krueger 2000:figure 2).

Figure 5.   "Sheepfold of Christ," cylindrical tankard (Schnelle), Siegburg stoneware (Krueger 1979:figure 26).

Figure 6.   "Law and Grace," stove-tile, polychromatic glazed red earthenware (Franz 1981:4).

Figure 7.   "Christ in Limbo," stove-tile, green glazed earthenware (Courtesy of Hansestadt Lüneburg, Stadtarchäologie).

Figure 8.   "Elector John Frederick I," stove-tile, black glazed earthenware. (Courtesy of Hansestadt Lüneburg, Stadtarchäologie).

PROTESTANT IMAGERY CREATED AT A LÜNEBURG POTTER'S WORKSHOP

Lüneburg was a city that had committed itself to the Protestant faith in 1530. Excavations carried out on a plot at "Auf der Altstadt 29" uncovered a potter's workshop that specialized in creating Protestant imagery. Stove-tiles depicting the Apostles' Creed, the Passion, and Protestant rulers constituted the majority of its output in the second half of the 16th century and early 17th century (Ring 2007a). The workshop would have primarily supplied the local market. The high quality of its products, however, may also have afforded the opportunity to market its wares further afield.

The Lüneburg potters also used central Reformation motifs including original sin and salvation (Ring 2007a:figure 3a) as is exemplified by a tile mold bearing the "law and grace" image and a stove-tile with polychrome glazing from Nuremberg with the same motif (Figure 6) (Franz 1981:83-84). Bisque fragments and wasters attest to the production of tiles bearing depictions of the Apostles' Creed by the same workshop. A waster showing Christ's descent into hell and a fragment of an inscription that reads "GESTIEGEN [...] Z HELLE [descended [...] into hell]" was clearly inspired by Albrecht Dürer's *Christ in Limbo* painting from the Great Passion series of 1510/1511 (Figure 7) (Strauss 1966:pl. 42,2).

The "cardinal and fool" motif already known from Siegburg funnel-necked beakers was also used on stove-tiles, as can be seen on a bisque fired example from the Lüneburg workshop (Ring 2007a:figure 2). This popular Reformation polemic was also used on other stove-tiles. All the examples published to date were found in northern Germany (Langenheim 1962; Busch 1987; Arnold et. al 1990:52-53; Rötting 1997:318).

PROTESTANT PRINCES

The range of products made by the potter's workshop at "Auf der Altstadt 29" in Lüneburg also included stove-tiles with portraits of Protestant princes from a defensive alliance called the Schmalkaldic League. Especially depicted were members of the House of Wettin with the older branch of the Ernestines and the younger branch of the Albertines. The series starts with the founder of the Schmalkadic League, the elector John Frederick I (1503-1554) (Figure 8). The portrait refers back to a 1551 painting by Lucas Cranach the Younger (1515-1586) (Christensen 1992:97, figure 31). John Frederick I is also depicted in another example with a short sword and a hat inspired by a medal minted in 1537 (Kat. Gotha 1994:23-24, cat. no. 4.22). The next members of the Ernestine succession were John Frederick II (1529-1595) and John William (1530-1573), whose portraits have survived on stove-tiles and on a mold (Ring 1996a:figures 16, 189). A large proportion of the prints the tiles were modeled on were created by Lucas Cranach the Younger.

The Albertine branch in Saxony is represented by Duke George (1471-1539) (Ring 2007a:figure 8). A painting by Lucas Cranach the Elder (1472-1553) dated 1534 can be identified as the inspiration (Kat. Nürnberg 1983:172-173, cat. no. 211). It is surprising that Duke George of Saxony is part of this series of portrait tiles, since he remained steadfastly opposed to religious changes up to the time of his death. His inclusion in this series would have been based not only on his family ties but also on his support for a disputation between Martin Luther (1483-1546) and Johann Eck (1494-1554), the Franconian reformer. The theological debate, known as the Leipzig Disputation, took place in 1519. Duke George himself sought for church reform to stop the prevalent commercialization and corruption. But he became Martin Luther's adversary due to Luther's commitment to Jan Hus.

Stove-tiles with portraits of the Princes of the Schmalkaldic League, the Protestant defensive alliance against the religious politics of Emperor Charles V, were extremely numerous and widespread. They have been found throughout the entire Baltic region, northern Germany, Hesse, and Thuringia (Stephan 1997; Hallenkamp-Lumpe 2006:238-240; Majanti 2007a:94-95, 2007b; Ose 2009:223-224). The most striking examples in respect to quality and heritage are the tiled stoves in Wilhelmsburg Castle in Schmalkalden, Thuringia.

A Stockholm stove-tile highlights the close connection between one of the Protestant sovereigns and Martin Luther (Majanti 2007c:214, cat. no. 179). Frederick the Wise, Elector of Saxony, and Martin Luther are depicted kneeling under Christ's Cross. A parallel find is known from Janovice Castle in the Czech Republic (Figure 9) (Menoušková 2008:81, no. 237). A similar depiction showing John Frederick the Magnanimous and Martin Luther can be seen in a woodcut by Lucas Cranach on the frontispiece of the 1547 bible print (Stievermann 1994:75, A 41).

REFORMERS

The Lüneburg potters also made ceramic objects bearing the portraits of reformers. One of the tile molds shows Martin Luther wearing the robes of a scholar (Figure 10). This motif could have been inspired by a copper engraving by Heinrich Aldegrever (1502-1555/1561) dating from 1540 (Wex 1996:22-24, cat. no. 13). Another reformer, Philipp Melanchthon (1497-1560), is portrayed on a ceramic relief (Figure 11) (Ring 2004). This relief, together with another depicting the elector John Frederick of Saxony and a portrait of Martin Luther, now lost, can be identified as the work of the Lüneburg artist Albert von Soest. An accomplished carver, he was best known for the wood reliefs he created for the great hall of the Lüneburg City Hall in the 1570s and 1580s, which measured approximately 49 × 35 cm. These were impressed in clay, which was then fired in the potter's workshop. Using these fired clay molds Albert von Soest produced a series of papier mâché reliefs. It remains uncertain whether the known ceramic reliefs had also been part of a series.

Figure 9.   "Elector Frederick the Wise and Martin Luther Kneeling under Christ's Cross," stove-tile (Menoušková 2008:81, no. 237).

Portraits of Luther on stove-tiles were very widespread. In the region of the Baltic Sea, examples are known from areas including Latvia (Figure 12), Estonia, Finland, and Mecklenburg-Western Pomerania, and further south from Lower Saxony and Hesse (Kollmann 2004:159; Hallenkamp-Lumpe 2006:pl. 173,1; Ose 2007:124; Hoffmann 2009:313-314). Stove-tiles bearing the portrait of the bohemian reformer Jan Hus (1369-1415) had a similar distribution area, but have been found in smaller numbers than the Luther tiles (Bencard and Kristiansen 2006:46-47; Hoffmann 2008:206). A stove-tile from Lüneburg shows the portrait of Johannes Hus in profile (Figure 13), which was widely known from medals minted around 1530 (Kat. Berlin 1983:380, F 17.1).

Another Lüneburg potter's workshop on Johann-Sebastian-Bach-Platz 2 yielded a pottery fragment of red, green-glazed earthenware with a male portrait in bas-relief (Figure 14) (Ring 2007b). This relief was

undoubtedly created with the aid of a mold. The distinct forehead and hair line allow us to positively identify the person as Philipp Melanchthon. It is a portrait *en face*. No print has yet been identified that could have inspired the depiction. While the ceramic fragment was made in a mold like a stove-tile, the size of the portrait itself suggests that it was not a fragment of a stove-tile. It was more likely a private memorial portrait that, produced in series, expressed reverence toward the scholar who had played an important part in the religious life of the town of Lüneburg, particularly in the years following the beginning of the Reformation in 1530.

Figure 10. (left) "Martin Luther," tile mold, red earthenware (Courtesy of Hansestadt Lüneburg, Stadtarchäologie).

Figure 11. (middle) "Philipp Melanchthon," ceramic relief, red earthenware (Courtesy of Hansestadt Lüneburg, Museum Lüneburg).

Figure 12. (right) "Martin Luther," stove-tile (Ose 2007:figure 3).

LAW AND GRACE

The central motif of the Reformation, original sin and salvation, or "law and grace," could only be depicted on narrow tile faces in a compressed form. Christ on the Cross is at the center of the image. Moses with the Tablets of the Law, the devil, and death are shown beneath the cross on the right, while John the Baptist can be seen on the left with a naked man kneeling in front of him (Franz 1981:color plate 4; Peine 2001:47; Kristiansen 2002:273; Ring 2007a:241-242). Another version also shows Christ on the Cross at the center, with the Sacrifice of Isaac on the left and the Brazen Serpent on the Cross on the right (Figure 15) (Stephan 1992:79; Hallenkamp-Lumpe 2006:165). Although Martin Luther considered the "law and grace" motif to be very important, relatively few stove-tiles decorated with this motif have been found to date.

THE TILED STOVE–A MEDIUM OF CONFESSIONALIZATION

The tiled stoves in burghers' houses were installed in rooms that were used for purposes of representation or business. Here, the stove served not just as a heater, but also as a medium to express one's world-views and religious beliefs (Ring 1996a:72). Tiled stoves bearing the motifs described above are often given the name "Reformation stove," a prime example of which was the tiled stove from Grafenegg Castle near Krems in Austria. It had originally stood in the town hall of Weißenkirchen on the Danube and was destroyed in 1945 (Strauss 1966; Hellenkamp-Lumpe 2007:324-325). Its imagery was composed of biblical scenes without inscriptions or with catechism quotes, portrait tiles of Saxon electors, polemic motifs, and references to the "law and grace" subject.

Stove-tiles with Reformation imagery have been found in large numbers in archaeological investigations and are known from vast areas of northern and central Europe, and from the Baltic to Transylvania (Stephan 2008:73).

Figure 13. (left) "Johannes Hus," stove-tile, green glazed earthenware (Courtesy of Hansestadt Lüneburg, Museum Lüneburg).

Figure 14. (right) "Philipp Melanchthon,"ceramic relief, green glazed earthenware (Courtesy of Hansestadt Lüneburg, Stadtarchäologie).

They played a central role in Protestant households as a medium of confessionalization. Archaeological assemblages that allow us to reconstruct a Reformation stove, however, are more rarely found. While the study of the Lüneburg potter's workshop at "Auf der Altstadt 29" revealed that the components for Reformation stoves had been produced on site, we have not yet been able to reconstruct such a stove from any particular household in the town.

The finds recovered from a burnt layer with stove-tiles in the Danish town of Ribe have allowed researchers there to reconstruct five tiled stoves (Bencard and Kristiansen 2006). Only two of them could actually be identified as Reformation stoves, however. Stove 3 had polychrome tiles bearing the motifs of *patientia*, "Joseph's dream" and "Joseph cast into the well" from the story of Joseph, Geometria, Atalanta, and a portrait of the reformer Jan Hus (Bencard and Kristiansen 2006:45-50). Another tiled stove showed scenes from the Passion of Christ as well as a number of parables, for example the subject of "the sheepfold of Christ," which is also known from a Siegburg jug. The stove also had one tile bearing the inscription "ANNO Lii," or "1552" (Bencard and Kristiansen 2006:50-62). The burnt layer can probably be associated with a conflagration that raged through the town in 1580. The reconstructed Reformation stoves stood in the house of a wealthy citizen, a merchant called Niels Thamsen.

Another Reformation stove can probably be reconstructed from tiles found in Lynge on the Island of Zealand in Denmark (Kristiansen 2002:270-273). While only three tiles have survived, two of them fit into this context, depicting "law and grace" based on the famous Cranach depiction and a portrait of Sibylle von

Figure 15.   *"Law and Grace," stove-tile, green glazed yellow earthenware (Stephan 1992:79, figure 111).*

Jülich-Kleve-Berg (1512-1554), the wife of the elector John Frederick I of Saxony, who is seen as the leader of the Schmalkaldic League.

WALL FOUNTAINS AND TABLEWARE

Similar to stove-tiles, glazed wall fountains were also adorned with decorations inspired by printed motifs. These box-shaped ceramic water containers were permanently built into wardrobes or alcoves. The central theme on a wall fountain from Görlitz is the "law and grace" motif with Christ on the Cross (Figure 16) (König 2008:103-104). The sacrifice of Isaac is shown on the left, the Brazen Serpent on the Cross can be seen on the right. A wall fountain from Luther's house in Wittenberg shows a crucifixion motif with John the Baptist and a naked person. This scene is reminiscent of the "law and grace" painting by Lucas Cranach the Elder, reduced here to the concept of "grace" (König 2008:101).

Besides the high-class tableware produced in Siegburg in the Rhineland mentioned at the outset, another type of tableware was manufactured in the Saxon town of Waldenburg. Stoneware production in Waldenburg was probably initiated by potters that had migrated there from the Rhineland. So-called beehive steins made of Waldenburg stoneware with applied relief decorations were excavated in Merseburg (Figure 17) and in Göttingen (Jarecki 2004). The central motif shows the

Figure 16. *"Law and Grace," wall fountain, green and yellow glazed earthenware (König 2008:figure 5).*

or "pole glass") from the Catholic Herford Abbey bears only a depiction of the Brazen Serpent. The glass, which was found in a cesspit, was probably used by the abbess of the aristocratic Imperial Abbey of Herford, which was very loyal to the Pope (Grewe and Wemhoff 1995; Gai 2006:60).

The example of the Brazen Serpent and the Crucified Christ shows the problems associated with identifying the creed behind Christian motifs on archaeological finds. In the case of Lüneburg, the combination of the Brazen Serpent and Christ on the Cross after the widespread acceptance of the Reformation in 1530 became a sign of commitment to the new creed in Luther's sense. The depiction was quite well known in Lüneburg, as is shown by a 1656 inventory of the Töbings, a Lüneburg patrician family, which lists an "emblem of the old and new testaments painted on wood by Lucas Kranach, but very old and brittle" (Ring 2007a:242). Owning a glass bearing such motifs in Paderborn would have been a more powerful expression of one's convictions during the process of confessionalization because, although the town was predominantly Protestant from 1525 onwards, Catholic resistance continuously flared up and a Counter-Reformation took place from 1580 onwards, which ultimately ended in the town losing its independence to the Catholic prince-bishop. In the Catholic Abbey of Herford, on the other hand, the depiction of the Brazen Serpent must be viewed as a symbol of salvation and as a typological precursor to the Christ on the Cross motif.

fall of Adam and Eve, flanked by two *en face* full figure images, undoubtedly depicting Martin Luther and Philipp Melanchthon.

Glass tableware with Reformational imagery is extremely rare. A goblet excavated in Lüneburg had been made in southern Germany or Bohemia in the second half of the 16th century (Figure 18) (Steppuhn 2003). It bears a motif from John 3:14-16, a passage from the bible that was important to the Lutheran creed, which spoke about the comparison between the Crucified Christ and the Brazen Serpent (which appears in the Book of Numbers 21:4-9). The serpent suspended from the cross as a means of survival on earth (as described in the Old Testament) is given a Christian meaning by referring to the mercy of eternal life that lies in the belief in the crucifixion of Christ. The translucence of the glass brings the two motifs closer together. The translucence of the glass brings the two motifs closer together. A footed beaker found in Paderborn also bears the same two motifs (Kruse 2002; Gai 2006:60-61). A so-called *stangenglas* (a tall, narrow, cylindrical drinking vessel,

Reformational images on vessels among the body of archaeological finds are still quite rare. They were predominantly high-quality objects that were not used in everyday life. The research on the production of ceramic vessels with explicitly Reformational imagery by Saxon potters' workshops is still in the early stages (Jarecki 2004). The central focal point of the process of confessionalization was the tiled stove, which in the Middle Ages was being used from the Netherlands to the State of the Teutonic Order and from the Duchy of Burgundy to Hungary and became a prestigious object of representation in the 16th century (Baeriswyl 2006:514-522). The Reformation stove with image tiles depicting Protestant polemics attacking the Catholic church, portraits of Reformers and Protestant princes, and the "law and grace" motif began to replace medieval devotional images and became an object of instruction (Ring 1998). It was an expression of a private religious practice, while at the same time attesting to the confessionalization of

Figure 17.   *"Martin Luther, Philipp Melanchton and the Fall of Man," stoneware, Waldenburg (Jarecki 2004:figure 2).*

the bourgeoisie. The demand for tiled stoves in bourgeois households was met by potters who specialized in the production of stove-tiles with the appropriate imagery as is exemplified by the finds recovered from a potter's workshop in Lüneburg (Ring 1996a). By extension, a potter's workshop in Flensburg may also be mentioned, which worked closely with the Flensburg bell founder Michel Dibler, who cast baptismal fonts for St. Nicholas' Church in Eckernförde in 1588 and for St. Mary's Church in Flensburg in 1591, both of which bear all-round relief depictions with scenes from the Passion of Christ (Kristiansen 2007; Ring 2007c:169).

THE PROCESS OF CONFESSIONALIZATION

The final question is whether archaeological finds can actually outline the spread of the Reformation in a differentiated chronological sequence of events (Scholkmann 2007:7). Under critical scrutiny it becomes evident that the imagery on archaeological finds does not reveal a chronological sequence of the Reformation in one particular place or region, due to a lack of precision in the dating of the objects. The prints that inspired the objects bearing biblical and religious motifs were largely created prior to the mid 16th century, while those that inspired the portraits date from the second half of the 16th century and from around 1600. This, however, only provides a *terminus post quem*.

May we in fact assume that Protestant households also had memorial portraits and images of better understanding, as Martin Luther mentioned? In order to identify such images and trace the process of the Reformation from the very first proclamation of the new doctrine to its visualization in churches, public houses, and particularly in private rooms, we must be able to study household inventories and catalogs of estates listing mainly furniture and movables, furnishings kept in museums, and archaeological finds. This can be demonstrated with some examples from Lüneburg. The information, however, only refers to the patrician social stratum. The inventory of the estate of the Patrician Margarete Grönhagen, compiled after her death in 1544, lists tiled stoves for both the study and the parlor (Terlau-Friemann 1991:86-89) with imagery that can be reconstructed thanks to the archaeological finds recovered on site. Another inventory, however, dating from 1656, provides yet further information about the furnishings of the parlor (Kühlborn 1999). This list mentions several paintings, including "a small round picture of the elector of Saxony." Perhaps this was also the original location of the "emblem of the old and new testaments" by Lucas Cranach? The inventories also list papier mâché pictures. We may assume that these were paper reliefs from the workshop of Albert von Soest, perhaps with portraits of reformers (Ring 1996b). The parlor was not, however, the actual living room of the family, but a room for the purpose of prestige where the head of the family could withdraw to tend to his business affairs (Terlau-Friemann 1991:88-89). The actual private room of the family was located on the ground floor of the wing behind the main building, which was heated by a fireplace. A small marriage casket dating from around 1565 that belonged to Johann Borcholt,

Professor of Law in Rostock and Helmstedt, and his wife Anna von Dassel, may have been kept in such a room (Figure 19). The lid bears prints showing the Crucifixion of Christ, the Brazen Serpent, Abraham's Sacrifice, and portraits of Luther and of the elector John Frederick of Saxony (Michael 1991:65 E 13.1).

The introduction of Protestant themes in private homes was a gradual process, often linked to a marriage or the construction of a house, which were occasions for acquiring chests or wall hangings, or having tiled stoves constructed.

Protestant images entered the private spheres of patrician households at an early stage in northern Europe,

Figure 18.   "Law and Grace," goblet with enamel ornamental painting (Steppuhn 2003).

Figure 19.   *Box depicting "Johann Friedrich I, Law and Grace, Martin Luther," wood, leather, and paper (Courtesy of Hansestadt Lüneburg, Museum Lüneburg).*

from around 1550 to 1580. The signs of a confession-alization in items of everyday use, which are mainly studied by archaeologists, would surely have developed in parallel. This process can be traced particularly well in stove-tiles and in high-quality drinking vessels and tableware.

REFERENCES

ARNOLD, VOLKER, THOMAS WESTPHAL, AND PAUL ZUBEK

1990   *Kachelöfen in Schleswig-Holstein. Irdenware—Gusseisen—Fayence* [*Tiled Stoves in Schleswig-Holstein. Earthenware—Cast Iron—Faience.*] Westholsteinische Verlangsanstalt Boysen & Co., Heide, Germany.

BAERISWYL, ARMAND

2006   Innovation und Mobilität im Spiegel der materialen Kultur: archäologische Funde und historische Fragestellung; ein Versuch [Innovation and Mobility Mirrored in Material Culture: Archaeological Finds and Historical Research Questions: An Attempt]. In *Europa im späten Mittelalter: Politik—Gesellschaft—Kultur*, Rainer C. Schwinges, editor, pp. 511-537. Historische Zeitschrift Beiheft Neue Folge No. 40. Oldenbourg, Munich, Germany.

BARNARD, FRANCIS PIERREPONT

1927   *Satirical and Controversial Medals of the Reformation. The Biceps or Double-Headed Series.* Oxford University Press, Oxford, England.

BENCARD, MOGENS, AND OLE KRISTIANSEN

2006   Niels Thamsens lutherfromme kakkelovne—et sluttet fund af monokrome og polykrome reformations-kakler i Ribe [Niels Thamsen's Luther-Pious Tiled Stove—A Find Complex of Monochrome and Polychrome Stove Tiles from the Reformation Period Found at Ribe]. *By, marsk og geest* 18:35-74.

BUSCH, RALF

1987   Narr und Kardinal [Fool and Cardinal]. *Braunschweigisches Landesmuseum. Informationen und Berichte* 2:18-19.

CHRISTENSEN, CARL C.

1992   *Princes and Propaganda: Electoral Saxon Art of the Reformation*. Sixteenth Century Essays & Studies No. XX. Kirkeville, MI.

FRANZ, ROSEMARIE

1981   *Der Kachelofen. Entstehung und kunstgeschichtliche Entwicklung vom Mittelalter bis zum Ausgang des Klassizismus* [*The Tiled Stove. Its Beginnings and Art-Historical Development from the Middle Ages to the Latter Stages of Classicism*]. Akademische Druck – und Verlagsanstalt, Graz, Austria.

GAI, SVEA

2006   Eine gemauerte Kloake am Schildern 1-7. Ein Blick auf den gläsernen Hausrat des 15. bis 17. Jahrhunderts [A Masonry Cesspit at Schildern 1-7. An Insight into 15th to 17th Century Household Glass]. In *Scherben der Vergangenheit. Neue Ergebnisse der Stadtarchäologie in Paderborn*, Sven Spiong and Matthias Wemhoff, editors, pp. 51-72. MittelalterStudien No. 8. Wilhelm Fink Verlag, Munich, Germany.

GAIMSTER, DAVID

1997   *German Stoneware 1200-1900. Archaeology and Cultural History*. British Museum Press, London, England.

GREWE, HOLGER, AND MATTHIAS WEMHOFF

1995   Die "Frau von Herford" und ihr Hausrat [The "Lady of Herford" and Her Household Effects]. In *Ein Land macht Geschichte*, Hein Günter Horn, editor, pp. 316-320. Verlag Philipp von Zabern, Mainz, Germany.

HALLENKAMP-LUMPE, JULIA

2006   *Studien zur Ofenkeramik des 12. bis 17. Jahrhunderts anhand von Bodenfunden aus Westfalen-Lippe* [*Studies on 12th to 17th Century Stove Ceramics Based on Archaeological Finds from Westphalia-Lippe*]. Denkmalpflege und Forschungen in Westfalen, No. 42. Philipp von Zabern, Mainz, Germany.

2007   Das Bekenntnis am Kachelofen? Überlegungen zu den sogenannten "Reformationskacheln" [The Confession of One's Faith via the Tiled Stove? Thoughts on the So-Called "Reformation Tiles"]. In *Archäologie der Reformation. Studien zu den Auswirkungen des Konfessionswechsels in der materiellen Kultur*, Carola Jäggi and Jörn Staecker, editors, pp. 239-258. Arbeiten zur Kirchengeschichte 104. Walter de Gruyter, Berlin, Germany.

HOFFMANN, CLAUDIA

2008   Lutherzeitliche Ofenkacheln aus dem Bestand des Kulturhistorischen Museums der Hansestadt Stralsund [Luther Period Stove-Tiles from the Collections of the Kulturhistorisches Museum der Hansestadt Stralsund]. In *Luthers Lebenswelten*, Harald Meller, Stefan Rhein, and Hans-Georg Stephan, editors, pp. 201-208. Tagungen des Landesmuseums für Vorgeschichte Halle, No. 1. Halle (Saale), Germany.

2009   Überlegungen zu Porträtdarstellungen auf Ofenkacheln des Spätmittelalters und der frühen Neuzeit aus Stralsund [Reflections on Stove-Tiles with Portraits from the Late Middle Ages and the Early Modern Period from Stralsund]. In *Zwischen Tradition und Wandel. Archäologie des 15. und 16. Jahrhunderts*, Barbara Scholkmann, Sören Frommer, Christina Vossler, and Markus Wolf, editors, pp. 305-315. Tübinger Forschungen zur historischen Archäologie, No. 3. Dr. Faustus, Tübingen, Germany.

JARECKI, HELGE

2004   In Szene gesetzt. Der Sündenfall auf renaissancezeitlicher Keramik [Staged. Original Sin on Renaissance Pottery]. *Zeitschrift für Archäologie des Mittelalters* 32:189-195.

KAT. BERLIN

1983   *Kunst der Reformationszeit* [*Art of the Reformation Period*]. Staatliche Museen zu Berlin, Capital City of the GDR, Exhibition in the Altes Museum from 16th August to 13th November 1983. Henschelverlag, Berlin, Germany.

KAT. BONN

2010   *Renaissance am Rhein* [*Renaissance on the Rhine*]. Exhibition in the LVR-Landesmuseum Bonn, 16th September 2010 to 6th February 2011. Cantz, Ostfildern, Germany.

KAT. GOTHA

1994   *Gotteswort und Menschenbild. Werke von Cranach und seinen Zeitgenossen* [*God's Word and the Conception of Man. Works by Cranach and His Contemporaries*]. Museen der Stadt Gotha. Schlossmuseum, Gotha, Germany.

KAT. NÜRNBERG

1983   *Martin Luther und die Reformation in Deutschland* [*Martin Luther and the Reformation in Germany*]. An Exhibition in Celebration of Luther's 500th Birthday. Insel-Verlag, Frankfurt, Germany.

KOLLMANN, KARL

2004   Ausgrabungen in der Wasserburg Aue im Jahr 2004 [Excavations in the Moated Castle of Aue in 2004]. *Hessen Archäologie* 2004:158-160.

KÖNIG, SONJA

2008   Wandbrunnen—Wandblasen—Wasserkästen [Wall Fountains—Wall Blisters—Water Boxes]. In *Luthers Lebenswelten*, Harald Meller, Stefan Rhein, and Hans-Georg Stephan, editors, pp. 101-111. Tagungen des Landesmuseums für Vorgeschichte Halle, No. 1. Halle (Saale), Germany.

KRISTIANSEN, OLE

2002   Danske kakkelovne og deres billedprogrammer i 1. halvdel af 1500-tallet [Danish Tiled Stoves and Their Iconographic Program in the First Part of the 16th Century]. In *Bolig og familie i Danmarks middelalder*, Else Roesdahl, editor, pp. 259-282. Jutland Archaeological Society publications, No. 33. Aarhus, Denmark.

2007   Ofenkachelmatrizen [Stove-Tile Matrixes]. In *Archäologie in Flensburg. Ausgrabungen am Franziskanerkloster*, Frauke Witte, editor, pp. 158-210. Gesellschaft für Flensburger Stadtgeschichte e. V. Schriftenreihe No. 57. Flensburg, Germany.

KRUEGER, INGEBORG

1979   Reformationszeitliche Bildpolemik auf rheinischem Steinzeug [Reformation Period Pictorial Polemics on Rhenish Stoneware]. *Bonner Jahrbücher* 179:259-295.

2000   Protestantisches Glaubensbekenntnis auch auf Steinzeug [Confessions of the Protestant Faith on Stoneware]. In *Lost and Found. Essays on Medieval Archaeology for H.J.E. van Beuningen*, D. Kicken, A.M. Koldeweij, and J.R. ter Molen, editors, pp. 247-256. Rotterdam Papers, No. 11. Rotterdam, the Netherlands.

KRUSE, PERNILLE

2002   Vom "Heil der Welt" [On the "Salvation of the World"]. *Archäologie in Deutschland* 2002:50.

KÜHLBORN, MARC

1999   Ein Papageu im blechern Bauer. Haushaltsinventare des 17. und 18. Jahrhunderts und ihre Aussagekraft zu Hausrat und Hausstruktur [Seventeenth – and Eighteenth-Century Household Inventories and the Information they Contain about Household Effects and Structure]. *Archäologie und Bauforschung in Lüneburg* 4:73-108.

LANGENHEIM, KURT

1962   Verzierte Ofenkacheln [Decorated Stove-Tiles]. *Lauenburgische Heimat Neue Folge* 38:58-61.

LUTHER, WA

1883–
2000   *D. Martin Luthers Werke, Kritische Gesamtausgabe* [*The Works of D. Martin Luther, Complete Critical Edition*]. Böhlau, Weimar, Germany.

MAJANTI, KIRSI

2007a   Ceramic Stove Tiles and the Start of Local Production in Turku. In *Pots and Princes. Ceramic Vessels and Stove Tiles from 1400–1700*, Kirsi Majanti, editor, pp. 93-96. Archaeologia Medii Aevi Finlandiae, No. XII. Turku, Finland.

2007b   Fashion-Consciousness or Support for Lutheran Faith? Portraits of Lutheran Princes on Finnish Stove-Tiles. In *Archäologie der Reformation, Studien zu den Auswirkungen des Konfessionswechsels in der materiellen Kultur*, Carola Jäggi and Jörn Staecker, editors, pp. 398-425. Arbeiten zur Kirchengeschichte 104. Walter de Gruyter, Berlin, Germany.

MAJANTI, KIRSI (EDITOR)

2007c   *Pots and Princes. Ceramic Vessels and Stove Tiles from 1400–1700*, Archaeologia Medii Aevi Finlandiae, No. XII. Turku, Finland.

MENOUŠKOVÁ, DANA (EDITOR)

2008   *Krása, která hřeje—výběrový katalog; gotických a renesančnich kachlů Moravy a Slezska* [*Beauty, which Warms—Selective Catalog: Gothic and Renaissance Dutch Stove Tiles of Moravia and Silesia*]. Slovácké Muzeum, Uherské Hradiště, Czech Republic.

MICHAEL, ECKHARD

1991   *Führer durch die Sammlungen* [*Guide to the Collections*]. Museum für das Fürstentum Lüneburg, Lüneburg, Germany.

OSE, IEVA

2007   Ceramic Tile Stoves in Latvia in the 16th and 17th Century. In *Pots and Princes. Ceramic Vessels and Stove Tiles from 1400–1700*, Kirsi Majanti, editor, pp. 127-130. Archaeologia Medii Aevi Finlandiae, No. XII. Turku, Finland.

2009   Rigaer Ofenkacheln des 16. Jahrhunderts und ihre Vorlagen [Sixteenth-Century Riga Stove-Tiles and Their Models]. In *The Hansa Town Riga as Mediator between East and West*, Andris Caune and Ieva Ose, editors, pp. 222-231. Riga, Latvia.

PEINE, HANS-WERNER

2001   Von qualmenden Herdfeuern und Wandkaminen zu rauchfreien Räumlichkeiten mittels Warmluftheizungen und Kachelöfen. Ein Beitrag zur Ofenkeramik des 12. bis 17. Jahrhunderts in Westfalen [From Smouldering Hearths and Fireplaces to Smoke-Free Rooms Thanks to Warm Air Heating Systems and Tiled Stoves. A Contribution on 12th – to 17th-Century Stove Ceramics in Westphalia]. In *Von der Feuerstelle zum Kachelofen. Heizanlagen und Ofenkeramik vom Mittelalter bis zur Neuzeit*, Manfred Schneider, editor, pp. 43-63. Stralsunder Beiträge zur Archäologie, Geschichte, Kunst und Volkskunde in Vorpommern, No. III. Stralsund, Germany.

RING, EDGAR

1996a   Eine Bilderwelt für die Stube. Die Produktion von Ofenkacheln [Imagery for the Parlor. The Production of Stove-Tiles]. In *Ton Steine Scherben. Ausgegraben und erforscht in der Lüneburger Altstadt*, Frank Andraschko, Hilke Lamschus, Christian Lamschus, and Edgar Ring, editors, pp. 71 – 91. De Sulte, No. 6. Deutsches Salzmuseum, Lüneburg, Germany.

1996b   "Zu trucken mit papir." Albert von Soest und die Herstellung von Papierreliefs ["To Print with Paper." Albert von Soest and the Creation of Paper Reliefs]. In *Ton Steine Scherben. Ausgegraben und erforscht in der Lüneburger Altstadt*, Frank Andraschko, Hilke Lamschus, Christian Lamschus, and Edgar Ring, editors, pp. 107-111. De Sulte No. 6. Deutsches Salzmuseum, Lüneburg, Germany.

1998   "Merkbilder"—Protestantische Themen auf Ofenkacheln ["Pictorial Memoranda"—Protestant Themes on Stove-Tiles]. In *Ton—in Form gebracht*, Kathrin Panne, editor, pp. 83-86. Bomann-Museum et al., Celle, Germany.

2004   Das Bild als Gegenstand renaissancezeitlicher Wohnkultur. Produktion von Kunst in Serie des Lüneburger Künstlers Albert von Soest [The Picture as Object of Renaissance Residential Culture. The Creation of Art in Series by the Lüneburg Artist Albert von Soest]. *Die Kunde* 55:33-44.

2007a   Die Reformation in Lüneburg im Spiegel archäologischer Funde [The Reformation in Lüneburg Reflected in the Archaeological Finds]. In *Archäologie der Reformation, Studien zu den Auswirkungen des Konfessionswechsels in der materiellen Kultur*, Carola Jäggi and Jörn Staecker, editors, pp. 239-258. Arbeiten zur Kirchengeschichte 104. Walter de Gruyter, Berlin, Germany.

2007b   Philipp Melanchthon—in Ton [Philipp Melanchthon—In Clay]. *Denkmalpflege in Lüneburg* 2007:25-30.

2007c   Ton, Bronze, Papier und Holz. Kooperation von Künstlern und Handwerkern in Lüneburg im 16. Jahrhundert [Clay, Bronze, Paper, and Wood. Cooperation of Artists and Craftsmen in 16th-Century Lüneburg]. In *Keramik auf Sonderwegen*. 37. Internationales Hafnerei-Symposion Herne 19. bis 25. September 2004, pp. 163-171. Denkmalpflege und Forschung in Westfalen No. 44. Verlag Philipp von Zabern, Mainz, Germany.

RÖTTING, HARTMUT

1997   *Stadtarchäologie in Braunschweig. Ein fachübergreifender Arbeitsbericht zu den Grabungen 1976–1992 [Urban Archaeology in Braunschweig. A Multi-Disciplinary Work Report on the Excavations Carried out from 1976 to 1992]*. Forschungen der Denkmalpflege in Niedersachsen 3. CW Niemeyer, Hameln, Germany.

SCHOLKMANN, BARBARA

2007   Forschungsfragestellungen, Möglichkeiten und Grenzen einer Archäologie der Reformation in Mitteleuropa [Research Questions, Possibilities and Limitations of Archaeological Studies on the Reformation in Central Europe]. In *Archäologie der Reformation, Studien zu den Auswirkungen des Konfessionswechsels in der materiellen Kultur*, Carola Jäggi and Jörn Staecker, editors, pp. 3-25. Arbeiten zur Kirchengeschichte 104. Walter de Gruyter, Berlin, Germany.

STEPHAN, HANS-GEORG

1992   *Keramik der Renaissance im Oberweserraum und an der Unteren Werra [Renaissance Pottery in the Upper Weser Area and on the Lower Werra]*. Zeitschrift für Archäologie des Mittelalters, Beiheft 7. Rheinland-Verlag, Cologne, Germany.

1997   Die Renaissanceöfen im landgräflich hessischen Schloß Wilhelmsburg in Schmalkalden/Thüringen [The Renaissance Stoves in the Landgraviate of Hesse Castle of Wilhelmsburg in Schmalkalden/Thuringia]. *Zeitschrift des Vereins für Hessische Geschichte und Landeskunde* 102:25-88.

2008   Luther-Archäologie: Funde und Befunde aus Mansfeld und Wittenberg. Gedanken und Materialien zur Erforschung der Lebenswelt des Reformators und zur Alltagskultur Mitteldeutschlands im 16. Jh. [Lutheran Archaeology: Finds and Features from Mansfeld and Wittenberg. Reflections and Materials on the Research into the World of the Reformer and on Everyday Culture in 16th-Century Central Germany]. In *Luthers Lebenswelten*, Harald Meller, Stefan Rhein, and Hans-Georg Stephan, editors, pp. 13-77. Tagungen des Landesmuseums für Vorgeschichte Halle, No. 1. Halle (Saale), Germany.

STEPPUHN, PETER

2003   Kat. Nr. 3.032 Kelchglas mit Christus-Darstellung [Glass Goblet with the Depiction of Christ]. In *Glaskultur in Niedersachsen. Tafelgeschirr und Haushaltsglas vom Mittelalter bis zur frühen Neuzeit*, Edgar Ring, editor, pp. 132-133. Archäologie und Bauforschung in Lüneburg No. 5. Husum Verlag, Husum, Germany.

STIEVERMANN, DIETER

1994   Lucas Cranach und der kursächsische Hof [Lucas
        Cranach and the Court of the Elector of Saxony].
        In *Lucas Cranach. Ein Maler-Unternehmer aus
        Franken*, Claus Grimm, Johannes Erichsen, and
        Evamaria Brockhoff, editors, pp. 66-77. Friedrich
        Pustet, Regensburg, Germany.

STRAUSS, KONRAD

1966   *Die Kachelkunst des 15. und 16. Jahrhunderts in
        Deutschland, Österreich und der Schweiz [The
        Art of Tile Making in Germany, Austria and
        Switzerland in the 15th and 16th Centuries]*. Ed.
        Heitz, Strasbourg, Austria.

TERLAU-FRIEMANN, KAROLINE

1991   Lüneburger Wohnkultur des 16. Jahrhunderts
        [Sixteenth-Century Lüneburg Domestic Culture].
        In *Raumkunst in Niedersachsen. Die Farbigkeit
        historischer Innenräume. Kunstgeschichte
        und Wohnkultur*, Rolf-Jürgen Grote and
        Peter Königfeld, editors, pp. 81-97. Deutscher
        Kunstverlag, Munich, Germany.

WEIMER, CHRISTOPH

1999   *Luther, Cranach und die Bilder. Gesetz und
        Evangelium—Schlüssel zum reformatorischen
        Bildgebrauch [Luther, Cranach and the Images.
        Law and the Gospel—Keys to the Reformational
        Utilization of Images]*. Arbeiten zur Theologie No.
        89. Calwer-Verlag, Stuttgart, Germany.

WEX, REINHOLD

1996   *Luthers und anderer Konterfei [Likenesses of
        Luther and Others]*. Herzog Anton Ulrich-
        Museum, Braunschweig, Germany.

Edgar Ring
Museumsstiftung Lüneburg
Stadtarchäologie
Wandrahmstr. 10
D-21335 Lüneburg
Germany

IBOLYA GERELYES

Ottoman Mosques and Cemeteries in the Hungarian Territories

ABSTRACT

The study examines the architectural work conducted in Hungarian towns within the Ottoman Empire. It explores three topics. In seven Hungarian towns it examines the issue of camis (Friday mosques) converted from Christian churches but still preserving medieval architectural features and those built entirely by the Ottomans. It surveys the changing numbers and ratios of camis and Christian churches, thus presenting the evolving dual Muslim-Christian aspect in townscapes. It also investigates the camis entirely built by the Ottomans and categorizes them architecturally. Finally, this study summarizes our knowledge concerning Hungary's Ottoman cemeteries.

MOSQUES

The Ottoman-Turks conducted significant building operations in central Hungary during the approximately 150 years of their presence there.[1] Research into this architectural legacy dates back more than a century, and successive generations of researchers have continually added to our knowledge of it (Gerő 1980:11-16, 2003b:17-22). Despite this, there are still unanswered questions in this field, as well as views in the specialist literature that have become established over the decades but that are questionable nevertheless. In relation to Ottoman *camis* (Friday mosques),[2] the research—in its generality and in the case of specific buildings—is still up against such basic questions as how many buildings were actually constructed, who commissioned them and when, their categorization within the cami genre, where exactly they stood, and what became of them subsequently.

Presentation of a realistic picture is vitiated by two basic problems. For a century now, Hungarian researchers have struggled with the task of reconciling data from two distinct provenances: the data from European sources and those from Ottoman sources. The identification of buildings bearing the designation "Turkish mosque" on surveys made by military engineers at the time of the reconquest, and on censuses of plots and houses made in the late 17th and early 18th centuries, began in the years after 1900. Even today Evliya Çelebi's travelog serves as the basis for identifications regarding the names of camis, their location within settlements, and the names of their founders. Those sections of his travelogue that relate to Hungary were published in Hungarian in two parts, in 1904 and in 1908 (Evliya 1904-1908). In the case of buildings maintained by the Ottoman state,

the information supplied by Evliya is augmented by the laconic notes to be found in the Ottoman Treasury records. A partial, selective Hungarian edition of these notes appeared as early as 1890 (Kincstári defterek 1890). When Evliya's descriptions are not entirely unequivocal, however, or when there are no other sources that identify a building's place within a settlement, it is extremely difficult, sometimes almost impossible, to identify a cami mentioned in the Ottoman sources with a building that features on a survey from the late 17th or early 18th century. As a result of this, the specialist literature of the last 100 years contains a mass of guesswork in relation to some camis. This is especially true for the towns of Fehérvár (today's Székesfehérvár) and Eger (Figure 1). As regards Buda, we are in a fortunate position since we have available to us a map made in 1686 by the military engineer Luigi Ferdinando Marsigli that gives names of particular camis and also their exact locations (Veress 1906:146-148).

Lajos Fekete's (1944:72-122) study clarifying the topography of buildings in Buda and Pest drew on the above-mentioned map, but also on broad analysis of Ottoman and European sources. In the early 21st century, nearer our own time, a significant step forward has been the archontological research conducted by Géza Dávid, namely the compilation of lists of names of Ottoman officials active on Hungarian territory and the identification of the locations in which they served. On the basis of the published lists, the identities of the founders of some buildings could be established, and hence the dating of the construction of these buildings (Dávid 2005:259-346). As well as those listed briefly above, many Ottoman and European sources do of

Figure 1. *Map with places mentioned in the text (all in Hungary, unless otherwise noted): (1) Baja; (2) Buda; (3) Eger; (4) Érd; (5) Esztergom: (6) Fehérvár; (7) Gyula; (8) Hatvan; (9) Kanizsa; (10) Lippa, Romania; (11) Mezõkeresztes; (12) Paks; (13) Pécs; (14) Pest; (15) Siklós; (16) Szigetvár; (17) Temesvár, Romania; and (18) Vienna, Austria. (Map provided courtesy of the Department of Prehistory and Medieval Archaeology, University of Vienna, Austria).*

course yield data. This is demonstrated by not only the above-mentioned work by Lajos Fekete, but also the analysis of the camis of Esztergom (Horváth et al. 1979).

Another highly significant problem of edifices of Ottoman origin in Hungary is the very small number that survive, in part or in whole. There is an obvious mismatch regarding the data in the sources and the number of monuments that we see today. This stems primarily from the fact that works of Turkish architecture have—with very few exceptions and for all intents and purposes—disappeared over the last 300 years.

With the ending of the Turkish era in Hungary, over a period of a few decades in the late 17th century and in the first third of the 18th century more than 90 percent of Ottoman architectural works created during the Turkish occupation were knocked down or perished in other ways. With some exaggeration we can say that what survived this period survives still. When we examine depictions from the 1730s and 1740s of Hungarian towns that played important roles in the one-time *vilayets* (provinces) of Buda, Eger, and Kanizsa before their recapture, we see almost no trace of the 150-year-long Ottoman presence.

BEHIND THE FIGURES

The numbers that emerge from the Ottoman sources reveal significant architectural activity on the part of the Turks, and the town surveys drawn up by army engineers at the time of the reconquest indicate likewise. Utilizing the source material on both sides, the latest research puts the number of camis operating on Ottoman-occupied Hungarian territory at 250-300 in all (Sudár 2009:639). The data from the different sources generate statistics that do not fully add up, however. With regard to the various settlements, we know of 186 camis on the basis of all the sources with the exception of Evliya Çelebi's descriptions. During his travels in Hungary between 1660 and 1666, Evliya described 160 camis, giving details and calling them by name. He mentioned 446 places of prayer in all (Sudár 2009:644-647). Even if we leave out the one or sometimes two camis in each castle and palisaded fort (these fortifications taken together numbered approximately 70), according to our present knowledge we can say that there were 93 camis operating in 12 Hungarian towns during the time of the Turkish occupation.

In contrast to this large number, we know of a total of eight camis surviving above ground, either wholly or in part, on the territory of today's Hungary; the memory of two more is preserved by freestanding minarets

(Gerő 1980:38-75). This picture is enriched slightly by excavations that have uncovered the foundations of another two cami buildings (Végh 1998; Gerelyes 2003). The possibility of conducting research in this field is, however, not fully excluded for the archaeologists and art historians of the future. The number of partially surviving buildings known will increase. This is because we are aware that many Christian churches contain some Turkish elements, having been either converted from camis built by the Turks or reconverted for Christian use after serving as camis during the Turkish period. These Turkish elements were incorporated into the buildings during reconstruction work in the 18th century. By way of examples, we may mention the Church of St. Catherine in the Tabán area of Buda, the Church of the Franciscans and the Parish Church of the Inner Town (both in Pest), and the Parish Church of the Water Town in Esztergom (Nagy 1975:221, 226; Horváth et al. 1979:123).

In what follows, we shall address the urban architecture of the Turks and changing townscapes under Ottoman rule by investigating the architectural activity of the Ottomans in seven of the Hungarian towns they occupied.

BUILDINGS CONVERTED FROM CHRISTIAN CHURCHES

Although it has been known in the specialist literature for a century now that some Turkish camis were converted Christian churches, the number of those created in this way has still not been investigated. Below we shall attempt to establish the proportion of such camis in the total stock of cami buildings.

Buda

The various sources mention eight camis on the territory of Buda Castle; Evliya Çelebi calls six such buildings by name. Marsigli's list, made when Christian forces recaptured the castle in 1686, also features six buildings. The Church of the Virgin Mary (today's Matthias Church) was converted into the Great Cami (called the Old Cami in some sources, the Süleyman Cami in others) directly after Buda Castle fell to the Turks in 1541. The Church of St. George was converted into the Orta Cami at the same time. Both were in

use throughout the Turkish occupation. By the time of Buda's recapture in 1686, another two camis established early on were already out of use: the Seray Cami (sometimes known as the Enderun—i.e., Inner—Cami) inside the palace building, converted from the Chapel of St. John the Almsgiver and often mentioned up to 1557; and the Hüsrev Pasha Cami, converted from the Church of St. Nicholas and mentioned as early as 1555. In 1596, to mark the Ottoman victory over a Habsburg-Transylvanian force at the Battle of Mezőkeresztes in that year, the Church of St. Mary Magdalene, hitherto used by the Christian population of the Buda Castle, was converted into the Fethiye Cami. Faced by the siege of 1598, Ahmed Mihalicli, the pasha of Buda, moved up to the palace in Buda Castle from his house in the Lower Town (Water Town) suburb next to the River Danube. It is probably from this time that use of the Franciscan order's Church of St. John as a cami (the Pasha Cami) can be dated. The only cami building in Buda Castle that was purely Turkish in origin was the Murad Pasha

Figure 2. *The Mustafa Pasha (Osman Bey) Cami, Buda. Aquarelle, 1770. Note the ogee arches and the building's general dilapidation (Budapest History Museum, Drawings Collection).*

Cami, built in 1651-1652 and sited in the Yeni Mahalle (Fekete 1944:86-88). The only Buda Castle cami whose origins are uncertain is the so-called Kirba Cami. Since at the time of Buda's recapture the Poor Clares asked that the building be given back to them, it is probable that in this case, too, the cami's origins were medieval.

At the time of Buda's recapture in 1686, a total of nine camis stood in the Lower Town and the Tabán suburb taken together. In the case of these camis, identification of the original buildings is much more difficult. The number of camis given by Marsigli corresponds to the number featured on depictions made at the time the town was won back (Rózsa 2005:32-35). By contrast, the number of camis mentioned by Evliya is smaller, namely a total of four. It is clear that the greater part of the building work undertaken in Buda by the Turks

was done in these two neighborhoods. Eminently important was the urban development work performed there by two *beylerbeys* (provincial governors) of Buda: Toygun Pasha (in office 1553-1556 and 1557-1558) and Sokollu Mustafa Pasha (in office 1566-1578) (Fekete 1944:94; Káldy-Nagy 1972:446-450). As outlined in the introduction, the identification problem with regard to Ottoman camis is well illustrated by the uncertain location of one such edifice founded by Sokollu Mustafa Pasha and thought to have been built by Sinan. On the basis of many considerations, the present author inclines to the view that the building recorded in 1686 as the Osman Bey Cami (it survived up to the 1770s) was in fact a Mustafa Pasha foundation (Figure 2). With regard to the building, we encounter many contradictions in the specialist literature. On the reverse of the picture published here as Figure 2, the following inscription can be read: "Mosquée dessinée à Bude en Hongrie l'an 1770. par F. I. Maître d'apres celle qui y ésistoit alors telle quelle est representée ici" ["Depicted here is a mosque drawn at Buda in Hungary in 1770 by the master F. I., after one still existing in unchanged form"] (Fekete 1944:327-328) (translation by author).

Of the nine places of prayer in the Lower Town and Tabán suburb, the Toygun Pasha Cami in the Lower Town and the Mustafa Pasha Cami in the Tabán suburb were undoubtedly built from Christian churches. The Toygun Pasha Cami was built on the site of an Augustinian cloister and the Mustafa Pasha Cami incorporated medieval elements (Fekete 1944:92, 95).

As regards the remaining seven buildings, we have no data. We can only surmise that the ecclesiastical buildings in the one-time St. Peter suburb, namely the Corpus Christi Chapel and the Carmelite cloister, were used similarly. Construction material from the Parish Church of St. Peter, which was destroyed in 1602, was surely used in the construction of the Çemberci Ağa Cami, which was built in the very same street (Gyürky 1971:229).

According to the data currently available to us, 15 camis were operating in Buda in 1686, of which 6 were certainly Christian churches originally.

Pest

The various sources mention five camis in Pest, the number given by Evliya Çelebi also, although the Turkish traveler does not name the individual buildings. The Great Cami, which was maintained by the Ottoman state, first features in the Treasury records in 1545 (Kincstári defterek 1890:37). Its location in the town we know exactly; indeed, we even have a picture of it, on the basis of which it may be regarded as a Turkish building. The second state-maintained cami (in some sources a prayer-house), the Ulema Pasha Cami, operated in a tower named after it. The Sinan Bey Cami was converted from the medieval Church of St. Peter. After the final recapture of Pest (likewise in 1686), this building was returned to the Franciscan order. The Parish Church of Pest was converted into a cami in the late Ottoman period. We do not know its name. Neither do we know the name of the cami likewise converted from a Christian church that stood on the site occupied by the present-day University Church (Fekete 1944:263; Nagy 1975:221). For the moment, no building can be

identified with the Pest cami established by Sokollu Mustafa Pasha (Káldy-Nagy 1972:446). In the case of Pest, out of the five edifices identifiable as camis, only one was Turkish-built from its foundations upwards.

Esztergom

Six camis feature in the different sources for Esztergom; Evliya mentions three, giving specifics of each. According to Evliya, directly after his capture of the town in 1543, Sultan Süleyman had the western half of St. Adalbert's Cathedral, a part that was still intact after the siege, turned into a cami. This building may, during the occupation period, have been the same as the state-maintained Great Cami in the castle (Kincstári defterek 1890:369-371; Hegyi 2007:739) mentioned by Evliya as the Kizil Elma Cami. The building suffered damage in 1594 during a siege by Christian forces. Nevertheless, 17th-century depictions and sources, as well as a survey made by an army engineer in 1683 (at the time of the town's final recapture by Christian forces), prove beyond doubt that the chapel built onto the south side of the cathedral by Archbishop Tamás Bakócz in the early 16th century functioned as a cami. Evliya's description is not completely clear and treats the two buildings as one. This probably stems from the fact that to begin with it was St. Adalbert's Cathedral that functioned as a cami with the Bakócz Chapel functioning as one only later on (Horváth et al. 1979:105; Evliya 1985: 310-313). A second state-maintained cami was the so-called City Cami (Kincstári defterek 1890:371-372) in the royal quarter of the town. This was converted into a cami from a medieval Franciscan church directly after the Ottoman capture of the town in 1543 (Török történetírók 1896:245).

The origins of the building in Esztergom's Water Town mentioned by Evliya as the Mehkeme Cami are uncertain. We cannot rule out entirely the possibility that it was converted from a medieval church: Evliya's remark that it was "built a long time ago" could indicate this. On the other hand, when the former Turkish cami was converted into the Parish Church of the Water Town in 1683, neither the time of the building's construction nor its original patron saint was known (Horváth et al. 1979:123).

The unusual Öziçeli Hacı İbrahim Cami, founded in 1605 and built with its west wall against the town wall, was clearly a Turkish building from its foundations upwards (Gerő 2009:256). Of the four camis that can be identified then, two were certainly Christian churches to begin with. Another may have been a Christian church while one was definitely a building of Turkish origin.

Eger

The sources mention a total of 11 cami buildings in the castle and town of Eger; for his part, Evliya mentions 9. The identification of camis in Eger is problematic for want of source material and standing buildings. The cami inside the castle was probably identical with St. John's Cathedral or else built using materials taken from it. In the Outer Castle, the Church of St. Peter was the precursor of the cami that stood "on the place of the Sultan's sacred flag." The Fethiye Cami, dedicated to Sultan Mehmed III when the Ottomans captured the town, was certainly a Christian church originally; it can be identified with the medieval Church of St. Michael (Molnár 1961:11). All three camis were maintained by the Ottoman state (Hegyi 2007:1509). Presumably, masonry from the medieval Church of St. Catherine was used for the building of the cami known in the specialist literature as the Kethüda Cami, which belonged together with the minaret that still stands. On the basis of data currently available to us, it is for all intents and purposes impossible to identify the camis listed by Evliya with buildings found when Christian forces recaptured the town. Likewise functioning as camis at the time of the town's recapture from the Ottomans were the medieval Church of the Virgin Mary and the Church of St. Demeter. Establishing the identities of the founders of these two camis has, however, proved impossible. Of the nine camis in Eger mentioned by Evliya, five were certainly converted Christian churches.

Pécs

Eleven cami buildings feature in the different sources for Pécs; seven particular examples are to be found in Evliya Çelebi's descriptions. On the survey made by the army engineer Joseph de Haüy in 1687, there are five buildings each indicated as a "mosqué," as well as another edifice oriented similarly but without this name. Two camis located outside the town walls did not feature on the map, while the cathedral and the Franciscan church were already shown as Christian places of worship.

The Romanesque cathedral standing on the territory of the castle of the bishop was converted into a cami in 1543 following the capture of the town by the Turks. It is later mentioned in the sources as the Süleyman Cami or Sacred Cami. The medieval Franciscan church features

as the Memi Pasha Cami. These two were in time followed by the Gazi Kasim Pasha Cami, constructed before 1566 beyond all doubt. Of the surviving works of Ottoman architecture in Hungary, this is the most monumental and the most significant. Featuring a square ground plan and covered by a dome, this cami was built by Kasim Pasha on the site of the medieval Church of St. Bartholemew, reusing the church's masonry. The Ferhad Cami built in the late 16th century was founded by Ferhad, pasha of Buda (1588-1590). According to archaeological excavations, this was a Turkish building from its foundations upwards, but we cannot be sure that during its construction the nearby church of the Dominican order was not utilized. The hypothesis that this church was indeed used is strengthened by the fact that after the recapture of Pécs in 1687 the Dominican order was given the building (Németh 1903:8). Already by 1620 a building known in the specialist literature as the Cami on Ágoston tér (Augustine Square) certainly stood very near the medieval Church of St. Nicholas or on its site; it was probably built using masonry taken from this church. Lastly, there was the Jakovali Hasan Pasha Cami constructed in the second third of the 17th century as a building that was Turkish from its foundations upwards. This is Hungary's best preserved cami (Sudár 2007:64).

In addition to the above, another three cami buildings can be identified in the sources as well as topographically. According to our present knowledge, none of them had a medieval antecedent and none made any use of medieval church buildings. Accordingly, of the cami buildings in Pécs, two were converted from Christian churches and three were made using materials from such churches.

Fehérvár

The various sources mention eight cami buildings in Fehérvár while Evliya Çelebi gives details of six. When the town fell to the Turks in 1543, the medieval Church of St. Peter underwent conversion. It is mentioned in the sources as the Great Cami or Holy Cami and features in Evliya as the Süleyman Cami. This cami's location within the town, and therefore its possible medieval origin, cannot be established. Among the camis established early on we must list the Veli Bey Cami in the castle since we know that its founder served as *sanjakbey* (district governor) of Fehérvár in 1556 and subsequently as sanjakbey of Hatvan around 1570.[3] The building was converted from the earlier church of the

Figure 3. *The Great Cami, Pest. Copper engraving after a drawing by Johann Bernhard Fischer von Erlach, 1721 (Hungarian National Museum, Historical Picture Gallery).*

Pauline order; next to it was built a minaret that was still standing in 1730 (Gerő 1977:108). For the present, we do not know when it was that a part of the royal basilica underwent alteration into a cami. The Veli Bey Cami features in Evliya as the Melias Cami. Of the three other camis mentioned by the Turkish traveler, the location and date of the so-called Palace Cami can be identified from a drawing made in 1601. As regards the two others, the Surut Cami and the Karakaş Cami, we know that the former stood on the territory of the

town. Because Evliya calls it "of old design," it may well have been converted from a Christian church. Since Evliya gives no other information, we may regard the cami founded by Karakaş Mehmed, pasha of Buda (1614, 1618-1621), as a Turkish building from its foundations upwards. Of the six cami buildings in the town that can be identified, four were converted from Christian churches. There are additional issues, too. We do not at present know the buildings identifiable with two camis mentioned as foundations of Sokollu Mustafa Pasha (Káldy-Nagy 1972:446). Likewise unclear is the function during the Turkish period of the Chapel of St. Anne, which was built around 1480 and which in its interior preserves traces of polychrome wall painting from the Turkish time.

Gyula

The sources mention six camis in Gyula, but the number in Evliya Çelebi's description is two. In Gyula, which fell to the Ottomans in 1566, three camis and three prayer-houses were standing as early as 1579 (Káldy-Nagy 1982:47-54). This number shows striking agreement with the number of Christian churches and chapels in the town at the time of its capture. Identification of the camis is, however, rather uncertain. We can exclude the castle chapel from Christian places of worship that may have been converted, since absolutely no trace of conversion has been found there by archaeologists. Also, the parish church in the Hungarian quarter of the town, the Church of the Franciscans, and the Chapel of St. Maurice can all be excluded. According to different hypotheses, the medieval Chapel of St. Alexis was converted into a cami by Pirsiz Ali, the sanjakbey (in office 1567-1571, 1581, and 1584). Also, we cannot rule out the possibility that one of the prayer-houses mentioned in the *sanjak* (district) register of 1579 is identical with the Chapel of St. Nicholas. Archaeological research has made it plain that the "Cami of the Sultanic Holy Hasse" stood on the territory of the Outer Castle; Evliya's "Süleyman Cami" was a Turkish building from its foundations upwards (Gerelyes 2003:173-177).

ARCHITECTURAL APPEARANCE: BUILDINGS THAT WERE TURKISH FROM THEIR FOUNDATIONS UPWARDS

In line with prescription, camis founded by beylerbeys and sanjakbeys were built on a square ground plan and surmounted by a dome. Each was supplied with a minaret and a vestibule featuring three or five cupolas.

Their interiors were faced neither with marble nor with Iznik wall-tiles; instead, plaster was used. For all intents and purposes they differed hardly at all from provincial buildings constructed with significant pecuniary

Figure 4.   The Kethüda Cami, Eger. Oleograph made by an unknown artist in the late 19th century on the basis of a black-and-white engraving from 1829 (Hungarian National Museum, Historical Picture Gallery).

assistance (Necipoğlu 2005:104, 439). In the view of earlier research, it was precisely this type of cami edifice that appeared in the occupied Hungarian territories. In his comprehensive book published almost 30 years ago but still considered a key work, Győző Gerő divides Turkish camis in Hungary that were Turkish from the foundations upwards and not converted from Christian churches into two large groups. The first featured buildings with an oblong ground plan that were covered by a gable roof and the second buildings with a square ground plan that were covered by a dome. In line with what was said above, neither marble nor wall-tile facing were used in these buildings. Gerő took the view that the majority of camis constructed on Hungarian territory belonged to the second group (Gerő 1980:41, 49). A reconsideration of this issue would, however, be in order, after supplementation of the older data with the findings of recent research.

As regards the architectural appearance of Turkish camis constructed in the Hungarian territories, there are three basic sources on which we can rely: buildings still standing in whole or in part, buildings demolished but with surviving foundations that can be excavated archaeologically, and a miscellany of contemporary depictions of buildings that vary in credibility.

According to the sources available to us, the building in Buda's Lower Town that was recorded in 1686 as the Osman Bey Cami belonged to the category constructed on a square ground plan and featuring a dome. So, too, did the Great Cami in Pest. Today neither building is standing, but creditable depictions have survived of each (Figures 2 and 3). Numerous camis in the Lower Town, which was next to the Danube, must have belonged to this category, if we can believe the schematic depictions made at the time of Buda's recapture (Rózsa 2005:32-35). For the moment we have no certain data on them because these buildings have perished.

To this category of square, domed buildings belong the above-mentioned camis in Pécs surviving wholly or in part that were not converted from Christian churches, as well as the Malkoç Bey Cami in Siklós and the Ali Pasha Cami in Szigetvár.

The original design of the Kethüda Cami in Eger is unclear. A depiction made in the late 19th century shows the building with a rectangular ground plan and a gable roof (Figure 4), while a description from the early 19th century speaks of a building with a dome (Molnár 1970-1971:232). Today only the well-known minaret of this building is standing; in like manner only the minaret of the cami founded in Érd by Hamza Bey now remains. There, archaeologists excavated a building with a rectangular ground plan (Fehér 1965:65).

The number of buildings differing from the classic type that feature a rectangular ground plan along with a gable roof is smaller but not insignificant. According to our present knowledge, also belonging to this category were the state-administered Süleyman Cami (inside Szigetvár Castle) (Molnár 1976:90) with its unusual ground plan and two mihrab niches; the Süleyman Cami at Gyula (Figure 5), which was likewise in state hands; the cami built at Székesfehérvár by Veli Bey, sanjakbey of Fehérvár and later of Hatvan (Gerő 1977:figure 4); the Öziçeli Hacı İbrahim Cami, built—unusually—against the town wall in Esztergom (Gerő 2009:figure 4); and the Mehkeme Cami, similarly in Esztergom, in the Water Town there (Figure 6). Lastly, there was the cami building of this type raised in Buda by Murad, pasha of Buda (Fekete 1944:plate L).

Despite their unorthodox ground plans and simpler execution, we can—on the basis of their orientation, their interior spaces, and their surviving relics—say that these buildings accord with the rules for Ottoman cami architecture. Buildings of this type were widespread in Turkish architecture in the Balkans (Ayverdi 1981). Győző Gerő has already called attention to parallels between camis in the Balkans and those in Hungary (Gerő 2003a:182).

According to the view that is generally accepted, this architectural solution is more characteristic of prayer-houses, although two cami buildings of this kind can be pointed out even in the work of Sinan. We should, however, note that these last-mentioned two buildings by Sinan were put up not for members of the ruling elite, but for tradesmen and those engaged in commerce (Necipoğlu 2005:502). As the above list shows, in the occupied Hungarian territories the founders of buildings of this kind could come even from the highest stratum of society.

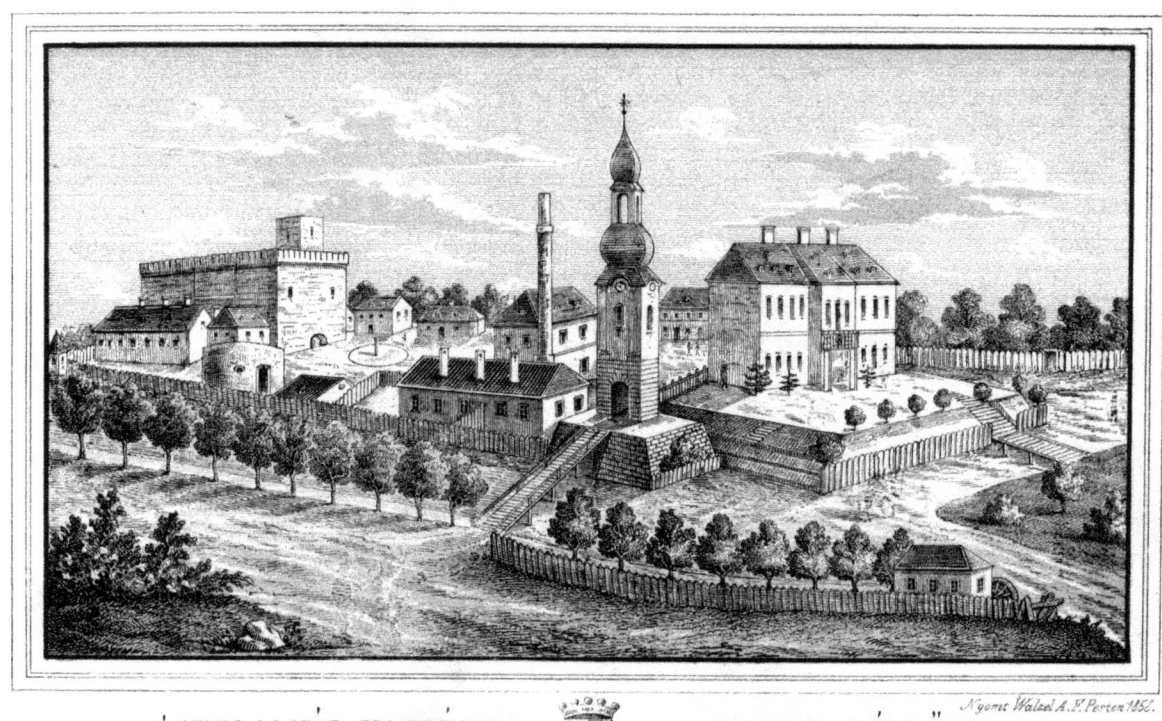

A'GYULAI-VÁR KASTÉLY   1745ᵇᵉⁿ   NYUGOT DÉLRŐL.

Nyomt. Walzel A. F. Pesten 1852.

Figure 5.   *View of Gyula in the 18th century. The Süleyman Cami, with its minaret, can be seen to the left of the gate tower in the center of the picture (Lithograph, Hungarian National Museum, Historical Picture Gallery).*

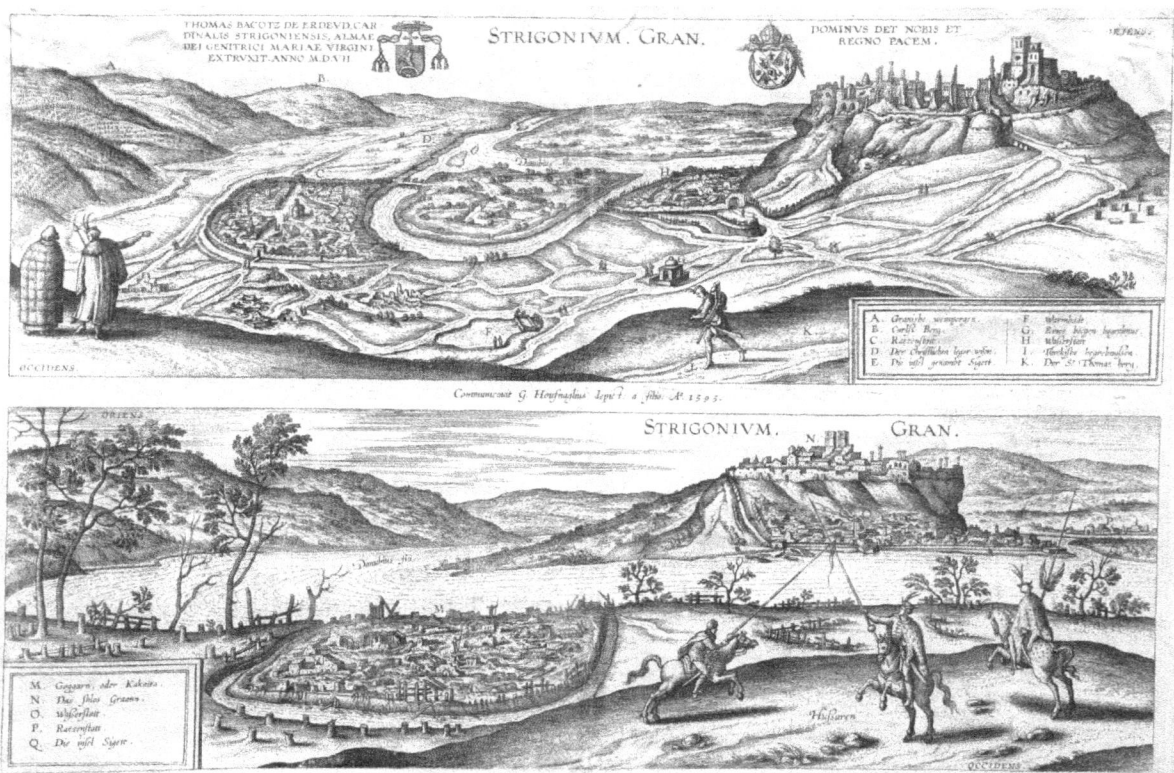

Figure 6.   *View of Esztergom. Engraving by Georgius Houfnaglius, 1598. A Turkish cemetery (marked "I") is shown on the far right of the uppermost picture; Strigonium and Gran were the names for Esztergom in Latin and German, respectively (Hungarian National Museum, Historical Picture Gallery).Historical Picture Gallery).*

LESSONS

Despite the uncertainties that exist, the above analysis yields a number of conclusions. When we look at the numbers we can see that of the 51 camis in the seven towns and castles investigated, 24 were converted from Christian churches and used in this form throughout the entire time of the occupation. With regard to the appearance of these camis, the data available to us is very scant. In the case of buildings that were Turkish from their foundations upwards, the existence of 10 with a square ground plan and a dome can be proved, as can that of 6 simpler buildings with a gable roof.

Among the various towns significant differences appear, in line with their geographical locations and the strategic-military roles of the settlements and of the castles belonging to them. Buda, the center of a vilayet, was of outstanding importance militarily (Hegyi 2007:423). On the territory of Buda Castle, medieval Christian churches used as camis preserved their medieval architecture. The townscape there changed little, and in 150 years only one cami was constructed that was Ottoman from its foundations upwards. This state of affairs is well shown by the depiction of Buda made in 1598 by the German engraver Hans Siebmacher (Figure 7). Much greater changes took place in Buda's Lower Town, in the one-time St. Peter suburb and in the tanners' quarter that developed next to it. These changes were in both cases primarily due to foundations established by Toygun Pasha and Sokollu Mustafa

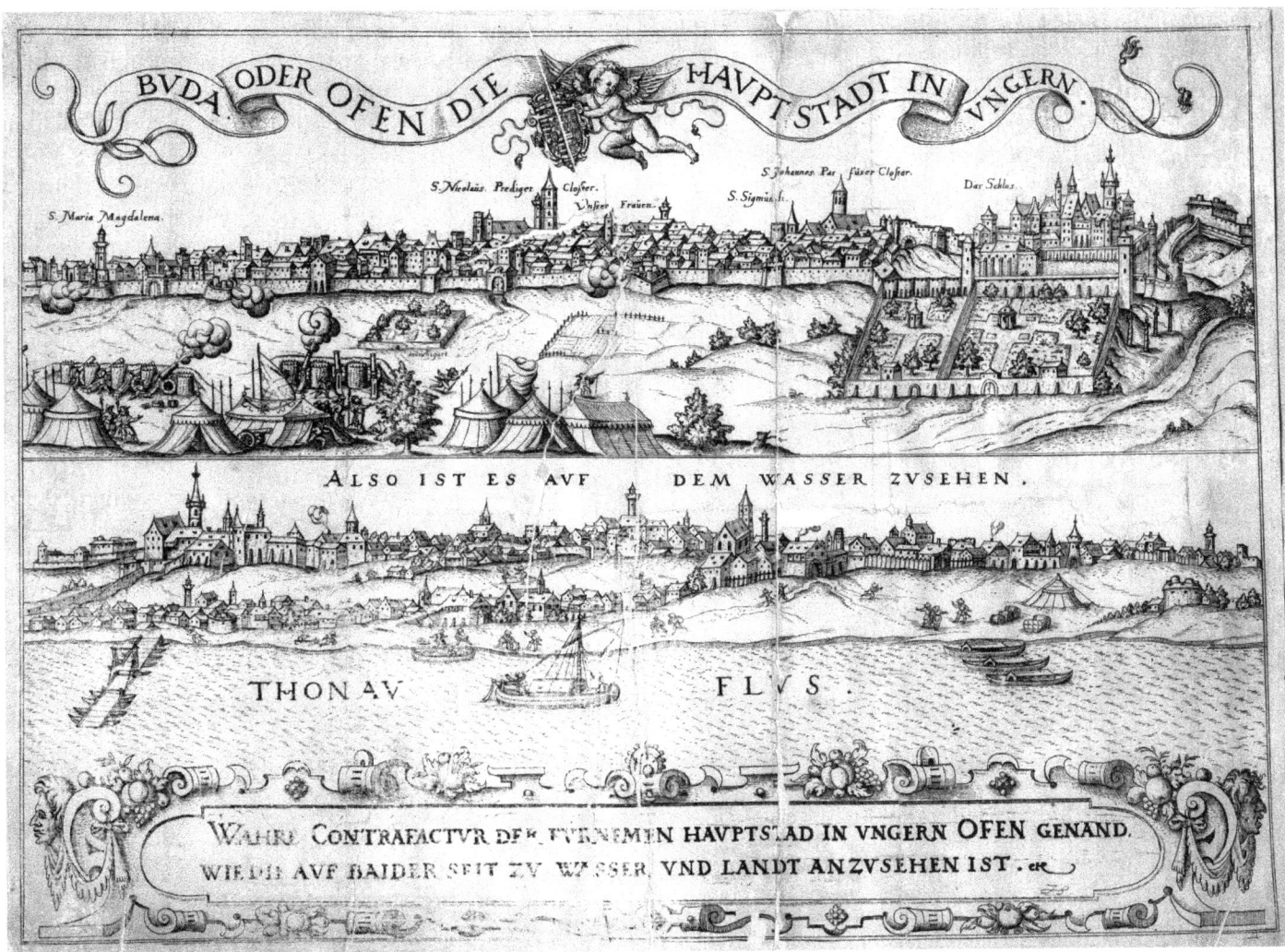

Figure 7.   *Buda seen from two different perspectives. Engraving by Hans Sibmacher, 1598 (Hungarian National Museum, Historical Picture Gallery).*

Pasha, respectively. We should not omit to mention that a great contributor to the transformation of the townscapes of these quarters was the fact that Turkish baths were built above hot-water springs there (springs that had been used in the Middle Ages also). These baths followed the prescriptions of Ottoman architecture.

A likewise significant role fell to Pest, on the opposite side of the Danube. In 1543 all the *martoloses* (Christian Ottoman soldiers) in Buda were transferred to Pest, which was home to the Danube flotilla's base and to a shipyard (Hegyi 2007:485). Of its five camis, one was certainly an Ottoman edifice from its foundations upwards. Located upstream from Buda, Esztergom was, as the defender of the overland and river routes to Vienna, of outstanding importance strategically and militarily. Its Hungarian population was obliged to move out; according to the census conducted in 1570, no one who lived there when the Turks captured the town (in 1543) still had a house there (Káldy-Nagy 1970:141). The castle was defended by a very large number of Ottoman soldiers (Hegyi 2007:687). Of its four camis, one was Ottoman from its foundations upwards.

The roles of Fehérvár, a sanjak center likewise highly important from the military point of view, and Gyula, a sanjak center with the second largest garrison in the Vilayet of Temesvár, may be appraised similarly. In Fehérvár, two camis that were Ottoman from their foundations upwards were built during the time of the occupation. In Gyula, only two camis have so far been identified, although the sanjak register for 1579 mentions three. One of the two was certainly Ottoman from its foundations upwards.

The architectural appearance in the Ottoman era of Eger Castle—which fell to the Turks in 1596, served as a vilayet center for almost a century, and housed a large number of soldiers—cannot be reconstructed now. Nor can that of the town. The number of cami buildings—14 according to some sources, 9 according to others—would indicate a significant transformation of the medieval townscape. At the same time, the number of camis converted from Christian churches (five) is, as in the case of Buda Castle, strikingly high. On the other hand, the number of newly built camis was similar to the numbers in Buda's Lower Town and in Pécs. This deserves notice because the period for which Eger was in Turkish hands was shorter by more than 50 years than in each of these two cases.

Of the settlements investigated in the present study, Pécs would seem to be special. After it fell to the Turks in 1543 a large force of soldiers was stationed in its castle, which, up until the late 1550s, was one of the most heavily garrisoned castles in the region. After 1566 the role of Pécs changed and it became a protected hinterland town behind the border-defense system established to the west (Hegyi 1999:93-94). It was in Pécs that perhaps the most significant Muslim cultural center in the whole of occupied Hungary developed (Ágoston 1991:201). This had a clear impact on Ottoman architecture in the town. Pécs had the highest number of camis that were Ottoman from their foundations upwards (seven). Of these, four indubitably belonged to the type featuring a square ground plan and a dome.

Based on the above, the following lessons can be drawn. In the case of militarily and strategically crucial castles and the towns belonging to them, we may speak of modest architectural activity and a significant use of standing Christian churches. A phenomenon accompanying this was the appearance of cami buildings of simpler execution architecturally that were probably created by local masters. Only in more protected settlements situated in the hinterland can we speak about significant construction work and the appearance of dome-supplied cami buildings in line with the prescriptions, and a real transformation of the townscape. The most significant examples of such transformation on Hungarian territory are Pécs and Buda's Lower Town, the latter thanks to the foundations and the urban construction activities of the pashas of Buda.

CEMETERIES

The researching of Turkish cemeteries is an overdue task for Hungarian archaeology. Following investigations that have grown more intense over the last two decades, the number of cemeteries in southern Transdanubia and on the southern edge of the Great Plain that can be linked to populations of Balkan origin settling in Hungarian villages has grown (Wicker 2008:11-21). Nevertheless, the burial places of Muslims living in the towns are for the most part unexcavated. Likewise awaited in Hungarian research is the linking together and writing up of Turkish sepulchral monuments indicative of cemeteries. We know of stray finds

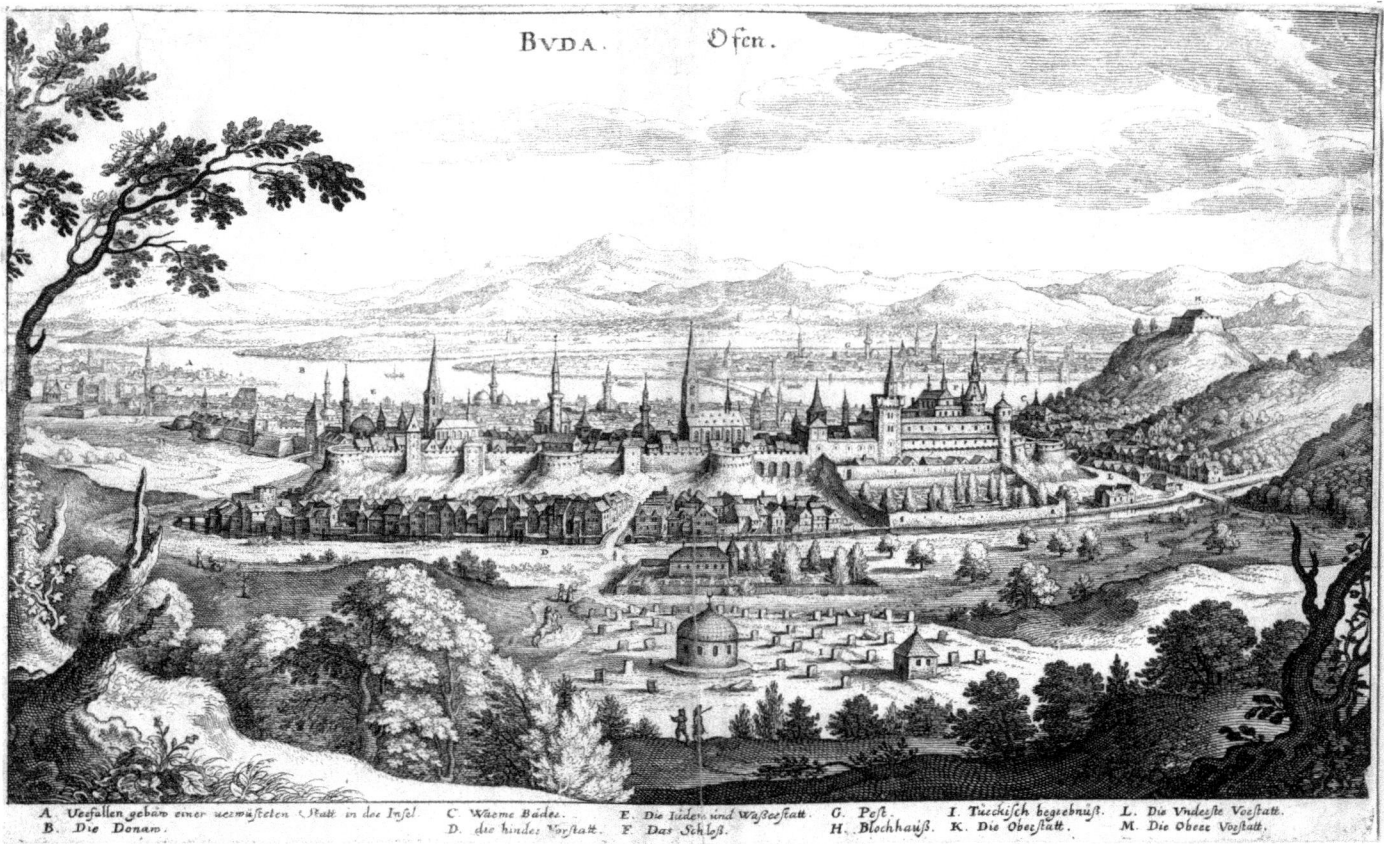

BVDA.   Ofen.

A. Vesfallen gebäw einer verwüsteten Statt in der Insel.   C. Warme Bäder.   E. Die Juden und Waßerstatt.   G. Pest.   I. Türckisch begrebnüß.   L. Die Vndeeste Vorstatt.
B. Die Donaw.   D. die hinder Vorstatt.   F. Das Schloß.   H. Blochhauß.   K. Die Oberstatt.   M. Die Obere Vorstatt.

Figure 8.   *View of Buda and Pest from the west, with a Turkish cemetery in the foreground. Engraving from the atelier of Matthaeus Merian, 1638 (Hungarian National Museum, Historical Picture Gallery).*

from Buda, Fehérvár, Lippa, Esztergom, Baja, and Paks.[4] Clearly, research is made more difficult by the fact that in some cases these monuments were deliberately destroyed at the time of the reconquest because of a need for the materials used to make them (e.g., at Eger).

With regard to the Turkish cemeteries of occupied Hungarian towns, we have not only sporadic archaeological data, but also surveys by army engineers, drawings, and the 18th-century sources. In addition, works on local history written in Hungarian in the 19th and early 20th centuries contain significant data. Compared to these works, this present account is rather sparse, recording as it does only the present state of the research. We have no data on the size of cemeteries, the arrangement of burials, or burial rites. Nor has there been any anthropological investigation of bones. Osteological analysis would be especially important since it would supply comparative data for the anthropological investigations continuing at the present time into the populations of Balkan origin that settled in Hungarian villages (Pálfi and Ardagna 2003).

Buda

On late 16th-century depictions of Buda, two Turkish cemeteries can be seen beyond any doubt. One was to the west of Castle Hill and the other to the north of the Lower Town. Especially striking is a watercolor made around 1600 by an unknown painter on which this latter cemetery can be seen, with tombstones and with a small *türbe* (mausoleum) in the middle (Rózsa 2005:24-25). Similarly, a cemetery around a *türbe* is depicted on a copper engraving from 1598 by Hans Sibmacher (Rózsa 2005:21), as well as on a view by Matthaeus Merian (Figure 8) that was published in 1638 and probably made on the basis of this Sibmacher engraving.

In depictions of the 1684 siege of Buda, a third cemetery is shown to the south of Castle Hill (Rózsa 2005:34-35, 37); all three cemeteries are outside the castle and town areas. On Marsigli's map, made at the time of the recapture of Buda in 1686, no cemeteries are indicated. On the other hand, a cemetery located to the north of the Lower Town is shown on a survey made by Andreas Magliar at the same time (Veress 1906:map following p.150).

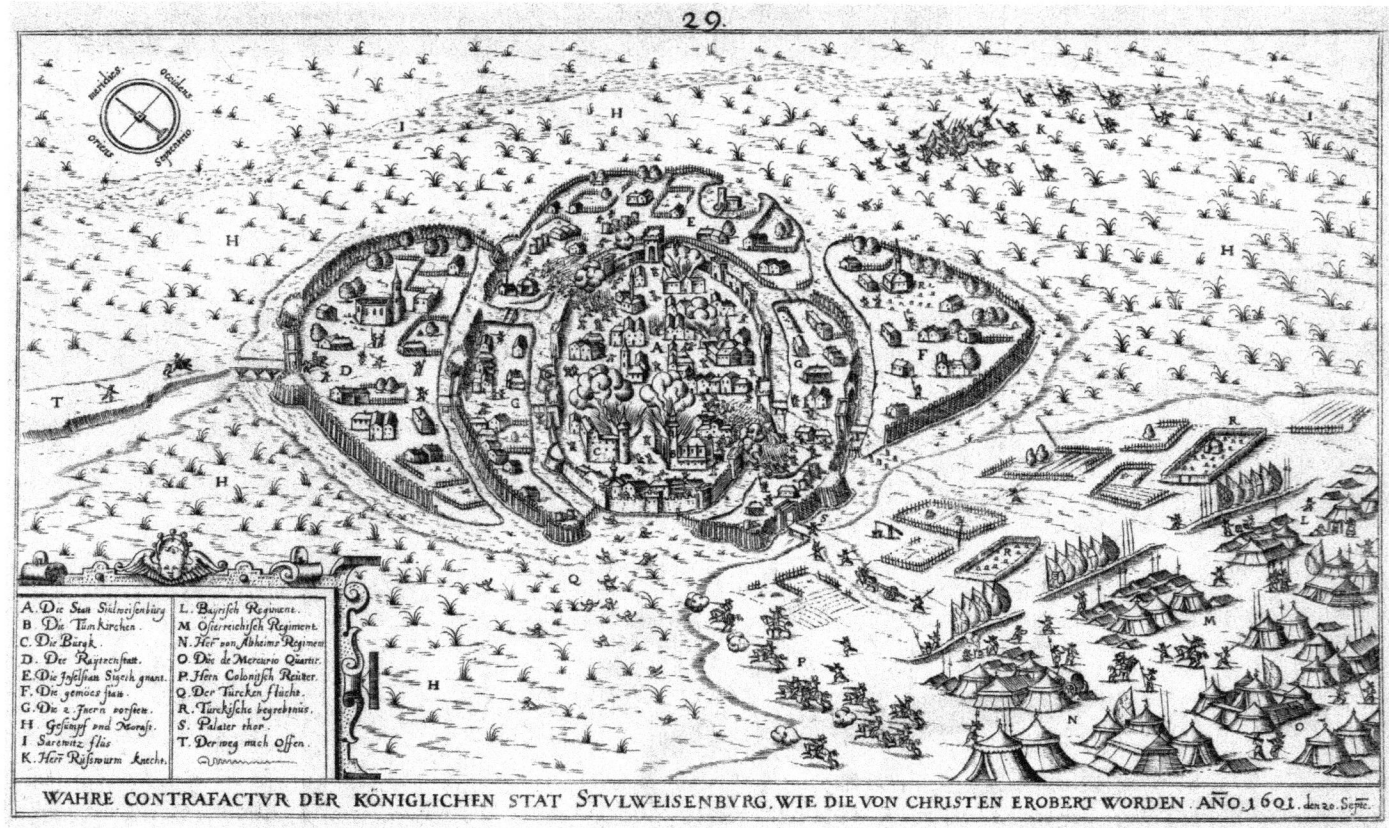

WAHRE CONTRAFACTVR DER KÖNIGLICHEN STAT STVLWEISENBVRG, WIE DIE VON CHRISTEN EROBERT WORDEN. AÑO 1601.

Figure 9. *Fehérvár (Stulweisenburg in German), 20 September 1601. Engraving by Hans Sibmacher, 1601. Reproduced here from a work published in Nuremberg in 1665. A Turkish cemetery, marked "R," can be seen on the right side of the picture (Hungarian National Museum, Historical Picture Gallery).*

Pest

On the basis of a depiction made during the 1684 siege, a cemetery for the Turkish inhabitants of Pest was located outside the town walls on a piece of ground the shape of a rounded arch to the east and north of the town (Rózsa 2005:32, 34). According to another depiction, various cemeteries were to be found in a ring around the town walls. Archaeologists have uncovered parts of the first-mentioned cemetery and of other cemeteries at a number of places in the present-day town, outside the line of the former town wall and near the sites of one-time town gates. To the north of the one-time Vác Gate, researchers happened upon part of a cemetery. They identified 31 regularly spaced burials in rows that were themselves regularly spaced. These burials, in coffins, were oriented in a southwest-northeast direction. No trace of any artifact—e.g., buttons or jewelry—was found (Írásné Melis 2003:165; Kovács 2003:119).

Esztergom

On the basis of engravings of Esztergom made in 1595, a domed türbe on four marble columns that was open at the sides once stood on the territory of what had been, in the Middle Ages, a royal free town. According to hypotheses, this structure stood on the edge of a Turkish cemetery of larger size (Horváth et al. 1979:161). One engraving shows a cemetery not near to the türbe but at a distance from it, to the west (see Figure 6).

Fehérvár

There was a cemetery in Fehérvár on the northern and eastern sides of the Süleyman Cami, the former Church of St. Peter. After the recapture of the town from the Ottomans, the incumbent, Father Lajos Martinus, had the "Turkish mausoleum" in the cemetery knocked down, between 1688 and 1690. Accordingly, in the cemetery surrounding the cami there stood a türbe that today no longer exists (Móra 1972:213-217). The name of the türbe's founder is unknown, as is the name of the person who reposed within it. We know of two cemeteries outside the town. One was probably located in the vicinity of the Palace Cami (Fitz 1966:39). Likewise, two Turkish cemeteries also feature on Hans Sibmacher's townscape engraved in 1601 (Figure 9).

Pécs

According to our present knowledge, in Pécs there was a Turkish cemetery around the one-time Ferhad Pasha Cami situated in the Inner Town. This is indicated not just by studies on local history that wrote up the historical monuments still visible in the late 19th century (Németh 1903:65), but also by rescue-type archaeological investigations conducted in the early 1980s such as that reported by Kárpáti (1980:111).

Eger

During excavations of the bishop's palace in Eger by archaeologists and historical monument protection specialists (it had been constructed in the 1470s, on the territory of the castle), a surprising number of Turkish tombstones and tombstone fragments came to light in sections of wall and in walled-up doorways linkable to reconstruction work in the 18th century, in the vicinity of the building and in the building itself (Kozák 1961:120, 127). In the Turkish period, the bishop's palace building was the residence of the pasha of Eger. The original site of the cemetery would need to be sought around the Inner Castle cami on the territory of the castle.

Gyula

Early 18th-century sources mention a cemetery in Gyula in the vicinity of the Ali Pasha Cami and a türbe that stood near to it (Scherer 1938:291).

CONCLUSIONS

Classifiable as sporadic, the above data are insufficient at the moment for drawing far-reaching conclusions. They say no more than what has been known hitherto, namely that Turkish cemeteries should be sought partly in the vicinity of camis (Fehérvár, Süleyman Cami; Pécs, Ferhad Pasha Cami) and partly outside settlements, in these cases each near a türbe (Buda, Veli Bey Türbe; Esztergom, Mehmet Bey Türbe).

NOTES

1. This can be dated from August 1541, when Sultan Süleyman the Magnificent seized Buda Castle, to September 1697, when Prince Eugene of Savoy defeated Ottoman forces at the Battle of Zenta. The southernmost region of the Kingdom of Hungary remained part of the Ottoman Empire until the Peace of Passarowitz in 1718.

2. Camis were used for the (noon) Friday prayers with sermon (hutba) to which all male Muslims were called, as well as for the prayers held five times daily. They differed from the smaller prayer-houses, which were not used for this Friday assembly. Only Friday mosques are discussed here. The identification of prayer-houses, which were rarely mentioned by name, exceeds the scope of the present study.

3. Sanjakbeys headed the districts into which vilayets were divided. At the head of each vilayet was a beylerbey (literally bey of beys or governor of governors), with authority over this larger area.

4. In the case of the last three towns, the material is in museum storage facilities and is unpublished. The earlier specialist literature relating to Hungary's known stones with inscriptions (among them tombstones) is given by Géza Fehér (1958:173-178).

REFERENCES

ÁGOSTON, GÁBOR
1991   Muslim Cultural Enclaves in Hungary under Ottoman Rule. *Acta Orientalia Academiae Scientiarum Hungaricae* 45:181-204.

AYVERDI, EKREM HAKKI
1981   *Avrupa'da Osmanlı Mimârî Eserleri. Yugoslavya II* [*Ottoman Architectural Monuments in Europe. Yugoslavia, Part II*], Vol. 3, Bk. 2. İstanbul Fetih Cemiyeti, İstanbul, Turkey.

DÁVID, GÉZA
2005   *Pasák és bégek uralma alatt* [*Under the Rule of Pashas and Beys*]. Akadémiai Kiadó-Magyar-Török Baráti Társaság, Budapest, Hungary.

EVLIYA ÇELEBI
1904-
1908   *Evlia Cselebi török világutazó magyarországi utazásai 1660-1664* [*Evliya Çelebi's Travels in Hungary 1660-1664*]. Translated from the Turkish by Imre Karácson, who also wrote the notes. Török-magyarkori Történelmi Emlékek. Második Osztály: Írók. Akadémia, Budapest, Hungary.

1985   *Evlia Cselebi török világutazó magyarországi utazásai 1660-1664* [*Evliya Çelebi's Travels in Hungary 1660-1664*]. Translated from the Turkish by Imre Karácson. With a foreword and glossary by Pál Fodor, who also revised the notes. Gondolat Kiadó, Budapest, Hungary.

FEHÉR, GÉZA
1958   Pierres Commémoratives à Inscriptions Turques en Provenance du Hongrie [Commemorative Tablets from Hungary with Turkish Inscriptions]. *Folia Archaeologica* 10:173-178.

1965   Érd–Ófalu [The Old Village District of Érd]. *Régészeti Füzetek* 18:65.

FEKETE, LAJOS
1944   *Budapest a törökkorban* [*Budapest in the Turkish Era*]. Budapest története III. Királyi Magyar Egyetemi Nyomda, Budapest, Hungary.

FITZ, JENŐ, LÁSZLÓ CSÁSZÁR, AND IMRE PAPP
1966   *Székesfehérvár* [*The City of Székesfehérvár*]. Műszaki Könyvkiadó, Budapest, Hungary.

GERELYES, IBOLYA
2003   Ottoman Architecture in the Town of Gyula. In *Archaeology of the Ottoman Period in Hungary*, Ibolya Gerelyes and Gyöngyi Kovács, editors, pp. 173-180. Hungarian National Museum, Budapest, Hungary.

GERŐ, GYŐZŐ
1977   Istolni Beograd építészeti emlékei [The Architectural Legacy of Turkish Székesfehérvár]. In *Székesfehérvár évszázadai 3. Török kor*, Alán Kralovánszky, editor, pp. 105-126. István Király Múzeum Közleményei. A. sorozat. 15. szám. Fejér Megyei Múzeumok Igazgatósága, Székesfehérvár, Hungary.

1980   *Az oszmán-török építészet Magyarországon (Dzsámik, türbék, fürdők)* [*Ottoman-Turkish Architecture in Hungary* [*Camis, Türbes, Baths*]]. Művészettörténeti Füzetek 12. Akadémiai Kiadó, Budapest, Hungary.

2003a   The History of Ottoman-Turkish Archaeological Research in Hungary. In *Archaeology of the Ottoman Period in Hungary*, Ibolya Gerelyes and Gyöngyi Kovács, editors, pp. 181-184. Hungarian National Museum, Budapest, Hungary.

2003b   Balkan Influences in the Mosque Architecture of Hungary. In *Archaeology of the Ottoman Period in Hungary*, Ibolya Gerelyes and Gyöngyi Kovács, editors, pp. 17-22. Hungarian National Museum, Budapest, Hungary.

2009   The Place of Esztergom's Öziceli Haci İbrahim Cami in the Ottoman Architecture of Hungary. In *Thirteenth International Congress of Turkish Art Proceedings*, Géza Dávid and Ibolya Gerelyes, editors, pp. 253-264. Hungarian National Museum. Budapest, Hungary.

GYÜRKY, KATALIN
1971   Adatok a budai Szent Péter külváros topográfiájához [Data on the Topography of Buda's Suburb of St. Peter]. *Budapest Régiségei. A Budapesti Történeti Múzeum Évkönyve* 21:223-243.

HEGYI, KLÁRA
1999   Pécs török katonasága [Pécs's Turkish Garrison]. In *Pécs a török korban*, Ferenc Szakály, editor, pp. 89-105. Tanulmányok Pécs történetéből 7. Pécs Története Alapítvány, Pécs, Hungary.

2007   *A török hódoltság várai és várkatonasága* [*Turkish Castles and Castle Garrisons in Hungary*]. História Könyvtár Kronológiák Adattárak 9. História-MTA Történettudományi Intézete, Budapest, Hungary.

HORVÁTH, ISTVÁN, MÁRTA H. KELEMEN, AND ISTVÁN TORMA
1979   *Komárom megye régészeti topográfiája.Esztergom és dorogi járás* [*The Archaeological Topography of Komárom County. Esztergom and the District of Dorog*]. Akadémiai Kiadó, Budapest, Hungary.

ÍRÁSNÉ MELIS, KATALIN
2003   Pest During the Ottoman Era. In *Archaeology of the Ottoman Period in Hungary*, Ibolya Gerelyes and Gyöngyi Kovács, editors, pp. 161-172. Hungarian National Museum, Budapest, Hungary.

KÁLDY-NAGY, GYULA
1970   *Harácsszedők és ráják. Török világ a XVI. századi Magyarországon* [*Tax Collectors and Taxpayers. A Turkish World in 16th-Century Hungary*]. Akadémiai Kiadó, Budapest, Hungary.

1972   Macht und Immobiliarvermögen eines Türkischen Beglerbegs im 16. Jahrhundert [The Power and Property of a Turkish Beylerbey in the 16th Century]. *Acta Orientalia Academiae Scientiarum Hungaricae* 25:443-450.

1982   *A gyulai szandzsák 1567. és 1579. évi összeírása* [*The 1567 and 1579 Registers for the Sanjak of Gyula*]. Békés megyei Levéltár, Békéscsaba, Hungary.

KÁRPÁTI, GÁBOR
1980   Pécs. Kazincy u.3/a [3a Kazincy Street, Pécs]. *Régészeti Füzetek* I 33:111.

KINCSTÁRI DEFTEREK
1890   *Magyarországi török kincstári defterek* [*Turkish Treasury Records for Hungary*], Vol. II, 1540-1639. Translated by Antal Velics with an introduction by Ernő Kammerer. M. Tud. Akadémia Történelmi Bizottsága, Budapest, Hungary.

KOVÁCS, ESZTER
2003   Budapest, V. József nádor tér [Palatine Joseph Square, Budapest, District V]. In *Régészeti kutatások Magyarországon*, p. 119. Kulturális Örökségvédelmi Hivatal–Magyar Nemzeti Múzeum, Budapest, Hungary.

KOZÁK, KÁROLY
1961   Az egri vár feltárása (1957-1961) I [Excavations at Eger Castle (1957-1961)]. *Az Egri Múzeum Évkönyve* I:119-171.

MOLNÁR, JÓZSEF

1961   Eger török műemlékei [Eger's Turkish Monuments]. Képzőművészeti Alap Kiadóvállalata, Budapest, Hungary.

1970-
1971   Az egri Kethüda dzsámi [The Kethüda Cami in Eger]. Az Egri Múzeum Évkönyve 9:231-247.

1976   Szülejmán szultán dzsámija Szigetvárott [The Sultan Süleyman Cami in Szigetvár]. Művészettörténeti Értesítő 1976(2):90-94.

MÓRA, MAGDA

1972   Források Fejér megye törökkori történetéhez [Sources for the History of Fejér County in the Turkish Period]. Fejér megyei Történeti Évkönyv 6:211-226.

NAGY, LAJOS

1975   Budapest története 1686-1790 [The History of Budapest 1686-1790]. In Budapest története a török kiűzésétől a márciusi forradalomig, Domokos Kosáry, editor, pp. 27-254. Akadémiai Kiadó, Budapest, Hungary.

NECIPOĞLU, GÜLRU

2005   The Age of Sinan. Architectural Culture in the Ottoman Empire. Reaktion Books, London, England.

NÉMETH, BÉLA

1903   A pécsi dominikánus ház története [The History of the Building of the Dominicans in Pécs]. Taizs Nyomda, Pécs, Hungary.

PÁLFI, GYÖRGY, AND YANN ARDAGNA

2003   Spinal Diseases and Tuberculosis from the Ottoman Period. Major Palaepathological Features of the Bácsalmás-Óalmás (Bácsalmás-Homokbánya) Sixteenth- to Seventeenth-Century Anthropological Finds. In Archaeology of the Ottoman Period in Hungary, Ibolya Gerelyes and Gyöngyi Kovács, editors, pp. 249-256. Hungarian National Museum, Budapest, Hungary.

RÓZSA, GYÖRGY

2005   The Finest Views of Budapest. HG & Társa, Budapest, Hungary.

SCHERER, FERENC

1938   Gyula város története [The History of Gyula Town], Vol. I. Gyula M. város, Gyula, Hungary.

SUDÁR, BALÁZS

2007   Megjegyzések a pécsi dzsámik történetéhez [Remarks on the History of the Camis in Pécs]. In Tanulmányok Pécs történetéből 19, Zoltán Kaposi and Mónika Pilkhoffer, editors, pp. 59-74. Pécs Története Alapítvány, Pécs, Hungary.

2009   Osmanlı Macaristan'ında Camiler ve Mescitler [Mosques in Ottoman Hungary]. In Thirteenth International Congress of Turkish Art. Proceedings, Géza Dávid and Ibolya Gerelyes, editors, pp. 637-650. Hungarian National Museum, Budapest, Hungary.

TÖRÖK TÖRTÉNETÍRÓK

1896   Török történetírók [Turkish Chroniclers], Vol. II. Translated from the Turkish by József Thury, who also wrote the notes. Török-magyarkori történelmi emlékek, M. Tud. Akadémia Történelmi Bizottság, Budapest, Hungary.

VÉGH, ANDRÁS

1998   Előzetes jelentés a budai Szentpétermártír külváros területén 1991-1995 között folytatott régészeti kutatásokról [Preliminary Report on the Archaeological Research Conducted in Buda's Suburb of St. Peter the Martyr between 1991 and 1995]. Budapest Régiségei 32:329-335.

VERESS, ENDRE

1906   Gróf Marsigli Alajos Ferdinánd olasz hadi mérnök jelentései és térképei Budavár 1684-86-iki ostromairól, visszafoglalásáról és helyrajzáról [The Reports and Maps of the Italian Military Engineer Count Luigi Ferdinando Marsigli Relating to the Sieges of Buda Castle in 1684 and 1686, and to the Recapture and Topography of the Castle]. Budapest Régiségei 9:105-170.

WICKER, ERIKA

2008   Rácok és vlahok a hódoltság kori Észak-Bácskában [Vlachs and Orthodox Serbs in the Northern Bácska/Bačka Region during the Turkish Period]. Bács-Kiskun megyei Önkormányzat Múzeumi Szervezete, Kecskemét, Hungary.

//

Ibolya Gerelyes
Magyar Nemzeti Múzeum
Múzeum krt. 14-16
H-1088 Budapest
Hungary

ARNE HOMANN

Battlefield Archaeology of Central Europe— With a Focus on Early Modern Battlefields

ABSTRACT

This paper discusses the development, current state, and methodological background of archaeological research on central European battlefields of the early modern period. From a purely historical perspective, the latter ends in the second half of the 18th century with the major social, economic, and technological changes caused by the French Revolution and the Industrial Revolution. But from an archaeological point of view, the invention of pointed or conical bullets in the 1830s and 1840s and their subsequent large-scale adoption by the military are of higher importance because such projectiles feature a massively higher analytical potential in battlefield-archaeological contexts than the traditional lead ball employed during the preceding centuries. Accordingly, the wars that took place in Europe between 1789 and 1815 are considered here too, since they were still fought with handheld firearms using traditional lead ball ammunition. Furthermore, when feasible, research history and case studies from other periods and/or regions of Europe and North America are included in the discussion. The subject in question encompasses military engagements of varying scales that were fought on dry, open land over short periods of time (a few days at most), by troops employing mostly mobile tactics. The term "battlefield archaeology" as used here thus emphasizes the "classic" concept of the pitched land battle. Due to theoretical and methodological differences between the study of land battlefields and other sites of armed conflict (naval battles, sieges, etc.), research on the latter is largely omitted. An up-to-date and concise overview of all aspects of battlefield archaeology in Germany has recently been published by the author in a special issue of Archäologie in Deutschland *(Brock and Homann 2011).*

HISTORICAL BACKGROUND

Warfare, history suggests, has been and may well always be one of mankind's signal activities. In early modern Europe in particular, military force was an all-too common instrument of power for the social and political elites of the time. Indeed, from the early 16th century to the early 19th century, wars were fought with such regularity and intensity across central Europe that today this period can be called "unusually belligerent" (Parker 1996:1). As a result, comparatively small regions may easily feature dozens of battlefields of varying sizes (Homann 2009a). Even if one counts only the conflicts with the most far-reaching consequences (especially in terms of population losses and destruction of infrastructure), any attempt at cataloging the dozens of small and large wars of early modern central Europe will result in a very long list (Phillips and Axelrod 2005).

Some wars, moreover, lasted decades, which means that the civilian populations of a number of territories again and again experienced periods of devastation and violent death. This is especially true for many of the German territories of the Holy Roman Empire during the infamous Thirty Years' War (1618-1648), the War of the Spanish Succession (1701-1714), the three Silesian Wars (1740-1742, 1744-1745, and 1756-1763, the last of which is more commonly known as the Seven Years' War), the Wars of the First and Second Coalition (1792-1797 and 1798-1801), and those of Napoleon (1803-1815). In the 16th and 17th centuries lengthy wars were also fought across the shifting borderlands between the Habsburg Monarchy and the Ottoman Empire. Still etched in popular memory is the most famous "event" of these conflicts, the massive Second Siege of Vienna (1683) (Figure 1). Poland and surrounding areas also saw much fighting from the 16th century to the 18th century, for instance in several wars against Russia and Sweden in the second half of the 17th century and in the Great Northern War, which lasted from 1700 to 1721.

During those centuries of military conflict Europe also saw the introduction of new instruments and methods of warfare. Whether or not one views the early modern period as a phase of military revolution (Eltis 1995;

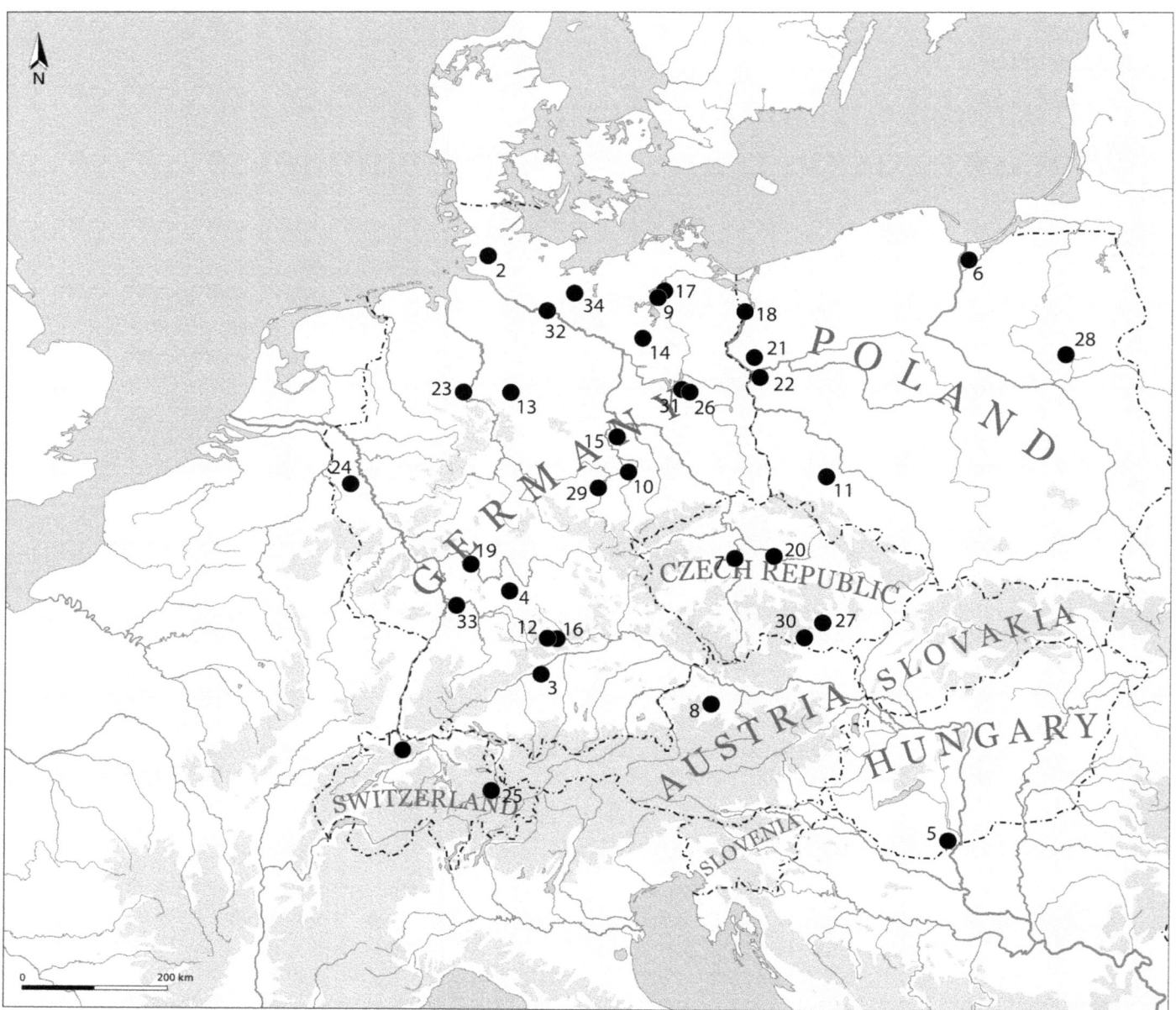

Figure 1.   Locations of early modern central European battlefields and other military-related sites mentioned in the text (in Germany unless otherwise noted; dates of corresponding events are in parentheses): (1) Dornach, Switzerland (1499); (2) Hemmingstedt (1500); (3) Leipheim (1525); (4) Lauda-Königshofen (1525) (5) Mohács, Hungary (1526); (6) Lübschau / Lubiszewo, Poland (1577); (7) White Mountain / Bílá hora, Czech Republic (1620); (8) Lambach, Austria (1626); (9) Benz near Gielow (1639); (10) Lützen (1632); (11) Liegnitz / Legnica, Poland (1634); (12) Nördlingen (1634); (13) Sarstedt (1634); (14) Wittstock (1636); (15) Latdorf near Bernburg (1644); (16) Alerheim (1645); (17) Heidenholz near Malchin (1659/60); (18) Stettin/Szczecin, Poland (1677); (19) Dettingen (1743); (20) Kolin / Kolín, Czech Republic (1757); (21) Zorndorf / Sarbinowo, Poland (1758); (22) Kunersdorf / Kunowice, Poland (1759); (23) Minden (1759); (24) Bedburg-Königshoven (1794); (25) Domat / Ems, Switzerland (1799); (26) Dahlewitz (18th century); (27) Jiríkovice-Austerlitz / Slavkov u Brna, Czech Republic (1805); (28) Puƚtusk, Poland (1806); (29) Jena and Auerstedt (1806); (30) Znaim / Znojmo, Czech Republic (1809); (31) Großbeeren (1813); (32) Lauenburg (Elbe) (1813); (33) Heidelberg (1622, 1633, 1634, 1635, 1689, 1693, 18th and 19th centuries); and (34) Battle of Gadebusch (1712). The locations of the Ukrainian battlefields of Zboriv / Zborów / Зборів (1648), Berestechko / Beresteczko / Берестечко (1651) and Poltava / Полтава (1709) are not marked (Map provided courtesy of the Department of Prehistory and Medieval Archaeology, University of Vienna).

Parker 1996), there can be no doubt that it was a time of fundamental changes in battlefield weaponry and tactics. At the beginning, in the late 15th and early 16th centuries, was the rise first of the Swiss *Reisläufer* and then the south German *Landsknecht* infantry who fought in the massed formation of the pike square. The Spanish next turned the pike square into the more versatile pike-and-shot infantry formation of the *Tercio*. At this time the handheld firearm assumed its role as the weapon that would dominate the battlefields of Europe and the world in the coming centuries. It was the chief fighting implement of the often uncontrollable mercenary troops of the Thirty Years' War, as well as of the highly drilled standing armies of the 18th century, the large French Revolutionary armies created by *levée en masse,* and of the soldiers of the Napoleonic Wars (Featherstone 1998; Black 1999; Starkey 2003; Ortenburg 2005a, 2005b, 2005c).

Given the multi-faceted background of political and social upheaval, military conflict, and technological innovation, battlefields offer one of the best approaches to the material legacy of early modern war, and thus should be expected to be widely studied archaeologically. Such, however, is not the case.

BATTLEFIELD ARCHAEOLOGY IN (CENTRAL) EUROPE: SUMMARY OF RESEARCH

The tradition of European archaeology studying ancient battlefields goes back to the 19th century. Famous examples include the fields of Marathon (490 B.C.) (Goette and Weber 2004), Alésia (52 B.C.) (Reddé et al. 1995), and the Teutoburg Forest (in Latin, *clades Variana,* A.D. 9) (Varusschlacht 2009). Yet unlike these battles of classical antiquity, Europe's early modern battlefields have long been neglected by archaeologists. This may be at least partly due to the much better historical documentation of most post-medieval battles. Over the centuries, the locations of many ancient and medieval battles were forgotten, and

Figure 2. *Bones of soldiers fallen in the battle of Poltava / Полтава (Ukraine, 1709), piled up next to their find spot. The photograph was taken during an excavation carried out by Swedish officers near the Lilla moraset (little morass) on 30 August 1911 (Bennedich 1913:53).*

there was (and is) often little or nothing in the way of written sources that might shed some light on these historical events. Researchers therefore had to carry out excavations to prove their theories about a given battle. Sometimes they only recommended doing so, as in the case of the battle of Mühldorf/Ampfing (Germany, 1322) (Erben 1923:68). An important exception was the archaeological excavation of several mass graves from the battle of Visby on Gotland (Sweden, 1361), which contained the skeletons of more than 1,000 members of a defeated Swedish force (Thordeman 1939-1940).

In contrast to this, the locations of early modern battles were usually well known, often with a sufficiently adequate supply of written or pictorial sources for researchers to investigate the events of their choice. So, there simply seemed to be no need for archaeological excavations of early modern battlefields. Another reason for this attitude seems to be primarily methodological. During the 19th and early 20th centuries, archaeological methods were not yet refined enough to generate useful new data on battles that may have been fought almost within living memory. In cases where ancient battlefields were subject to archaeological examination, exact location was often a matter of dispute. Disputes of this sort, it was hoped, could be resolved if excavations were to uncover battle relics. For early modern battlefields this incentive to explore the ground did not exist. One exceptional case was a concerted search for and excavation of burials dating from the battle of Poltava/Полтава (Ukraine, 1709) conducted in 1911 (Bennedich 1913) (Figure 2). But usually, material remains found during construction or agricultural work were, at best, regarded as antiquarian curiosities and publicly exhibited as such. At worst, and most frequently, finds were sold to tourists or private collectors, recycled, or simply thrown away (Baumann 2004; Foard 2004:343-379).

It was not until several east-central and eastern European governments decided in the late 1950s to commemorate the anniversaries of historical battles of national significance that this status quo began to change. In preparation for official celebrations large-scale archaeological surveys and excavations were conducted at medieval battle sites such as Liegnitz/Legnicą (Poland, 1241) (Siedlak 1961; Boruta 2007; Wolski 2008:27-43), Tannenberg/Grunwald/ Žalgiris (Poland, 1410) (Ekdahl 1982:320-344; Boruta 2007; Wolski 2008:57-109), and Varna/ Варна (Bulgaria, 1444) (Dzingov 1969). The Polish projects in particular drew on the latest archaeological methods of the time, including soil phosphate testing and the use of metal-detectors and helicopters provided by the military (Figure 3). The first systematic archaeological investigation of an early modern battlefield at Mohács (Hungary, 1526) took place in a similar context (Papp 1960, 1962; Zoffmann 1982). While it is true that most of these projects aimed primarily at discovering battle relics for exhibitions, the participating archaeologists nonetheless hoped to gain some insight into the course of the battles whose material remains they were excavating (Rajewski 1964:101; Dzingov 1969:310).

Among western archaeologists these early examples of battlefield archaeology went largely unnoticed. Here is not the place to speculate on the reasons for this oversight. It is, however, possible that the projects did not conform to western notions of independent research. In addition, medieval archaeology, not to mention the archaeology of early modern times, was then still in its infancy. In the case of the two German states and Austria there were also other reasons. After the man-made disasters of the two World Wars, military history was generally viewed with suspicion (Junkelmann 2004:8). Accordingly, most archaeologists (and historians) would focus on more distant ages and/or less bellicose research topics.

Starting in the 1960s the new east-central European focus on battlefield archaeology was carried on primarily in Poland. Work at Tannenberg/Grunwald/Žalgiris (Poland, 1410) continued well into the mid-1980s, while

Figure 3.   Tannenberg / Grunwald / Žalgiris (Poland)–archaeological survey on the battlefield of 1410 assisted by Polish army soldiers equipped with mine detecting devices. Photograph undated but most likely taken between 1958 and 1960 (Boruta 2007:25) (Courtesy of Państwowe Muzeum Archeologiczne [State Archaeological Museum, Poland]).

several smaller projects were initiated at Zehden/ Cedynia (972), Schwetzin/Świecino/Zarnowitz/ Żarnowiec (1462), and Lübschau/Lubiszewo (1577) (Nowakowski 1968; Głosek and Łuczak 1983; Filipowiak 1988; Wolski 2008:13-26, 110-135). In neighboring Ukraine an important project targeted Berestechko/ Beresteczko/Берестечко (1651), the site of a large Polish-Lithuanian battle against a Cossack-Tartar army (Swiesznikow 1992, 1993, 1996; Mandzy 2007:196). Also worth mentioning here is a special branch of battlefield archaeology that emerged in Czechoslovakia during the 1980s. Its chief subject of research was early modern field fortification. Military earthworks from the Thirty Years' War in particular have become a self-contained sub-field—the so-called "archaeology of war"—on which research continues today, though it appears that new methodological approaches from the United States mentioned below have not yet been tested extensively in this context (Grabolle et al. 2009).

While medieval and early modern battlefields thus became regular subjects of archaeological research in east-central Europe, battlefield projects were slow to develop elsewhere on the continent. Minor investigations did occur sporadically, but were carried out mostly by dedicated amateur archaeologists. For example, in Germany in the early 1980s Herbert Matejka, a local historian licensed for metal detecting, probably located the site of the battle of Mühldorf/Ampfing (1322) by mapping find spots of weapons and other 14th-century objects he found with a metal detector (Scherff 1993). Similar work has been done since the late 1990s on the battlefield of Idstedt (1850) (Weise 2009; Homann and Weise 2010). Most famous are the excavations at Kalkriese, the likely location of part of the clades Variana (A.D. 9), which were jumpstarted by the 1987 discoveries by the amateur archaeologist and metal detectionist Tony Clunn (Rost and Wilbers-Rost 2009:68-69). Even though at least parts of the German archaeological community recognized the research potential of both ancient and more recent battle sites (Kunow 1996:320-321; Junkelmann 2004:6), the foregoing cases long remained isolated examples of battlefield research.

This situation began to change in the late 1990s when methodological approaches developed by Connor, Fox, and Scott at the site of the battle of the Little Bighorn (United States, 1876) (Scott 2009) were gradually being adopted by European archaeologists. New projects focused initially on medieval and early modern battlefields in the United Kingdom (Pollard and Oliver 2002; Foard 2004, 2007, 2009), where in 2000 the first "Fields of Conflict" conference was held (Glasgow), and Sweden (Knarrström 2009:187). A major example in this context is the ongoing project at Towton (England, 1461), which

was initiated in 1996 following the accidental discovery of a medieval mass grave (Sutherland 2009). Since 2006 systematic archaeological investigations of early modern battlefields have also become more common in central and east-central Europe. In Poland, archaeologists have been working at Pułtusk (1806) (Wrzosek 2007), Zorndorf/Sarbinowo (1758) (Podruczny and Wrzosek 2011), and Kunersdorf/Kunowice (1759) (Wrzosek 2010). In the Ukraine, the site of another Polish battle at Zboriv/Zborów/Зборів (1648) has recently become a subject of archaeological research (Mandzy 2007). In Germany, there are currently projects on the battlefields of Lauda-Königshofen (1525) (Michael Bletzer 2009, pers. comm.), Lützen (1632) (Schürger 2011), Wittstock (1636) (Grothe and Jungklaus 2009; Eickhoff and Schopper 2012), Gadebusch/Wakenstädt (1712) (ongoing project by author), Minden (1759) (on-going project by author), and Großbeeren (1813) and Lauenburg (Elbe, 1813) (Homann 2009b, 2009c; Homann and Weise 2009, 2010). Reflecting this new trend, the first central European conference to focus exclusively on the whole range of battlefield archaeology from ancient times to the 20th century was held at Halle (Saale) in Germany in October 2008 (Meller 2009).

SOME ASPECTS OF BATTLEFIELD RESEARCH

Over the course of the time span considered here, European military weaponry and tactics underwent several fundamental changes. The material record relating to these changes has profound implications for the archaeology of modern period battlefields. During the early 16th century, for instance, compact square formations of foot soldiers (mainly pikemen) dominated battlefields. Pike tactics had been perfected in the later 15th century by the Swiss. Fighting in *Gewalthaufen*, their pikemen and halberdiers ultimately broke the power of feudal cavalry and heralded the epoch of infantry on the European continent. This development had started in the 14th century. During the 16th century further changes occurred, the most important of which was the spread of handheld firearms. Gunpowder artillery had been in use since the 14th century, but now the percentage of foot soldiers equipped with handguns increased rapidly. Expanding on the earlier practice of adding handgunners to pike squares, the Spanish developed the *Tercio*—a large, more diverse formation of infantry carrying handheld firearms as well as pikes, other polearms, and bladed weapons. The Tercio quickly became a decisive element in land battles and in variations was used well

into the Thirty Years' War. Also, from the 16th century onwards field fortifications were more frequently employed in open-field engagements, though in general this happened not all too often. By the mid-18th century, handheld firearms ultimately replaced most other kinds of infantry weapons. Now frequently, yet not as a rule, cavalry and artillery played only minor roles on the battlefield. But the skillful cooperative action of all arms was still reckoned a basic element of the art of war. Also, in this time the development of standing armies that had slowly been initiated in the first half of the 17th century was completed. The armies of Europe now chiefly consisted of highly drilled and disciplined infantry units fighting in broad, complex line formations. The final major changes happened after 1789 as the French utilized the *levée en masse* to raise large armies of often untrained yet highly motivated citizens. These armies again and again defeated aggressive mercenary forces of the old order monarchies. Thereby they established the concept of general conscription on the continent, which directly led to the huge armies fielded during the Napoleonic wars (Featherstone 1998; Black 1999; Starkey 2003; Ortenburg 2005a, 2005b, 2005c).

These numerous serious changes in military weaponry and tactics resulted in different kinds of artifacts and features that were left on Europe's battlefields and can be found there today. Such relics offer varying potentials for historical-archaeological reconstructions of the events that once took place on a given battlefield, depending on the battlefield's chronological and cultural background.

ENCAMPMENTS

On campaign, each military force needed places where the soldiers could rest and recover—cook, eat, sleep, or prepare for combat. Here, they are summarized under the term "encampments." In the context of battlefield archaeology encampments are well worth a look because they usually were built immediately before a battle and can therefore be useful in narrowing down the possible position of a hitherto unlocated battlefield. Up to now, however, only few corresponding sites from battle contexts have been subjects of archaeological research.

In early modern central Europe, encampments could take different forms according to their intended purpose. On the march, encampments often comprised nothing more than a few fireplaces and some makeshift windbreaks in the open, to be used only for a couple of hours or overnight. There were no encampments at all if soldiers were billeted in, or simply occupied, civilian buildings. But encampments also regularly covered large areas with hundreds of tents or even semi-permanent

Figure 4. *Royal Swedish encampment of 1631 near Werben/ Elbe (Germany). Detail of a contemporary engraving. Pictured are the city of Werben (lower left) and the Swedish encampment consisting of tents and huts and fortified by walls and ditches (upper half). In the middle of the right half of the picture, the commander's cruciform tent can be seen. It is protected by an additional wall and ditch. Along the lower river bank, clouds of smoke indicate places for cooking food. Also, in front of the main defensive system and below the windmills (lower right), there is a fortified ditch manned with soldiers (Wollesen 1898:144-145).*

barracks that were protected by complex defensive systems of walls and ditches, and sometimes existed for months (Ortenburg 2005a:138-151, 2005b:160-172, 2005c:181-194) (Figure 4). Finds and features associated with military encampments can thus be expected to vary with camp function, length of occupation, and historical context. From an archaeological perspective, the basic assumption is that a military force that built and used a camp always left behind varying numbers of objects. Thus, artifacts of a military but not necessarily battle-related nature (e.g., unused musket balls, buckles, buttons, etc.) or of civilian origin (e.g., sherds of pottery, clay pipes) may point to the location of such an encampment (Sivilich 1996; Straßburger 2007, 2009).

An example of the archaeological "footprint" of a 17th-century camp site was recorded in the woodland of Heidenholz near Malchin, Germany. There, more than a hundred metal artifacts of more or less apparent military origin were recovered during prospecting. The objects included pieces of horse gear and bladed weapons. In 1659/1660 during the Second Northern War, several thousand troops of the German emperor reportedly camped in the area for a total of 42 weeks. It seems likely, therefore, that the artifacts found here were lost during this period (Schoknecht 2005). A similar number of metal objects was discovered in the woodland of Benz near Gielow, Germany. They again included bits of horse gear, but also fragments of 17th-century firearms. The area where these objects were found is known to have served as an encampment during the Thirty Years' War. Some historical sources claim that an 80,000-strong imperial army had lain there for seven weeks in 1639 (Schoknecht 2006). The two examples are, however, exceptional in that these sites were occupied for comparatively long periods of time. Encampments built on the verge of battle were generally used only for a few days at most. Given this, relatively large numbers of objects such as those found at Benz and Heidenholz are less likely to have been left in "normal" battlefield encampments.

Larger encampments used for more than just a few hours usually contained different kinds of features that can

Figure 5. *Examples of tent ditches from an 18th-century military maneuver encampment found near Dahlewitz, Germany, in 2003/2004. The upper half of the image shows 2 of the 19 circular ditches; the lower half shows 1 of the 3 oval ditches during excavation (Photo by Frauke Arndt M.A., Brandenburgisches Landesamt für Denkmalpflege und Archäologisches Museum [BLDAM], ca. 2003-2004; courtesy of BLDAM).*

be documented archaeologically (see Figure 4). Such features include, among other things, deep latrines and cooking pits dug in the ground. Examples of the latter come from Sarstedt in Germany where several rectangular pits were discovered during the 1989 excavation of a Bronze Age burial ground. The pits' clay walls had changed to brick under the influence of heat. The pit fill contained fragments of charcoal, horse bones, and 17th-century artifacts (iron door fittings, clay pipe fragments, and ceramic sherds). The excavator interpreted these features as cooking pits that were built there in 1634, after a historically known engagement during the Thirty Years' War (Cosack 2006).

Traces of another encampment were encountered near Dahlewitz, Germany. Here, 19 circular and 3 shallow oval ditches (10-60 cm wide) were excavated in 2003/2004. Arranged in two rows, the ditches enclosed areas measuring between 5.5 m and 5.8 m in diameter (circular), and up to 10 m in length (oval) (Figure 5). The ditch fill contained early modern artifacts. The excavator interpreted these features as ditches dug around tents that had been erected during a military maneuver (Arndt 2004). Although the ditches from Dahlewitz are considered the result of a training exercise, there is no

doubt that similar tents and ditches were regularly erected/dug in the context of 18th-century battlefield encampments.

In encampments of longer occupation, the most notable features were often defensive earthworks (deep ditches and ramparts) and permanent buildings for supreme commanders (see Figure 4). While such structures were not usually constructed close to actual engagements, they are nonetheless of interest as they could, and at times did, become parts of battlefields. One such permanent encampment was examined archaeologically near Latdorf, Germany. There, in late autumn 1644, a Swedish and an imperial army stood almost in sight of each other for two months. Parts of the Swedish encampment were excavated in 2006/2007, revealing for example a section of wall and ditch with a bastion, several human and horse burials, and a pit that contained the remains of a 17th-century tiled stove likely used to heat a tent or some other kind of lightly constructed building (Fahr et al. 2009). Given their structural complexity, features of extensive permanent encampments may also often be located via crop marks (Kerscher 1995).

A special case of military encampments used not only once but on different occasions has recently been examined by Martin Straßburger near Heidelberg, Germany. Between 1962 and 1984, United States army personnel surveyed the 1622 siege camps of the imperial army around the city using metal-detectors, recovering more than 3,000 artifacts from the 17th, 18th, and 19th centuries. All finds were handed over to the Kurpfälzische Museum in Heidelberg where they were documented and archived. The extensive siege-fortifications have been recorded archaeologically since 2007. In the past the finds were seen in connection with the events of 1622 (Benner 1998; Ludwig 2004). This is now being questioned, however, as Heidelberg was besieged repeatedly in 1633, 1634, 1635, 1689, 1693, and also in the 18th and 19th centuries. Historical records and the recovered artifacts indicate the existence and reuse of several camps in the same locations (Figure 6). A joint historical-archaeological analysis of finds, earthworks, and historical sources can be expected to help resolve the remaining questions (Straßburger 2007, 2009).

While the encampments near Heidelberg were built during several sieges, comparable problems may also surface while researching similar features in battlefield contexts.

PATTERNS OF ARTIFACT DISTRIBUTION

Modern archaeological studies of battlefields rely primarily on distributional analyses of identified battle relics. In and after military engagements, objects that had been lost, used (fired), struck off, or otherwise discarded entered the ground. It can be assumed that the post-combat distribution of such objects largely represents the course of fighting. Zones of heavy combat should be represented by relatively large numbers of objects, zones of minor or no combat by only few artifacts or no artifacts at all. By mapping find spots of battle relics it should be possible to create a distribution map—an archaeological fingerprint that may be interpreted historically and archaeologically to reconstruct the course of events long lost to history. One of the first analyses of artifact distributions on early modern battlefields in a broader sense of the word was undertaken in the United States during the 1970s by Ferguson who mapped find spots of musket balls and other ordnance found at Fort Watson (1780-1781) (Ferguson 1977). During the 1980s Connor, Fox, and Scott perfected this approach in their study of the late modern site at the Little Bighorn (United States, 1876) (Scott 2009). On European early modern battlefields the method was first employed in the 1970s in Great Britain (Foard 2007).

As battlefields usually encompass areas of often several square kilometers or more, excavations to recover battle relics are usually not feasible due to time and cost constraints. For a variety of reasons, conventional survey methods (shovel pit testing, etc.) are also problematic. It has been shown that, at present, use of metal detectors is the only viable method for locating battle relics in a timely and effective manner. There are no basic methodological problems with this; most artifacts lost in early modern combat (arms, armament, projectiles, etc.) and encountered on battlefields today are of metal. While the various methodological approaches used in metal detecting surveys cannot be discussed here in detail, some basic points must be emphasized. First, survey areas should be searched evenly if statistically relevant artifact distribution patterns are to be identified. Areas with few or no finds are as significant as areas with numerous artifacts. If only the most productive parts of battlefields are repeatedly searched, the number of finds will grow over time, especially where the battle site has been turned into farmland subject to regular plowing. Such an approach, however, can severely bias both archaeological recognition of the battle area and historical reconstruction of the battle itself. In addition, there is a strong correlation between

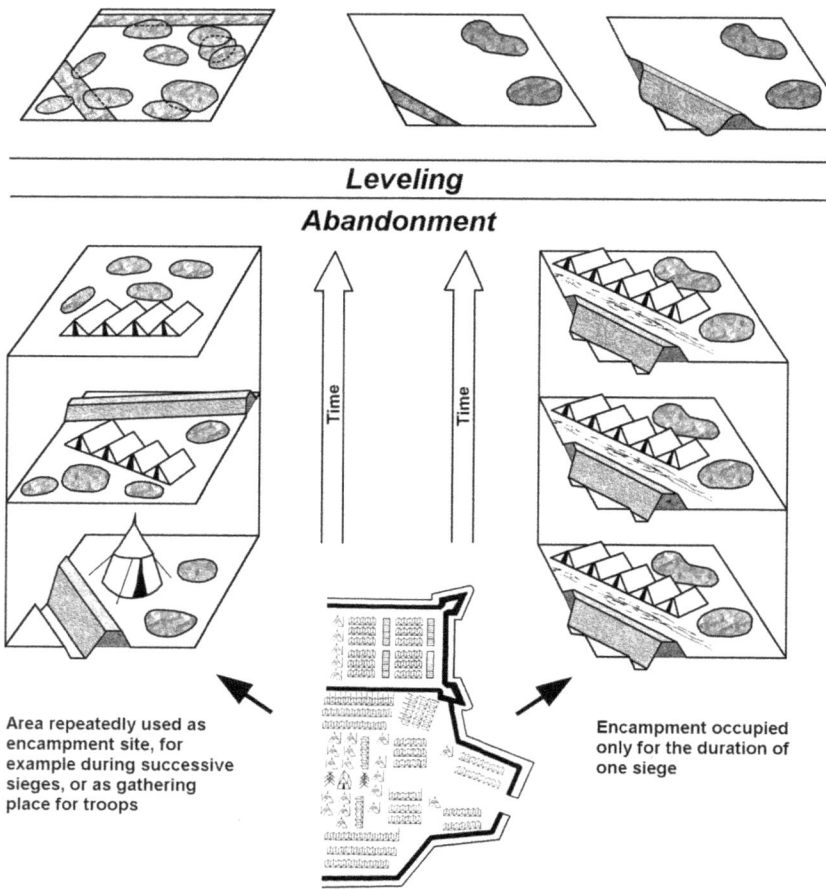

Current archaeological situation

Leveling

Abandonment

Area repeatedly used as encampment site, for example during successive sieges, or as gathering place for troops

Encampment occupied only for the duration of one siege

Figure 6.   *Different developmental patterns of early modern encampment sites occupied on one, two, or more occasions (adapted from Straßburger 2007:60) (Courtesy of Martin Straßburger M.A.).*

number of finds and amount of time spent prospecting in a given area (Moosbauer 2005:95-96; Foard 2007:148). Finally, the amount of relics recovered depends on the type of metal detector used and the experience of the person operating it. During archaeological field work, all these factors should be documented and included in interpretations of artifact distributions.

The largest group of metal relics encountered on early modern battlefields in Europe (except for early 16th-century sites) are projectiles of handheld firearms (lead balls). Armies of the time usually carried large quantities of such balls into battle, discharging and scattering them over the battlefield in large numbers. Much information can be gathered from such projectiles. The presence of marks and deformations on them may allow one to determine if a ball was used (loaded and fired) or not. And mapping their find spots may indicate the extent of a battlefield or positions of units during combat. Other potential data from analyses of lead balls will be discussed below. The second-largest group of battlefield relics are metal parts of uniforms and other accoutrements (buttons, buckles, etc.). Their interpretative potential varies strongly according to the period in which they were lost. Especially during

the first two centuries of the early modern period such items were rarely produced in centralized factories. As a result, it can be difficult to assign buttons or buckles to specific military forces, which leaves general identification of the battle zone as the primary function of such items. Compounding this problem is the fact that publications that can help archaeologists to distinguish military from civilian accoutrements are few and far between (Dienst der Publieke Werken 1977; Lenting et al. 1993). Standardization of military equipment only began to take shape in the first half of the 18th century. Subsequently, metal parts of uniforms and accoutrements assumed distinctive characteristics, for example buttons showing numerals or heraldic images that often represented specific army units (Bottet 1908; Krause 1983; Pétard 1984-1994; Rastatt and Koblenz 1986; Bingeman and Mack 1997).

In general, then, the extent of a given battlefield may be reconstructed via battle relics. A well-known example of this is the Towton battlefield (England, 1461). Mapping of weapons and armor fragments and of other accoutrements revealed the size of the area in which the battle took place. Although Towton dates from the late medieval period, the results can be considered representative

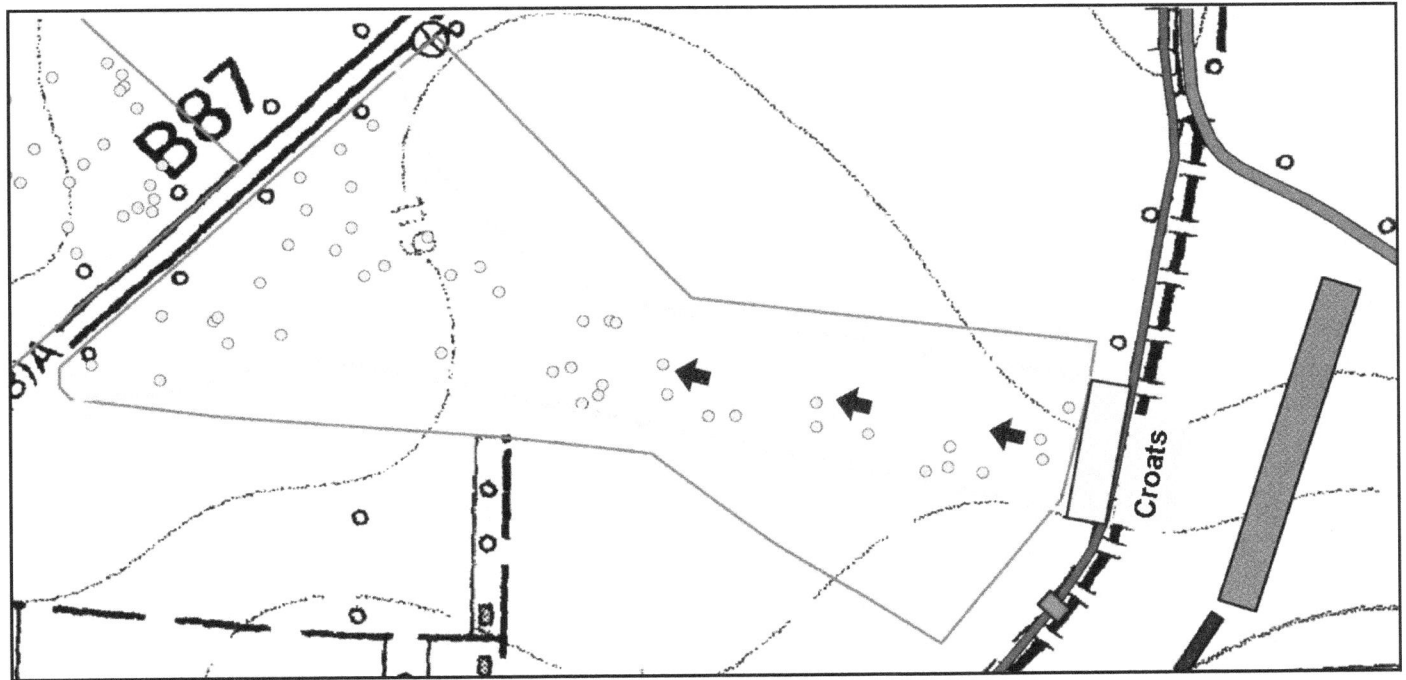

Figure 7. Battlefield of Lützen (Germany, 1632): one of several surveyed areas on the left wing of the imperial army's position. A concentration of lead balls (grey-filled circles) probably reflects the movement path of an imperial unit (yellow-filled rectangle) retreating from combat with Swedish units (blue-filled rectangles). No lead balls were found in the remaining parts of this particular surveyed area (extent marked in red) (adapted from Schürger 2009:139) (Courtesy of André Schürger M.A.).

for early 16th-century sites, since by then handheld firearms still often played a comparatively minor role in pitched battles (Sutherland 2006:251). An example from early modern times is the English Civil War battlefield of Marston Moor (1644). Again, mapping of finds, in this case predominantly lead balls fired from pistols, carbines, and muskets, clearly demonstrated the limits of the combat zone and indicated several distinct artifact concentrations (Foard 2007:146).

If areas of combat can be identified through distribution patterns of different kinds of metal battle relics, reconstructing the actual course of fighting requires a closer look at the artifacts recovered. Projectiles carry the highest informative potential, especially projectiles fired from handheld guns with which larger parts of European armies had been equipped since the 16th century at the latest. Lead balls or parts of them can be found on most early modern battlefields, often in fairly large numbers. As mentioned, an important distinction is between fired and unfired balls, for this may enable the archaeologist to locate areas in which forces stood in readiness or were involved in combat. Projectiles fired by soldiers of one unit hit their opponents or the ground held by them, while some of the opponent's own unused balls and/or other metal accoutrements may have been lost in the same space. Weight and caliber differences may also indicate type of weapon and affiliation with one or more parties involved in the battle. In a best-case scenario, both the unit that stood at the find spot of a battle relics concentration and the unit that fired at it can be identified (Haecker and Mauck 1997; Sivilich and Wheeler Stone n.d.). In theory, at least, such levels of identification promote detailed historical-archaeological battle reconstructions.

Despite sporadic 17th-century attempts at standardizing military armaments, above all handheld firearms, many European armies continued to rely primarily on non-standardized equipment well into the 18th century. For a long time, arms production was not organized by governments. Ordnance departments or even individual commanders ordered weapons they needed from private contractors who worked in large civilian production centers (for example, Suhl or Lüttich). Buyers usually defined gun types and general specifications, but actual production could vary significantly. As a result, infantry units belonging to one army would often be equipped with muskets of different bores that fired lead balls of different calibers. For the archaeologist this means that it can be extremely complicated or even impossible to assign balls found on modern period battlefields to different troop contingents and thus trace the course of combat with the help of artifact scatters. It may often only be possible to say whether balls were produced for infantry muskets, cavalry pistols, or cavalry carbines (Engerisser 2007; Foard 2009).

Yet despite problems of this kind, it can be possible to identify discrete concentrations of lead balls and to interpret them successfully. Work on the Thirty Years' War battlefield of Lützen (Germany, 1632), for instance, has since 2006 produced more than 10,000 metal artifacts, about a third of which can be assigned to the events of 1632. The artifacts include 1,881 lead balls of varying sizes, plus several hundred other objects (buttons, buckles, parts of military accoutrements). One survey area on the left wing of the imperial army's position produced a distinct concentration of lead balls (Figure 7). Based on this pattern, archaeologists assume that here a cavalry unit of the imperial army retreated during skirmishing in the opening stages of the battle. The total area surveyed to date at Lützen stands at 1 km², which makes this one of the most extensive archaeological surveys of an early modern battlefield in central Europe (Schürger 2009, 2011).

On battlefields dating from the first half of the 18th century at the latest onwards, the likelihood of assigning balls to different armies or units is better. By this time most European armies were increasingly being equipped with standardized weapons produced in officially controlled factories (Wirtgen 1976, 1986; Müller 2001:30-37). Also, bores were now of a more uniform caliber as were the lead balls to be fired from muskets and pistols (Ortenburg 2005b:57). If too big, balls were hard or even impossible to load; if too small, the guns fired even less accurately than they did already. Given this, lead balls for handheld firearms found on battlefields of the 18th and early 19th centuries can usually be assigned with some confidence to different types of muskets, pistols, etc., and to the army units that were equipped with those weapons. Identifications of this kind were successfully made during recent archaeological research on the Polish battlefields of Pułtusk (1806) (Wrzosek 2007), Zorndorf/Sarbinowo (1758) (Podruczny and Wrzosek 2011), and Kunersdorf/Kunowice (1759) (Wrzosek 2010).

Another example of the interpretive potential of lead balls from this period comes from the site of the engagement of Lauenburg (Germany, 1813), which has been

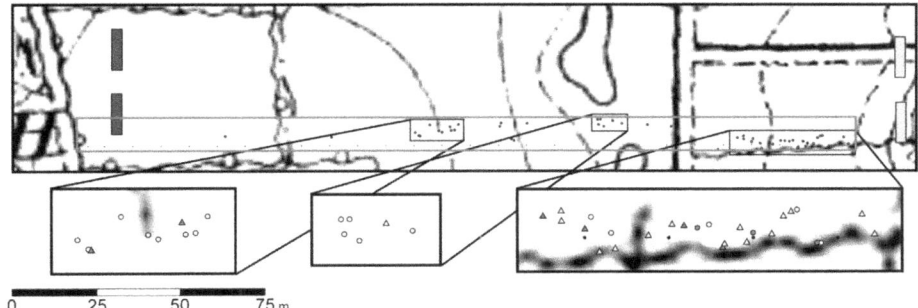

△ French musket-ball, fired   ○ Lützower rifle-ball, fired

▲ French musket-ball, unfired   ◉ Lützower rifle-ball, unfired

0   25   50   75 m

N

Figure 8.   Distribution of lead balls recovered in 2008 at the site of the engagement of Lauenburg (Germany, 1813). The approximate extent of the survey area is marked in red. Blue-filled rectangles indicate the assumed main position of the French; green-filled rectangles indicate the assumed advanced positions of the Lützower Jäger to the west of their main position (Graphic by author, 2009).

researched archaeologically since 2007. Here, parts of Lützow's Prussian Jäger free corps and Russian Cossacks fought for almost three days against a superior French force that had marched east from Hamburg. In 2008 a central part of this small battlefield was surveyed with metal detectors. Among the artifacts recovered were 66 lead balls, most of which probably date from 1813. Their weight distribution shows two clusters around 17 g and 24 g. Those in the lighter cluster were identified as balls for rifles (Büchsen), which fired projectiles of this weight and size and were used by the Jäger troops. The bore of this kind of gun had several incised grooves, which allowed for more precise shooting. The lead ball was wrapped in a greased textile patch to ensure tight fit in the barrel and then rammed down the bore with hammer and ramrod. Due to this process, loaded balls usually show deep dents and strong deformations caused by hammer and ramrod, as well as impressions of the textile patch. The cluster of heavier balls represents the French standard for military musket balls, which was about 24.5 g per piece at the time of Napoleon. Furthermore, due to the different loading process of military muskets without rifling, these balls show only faint ramrod dents and no textile impressions. With these findings, the distribution of balls across the survey area can be interpreted (Figure 8). There are three clearly visible concentrations: an eastern one that consists of fired and unfired balls of both the Prussian Jäger troops and the French. These balls point to long and intense fire-fights in this area, which may represent the historically known main combat zone of 1813. A second concentration lies in the middle of the survey area and

consists almost exclusively of fired Jäger rifle balls. It can be assumed that this concentration represents an area through which the French (who advanced from the west) had to cross on their way to the main combat zone in the east. At this point they came within shooting range of forward Jäger positions and were fired upon. The third and last concentration in the west may again be interpreted differently. It is known from historical sources that the main body of French troops camped somewhere in this area, and that from here they launched their attacks against Lützow's Jäger to the east. At least two times, however, the latter also attacked the main position of the French. It is thought, therefore, that the western concentration of fired Jäger rifle balls and two unfired French musket balls may represent the position of a French unit that defended its encampment against one of the two Jäger attacks (Homann 2009c; Homann and Weise 2009, 2010).

To conclude, a short word on artillery projectiles (cannon balls, shell fragments, grape shot, etc.), which also have good archaeological research potential, is in order. An example of this from the United States comes from the Monmouth (1778) project where Sivilich and Wheeler Stone mapped, among other battle-relics, the find spots of fired and unfired American grape and canister shot. In doing so, they were able to track the area where a British infantry unit stood when fired upon by American artillery, as well as the position of one of the field guns (Sivilich and Wheeler Stone n.d.). Until now only few corresponding results from central European battlefields exist (Homann 2008, 2009b; Homann and Weise 2010), though Polish research conducted at Pułtusk (1806) (Wrzosek 2007) and Kunersdorf/Kunowice (1759) has produced interesting findings (Wrzosek 2010).

Despite the research potential distributional analyses of battle relics offer, archaeologists face several methodological problems. Since interpretations of artifact scatters represent the most common method for reconstructing battle events, undocumented removal of relics can severely impact archaeological interpretations. Most central European battles took place in populated

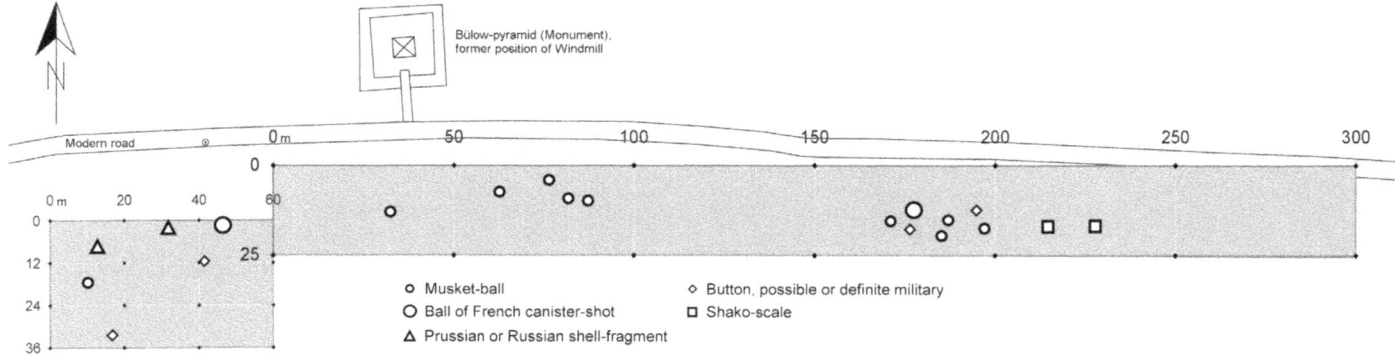

Bülow-pyramid (Monument), former position of Windmill

Modern road

∘ Musket-ball
◦ Ball of French canister-shot
△ Prussian or Russian shell-fragment

◇ Button, possible or definite military
□ Shako-scale

Figure 9.   *Distribution of battle-relics from 1813 recovered at Großbeeren, Germany, in 2006 (Graphic by author, ca. 2009).*

areas, which means that many battlefields have been altered more or less extensively after the combat ended. A range of factors can deplete the number of battle relics left on or in the ground, in extreme cases to the extent that all traces of the "original" distribution of artifacts are obliterated. One such factor often began right during combat and could last for days: the looting of the battlefield as soldiers and members of the baggage train of the winning side collected the spoils of victory. Weapons, ammunition, uniform parts, and other accoutrements were recycled or sent home as trophies. Needless to say, another motivation behind looting was personal enrichment. As a rule, the dead, the wounded, and those taken prisoner were stripped of their belongings—often literally down to the last shirt. For a long time, this practice was the legal right of the victor and part of, or even substitute for, pay (which all too often was forthcoming only sporadically or not at all). After the troops finally left, civilians from surrounding villages usually appeared on the scene. During military campaigns, civilians frequently had to endure massive looting and destruction of their property. Now they took the opportunity at hand to make up for at least part of their own losses by collecting material from those who may have previously harmed them. A detailed description of looting by civilians after the twin battle of Jena and Auerstedt (Germany, 1806) can be found in a contemporary account by the pastor Tieze from the small village of Hassenhausen: "Many people from the villages walked around the battlefield, who collected bread, meat, clothes, black powder, lead balls, and struck-off musket butts and carried away baskets filled with them. Over a span of 14 days the battlefield was picked so cleanly that one could not even find a playing card anymore; because these had been picked up and carried away, too" (Verein Gedenkstätte Hassenhausen 1996:13-14) (translated from the German by the author).

In the years and centuries following a battle, more relics were removed by farmers who used the land agriculturally. Such finds were most often recycled as scrap metal or sold as antique curios to collectors and tourists. The latter practice began especially after the rise of modern "battlefield tourism" during the early 1800s (Seaton 1999; Baumann 2004; Foard 2004:343-379).

A more recent and serious challenge to archaeological research on battlefields is the modern looting of these sites by illegal metal-detecting. In central Europe this became a general problem for archaeology during the 1980s (Bérenger 2006; Biel 2006). One can easily imagine the damage done when an area is stripped repeatedly of relics by individuals acting out of "historical interest" or for personal gain (Legg and Smith 2007). It is thus of utmost importance for researchers to collect and document information about such activities by consulting the local population and public authorities.

Landscape changes due to construction or agriculture also influence conservation and the possibility of detecting battle relics. Farmers often use soil excavated in construction works on their fields. This may cover metal artifacts to a depth that can no longer be penetrated by standard-issue metal detectors. Similar problems can derive from past construction work, whose impact often is not readily visible in the present-day landscape (e.g., leveled field paths, filled irrigation ditches, etc.). Recent research at the site of the battle of Großbeeren (Germany, 1813), for instance, revealed two clearly distinguishable artifact concentrations within the large rectangular survey area (Figure 9). The two concentrations initially appeared to reflect the course of combat in the area, indicating, perhaps, two fighting units separated by open ground. A closer look, however, revealed the real reason for the artifact-free zone between the two concentrations. At some point after the battle an earth dam had been built, but this was leveled in the 20th century and is therefore largely invisible on the field today. The earth used in the dam's construction was probably taken from a distant location and now covers relics of 1813 in the area where the dam once stood (Homann 2008, 2009b; Homann and Weise 2010).

When interpreting the course of combat from distributions and clusters of battle-relics, archaeologists should keep in mind the negative factors listed above and consider the potential problems caused by them. For example an area with few finds may not necessarily have seen only sporadic fighting, but may have been more recently stripped of artifacts by illegal metal-detecting. Notwithstanding these factors and their repercussions, if one is aware of them and considers their potential impact in analyses and interpretations of artifact distributions, erroneous conclusions can be avoided.

FIELD FORTIFICATIONS

On the "classic" early modern European battlefield as defined above, warfare was based mainly on the firepower of infantry units, with artillery and cavalry acting in their support. Although permanently fortified places frequently became part of a combat zone, they usually played only minor roles in pitched battles. Especially during the 17th century, however, field fortifications were built just before, or even during, an engagement on the chosen battleground. That such fortifications could be built on short notice if enough manpower was available has been shown by Czech experimental archaeologists. In 2002 and 2004 a group of just 100 persons built a small 17th-century redoubt in a mere two days (Grabolle et al. 2009:176).

Field fortifications usually had a wall and ditch and could vary in form (Figure 10). According to their intended purpose, there were closed quadrangular or polygonal fortifications or constructions open to one or more sides (Ortenburg 2005a:152-156, 2005b:174-178, 2005c:198-202). Sometimes there were fortified trenches, for instance at Lützen (Germany, 1632) (Schürger 2009:138-141). The primary function of this group of earthworks was to strengthen points of strategic importance during a single battle, afterwards they were usually abandoned.

While field fortifications may be more or less invisible in the landscape, they have regularly attracted the attention of European military historians. In the case of the earthworks from the battle of Nördlingen (Germany, 1634) on the Albuch-Plateau, this interest began back in 1834. Yet often no archaeological excavations ensued, and sketches made of the more prominent features were of questionable quality (Engerisser and Hrnčiřík 2009:177). In central Europe, the development of archaeological interest in early modern field fortifications was mainly linked to the attention battlefield archaeology received in general. As mentioned above, the Czech "archaeology of war" began

Figure 10.   *Different types of early modern field fortifications (idealized depiction) in use during the battle of Nördlingen (Germany, 1634). Detail of a contemporary engraving (adapted from Oraeus 1639, 272-273).*

to look at these sites in the 1980s (Grabolle et al. 2009). More recently, research was carried out in 2003/2004 on the earthworks at Nördlingen (Engerisser and Hrnčiřík 2009:177-184). And in Poland, earthworks built by a Prussian army near Kunersdorf/Kunowice in 1759 and subsequently used by Austro-Russian forces in the battle of the same name later that year were examined in 2009 (Wrzosek 2010). Comparable fortifications built not just for one battle but to permanently block strategically important points have attracted archaeological interest in central Europe for some time (Aßmann 1938; Biermann and Gebuhr 1997, 2000).

Identifying field fortifications can be important for archaeological battle reconstructions. The landscapes of many European battlefields have been dramatically altered by humans in recent centuries. So it is often difficult (and sometimes downright impossible) to find battle sites known from historical sources and to narrow down areas of possible archaeological importance prior to a metal-detecting survey. This dilemma can be at least partly remedied by locating field fortifications, if such exist. Not only can they provide vital clues as to where the fighting took place, but recognizing their extent and orientation can also help in determining battlefield boundaries and in the interpretation of other kinds of battle relics such as burials or the distribution of metal objects. Owing to their more permanent nature compared to other traces of combat, field fortifications may even be the only historically known sites of battle-relevance clearly identifiable today on a site of combat.

A recent example of archaeological research on early modern field fortifications is the search for fortified trenches allegedly dug by imperial troops before the battle of Lützen (Germany, 1632). According to historical sources the supreme commander of the Emperor's army, Wallenstein, ordered his infantry to fortify and man two already extant roadside ditches. Excavations undertaken in the left wing of the imperial troops in 2007 showed these ditches to have been not very deep and probably unmodified. On the basis of these findings, the excavator came to the conclusion that no fortified ditches existed at least in that part of the battlefield subject to survey (Schürger 2009:138-141).

ARCHAEOLOGICAL EVIDENCE OF TREATMENT OF WOUNDED

Aside from the actual field of combat, there are certain concomitant features or aspects of a battle that may be traceable in the archaeological record. One such feature is the field hospital, or more generally the treatment of the wounded. However rudimentary the service may have been, European armies during the early modern period provided their soldiers with some sort of medical care. But this was mainly a development of the 18th century. During the 16th and 17th centuries little in the way of organized care existed; usually recourse to medical help was a private affair, with spotty availability and of questionable quality (Figure 11). The spread of handheld firearms during this period posed major challenges to medical practitioners, as the key problem of non-existent hygiene was exacerbated by projectiles inflicting deep penetrating wounds that were extremely difficult to treat and heal. The development of standing armies in the 18th century slowly changed this situation as the first steps toward modern military medicine were taken in the form of organized transport of the wounded, mobile first aid stations, and better-trained physicians (Gabriel and Metz 1992).

In theory, there are several conceivable ways to identify the possible treatment of wounded in the

Figure 11. *Military surgery in a field hospital during the first half of the 18th century. Contemporary engraving entitled "Die Verrichtungen des Feldscheers" (The Duties of the Field Surgeon) (von Fleming 1726:320-321).*

archaeological record. Most straightforward, perhaps, is the discovery of battlefield burials with skeletons exhibiting unhealed traces of surgery. A good example of this is a mass grave discovered at Jiríkovice in the Czech Republic in 1994. The grave pit contained the remains of 22 individuals who had died during or after the battle of Austerlitz/Slavkov u Brna (1805). Three bones showed fresh traces of amputation, for example a femur that had been cut with a saw (Horácková and Benešová 1997; Horácková and Vargová 1999). More difficult to identify are burials of soldiers who died some time after a battle in more permanent hospitals. Daily losses in a hospital/infirmary setting would be much lower than in the immediate battle context, except during epidemics. Accordingly, casualties could be buried individually or in smaller groups of two or three in isolated grave pits. Such a small cemetery with 43 burials containing the skeletons of 58 likely French soldiers was excavated at Bedburg-Königshoven (Germany). It is thought to date from the 1794 invasion of the Rhineland by France's revolutionary forces (Schleifring 1987; Schwellnus 1987).

Archaeological approaches for verifying the existence of first aid stations and field hospitals are more complicated as those installations were usually set up in tents, existing civilian buildings, or out in the open (Gabriel and Metz 1992:45-213). Accordingly, identifiable traces of medical installations only rarely can be expected to survive in the ground. An example of a characteristic assemblage comes from an American Civil War battlefield in the form of artifact scatters comprising, among other things, pharmaceutical bottles, buttons from soldier's underwear and uniforms, and the metal fittings of other military equipment (Geier 1994:204-208). Surgical instruments, however, should not be expected in such contexts because these were expensive implements normally looked after by their owners. Other potentially distinctive objects are lead balls that were surgically removed from bodies and therefore show marks from surgical instruments, or the so-called "biting bullets" on which wounded reportedly chewed during surgery (Sivilich 2005:11-14, 2007:91-93).

ARCHAEOLOGICAL EVIDENCE OF TREATMENT OF THE DEAD

During the approximately 300 years of central European warfare considered here, uncounted numbers of people, soldiers as well as civilians, died directly or indirectly as a result of armed conflict—several millions during the Thirty Years' War alone. Death occurred in every form everywhere—from wounds on the battlefield, by epidemics in encampments and hospitals, or from exhaustion during some interminable march to a distant theater of war. Without doubt, a battlefield after combat ranked among the most unpleasant sights of war: "This was the ground we pitched our tents on after the battle and tho we removed many dead bodies out of the way, in the morning on the ground in our tents was pools of Blood and pieces of Brains." Thus wrote British lieutenant Richard Browne after the battle of Minden (Germany, 1759) (Starkey 2003:91). His is only one of many contemporary testimonials of carnage. Of course, the corpses of the fallen had to be disposed of, if only because most early modern battles in central Europe took place in more or less densely inhabited areas. In most cases, the dead were simply buried in mass graves near where they had been killed (Figure 12). Only officers or isolated dead would receive single burial—the former in regular graveyards or in churches (Baumann 2004:271), the latter where they were found. A fairly large number of early modern battlefield burials have so far been discovered in central Europe, but of these only a few have seen any archaeological and anthropological analysis.

Up until the second half of the 20th century discoveries of human remains on old battlefields were only sporadically deemed worthy of note. An example of an early reference comes from Stettin/Szczecin (Poland), where in or before 1868 skeletons of six Swedish sappers who had been accidentally buried alive in 1677 were discovered. A mining lamp found with them received more attention than the dead (Anonymous 1868:398). While rare,

Figure 12. *"Battle of Antietam—The 130th Pennsylvania Regiment of Volunteers Burying the Rebel Dead, Friday, Sept. 19 (…)." Detail of a contemporary engraving after a sketch made on-site. Comparable scenes were a common sight on central European battlefields of the early modern period (Schell 1862:52).*

concerted searches for battlefield burials occasionally did occur, as at Poltava/Полтава (Ukraine, 1709) in 1911 (Bennedich 1913) (see Figure 2). If these projects were successful, the bones found were often seen primarily as objects of anthropological study (Bennedich 1913; Gejvall 1957). Most often burials were discovered by chance, especially during construction work. If archaeologists got wind of such discoveries, more or less professional excavations sometimes followed (Fremersdorf 1950). But far more often, and sometimes even after archaeological excavation, human remains were just reburied without further scientific research at local cemeteries or the spot where they had been found (Jäger 1952). Fortunately, however, over the last few decades awareness of the significance of mass graves has become engrained enough to limit such casual treatment of burials.

In the context of the time and region considered here, corpses on the battlefield were usually buried in variable numbers in pits without intentional manipulation (such as cremation) before or during the process of interment. This was in accordance with Christian tradition of the time and also the most practical and hygienic solution available. Occasionally, though, there were exceptions to this pattern, so, for example, the burning of tens of thousands of corpses by the Russians during and after the retreat of Napoleon's *Grande Armée* in the winter of 1812/1813. In this case, the overwhelming sanitary problems presented by the huge numbers of dead men and animals left the Russians with no other way of disposing of the corpses (Hartley 2008:122).

If conditions were right, namely after a "decisive" victory, soldiers of the triumphant army could remain on the battlefield to bury the dead. This is known to have happened after the battles of Dettingen (Germany, 1743) (Handrick 1991:214; Winter 1993) and Minden (Germany, 1759) (von Westphalen 1871:518). Often local gravediggers and other civilians were ordered to help with burials. And at times, civilians would be enlisted to clean up the battlefield more or less on their own, as after the battles of Liegnitz/Legnica (Poland, 1634) (zum Winkel 1916:51), Alerheim (Germany, 1645) (Berg-Hobohm 2008:22; Misterek 2012), or Jena and Auerstedt (Germany, 1806). After the Jena and Auerstedt battle the local pastor Tieze (mentioned above) organized the burial of the dead lying in the fields around his village. He subsequently reported that 501 naked bodies had been interred in several deep pits (Verein Gedenkstätte Hassenhausen 1996:14-15).

Though there was something like a standard approach to dealing with the fallen, details of burial could vary widely. For example, peasants killed by troops of the Swabian League near Leipheim (Germany) in April 1525 seem to have been thrown without order and care into hastily dug holes (Ambs et al. 1994). In contrast to this, the skeletons in a mass grave discovered in 2007 on the battlefield of Wittstock (Germany, 1636) lay in almost perfect order—very much "in file," as noted by the excavators (Figure 13). These dead had probably been buried by the victorious Swedes who prepared a proper military burial for the fallen (Grothe and Jungklaus 2009; Eickhoff and Schopper 2012). If available, suitable natural or cultural features could also be used for burial. At Domat/Ems (Switzerland), for instance, an

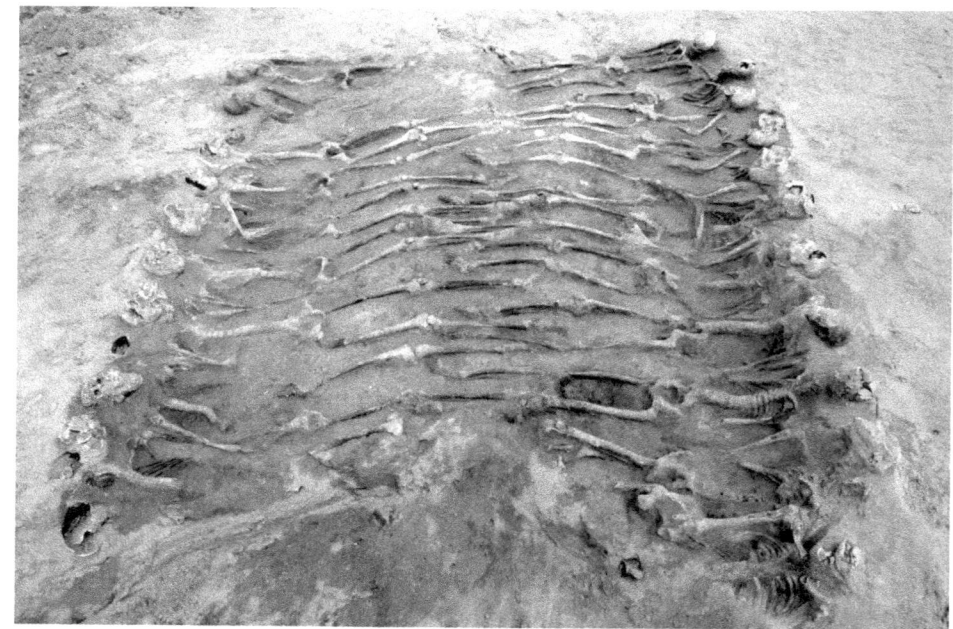

Figure 13. Mass grave from the battle of Wittstock (Germany, 1636) during archaeological excavation in 2007. The rectangular pit contained the skeletons of 125 persons, of which 88 could be documented in situ. Pictured is a burial layer that consisted of two rows of skeletons orderly arranged (Photo by Anja Grothe M.A., BLDAM, 2007; courtesy of Anja Grothe M.A.).

Figure 14.   Mass grave from the battle of Alerheim (Germany, 1645) during archaeological excavation in 2008. The rectangular pit contained the remains of an estimated 70 persons. The uppermost layer (visible here) consisted of numerous intermingled, disarticulated bones. Only the lower part of the pit contained any more-or-less complete skeletons (Berg-Hobohm 2008:22).

abandoned lime kiln rediscovered in 2007 contained the skeletal remains of the members of a peasant militia killed by French forces in 1799 (Berther et al. 2007).

Yet what happened when there was no one around to clean up the areas of fighting, when all surviving combatants had left the field and no civilians were available for burial duty? Under such circumstances, quick burial was impossible. Needless to say, the effects could be gruesome. The 2008 excavation of a mass grave near Alerheim in Germany documented the result of just such a scenario. The pit contained the heavily fragmented and decayed remains of some 70 persons killed in combat and buried there in 1645, after apparently being exposed to summer heat and wild animals for at least several weeks (Figure 14). This was all that those men who were paid to undertake that sad duty could put into the grave they had dug (Berg-Hobohm 2008:22; Misterek 2012).

Archaeologists need to be aware that various factors might prevent burial or make burials disappear over time. One key factor is soil chemistry. In conditions of extreme soil acidity skeletal remains are susceptible to severe mineral loss and structural dissolution. This can be seen at the Kalkriese site, a likely part of the battle zone of the clades Variana (A.D. 9) (Tolksdorf-Lienemann and Lienemann 2004; Grosskopf 2009). Archaeologists also have to consider the chances of grave pits having been destroyed through agricultural land-use, soil erosion, modern development, or various combinations thereof.

Finally, there is the possibility that battle victims were not interred at all. At Dornach in Switzerland (1499), for instance, the victorious Swiss left their fallen enemies unburied for years (Leutenegger 1999:228). A year later at Hemmingstedt, Germany, the victorious Dithmarsians reportedly showed the same indifference to the enemy's fallen knights, but not to foot soldiers and mercenaries who received "proper" burial where they had died (Lammers 1987:182). Common to most recorded mass graves is a general lack of artifacts associated with the skeletal remains. This reflects the prevailing custom of stripping the dead of their belongings and burying them completely or almost naked. Examples of mass graves yielding at least small amounts of artifacts (musket balls, buttons, buckles and other clothing accoutrements, and coins) come from the battlefields of White Mountain/Bílá hora (Czech Republic, 1620) (Janská 966), Lambach (Austria, 1626) (Pertlwieser 1996), Wittstock (1636) (Eickhoff and Schopper 2012), Alerheim (Germany 1645) (Misterek 2012), Kolin/Kolín (Czech Republic, 1757) (Murrer 2007), and Znaim/Znojmo (Czech Republic, 1809) (Kovárník et al. 2006).

For a reconstruction of events during combat, however, battlefield burials tend to be of limited use. Individual mass graves, even if they contain dozens of bodies, usually hold only a fraction of the recorded or estimated battle dead. A large-scale excavation of a battlefield might reveal a burial distribution approximating, perhaps, the course of fighting, but this is a largely hypothetical best-case scenario. Among the few sites where such a distribution has been recorded is the 1st-century Roman battlefield of Gelduba/Krefeld-Gellep (Germany, A.D. 69) with its series of distinctive horse burials (Reichmann 2009). Also, as the example of the battlefield of Lübschau/Lubiszce (Poland, 1577) shows, the spatial distribution of graves can indicate key strategic points whose positions were lost to history (Głosek and Łuczak 1983; Wolski 2008:121-135). Large mass graves or dense burial clusters may mark zones of heavy combat, as at Mohács (Hungary, 1526) where between 1960 and 1977 five mass graves with an estimated 700 to 1,000 skeletons were discovered (Papp 1960; Zoffmann 1982). It must be emphasized, however, that these examples are rare exceptions in what is still only an incipient record of battlefield research.

Nonetheless, the physical remains of battle victims obviously may provide the only "hard" evidence available for examining issues relating to age, health, subsistence, regional origins, or manner of death of soldiers engaged in a battle. The mass grave at Wittstock in Germany, for instance, contained the skeletal remains of some 125 soldiers killed in the eponymous Thirty Years' War battle of 1636 (see Figure 13). The remains of 88 persons were documented in situ and underwent extensive paleopathological and anthropological analyses. These provided a wealth of data on health status and cause of death for each individual. More recent strontium and oxygen isotope analysis of dental enamel samples provided further data on lifetime diets and geographical origins of the fallen (Pate 2008; Grothe and Jungklaus 2009; Eickhoff and Schopper 2012).

Patterns emerging from such data can be used to draw inferences about age and health structure of combatants. These patterns in turn may throw some light on what conditioned the outcome of a given battle. A mass grave at Hemmingstedt (Germany, 1500), for example, contained the remains of eight male individuals, presumably members of the beaten Danish-Holsteinian army. Since one of them was identified anthropologically as about 13 years of age and another as between 50 and 60 years old, and since the bones of several individuals showed signs of illness and attrition, it was assumed that these dead had belonged to one of the historically recorded militia units of the defeated army, and that those units had provided little combat value (Masemann 1997; de Albuquerque Leinenbach et al. 2000). Moreover, analysis of perimortem injury records is indispensable for reconstructing fighting methods, use of arms and armor, and the treatment of fleeing enemies, prisoners, and the dead (e.g., "overkill," mutilations, etc.) (Zoffmann 1982; Cooper 2008).

CONVERGENCE OF HISTORICAL AND ARCHAEOLOGICAL DATA

Reconstructions of past events based solely on interpretations of written and pictorial sources, it is widely acknowledged today, can only approximate historical reality. During the last three decades, archaeological studies of battlefields carried out mainly in the United States and Great Britain have repeatedly illustrated the problem of the all-too-often insufficient and confusing historical documentation of past battles and other military actions. In doing so, these studies

demonstrate that joint historical-archaeological investigations provide a more factual picture of the past by cross-checking established "truths." Significantly, too, from a socio-political perspective, the subject—though it may be an event or events long in the past—may still arouse emotions and may even be exploited for political and other purposes. Given this potential for exposure, archaeology must make every possible effort to contribute to a better understanding of causes, courses, and effects of past wars. At times, archaeological research may also have a major impact on historical interpretations, as, for instance, in the case of the Little Bighorn (United States, 1876) (Scott 2009). Even the documentation of a single mass grave, however, can still be relevant today by allowing adequate remembrance of a long-forgotten conflict and its victims.

OUTLOOK

Archaeological work on early modern battlefields in central Europe offers a complex and fascinating field for joint historical-archaeological research with a strong potential for generating important new data. Battlefields are still not widely recognized as subjects of archaeological studies, but at least the number of corresponding projects is growing, especially in Poland, the Czech Republic, and Germany. Eventually, one may hope, the scope of battlefield research reaches a level that adequately reflects the historical and cultural importance of these places. Indeed, battlefield archaeology is not just about collecting bullets and buttons. It is about reconstructing historical events lost in time, about comparing historical tradition with archaeological data to prove or disprove old and often vague views of past battles. And such research can definitely provide the foundation for protecting battlefields as historically and archaeologically important places and encourage their appropriate treatment as memorial landscapes. In this, one should always bear in mind that battlefield archaeology deals with the material remains of events that adversely affected the lives of innumerable human beings. No doubt many of those caught up in these events felt like British infantry officer Lieutenant Thomas Thomson, who after being wounded in the battle of Minden (Germany, 1759) ended a letter he wrote home from the hospital with the following bitter words: "I hope the nation is now satisfied as there was plenty of blood for their money" (Field 1934:103; Moir 1969:28).

ACKNOWLEDGMENTS

The author is grateful to many of the colleagues cited above, who generously supplied literature or information or granted permission to use pictures. He extends special thanks to Michael Bletzer (New York), who made the manuscript more readable, and Kathrin Misterek (Berlin), who was always willing to discuss different aspects and problems of battlefield archaeology.

REFERENCES

AMBS, R., P. SCHRÖTER, AND B. ZIEGAUS

1994   Spuren der Bauernschlacht von Leipheim: Landkreis Günzburg, Schwaben [Traces of the Peasant Battle of Leipheim: Landkreis Günzburg, Schwaben]. *Das archäologische Jahr in Bayern* 1994:176-180.

ANONYMOUS

1868   Sitzungs-Protokolle [Minutes of the Meeting]. *Zeitschrift für Preußische Geschichte und Landeskunde* 5:397-400.

ARNDT, FRAUKE

2004   Grabungsbericht zur archäologischen Hauptuntersuchung des Bodendenkmals Dahlewitz 16 im Zuge des Neubaus der B 96n/OU Dahlewitz, Landkreis Teltow-Fläming. Dokumentations-Nr.: GV 2000:170/4G [Excavation Report of the Major Archaeological Investigation of the Ground Monument Dahlewitz 16 in the Course of the New Construction of the B 96n/OU Dahlewitz, Landkreis Teltow-Fläming. Documentation Number: GV 2000: 170/4G]. Brandenburgisches Landesamt für Denkmalpflege und Archäologisches Landesmuseum. Wünstorf, Germany.

ASSMANN, GUSTAV

1938   Die Schwedenschanze bei Neuhof [The Swedish Redoubt at Neuhof]. *Elbinger Jahrbuch* 15:208-213.

BAUMANN, KARL

2004   Die Schlacht von Blindheim bei Höchstädt am
        13. August 1704: Spuren bis in die Gegenwart
        [The Battle of Blindheim near Höchstädt on 13th
        August 1704: Traces to the Present]. *Jahrbuch
        des Historischen Vereins Dillingen an der Donau*
        105:269-425.

BENNEDICH, CARL

1913   Om den Svenska planläggningen af slaget vid
        Poltava och stridsledningen [On the Swedish
        Planning of the Battle of Poltava and Battle
        Management]. *Karolinska Förbundets årsbok*
        1913:1-58.

BENNER, MANFRED

1998   Ein ungewöhnlicher, genau datierter
        Fundkomplex—Trinkgeschirr der kaiserlichen
        Belagerungsarmee vor Heidelberg, 1622 [An
        Unusual, Precisely Dated Find Deposit—
        Drinking-Tableware of the Imperial Siege-Army
        around Heidelberg, 1622]. *Archäologische
        Nachrichten aus Baden* 58:39-44.

BÉRENGER, DANIEL

2006   Raubgräber und Metallsondengänger—die
        Situation in Westfalen [Criminal Diggers
        and Metal Detectorists—The Situation in
        Westphalia]. *Archäologisches Nachrichtenblatt*
        11(2):189-193.

BERG-HOBOHM, STEFANIE

2008   Ein anderer Blick auf die Schlacht von Alerheim:
        Massengrab aus dem Dreißigjährigen Krieg
        entdeckt [A Different View on the Battle of
        Alerheim: Mass Grave from the Thirty Years' War
        Discovered]. *Denkmalpflege Informationen* 140
        (July):21-22.

BERTHER, IVO, CHRISTINA PAPAGEORGOPOULOU, AND
MATHIAS SEIFERT

2007   Domat/Ems, Tuleu bel: Rätsel um historisches
        Massengrab gelöst [Domat/Ems, Tuleu bel:
        Mystery around Historical Mass Grave Solved].
        *Jahresbericht des Archäologischen Dienstes
        Graubünden und der Denkmalpflege Graubünden*
        2007:25-35 <http://www.archaeologie.gr.ch/
        uploads/media/2007_Jahresbericht_02.pdf>.
        Accessed 22 July 2012.

BIEL, JÖRG

2006   Sondengänger und Archäologische
        Denkmalpflege [Metal Detectorists and
        Archaeological Heritage Management].
        Archäologisches Nachrichtenblatt 11(2):184-188.

BIERMANN, FELIX, AND RALF GEBUHR

1997   Bodendenkmale der Befreiungskriege [Ground
        Monuments of the Wars of Liberation].
        Archäologie in Berlin und Brandenburg 1997:26-
        28.

2000   Untersuchungen zu Befestigungen des 16.-
        19. Jahrhunderts in Brandenburg. Vorbericht
        zu einem Projekt am Lehrstuhl für Ur – und
        Frühgeschichte der Humboldt-Universität zu
        Berlin [Studies on Fortifications of the 16th-19th
        Century in Brandenburg. Preliminary Report
        on a Project at the Institute of Prehistory and
        Early History of the Humboldt University Berlin].
        Archäologisches Nachrichtenblatt 5(1):267-273.

BINGEMAN, JOHN M., AND ARTHUR T. MACK

1997   The Dating of Military Buttons: Second Interim
        Report Based on Artefacts Recovered from the
        18th-Century Wreck *Invincible*, between 1979
        and 1990. *International Journal of Nautical
        Archaeology* 26(1):39–50.

BLACK, JEREMY (EDITOR)

1999   *European Warfare: 1453-1815*. Macmillan Press,
        Houndmills Basingstoke Hampshire, England.

BORUTA, MAREK

2007   Badania archeologiczne pól bitewnych pod
        Grunwaldem i Legnicą [Archaeological Research
        on the Battlefields of Tannenberg and Liegnitz].
        Z otchłani wieków 62(1-4):22-33.

BOTTET, MAURICE

1908   *Le bouton de l'Armée Française* [*The Button of the
        French Army*]. J. Leroy, Paris, France.

BROCK, THOMAS, AND ARNE HOMANN

2011   *Schlachtfeldarchäologie: Auf den Spuren
        des Krieges* [*Battlefield Archaeology: In the
        Footsteps of War*]. Special issue of the magazine
        Archäologie in Deutschland 2011(2). Konrad
        Theiss Verlag GmbH, Stuttgart, Germany.

COOPER, CHRISTINE

2008   Kriegsverletzungen an historischen Skeletten
        aus der Schweiz [War Injuries on Historic-
        Period Skeletons from Switzerland]. In
        *Traumatologische und pathologische
        Veränderungen an prähistorischen und
        historischen Skelettresten—Diagnose,
        Ursachen und Kontext*, Jürgen Piek, editor,
        pp. 113-123. Interdisziplinärer Workshop in
        Rostock-Warnemünde, 17.-18. November 2006.
        Archäologie und Geschichte im Ostseeraum, 3.
        Leidorf, Rahden, Germany.

COSACK, ERHARD

2006   Spuren eines Heerlagers vor den Toren von
        Sarstedt, Ldkr. Hildesheim [Traces of a Military
        Camp in Front of the Gates of Sarstedt, Ldkr.
        Hildesheim]. *Nachrichten aus Niedersachsens
        Urgeschichte* 75:241-252.

DE ALBUQUERQUE LEINENBACH, GISELLY, VICTORIA MÁLYUSZ, AND INGE SCHRÖDER

2000   Anthropologische Befunde zur Schlacht bei Hemmingstedt [Anthropological Findings Relating to the Battle of Hemmingstedt]. *Archäologische Nachrichten aus Schleswig-Holstein* 11:58-83.

DIENST DER PUBLIEKE WERKEN/AMSTERDAMS HISTORISCH MUSEUM, AFDELING ARCHEOLOGIE (EDITORS)

1977   *Opgravingen in Amsterdam. 20 jaar stadskernonderzoek [Excavations in Amsterdam. Twenty Years of City Center Research]*. Fibula-Van Dishoeck, Amsterdam, the Netherlands.

DZINGOV, GEORGI

1969   Опит за археологическо проучване на бойното поле от 1444 г. край Варна (Un essai de recherche archeologique du champ de bataille de 1444 pres de la ville de Varna) [A Test of Archaeological Research on the Battlefield of 1444 Close to the Town of Varna]. In *Варна 1444: Сборник от изследвания и документи в чест на 525-та годишнина от битката край гр. Варна*. Националнен Военноисторически Музей—София, editor, pp. 284-312. Държавно военно издателство, Sofia, Bulgaria.

EICKHOFF, SABINE, AND FRANZ SCHOPPER (EDITORS)

2012   1636—ihre letzte Schlacht: Leben im Dreißigjährigen Krieg [1636—Their Last Battle: Like in the Thirty Years' War]. Konrad Theiss Verlag GmbH, Stuttgart.

EKDAHL, SVEN

1982   *Die Schlacht bei Tannenberg 1410: Quellenkritische Untersuchungen. Band I: Einführung und Quellenlage [The Battle of Tannenberg 1410: Critical Analyses of the Sources. Volume I: Introduction and State of Sources]*. Berliner historische Studien: 8; Einzelstudien, I. Duncker & Humblot, Berlin, Germany.

ELTIS, DAVID

1995   *The Military Revolution in Sixteenth-Century Europe*. Tauris, London, England.

ENGERISSER, PETER

2007   Kalibertabellen und – abmessungen für Feuerwaffen von 1600 bis 1650. Frühe Neuzeit und Dreißigjähriger Krieg [Caliber Tables and Dimensions for Firearms from 1600 to 1650. Early Modern Period and Thirty Years' War], <http://www.engerisser.de/Bewaffnung/Kaliber.html>. Accessed 22 July 2012.

ENGERISSER, PETER, AND PAVEL HRNČIŘÍK

2009   *Nördlingen 1634: Die Schlacht bei Nördlingen— Wendepunkt des Dreißigjährigen Krieges [Nördlingen 1634: The Battle of Nördlingen— Turning Point of the Thirty Year's War]*. Heinz Späthling, Weißenstadt, Germany.

ERBEN, WILHELM

1923   *Die Schlacht bei Mühldorf, 28. Sept. 1322: historisch-geographisch und rechtsgeschichtlich untersucht [The Battle of Mühldorf, 28 Sept. 1322: Examined Historically-Geographically and Legally-Historically]*. Veröffentlichungen des historischen Seminars der Universität Graz, 1. Leipzig, Leuschner & Lubensky, Graz, Austria.

FAHR, JOCHEN, CORNELIA MÜLLER, AND PETER PACAK

2009   Das schwedische Feldlager von Latdorf bei Bernburg von 1644 (Salzlandkreis, Sachsen-Anhalt)—Ergebnisse der Ausgrabungen am Kalkteich 22 und an der der L73 [The Swedish Military Camp of Latdorf near Bernburg of 1644 (Salzlandkreis, Saxony-Anhalt)—Results of the Excavations at Kalkteich 22 and at the L73]. In *Schlachtfeldarchäologie, Battlefield Archaeology*, Harald Meller, editor, pp. 151-162. Tagungen des Landesmuseums für Vorgeschichte Halle, 2. Landesamt für Denkmalpflege und Archäologie Sachsen-Anhalt und Landesmuseum für Vorgeschichte, Halle, Germany.

FEATHERSTONE, DONALD

1998   *Armies and Warfare in the Pike-and-Shot Era.* Constable, London, England.

FERGUSON, LELAND G.

1977   An Archaeological-Historical Analysis of Fort Watson: December 1780-April 1781. In *Research Strategies in Historical Archaeology*, Stanley South, editor, pp. 41-71. Studies in Archaeology. Academic Press, New York, NY.

FIELD, CYRIL

1934   *Echoes of Old Wars: Personal and Unofficial Letters, and Accounts of Bygone Battles, both by Land and on Sea; By Those That Were There 1513 to 1814. A Martial Anthology*. Herbert Jenkins Limited, London, England.

FILIPOWIAK, WŁADYSLAW

1988   Cedynia 972—Le champ de bataille à la lumière de l'analyse isotope C14 [Cedynia 972—The Battlefield in Light of C14 Analysis]. *Fasciculi Archaeologiae Historicae* 2:11-14.

FOARD, GLENN

2004   *Naseby: The Decisive Campaign*. New edition. Pen & Sword, Barnsley, England.

2007   English Battlefields 991-1685: A Review of Problems and Potentials. In *Fields of Conflict: Battlefield Archaeology from the Roman Empire to the Korean War*. Vol. 1: Searching for War in the Ancient and Early Modern World, Douglas Scott, Lawrence Babits, and Charles Haecker, editors, pp. 133-159. Praeger, Westport, CT.

2009   The Investigation of Early Modern Battlefields in England. In *Schlachtfeldarchäologie, Battlefield Archaeology*, Harald Meller, editor, pp. 117-125. Tagungen des Landesmuseums für Vorgeschichte Halle, 2. Landesamt für Denkmalpflege und Archäologie Sachsen-Anhalt und Landesmuseum für Vorgeschichte, Halle, Germany.

FREMERSDORF, FRITZ
1950   Ein napoleonisches Massengrab von 1813 in der Nähe von Mainz [A Napoleonic Mass Grave from 1813 near Mainz]. *Mainzer Kalender* 1950:58-64.

GABRIEL, RICHARD A., AND KAREN S. METZ
1992   *A History of Military Medicine*. Volume 2: From the Renaissance through Modern Times. Contributions in Military Studies, 124. Greenwood Press, Westport, CT.

GEIER, CLARENCE R., JR.
1994   Towards a Social History of the Civil War: The Hatcher-Cheatham Site. In *Look to the Earth: Historical Archaeology and the American Civil War*, Clarence R. Geier, Jr., and Susan E. Winter, editors, pp. 191-214. University of Tennessee Press, Knoxville.

GEJVALL, NILS-GUSTAV
1957   Skelettfynd från Poltava: En antropologisk och medecinisk-anatomisk studie av några från slagfältet hemförda kraniefragment [Skeleton Finds from Poltava: An Anthropological and Medical-Anatomical Study on Some Skull Fragments Brought Home from the Battlefield]. *Föreningen Armémusei vänner. Meddelanden* 18:39-65.

GŁOSEK, MARIAN, AND BOGDAN ŁUCZAK
1983   Bitwa pod Lubiszewem (17 Kwietnia 1577 r.) w świetle badań archeologicznych [The Battle near Lubiszewo (17 April 1577) in Light of Archaeological Investigations]. *Studia i Materiały do Historii Wojskowości* 25:81-100.

GOETTE, HANS RUPPRECHT, AND THOMAS MARIA WEBER
2004   *Marathon: Siedlungskammer und Schlachtfeld—Sommerfrische und olympische Wettkampfstätte* [*Marathon: Settlement Cluster and Battlefield—Summer Resort and Olympic Competition Site*]. Zaberns Bildbände zur Archäologie; Sonderbände der Antiken Welt. Von Zabern, Mainz, Germany.

GRABOLLE, ROMAN, VÁCLAV MATOUŠEK, PETR MEDUNA, AND ZDENĚK ZMRŽ
2009   Die Schlacht bei Třebel/Triebl im Jahr 1647 und weitere Untersuchungen zur Archäologie des Krieges in der Tschechischen Republik [The Battle of Třebel/Triebl in the Year 1647 and Further Investigations on the Archaeology of War in the Czech Republic]. In *Schlachtfeldarchäologie, Battlefield Archaeology*, Harald Meller, editor, pp. 173-186. Tagungen des Landesmuseums für Vorgeschichte Halle, 2. Landesamt für Denkmalpflege und Archäologie Sachsen-Anhalt und Landesmuseum für Vorgeschichte, Halle, Germany.

GROSSKOPF, BIRGIT
2009   Kalkriese—Schlachtfeld ohne Massengräber? [Kalkriese—Battlefield without Mass Graves?]. In *Schlachtfeldarchäologie, Battlefield Archaeology*, Harald Meller, editor, pp. 81-87. Tagungen des Landesmuseums für Vorgeschichte Halle, 2. Landesamt für Denkmalpflege und Archäologie Sachsen-Anhalt und Landesmuseum für Vorgeschichte, Halle, Germany.

GROTHE, ANJA, AND BETTINA JUNGKLAUS
2009   In Reih' und Glied—Archäologische und anthropologische Aspekte der Söldnerbestattungen von 1636 am Rande des Wittstocker Schlachtfeldes [In Rank and File—Archaeological and Anthropological Aspects of the Mercenary Burials from 1636 on the Border of the Wittstock Battlefield]. In *Schlachtfeldarchäologie, Battlefield Archaeology*, Harald Meller, editor, pp. 163-171. Tagungen des Landesmuseums für Vorgeschichte Halle, 2. Landesamt für Denkmalpflege und Archäologie Sachsen-Anhalt und Landesmuseum für Vorgeschichte, Halle, Germany.

HAECKER, CHARLES M., AND JEFFREY G. MAUCK
1997   *On the Prairie of Palo Alto: Historical Archaeology of the U.S.-Mexican War Battlefield*. Texas A&M University Military History Series, 55. Texas A&M University Press, College Station.

HANDRICK, WOLFGANG
1991   *Die Pragmatische Armee 1741 bis 1743: Eine alliierte Armee im Kalkül des Österreichischen Erbfolgekrieges* [*The Pragmatic Army 1741 to 1743: An Allied Army in the Calculus of the War of the Austrian Succession*]. Beiträge zur Militärgeschichte, 30. R. Oldenbourg, Munich, Germany.

HARTLEY, JANET M.
2008   *Russia, 1762-1815: Military Power, the State, and the People*. Studies in Military History and International Affairs. Praeger, Westport, CT.

HOMANN, ARNE

2008   Historische Schlachtfelder als archäologische
        Quelle: Studien zu Möglichkeiten und Grenzen
        ihrer Erforschung [Historical Battlefields as
        Archaeological Source: Studies on Opportunities
        and Limits of Their Investigation]. Unpublished
        Master's thesis, Universität Hamburg, Germany.

2009a   Historische "Schlachtfelder" Norddeutschlands:
        Potentiale und Probleme ihrer archäologischen
        Erforschung [Historical "Battlefields" of
        North Germany: Potentials and Problems
        of Their Archaeological Investigation]. In
        Schlachtfeldarchäologie, Battlefield Archaeology,
        Harald Meller, editor, pp. 217-221. Tagungen
        des Landesmuseums für Vorgeschichte Halle, 2.
        Landesamt für Denkmalpflege und Archäologie
        Sachsen-Anhalt und Landesmuseum für
        Vorgeschichte, Halle, Germany.

2009b   Großbeeren, 23. August 1813: Ein neuer Blick auf
        eine altbekannte Schlacht der Befreiungskriege
        [Großbeeren, 23 August 1813: A New View on a
        Well-Known Battle of the Wars of Liberation]. In
        Schlachtfeldarchäologie, Battlefield Archaeology,
        Harald Meller, editor, pp. 223-226. Tagungen
        des Landesmuseums für Vorgeschichte Halle, 2.
        Landesamt für Denkmalpflege und Archäologie
        Sachsen-Anhalt und Landesmuseum für
        Vorgeschichte, Halle, Germany.

2009c   Lauenburg, 17. bis 19. August 1813: Eine
        historisch-archäologische Untersuchung des
        Gefechtsfelds bei Lauenburg (Elbe). Erste
        Resultate [Lauenburg, 17 to 19 August 1813: A
        Historical-Archaeological Investigation of the
        Battlefield near Lauenburg (Elbe). First Results].
        Unter Mitarbeit von Carsten M. Walczok
        und Jochim Weise. Lauenburgische Heimat
        182(September):28-42.

HOMANN, ARNE, AND JOCHIM WEISE

2009   Lützows Jäger gegen französische Infanterie:
        Das Gefecht bei Lauenburg (Elbe) vom 17. bis
        19. August 1813 [Lützow's Huntsmen against
        French Infantry: The Engagement near
        Lauenburg (Elbe), 17 to 19 August 1813]. In
        Schlachtfeldarchäologie, Battlefield Archaeology,
        Harald Meller, editor, pp. 227-229. Tagungen
        des Landesmuseums für Vorgeschichte Halle, 2.
        Landesamt für Denkmalpflege und Archäologie
        Sachsen-Anhalt und Landesmuseum für
        Vorgeschichte, Halle, Germany.

2010   The Archaeological Investigation of Two Battles
        and an Engagement in North Germany from the
        19th Century: A Summary of Work Carried Out at
        Idstedt, Grossbeeren and Lauenburg. Journal of
        Conflict Archaeology 5:27-56.

HORÁČKOVÁ, LADISLAVA, AND LENKA BENEŠOVÁ

1997   Findings of War-Time Injuries from the Battle of
        Austerlitz. Anthropologie 35(3):283-289.

HORÁČKOVÁ, LADISLAVA, AND LENKA VARGOVÁ

1999   Bone Remains from a Common Grave Pit from
        the Battle of Austerlitz (Anthropology and
        Paleopathology). Journal of Paleopathology
        11(3):5-13.

JÄGER, FRANZ

1952   Das Gallneukirchner Franzosengrab vom Jahre
        1742 [The Frenchmen-Grave from the Year 1742 of
        Gallneukirch]. Oberösterreichische Heimatblätter
        6(3):363-366.

JANSKÁ, EVA

1966   Hromadný hrob bělohorských bojovníků [Mass
        Grave of White Mountain Warriors]. Staletá
        Praha 2:107-110.

JUNKELMANN, MARCUS

2004   Das greulichste Spectaculum: Die Schlacht von
        Höchstädt 1704 [The Most Ghoulish Spectacle:
        The Battle of Höchstädt 1704]. Hefte zur
        bayerischen Geschichte und Kultur, 30. Haus der
        Bayerischen Geschichte, Augsburg, Germany.

KERSCHER, HERMANN

1995   Zur Topographie und Befestigung des
        kaiserlichen Beobachtungslagers bei
        Wittislingen im Jahr 1703 [On Topography
        and Fortification of the Imperial Surveillance
        Camp near Wittislingen in the Year 1703].
        Landkreis Dillingen a. d. Donau, Schwaben. Das
        archäologische Jahr in Bayern 1995:185-187.

KNARRSTRÖM, BO

2009   Battlefield Research in Scania, South Sweden:
        Epic Battles and Small Scale Skirmishes
        in the Scope of Battlefield Archaeology. In
        Schlachtfeldarchäologie, Battlefield Archaeology,
        Harald Meller, editor, pp. 187-198. Tagungen
        des Landesmuseums für Vorgeschichte Halle, 2.
        Landesamt für Denkmalpflege und Archäologie
        Sachsen-Anhalt und Landesmuseum für
        Vorgeschichte, Halle, Germany.

KOVÁRNÍK, JAROMÍR, LADISLAVA HORÁČKOVÁ, LENKA
VARGOVÁ, LADISLAVA MUCHA, AND ALENA VACHUNKOVÁ

2006   Hromadné hroby vojáků na Brněnské ulici z bitvy
        u Znojma v roce 1809 [Mass Graves of Soldiers in
        Brněnská Street from the Battle of Znojmo]. Ve
        službách archeologie 7:313-328.

KRAUSE, GISELA

1983   Altpreußische Militärbekleidungswirtschaft:
        Materialien und Formen, Planung und Fertigung,
        Wirtschaft und Verwaltung [Old Prussian
        Military Clothing Economy: Materials and
        Forms, Planning and Production, Economy
        and Management]. Das altpreußische Heer, 7:
        Heeresverfassung, 1. Biblio Verlag, Osnabrück,
        Germany.

KUNOW, JÜRGEN

1996   Zu den Aufgaben und Zielen der Bodendenkmalpflege bei Objekten aus unserer jüngsten Vergangenheit: Fallbeispiele des 20. Jahrhunderts aus dem Land Brandenburg [On the Tasks and Goals of the Preservation and Care of Field Monuments Regarding Objects from our Recent Past: Case Studies of the 20th Century from Brandenburg]. *Archäologisches Nachrichtenblatt* 1:315-326.

LAMMERS, WALTHER

1987   *Die Schlacht bei Hemmingstedt: freies Bauerntum und Fürstenmacht im Nordseeraum; eine Studie zur Sozial-, Verfassungs – und Wehrgeschichte des Spätmittelalters* [*The Battle of Hemmingstedt: Free Peasantry and Princely Power in the North Sea Region; A Study on the Social-, Constitutional – and Military History of the Late Middle Ages*]. 3rd edition. Westholsteinische Verlagsanstalt Boyens & Co., Heide in Holstein, Germany.

LEGG, JAMES B., AND STEVEN D. SMITH

2007   Camden: Salvaging Data from a Heavily Collected Battlefield. In *Fields of Conflict: Battlefield Archaeology from the Roman Empire to the Korean War.* Vol. 1: Searching for War in the Ancient and Early Modern World, Douglas Scott, Lawrence Babits, and Charles Haecker, editors, pp. 208-233. Praeger, Westport, CT.

LENTING, J. J., H. VAN GANGELEN, AND H. VAN WESTING (EDITORS)

1993   *Schans op de grens: Bourtanger bodemvondsten 1580-1850* [*Redoubt on the Border: Archaeological Finds from Bourtange 1580-1850*]. Stichting Vesting Bourtange, Sellingen, the Netherlands.

LEUTENEGGER, MARCO A. R.

1999   Nach geschlagener Schlacht: Kein "einzig Volk" von Siegern; Das Schicksal der Beute von Dornach [After the Battle was fought: No "One Nation" of Winners; The Fate of the Loot of Dornach]. *Jahrbuch für Solothurnische Geschichte* 72:219-245.

LUDWIG, RENATE

2004   "Lacrumae Haidelbergensis": Die archäologische Überlieferung zur Belagerung 1622 ["Lacrumae Haidelbergensis": The Archaeological Tradition Regarding the Siege of 1622]. In *Der Winterkönig: Heidelberg zwischen höfischer Pracht und Dreißigjährigem Krieg*, Anette Frese, Frieder Hepp, and Renate Ludwig, editors, pp. 55-64. Exhibition Kurpfälzisches Museum der Stadt Heidelberg, 21.11.2004-27.05.2005. Greiner, Remshalden, Germany.

MANDZY, ADRIAN

2007   Tatars, Cossacks, and the Polish Army: The Battle of Zboriv. In *Fields of Conflict: Battlefield Archaeology from the Roman Empire to the Korean War.* Vol. 1: Searching for War in the Ancient and Early Modern World, Douglas Scott, Lawrence Babits, and Charles Haecker, editors, pp. 193-207. Praeger, Westport, CT.

MASEMANN, ULLRICH

1997   Archäologische Forschungen in Meldorf und auf dem Hemmingstedter Schlachtfeld [Archaeological Research in Meldorf and on the Battlefield of Hemmingstedt]. *Archäologische Nachrichten aus Schleswig-Holstein* 8:139-158.

MELLER, HARALD (EDITOR)

2009   *Schlachtfeldarchäologie, Battlefield Archaeology*. Tagungen des Landesmuseums für Vorgeschichte Halle, 2. Landesamt für Denkmalpflege und Archäologie Sachsen-Anhalt und Landesmuseum für Vorgeschichte, Halle, Germany.

MISTEREK, KATHRIN

2012   Ein Massengrab der Schlacht von Alerheim am 3. August 1645 [A Mass-Grave from the Battle of Alerheim on 3 August 1645]. *Bericht der Bayerischen Bodendenkmalpflege* 53 (2012):361-392.

MOIR, GUTHRIE

1969   *The Suffolk Regiment (The 12th Regiment of Foot)*. Famous Regiments. Leo Cooper Ltd., London, England.

MOOSBAUER, GÜNTHER

2005   Der römische Kampfplatz bei Kalkriese, Stadt Bramsche, Ldkr. Osnabrück [The Roman Battle-Site at Kalkriese, City of Bramsche, Ldkr. Osnabrück]. In *Archäologie der Schlachtfelder— Militaria aus Zerstörungshorizonten*, Werner Jobst, editor, pp. 89-98. Akten der 14. Internationalen Roman Military Equipment Conference (ROMEC). Carnuntum-Jahrbuch 2005. Verlag der Österreichischen Akademie der Wissenschaften, Vienna, Austria.

MÜLLER, HEINRICH

2001   *Die Bewaffnung* [*The Armament*]. Second edition. Das Heerwesen in Brandenburg und Preußen von 1640 bis 1806. Brandenburgisches Verlagshaus, Berlin, Germany.

MURRER, ERNST G. F.

2007   Nach 250 Jahren... [After 250 Years...]. *Österreichisches Schwarzes Kreuz. Kriegsgräberfürsorge. Mitteilungen und Berichte* 124(1):34-35.

NOWAKOWSKI, ANDRZEJ

1968   Badania na pobojowisku z Wojny Trzynastolectniej pod wsią Świecino powiat Puck [Research on the Battlefield of the Thirteen Years' War near the Village of Świecino District Puck]. *Pomorania Antiqua* 2:315-319.

ORAEUS, HEINIRICH

1639   *Theatrum Europaeum, oder Außführliche und warhafftige Beschreibung aller und jeder denckwürdiger Geschichten so sich hin und wider in der Welt fürnämlich aber in Europa und Teutschlanden...zugetragen: Continuation 3 ... Von Anno 1633 biß 1638...[European Theater, or detailed and true description of all and each memorable stories that befell from time to time in the world but particularly in Europe and Germany: 3rd continuation: from the year 1633 to 1638].* Merian, Franckfurt am Mayn (Germany).

ORTENBURG, GEORG

2005a   *Waffen der Landsknechte: 1500-1650 [Weapons of the Landsknechte: 1500-1650].* Heerwesen der Neuzeit: Abt. 1; Das Zeitalter der Landsknechte 1500-1650, 1. Bechtermünz, Augsburg, Germany.

2005b   *Waffen der Kabinettskriege: 1650-1792 [Weapons of the Cabinet Wars: 1750-1792].* Heerwesen der Neuzeit: Abt. 2; Das Zeitalter der Kabinettskriege 1650-1792, 1. Bechtermünz, Augsburg, Germany.

2005c   *Waffen der Revolutionskriege: 1792-1848 [Weapons of the Revolutionary Wars: 1792-1848].* Heerwesen der Neuzeit: Abt. 3; Das Zeitalter der Revolutionskriege 1792-1848, 1. Bechtermünz, Augsburg, Germany.

PAPP, LÁSZLÓ

1960   A mohácsi csatahely kutatása (Die Forschung des Schlachtfeldes von Mohács) [Research on the battlefield of Mohács]. *Janus Pannonius Múzeum Évkönyve* 1960:197-252.

1962   Újabb kutatások a mohácsi csatatéren (Neuere Ausgrabungen auf dem Schlachtfeld von Mohács) [Newer Excavations on the Battlefield of Mohács]. *Janus Pannonius Múzeum Évkönyve* 1962:199-220.

PARKER, GEOFFREY

1996   *The Military Revolution. Military Innovation and the Rise of the West, 1500-1800.* Second edition. Cambridge University Press, England.

PATE, DONALD

2008   Geographic Origin and Mobility Recorded in the Chemical Composition of Human Tissue. In *Forensic Approaches to Death, Disaster and Abuse*, Marc Oxenham, editor, pp. 177-188. Australian Academic Press, Brisbane, Australia.

PERTLWIESER, MANFRED

1996   Die Toten von Lambach [The Dead of Lambach]. *Archäologie Österreichs* 7(2):49-59.

PÉTARD, MICHEL

1984-
1994   *Equipements militaires de 1600 a 1870 [Military Equipment from 1600 to 1870].* 10 vols. [No publisher].

PHILLIPS, CHARLES, AND ALAN AXELROD (EDITORS)

2005   *Encyclopedia of Wars.* Three vols. Facts on File Library of World History. Facts on File, New York, NY.

PODRUCZNY, GRZEGORZ, AND JAKUB WRZOSEK

2011   Odwrót przez Dworskie Łęgi—jeden z epizodów bitwy Sarbinowem stoczonej 25 sierpnia 1758 roku w świetle przekazów historycznych i badań archeologicznych [Retreat through the Hofbruch/Dworskie Łęgi—An Episode of the Battle of Zorndorf/Sarbinowo (August 25, 1758) in Light of Historical Tradition and Archaeological Research]. In *Nowa Marchia—Prowincja Zapomniana—Ziemia Lubuska—Wspólne Korzenie; Materiały z sesji naukowych zorganizowanych przez Wojewódzką i Miejską Bibliotekę Publiczną im. Zbigniewa Herberta w Gorzowie Wlkp. Wspólnie ze Stiftung Brandenburg w Fürstenwalde*, Edward Jaworski/ Grażyna Kostwiewicz-Górska/ Magdalena Matuszewska, editors, pp. 105-121. Zeszyty Naukowe/Wojewódzka i Miejska Biblioteka Publiczna Im. Zbigniewa Herberta [Gorzów Wielkopolski], 9. Sonar Sp. Z o.o., Gorzów Wlkp, Poland.

POLLARD, TONY, AND NEIL OLIVER

2002   *Two Men in a Trench: Battlefield Archaeology—The Key to Unlocking the Past.* Joseph, London, England.

RAJEWSKI, ZDZISŁAW

1964   Muzealny pokaz pól bitewnych; Музейный показ полей битв; A Memorial Display of Historical Battle Fields. *Wiadomości Archeologiczne* 30(1/2):96-101.

RASTATT AND KOBLENZ

1986   *Die Bewaffnung und Ausrüstung der Armee Friedrichs des Großen [Armament and Equipment of Frederick the Great's Army].* Vereinigung der Freunde des Wehrgeschichtlichen Museums Schloß Rastatt e.V.; Verein der Freunde und Förderer der wehrtechnischen Studiensammlung Koblenz e.V. (editors). [No publisher].

REDDÉ, MICHEL, SIEGMAR VON SCHNURBEIN, PHILIPP BARRAL, JACKY BÉNARD, VÉRONIQUE BROUQUIER-REDDÉ, AND RENÉ GOGUEY

1995   Neue Ausgrabungen und Forschungen zu den Belagerungswerken Caesars um Alesia (1991-1994) [New Excavations and Research on Caesars Siegeworks around Alesia (1991-1994)]. *Bericht der Römisch-Germanischen Kommission* 76:73-158.

REICHMANN, CHRISTOPH

2009   Die Schlacht bei Gelduba (Krefeld-Gellep) im Herbst 69 n. Chr [The Battle of Gelduba (Krefeld-Gellep) in the Autumn of A.D. 69]. In *Schlachtfeldarchäologie, Battlefield Archaeology*, Harald Meller, editor, pp. 99-108. Tagungen des Landesmuseums für Vorgeschichte Halle, 2. Landesamt für Denkmalpflege und Archäologie Sachsen-Anhalt und Landesmuseum für Vorgeschichte, Halle, Germany.

ROST, ACHIM, AND SUSANNE WILBERS-ROST

2009   Kalkriese—Die archäologische Erforschung einer antiken Feldschlacht [Kalkriese—The Archaeological Investigation of an Antique Field Battle]. In *Schlachtfeldarchäologie, Battlefield Archaeology*, Harald Meller, editor, pp. 67-79. Tagungen des Landesmuseums für Vorgeschichte Halle, 2. Landesamt für Denkmalpflege und Archäologie Sachsen-Anhalt und Landesmuseum für Vorgeschichte, Halle, Germany.

SCHELL, F. H.

1862   Battle of Antietam—The 130th Pennsylvania Regiment of Volunteers Burying the Rebel Dead, Friday, Sept. 19—This Spot Was the Scene of One of the Most Desperate Conflicts of the Day. From a Sketch by our Special Artist, Mr. F. H. Schell. *Frank Leslie's Illustrated Newspaper* XV(368 [18 October]:52.

SCHERFF, BRUNO

1993   Mühldorf 1322 und die Archäologie [Mühldorf 1322 and the Archaeology]. In *Die Schlacht bei Mühldorf, 28. September 1322: Ursachen—Ablauf—Folgen*, Josef Steinbichler, editor, pp. 69-82. Heimatbund Mühldorf, Mühldorf am Inn, Germany.

SCHLEIFRING, JOACHIM H.

1987   Anthropologische Untersuchungen in einem französischen Soldatenfriedhof [Anthropological Research on a French Soldiers' Cemetery]. *Archäologie im Rheinland* 1987:167-168.

SCHOKNECHT, ULRICH

2005   Der Sporkenkeller im Heidenholz bei Malchin [The Sporkenkeller in the Heidenholz near Malchin]. *Archäologische Berichte aus Mecklenburg-Vorpommern* 12:187-198.

2006   Ein Heerlager in der Benz bei Gielow, Ldkr. Demmin [A Military Camp in the Benz near Gielow, Ldkr. Demmin]. *Archäologische Berichte aus Mecklenburg-Vorpommern* 13:230-244.

SCHÜRGER, ANDRÉ

2009   Die Schlacht von Lützen 1632: Archäologische Untersuchungen auf dem linken kaiserlichen Flügel [The Battle of Lützen 1632: Archaeological Research on the Imperial Left Wing]. In *Schlachtfeldarchäologie, Battlefield Archaeology*, Harald Meller, editor, pp. 135-149. Tagungen des Landesmuseums für Vorgeschichte Halle, 2. Landesamt für Denkmalpflege und Archäologie Sachsen-Anhalt und Landesmuseum für Vorgeschichte, Halle, Germany.

2011   Die ersten Minuten der Schlacht von Lützen am 16.11.1632: Isolanis Kroaten und Stålhandskes finnische Reiter aus archäologischer Sicht [The First Minutes of the Battle of Lützen on 16 November 1632: Isolani's Croats and Stålhandske's Finnish Horsemen from an Archaeological Perspective]. In *Leben und Sterben auf dem Schlachtfeld von Lützen*, Maik Reichel and Inger Schuberth, editors, pp. 103-120. Lützener Gespräch, 5. Heimat – und Museumsfreunde Lützen e.V. and Stiftelsen Lützenfonden Göteborg, Lützen, Germany.

SCHWELLNUS, WINRICH

1987   Archäologische Beobachtungen zur französischen Besetzung des Rheinlands im Jahre 1794 [Archaeological Observations Relating to the French Occupation of the Rhineland in 1794]. *Archäologie im Rheinland* 1987:164-166.

SCOTT, DOUGLAS D.

2009   Battlefield Archaeology: Some New Insights into Custer's Last Stand. In *Schlachtfeldarchäologie, Battlefield Archaeology*, Harald Meller, editor, pp. 253-258. Tagungen des Landesmuseums für Vorgeschichte Halle, 2. Landesamt für Denkmalpflege und Archäologie Sachsen-Anhalt und Landesmuseum für Vorgeschichte, Halle, Germany.

SEATON, ANTHONY V.

1999   War and Thanatourism: Waterloo 1815-1914. *Annals of Tourism Research* 26:130-158.

SIEDLAK, STANISŁAW

1961   Badania archeologiczne w 720 rocznicę bitwy pod Legnicą [Archaeological Research prior to the 720th Anniversary of the Battle of Legnica]. *Z Otchłani Wieków* 27(3):203-209.

SIVILICH, DANIEL M.

1996   Analyzing Musket Balls to Interpret a Revolutionary War Site. *Historical Archaeology* 30(2):101-109.

2005   Revolutionary War Musket Ball Typology—An Analysis of Lead Artifacts Excavated at Monmouth Battlefield State Park. *Southern Campaigns of the American Revolution* 2(1):7-19, <http://www.southerncampaign.org/newsletter/v2n1.pdf>. Accessed 22 July 2012.

2007 What the Musket Ball Can Tell: Monmouth Battlefield State Park, New Jersey. In *Fields of Conflict: Battlefield Archaeology from the Roman Empire to the Korean War*. Vol. 1: Searching for War in the Ancient and Early Modern World, Douglas Scott, Lawrence Babits, and Charles Haecker, editors, pp. 84-101. Praeger, Westport, CT.

SIVILICH, DANIEL M., AND GARY WHEELER STONE

n.d. The Battle of Monmouth: The Archaeology of Molly Pitcher, the Royal Highlanders, and Colonel Cilley's Light Infantry. Society for American Archaeology, "Archaeology for the Public, Metal Detecting in Archaeology," <http://www.saa.org/publicftp/public/resources/MonmouthBravo.pdf>. Accessed 22 July 2012.

STARKEY, ARMSTRONG

2003 *War in the Age of Enlightenment: 1700-1789.* Studies in Military History and International Affairs. Praeger, Westport, CT.

STRASSBURGER, MARTIN

2007 Archäologische Nachweise zur Belagerung Heidelbergs im Dreißigjährigen Krieg [Archaeological Proof of the Siege of Heidelberg in the Thirty Years' War]. *Archäologische Nachrichten aus Baden* 74/75:56-61.

2009 Haydelberga vt capitur: Archäologie der Belagerungen Heidelbergs im 17. Jahrhundert [Haydelberga vt Capitur: Archaeology of the Sieges of Heidelberg in the 17th Century]. *Militär und Gesellschaft in der frühen Neuzeit* 13(1):143-146.

SUTHERLAND, TIMOTHY

2006 The Battle of Agincourt: An Alternative Location? In *Past Tense: Studies in the Archaeology of Conflict*, Tony Pollard and Iain Banks, editors, pp. 245-263. Journal of Conflict Archaeology, 1. Brill, Leiden, the Netherlands.

2009 Archaeological Evidence of Medieval Conflict—Case Studies from Towton, Yorkshire, England (1461) and Agincourt, Pas de Calais, France (1415). In *Schlachtfeldarchäologie, Battlefield Archaeology*, Harald Meller, editor, pp. 109-116. Tagungen des Landesmuseums für Vorgeschichte Halle, 2. Landesamt für Denkmalpflege und Archäologie Sachsen-Anhalt und Landesmuseum für Vorgeschichte, Halle, Germany.

SWIESZNIKOW, IGOR

1992 Bitwa pod Beresteczkiem 1651 r. w świetle źródeł historycznych i archeologicznych [The Battle of Beresteczko in 1651, in Historical and Archaeological Sources]. *Muzealnictwo Wojskowe* 5:66-98.

1993 *Битва під Берестечком* [*The Battle of Berestechko*]. Львів, Слово, Lviv, Ukraine.

1996 Bitwa pod Beresteczkiem w świetle źródeł kartograficznych i archeologicznych [The Battle of Beresteczko in Light of Cartographic and Archaeological Sources]. In *Kartografia wojskowa krajów strefy bałtyckiej XVI-XX w.*, Stanisław Alexandrowicz, Zbigniew Karpus, and Waldemar Rezmer, editors, pp. 35-49. Materiały Konferencji Naukowej; Toruń, Uniwersytet Mikołaja Kopernika, 20-22 października 1994 r. Uniwersytet Mikołaja Kopernika, Toruń, Poland.

THORDEMAN, BENGT

1939-
1940 *Armour from the Battle of Visby 1361.* In Collaboration with Poul Nörlund. Stockholm, Kungl. Vitterhets Historie och Antikvitets Akademien, 1939-1940. (Archaeological monographs/Kungl. Vitterhets Historie och Antikvitets Akademien, 27).

TOLKSDORF-LIENEMANN, EVA, AND JÖRG LIENEMANN

2004 Phosphatkartierung: Bodenkunde angewandt in Archäologie und Siedlungsforschung [Phosphate Mapping: Soil Science Applied in Archaeology and Settlement Research]. In *Archäologie Land Niedersachsen: 400 000 Jahre Geschichte*, Mamoun Fansa, Frank Both, and Henning Haßmann, editors, pp. 77-82. Theiss, Stuttgart, Germany.

VARUSSCHLACHT IM OSNABRÜCKER LAND GMBH—MUSEUM UND PARK KALKRIESE (EDITOR)

2009 *Konflikt. 2000 Jahre Varusschlacht [Conflict. 2000 Years Varus Battle].* 2000 Jahre Varusschlacht, Vol. 2. Wissenschaftliche Buchgesellschaft, Darmstadt, Germany.

VEREIN GEDENKSTÄTTE HASSENHAUSEN (EDITOR)

1996 *Zuverlässige Nachrichten des Pfarrer Tieze. Joh. Chr. David von 1785 bis 1823 Pfarrer zu Hassenhausen [Reliable Messages of the Pastor Tieze. Joh. Chr. David, Pastor at Hassenhausen from 1785 to 1823].* Schriftenreihe der Gedenkstätte Hassenhausen. Bad Kösen, Germany.

VON FLEMING, HANS FRIEDRICH

1726 *Der Vollkommene Teutsche Soldat: welcher die gantze Kriegs-Wissenschafft, [...] deutlich vorträgt, [...]; Nebst einem Anhange Von gelehrten Soldaten, Adel und Ritterstande, [...] [The Complete German Soldier: Who Precisely Reports the Whole Science of War; along with an Annex on Scholarly Soldiers, Gentry, and Knighthood].* Martini, Leipzig, Germany.

von Westphalen, Christian Heinrich Philipp

1871   *Geschichte der Feldzüge des Herzogs Ferdinand von Braunschweig-Lüneburg* [*History of the Campaigns of Duke Ferdinand of Braunschweig-Lüneburg*]. Urkundliche Nachträge zu dem nachgelassenen Manuscript von Christian Heinrich Philipp Edler von Westphalen. Zusammengestellt aus Materialien seines Nachlasses und des Kriegs-Archivs des Herzogs Ferdinand, und herausgegeben von F. O. W. H. v. Westphalen. Vol. III. (1757, 1758, 1759.). Ernst Siegfried Mittler & Sohn, Berlin, Germany.

Weise, Jochim

2009   Idstedt, 23/24. Juli 1850: "Die größte Schlacht nördlich der Elbe seit Menschengedenken" [Idstedt, 23-24 July 1850: "The Largest Battle North of the River Elbe within Living Memory"]. In *Schlachtfeldarchäologie, Battlefield Archaeology*, Harald Meller, editor, pp. 231-235. Tagungen des Landesmuseums für Vorgeschichte Halle, 2. Landesamt für Denkmalpflege und Archäologie Sachsen-Anhalt und Landesmuseum für Vorgeschichte, Halle, Germany.

Winter, Helmut

1993   Die Schlacht bei Dettingen, am 27. Juni 1743 [The Battle of Dettingen, on 27 June 1743]. *Unser Kahlgrund* 38:4;18-23.

Wirtgen, Arnold

1976   *Die preußischen Handfeuerwaffen: Modelle und Manufakturen; 1700-1806* [*The Prussian Handguns: Models and Manufacturing; 1700-1806*]. 2 vols. Biblio-Verlag, Osnabrück, Germany.

1986   Die Handfeuerwaffen der preußischen Armee 1740-1786: Manufakturen und Güteprüfung [The Handguns of the Prussian Army 1740-1786: Manufactures and Quality Testing]. In *Die Bewaffnung und Ausrüstung der Armee Friedrichs des Großen*, Vereinigung der Freunde des Wehrgeschichtlichen Museums Schloß Rastatt e.V.; Verein der Freunde und Förderer der wehrtechnischen Studiensammlung Koblenz e.V., editors, pp. 35-49. [No publisher].

Wollesen, Ernst

1898   *Chronik der altmärkischen Stadt Werben und ihrer ehemaligen Johanniter-Komturei* [*Chronicle of the City of Werben in the Altmark and Her Former Hospitaller Commandery*]. Werben a. d. Elbe, Germany.

Wolski, Krzysztof

2008   *Polskie pola bitew w świetle archeologii: Średniowiecze i okres wczesnonowożytny* [*Polish Battlefield in Light of Archaeology*]. Wydawnictwo i Agencja Informacyjna WAW Grzegorz Wawoczny, Racibórz, Poland.

Wrzosek, Jakub

2007   Bitwa pod Pułtuskiem w świetle dotychczasowych badań archeologicznych [The Battle of Pultusk in Light of Archaeological Research]. *Z otchłani wieków, Rocznik* 62(1-4):62-69.

2010   Wyniki badań archeologicznych przeprowadzonych w sezonie 2009 na polu bitwy pod Kunowiciami [The Results of the Archaeological Research Carried out on the Battlefield of Kunersdorf during the 2009 Season]. In *Kunersdorf 1759. Kunowice 2009: Studien zu einer europäischen Legende – Studium pewnej europejskiej legendy*, Werner Benecke und Grzegorz Podruczny, editors, pp 95-101. Thematicon, 15. Logos Verlag, Berlin.

zum Winkel, Arnold

1916   Die Schlacht bei Liegnitz am 13. Mai 1634 [The Battle of Liegnitz on 13th May 1634]. *Zeitschrift des Vereins für Geschichte Schlesiens* 50:28-56.

Zoffmann, Zsuzsanna K.

1982   *Az 1526-os Mohácsi csata 1976-ban feltárt Tömegsírjainak embertani vizsgálata* [*The Battle of Mohács in 1526, Anthropological Study of Mass Graves Discovered in 1976*]. Biológiai Tanulmányok, 9. Budapest, Hungary.

///

Arne Homann
Horner Weg 38a
D-20535 Hamburg
Germany

MIKE BELASUS

The Great Northern War Underwater: A Swedish Ship Barrier of 1715 in Northeast Germany

ABSTRACT

The Swedish ship barrier is an important archaeological and historical monument of the Great Northern War in northern Germany. It is protected by the Heritage Protection Act of the German federal state of Mecklenburg-Western Pomerania. As a part of the defense system of Swedish Pomerania, requisitioned ships were deliberately sunk at the eastern entrance of the Bay of Greifswald in 1715. Today the monument is threatened by the building of a gas pipeline, and one wreck had to be excavated and recovered. Due to current legislation, all archaeological actions had to be financed by the builder of the pipeline.

INTRODUCTION

The ship barrier of 1715 is one of many underwater archaeological sites on the Baltic coast of the German federal state of Mecklenburg-Western Pomerania (Figure 1). From the air it is still visible today. Like a string of pearls, each dark spot on the sandy bottom of the Bay of Greifswald represents one shipwreck (Figure 2). The discovery of this magnificent site was only possible after German reunification when aerial surveys could be carried out in the early 1990s. Later, in 1996 volunteer divers confirmed the spotted anomalies as being the remains of old shipwrecks that corresponded to 18th-century historical sources. Now a pipeline is planned through the Baltic Sea from Russia

to Germany to supply western Europe with gas. After crossing the waters of Finland, Sweden, and Denmark the pipeline enters the German territory and will cross the ship barrier (Figure 3).

The site is situated on a natural shoal at the eastern entrance of the Bay of Greifswald between the Rügen Island's Mönchgut Peninsula in the northwest and the small island of Ruden in the southeast (Figure 4). Fourteen verified wreck sites stretch in a line for almost 1 km from the west to the east. This site—lying at a depth of only 3-4 m—is regarded as one of the most impressive visible underwater monuments of Germany.

THE GREAT NORTHERN WAR AND THE DEFENSE OF STRALSUND

The wrecks commemorate a very important event in the history of northern Europe (Frost 2000). They are a monument to the struggle for supremacy in the Baltic Sea during the Great Northern War from 1700 to 1721. In this period the Russian Empire fought together with Saxony-Poland and Denmark-Norway against the Swedish kingdom. During that time Sweden reined over large parts of Pomerania on the southern Baltic coast. The war took place foremost around and in the Baltic Sea and reached Pomerania in August 1711 when Danish troops entered the country from Mecklenburg. Later the forces where joined by troops from Saxony and Russia and outnumbered the Swedish troops. This situation forced the Swedish troops to concentrate on the defense of the fortresses of Stralsund and Stettin and Rügen Island. In the following time the fortress of Stralsund suffered four sieges by the allied troops. The besieging armies had

serious problems with supplies and the transport of heavy siege artillery. The town of Greifswald was at that time the only suitable harbor to bring the much needed artillery on land but it was still blocked by the Swedish who ruled over the Bay of Greifswald. After the fortress of Stettin had to surrender in September 1713 only Rügen Island and Stralsund remained in Swedish hands. The last siege of Stralsund began in the end of 1714. This time troops from Denmark, Russia, Saxony, and recently joined Prussia tried to break the Swedish defense. The Swedish still had Rügen Island under control to defend the waterways to the town of Stralsund from land with heavy gun batteries. This strategic advantage also prevented the landing of the urgently needed artillery. Heavy artillery was placed on the narrow western entrance into a narrow strait between the mainland and Rügen Island called the Strelasund. More complicated was the situation at the eastern

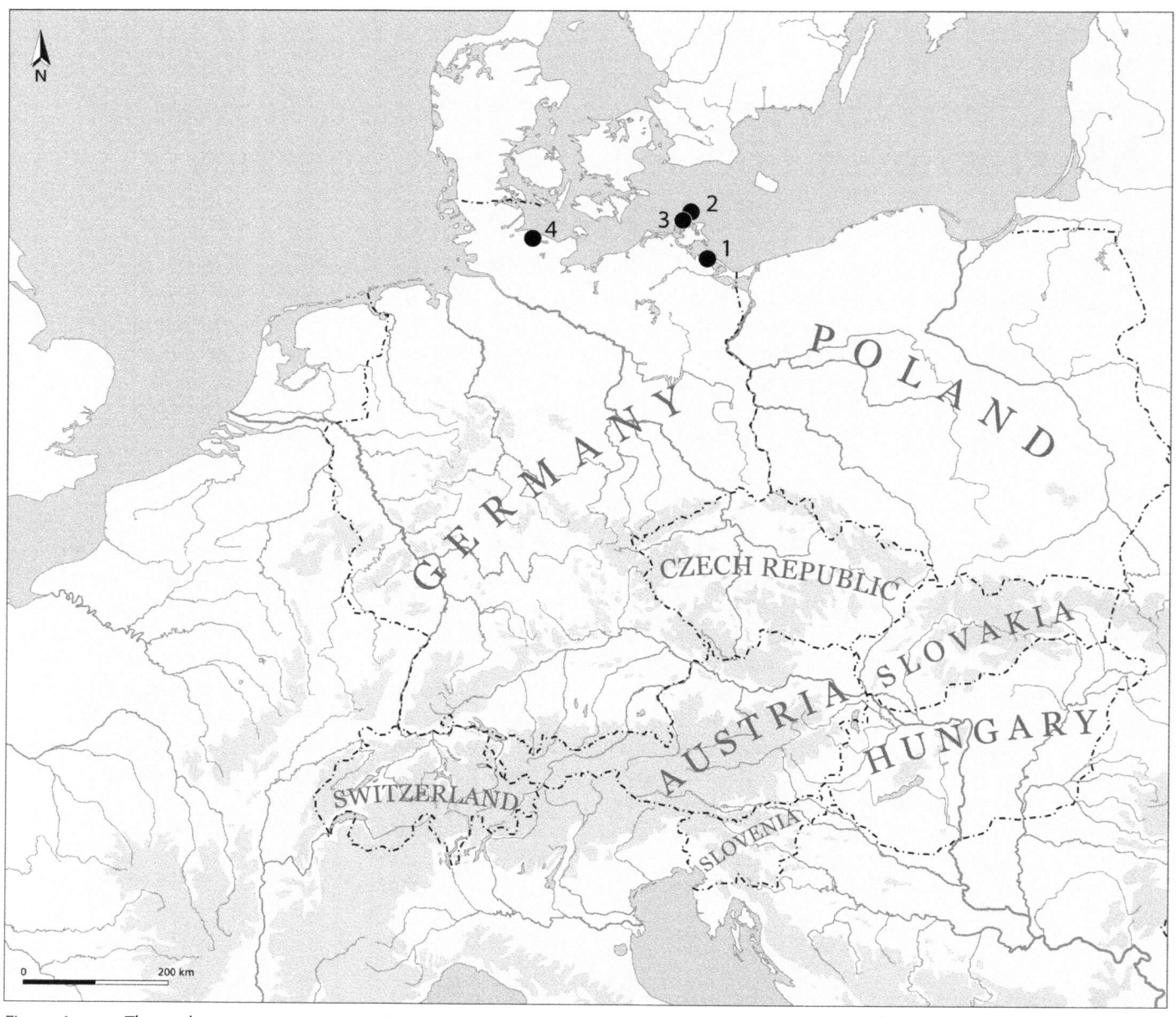

Figure 1. The underwater sites connected to the Great Northern War in northern Germany: (1) the Swedish ship barrier of 1715 at the entrance of the Bay of Greifswald; (2) the small Danish frigate Mynden lost in 1718 at Cape Arkona; (3) the lost Swedish support fleet of 1715 on the west coast of Rügen Island; and (4) the lost Swedish fleet of 1715 in the Kiel Bay (Map provided courtesy of the Department of Prehistory and Medieval Archaeology, University of Vienna, Austria).

entrance to the Bay of Greifswald. Guns were placed on Rügen Island's Mönchgut Peninsula, the small island of Ruden, and on the northwestern tip of the island of Usedom. The water between the Mönchgut Peninsula and the small island of Ruden is very shallow because of natural shoals. In 18th-century sources these shoals are also called the Ruden reef. The access of bigger ships into the bay was only possible by a few passages. One of these passages, the so called *Mitteltief* (middle deep), was out of reach for the land batteries. For this reason the Swedish decided in 1715 to block this passage with an artificial barrier to force every ship to

pass into the bay within reach of their guns. For this purpose the Swedish requisitioned several small and medium sized vessels from the harbors in the area. The ships were loaded with cobblestones and sunk across the Mitteltief passage together with big anchors. In July 1715 the Danish fleet approached and attacked this defense system for the first time, but they were beaten back by the artillery at the small island of Ruden. The Swedish plan seemed to work, but already in September 1715 another attack followed. According to some historical sources a local pilot who was treated badly by the Swedes ran over to the Danes (Krüger 2002:189) and

Historical Archaeology in Central Europe

guided the Danish ships to a secret passage in the barrier. During the night the Danish dragged their ships through this passage using anchors that were brought out by the boats. This sudden change of the situation caused confusion among the commanders of the Swedish ships within the bay. Some tried to flee toward Sweden while others burned their own ships to avoid having them captured by the Danes. The heavy siege artillery was subsequently brought ashore in the harbor of Greifswald and positioned in front of the besieged fortress of Stralsund. In November 1715 Rügen Island was conquered by a joint Danish-Prussian army. The fortress of Stralsund surrendered in December 1715 just one day after the Swedish King, who resided there, secretly escaped to Sweden. After the war was over the barrier was gradually forgotten. The anchors were most probably salvaged, but the shipwrecks with their cargoes of stones remained a hazard to shipping at least until the mid-19th century. Then they were forgotten for the next 150 years until they were rediscovered in 1996 (Förster et al. 2002; Krüger 2002; Scherer 2003).

THE MONUMENT

Today the remains of the ships are regarded as a unique archive of local shipbuilding traditions of the late 17th century and an important historical monument of European history. The surveys of the previous years showed that the ships were built using carvel and clinker (or lapstrake) building techniques—the former characterized by planks set edge-to-edge and the latter by overlapping planks. The remains of the vessels vary in length from 11.5 m to almost 20 m. Some are up to 7 m wide. The dimensions are not related to the building technique: clinker-built ships are among both the smaller and larger wrecks. All dated ships were built in the last quarter of the 17th century. The origin of the oak that was used for the ships is from around the area. There is almost no sedimentation around the wrecks because of currents caused by the wind. Therefore the ballast mounts that cover each wreck are the only protection for the timbers. Only the lowest parts of the ships have survived beneath the cobblestones. Some test trenches

Figure 2. The ship barrier of 1715 is almost 1 km long and visible from above in the shallow water of the eastern entrance of the Bay of Greifswald (Image by Otto Braasch, 2006; courtesy of Landshut/Landesamt für Kultur und Denkmalpflege, Schwerin).

on selected wrecks of the monument were excavated in the past. They gave some information on the construction, but finds were rather scarce. In some wrecks split trunks of young conifer trees were placed under the heavy ballast, probably to prevent any destruction that could be caused by the stones (Förster et al. 2002:378). Two deadeyes were found in the vicinity of one wreck. The most spectacular find was a silver coin minted in 1679 in Brandenburg that was still placed in the mast step of a vessel (Förster et al. 2002:378).

LEGISLATION AND THE PRESERVATION OF MONUMENTS

The site is protected by state heritage legislation today. This protection by the Monument Protection Act of the German federal state of Mecklenburg-Western Pomerania has existed since 1993. Until 1990 this part of Germany belonged to the territory of the former German Democratic Republic (GDR). Diving in the coastal waters of the GDR was very limited because of strict border regulations. For this reason the underwater heritage remained almost undisturbed until the early 1990s. With the political

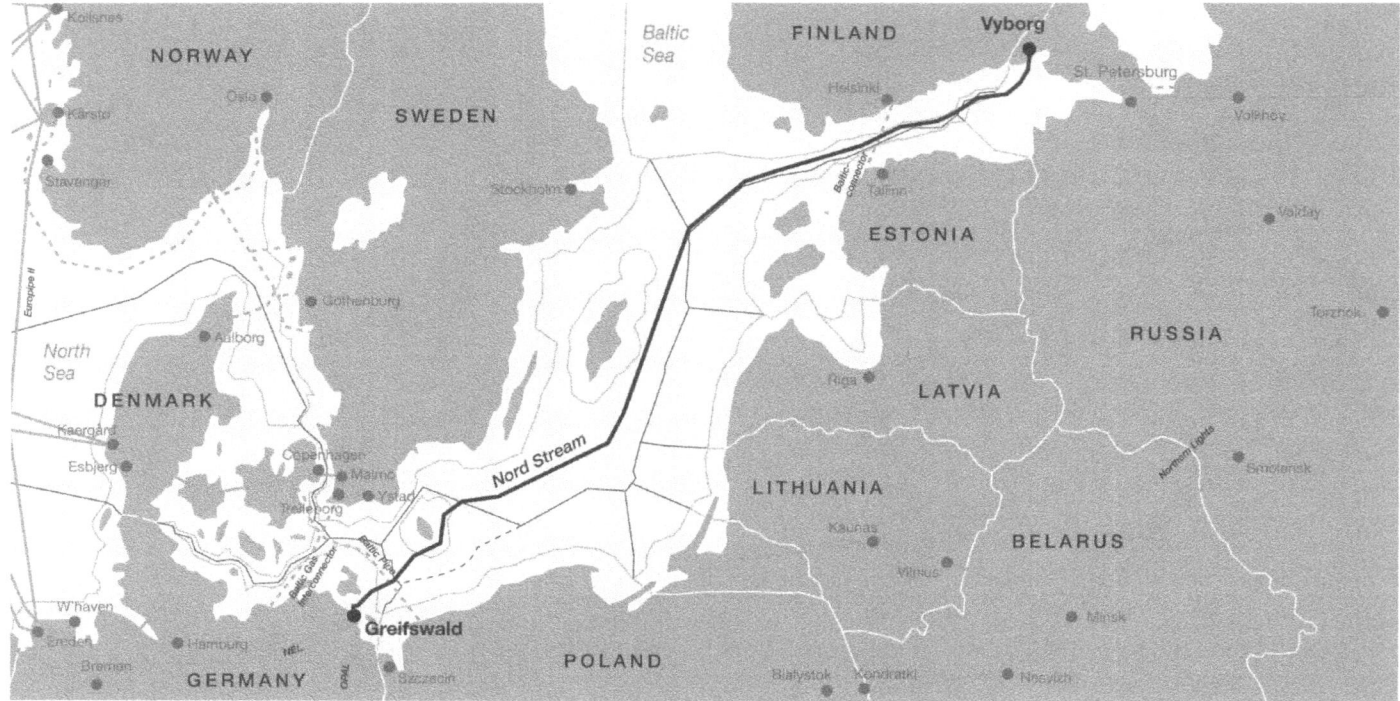

Figure 3.   The gas pipeline corridor between Vyborg in Russia and Lubmin at the Bay of Greifswald in northern Germany (Company press release, Nord-Stream AG, 2008).

change activities of many kinds were increasing in the waters of the state. For this reason regulatory legislation was urgently needed. Today the Monument Protection Act of Mecklenburg-Western Pomerania considers underwater cultural heritage in particular. Furthermore it is regulated that any costs related to interference at a monument, including maintenance, professional restoration, recovery, and documentation of the monument shall be borne by the entity that causes the interference. This means that any archaeological work has to be financed by the entity that might disturb an archaeological site.

After the reunification of Germany the establishment of a modern infrastructural network was needed in the former GDR. The heritage legislation proved its necessity because wherever building took place archaeological sites turned up on land and underwater. In the beginning the acceptance of archaeology as a fixed component of the planning of building projects was hard to achieve. Today the Authority for Culture and Preservation of Monuments (the Authority) has established a permanent position within these processes in Mecklenburg-Western Pomerania and is widely accepted by the public.

One of the main tools for the management of cultural heritage in Mecklenburg-Western Pomerania is a GIS

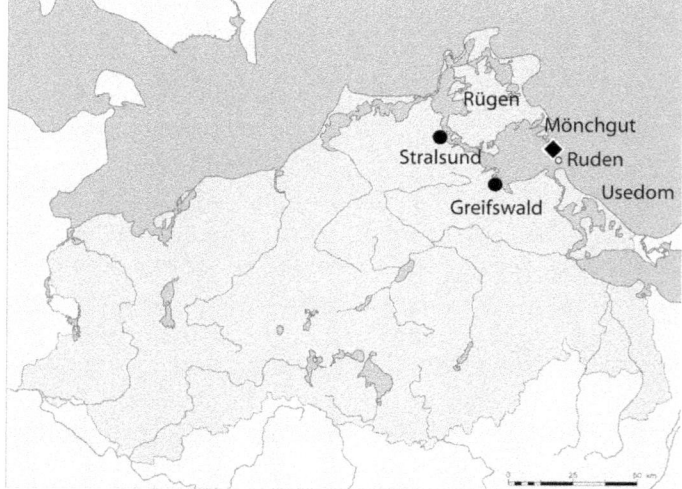

Figure 4.   The federal state of Mecklenburg-Western Pomerania, Germany, and places mentioned in the text. The rhombus at the eastern entrance of the Bay of Greifswald indicates the site of the Swedish ship barrier of 1715. (Image by author, 2009; courtesy of Landesamt für Kultur und Denkmalpflege, Schwerin.)

database for the collection of all available data. The data on underwater heritage are collected from historical archives, water-related authorities, aerial photography, information from the public, and the work of the Society for Underwater Archaeology of Mecklenburg-Western Pomerania. This society is a sport diving association with archaeological interest and is cooperating very closely with the Authority. Together with archaeologists the members of the society participate in surveys and in some excavations. All data collected by the society are added to the database.

One major source of data about potential archaeological sites in the waters of Mecklenburg-Western Pomerania is the aerial survey of the coast. Due to the geological conditions on the southern Baltic coast fine sediments create long beaches and shallow waters with moving sands. These circumstances caused many ships to founder on the shoals. Today the light sandy ground enables archaeologists to find sites from above. Anomalies are visible from a height of 300 m down to a water depth of about 6 m in good conditions. In many cases these sites are easily identified as shipwrecks. Today the number of the potential underwater archaeological sites in the database of the Authority exceeds 1,400.

Fourteen among these sites are found in the ship barrier of 1715. The ship barrier remained undisturbed for almost 300 years. The 1-km-long barrier was constructed to close an important shipping passage, and considering the narrow entrance to the Bay of Greifswald it was only a matter of time before this monument would be threatened by building projects.

FIELDWORK AND RESULTS 2006–2009

The pipeline planned within the North-European-Gas-Pipeline-Project (NEGP) will connect Russia and Germany from Vyborg to Lubmin near the town of Greifswald at the Bay of Greifswald though the Baltic Sea. It will be 1,220 km long. The modern shipping canal at the eastern entrance to the bay and the nature preserves of Ruden Island leave no other route into the bay except through the ship barrier. The planned building of a dual pipe pipeline means an enormous impact on the seabed. The Authority was included in the negotiations from the beginning along with similar groups in Finland, Sweden, and Denmark, through which the pipeline will pass. Necessary actions were planned very early with the builders, Nord-Stream AG. Planning also included geophysical surveys of the whole pipeline route within German waters to locate previously unknown potential archaeological sites and objects. The results of these surveys will be the basis for the determination of future archaeological activities. Some areas of archaeological significance, such as the ship barrier of 1715, were already in the underwater database, and first steps could be prepared at an early stage of the process.

The first fieldwork campaign was launched in 2006 to get more detailed information about the barrier in the area of the pipeline corridor. This campaign included a geophysical survey and diving examinations of the wrecks. The goal was to find out if there were ways to pass the monument without any disturbance and if not, how to limit the interference. For this purpose side scan data were collected to give an overview of the sites (Figure 5). A seismic survey with two different frequencies was carried out to give more information about bathymetry, correct position, and possible hidden parts of the barrier in the sediment. Considering all collected data the decision was made to recover one of the wrecks to guarantee better protection of the adjacent wrecks. To keep the interference as small as possible the smallest and most disturbed site, Ostseebereich VII, Mönchgut, Fpl. 67 (Mönchgut 67), was chosen to be excavated and recovered.

In 2008 a second fieldwork campaign was launched to gather further information from the chosen site for the

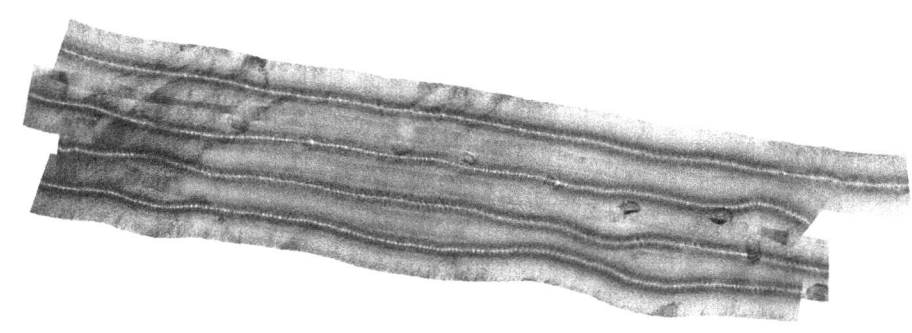

Figure 5. A side scan overview of a ca. 300-m long section of the ship barrier of 1715 in the Bay of Greifswald. The shadows of the shipwrecks are visible along the length of the scan (Image by INNOMAR, Rostock, 2006; courtesy of Landesamt für Kultur und Denkmalpflege, Schwerin).

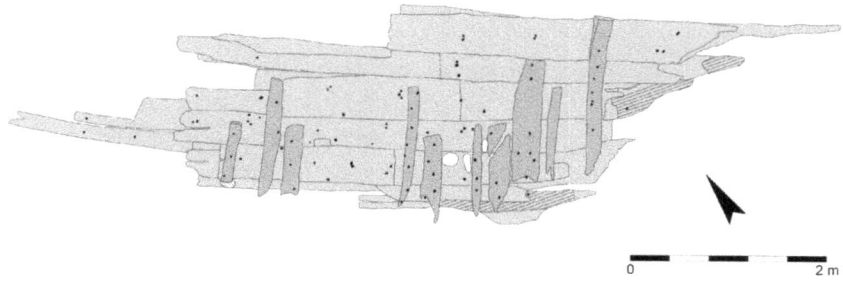

Ostseebereich VII, Mönchgut, Fpl. 67

Figure 6. *Site plan of the wreck Mönchgut 67 (Drawing by Roman Scholz, 2010; courtesy of Landesamt für Kultur und Denkmalpflege, Schwerin).*

planned recovery of the wreck. Detailed documentation of the site was done, and test trenches were excavated. The examination of the site revealed the remains of one side of a ship 9 m long and 4.7 m wide (Figure 6). The wreck lay on top of the sediment protected only by a small ballast mount of cobblestones (Figure 7). Most parts of the ship were gone. Parts of the outer planking, frames, and ceiling planking survived under the ballast, but there were no signs of the keel, keelson, or the posts. The visible parts showed overlapping oak planks connected by rivets in clinker technique.

In summer 2009 the full excavation of the site and recovery of all timbers of the wreck was carried out. Each timber was documented in detail in 1:1 scale after the recovery. The wreck represents a rather small vessel. During the work it was discovered that a second layer of planks was added to the clinker planking of the hull in the carvel manner. For this purpose the steps in the clinker planking where smoothed with an axe or adze. While the planks within the strakes of the clinker planking were joined by 20-25-cm-long lashes, the planks of the outer carvel planking were but-end joined within the strakes. The timbers were dated by dendrochronology to after 1658 A.D. and were most probably cut in the area. There was almost no difference in date between the clinker and the carvel planking of the outer hull. This could suggest that the construction

of both layers occurred when the vessel was first built, but the first clinker-built planking showed repairs, and the technical features were very different in addition to the fact that one was clinker-built and the other carvel. The pattern of the framing gave further reason to suggest that extra framing was added to the hull during a major rebuilding of the vessel. While the first layer of planking was hardly distinguishable from late medieval clinker hulls, the second flush-laid planking was comparable to that of Dutch-influenced early modern shipbuilding. Ships with a first clinker-built and second carvel-built outer planking are known from the archaeological record on the southern Baltic coast (Ossowski 2006; Grundvad Nielsen 2010). All of them are post-medieval with the earliest example built around 1550 (Mäss 1994). There are several reasons for a second layer of planks. It could be a rebuilding of an old vessel but also a protection against ice or a strengthening for heavy cargos. It also could be an improvement for fishing vessels because a clinker-built hull can cause problems when working with a net (Eichler 1990:218).

Figure 7. *The few preserved timbers of Mönchgut 67 were covered with ballast stones (Photo by James McClean, 2008; courtesy of Landesamt für Kultur und Denkmalpflege, Schwerin).*

Among the scarce number of finds were a part of a leather shoe representing life on board and a bar shot as evidence for warfare (Heinze 2010). After the recovery and detailed documentation the timbers were stored in water tanks. To prevent a loss of information through possible accidents during the pipeline building process the adjacent wrecks of the barrier on both sides of the planned pipeline were documented in situ. During construction in the vicinity of the monument, the adjacent wrecks will be marked with buoys. Archaeologists will be on site to observe the construction. After the pipeline is finished the sites next to the pipeline will be surveyed. To preserve the visual effect of the entirety of this unique monument for the public, the shape of the wreck site will be recreated to reconstruct the appearance of the barrier as seen from the air.

OTHER MARITIME EVIDENCE OF THE GREAT NORTHERN WAR

The Swedish ship barrier of 1715 is not the only underwater site related to the Great Northern War in northern Germany. In Mecklenburg-Western Pomerania there are two more sites connected to this historical event. Research on a shipwreck at the northern point of Rügen Island could identify it to be the small Danish frigate *Mynden*. The ship sank within minutes after hitting an uncharted rock near Cape Arkona in 1718 (Auer 2004). The remains of two other vessels were found on the west coast of the same island. The results of a survey of these sites and the recovery of one of them in 2003 gave reason to connect these wrecks with an incident of the Great Northern War. In 1715 the Danes prevented the landing of a Swedish supply fleet in this area and destroyed many of the enemy's vessels by setting them on fire (Kleingärtner and Nakoinz 2005). Additional archaeological evidence of this war turned up in the Bay of Kiel in the state of Schleswig-Holstein. A huge area with scattered gunshot was found close to the shore. Later an 18th-century gun barrel was found further out in the bay. The site was identified as a place were Swedish ships were deliberately grounded after the Battle of Colberger Heide in 1715 west of the island of Fehmarn. Total destruction of the fleet was prevented by the Danes, and all except the heavily damaged flagship *Hedwig Sophia* were taken as a prize (Belasus 2002). In 2008 the wreck of the abandoned *Hedwig Sophia* was found in the same area, and surveys were carried out in 2009 and 2010 by the Archaeological State Authority of Schleswig-Holstein together with the Maritime Archaeological Programme at the University of Southern Denmark in Esbjerg and the University of Kiel (Auer 2011).

CONCLUSION

The Swedish ship barrier of 1715 is a unique monument in itself but just one part of the enormous cultural value buried along the German Baltic coast. Opportunities for high standard archaeological access to this vast archive are currently controlled by the state heritage protection program and are only possible when potential sites are threatened by human interference. Until today no research institution or university has been permanently involved in the underwater archaeology of Germany, and for this reason comprehensive research is currently very limited in this field.

The ship barrier represents only a short period in time, but this and the fact that all ships were requisitioned in the same area and sunk at the same time makes them a very important resource. It gives us the unique opportunity to study the ships and their building traditions and how they appeared next to each other in the harbors around the Bay of Greifswald and the island of Usedom. They have the potential to give us a glimpse into the human mind about 300 years ago, to analyze the technical understanding of those days and what might have influenced it. Carvel flush-built hulls lay next to clinker-built vessels, and in the wreck recently excavated both techniques seem to have been combined.

The excavation of the site Mönchgut 67 showed that even small remains of a ship can reveal important information. The clinker building tradition in this area seems to have survived unaltered from the late medieval period to the late 17th century or even early 18th century. It is the supplementation of a flush-laid second skin with clear technical details of the Dutch-influenced carvel building tradition that makes the early modern context most likely. The people that were practicing different shipbuilding traditions in the region not only lived next to each other but also engaged in a certain degree of technical exchange. Yet they stuck to their own shipbuilding philosophies. Obviously there was no need for a major change in shipbuilding in general. For some purposes or people the older clinker technique was still accepted as a good solution, even until today as clinker-built boats are still used in fisheries along the Baltic coast.

The shipyards, where the small and medium sized vessels of the ship barrier were built, were most probably not using any drawings at that time. Therefore, unlike in the building of many navy vessels, we do not know much about the building of this kind of vessel during that period. A detailed survey of all wrecks within the barrier would be desirable to shed more light on this piece of unwritten history and to uncover the social and economic background that influenced the development of shipbuilding or led to the maintenance of old solutions for centuries.

The remaining ships of the barrier will be preserved underneath their stone ballast for other archaeologists to come, thanks to heritage legislation in Mecklenburg-Western Pomerania and the growing acceptance of it among the public. Our common underwater heritage will be safe for future generations.

REFERENCES

AUER, JENS

2004   Fregatten Mynden. A 17th-century Danish Frigate Found in Northern Germany. *International Journal of Nautical Archaeology* 33(2):264-280.

2011   Prinsessan Hedvig Sophia 2010. Fieldwork Report. *Esbjerg Maritime Archaeology Reports* 3. Maritime Archaeological Programme, University of Southern Denmark, Esbjerg, Denmark.

BELASUS, MIKE

2002   Ein Schiffsgeschütz aus der Kieler Förde [A Naval Gun from Kiel Fjord]. *Starigard* 2002:30-35.

EICHLER, CURT W.

1990   *Holzbootsbau und der Bau von stählernen Booten und Yachten* [Wooden Boat Building and the Building of Steel Boats and Yachts]. RKE Verlag, Kiel, Germany.

FÖRSTER, THOMAS

2000   Schiffbau und Handel an der südwestlichen Ostsee. Untersuchungen an Wrackfunden des 13.-15. Jahrhunderts [Ship Building and Trade in the Southwest Baltic Sea. The Examination of Wreck Finds of the 13th-15th Centuries]. In *Schutz des Kulturerbes Unterwasser. Veränderungen europäischer Lebenskultur durch Fluß – und Seehandel*, Friedrich Lüth, Ulrich Schoknecht, editors, pp. 221-236. Landesamt für Bodendenkmalpflege, Lübstorf, Germany.

FÖRSTER, THOMAS, JOACHIM KRÜGER, AND THOMAS SCHERER

2002   Die schwedische Schiffssperre von 1715—taucharchäologische Untersuchungen im Greifswalder Bodden [The Swedish Ships Barrier of 1715—Underwater Archaeological Examination in Greifswald Bay]. In *Forschungen zur Archäologie und Geschichte in Norddeutschland*, Ulrich Masemann, editor, pp. 371-388. Archäologischen Gesellschaft im Landkreis Rotenburg/Wümme e.V., Rotenburg/Wümme, Germany.

FROST, R. I.

2000   *The Northern Wars: War, State and Society in Northeastern Europe 1558-1721*. Longman, Harlow, England.

GRUNDVAD NIELSEN, BENTE

2010   Converted Clinker Vessels from the 16th-17th Century. A Case Study of the Ostsee Bereich IV, Fischland, FPL 77. Master's dissertation, Maritime Archaeological Programme, University of Southern Denmark, Esbjerg, Denmark.

HEINZE, JANA

2010   Bericht zur Hauptuntersuchung der Unterwasserfundplatzes Mönchgut 67 im Rahmen des Ostseegaspipelinebaus von Vyborg nach Lubmin [Report on the Excavation of the Underwater Site Mönchgut 67 in Connection to the Baltic Sea Gas Pipeline Construction from Vyborg to Lubmin]. Landesamt für Kultur und Denkmalpflege, Schwerin, Germany.

KLEINGÄRTNER, SUNHILD, AND OLIVER NAKOINZ

2005   Zwei Neuzeitliche Schiffswracks vor Dranske, Gem. Wittow, Kr. Rügen [Two Early Modern Shipwrecks off Dranske, Community Wittow, County of Rügen]. *Jahrbuch Bodendenkmalpflege Mecklenburg-Vorpommern* 53(2005):315-346.

KRÜGER, JOACHIM

2002   Die Schiffssperre im Greifswalder Bodden von 1715 und ihr historischer Hintergrund [The Ships Barrier in Greifswald Bay of 1715 and its Historical Background]. In *Maritime Archäologie heute*, Carl-Olof Cederlund and Kersten Krüger, editors, pp. 186-193. Ingo Koch Verlag und Co. KG, Rostock, Germany.

MÄSS, VELLO

1994   A Unique 16th Century Estonian Ship Find. In *Crossroads in Ancient Shipbuilding. Proceedings of the Sixth International Symposium on Boat and Ship Archaeology* (Roskilde 1991), Christer Westerdahl, editor, pp. 189-194. Oxbow, Oxford, England.

OSSOWSKI, WALDEMAR

2006   Two Double-Planked Wrecks from Poland. In
        *Connected by the Sea. Proceedings of the Tenth
        International Symposium on Boat and Ship
        Archaeology* (Roskilde 2003), Lucy Blue, Frederic
        M. Hocker, and Anton Englert, editors, pp. 259-
        265. Oxbow, Oxford, England.

SCHERER, THOMAS

2003   Vier untersuchte Klinkerschiffe einer
        schwedischen Schiffssperre von 1715 im
        Greifswalder Bodden [Four Examined Clinker
        Ships in a Swedish Ships Barrier of 1715 in
        Greifswald Bay]. Magister dissertation, University
        of Bamberg, Germany.

Mike Belasus
Deutsches Schiffahrtsmuseum
Hans-Scharoun-Platz 1
D-27568 Bremerhaven
Germany

CLAUDIA THEUNE

Archaeology and Remembrance:
The Contemporary Archaeology of Concentration Camps, Prisoner-of-War Camps, and Battlefields

ABSTRACT

Archaeological research at places of recent history is of important socio-political significance that can only be compared in a limited way to research of older (prehistoric) periods. The research relates to current issues of cultural memory of the 20th century and shows clearly the political dimension of our profession. The differently motivated archaeological works in former concentration camps, prisoner-of-war camps, or on battlefields in Europe are of great importance for the collective national or even European memory. Connected to this memory is also admonishment and commemoration of the victims of the terror of the world wars and the Holocaust. In the past, remembrance, commemoration, and admonishment were carried on by the survivors and witnesses. In the future, archaeological finds and findings will play an important role in this. By the haptic engagement with the objects (and thus also with the witnesses), which carry with them the history and the structure of these places and the objects' former owners, we archaeologists and the general population learn about these places and systems.

INTRODUCTION

The archaeology of sites from the recent past is indisputably part of historical archaeology, yet English-language synopses from the field in recent years have included few references to research from the 20th century (Hall and Silliman 2006; Hicks and Beaudry 2006; Majewski and Gaimster 2009). They have been mostly limited to the early modern and modern periods. Case studies from the National Socialist period or about the Holocaust are included only rarely and sometimes not at all, even in publications about contemporary archaeology (Russell and Flemming 1991; Buchli and Lucas 2001). Instead, these collections feature contributions about the battlefields of World War I (De Meyer 2010) and about sites in the British or French parts of the world (Schofield and Johnson 2006). Schofield (2005) offers an exhaustive analysis from an Anglophone standpoint, with a broad methodological and theoretical approach and many examples from the 20th century drawn from across Europe that stress the importance of remembrance.

A continental European viewpoint can contribute other facets, in particular through archaeological research from sites that have to do with National Socialism. At issue are forms of cultural memory and the changes they go through (Assmann 1999). Remembrance and cultural memory have changed at these places since the end of World War II and in particular since the 1980s. Sites such as former concentration or extermination camps, but also, for example, the place in Berlin where a Gestapo prison, SS headquarters, and the Reich Security Department were found—known today under the title "The Topography of Terror"—are particularly important in this regard. These places were previously confined to the edges of cultural memory, but have now taken up a central position. These—for Germany at least—"traumatic places" or "reluctant" places of memory (Assmann 1999:328-330) play a role very different in the remembrance of survivors and their relatives than for young people or tourists today. They have distinct connotations for different groups, societies, and nations (Moshenska 2006). These places, which exist across Europe, now have an important function as memorials and places of admonition, remembrance, and learning at the scenes of past crimes. They are memorials and places of admonition for the victims, the survivors, and their descendants. Survivors and their immediate descendants remember there the victims of war or of National Socialism and hand on this tradition. They are also historical and political places of learning for young people (Engelhardt 2004). Those who did not experience the misery of war or the terror of the so-called Third Reich at first hand, and who have not learned of these things through the stories of the

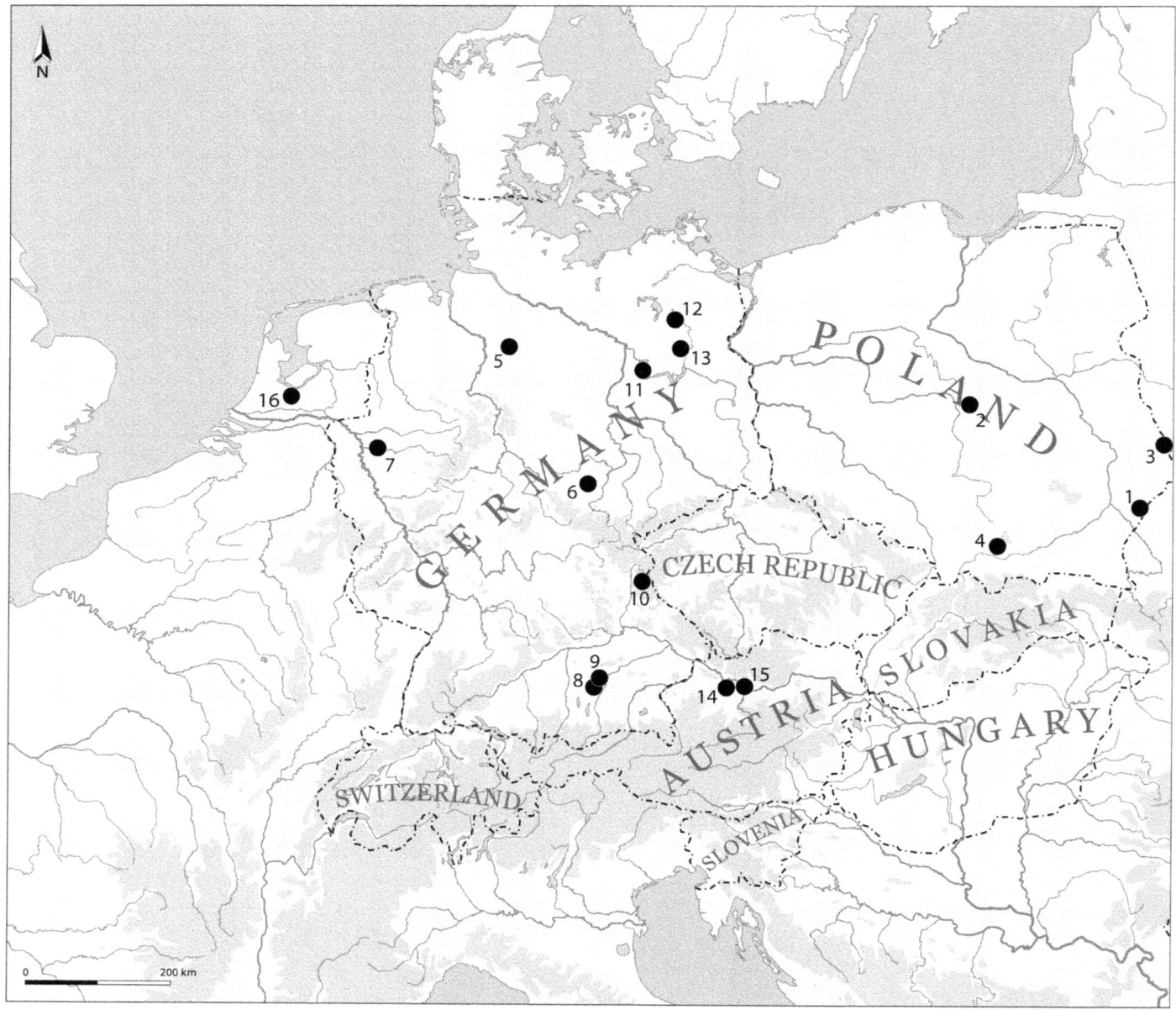

Figure 1. The underwater sites connected to the Great Northern War in northern Germany: (1) the Swedish ship barrier of 1715 at the entrance of the Bay of Greifswald; (2) the small Danish frigate Mynden lost in 1718 at Cape Arkona; (3) the lost Swedish support fleet of 1715 on the west coast of Rügen Island; and (4) the lost Swedish fleet of 1715 in the Kiel Bay (Map provided courtesy of the Department of Prehistory and Medieval Archaeology, University of Vienna, Austria).

first or second generations, are taught about National Socialism at these places with the help of eyewitness accounts, documents, and large and small objects. Such places can become places of remembrance (*lieu de mémoire* [Nora 1998]) and enter into collective memory. Archaeological research at such former crime scenes has helped to ensure that this remembrance can be preserved and continue to be passed on.

Places directly associated with the 20th-century world wars or with the National Socialist dictatorship have begun to be analyzed by archaeologists from Germany,

Poland, and Austria in the last 15-20 years. Excavations have taken place on battlefields and at prisoner-of-war camps, as well as at firing squad sites, concentration camps, and death camps. The publications of heritage organizations regularly contain a large number of smaller and larger excavations, some of which take place as a routine response to legal guidelines, others of which are part of designed research projects.

The study of the history of these places was traditionally the sole preserve of historians. The sources used were written records or oral history accounts. They were official records from the period or private letters and other contemporary documents, but they also included later court records and eyewitnesses accounts, which reflected personal experiences and memories, but at differing intervals of time from the events. It was presumed that these sources offered comprehensive information about the events, the structures, and the historical processes involved. Pictures, above all photos, and objects played only a secondary role in this historical research and were mostly used to illustrate the written or spoken word.

Recently, however, it has become increasingly clear in the historical sciences that both written and oral sources throw light on only very specific and sometimes contradictory views of the past, thus only telling part of the story. Written records prepared by official sources, in particular, often reflect a solely bureaucratic view, while personal memoranda disclose only those recollections and experiences that are most present in memory. Photographs as pictorial sources are framed by the photographer, the motif is often stage-managed and people and objects arranged. Closer examination reveals details of the motif's surroundings, a date can pin down the subject in time. If a photo is understood in its context, then new interpretations of its meanings are possible. Objects accompany us everywhere. We cannot function without them and they are part of everyday life. The objects may not speak for themselves, but they nevertheless reveal their own history and biography, their specific use in a particular context, and in this way their cultural meaning.

Moreover, there are only very few written or oral sources for some structures, places, and events of the recent past, for example the Nazi death camps in eastern Poland. A first study of part of the Mauthausen concentration camp in Austria has shown that the explanatory potential of the sources can be raised through their combined analysis. The testimony of individual sources can be falsified, verified, modified, or supplemented (Dejnega and Theune in press). All sources have to be used if comprehensive research is to be carried out.

ARCHAEOLOGY AND MODERN/CONTEMPORARY HISTORY

Traditionally, archaeology limited itself to periods and epochs in which material sources were the only or at least the most important basis for cultural insights. The medieval period was increasingly taken on board during the second half of the 20th century, as it was realized that archaeological sources can tell us a great deal about everyday life. Written records or art, strongly influenced as they were by Christianity, do not have the same potential. Readiness to glance over the borders of a particular period led in further course to an extension of interest to post-medieval times, to the early modern period, the era of industrialization, and the modern period. The removal of temporal restrictions for archaeological research by the Convention of Valetta/Malta in 1992 (Council of Europe 1992) prompted the adaptation of the relevant laws in many countries. Article 1 of the convention also explicitly defined archaeological heritage as a source of common European memory. This means that archaeological research at places of recent history is among the responsibilities of arts and monuments organizations and is within the field of research of the archeological sciences at European universities.

The use for political education at memorial sites of artifacts and material remains brought to light by excavations has also increased. There are ever fewer eyewitnesses to talk in schools about their awful experiences or the conditions of survival in the camps. Archaeological finds will therefore play an important role in the instruction of young people in the future, ensuring that memorial sites and places of remembrance continue to be places of learning and historical-political education about National Socialism.

The following text deals with archaeological research projects at sites from the first half of the 20th century (Figure 1). Its focus is on historical research to do with the National Socialist dictatorship, but commemoration of the victims of World War I also plays an important role for contemporary remembrance culture.

An impressive amount of archaeological research now exists that deals with objects directly connected to World Wars I and II, the Holocaust, and to other sites of National Socialist crimes. Some of these are crime sites, which were knowingly or unknowingly forgotten in the postwar period and which are now scheduled to become memorial sites again. Archaeological finds and features have to be seen as an important source if we are to learn more about these sites.

The extensive archaeological and forensic archaeological excavations of mass graves and terror sites from the second half of the 20th century, for example in those parts of former Yugoslavia affected by war (Russell and Flemming 1991), in Iraq, Darfur, or Sudan, should at least be mentioned at this point.

WORLD WAR I

World War I was one of the greatest catastrophes of recent history. Hegemonic aspirations, nationalism, imperialism, and political and economic ambitions/contradictions are among the reasons for its outbreak. World War I, or the Great War as it is known in France and Great Britain, was characterized by unprecedented industrialization and an immense utilization of materials. The war led to the deaths of around 17 million people, substantial numbers of these through poison gas. The particularly costly trench war on the Western Front and the battle at Verdun are symbols in today's remembrance culture for this early 20th-century disaster. After the war the monarchy collapsed in large parts of Europe, many borders were redrawn, republics were proclaimed in Germany and Austria, and the Soviet Union was founded in formerly Tsarist Russia. A new epoch began, which has been called the "short 20th century" (Hobsbawm 1998).

Archaeological projects initiated by central and western European archaeologists at sites associated with World War I take place across much of the world (Tarlow 1997; Saunders 2004, 2007). They are often concerned with battlefields, however, and are therefore carried out at places of remembrance; that is, also tourist sites on the Western Front, above all in northern France (Brown 2005; Adam 2006) and in Belgium (De Meyer 2010). Their aim is to add to knowledge about the events (Association for World War Archaeology 2007; Great War Archaeology Group 2012). In the Flemish part of Belgium, archaeological activity in this subject area led in 2003 to the foundation of a special department for the archaeology of World War I in the former "Instituut voor het Archeologisch Patrimonium" (now Vlaams Instituut voor het Onroerend Erfgoed) (Dewilde et al. 2004). Extensive research has taken place on the battlefields around Ypres (1914, 1915, 1917) (Saunders 2001a, 2007). A motorway was planned through the middle of the battlefield area and the building work was accompanied by a great deal of archaeology. Various complexes of connected trenches, bunkers, and artillery emplacements were revealed, several dead soldiers recovered, and numerous objects, either military equipment or personal possessions, excavated (De Meyer and Pype 2004; Dewilde and Saunders 2007). Detailed prospection including the use of aerial photos,

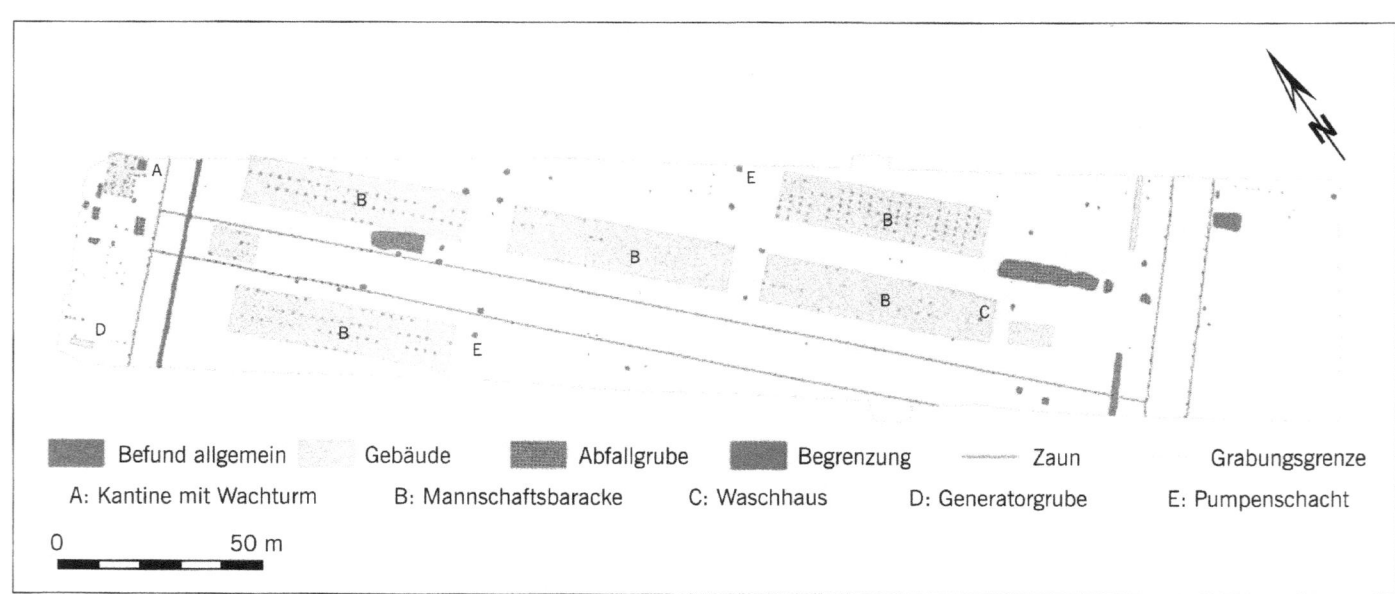

Befund allgemein   Gebäude   Abfallgrube   Begrenzung   Zaun   Grabungsgrenze

A: Kantine mit Wachturm   B: Mannschaftsbaracke   C: Waschhaus   D: Generatorgrube   E: Pumpenschacht

0   50 m

Figure 2.   *Excavation at the prisoner-of-war camp in Quedlinburg (Saxony-Anhalt, Germany) showing traces of the barracks (Befund allgemein/feature; Gebäude/building; Abfallgrube/garbage pit; Begrenzung/boundary; Zaun/fence; Grabungsgrenze/ excavation boundary; Kantine mit Wachturm/canteen with watch tower; Mannschaftsbaracke/barracks for prisoners of war; Waschhaus/washhouse; Generatorgrube/generator pit; Pumpenschacht/pump shaft) (Demuth 2009a:261).*

maps, eyewitness reports, and other documents, made large-scale research possible and created a solid basis for interpretation. The research was also understood as landscape archaeology connected to the culture of remembrance around World War I (Dendooven 2001; Saunders 2001b; Holtorf and Williams 2006).

Another highway construction project near Quedlinburg (Saxony-Anhalt, Germany) led to the excavation of a prisoner-of-war camp from World War I (Demuth 2009a, 2009b). The features excavated included 5 of the former 48 barrack buildings measuring ca. 50 × 15-20 m, as well as barbed wire fences and other boundaries dividing the camp into different zones (Figure 2). The numerous finds included beer bottles from French brewers and French porcelain, which indicate that French prisoners were sent packets of provisions from home (Figure 3). French prisoners-of-war were visible in the archaeological record in this way, but in a methodological note it has to be pointed out that many more nationalities were present among the prisoners, about whom we would know almost nothing if it were not for the written sources. There were also hints about the food situation and the menu—numerous animal bones were found from cattle and pigs, but also from saltwater fish and stingrays.

There are various other archaeological projects with a direct connection to World War I in Europe (Saunders 2007; Saunders and Cornish 2009), but there is also global commitment, for example investigations into the early 20th-century Arab rebellion against the Ottoman Empire (Saunders 2007).

Figure 3.   Finds of French origin from the prisoner of war camp in Quedlinburg (after Demuth 2009a:264).

WORLD WAR II AND THE HOLOCAUST

The National Socialist assumption of power in Germany in March 1933 led to systematic terror and to the racist persecution and annihilation of several million Jews and members of numerous other groups. It further led in 1938 and 1939 to the *Anschluss*, or annexation of Austria, the Sudetenland, Memel, and later Bohemia and Moravia, as well as the other areas occupied during the war. It also meant World War II, which brought devastation, destruction, and death to Europe and many other parts of the world. From 1933 onwards concentration camps were built in which people were subjected to forced labor in inhumane conditions, stripped of their human rights, mistreated, tortured, and murdered. This is a dark chapter of German history that has left traces across the whole of Europe, and today it is important to throw light on the period, to preserve the memory of it and to honor the victims. This can happen in a systematic way only if many sciences collaborate and among these is historical archaeology.

The concentration camps and the death camps are the main subject of archaeological research from the period of the National Socialist dictatorship. This has been the case in Poland and Germany for almost 20 years and in Austria for around 10 years (Stensager 2007; Theune 2010c). Only a few research projects have taken place in the neighboring western countries, although there were numerous concentration camps or sub-camps in the Netherlands, Belgium, France, on the occupied

Channel Islands (Alderney), in Denmark, and in Norway (Jasinski [2010]). Research is now starting slowly, for example with a trial excavation at Amersfoort in the Netherlands (Schute and Wijnen 2010). A fortification from 1938 has been excavated in the Czech Republic (Vařeka 2010). The reason for the delayed beginning of investigations in countries other than Poland and Germany might be seen in a different nexus of cultural memory regarding the Holocaust and National Socialist regime.

Parallel to such projects and due in no small part to changes in protection of monuments legislation (for example in Germany and Austria) research has also been taking place at other sites associated with the National Socialist dictatorship and World War II. These excavations often take place in advance of construction projects and are carried out by archaeological heritage departments. Architectural structures are recorded and considerable finds salvaged. Projects in Germany include excavations in prisoner-of-war camps at Luckenwalde, Brandenburg (Antkowiak 2001), Fürstenberg, Brandenburg (Drieschner et al. 2001; Drieschner and Schulz 2002, 2008), Mönchengladbach, North Rhine-Westphalia (Frank 2005), Retzow, Mecklenburg-Western Pomerania (Jantzen 2004), and in the Hassel Forest, North Rhine-Westphalia (Kamps et al. 2007); in forced labor camps at Groß Schönebeck, Brandenburg (Grothe 2006) and Jülich,

North Rhine-Westphalia (Perse 2005); at a firing squad site near Dachau, Bavaria (David 2003); on battlefields from April 1945 at Kausche und Horno, Brandenburg (Beran 2005) and Hürtgenwald/Nideggen, North Rhine-Westphalia (Schmid-Hecklau and Schönfelder 2007; Wegener 2007); on the Siegfried Line (Wegener 2006; Smani and Tutlies 2007) (Figure 4); in armaments' factories in Kleinmachnow, Brandenburg (Antkowiak 2002); at bunkers in Essen, North Rhine-Westphalia (Hopp and Przybilla 2007) and Berlin (Kernd'l 1995); and the Gestapo prison in Berlin (Hesse et al. 2010). A bunker has also been recorded in Vienna, Austria (La Speranza 2000), and there is also work at the anti-aircraft towers in that city (Bauer 2010). Research into the Cossacks and their forced deportation to the Soviet Union in May 1945 should also be mentioned (Stadler 2005; Stadler and Stepanek, this volume).

The commemoration of (one's own) victims is the priority in Poland, a land that suffered particularly severely under National Socialism and in World War II. The creation of memorial sites for victims is a frequent reason for excavations there. This applies not only to crime sites of the National Socialist regime, but also to places associated with the Stalinist terror. In this way some of the earliest contemporary period archaeological excavations took place in Katyn and at other sites of mass graves where Polish elite were murdered by the NKVD of the Soviet home office (People's Commissariat for Internal Affairs; precursor to the KGB) in early 1940 (Cienciala et al. 2007). The mass graves were discovered during World War II; an investigation by a commission consisting of forensic pathologists from different European countries, Polish exiles, and the Red Cross was able to clear up the question of guilt by finding objects such as Soviet munitions. Excavations by archaeologists from the University of Torun, Poland, in the late 1980s took place largely because of the importance of the sites as a memorial place for Polish victims (Koła 2005, 2009; Metz 2005). In Katyn and at other places the mass graves were localized in the wooded areas with the help of aerial

Figure 4.   Part of the so-called Siegfried Line in Germany near the Dutch and Belgian border. These concrete structures known as "dragon's teeth" were designed to block the passage of tanks (Wegener 2006:282).

photographs. In the next, more precise stage bore holes were drilled at regular intervals across each site in order to calculate the size of the graves. On this basis an estimated total of 16,000 murdered people has been suggested in Katyn, Miednoje, and Charkiv. Around 8,000 bodies have been exhumed to date. Anthropological investigations of the human remains were carried out in order to gather information and evidence about the cause of death. The victims had been shot at close range in the back of the head, broken hands and ribs and fractured skulls were found in some cases. Three thousand

of the dead could be identified through personal possessions found with the bodies. The excavations at the massacre sites found evidence of the exhumations carried out by the National Socialists and the international commission in 1943 and also proved that the graves had been opened by the Soviet secret services, who had aimed to erase the killers' traces. In some cases original Soviet bullets in bodies from the upper layer had been replaced by German bullets, and German newspapers had been placed among the dead.

NATIONAL SOCIALIST DEATH CAMPS IN POLAND

There has also been great support from Polish quarters for contemporary archaeology at memorial sites in the National Socialist death camps. There are no (or very few) written or pictorial contemporary sources for the eastern Polish death camps such as Bełżec and Sobibór (Benz and Distel 2008), and the Nazis blurred and removed their traces after the camps were abandoned. There were very few survivors who were, or are, able to tell us about the camps. The death camp at Bełżec was built in the winter of 1941/1942 on a site of somewhat more than 7 ha and included a fitted gas chamber from the beginning. Significant renovation work took place during the life of the camp. Approximately 600,000 people were murdered there between March and December 1942. The extermination camp at Sobibór was built in early 1942 on a site of initially 12 ha and later 60 ha, and it included several distinct zones. The actual extermination center was situated on the Camp III site, where 250,000 people were murdered in an industrial fashion between May and October 1942. Only very few prisoners survived a revolt and mass flight in October 1943.

At Bełżec an authentic contemporary plan of the camp in which the various buildings are marked is absent. A local resident drew a plan from memory after the war, and a second plan was created—also from memory—by a survivor, but the plans contradict each other (Koła 2000:figure 2-4). The archaeologists' first task was to arrive at an overview of the camp's structures.

It was hoped therefore that archaeology could supply primary knowledge about the position and size of individual buildings and also locate the gas chamber. Excavations of different magnitude (Gileadi et al. 2009) took place in Bełżec (Koła 2000), Chełmno (Golden 2003; Pawlicka-Nowak 2004), and Sobibór (Koła 2001).

This research has continued at some places, for example at Bełżec (O'Neil and Tregenza 2006), while new investigations have begun in Auschwitz (A. Koła 2010, pers. comm.).

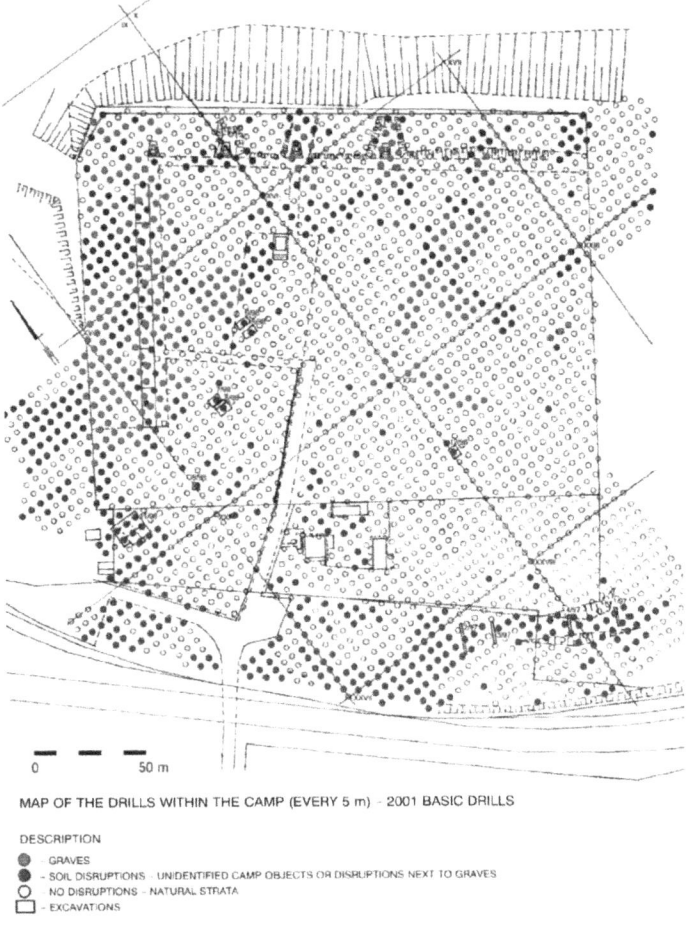

MAP OF THE DRILLS WITHIN THE CAMP (EVERY 5 m) - 2001 BASIC DRILLS

DESCRIPTION
- ● GRAVES
- ● - SOIL DISRUPTIONS - UNIDENTIFIED CAMP OBJECTS OR DISRUPTIONS NEXT TO GRAVES
- ○ NO DISRUPTIONS - NATURAL STRATA
- ▢ - EXCAVATIONS

Figure 5.   *Map of the death camp of Bełżec, Poland, showing the locations of the core drillings (Koła 2000:70).*

At Bełżec core drillings across the entire area of the camp helped make the structures still preserved below ground visible (Figure 5). In this way, it was possible to locate the remains of the buildings and the mass graves. The camp was modified during its lifetime when the gas chambers were installed in several phases. In the first phase the building with the gas chamber was situated in the center of the camp, while in a second phase it lay in the northern area. The camp did not have a crematorium, and the people were at first laid uncremated in mass graves, cremation starting only later.

In these cases, archaeology helped make the sites of the Holocaust visible and made possible the setting up of memorial sites on the basis of archaeological evidence. A large, dignified memorial has existed at Bełżec since 2004.

ARCHAEOLOGY IN CONCENTRATION CAMPS IN GERMANY

Remembrance at the sites of the crimes was given special emphasis in Germany by the successor state of the so-called Third Reich. Memorials and places of admonition at former concentration camps have existed for decades in that country. They are learning places for the younger generation, who have no knowledge of the National Socialist terror, either through their own experiences or through their parents' stories. A great deal of archaeological research is concentrated at these sites.

Many excavations have now taken place, for example in the former concentration camps at Buchenwald and Sachsenhausen. The collapse of the German Democratic Republic (GDR) made it politically necessary to revise the exhibitions and the concepts behind the memorials. New ideas led to renovations and reorganization, prompting further excavations and the recovery of finds. On the other hand there were large numbers of sub-camps of the main concentration camps in Germany that have been forgotten or about which very little is known. Excavations at these sites help bring the scenes of the National Socialist crimes back into public memory.

The camp in Witten-Annen, a sub-camp of Buchenwald, was a forgotten place (Isenberg 1995). Back in 1988 the city of Witten asked the Office for the Preservation of Ancient Monuments to carry out excavations in the area of the camp. Before this, pupils from Witten visiting the Buchenwald memorial saw on a memorial plate that Witten-Annen, their home town, was listed as a sub-camp, a fact they had not known. So interest in this forgotten place and in making it visible began to increase. The aim was to determine the extent of the remains of the camp, study living conditions there, and place the remains under protection. At the same time, written sources were investigated in order to explore the history of the camp as comprehensively as possible.

Sachsenhausen

The most extensive excavations at former concentration camps in Germany have taken place at Sachsenhausen near Berlin and at Buchenwald near Weimar. The camp at Sachsenhausen, north of Berlin, was built in 1936 while the Olympic Games were being held in Berlin itself (Benz and Distel 2006a; Morsch 2008). The triangular shape of the camp was considered to be perfect for control purposes, representing the geometry of terror. The entire inner semicircle could be seen from Tower A on the southeastern edge of the camp. The headquarters and the SS area were situated south of the camp. There were numerous extensions of the complex beginning in 1938. The camp was liberated on 22-23 April 1945. Later, from August 1945 until 1950, it was a Soviet special (detention) camp. The Soviets used all the facilities except the killing area, the so-called "Station Z" of the Nazis. The Nazis used the two designations—"Tower A" as the beginning and the entrance of the camp and "Station Z" as the killing area and the absolute end—completely deliberately.

From 1950 to 1960 the camp was used by the Nationale Volksarmee (GDR army) and many buildings fell into disrepair. Station Z was blown up in 1952-1953, and the national memorial of the GDR was located on its site from 1961 onwards.

The varied history of the site means that many buildings have been altered and that many other buildings have been demolished. The (new) memorial and Sachsenhausen museum were established there in 1993. One of the conceptual aims for the site is to show all aspects of the National Socialist concentration camp, the Soviet special camp, and the GDR memorial.

The excavations covered the area around Station Z (Weishaupt 2005). It has to be stressed, however, that the killing area, which was built during the winter of

1941/1942, the gas chamber, built in 1943, the execution facilities, and the crematorium were not substantially affected by the excavations. The paving formerly leading to the gas chamber was uncovered, revealing teeth of the victims between the bricks. The ash container was situated behind the crematorium. The structure connecting the furnaces in the building with the ash container was found outside the complex. The ash from the furnaces was deposited in the ash container, and when the container was full the cremated remains were dumped in large pits (Figure 6).

Photographs taken in May 1945 show that large deposits of cremated human remains were stored in Station Z. Jewish religious burial customs have to be respected when excavating human remains in former concentration camps. One of the most fundamental Jewish beliefs, the sanctity of the sleep of the dead, determines that graves last forever. It is forbidden to disturb a Jewish grave in the "house of eternity." This principle is respected as much as possible during excavations in the former concentration camps and means that anthropological analysis of the cremated or skeletal remains is never carried out and that the remains are rapidly re-buried.

Large pits were discovered during the pre-planning phase of a museum for the victims of the Soviet special camp. In 2000 geophysical survey revealed a very large garbage pit of 30 × 5.6 m and 2–3 m depth. The contents of the pit could not be excavated properly, but an excavating machine brought the contents to the industrial area of the memorial, depositing them in 13 large heaps. The finds were recovered from these heaps in a four-week campaign. A sorting machine with different strengths processed the material through 10 cm and 5 cm screens. The remaining soil was sieved again through even smaller screens. Small finds such as coins or buttons were collected in this way (Theune 2006; Müller 2010).

All in all, there were finds with a total weight of 5,556.3 kg. As is often the case in archaeology, a first sorting criterion was the material of the artifacts. The weight of the iron objects was about 3,000 kg, bottles and other glass objects weighed 800 kg, and porcelain weighed nearly 300 kg. It soon became clear, however, that these material-based groups were not suitable for the evaluation of camp life or the general circumstances of either the perpetrators or the victims, and a functional classification was established instead. The following groups were formed: construction, clothing, toiletries, household, militaria, coins, and other. Each group was further divided into several sub-groups.

The clothing group contains belts, shoes, buttons, and gloves; included in the toiletries group are, among other things, medicinal objects such as phials, ampoules, tablets, prostheses, medical dishes and similar things, but also eyeglasses and hygiene articles such as combs, toothbrushes, and shaving equipment. The household articles group is particularly wide-ranging. It includes candlesticks, flower pots, eating and drinking vessels, cooking and storage vessels of various materials, and also toys and games, jewelry, smoking utensils, pocket knives, and many accessories. The objects can be assigned to perpetrators or victims with relative ease. Homemade combs and small vessels belonged

Figure 6.   Excavation at Sachsenhausen in front of the crematorium with the ash container (Photo by Johannes Weishaupt, Löwenberger Land, 2005; courtesy of Johannes Weishaupt).

Figure 7. Part of a mess kit from Sachsenhausen, Germany, with the name Arnold (Photo by Anne-Kathrin Müller, Berlin, 2006; courtesy of Anne-Kathrin Müller).

without doubt to the victims/prisoners. The same is true of most of the large number of aluminum spoons. On the other hand, only a few forks or knives were found, and these were mostly of better material. Knives of high-grade steel or even precious metals with skillfully engraved initials can be assigned to the perpetrators.

Many objects are decorated and some of them can give a clue to the identity of the prisoner (Figure 7). Some also hint at whether they were used during the concentration camp period or during the period of the Soviet special camp. Finds from this latter period are often marked with the year.

The artifacts also have to be seen in terms of memory. It is clear that objects are also carriers of a history of the events and in this way of memory (Veit 2003; Hahn 2006; Woodward 2007). This memory is directly connected to the meaning that the objects had during their period of use. The history and the significance of the objects, but also their owner or owners, are stored through space and time, from their manufacture, through their use, possible repairs, and other changes, until they became garbage. Artifacts have great permanence and a distinct life of their own, by being handed down they can become part of other cultural environments. They are symbols of structures that we recognize, but also of structures that are initially invisible, that is, carriers of meaning for non-obvious information. This also applies to objects from the concentration camps. The objects—whether they be the buildings of the SS, the walls of the camp, or the barracks of the prisoners, or whether they are the eating and drinking vessels of the guards

or of the guarded—all carry history. They thus become for us today symbols of the structures and events of the terror. Some of the finds belonged to prisoners and record powerlessness, oppression, and humiliation, but also perhaps self-assertion and self-respect. There are also numerous objects connected to the perpetrators, however, and these have to be regarded as objects of power (Freund and Greifeneder 2004).

Buchenwald

The concentration camp in Buchenwald was built on the Ettersberg Heights above Weimar in 1937 (Benz and Distel 2006a). It was divided into three parts, the main camp, the so-called tent camp, and the "small camp," which was built in 1938, became the quarantine area in 1942, and was known in the final phase as the dying area. The prisoners were forced to work in, among other places, a quarry or in armaments factories. Considerably more than 100 sub-camps and detached work groups were part of the Buchenwald complex. A Soviet special camp was set up on the site after liberation in April 1945 and lasted until 1950. In 1958 the national memorial of the GDR was established there. The concept behind the memorial was revised in Buchenwald from 1991 onwards, in a process similar to Sachsenhausen.

Archaeological excavations and the salvaging of finds took place within the framework of working camps as early as the first years of the 1990s at several sites in Buchenwald. These were in part to do with the redesign of the memorial after the collapse of the GDR (Hirte 2000). Particular attention was paid to a garbage heap in the small camp, which was excavated from 1996 onwards. Dealing with garbage had been a great problem in the camp, as was also clear in Sachsenhausen. This was particularly true for the last period, the liberators reporting that large garbage heaps could be found throughout the complex (Hirte 2000:25-28). Around 2,500 objects and almost 4,000 buttons were salvaged from an area of only 4 × 4 m. The successful work with young people at this place of remembrance led to the decision to record the finds in an object data base (Buchenwald and Mittelbau-Dora Memorials Foundation [2012]). This is accessible on the web and is used in Buchenwald for educational work. Functional criteria are used in this case as well, but the terms used are different from the classification employed for the Sachsenhausen finds (camp, international, location, work, health, hygiene, food, jewelry, religion, leisure, prisoners' functionaries, women, children, numbers, name, transport, and death).

Excavations have been carried out in many other concentration camps in Germany. The motivation behind the projects varies, but usually the intention is to make symbolically important points visible again through excavation. This is the case with the so-called "death ramp" in Flossenbürg, Bavaria, for example (Figure 8). The excavations were also aimed at increasing knowledge about that site (Ibel 2002). At other places there has been intensive work with youth camps as was the case in Buchenwald. The boundaries of the camp at Bergen-Belsen, Lower Saxony, were archaeologically investigated with the help of such groups (Assendorp 2003). Sometimes a further aim is to establish the condition of the remains in the ground, as has been the case in Dachau, Bavaria, for example (David 2001).

The Firing Squad Complex at Hebertshausen near Dachau

The firing squad site at Hebertshausen is closely related to the nearby concentration camp at Dachau. Soviet prisoners-of-war were shot there in autumn 1941 and in the following winter. The excavations carried out at Hebertshausen in 2001 indicate violence and death in concentration camps in a very specific way. The site of the mass shootings is defined by two walls. The border is a wooden wall and a bullet trap. In front of the wooden wall, the ruins of which were detected, there were still traces of the posts to which the prisoners had been tied.

Figure 8.   Excavation of the so-called death ramp at Flossenbürg, Germany (after Ibel 2002:149).

Small pieces of human bone lay around these objects, traces of the firing squads' victims (David 2003).

ARCHAEOLOGY IN CONCENTRATION CAMPS IN AUSTRIA

In the concentration camp at Mauthausen historical and archaeological research became necessary in context of the renewal of the memorial and of the exhibitions, as had been the case at the German memorial sites. The construction of the camp began in summer 1938; it was initially intended to be a camp for Austrian prisoners (Benz and Distel 2006b). The prisoners were forced to do heavy labor in the nearby quarry. Many of them died due to the exhausting conditions, of malnutrition, and through the arbitrary despotism of the SS; many others died in the gas chamber. The Soviet occupiers returned the camp at Mauthausen to Austria as early as 1947 with the proviso that a memorial was to be installed (Perz 2006). The aim at that time was to show the central parade ground with the SS utility buildings (laundry building, kitchen building, prison,

hospital) on one side and the first row of prisoners' barracks on the other. In the view at that time these areas were of high symbolic meaning for the suffering of the prisoners. A stone sarcophagus was set up between these buildings as a central monument. The other barrack buildings and the outer reaches of the camp were explicitly seen as not being of sufficient historical value to be preserved. The barracks had been used after the war, before being dismantled and re-assembled in other contexts elsewhere. Over the course of time aboveground traces of the outer areas became invisible to all but the practiced eye of an archaeologist. The visitors' time at the camp was thus limited to the central buildings around the parade ground and the exhibition. The recently announced new plan for the camp intends to make the entire area of the complex visible. The day of liberation, 5 May 1945, is the reference point for the careful changes to the buildings that are necessary in some places (Mauthausen Memorial neu gestalten 2009).

In its final phase the concentration camp at Mauthausen consisted not only of the main camp (Lager I) with 20 prisoners' barracks, but also of additional areas within the camp walls (the Special Camp, Lager II); the so-called Russian hospital camp (to the southwest of the main camp) with 10 barrack huts, a kitchen building, and hospital building; Lager III (to the southeast); and a tent camp with five large tents on the northern perimeter. There were also various SS buildings that served as accommodation or workshops. A new visitor center was built in the SS workshop area in the early years of the last decade, and the construction was accompanied by archaeological studies (Artner et al. 2003).

The first step in the present research project took the form of large-scale geophysical survey work in the entire hospital and tent camps and in an SS workshop area. The aim was to find out which parts of the outer areas were still preserved below ground (Neubauer and Löcker 2010). It was thus possible to establish the exact position of the barracks and other buildings in the hospital camp (Figure 9), as well as of the tents in the tent camp and of many workshops in the northern area. The northern area of the camp included the camp's execution area, which was only little known from other sources. Until now excavations were carried out at several sites. They give a deep insight into the conditions of being a prisoner in Mauthausen. Renovation work for the new museum is accompanied by archeological activity on a regular basis.

The aim of the first excavation in summer 2009 was to investigate the condition of the remains and objects preserved below ground (Theune 2010a, 2010b). The head of a barracks building in the hospital camp was uncovered. The barracks there were around 55 m long and 9.5 m wide, and in this case the base of the walls and their stone rubble foundations survived in good condition. The carefully cobbled entrance area was found in the middle of the side end. The interior was divided by posts into three aisles, and the foundations of a stove were also found. A complete stove was salvaged from a pit in the vicinity of another barracks. Construction debris from the barracks buildings formed a large part of the finds, but there were also personal objects that can be attributed to prisoners, for example eating vessels, cutlery, prisoners' identification tags, buttons, and many other things.

A small excavation has also taken place on the path that leads from the main camp to the quarry. Today this is an uneven and irregularly cobbled route, the sides of which are overgrown with grass. The investigation aimed to find out if this surface was from the Nazi or the postwar period. In fact two phases were found, both of which date to the 1930s and 1940s. The second phase was founded on large pieces of stone rubble, so that the path could support heavy loads, while the first phase employed only simple slabs and was without further foundations. The uncovering of the path's edges revealed the entire breadth of the route in the Nazi period, which was substantially wider than its visible extent in the recent past. An open concrete drain was found on both sides of the road.

Core drilling has taken place in the so-called "ash heap." Today this a semicircular surface on which a stone monument stands, within an area of ca. 12 m² surrounded by a hedge. Behind this memorial is a steep slope. The aim of the drilling was to establish the extent and volume of the ash deposits. Fourteen boreholes were sunk inside the hedge and two outside with a drill of 10-cm diameter, stopping only after the natural layers had been reached. The drill cores were scrutinized, the finds retrieved, and afterwards the material from the core (earth, burnt human bone, and ash) was redeposited on the spot. It became apparent that the Nazis had prepared and leveled the site in preparation for the deposition of ash. Later leveling layers were also recorded. Not only the burnt human bone of the murdered prisoners was found, but also various objects, including prisoners' personal possessions and ash from sources other than the crematorium. The ash layers became deeper further down the slope.

Structural archaeological research is also taking place (Mitchell and Buchinger 2009). All standing buildings are being investigated in their construction phases and their historical role during the time of the camp and the postwar period. Detailed analyses have been submitted for the "killing area," which includes execution sites 2 and 3, the gas chamber, the cremation ovens, the camp brothel, the kitchen and other buildings.. Changes that occurred when the memorial was set up after the war, for example in the interior decoration and in the room plan, are very clear. The partially uncovered colored trimmings and the wall and ceiling colors of the brothel are

Figure 9.   *Georadar map from the hospital camp at Mauthausen showing the foundations of the barracks (Graphic by Archaeo Prospections, 2008; courtesy of Archaeo Prospections).*

remarkable. This color scheme, which was painted over after the war, seems to have been intended to make the rooms a little friendlier (Mitchell and Buchinger 2009).

Other excavations took place at the tent camp or in some sub-camps of Mauthausen such as in Loibl, a mountain pass in Carinthia, or Gunskirchen in Upper Austria.

Hartheim

A very successful excavation was carried out in Hartheim in Upper Austria. This was a Nazi euthanasia center in

1940-1944 (Klimesch 2002; Klimesch and Rachbauer 2008). Here, the question was again what remains were still in situ after the war, because it was known that there had been many changes. First, a buildings archaeological analysis noted massive interference with the structures. Significant finds of the victims and many cremated remains were later found in a trench during an archaeological investigation. The personal belongings of the murdered were found in a pit. The contents of the pit were dug *en bloc* and placed in the present memorial.

CONCLUSION

In part at least, new perspectives in the understanding of the war and extermination sites are being opened thanks to the numerous archaeological investigations that have been, and are, taking place. Archaeology's strength—research into everyday life—can reveal many new facets of the crime sites. The archaeological

research of recent sites with its comprehensive and plentiful record is immensely important for wide-ranging analyses.

The interplay of archaeological heritage and memory is an interesting aspect. Places of remembrance are traditionally points at which national inheritance, one's own united tradition, a splendid history, and identity are made manifest (Assmann 1999). These places are usually positive reference points in collective national memory. Battle sites, at which victories were won or defeats suffered, can achieve such a status. Cultural assets and sites become collective places of remembrance when they are attributed symbolic meaning for past events. Then monuments are erected, which pass on the memory of persons or events (Van Dyke and Alcock 2003; Pollak 2010).

Former concentration camps or other places in Germany associated with the National Socialist terror do not fulfill these positive connotations. Instead, they are "evil places" (Porombka and Schmundt 2005) or "reluctant" places of memory (Assmann 1999:328-330). Nevertheless, in Germany these sites are often preserved as monuments and places of remembrance. There, the victims will continue to be remembered and young people, tourists, and others will be educated about National Socialism. Archaeology will play its part.

REFERENCES

ADAM, FRÉDÉRIC
2006   *Alain-Fournier et ses compagnons d'arme: Une archéologie de la Grande Guerre [Alain-Fournier and his Comrades. An Archaeology of the Great War]*. Editions Serpenoise, Metz, France.

ANTKOWIAK, MATTHIAS
2001   Kriegsgefangene in Brandenburg I. Das Stalag III A in Luckenwalde, Landkreis Teltow-Fläming [Prisoners-of-War in Brandenburg I. Stalag III A in Luckenwalde, Teltow-Fläming County]. *Archäologie in Berlin und Brandenburg* 2001:170-172.

2002   Struktur eines Rüstungsbetriebes. Barackenlager in Kleinmachnow. Landkreis Potsdam-Mittelmark [The Structure of an Armaments Factory. Barracks Camp in Kleinmachnow. Potsdam-Mittelmark County]. *Archäologie in Berlin und Brandenburg* 2002:165-167.

ARTNER, GOTTFRIED, CHRISTA FARKA, NIKOLAUS HOFER, AND MARTIN, KRENN
2004   Archäologische Untersuchungen im ehemaligen Konzentrationslager von Mauthausen [Archaeological Investigations in the Former Concentration Camp at Mauthausen]. In *Das Gedächtnis von Mauthausen*, Bundesministerium für Inneres, editor, pp. 26-29. Wien: Bundesministerium für Inneres, Vienna, Austria.

ASSENDORP, JAN JOST
2003   KZ Bergen-Belsen. *Archäologie in Niedersachsen* 2003:78-81.

ASSMANN, ALEIDA
1999   *Erinnerungsräume. Formen und Wandlungen des kulturellen Gedächtnisses [Rooms of Memory. Forms of and Changes in Cultural Memory]*. Beck, Munich, Germany.

ASSOCIATION FOR WORLD ARCHAEOLOGY
2007   Association for World Archaeology (AWA) website, http://www.a-w-a.be/. Accessed 18 September 2012.

BAUER, U. (EDITOR)
2010   *Erinnerungsort Flakturm. Der ehemalige Leitturm im Wiener Arensbergpark [The Anti-aircraft Tower as a Place of Memory]*. Phoibos, Vienna, Austria.

BENZ, WOLFGANG, AND BARBARA DISTEL (EDITORS)
2006a   *Der Ort des Terrors [The Site of Terror]*, Vol. 3: Sachsenhausen, Buchenwald. Beck, Munich, Germany.

2006b   *Der Ort des Terrors [The Site of Terror]*, Vol. 4: Flossenbürg, Mauthausen, Ravensbrück. Beck, Munich, Germany.

2008   *Der Ort des Terrors [The Site of Terror]*, Vol. 8: Riga, Kaunas, Vaivara, Plasów, Klooga, Chełmo, Bełżec, Treblinka, Sobibór. Beck, Munich, Germany.

BERAN, JONAS
2005   Der April 1945 im archäologischen Befund. Beobachtungen in Kausche und Horno, Niederlausitzer Braunkohlerevier [April 1945 in Archaeological Contexts. Observations in Kausche and Hornao, Lower Lusatian Soft Coal Area]. *Archäologie in Berlin und Brandenburg* 2005:160-165.

BROWN, MARTIN
2005   Journey Back to Hell: Excavations at Serre on the Somme. *Current World Archaeology* 10:25-33.

BUCHENWALD AND MITTELBAU-DORA MEMORIALS FOUNDATION
[2012] Buchenwald Memorial, Digital Collection, Found Objects, http://www.buchenwald.de/media_de/fr_content.php?nav=fundstuecke&view=ct_digisammlung_fundstuecke.html. Accessed 18 September 2012.

BUCHLI, VICTOR, AND GAVIN LUCAS (EDITORS)
2001   *Archaeologies of the Contemporary Past*. Routledge, London, England.

CIENCIALA, ANNA M., NATALIA S. LEBEDEVA, AND WOJCIECH MATERSKI

2007　*Katyn a Crime without Punishment.* Yale University Press, New Haven, CT.

COUNCIL OF EUROPE

1992　European Convention on the Protections of the Archaeological Heritage (revised). Valetta, 16.1.1992. Council of Europe, http://conventions. coe.int/treaty/en/treaties/html/143.htm. Accessed 18 September 2012.

DAVID, WOLFGANG

2001　Archäologische Ausgrabungen im ehemaligen Konzentrationslager Dachau (18.9.–6.10.2000) [Archaeological Excavations in the Former Concentration Camp at Dachau, 18 September–6 October 2000)]. Unpublished report, München, Germany.

2003　*Archäologische Ausgrabungen in der ehemaligen SS-Schießanlage bei Hebertshausen 2001 [Archaeological Excavations at the Former SS Firing Squad Site at Hebertshausen 2001].* Unpublished report, München, Germany.

DEJNEGA, MELANIE, AND CLAUDIA THEUNE

in press　Das Sanitätslager in Wort, Bild und Objekt. Warum die Zusammenarbeit von HistorikerInnen und ArchäologInnen Sinn macht [The Hospital Camp in Words, Pictures and Objects. Why Historians and Archeologists Should Work Together]. In *Leben und Überleben in Mauthausen. Mauthausen überleben und erinnern*, Bd. 2, Alexander Prenninger, Regina Fritz, Gerhard Botz, and Eva Brücker, editors.

DE MEYER, MATHIEU

2010　Great War Archaeology in Belgium and France: A New Challenge for Battlefield Archaeology. In *The Historical Archaeology of Military Sites: Method and Topic*, Clarence R. Geier, Lawrence E. Babits, and Douglas D. Scott, editors, pp. 135-148. Texas A&M University Press, College Station, TX.

DE MEYER, MATHIEU, AND PEDRO PYPE

2004　*The A19 Project. Archaeological Research at Cross Roads.* AWA, Zarren, Belgium.

DEMUTH, VOLKER

2009a　"Die das Schlachtfeld überlebten..." Archäologische Untersuchungen in einem Kriegsgefangenenlager des Ersten Weltkrieges bei Quedlinburg ["Those who Survived the Battlefields..." Archaeological Investigations in a Prisoner-of-War Camp near Quedlinburg (Harz/Germany) from the First World War.] In *Schlachtfeldarchäologie—Battlefield Archaeology*, Harald Meller, editor, pp. 259-267. Landesamt für Denkmalpflege und Archäologie Sachsen-Anhalt, Halle/Saale, Germany.

2009b　"Those Who Survived the Battlefields" Archaeological Investigations in a Prisoner of War Camp near Quedlinburg (Harz/Germany) from the First World War. *Journal of Conflict Archaeology* 5/1:163-181.

DENDOOVEN, DOMINIEK

2001　*Ypres as Holy Ground: Menin Gate & Last Post.* De Klaproos, Koksijde, Belgium.

DEWILDE, MARC, PEDRO PYPE, MATHIEU DE MEYER, FREDERIK DEMEYERE, WOUTER LAMMENS, JANIEK DEGRYSE, FRANKY WYFFELS, AND NICHOLAS J. SAUNDERS

2004　Belgium's New Department of First World War Archaeology. *Antiquity* 78(301), http://antiquity. ac.uk/projgall/saunders/index.html#saunders. Accessed 18 September 2012.

DEWILDE, MARC, AND NICHOLAS J. SAUNDERS

2007　Archaeology of the Great War: The Flemish Experience. In *Contested Objects: Material Memories of the Great War*, Nicholas J. Saunders and Paul Cornish, editors, pp. 252-265. Routledge, Abingdon, England.

DRIESCHNER, AXEL, CHRISTOF KRAUSKOPF, AND BARBARA SCHULZ

2001　Kriegsgefangene in Brandenburg II. Das M Stalag III B in Fürstenberg/Oder, heute Eisenhüttenstadt, Landkreis Oder-Spree [Prisoners-of-War in Brandenburg II. Stalag III B in Fürstenberg on the Oder, Today Eisenhüttenstadt, Oder-Spree County]. *Archäologie in Berlin und Brandenburg* 2001:173-174.

DRIESCHNER, AXEL, AND BARBARA SCHULZ

2002　Fotos an Befunden überprüft. Das Kriegsgefangenlager M Stalag III B in Fürstenberg. Landkreis Oder-Spree [Photos Checked with Features. Prisoners-of-War Camp Stalag III B in Fürstenberg, Oder-Spree County]. *Archäologie in Berlin und Brandenburg* 2002:168-171.

2008　Ungebetene Befunde. Archäologische Grabung zum Stalag III B in Fürstenberg (Oder), heute Eisenhüttenstadt [Unwelcome Features. An Archaeological Excavation at Stalag III B in Fürstenberg on the Oder, today Eisenhüttenstadt, Oder-Spree County]. In *Einvernehmliche Zusammenarbeit? Wehrmacht, Gestapo, SS und sowjetische Kriegsgefangene*, Johannes Ibel, editor, pp. 181-199. Metropol, Berlin, Germany.

ENGELHARDT, ISABELLE

2004　Umstrittenes Gedächtnis: Erinnerungskultur in KZ-Gedenkstätten [Controversial Memory. The Culture of Memory in Concentration Camp Memorials]. In *Das Gedächtnis von Mauthausen*, Bundesministerium für Inneres, editor, pp. 9-25. Bundesministerium für Inneres, Vienna, Austria.

FRANK, KLAUS
2005   Das Kriegsgefangenenlager Mönchengladbach-Wickrathberg [The Prisoner-of-War Camp at Mönchengladbach-Wickrathberg]. In *Von Anfang an. Archäologie in Nordrhein-Westfalen*, Heinz Günter Horn, Hansgerd Hellenkemper, Gabriele Isenberg, and Jürgen Kunow editors, pp. 573-577. Römisch-Germanisches Museum, Cologne, Germany.

FREUND, FLORIAN, AND HARALD GREIFENEDER
2004   Objekte erzählen Geschichte [Objects Reveal History]. In *Das Gedächtnis von Mauthausen*, Bundesministerium für Inneres, editor, pp. 46-57. Bundesministerium für Inneres, Vienna, Austria.

GILEADI, ISAAC, YORAM HAIMI, AND WOJCIECH MAZUREK
2009   Excavating Nazi Extermination Centres. *Present Pasts* 1:10-39.

GOLDEN, JULIET
2003   Remembering Chełmno. Heart-Wrenching Finds from a Nazi Death Camp. *Archaeology* 2003(January-February):50-54.

GREAT WAR ARCHAEOLOGY GROUP
2012   Great War Archaeology Group (GWAG) website, http://www.gwag.org/. Accessed 18 September 2012.

GROTHE, ANJA
2006   Erzwungene Dienstleistung. Arbeitslager und Wirtschaftsbetrieb bei Groß Schönebeck, Lkr. Barmin [Forced Services. Labor Camp and Business]. *Archäologie in Berlin und Brandenburg* 2006:129-131.

HAHN, HANS PETER
2006   *Materielle Kultur. Eine Einführung [Material Culture. An Introduction]*. Reimer, Berlin, Germany.

HALL, MARTIN, AND STEPHEN W. SILLIMAN (EDITORS)
2006   *Historical Archaeology*. Blackwell, Malden, Oxford, England.

HESSE, KLAUS, KAY KUFEKE, AND ANDREAS SANDER
2010   *Topography of Terror. Gestapo, SS and Reich Security Main Office on Wilhelm – and Prinz-Albrecht-Straße. A Documentation*. Stiftung Topographie des Terrors, Berlin, Germany.

HICKS, DAN, AND MARY C. BEAUDRY
2006   *The Cambridge Companion to Historical Archaeology*. Cambridge University Press, Cambridge, England.

HIRTE, RONALD
2000   *Offene Befunde. Ausgrabungen in Buchenwald. Zeitgeschichtliche Archäologie und Erinnerungskultur [Open Contexts. Excavations in Buchenwald. Contemporary Archaeology and Memory Culture]*. Hinz und Kunst, Braunschweig, Germany.

HOBSBAWM, ERIC
1998   *Das Zeitalter der Extreme. Weltgeschichte des 20. Jahrhunderts [Age of Extremes. The Short Twentieth Century 1914-1991]*. Dtv, Munich, Germany.

HOLTORF, CORNELIUS, AND HOWARD WILLIAMS
2006   Landscapes and Memories. In *The Cambridge Companion to Historical Archaeology*, Dan Hicks and Mary C. Beaudry, editors, pp. 235-254. Cambridge University Press, Cambridge, England.

HOPP, DETLEF, AND HEINZ-JÜRGEN PRZYBILLA
2007   Auch "Für russische Arbeiter" ["For Russian Workers" as Well]. *Archäologie im Rheinland* 2007:184-185.

IBEL, JOHANNES
2002   Konzentrationslager Flossenbürg: Ausgrabungen und Funde [Flossenbürg Concentration Camp. Excavations and Finds]. *Das Archäologische Jahr in Bayern* 2002:147-149.

ISENBERG, GABRIELE
1995   Zu den Ausgrabungen im Konzentrationslager Witten-Annen [Excavations in the Concentration Camp Witten-Annen]. *Ausgrabungen und Funde* 40: 33-37.

JANTZEN, DETLEF
2004   Retzow, Lkr. Müritz [Retzow, Müritz County]. *Bodendenkmalpflege Mecklenburg-Vorpommern* 52:710.

JASINSKI, MAREK E.
[2010]   Painful Heritage: Cultural Landscape of the Second World War. Phenomenology, Lessons and Management Systems. Painful Heritage, an interdisciplinary research project of NTNU Vitenskapsmuseet and Falstad Center, financed by The Research Council of Norway, http://painfulheritage.no/eng/Revidert_Painful_Heritage_4-1.pdf. Accessed 18 September 2012.

KAMPS, BERN, GABY SCHULENBERG, AND PETER SCHULENBERG
2007   Verdrängt und vergessen—Ein Lager im Hasseler Forst [Suppressed and Forgotten—A Camp in the Hassel Forest]. *Archäologie im Rheinland* 2007:182-184.

KERND'L, ALFRED
1995   "Fahrerbunker" und andere Bodendenkmäler aus dem 20. Jahrhundert im Zentrum der Hauptstadt [The "Drivers' Bunker" and Other Earthfast Monuments from the 20th Century in the Capital's Center]. *Ausgrabungen und Funde* 40:29-33.

KLIMESCH, WOLFGANG

2002   Veritatem dies aperit! Vernichtet—Vergraben—
        Vergessen. Archäologische Spuren im
        Schloss Hartheim [Exterminated—Buried—
        Forgotten. Archaeological Traces in Schloss
        Hartheim]. *Jahrbuch des Oberösterreichischen
        Musealvereines Gesellschaft für Landeskunde*
        147(1):411-434.

KLIMESCH, WOLFGANG, AND MARKUS RACHBAUER

2008   Archäologische Spurensuche in Schloss
        Hartheim [Archaeological Traces in Schloss
        Hartheim]. In *Tötungsanstalt Hartheim*,
        Oberösterreichisches Landesarchiv/Lern – und
        Gedenkort Schloss Hartheim, editor, pp. 499-522.
        Verlag Oberösterreichisches Landesarchiv, Linz,
        Austria.

KOŁA, ANDRZEJ

2000   *Bełżec, The Nazi Camp for Jews in the Light of
        Archaeological Sources, Excavations 1997-1999.*
        Council of Protection of Memory of Combat and
        Martyrdom, Warsaw, Poland.

2001   Badania archeologiczne terenu byłego obozu
        zagłady Żydów w Sobiborze. Przeszłość i
        Pamięć [Archaeological Research in the Former
        Extermination Camp for Jews in Sobibor. Past
        and Memory]. *Biuletyn Rady Ochroni Pamięci
        Walk i Męczeństwa* 4:115-122.

2005   *Archeologia zbrodni. Oficerowie polscy
        na cmentarzu ofiar NKWD w Charkowie
        [Archaeology Crime. Polish Officers in the
        Cemetery of the Victims of the NKVD in Kharkiv].*
        Uniw. Mikołaja Kopernika, Toruń, Poland.

2009   Archäologie des Verbrechens. Das archäologische
        Know-how im Dienste der Aufklärung von
        Geheimnissen der jüngsten Vergangenheit—am
        Beispiel exhumierter Opfer des Stalinismus aus
        Massengräbern von Charkow und Kiew [The
        Archaeology of Crime. Archaeological Know-
        how as Part of the Investigation of the Recent
        Past—The Example of Exhumed Victims of
        Stalinism from Mass Graves in Charkov und
        Kiev]. *Jahrbuch des Wissenschaftlichen Zentrums
        der Polnischen Akademie der Wissenschaften in
        Wien* 2009:107-116.

LA SPERANZA, MARCELLO

2000   Luftschutzeinrichtungen in den Kellern der
        Wiener Innenstadt [Air Raid Shelters in the
        Cellars of Downtown Vienna]. *Fundort Wien*
        3:186-195.

MAJEWSKI, TERESITA, AND DAVID GAIMSTER (EDITORS)

2009   *International Handbook of Historical
        Archaeology.* Springer, New York, NY.

MAUTHAUSEN MEMORIAL NEU GESTALTEN

2009   Mauthausen Memorial neu gestalten.
        Rahmenkonzept für die Neugestaltung
        der KZ-Gedenkstätte Mauthausen. Hrsg.
        Bundesministerium für Inneres [Redesigning
        the Mauthausen Memorial. Framework
        Document for the Redesign of the Mauthausen
        Concentration Camp Memorial]. Abteilung IV/7
        Bundesministerium für Inneres, Vienna, Austria.

METZ, DANUTA

2005   Zeitgeschichtliche Archäologie in Polen am
        Beispiel von Exekutionsstätten des Zweiten
        Weltkrieges [Contemporary Archaeology
        in Poland. Two Execution Places from the
        Second World War]. Senatsverwaltung für
        Stadtentwicklung und Umwelt, Berlin, Germany,
        http://www.stadtentwicklung.berlin.de/
        denkmal/archaeologentag/2005/vortrag_metz.
        pdf. Accessed 18 September 2012.

MITCHELL, PAUL, AND GÜNTHER BUCHINGER

2009   Die Baugeschichte von Block 1, Lager I, KL
        Mauthausen [The Architectural History of Block
        1, Camp 1, Mauthausen]. Unpublizierter Bericht
        der bauarchäologischen Untersuchungen Vienna,
        Austria.

MORSCH, GÜNTER (EDITOR)

2008   Mord und Massenmord im Konzentrationslager
        Sachsenhausen 1936–1945. [Murder and Mass
        Murder in Sachsenhausen Concentration
        Camp 1936-1945]. *Schriftenreihe der Stiftung
        Brandenburgische Gedenkstätten* 13(2).

MOSHENSKA, GABRIEL

2006   Scales of Memory in the Archaeology of the
        Second World War. *Papers of the Institute of
        Archaeology* 17:58-68.

MÜLLER, ANNE KATHRIN

2010   Entsorgte Geschichte—Entsorgte Geschichten.
        Die Funde aus einer Abfallgrube auf dem
        Gelände der Gedenkstätte Sachsenhausen und
        die Bedeutung zeitgeschichtlicher Archäologie
        [History Disposed of—Histories Disposed of. The
        Finds from a Garbage Pit at the Sachsenhausen
        Memorial and the Importance of Contemporary
        Period Archaeology]. Unpublished Magister
        thesis, Humboldt-Universität zu Berlin, Germany.

NEUBAUER, WOLFGANG, AND KLAUS LÖCKER

2010   Archäologisch-geophysikalische Prospektion.
        Ehemaliges Konzentrationslager Mauthausen
        [Archeological-Geophysical Survey. Former
        Concentration Camp Mauthausen]. Unpublished
        report, Vienna, Austria.

NORA, PIERRE

1998   *Zwischen Geschichte und Gedächtnis [Between
        History and Memory].* Klaus Wagenbach, Berlin,
        Germany.

O'NEIL, ROBIN, AND MICHAEL TREGENZA
2006 Archaeological Investigations. A Review by Historians. Holocaust Education & Archive Research Team, http://www.holocaustresearchproject.org/ar/modern/archreview.html. Accessed 18 September 2012.

PAWLICKA-NOWAK, LUCJA
2004 Archaeological Research in the Grounds of the Chełmno-on-Ner Extermination Center. In *The Extermination Center for Jews in Chełmno-on-Ner in the Light of Latest Research, Symposium Proceedings September 6-7*, Lucja Pawlicka-Nowak, editor, pp. 42-67. District Museum of Konin, Konin, Poland.

PERSE, MARCELL
2005 Ein Denkmal offener Fragen—Das Zwangsarbeiterlager Jülich-Süd [A Monument with Open Questions. The Forced Labor Camp Jülich South]. In *Von Anfang an. Archäologie in Nordrhein-Westfalen*, Heinz Günter Horn, Hansgerd Hellenkemper, Gabriele Isenberg, and Jürgen Kunow, editors, pp. 571-572. Römisch-Germanisches Museum, Cologne, Germany.

PERZ, BERTAND
2006 *Die KZ-Gedenkstätte Mauthausen 1945 bis zur Gegenwart* [*The Mauthausen Memorial 1945 to the Present Day*]. Studienverlag, Innsbruck, Austria.

POLLAK, MARIANNE
2010 *Vom Erinnerungsort zur Denkmalpflege. Kulturgüter als Medien des kulturellen Gedächtnisses* [*From Place of Remembrance to Protection of Monuments. Cultural Assets as Transmitters of Cultural Memory*]. Böhlau, Vienna, Austria.

POROMBKA, STEPHAN, AND HILMAR SCHMUNDT (EDITORS)
2005 *Böse Orte. Stätten nationalsozialistischer Selbstdarstellung—heute* [*Evil Places. Sites of National Socialist Self-Projection*]. Claassen Verlag, Berlin, Germany.

RUSSELL, S., AND M.A. FLEMMING
1991 A Bulwark in the Pacific: An Example of World War II Archaeology on Saipan. In *Archaeology Studies of World War II*, Raymond Wood, editor, pp. 13-28. University of Missouri, Columbia.

SAUNDERS, NICHOLAS J.
2001a Excavating Memories. Archaeology and the Great War 1914-2001. *Antiquity* 76:101-108.

2001b Matter and Memory in the Landscapes of Conflict: The Western Front 1914-1999. In *Contested Landscapes: Movement, Exile and Place*, Barbara Bender and Margot Winer, editors, pp. 37-53. Berg, Oxford, England.

2007 *Killing Time: Archaeology and the First World War*. Stroud, Sutton, England.

SAUNDERS, NICHOLAS J. (EDITOR)
2004 *Matters of Conflict: Material Culture, Memory and the First World War*. Routledge, London, England.

SAUNDERS, NICHOLAS J., AND PAUL CORNISH (EDITORS)
2009 *Contested Objects. Material Memories of the Great War*. Routledge, London, England.

SCHMID-HECKLAU, A., AND U. SCHÖNFELDER
2007 Archäologische Untersuchungen am Westwallabschnitt Niederkrüchten [Archaeological Investigations on the Siegfried Line at Niederkrüchten]. *Archäologie im Rheinland* 2007:176-178.

SCHOFIELD, JOHN
2005 *Combat Archaeology. Material Culture and Modern Conflict*. Duckworth, London, England.

SCHOFIELD, JOHN, AND W. JOHNSON
2006 Archaeology, Heritage and the Recent and Contemporary Past. In *The Cambridge Companion to Historical Archaeology*, Dan Hicks and Mary C. Beaudry, editors, pp. 104-122. Cambridge University Press, Cambridge, England.

SCHUTE, IVAR, AND JOBBE A. T.WIJNEN
2010 Archeologisch onderzek in een "schuldig landschap": Concentratiekamp Amersfoort [Archaeological Research in a "Guilty Landscape": Concentration Camp Amersfort]. *RAAP-Rapport 2197* 2010:7-89.

SMANI, RIZA, AND PETRA TUTLIES
2007 Auf den Spuren der jüngsten Vergangenheit—Unerwartete Relikte des Zweiten Weltkrieges [On the Trail of the Recent Past—Unexpected Remains of the Second World War]. *Archäologie im Rheinland* 2007:174-181.

STADLER, HARALD
2005 Zur Archäologie der Kosaken in Osttirol [The Archaeology of the Cossacks in Eastern Tyrol]. In *Flucht in die Hoffnungslosigkeit. Die Kosaken in Osttirol*, Harald Stadler, Martin Kofler, and Karl C. Berger, pp. 39-54. Studienverlag, Innsbruck, Austria.

STENSAGER, ANDERS OTTE
2007 *Holocaustarkæologi—en arkæologisk funktionsanalyse af udryddelseslejrene in Polen 1941–1945* [*Holocaust Archaeology, an Archaeological Analysis of the Extermination Camps in Poland 1941-1945*]. Magister thesis, University Kopenhagen, Denmark, http://www.diis.dk/sw36111.asp. Accessed 18 September 2012.

TARLOW, SARAH
1997 An Archaeology of Remembering: Death, Bereavement and the First World War. *Cambridge Archaeological Journal* 7(1):105-121.

THEUNE, CLAUDIA

2006   Vier Tonnen Funde geborgen. Bergung von Funden aus einer Müllgrube im ehemaligen Konzentrationslager von Sachsenhausen, Stadt Oranienburg, Landkreis Oberhavel [Four Tons of Finds! The Recovery of Finds from a Garbage Pit in the Former Concentration Camp at Sachsenhausen/Orabienburg, Oberhavel County]. *Archäoloie in Berlin und Brandenburg* 2006:131-133.

2010a   Archäologische Relikte und Spuren von Tätern und Opfern im ehemaligen Konzentrationslager Mauthausen [Archaeological Remains and Traces of Perpetrators and Victims in the Former Concentration Camp at Mauthausen]. In Mauthausen Memorial neu gestalten. Tagungsbericht zum 1. Dialogforum Mauthausen 18.-19. Juni 2009, pp. 33-38. Bundesministerium des Inneren, Vienna, Austria.

2010b   Zeitschichten—Archäologische Untersuchungen in der Gedenkstätte Mauthausen [Archeological Investigations in Mauthausen Memorial]. In KZ Gedenkstätte Mauthausen Mauthausen Memorial 2009. Forschung, Dokumentation, Information, pp. 25-30. Bundesministerium des Inneren, Vienna, Austria.

2010c   Historical Archaeology in National Socialist Concentration Camps in Central Europe. *Historische Archäologie* 2010(4).

VAN DYKE, RUTH M., AND SUSAN E. ALCOCK

2003   *Archaeologies of Memory: An Introduction.* Blackwell, Malden, Oxford, England.

VAŘEKA, PAVEL

2010   An Archaeological Perspective on Czechoslovakian Mobilization in 1938: The "Toužim Treverse" Fortification Line Project. *Society for Historical Archaeology Newsletter* 43(4):16-17.

VEIT, ULRICH

2003   Menschen—Objekte—Zeichen. Perspektiven des Studiums materieller Kultur [People—Objects—Signs. Perspectives in the Study of Material Culture]. In *Spuren und Botschaften. Interpretation materieller Kultur*, Ulrich Veit, Tobias Kienlin, Christoph Küpmmel, and Sascha Schmid, editors, pp. 17-28. Tübinger Archäologische Taschenbücher 4. Waxmann, Münster, Germany.

WEGENER, WOLFGANG

2006   Der Westwall. Denkmal und Mythos [The Siegfried Line. Monument and Myth]. *Rheinische Heimatpflege* 43(4):279-292.

2007   Schlachtfelder des Zweiten Weltkrieges— eine neue Herausforderung für die Bodendenkmalpflege [Battlefields of the Second World War. A New Challenge for the Archaeological Heritage Organizations]. *Archäologie im Rheinland* 2007:176-181.

WEISHAUPT, JOHANNES

2005   Zeugnisse des Terrors. Archäologischer Beitrag zur Aufarbeitung im KZ-Sachsenhausen [Witnesses of Terror. The Archaeological Contribution to Analysis in Sachsenhausen Concentration Camp]. *Archäologie in Berlin und Brandenburg* 2005:156-160.

WOODWARD, IAN

2007   *Understanding Material Culture.* Sage, Los Angeles, CA.

Claudia Theune
Institut für Ur – und Frühgeschichte
Universität Wien
Franz Klein Gasse 1
A-1190 Wien
Austria

HARALD STADLER / FRIEDRICH STEPANEK

The Drau Valley Tragedy: The Historical Archaeology of World War II Cossacks in East Tyrol

ABSTRACT

In June 1945 British occupation forces forcibly handed over to the Soviet Union around 25,000 Cossacks and Caucasians who had fought for Hitler's Germany and were stranded in East Tyrol. The University of Innsbruck has taken an interest in this story—known as the "Drau Valley Tragedy"—since 2003. This article talks about the motives, methods, and results to date of this interdisciplinary (archaeology, contemporary history, folklore studies) project.

ARCHAEOLOGY AND CONTEMPORARY HISTORY

The founder of modern methodology in the historical sciences, Johann Gustav von Droysen (1808-1884), wrote as early as 1868 in his book *Outline of the Principles of History* that the material that a historian analyzes in order to answer his or her questions sometimes only survives in fragments. Not only written sources are meant here, but also "other things, which have perhaps been salvaged from the earth, or have survived among the trash and junk of old churches or long abandoned castles" (Hübner 1974:38). Although in theory the value of such sources does not depend on the age of the object, in German language archaeological practice material objects from the recent past have often not been treated the same way as pre – or early historic artifacts, but instead have been seen as insignificant, unscientific, and uninteresting.

In Germany, the Brandenburg region has pioneered contemporary period archaeology by consciously refusing to set temporal limits for the definition of a monument. Frequently, excavations in concentration camps have proven the only way of obtaining new results about questions of detail, as the pertinent records were destroyed at the end of the war (Antkowiak 2005; Theune 2006). Contemporary period archaeology is in its infancy in Austria: the field is still dominated by private militaria collectors; popular-scientific monographs and articles are the rule (Enigl 2007). Only a few objects, most of them above-ground complexes such as the anti-aircraft towers in Vienna (Stadtentwicklung Wien 2002), are seen as worthy of preservation, although in this case the size and indestructibility of the buildings (the United States army has repeatedly, and unsuccessfully, tried to blast away the buildings) may have meant that a virtue has been made of necessity. The situation has improved recently through a new focus at the Department of Prehistoric and Historical Archaeology at Vienna and also at Austrian Department of Monuments, which since 2008 has taken up the archaeological traces of contemporary history (Klimesch and Rachbauer 2008; Theune 2010).

PROJECTS ABOUT THE RECENT PAST AT THE UNIVERSITY OF INNSBRUCK

Modern-period archaeology has become increasingly important at the Department of Archaeology at Innsbruck (formerly the Department for Pre – and Early History, Medieval and Modern-period Archaeology) in the last 20 years. Examples include the documentation of the corpse of a poacher found preserved in a glacier who was the victim of an accident in 1839, the recovery of a Ju 52 airplane that made an emergency landing on an East Tyrolean glacier in 1941 (Stadler 2006; Falch, this volume), and the detailed company histories of the ceramics manufactory Julius Paul & Son in Bunzlau, Lower Silesia (1893-1945) (Lippert et al. 2002) and of the small pottery business Höfer-Troger-Steger in Abfaltersbach, East Tyrol (Stadler 2002).

These research projects have consistently shown that an archaeological approach to the recent past can reveal

Figure 1.　Map with places mentioned in the text (in Austria, unless otherwise noted); the East Tyrol area is shown in dark grey: (1) Ainet; (2) Lienz-Peggetz; (3) Lavant; and (4) Tolmezzo, Italy (Map provided courtesy of the Department of Prehistory and Medieval Archaeology, University of Vienna, Austria).

information about both socio-structural phenomena and particular individuals, and that the analysis of

objects leads to the emergence of questions that had previously not even been thought of.

THE LIENZ COSSACKS

The term Cossacks is used to describe free "armed peasants"—peasants who were obligated to military service by their lords, receiving certain rights in return—who, at the end of the 15th century, settled in border areas of the Muscovite Empire[1] that had been devastated by repeated Tartar raiding and in which centralized authority was lacking. They organized themselves militarily in cavalry units and were

granted increasing privileges over time. The Cossacks were not a homogenous ethnic group, but were instead a combination of runaway serfs, peasants, and criminals variously of Russian, Ukrainian, and Turkish-Tartar origin (Stökl 1953; Hobsbawm 2007:91-104). In this article the term is used to describe those men, women, and children who in World War II attached themselves to the German Wehrmacht as the Cossack "Stan,"[2] despite the fact that on the one hand the "Cossacks" were a historically outdated concept by that time and on the other that the "Stan" consisted not only of Cossacks, but also of Kalmucks, Ukrainians, Georgians, and people of other nationalities who had been forced to flee (Newland 2005:131-137).

HISTORY OF THE COSSACKS IN EAST TYROL

During the attack on the Soviet Union in 1941, as the German army advanced eastwards they were greeted in many places as liberators from the "Bolshevik yoke" (Neulen 1985:315). This reception was particularly pronounced in the traditionally Cossack regions on the rivers Don, Terek, and Kuban as the "Whites"[3] had held on longest in these areas during the Russian Civil War (1917-1920) and the population had suffered greatly under the "liquidation of the Kulaks"[4] (Ziegler 1993:189-200). The brutality of National Socialist oppression was soon to be felt in the Ukraine, but the Wehrmacht allowed the inhabitants of the Caucascus foothills a certain amount of autonomy (Newland 2005:127-131).

The German army was forced to withdraw from the Caucasus after the battle of Stalingrad in 1942/1943. Many civilians accompanied it (R. Müller 1994), choosing an uncertain future instead of the repression they feared at the hands of the Red Army. This profound fear was not unjustified, for on 24 June 1942 Stalin had decreed that family members would be held responsible for the actions of traitors to their country (Goeken-Haidl 2006:17-18), and among the Cossacks and the peoples of the Caucasus tens of thousands had voluntarily joined the Wehrmacht.

The Cossack Stan, which now emerged, moved westwards via transit camps in Byelorussia and Poland before finally being compulsorily settled by the "Ministry for the Occupied Eastern Territories" in the region around the North Italian town of Carnia in Summer 1944 (Wedekind 2003:343). The families lived in confiscated houses in the Tolmezzo area, above all in the Tagliamento and Degano river valleys. The male Cossacks were attached to the Trieste police and were deployed in the fight against partisans in that area. They rapidly became feared because of the atrocities they committed (Koschat 2003:2040-2215).

Fear of mistreatment meant that the Cossacks refused to surrender to the Italian partisans at the end of the war. They decided to move through the Plöcken pass into Austria instead and were allocated a bivouac area in the Drau valley east of Lienz, where they waited to be taken

prisoner by the British army (Figure 1). At first the estimated 25,000 people were treated in a friendly fashion by the British and not as prisoners-of-war, but their fate had already been decided at the 1945 Yalta conference. At Yalta the United States and Great Britain had signed a secret supplementary accord that regulated the repatriation of Soviet citizens (Polian 2001:60-69). Many of the Cossacks had never been citizens of the Soviet Union, having emigrated many years previously, and it had not been decided what would be done if repatriation was resisted, but the British government was determined to demonstrate its goodwill toward the Soviet Union by handing over all of the Cossacks, thus "over-satisfying" the Yalta agreement (Tolstoy 1987:343-384).

The British disarmed the Cossacks under false pretenses. Their officers were led away, incarcerated, and then handed over to the Soviets. The remaining men, women, and children heard about their planned extradition and chose to resist non-violently, but British soldiers nevertheless began to load Cossacks onto trucks by force. Terrible scenes occurred in the early hours of 1 June 1945, particularly in the camp at Peggetz near Lienz: a mass panic broke out and children and women were trampled to death. Some Cossacks committed suicide rather than be deported to the Soviet Union, and women plunged with their children into the river Drau, which was swollen with floodwater at the time. Some Cossacks managed to flee (Wilding 1999:78-85), but the exact number of people who died in the East Tyrol area during and after the events remains unknown today.

Many people in East Tyrol saw or heard these events, which became known as the "Drau Valley Tragedy." They were predictably shocked by the behavior of the occupying soldiers and felt sorry for the deportees (Berger 2005). Afterwards the personal effects remaining in the abandoned Cossack camps were plundered (Wilding 1999:95), so that local people in the upper Drau valley often possessed and still possess not only vivid memories of those events at the end of the war in 1945, but also sometimes objects that formerly belonged to the Cossacks.

Figure 2.   Cossack cemetery in the Peggetz neighborhood of Lienz, Austria (Photo by Alexander Duwakin, New Zealand, 1949; courtesy of Alexander Duwakin).

The ultimate fate of those Cossacks, who had camped in East Tyrol, remains unclear even today. Many fled to the hills, were taken in by farmers, or hid in alpine huts, and although more than 1,350 Cossacks were recaptured by British patrols (Cowgill 1990:343-359) a few were nonetheless successful and scattered across the world. Some of the Cossacks even remained in Lienz, their descendants living there to this day (Wilding 1999:105-109).

The most important leaders of the Cossack deportees were executed in Moscow in January 1947 after a show trial. Most appear to have been sent to "screening camps" and were compelled to forced labor east of the Urals (Goeken-Haidl 2006:455-458). Their rate of survival is unknown. The initial fate of one group of Cossacks consisting of 807 women and children and one man has been exactly researched, however. Although more than half of this group was aged less than 21, those involved were sent as so-called "Vlasov-people"[5] to a camp in the mining district at Stalinsk in Siberia. The death rate there was around 10 percent. What happened to the survivors after the camp was dissolved in 1949 is unknown, however (Karner and Ruggenthaler 2005:248-255).

A remembrance ceremony has taken place at the little Cossack cemetery in the Peggetz neighborhood of Lienz every year since 1953 (Figure 2). Many local people remember the Drau Valley Tragedy, the only time East Tyrol has ever been "part of world history" (Kofler 2005:21; Karner 2008) and not only because of its presence in the local media. There are still East Tyroleans who possess a Cossack object into which, as it were, a memory has been placed, and which today, surrounded by an "aura of originality" (Kuntz 1995:356), serves as a little monument of its own.

As early as 2002 an unsuccessful attempt was made to win the support of local politicians for an exhibition about the Cossacks in East Tyrol based on a contemporary historical/archaeological approach. The original idea, the installation of a presentation in the spacious old locomotive shed at Lienz railroad station in "Memorial Year (2005)" and on the 60th anniversary of the Drau Valley Tragedy, had to be abandoned for financial reasons. That site would have been an ideal location as on-site period railroad cars belonging to the "Friends of the Railroad" organization could have been used to illustrate the forced extradition theme.

Instead preparatory university classes, working with students, have proved to be an inexpensive but no less scientific way of organizing an exhibition. Karl Berger from the Department of European Ethnology/Folklore at the University of Innsbruck agreed to work for the project on an interdisciplinary basis. University classes were held at the scene of the events in Lienz in 2003-2004 in order to find as many original sources as possible and to deepen knowledge of the subject matter.

Students were schooled in the theory and practice of interviewing and the subsequent evaluation of the interviews in classes at the Department of European Ethnology/Folklore. As an introduction 14 interviews with contemporary witnesses, which had been carried out by members of the Dölsach theater workshop in 2001 as part of preparations for the theater production "Run Katinka," and which were made available by the Austrian Contemporary Witnesses archive, were

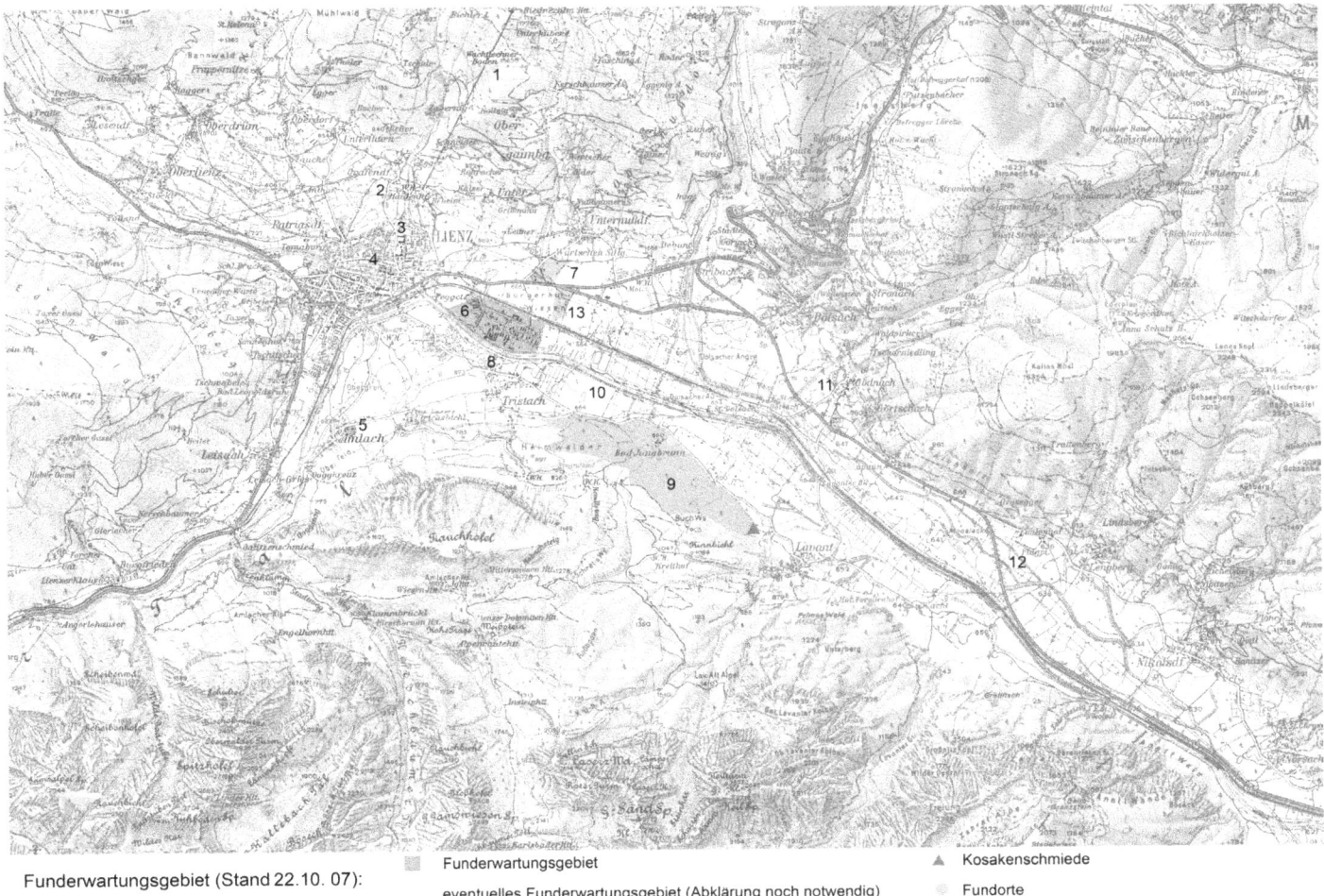

Funderwartungsgebiet (Stand 22.10. 07):

▨ Funderwartungsgebiet
eventuelles Funderwartungsgebiet (Abklärung noch notwendig)
▲ Kosakenschmiede
◌ Fundorte

Figure 3. Areas where Cossack finds are likely to occur in the valley around Lienz. The areas shaded pink (Funderwartungsgebiet) and yellow (eventuelles Funderwartungsgebiet) are zones of known and suspected sensitivity, respectively. The green dots (Fundorte) are find spots, and the red triangle (Kosakenschmiede) is a blacksmith shop (Illustration by M. Schick, 2009; courtesy of the Department of Archaeology, University of Innsbruck, Austria).

Figure 4. *Identification tag from an unknown member of the Cossack Stan regiment from the Cossack smithy in Lavant. Scale 1:1 (Photo by M. Schick, 2004; courtesy of the Department of Archaeology, University of Innsbruck, Austria).*

transcribed and evaluated. Later the students themselves questioned more than 60 people who still had vivid memories of those days in May 1945.

A critical analysis of fieldwork methods in folklore studies also took place in order to be as well prepared as possible for the three field trips to Lienz and to profit by this "learning through research."

Students from both the Department of Pre – and Early History, Medieval and Modern-period Archaeology and the Department of European Ethnology/Folklore took part in the field trips. This interdisciplinary teamwork meant that the students were encouraged to see beyond the end of their own noses and to gain experiences outside of their own discipline. Archaeology students were thus introduced to the theory and practice of interviewing contemporary witnesses, while students of European Ethnology/Folklore accompanied their archaeological colleagues in the investigation of possible find spots and observed them as they photographed and drew Cossack objects, whether newly salvaged or provided by local people. All sites mentioned in the conversations were localized and entered on a map to show possible find spots (Figure 3), which has not yet been systematically used.

For the students these differing approaches to the complex subject of the Cossacks in East Tyrol have amounted to new forms of cognitive learning and contrast immensely to the more usual "force feeding" of lecture theaters. The students reacted positively with a high degree of motivation.

An archaeological training excavation took place at the site of the "Cossack field smithy" in Lavant in spring 2005. A conversation with a contemporary witness led

Figure 5. *Diary of Iwan Nikolajewitsch Tscherenkow with a reconstruction of his journey from the Ukraine to Upper Italy, discovered in a loft at Nußdorf (Photo by M. Schick, 2004; courtesy of the Department of Archaeology, University of Innsbruck, Austria).*

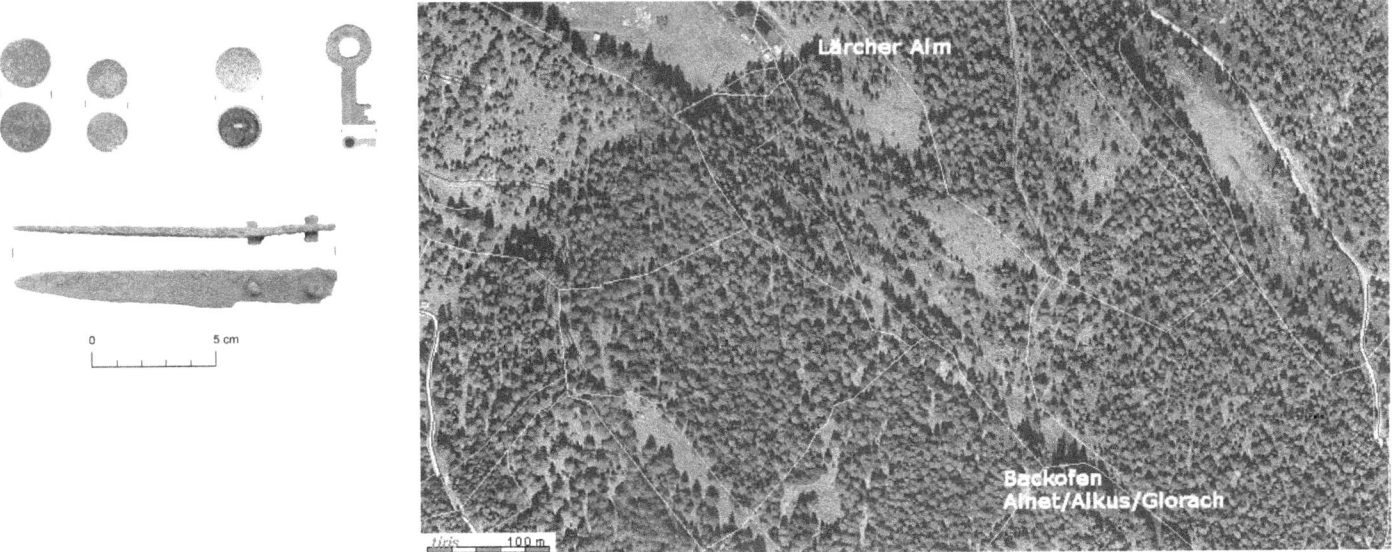

Figure 6. Cossack bivouac site on the alpine pasture "Larcher Alm," part of Ainet villageship, with the site of an oven (Backofen) to the south. Typical finds from the site, shown on the left, include coins, a military button, a key, and a knife (Illustration by M. Schick, 2008; courtesy of the Department of Archaeology, University of Innsbruck, Austria).

to the identification of the stone on which the forge had stood. Four trial trenches probed the boulder and its surroundings. The excavations and the prospection of the surrounding plots led to the discovery of horseshoes, parts of horses' harnesses, uniform parts, and other objects. Among the most important discoveries were two identification tags from soldiers of the Cossack regiments (Figure 4) and a hoard of German, Polish, and Italian coins, effectively a record of the route the Cossacks traveled (F. Müller and Stadler 2005).

Conventional excavations were not the only means by which Cossack objects were collected for the future exhibition—"loft archaeology" also played a role. Through the local media people from the area were encouraged to make Cossack objects they owned available for scientific recording and research while the field team was in town. True to the motto "the loft is the Austrian's archive" (Rauscher 2007), this form of "archaeology above the sod" (Atzbach and Ericsson 2005) proved particularly effective because objects are kept in countless East Tyrol households, their owners unaware of their significance.

Around 300 objects appeared including everyday items such as cooking pots, but also many unusual objects such as jewelry and showpiece weapons. The most surprising finds included a completely preserved *Panjewagen*[6] and the diary of the Cossack Iwan Nikolajewitsch Tscherenkow (Figure 5), which East Tyrol children had re-used as a school book. The diary is the unique documentation of an ordinary Cossack and his journey from recruitment by the Red Army, through desertion and defection to the Wehrmacht, up to his stopover in northern Italy.

Exhibitions in 2005 and 2010 produced a variety of Cossack material remains that were loaned for scientific research, or even gifted, by local people and by Cossack descendants from across the world. The exhibition team was able to analyze and employ a total of 12 Cossack estates. Numerous photographs and useful pieces of information were contributed. Contemporary witnesses also emerged, who were able to localize Cossack hideouts in the forest (Figure 6) or in the high mountains.

THE ARCHAEOLOGICAL APPROACH

In 1995 several modern period graves were found east of the chancel of St. Ulrich's church in Lavant. The result was an excavation in which it was hoped the early Christian predecessor of the present church would be revealed. Instead finds that accompanied one skeleton, Italian coins from 1940 and 1941, and

information from the local population about Cossack funerals outside the church with burial goods of coins and accompanying meals, led to a very different reconstruction of events. The same local sources also remembered wooden crosses with Cyrillic inscriptions, which had rotted away in the intervening period. Sadly,

Figure 7. (above) Cossack graves excavated in the churchyard at Lavant, to the east of St. Ulrich's Church. Detail shows two coins excavated from the graves (Illustration by M. Schick and M. Tschurtschenthaler, 2004; courtesy of the Department of Archaeology, University of Innsbruck, Austria).

Figure 8. (above, right) Pyramid-shaped pendant, the property of Sonja Walder, Kartitsch (Illustration by M. Schick, 2004; courtesy of the Department of Archaeology, University of Innsbruck, Austria).

Figure 9. (below) Marked iron cauldron from the Bad Jungbrunn site, Lavant (Photo by M. Schick, 2004; courtesy of the Department of Archaeology, University of Innsbruck, Austria).

Figure 10. (right) Hoard of watches found with a metal detector at the Bad Jungbrunn site, Lavant (Photo by H. Stadler, 2008; courtesy of the Department of Archaeology, University of Innsbruck, Austria).

the late antique focus of the excavation meant that anthropological analyses aiming at establishing the age, sex, and DNA of the dead were not even considered. In any case eccentric burial practices were recorded during the excavation (coins and remains of meals placed in the graves) (Figure 7), which have still to be explained.

It may be surprising that specialists for medieval and post-medieval archaeology should be interested in this subject, but in fact the study of the events in the valley around Lienz in 1945 raises a number of particular issues that can be satisfactorily addressed with an archaeological approach.

First, archaeology has the clear advantage in this case in that it approaches the material through the objects involved and is thus objective and unprejudiced and not caught up in the preceding victim-perpetrator discourse, in which the Cossacks are exclusively understood as the playthings of Churchill, Roosevelt, and Stalin.

Second, the passage from the Caucasus foothills through the Ukraine, Byelorussia, Poland, and Italy to East Tyrol on the one hand and the heterogenic composition of those involved—Cossacks, Ukrainians, Byelorussians, and Kalmucks—on the other, offers a very obvious comparison to the semi-nomadic bands of the migration period. In contrast to the roaming tribal groups of the early Middle Ages, however, written records and the oral accounts of contemporary witnesses can be called upon in this case, making a close examination of archaeological methods as they are applied in early history possible in turn. Some researchers, for example, have questioned how far it is possible to prove archaeologically the presence of groups of

mounted nomads, who were only in a particular region for a short period of time (Parzinger 1993:216). The Cossacks around Lienz show very clearly that this is possible. Astonishingly, some of the material remains involved can even be compared to early medieval objects. Research in advance of the 2005 exhibition, for instance, turned up an earring in the form of a pointed pyramid (Figure 8) that strongly resembles a Byzantine product common among the Avars from the 6th and 7th centuries onwards. A cast iron cooking pot without handles (Figure 9), a very strange object to local Tyroleans, calls to mind shapes from the early historical Przeworsk culture in Poland.

Third, archaeological sources bring insights into social relationships and the position of individuals in society. Thus they can reveal evidence of social stratification within the Cossack Stan, for example of the presence of watchmakers: pocket watches and wristwatches (Figure 10), and replacement parts (Figure 11) were

Figure 11. Replacement parts for watches found in a tin can with a metal detector at the Bad Jungbrunn site, Lavant. Scale ca 1:1 (Illustration by M. Schick, 2004; courtesy of the Department of Archaeology, University of Innsbruck, Austria).

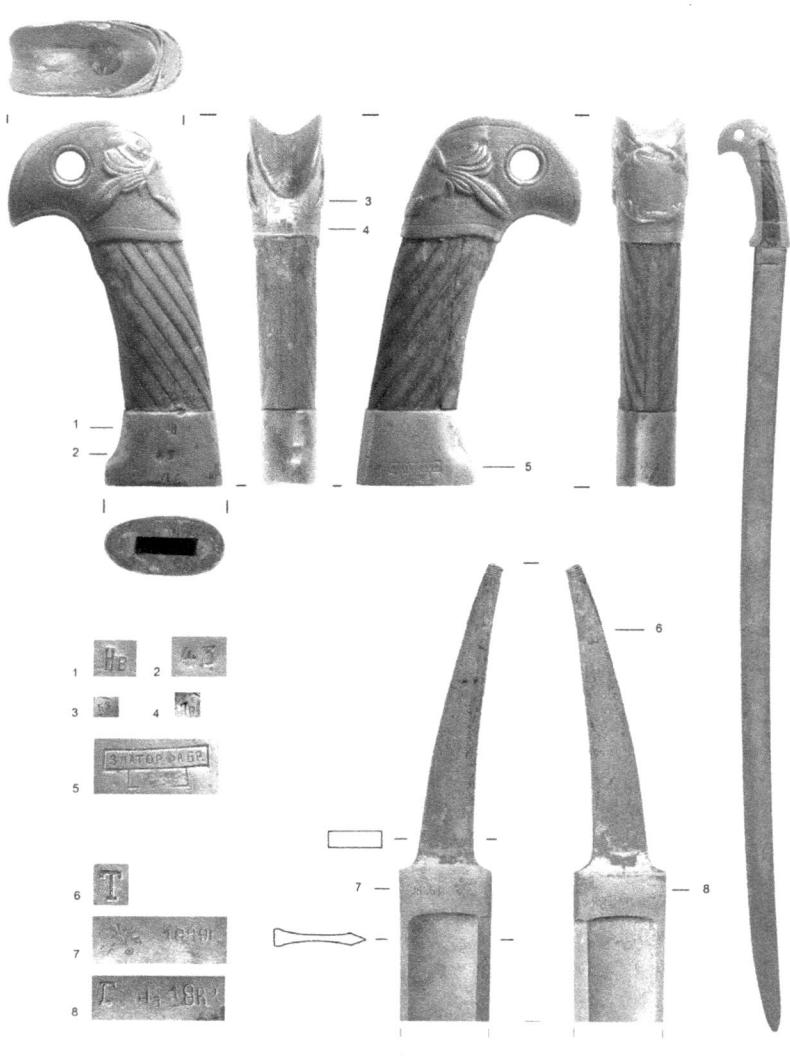

Figure 12.   (left) chaschka (Circassian saber) from Lienz, Peggetz neighborhood (Illustration by A. Blaickner, 2008; courtesy of the Department of Archaeology, University of Innsbruck, Austria).

Figure 13.   (below) Porcelain carving plate made in the Ukraine and bartered for food, from Nußdorf-Debant (Photo by A. Blaickner, 2005; courtesy of the Department of Archaeology, University of Innsbruck, Austria).

found wrapped in a blanket and hidden in a crevice. This is a particularly interesting historical issue that has not yet been investigated, presumably because there is a lack of pertinent written sources. Only different occupations are known, one Cossack regiment being said to have contained "every occupation, from engine driver to watchmaker" (Blaese 1982, quoted in Neulen 1985:315).

Fourth, through archaeology, small finds of a personal nature reveal the fates of individuals. The objects found are often silent witnesses, which when given a voice through archaeological analysis and historical interpretation tell the stories of individual people and have a strong emotive power. Individuals about whom we have no written records can be raised out of anonymity and made tangible. Archaeological features and finds such as watches, weapons (Figure 12), and pottery (which was bartered for food) (Figure 13) as well as documents, shed light on an individual biography,

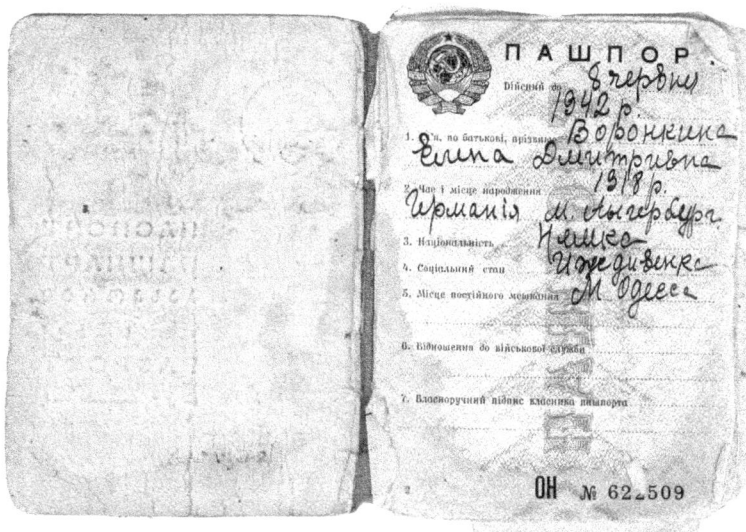

Figure 14.   Passport stamped with the word "Germania" from Dölsach, in the personal possession of M. Rainer, Dölsach. Slightly smaller than original size (Photo by M. Schick, 2004; courtesy of the Department of Archaeology, University of Innsbruck, Austria).

which sometimes can be attached to a name and further researched, if, for example, an identification tag (see Figure 4) is found.

Figure 15.   Medallion of non-ferrous metal with a religious motif, found with a metal detector at the Bad Jungbrunn site, Lavant. Scale 2:1 (Photo by M. Schick, 2004; courtesy of the Department of Archaeology, University of Innsbruck, Austria).

There are also the usually anonymous features from bivouac sites in rough terrain or from hideouts in caves (so-called "Cossack holes") and rock shelves in the high mountains. Many Cossacks chose to flee over the high dairy pastures north of Lienz, where food was likely to be had. Information from local sources led in one case to the discovery and recording of a bivouac site, which included a self-built bread oven in a gorge (see Figure 6).

Fifth, new questions often first emerge in the course of the intensive analysis of an object. For example, in the course of the research a Soviet passport appeared on which the word "Germania" had been stamped (Figure 14). The question in this case is whether those Cossacks who attached themselves to the German army automatically received German citizenship. The search for objects also led to written sources, for instance to the diary of Iwan Nikolajewitsch Tscherenkow (see Figure 5). Further research turned up the daughters of the author and so his fate could be reconstructed from his extradition from Lienz to his exile in Siberia and ultimately to his death and his grave. A publication of this individual story, which will include the diary, is in preparation. One of his daughters was even found alive in the village of Moschaiowko, Rostov on the Don province, not far from the eastern border of the Ukraine.[7]

Last but not least an archaeological approach guarantees the protection of strange and valuable cultural artifacts (Figure 15) that would otherwise be lost to science since succeeding generations usually do not realize the significance of the Cossack objects they possess. Disinterest often leads to the material remains of the Cossacks landing in the second-hand goods trade or on the garbage heap.

OUTLOOK

An interdisciplinary team of archaeologists, European ethnologists, and contemporary historians is ready to begin the remaining tasks as soon as a further project is financed. The value for European ethnology lies in the way the East Tyrol population related to the strangers, how they dealt with the Drau Valley Tragedy, and in the symbolism of the material remains. The task for contemporary history is the heuristic evaluation of the relevant source material and the historical placement of the themes involved in an international context (Grelka 2008).

A range of surveys has localized previous and future areas where archaeological finds are possible, such as bivouac sites or pits that the British dug in May 1945 to dispose of the vehicles and household effects left behind, and tested them with metal detectors. As was the case before the exhibitions, the local population will again be encouraged to make Cossack objects available for scientific documentation. All objects, whether found above – or below ground, will be examined with the appropriate methods, included in a database, and linked to the testimonies of witnesses, written records, and pictorial sources. The analysis of all sources relevant to the East Tyrol question marks the end of the process.

In the long-term there are plans for an architecturally modern memorial and museum in the form of a "bridge of memory" not far from the Cossack cemetery and thus the original site of the Drau Valley Tragedy. The historical awareness of the grandchildren and great-grandchildren of contemporaries will be fostered by, among other things, Cossack objects, which are particularly suitable for didactic purposes because of their inherent emotiveness.

The presentation of the results of the interdisciplinary research will demonstrate that archaeological sources are not only a source of exhibits, but that they also possess value as sources in their own right and can yield new testimony—even in the richly sourced field of contemporary history.

NOTES

1. This is the unofficial term for the Principality of Moscow, which formed the core of the unified Russian state.
2. The Cossack "Stan" includes the entire family of the Cossacks and not only the military personnel.
3. The white army, white troops, or white guards (Russ. Белая армия, *belaja armija*) is the term used in historical writing for the soldiers of the Russian White Movement, who fought in the Russian Civil War against the results of the October Revolution and formed the main opposition to Bolshevik Soviet Russia.
4. The liquidation of the Kulaks (Russ. раскулачивание, *raskulatschiwanije*) was a campaign of repression in the Soviet Union between 1929 and 1932 against the so-called Kulaks and which included mass arrests, numerous

executions, and deportations. In Russia prior to 1917 Kulak (Russ. кулак, "fist") was a derogatory word used for middlemen, profiteers, and swindlers. The term "Kulak" was extended to include all rural "exploiters" after the 1917 October Revolution and in particular during the collectivization of agriculture from 1928 to 1932.

5. Andrei Andreyevich Vlasov (Russ. Андрей Андреевич Влáсов) was a Russian former general of the Soviet army who collaborated with Nazi Germany during the World War II.

6. A small, simple wooden cart with four wheels, usually pulled by a horse and used in several eastern European countries.

7. A publication in Russian and German is being prepared by Anatoly Zaretskow/Rostov on the Don and Harald Stadler/Innsbruck.

REFERENCES

ANTKOWIAK, MATTHIAS
2005   Archäologie, Stumme Zeugen [Archaeology. Silent Witnesses]. *Zeit Online* 20/2005:48, http://www.zeit.de/2005/20/KZ-Arch_8aologie. Accessed 21 September 2012.

ATZBACH, RAINER, AND INGOLF ERICSSON (EDITORS)
2005   *Depotfunde aus Gebäuden in Zentraleuropa [Concealed Finds from Buildings in Central Europe].* Bamberger Kolloquien zur Archäologie des Mittelalters und der Neuzeit, No. 1, Archäologische Quellen zum Mittelalter, No. 2. **Scrîpvaz** , Berlin, Germany.

BERGER, KARL C.
2005   Schwieriges Erinnern. Eine volkskundliche Skizze [Difficult Memories]. In *Flucht in die Hoffnungslosigkeit. Die Kosaken in Osttirol,* Harald Stadler, Martin Kofler and Karl C. Berger, editors, pp. 28-38. Nearchos Sonderheft, No. 13. Studienverlag, Innsbruck, Austria.

BLAESE, HERMANN
1982   Don-Kosaken-Regiment 5 Nr. [5th Don Cossack Regiment]. *Nachrichten der Kameradschaft des XV. Kosaken-Kavallerie-Korps* 40:9.

COWGILL, ANTHONY
1990   *The Repatriations from Austria in 1945. Cowgill Inquiry. The Documentary Evidence Reproduced in Full from British, American, German and Yugoslav Sources.* Sinclair-Stevenson, London, England.

DIETRICH, STEFAN
2006   Flucht ins Verderben [Flight into Disaster]. *Abenteuer Archäologie* 3:40-43.

ENIGL, MARIANNE
2007   1073 Liter Wein [1073 Liters of Wine]. *Profil Nr.* 13:34-41.

GOEHRKE, CARSTEN
1977   Historische Selbststilisierung des Kosakentums: Ständische Tradition als Integrationsideologie [The Historical Self-Image of the Cossacks. Hierarchical Tradition as an Ideology of Integration]. In *Osteuropa in Geschichte und Gegenwart. Festschrift für Günther Stökl zum 60. Geburtstag,* Hans Lemberg, Peter Nitsche, and Erwin Oberländer, editors, pp. 359-375. Böhlau, Cologne, Germany.

GOEKEN-HAIDL, ULRIKE
2006   *Der Weg zurück. Die Repatriierung sowjetischer Zwangsarbeiter und Kriegsgefangener während und nach dem Zweiten Weltkrieg [The Way Back. The Repatriation of Soviet Forced Laborers and Prisoners-of-War during and after World War II].* Klartext, Essen, Germany.

GRELKA, F.
2008   "Zwischen Kollaborationismus, Kriminalisierung und Kanonenfutter" Zur kosakischen und ukrainischen Rolle vom Ersten zum Zweiten Weltkrieg ["Collaboration, Criminalization, and Cannon Fodder." The Role of the Cossacks and the Ukrainians from World War I to World War II]. In *Die Kosaken im Ersten und Zweiten Weltkrieg,* Harald Stadler, Rolf Steininger, and Karl C. Berger, editors, pp. 93-111. Archäologisch-Militärhistorische Forschungen, No. 3. Studienverlag, Innsbruck, Austria.

HOBSBAWM, ERIC
2007   *Die Banditen. Räuber als Sozialrebellen [Primitive Rebels].* 2nd edition. Carl Hanser, Munich, Germany.

HÜBNER, RUDOLF (EDITOR)
1974   *Johann Gustav von Droysen: Historik [Outline of Principles of History].* 7th edition. Wissenschaftliche Buchgesellschaft, Darmstadt, Germany.

KARNER, STEFAN
2008   Zur zwangsweisen Übergabe der Kosaken an die Sowjets 1945 in Judenburg [The Forcible Extradition of the Cossacks to the Soviets in Judenburg in 1945]. In *Die Kosaken im Ersten und Zweiten Weltkrieg,* Harald Stadler, Rolf Steininger, and Karl C. Berger, editors, pp. 141-151. Archäologisch-Militärhistorische Forschungen, No. 3. Studienverlag, Innsbruck, Austria.

KARNER, STEFAN, AND PETER RUGGENTHALER

2005 (Zwangs-)Repatriierungen sowjetischer Staatsbürger aus Österreich in die UdSSR [The Forced Repatriation of Soviet Citizens from Austria to the USSR]. In *Die Rote Armee in Österreich. Sowjetische Besatzung 1945-1955. Beiträge*, Stefan Karner and Barbara Stelzt-Marx, editors, pp. 243-274. Veröffentlichungen des Ludwig-Boltzmann-Instituts für Kriegsfolgen-Forschung, Sonderband, No. 4. Verein zur Förderung der Forschung von Folgen nach Konflikten und Kriegen, Graz, Austria.

KLIMESCH, WOLFGANG, AND MARKUS RACHBAUER

2008 VERITATEM DIES APERIT Vernichtet-Vergraben-Vergessen Archäologische Spurensuche in Schloss Hartheim [Exterminated—Buried—Forgotten. Archaeological Traces in Schloss Hartheim]. *Studien zur Kulturgeschichte von Oberösterreich* 17:177-189.

KOFLER, MARTIN

2005 Osttirol 1945—Zwischen Chaos und Neubeginn [East Tyrol in 1945—Chaos and a New Beginning]. In *Flucht in die Hoffnungslosigkeit. Die Kosaken in Osttirol*, Harald Stadler, Martin Kofler, and Karl C. Berger, editors, pp. 21-27. Nearchos Sonderheft, No. 13. Studienverlag, Innsbruck, Austria.

KOSCHAT, MICHAEL

2003 Die italienischen "Partisanenrepubliken" im Sommer und Herbst 1944. Improvisation oder historisches Modell? Die "Repubblica Partigiana della Carnia e del Friuli" ["Partisan Republics" in Italy in Summer and Autumn 1944. Improvisation or a Historical Model. The "Repubblica Partigiana della Carnia e del Friuli"], Vol. 4. Doctoral dissertation, Institut für Geschichte, Geisteswissenschaftliche Fakultät, Universität Wien, Austria.

KUNTZ, ANDREAS

1995 Symbolisch?—Original, Migrationsgeschichte, Folklorismus [Symbolic—Original, Migration History, Folklore]. In *Lokale und biographische Erfahrungen. Studien zur Volkskunde*, Andreas Kuntz, editor, pp. 351-366. Waxmann, Münster, Germany.

LIPPERT, INGE, KONRAD SPINDLER, WERNER ENDRES, AND EKKEHARD LIPPERT

2002 *Bunzlauer Keramik. Die Feinsteinzeugfabrik Julius Paul & Sohn in Bunzlau 1893-1945 [Bunzlau Pottery. The Julius Paul & Son Fine Stoneware Factory in Bunzlau 1893-1945].* 3 vols. Nearchos 8-10. Arnoldsche, Innsbruck, Austria.

MÜLLER, FLORIAN MARTIN, AND HARALD STADLER

2005 KG Lavant, OG Lavant, VB Lienz. *Fundberichte aus Österreich* 44:639-640.

MÜLLER, ROLF DIETER

1994 Es begann am Kuban… Flucht und Deportationsbewegungen in Osteuropa während des Rückzuges der deutschen Wehrmacht 1943/44 [It Began on the Kuban… Flight and Deportation in Eastern Europe during the German Army's Retreat 1943/44]. In *Flucht und Vertreibung. Zwischen Aufrechnung und Verdrängung*, Robert Streibel, editor, pp. 42-76. Picus, Vienna, Austria.

NEULEN, HANS WERNER

1985 *An deutscher Seite. Internationale Freiwillige von Wehrmacht und Waffen-SS [On the German Side. International Volunteers for the Wehrmacht and the SS].* Universitas, Munich, Germany.

NEWLAND, SAMUEL J.

2005 *Cossacks in the German Army 1941-1945.* Frank Cass, New York, NY.

PARZINGER, HERMANN

1993 Vettersfelde-Mundolsheim-Aspres-lès-Corps. In *Kulturen zwischen Ost und West. Das Ost-West-Verhältnis in vor und frühgeschichtlicher Zeit*, Amei Lang, Hermann Parzinger, and Hansjörg Küster, editors, pp. 203-238. Akademie Verlag, Berlin, Germany.

POLIAN, PAVEL

2001 *Deportiert nach Hause. Sowjetische Kriegsgefangene im "Dritten Reich" und ihre Repatriierung [Deported Home. Soviet Prisoners-of-War in the "Third Reich" and their Repatriation].* Oldenbourg, Munich, Germany.

RAUSCHER, HANS

2007 "Der Stammtisch soll sich aufregen" ["The Bar-Room Politicians Won't Like It"]. *Der Standard* 27/28(October):9.

STADLER, HARALD

2002 *Untersuchungen zur neuzeitlichen Keramikproduktion im Pustertal am Beispiel der Hafnerei Höfer-Troger-Steger in Abfaltersbach, Osttirol. Bd. 1 Die Familiengeschichte, die Baulichkeiten und das hafnereitechnische Inventar [Post-Medieval Pottery Production in the Puster Valley. The Höfer-Troger-Steger Pottery in Abfaltersbach, East Tyrol. Volume 1, Family History, the Buildings and the Pottery's Technical Equipment].* Nearchos 11. Golf, Innsbruck, Austria.

2006 Suchschnitte in die Zeitgeschichte. Aktuelle Forschungen der Neuestneuzeitarchäologie in Tirol [Trial Trenches into Contemporary History. Current Research in the Most Recent Modern Archaeology]. In *Bericht über den 24. Österreichischen Historikertag in Innsbruck*, Tiroler Landesarchiv, editor, pp. 625-636. Veröffentlichungen des Verbandes Österreichischer Historiker und Geschichtsvereine, No. 33. Verlag Österreichisches Staatsarchiv, Innsbruck, Austria.

STADTENTWICKLUNG WIEN
2002   *Wiener Flaktürme. Untersuchung zur Klärung der Nutzungsmöglichkeiten im Auftrag der Magistratsabteilung 18* [The Vienna Flak Towers. Research into Possible uses for Local Authority Department 18]. Stadtentwicklung Wien, Werkstattberichte, No. 53. Vienna, Austria.

STÖKL, GÜNTHER
1953   *Die Entstehung des Kosakentums* [The Birth of the Cossacks]. Isar, Munich, Germany.

THEUNE, CLAUDIA
2006   Vier Tonnen Funde geborgen. Bergung von Funden aus einer Müllgrube im ehemaligen Konzentrationslager von Sachsenhausen, Stadt Oranienburg, Landkreis Oberhavel [Four Tons of Finds! The Recovery of Finds from a Garbage Pit in the Former Concentration Camp at Sachsenhausen/Oranienburg, Oberhavel County]. *Archäologie in Berlin und Brandenburg* 2006:131-133.

2010   Zeitgeschichtliche Archäologie –Denkmalpflege und Forschungen in der Gedenkstätte Mauthausen [Contemporary Archaeology— Conservation and Research in the Mauthausen Memorial]. *Archäologie Österreichs* 21(2):30-33.

TOLSTOY, NIKOLAI
1987   *Die Verratenen von Jalta* [Those Betrayed at Yalta]. Ullstein, Frankfurt, Germany.

WEDEKIND, MICHAEL
2003   *Nationalsozialistische Besatzungs – und Annexionspolitik in Norditalien 1943-1945. Die Operationszonen "Alpenvorland" und "Adriatisches Küstenland"* [National Socialist Occupation and Annexation Policy in Northern Italy 1943-1945. The Operational Zones "Alpine Foothills" and "Adriatic Coast"]. Militärgeschichtliche Studien, No. 38. Oldenbourg, Munich, Germany.

WILDING, ARMIN
1999   *Die Kosaken im oberen Drautal und ihre Auslieferung an die Sowjetunion 1945* [The Cossacks in the Upper Drau Valley and their Extradition to the Soviet Union 1945]. Studia Carinthiaca, No. 14. Hermagoras/Mohorjeva, Klagenfurt, Austria.

ZIEGLER, GUDRUN
1993   *Auf dem wilden Feld* [In the Wild Country]. Carlsen, Hamburg, Germany.

Harald Stadler
Institut für Archäologien
Universität Innsbruck
Langer Weg 11
A-6020 Innsbruck
Austria

Friedrich Stepanek
Institut für Geschichte und Europäische Ethnologie
Universität Innsbruck
Innrain 52
A-6020 Innsbruck
Austria

III. Technology, Industry, and Modernization

ANDREAS HEEGE

Craftsmen's Pottery Kilns in Belgium, The Netherlands, Germany, Austria, and Switzerland

ABSTRACT

The topic of the paper focuses on the history of non-industrial ceramic technology in the German-speaking parts of Europe, in Belgium, and in the Netherlands on the basis of excavated pottery kilns. Kilns are the most important part of the pottery production process. In Europe two basic kiln types have been identified archaeologically: updraft kilns and crossdraft kilns. These basic types can be further differentiated on the basis of their ground plans and various construction details. Vertical and horizontal kilns coexisted for a long time. Vertical updraft kilns with circular ground plans for the production of earthenware remained in use alongside crossdraft kilns into the 14th century in almost all regions of the area investigated. Further development of this kiln type only took place on both sides of the English Channel and led in the end to the well known "bottle kilns" of the English ceramic industries. Horizontal crossdraft kilns could be used for the production of earthenware or stoneware. There are several different types, which had been developed since the 12th or 13th century. One of the latest developments for Rhenish earthenware production was mixed crossdraft/downdraft earthenware kilns of the early 19th century.

INTRODUCTION

Pottery kilns are the most important part of the pottery production process. The way they are built decisively influences the final product and its technological properties. The control of the firing process, the steering of an oxidized or reduced kiln atmosphere, and the possibility of reaching the top temperatures necessary for the production of stoneware or porcelain is dependent upon developments and technological progress in kiln construction. The following essay begins with the late medieval foundations of kiln technology in order to better understand the kiln types found between the 15th and 20th centuries (for references and extended bibliography see Heege 2007).

Archaeological finds of kilns occur relatively frequently in the areas investigated (Germany, Belgium, the Netherlands, Austria, and Switzerland; kilns from France, England, or the Mediterranean/Arabic world were not included in the project). A database of 316 datable pottery kilns from the 15th to the 20th centuries was compiled between January 2005 and March 2007. The largest number of kilns—245 examples—was found in Germany (Figure 1).

KILN TYPES

Two basic types of kilns were identified archaeologically:

- Updraft kilns. These are characterized by a horizontal separation of superimposed furnace and firing chamber through a raised kiln floor, designed as domed or open-top kilns (Figure 2).

- Crossdraft kilns. The essential criterion of this type is the more or less horizontal or upward sloping arrangement of the furnace and firing chamber, which are placed on one level, one behind the other. They may be separated by a pronounced step, mostly combined with a fire grate of crock or clay columns, or vertically separated by a latticework of bricks. The separating element acts as an openwork fire-protection wall or a fireguard. The kiln draft is diagonal to almost horizontal and includes vents in the kiln vaulting or at the rear of the kiln. An exhaust vent or chimney is not absolutely necessary, but when present ensures an optimum draft (Figure 3).

These basic types can be further differentiated on the basis of their ground plans and various construction

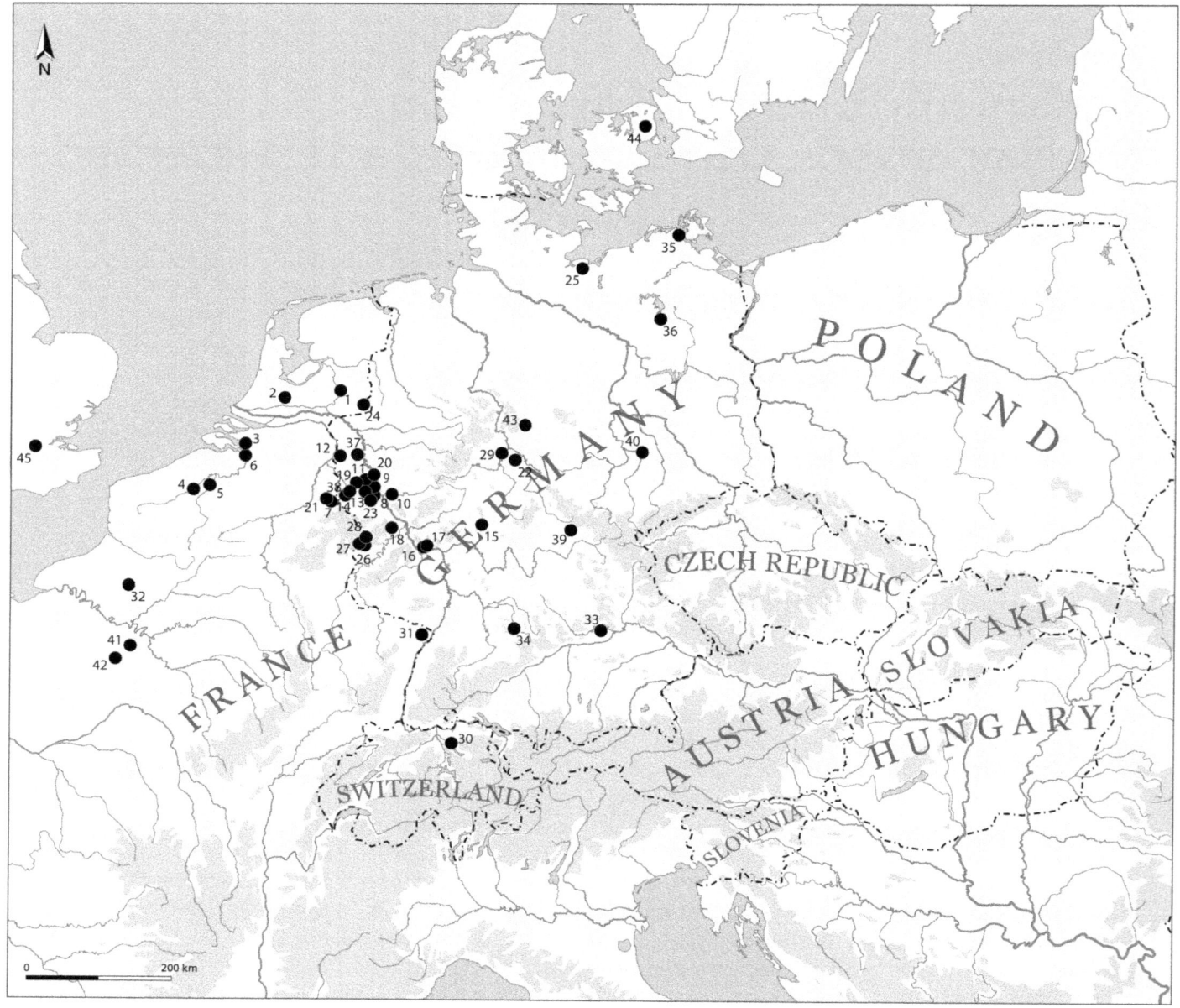

Figure 1. Map with sites mentioned in the text (in Germany, unless otherwise noted): (1) Deventer, the Netherlands; (2) Utrecht, the Netherlands; (3) Bergen op Zoom, the Netherlands; (4) Kortrijk, Belgium; (5) Oudenaarde, Belgium; (6) Antwerp, Belgium; (7) Raeren, Belgium; (8) Badorf; (9) Pingsdorf; (10) Siegburg; (11) Hürth; (12) Brüggen; (13) Brühl; (14) Langerwehe; (15) Aulendiebach; (16) Aulhausen; (17) Marienthal; (18) Mayen; (19) Frechen; (20) Cologne; (21) Aachen; (22) Großalmerode; (23) Bornheim-Sechtem; (24) Vreden; (25) Grenzhausen; (26) Binsfeld; (27) Herforst; (28) Bruch; (29) Möncheberg; (30) Zürich, Switzerland; (31) Oberbetschdorf, France; (32) Beauvais, France; (33) Sandersdorf; (34) Wildenhäusle; (35) Stralsund; (36) Rheinsberg; (37) Neuss; (38) Bedburg; (39) Coburg; (40) Leipzig; (41) Saint-Maurice-Montcourconne, France; (42) Rionville-sous Dourdan, France; (43) Fredelsloh; (44) Fraum Lillevang, Denmark; and (45) Woolwich, Great Britain (Map provided courtesy of the Department of Prehistory and Medieval Archaeology, University of Vienna, Austria).

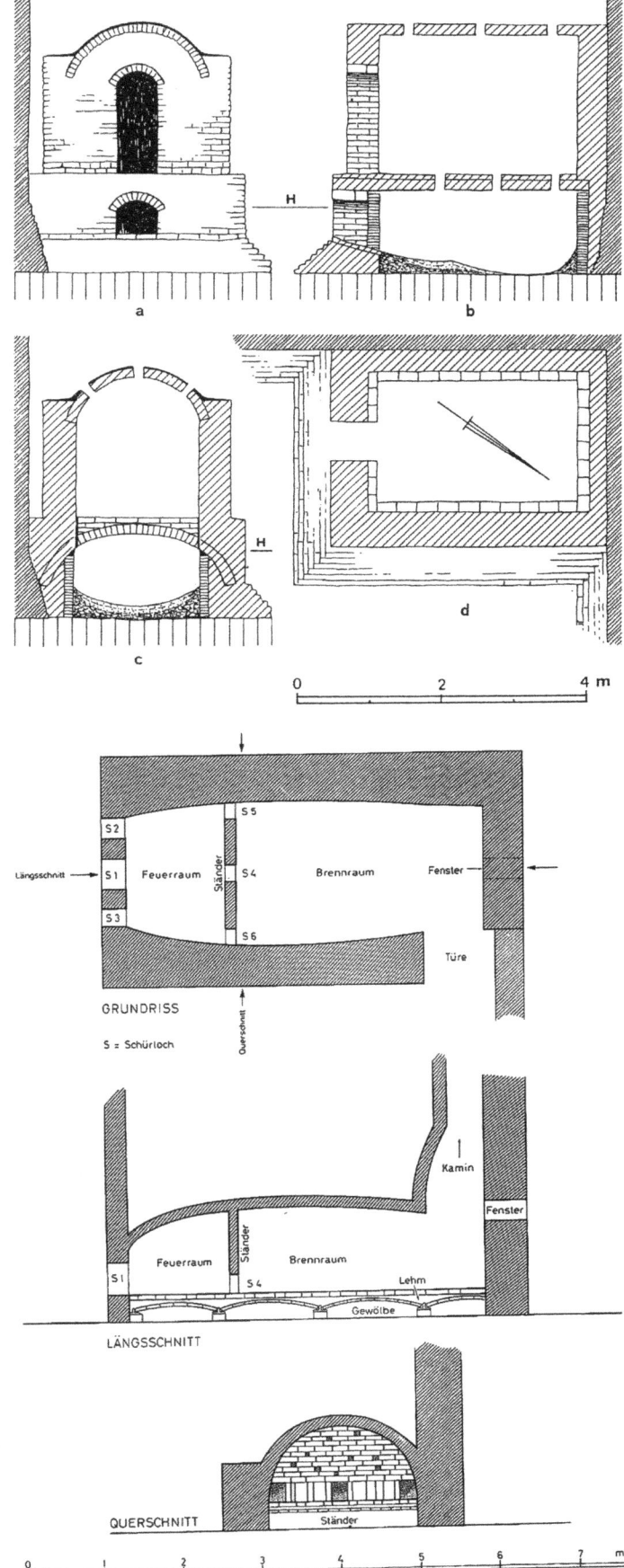

Figure 2. *(right, top)* Reconstruction of a vertical updraft majolica kiln with a rectangular ground plan; the furnace and superimposed firing chamber are separated by a raised kiln floor ("Piccolpasso type"). This example is in Deventer, the Netherlands, Klooster noord, and its production period was 1624-1637 (Lubberding et al. 1985:32).

Figure 3. *(right, bottom)* Ground plan (Grundriss), longitudinal section (Längsschnitt), and cross section (Querschnitt) of crossdraft kiln with furnace (Feuerraum) and firing chamber (Brennraum) positioned one behind the other. Other features depicted are the fire observation hole (Fenster), the kiln door (Türe), the vertical fire grate (Ständer), the chimney (Kamin), and the domed kiln floor (Gewölbe) with clay (Lehm) supports. This example is in Wildenhäusle, Baden-Württemberg, Germany (Stachel 1983:figure 9).

details, which vary according to the type of ware to be produced (i.e., earthenware, stoneware, majolica/faïence, or porcelain). There are two groups of updraft kilns with either circular or rectangular ground plans, both of which have roots in the Roman period. Updraft kilns with rectangular ground plans are typical kiln types in the production of majolica and faïence. In Switzerland, Austria, and southern Germany they were used for earthenware production as well.

As far as crossdraft kilns are concerned, late medieval specimens with fireguards form the basis of two continuing lines of development: Rhineland oval stoneware kilns with sunken furnaces and crossdraft earthenware and stoneware kilns with elongated oval ground plans. The latter type is widespread in Lower Saxony, Saxony, Thuringia, and Bavaria. Two further types of crossdraft earthenware kilns with rectangular ground plans were developed in the 18th century.

Updraft Kilns

Vertical Updraft Kilns with Circular Ground Plans

Vertical updraft kilns with circular ground plans and vertical flues from the Celtic and Roman (later Frankish or Roman) areas of German-speaking central Europe (as well as in Italy and southern France) were the starting point in the further development of kilns. To what extent Islamic kiln building influenced French or Italian kiln traditions is unclear. Updraft kilns of this basic type, with structural variations over time, remained in use alongside crossdraft kilns into the 14th century in almost all regions of the area investigated. The later examples were built in brick, and the Dutch and Belgian findings from Utrecht (the Netherlands) as well as Kortrijk and Oudenaarde (Belgium) are particularly

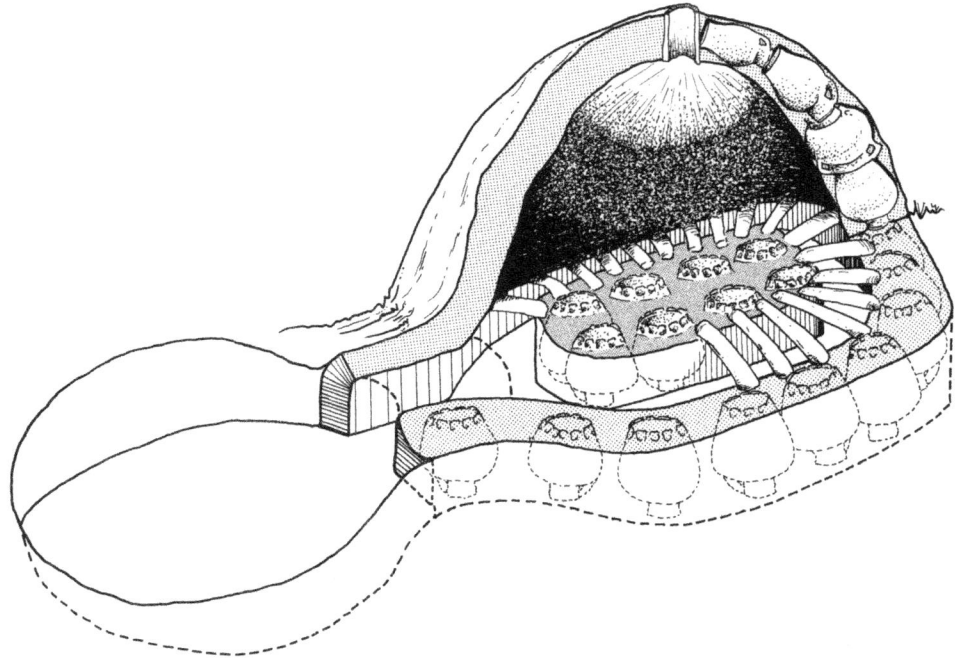

Figure 4. *Reconstruction of a vertical updraft kiln with circular ground plan and a raised kiln floor consisting of a central pillar and movable fire bars. The kiln superstructure is a permanent dome made of crocks. This example is in Oudenaarde-Pamele, Belgium, kiln D, and it dates to the second half of the 14th century (De Groote 1993:figure 21).*

roots (Italy, Spain, southern France). Corresponding to the well-known construction drawings from the Piccolpasso manuscript of 1558 (Figure 6) (Lightbown and Caiger-Smith 1980), kilns of this construction type were initially introduced north of the Alps by Italian majolica potters by 1500 at the latest (see Figure 2). With small modifications in its construction, this kiln type became the technological foundation of all European faïence manufacture (even in England and France). This type, with adaptations to the flue (i.e., grate and air supply) was also adopted by European porcelain manufacturers as glow or bisque firing kilns. The rapid and seemingly technologically unproblematic acceptance

noteworthy for their good archaeological preservation (Figure 4) (De Groote 1993).

Despite the continuous presence of pottery in the archaeological record, there is a gap of more than 200 years between these kilns and the younger vertical updraft kilns as typified by excavated examples from Bergen op Zoom (the Netherlands) and Arras in northeastern France. A technological relationship is nevertheless likely. The younger updraft kilns of "Bergen op Zoom-type" (Figure 5), which occur in the 17th and 18th centuries, were made from bricks with double opposed flues (twin stoke holes) and a raised oven floor made of a central pillar and movable fire bars (Groeneweg 1992). On both sides of the English Channel this type of kiln seems to have combined twin stoke holes with elements from stoneware-kiln technology (movable fire bars) and from early industrial cylindrical updraft kilns, although it is not clear where the invention of the early round updraft kiln took place. Knowledge of the described kiln construction technology reached North America in the late 17th century (Noël Hume 2001:30).

Vertical Updraft Kilns with Rectangular Ground Plan ("Piccolpasso Type")

Vertical updraft kilns with a rectangular ground plan can also be traced back to Roman-Mediterranean

of this type of kiln may have also been influenced by the fact that, in Utrecht and Switzerland for instance, similar kilns with raised floors on transverse arches, in which roof tiles and glazed floor slabs were made, had already existed in the 14th and 15th centuries.

Vertical updraft kilns with rectangular ground plans, but with a frontal stoke-hole and later with a second smoke dome, are found regularly in Switzerland as "standard kilns" from the mid-16th century onwards (Figure 7). They were used for the manufacture of faïence ceramics and faïence stove-tiles, and for the production of simple glazed earthenware. A few examples, based on technology transfer by wandering journeymen in the 19th and 20th centuries, subsequently spread (as earthenware kilns) to southern Germany and South Tyrol and East Tyrol in Austria.

Crossdraft Kilns

The second group of kilns is that of the horizontal crossdraft kilns (see Figure 3). Until now, the medieval development of the horizontal kiln type could only be hypothesized. One possible starting point of their development may have been the "prehistoric looking" single chamber kilns of the 8th-10th centuries in France, for example in Saint-Maurice-Montcourconne

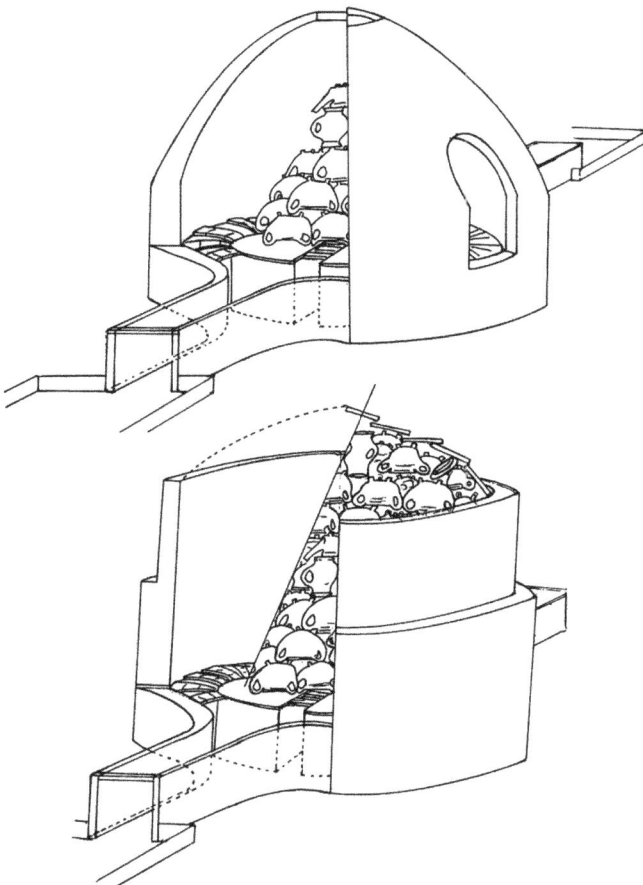

Figure 6. Vertical updraft kiln with a rectangular ground plan for Majolica production in Italy, from Cipriano Piccolpasso's The Three Books of the Potter's Art, 1558 (Lightbown and Caiger-Smith 1980:book 1, folio 35r, figure 100).

Figure 5. Vertical updraft kiln made from bricks, with double opposed flues and a raised kiln floor consisting of a central pillar and movable fire bars. This example is from Bergen op Zoom, the Netherlands, Steenbergen workshop, with production dates before 1765. Below the photograph of the kiln, drawings show alternate reconstructions as a domed (middle) and open-top (bottom) kiln (Groeneweg 1992:figures 78, 80-81).

Figure 7. Vertical updraft kiln with a rectangular ground plan, 16th century. The kiln base with stoke hole and combustion chamber are shown; the raised kiln floor and the firing chamber are not preserved. This example is in Zürich, Switzerland, Augustinergasse 46 (Heege 2007:284, figure 8).

or Rionville-sous Dourdan (Bourgeau 1987; Goustard 2002). A separating element between the furnace and firing chamber was perhaps developed in a second stage, from the 11th and 12th centuries onwards. This consisted of individual or multiple clay or crock columns. These distributed the flames (by acting as fire grates or flame separators), supported the transition between the furnace area and the kiln dome, and prevented the shifting of the kiln load. In Rhineland and northern Germany, kilns of this type became the starting point for the subsequent development of stoneware kilns.

There has been no verified occurrence of this type of kiln in Belgium or the Netherlands, nor is it known in southern Germany (Bavaria, Baden-Württemberg). Instead, it is known in the Rhineland and in the Rhineland-Palatinate in the 12th and 13th centuries. Further development can be followed relatively well until the 14th century. An increasingly lower setting of the furnace in combination with a sloping or vertical positioning of the transition point from the furnace to the firing chamber, a sloping firing chamber floor, and a massive fire grate of thick, mainly horizontally braced clay columns can be observed. Such kilns are known from North Rhine-Westphalia, Germany: at Badorf, Pingsdorf, Siegburg-Galgenberg and Siegburg-Aulgasse, Hürth-Fischenich, and Brüggen-Elmpt. At first, from the 13th century onwards, open flue-like structures in the middle or at the edge of the firing chamber floor were also developed (Ulbert 2004) in order to ensure a better circulation of the heating gases under the kiln load (the best example is a kiln in Brühl, Germany, Figure 8). Only with the most recent find of this kiln type in Langerwehe, Germany (ca. 1400), have fixed, built-on flue covers, so-called "immovable fire bars," been verified (Figure 9). Kilns with sunken furnaces and fire grates were also known in the 13th and 14th centuries in Germany in the Hesse region north of the Rhine (Aulendiebach, Aulhausen, and Marienthal), as well as in Rhineland-Palatinate (Mayen and the Westerwald).

Sunken Crossdraft Stoneware Kilns with Oval Ground Plan and a Sunken Stoking-Pit, Vaulting Supporting the Kiln Floor ("Frechen Type")

At the present time we can only speculate that the kiln type described above was further developed into the sunken oval stoneware kiln ("Frechen type") during the following 100 years, since late 14th – and 15th-century kiln finds in the Rhineland are scarce. Kiln construction materials changed at the same time, up to the first

Figure 8. *Horizontal crossdraft kiln with a vertical fire grate of clay columns as a dividing element between the stoking pit (background) and the firing chamber (foreground), a low-lying furnace, and a sloping firing chamber floor. Open flue-like structures were additionally placed in the middle or at the periphery of the firing-chamber floor, in order to provide for better distribution of the heating gases under the kiln load. This example is in Brühl, North Rhine-Westphalia, Germany, Franziskanerhof kiln 256, and it dates to the second half of the 13th century (Ulbert 2004:figure 159).*

half of the 16th century (brick or fire-resistant argillite replaced domes of clay wickerwork or domed crocks). This kiln type has a sunken furnace and a horizontal or slightly sloping firing chamber floor, which was formed by "fire bars" that covered the three flues below (Figure 10). Based on construction drawings, it has been shown that in Frechen, Germany, this kiln type was built and operated virtually unchanged into the late 19th century (Koch 1998). Only then did recognizable changes in stoneware kilns take place, primarily the building of additional chimneys.

Figure 9.   (left) Horizontal crossdraft kiln with elongated ground-plan, low-lying furnace, and upright vertical step as the rear part of a sunken furnace. The remains of a vertical fire grate and a firing chamber with three flues and permanent built-on flue covers (so-called "immovable fire bars") can be seen. This example is in Langerwehe, North Rhine-Westphalia, Germany, Hauptstraße 78, kiln 1, and it dates to the second half of the 14th century (Heege 2007:79, figure 130).

Figure 10. (right) Sunken crossdraft stoneware kiln with oval ground plan and a sunken stoking pit with vaulting under the kiln floor and a slightly sloping firing chamber floor formed by "fire bars" that covered the three flues below. This Frechen-type kiln is from Frechen, North Rhine-Westphalia, Germany, Franzstraße/Mühlenbach, kiln 1, and it dates to ca. 1600 (Koch 1998:figure 131).

Based on recent excavations, it has become clear that in the second half of the 16th century kilns for earthenware production in Frechen (and perhaps in the rest of Rhineland), hardly differed from stoneware kilns. They were somewhat more elongated and probably had a chimney at the end of the firing chamber.

Identical stoneware and earthenware kilns from the late 15th and early 16th centuries are also known from Cologne, Germany. To the west, the distribution of this type of kiln reached as far as Langerwehe and the Aachen (Germany) and Raeren (Belgium) region. This is not surprising considering the typological kiln forerunner in Langerwehe (see above, Figure 9). To the east of the Rhineland, this type of kiln spread in Germany via Bornheim-Sechtem at least as far as Siegburg. Thanks to migrating Frechen potters, this kiln type reached the Westphalian stoneware centers at Vreden/Stadtlohn

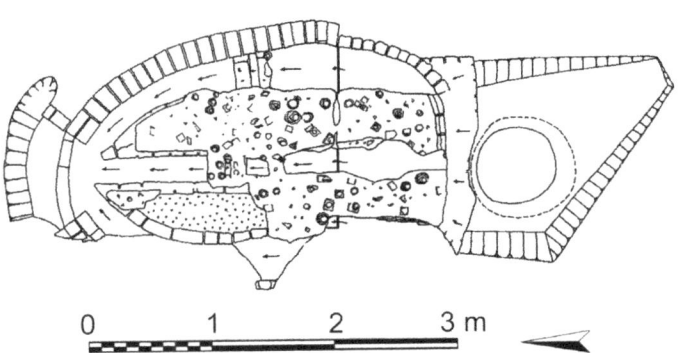

0   1   2   3 m

Figure 11.   Sunken crossdraft stoneware kiln with oval ground plan and a sunken semi-circular stoking pit with vaulting under the kiln floor, Frechen type. This example is from Woolwich, Great Britain, near London, and dates from 1640 to ca. 1660 (Pryor and Blockley 1973:figure 4).

and also England, where the mid-17th-century kiln from Woolwich is the only known example (Pryor and Blockley 1973) (Figure 11).

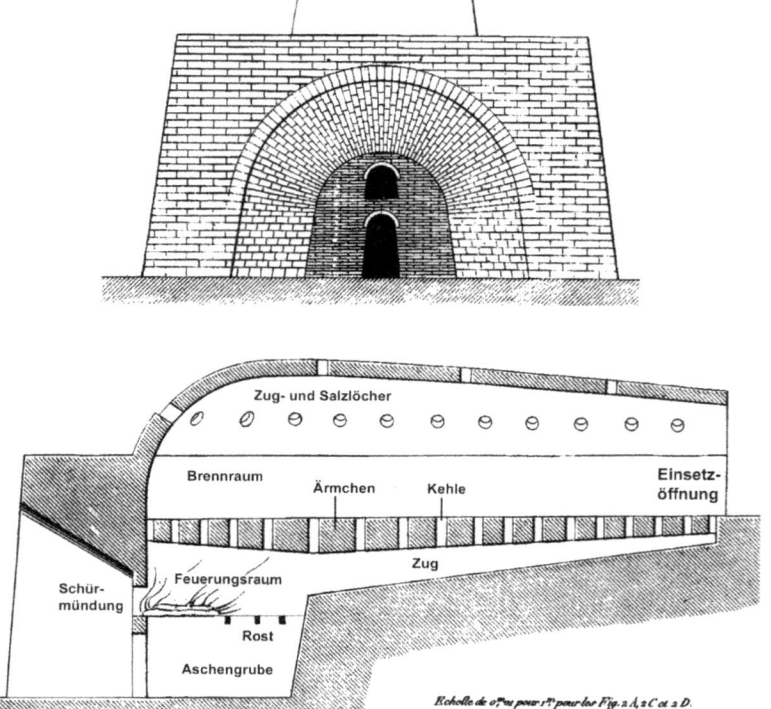

Crossdraft Stoneware Kilns, Built in a Sloping Position above Ground with a Rectangular Ground Plan ("Westerwald Type")

The technological connection between stoneware kilns from Frechen and those in the area where the Westerwald potters later dispersed is unfortunately unclear, since there have been no relevant excavations in the Westerwald. In the light of the Rhenish bases of kiln technology in Rhineland-Palatinate and the immigration of potters from Raeren (Belgium) and Siegburg (Germany) in the second half of the 16th century, kilns with sunken furnaces such as those in Frechen or Raeren are likely in the Westerwald from the 16th to 18th centuries.

Due to the inclination of the slope, however, they had to be constructed differently, and the ground plan was changed to the well-known elongated rectangular shape. Development could just as well have originated in the pottery region of Raeren, for example, where stoneware kilns have been found, originally with oval ground plans and then in the 19th century with rectangular ground plans.

The oldest verified example of a stoneware kiln with a rectangular ground plan, a sunken furnace, and only two flues comes from Sandersdorf in Bavaria (construction plan dated 1831). The construction principle occurring here could, however, be older (kiln find from Grenzau bei Grenzhausen, Germany). This kiln construction type (Figure 12) was also used until the late 19th century in all the migration and influence areas of the Westerwald potters, above all in the southern Eifel area (Binsfeld, Herforst, and Bruch, Germany), in Raeren (Belgium), in Oberbetschdorf in Alsace (France), and around Beauvais in northern France (Brongniart 1877). The kilns of the stoneware potters Crolius and Remmey, who emigrated from the Westerwald to Manhattan in 1718 and 1731, respectively, were used there until ca. 1831 and were probably similar (Baaden 1994:3).

The Westerwald stoneware kilns appear to have switched to coal and to firing with a horizontal grill

Figure 12. Crossdraft stoneware kiln with a rectangular ground plan, one sunken furnace, and two flues, Westerwald type. Features shown are the stoke hole (Schürmündung); the combustion chamber (Feuerungsraum); the hearth (Rost), which was built with iron fire bars or bricks as a horizontal separation between the underlying ashpit and the combustion chamber; the ashpit (Aschengrube); the flue channel (Zug); the immovable fire bar (Ärmchen), which covered the flue; the space between the flue covers (Kehle); the firing chamber (Brennraum), the kiln door (Einsetzöffnung); and vents (Zug- und Salzlöcher) for draft-control or salting of the stoneware kiln. This example is in Voisinlieu near Beauvais, France (Brongniart 1877:table 38, figure 2).

as early as the first half of the 19th century, leading to construction changes. Kilns with one furnace per flue were constructed a little later. Stoneware kilns with three furnaces and three flues were constructed (even in the Westphalian stoneware centers) possibly in the late 19th century, but certainly before World War I. After a switch to two flues per furnace and the introduction of movable "fire bars," technological development ceased shortly before World War II. After ca. 1970-1980 all firing of this type of stoneware kiln stopped, due to rapid changes in the methods of preserving food (refrigerators). Stoneware of Westerwald-type was no longer a mass-product and is almost completely out of use today. The last "experimental" firings took place in Höhr-Grenzhausen, Westerwald, in 2004 in one of the last existing kilns of this type (Figure 13).

Figure 13.   Interior of a 50-cubic-meter, Westerwald-type crossdraft stoneware kiln with a rectangular ground plan, three exterior stoking pits, six flues (two flues per furnace), and a firing chamber floor formed of movable "fire bars." The kiln load is partially placed for firing. This example is from Höhr-Grenzhausen, Germany, Bergstr. 3, 2004 (Heege 2007:33, figure 43).

Figure 14.   Horizontal crossdraft kiln with a vertical fire grate of clay columns, stoking pit (excavated) in the foreground, and combustion chamber behind the fire grate. This example is from Rheinsberg, Brandenburg, Germany, and dates to the 13th century (Heege 2007:97, figure 162).

Horizontal Crossdraft Kilns with a Vertical Fire Grate of Pottery or Crock-Columns as a Dividing Element Between Stoking Pit and Firing Chamber: Northwest and Northeast Germany

A further line of technological development began in the 13th century with the horizontal crossdraft kilns with clay or crock columns from the federal states of Hamburg, Mecklenburg, Brandenburg, Saxony-Anhalt, Thuringia, Saxony, Lower Saxony, and (north) Hesse. These kilns had a sloping or almost horizontal firing chamber that was separated from the stoking pit by a variably sloping pronounced step with a fire grate of crock or clay columns (Figure 14). They predominantly date to the late 12th to mid-14th centuries, as is also true of comparable findings from Denmark.

The further technological development of this type of kiln can be seen in southern Lower Saxony, North Hesse,

Saxony, and Denmark. The relevant kilns (for example from Fredelsloh, Leipzig, and Farum Lillevang) date to the late 13th or early 14th centuries (Liebgott 2001; Lönne 2007; Ronnefeldt 2007). The pronounced sloping step with crock or clay columns was further developed into an upright vertical step, on top of which a vertical fire grate sometimes stood. The form, construction type, and size of this fire grate are, however, currently unknown. It cannot be ruled out that a first row of rigidly fixed built-in vessels functioned as a fire grate and was subsequently disposed of as wasters. These kilns are characterized by elongated, slightly bulging ground plans.

Figure 15. *Horizontal crossdraft kiln with elongated, slightly bulging ground plan and upright vertical step as the rear part of a sunken furnace. Traces of a vertical partition wall or fire grate built of bricks can be seen on top of the sunken furnace. This example is in Leipzig, Saxony, Germany, Grimmaische Vorstadt, kiln VII, and dates to the 16th century (Heege 2007:figure 171, 101).*

Horizontal Crossdraft Earthenware and Stoneware Kilns with a Vertical Fire Grate and an Elongated Oval Ground Plan ("Kassel-Type")

From the late 15th century until the 17th century evidence for the appearance of kilns is limited to a few regionally, widely separated kilns in northern Germany, North Hesse, Saxony, and Bavaria. These kilns appear as a brick version of the above-mentioned older kilns (Figure 15). They have an elongated oval ground plan, a sunken brick-built furnace, and probably a vertical partition wall or fire grate between it and the horizontal firing chamber. Contrary to the stone – and earthenware kilns from Frechen and Cologne (see Figure 10), they do not have sunken flues. Whether there was a chimney, necessary for a genuinely horizontal flue, is not known.

The probable line of development led in the 18th century to kiln types with a deeply sunken furnace, a vertical partition wall, a horizontal or near-horizontal firing chamber floor, a chimney, and an oval to spindle-shaped ground plan. These tended to be called "Kassel-type kilns" from the second half of the 19th century onwards. The name was taken from the "Kasseler Flamm-Ziegelofen," used for bricks, roof tiles, and pipes, developed in 1827 in Möncheberg near Kassel, Germany, but only published in 1855 (Wiegand 2000). The development of this type of brick kiln demonstrates the technological interaction between traditional earthenware pottery, stoneware, faïence, and porcelain production and the brick industry in the early 19th century.

When historical news items, reports and excavation finds, construction drawings, and still-standing kilns or remains thereof from the German states of Lower Saxony, Hesse, Brandenburg, Saxony, Thuringia, and Bavaria are taken together, an independent southern Lower Saxony-northern Hessian-central German-eastern Bavarian kiln region can be posited, which spans the period from the 16th to the 20th centuries. Kilns with a pointed to elongated oval ground plan (Figure 16) in which stoneware and earthenware could both be manufactured, sometimes even in one and the same firing, were built in this area.

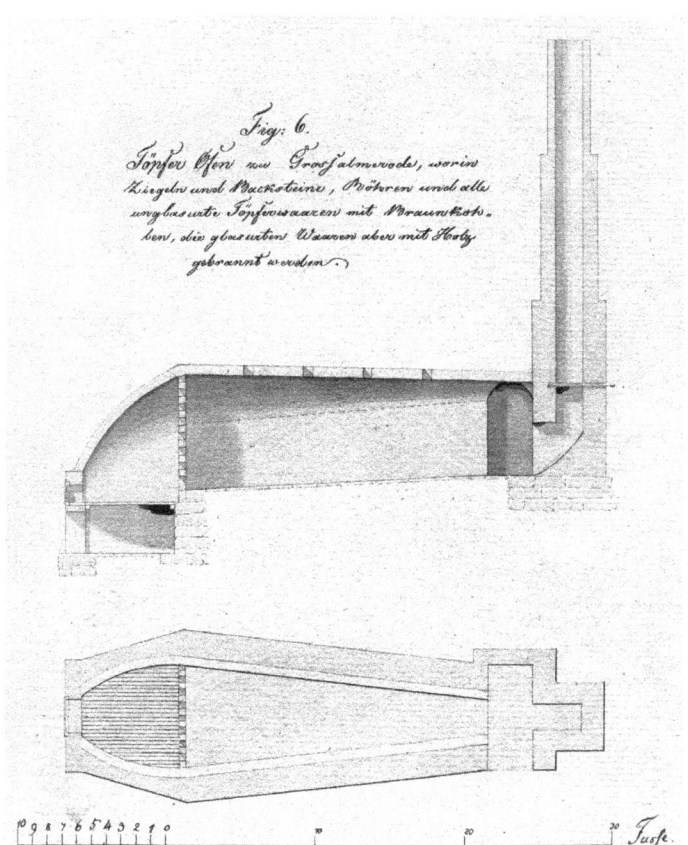

Figure 16. (left) Horizontal crossdraft stone- or earthenware kiln with a deeply sunken furnace, a vertical partition wall, a horizontal or near-horizontal firing-chamber floor, a chimney, and an oval to spindle-shaped ground plan: "Kasseler Ofen." The inscription reads: "Pottery kiln from Großalmerode for the production of bricks, roof tiles, drain pipes and unglazed earthenwares by means of brown coal, the glazed earthenwares will be fired with wood." This example is from Großalmerode, Hessen, Germany, and dates to 1851 (Wiegand 2000:37).

Figure 17. (bottom) Mixed crossdraft/downdraft earthenware kiln with a raised kiln floor on a double vault. This example is from Frechen, North Rhine-Westphalia, Germany, Alte Straße 67-73 (Heege 2007:418, Figure 6).

Horizontal Crossdraft Earthenware Kilns with a Vertical Fire-Grate and a Rectangular Ground Plan

In contrast to the kiln group just described, horizontal crossdraft kilns with a rectangular ground plan and chimney and variable furnaces (sunken or on the same level as the firing chamber, with or without a hearth) and firing chambers (with or without temporarily installed flues, firing-chamber floor mostly level or slightly sloping, firing chamber interior occasionally slightly tapered) seem to occur considerably more frequently (see Figure 3). They are evenly scattered between the North Sea and the Alps, and are the "classic" 18th – to 20th-century earthenware kiln. They are usually referred to as "Kassel kilns." In the second half of the 19th century, they are also encountered as firing and glazing or reduction/smoking kilns for roof tiles and bricks. There is currently no evidence of kilns of this type from Belgium, Switzerland, and Austria. In the Netherlands, they are only known in the area bordering on Germany.

How this type of kiln developed technologically until the first evidence for it in the late 18th century has not yet been clearly established. What is certain, on the basis of the oldest dates, is that it is not a successor, but instead a forerunner of the "Kasseler Flamm-Ziegelofen" (brick kiln). The two oldest examples of a horizontal crossdraft kiln with a rectangular ground plan functioning as an earthenware kiln come from Stralsund (built 1784) and Neuss (planning application dated 1786), Germany. They also existed until the middle of the 20th century,

however, in Schleswig-Holstein, Mecklenburg-Western Pomerania, Lower Saxony, North Rhine-Westphalia and the eastern part of the Netherlands, Hesse, Thuringia, Rhineland-Palatinate, Bavaria, Baden-Württemberg, and Alsace (France). The development of wood-fired earthenware kilns came to an end in the 20th century with this type of kiln. In the still-existing potteries, they were at first either converted to gas – or oil-firing at the end of World War II, or replaced by smaller electric kilns.

Mixed Crossdraft/Downdraft Earthenware Kilns

One last kiln type remains to be described, based on excavation finds and historical construction drawings from Frechen, Bedburg, Siegburg, and Coburg, Germany. This is a crossdraft kiln with a chimney and horizontal grate of bricks or iron, a vertical partition wall, and, as a characteristic feature, a raised kiln floor supported by a double arch (Figure 17). The chimney guaranteed an optimum diagonal or downdraft. Since the two supporting arches were open to the stoking pit, the flames were distributed under the kiln load, and were also extracted through the partition wall and the kiln floor. The oldest example of this type of kiln is known from Frechen and dates to ca. 1800. Comparable finds from faïence and porcelain manufacture can be taken as a firm indication of the basis on which this very specific kiln type was developed in the Rhineland.

CONCLUSIONS

All known kiln types are a functional adaptation of the thermodynamic and physical properties of fire. Amongst other things, this led to the independent emergence of similar or identical ceramic firing methods and kiln types in Latin America, Asia, and Europe (vertical and horizontal kilns). As regards the various peculiarities of the kilns dealt with here, the spread of specific kiln types can also be traced back to cultural contacts and technology transfer.

Kiln types provide evidence of technology transfer by migrant potters and their still-existing contacts to home. One example of this, oval stoneware kilns of the Frechen pattern, can be seen in Westphalia, Germany, and in Woolwich, England. It is noteworthy that this kiln type was not adopted by English potters later on. Evidence of technology transfer can be seen as well with the rectangular stoneware kilns in the

emigration area of the Westerwald potters, or of the oldest vertical majolica kiln brought by Italian potters to Antwerp, Belgium.

Kiln types also provide evidence of technology transfer by adoption (which could well be in the way of espionage). Examples here are the spread of vertical majolica and faïence kilns in the Netherlands and the rest of northwestern Europe, which are used by Dutch and, later on, German faïence potters.

Kiln types additionally provide proof of technology transfer by adoption without, however, taking on the original specific production methods or product range for the type of kiln concerned. Examples of this type are the "Italian" vertical majolica kilns in Switzerland and their further development, which were primarily used in normal earthenware and stove-tile production.

With regard to the date of technological "innovations," we can conclude that the tendency was toward relatively long and continuous lines of development, during the course of which several different kiln types existed coincidently. Vertical and horizontal kilns coexisted for a long time.

On the other hand, kiln types that had reached a mature state were erected and used for centuries virtually unchanged. Good examples of this are the horizontal, oval, sunken stoneware kilns from the Rhineland and the vertical kilns with a rectangular ground plan of the "Piccolpasso" type. In the first case, the technological foundations were developed between the 12th and 14th centuries, and in the latter as early as the Roman period. The same seems to have been the case for the horizontal earthenware and stoneware kilns with an elongated oval ground plan from the Lower Saxony-Saxony-Bavaria region in Germany. Their development started in the 12th century and essentially seems to have ended around 1500 in a perfect technological state. In comparison, horizontal kilns with a rectangular ground plan and horizontal kilns with a firing chamber floor on a double arch only seem to have been developed from the 18th century onwards.

REFERENCES

BAADEN, FRANZ
1994   Aufbruch in die Neue Welt. Die Auswanderung aus dem Kannenbäckerland [Brake-up to the New World. Emigration from the Kannenbäckerland.] *Jahresbericht 1994 der Volksbank Westerwald,* 1994:1-22.

BOURGEAU, LAURENT
1987   La production de céramique médiévale dans la région de Dourdan (Essonne) [Medieval Ceramic Production in the Region of Dourdan (Essonne)]. In Jean Chapelot, Henri Galinie, and Jacqueline Pilet-Lemiere, editors, pp. 77-86. *La céramique (Ve-XIXe s.). Fabrication-Commercialisation-Utilisation.* Actes du premier congrès international d'archéologie médiévale (Paris, 4-6 octobre 1985). Societe d'archéologie médiévale, Caen, France.

BRONGNIART, ALEXANDRE
1877   *Traité des arts céramiques ou des poteries considérées dans leur histoire, leur pratique et leur théorie* [A Study of the Potters' Skills and of Pottery Considered in Their History, Praxis and Theory]. 3rd edition. Paris, France.

DE GROOTE, KOEN
1993   De middeleeuwse ambachtelijke wijk van Pamele (stad Oudenaarde, Oost-Vlaanderen). Het onderzoek in het Huis de Lalaing, 1. De pottenbakkersovens [The Medieval Craftmen's Quarter of Pamele (Town of Oudenaarde, East-Flanders). The Archaeological Excavation in the House de Lalaing, 1. The Pottery Kilns]. *Archeologie in Vlaanderen* 3:359-399.

GOUSTARD VINCENT
2002   Un centre de production de céramique carolingienne á Saint-Maurice-Montcourconne (Essonne, France). Milieu VIIIe-IXe siècle [A Center for the Production of Carolingian Pottery at Saint-Maurice-Montcourconne (Essonne, France). Middle of the 8th to the 9th Centuries]. In Guido Helmig, Barbara Scholkmann, and Matthias Untermann, editors, pp. 299-306. *Centre—Region—Periphery. Medieval Europe 2002.* 3rd International Conference of Medieval and Later Archaeology Basel (Switzerland) 10-15 September 2002, Vol. 3. Folio Verlag, Hertingen, Germany.

GROENEWEG, GERRIT
1992   Bergen op Zooms aardewerk. Vormgeving en decoratie van gebruiksaardewerk gedurende 600 jaar pottenbakkersnijverheid in Bergen op Zoom [Earthenware from Bergen op Zoom. Shape and Decoration of Household Ceramics during 600 Years of Ceramic Production in Bergen op Zoom]. Bijdragen tot de Studie van het Brabantse Heem 35, Waalre, the Netherlands.

HEEGE, ANDREAS
2007   *Töpferöfen-Pottery kilns-Fours de potiers.* Basler Hefte zur Archäologie 4. Welt und Erde Verlag Kerpen-Loogh, Basel, Switzerland.

KOCH, WILFRIED MARIA
1998   Der Frechener "Prachtofen" [The "Splendid Kiln" from Frechen]. *Archäologie im Rheinland* 1998:153-155.

LIEBGOTT, NIELS-KNUD
2001   Farum Lillevangovnene [The Kilns from Farum Lillevang]. *Hikuin* 28:53-62.

LIGHTBOWN, RONALD, AND CAIGER-SMITH, ALAN
(TRANSLATORS)

1980   Cipriano Piccolpasso, I tre libri dell'arte del
        vasaio [The Three Books of the Potter's Art].
        Facsimile of the Manuscript in the Victoria and
        Albert Museum, London. Scolar Press, London,
        England.

LÖNNE, PETRA

2007   Ein Töpfereistandort der Zeit um 1300 in
        Fredelsloh, Lkr. Northeim, Niedersachsen D
        [A Potting Center of around 1300 in Fredelsloh,
        Northeim County, Lower Saxony, Germany].
        In Töpferöfen-Pottery kilns-Fours de potiers,
        Andreas Heege, pp. 367-374. Basler Hefte zur
        Archäologie 4. Welt und Erde Verlag Kerpen-
        Loogh, Basel, Switzerland.

LUBBERDING, H., DEBEER, H., KORF, D., AND BRUIJN, A.

1985   De Deventer Majolica Oven. Mededelingenblad
        nederlandse vereniging van vrienden van de
        ceramiek 119-120:3-56.

NOËL HUME, IVOR

2001   If These Pots Could Talk. Collecting 2000 Years
        of British Household Pottery. University Press of
        New England, Milwaukee, WI.

PRYOR, SYLVIA, AND BLOCKLEY, KEVIN

1973   A 17th-Century Kiln Site at Woolwich. Post-
        Medieval Archaeology 12:30-85.

RONNEFELDT, CHRISTIAN

2007   Töpferöfen in der Grimmaischen Vorstadt
        in Leipzig, Sachsen D [Pottery Kilns in the
        Grimma-Suburb in Leipzig, Saxony, Germany].
        In Töpferöfen-Pottery kilns-Fours de potiers,
        Andreas Heege, pp. 385-397. Basler Hefte zur
        Archäologie 4. Welt und Erde Verlag Kerpen-
        Loogh, Basel, Switzerland.

STACHEL, GÜNTER

1983   Ein spätmittelalterlicher Töpferofen von Mistlau,
        Gemeinde Kirchberg/Jagst, Lkr. Schwäbisch
        Hall [A Late Medieval Potters' Kiln from
        Mistlau, Kirchberg/Jagst Township, Schwäbisch
        Hall County]. Forschungen und Berichte
        der Archäologie des Mittelalters in Baden-
        Württemberg 8:281-299.

ULBERT, CORNELIUS

2004   Öfen ohne Ende [Countless Kilns]. Archäologie
        in Deutschland 2004(1):48-49.

WIEGAND, THOMAS

2000   Ofenreise. Der Kasseler Flammofen und die
        Großalmeroder Tonwarenindustrie [Kiln Journey.
        The Kassel, Flame Kiln, and the Großalmerode
        Ceramics Industry]. Jenior Verlag, Kassel,
        Germany.

///

Andreas Heege
Im Roetel 3
CH-6300 Zug
Switzerland

RALF KLUTTIG-ALTMANN

New Technologies in the Manufacture of Clay Tobacco Pipes in Central Europe

ABSTRACT

Ten years ago production marks were found on clay tobacco pipes from Upper Lusatia in eastern Germany that indicated previously unknown methods of manufacture. These include the manual and separate production of bowls and stems without the customary assistance of two-part molds, the fitting of bowl and stem before firing, and the manufacture of bowls on the potter's wheel. Resulting publications on this theme led to the identification of many finds manufactured in this way in an area comprising central Germany, Bavaria, the Czech region, and western Poland and to the recognition of various different types manufactured with this technology. Even finds from widely spaced locations are very similar and imply common places of origin. Bernstadt in Upper Lusatia is the only production site identified to date, as a pipe of this type has been found bearing that location's name. Further investigations will undoubtedly soon expand our knowledge of this recent development in the history of clay pipe research.

IDENTIFICATION OF NEW PIPE TYPES

The manufacture of clay tobacco pipes in a two-part mold, which included the stem, was developed in England before 1600 and afterwards became a mass production technology in the Netherlands. Until the late 1990s it was believed that from the 16th to 19th centuries this was the only imaginable and economically sensible method of clay pipe manufacture and therefore the only one employed. Historical written sources that did not conform to this dogma were seen as inaccurate (Kügler 1995:43).

Two new technologies, used in the standard production of clay pipes, have been known in the German language area for a few years now. Through lucky circumstance this author was able to observe technological traces on a handful of clay pipes from Görlitz and nearby Bernstadt in 2002 and to confirm those observations with a finds complex from Zittau (all locations in Upper Lusatia; Figure 1). Production marks on these clay pipes could not be explained in the usual way and implied the existence of not only one but several previously unknown clay pipe technologies. These pipes stood out, not only due to the newly recognized production marks, but also because in their generally crude fabrication, unknown ornamentation, and unusual shape they were different from "normal" clay pipes.

The pipes possessed a number of particular features, as follows:

1. Manual ornamentation on the bowl (roulette, scratched marks) that differed from the more commonplace "bordering" decorations.

2. Turning grooves on the inside of the bowl resulting from the use of a potter's wheel.

3. A great number of distorting finger marks on the base of the bowl, often with a prominent break at this point, suggesting the stem was fitted on after the bowl's manufacture.

4. The hole from the wire used to pierce the stem not at the base of the firing chamber as usual, but in the upper zone of the bowl or nonexistent, suggesting secondary bending of the stem into the desired bowl-stem angle after piercing.

5. Badly-formed, irregular heels without a mark, suggesting heels were manually formed after the joining of the bowl and stem.

6. Narrow bridge between the bowl and the stem (bowl-stem fitting) or the bowl emerging seamlessly from the stem also suggesting bowl-stem junctures were secondarily bent.

7. Crumpled ornamentation caused by the bowl and stem being fitted together after ornamentation.

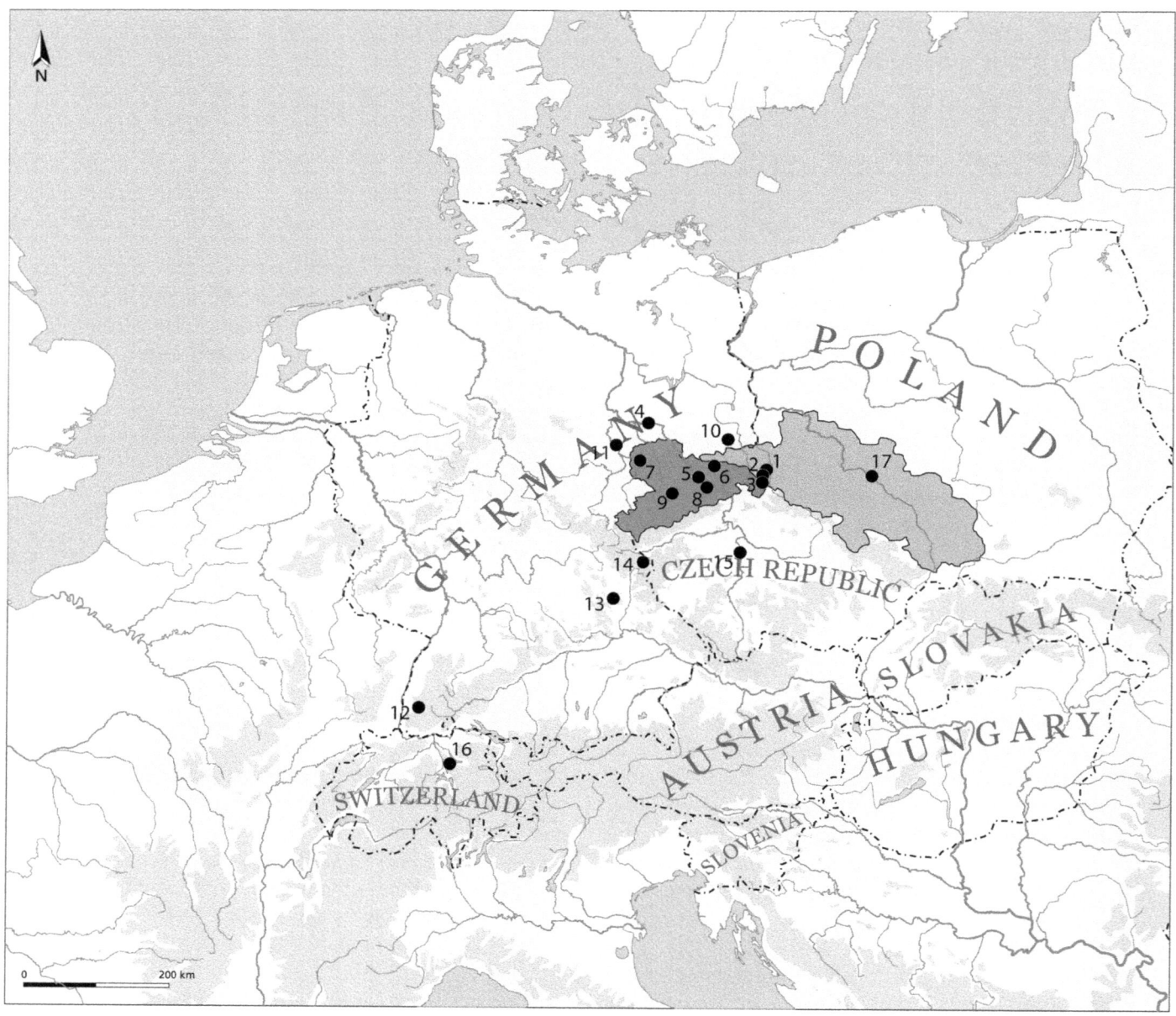

Figure 1.   *Map with places mentioned in the text (in Germany, unless otherwise noted): (1) Görlitz; (2) Bernstadt; (3) Zittau; (4) Wittenberg; (5) Dresden; (6) Kamenz; (7) Leipzig; (8) Pirna; (9) Freiberg; (10) Drebkau; (11) Halle/Saale; (12) Freiburg im Breisgau; (13) Amberg; (14) Bärnau; (15) Prague, Czech Republic; (16) Zug, Switzerland; and (17) Wrocław, Poland. The area of Saxony is marked dark grey, the area of Silesia light grey (Map provided courtesy of the Department of Prehistory and Medieval Archaeology, University of Vienna, Austria).*

8. Not polished, and no appearance of mold lines, suggesting two-part molds were not employed.

What was new to researchers was that individually finished bowls and stems were connected as entire pipes before firing and that these components were produced without molds, some of the bowls being thrown on the potter's wheel. The use of a mold for the manufacture of a bowl cannot always be ruled out with certainty. Some ornamentation at the base of a bowl seems to indicate a mold, but the lines that almost inevitably accompany the employment of molds have not yet been observed on these pipes. The pipes demonstrating the above-mentioned features in different combinations can be provisionally divided into the following simple groups:

1. Heeled pipes. A (small) bowl was formed by hand or with a mold and mounted on a separately produced stem (features 3, 5, 6, 7, 8; 1 and 4 possible) (examples from Zittau, Bernstadt, Wittenberg, and Dresden) (Figures 2-6).

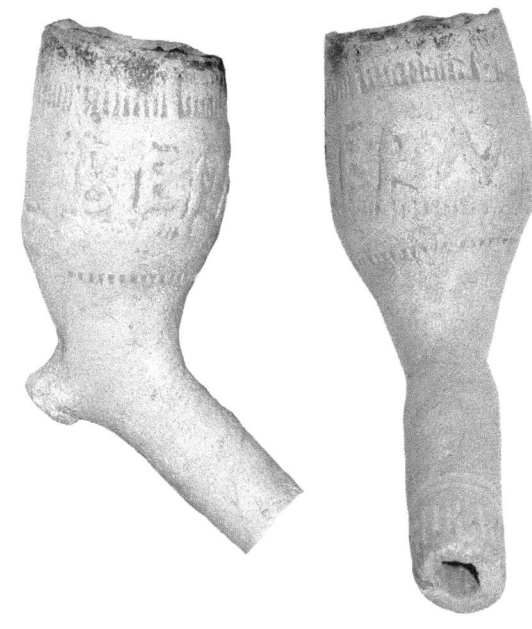

Figure 2.   (top, left) Pipes from Zittau, Salzhaus, with roulette ornamentation and a typical impression on the joint between bowl and stem (Photo by M. Kügler, 2004).

Figure 3.   (top, right) Two sides of a pipe from Bernstadt, Folk Museum, with raised lettering "BERNSTA" on the bowl, above and below this a simple roulette ornamentation. Roulette marks are also on the base of the stem (Photo by M. Kügler, 2004).

Figure 4.   (middle, left) Two sides of a pipe bowl fragment from Wittenberg, Bürgermeisterstr. 5. This handmade pipe has a manually stepped bowl wall, possible roulette ornamentation, and angularly formed heel. The inner side of the bowl wall with the puncture mark of the piercing rod proves that bowl and stem were at a very shallow angle to each other at the moment of piercing. Height from the bowl rim to the front edge of the heel is 3.4 cm (Photo by author, 2010; courtesy of LDA Sachsen-Anhalt).

Figure 5.   (middle, right) Pipe bowl fragment from Wittenberg, Bürgermeisterstr. 5 with combed/scored ornamentation. Height 2.7 cm (Photo by author, 2010; courtesy of LDA Sachsen-Anhalt).

Figure 6.   (right) Pipe bowl fragment from Wittenberg, Bürgermeisterstr. 5 with knobbly ornamentation. Height 2.4 cm (Photo by author, 2010; courtesy of LDA Sachsen-Anhalt).

2. Long-necked pipes. The term "long-necked pipe" *(Langhalspfeife)* is suggested for this pipe type as it cannot otherwise be fitted into the conventional Low Countries pipe terminology and its most obvious feature is the long, curved "neck" or stem base (Kluttig-Altmann 2009:125, footnote 2). A bowl produced on a potter's wheel is mounted on a separately produced stem and the complete pipe is afterwards bent into the desired angle (features 1, 2, 4, 6, 8; 3 and 7 possible) (examples from Görlitz and Bernstadt) (Figure 7).

3. Long-necked pipes. A (large) bowl emerges seamlessly from the stem. In this case bowl and stem have apparently not been fitted to each other, but instead the pipe was produced as one piece without the use of a mold and entirely by hand, and afterwards bent into the desired angle (features 1, 2, 4, 6, 8; 7 possible) (examples from Zittau, Kamenz, Dresden, and Pirna) (Figures 8-11).

The pipes, particularly those of groups 1 and 2, are not very attractive due to the suboptimal course of the individual production stages—the roulette or notched ornamentation of the bowls was regularly smeared as the stem was fitted on. The pipes are unpolished.

Group 2, with a markedly cylindrical bowl shape and turning grooves on the inside, is particularly interesting in historical terms. This type is a "missing link" that proves that the bowls of clay pipes could also be produced on the potter's wheel. It means that the pipe maker's craft did not only emerge autonomously in the 17th century, but that in some places potters were at least partly able to satisfy demand for the new product "clay pipe" by employing their own methods and tools. The pipes with wheel-thrown bowls would be a good reason for regional studies into the little-understood interaction between clay pipe manufacture and the pottery industry in the 17th century.

The publication of these results and of the characteristics by which the pipes could be identified (Kluttig-Altmann and Kügler 2003) led to a great response in clay pipe research circles. This response led to both the observation of new found objects and the re-evaluation of old finds. "Exceptional objects," which differed in design from the general pattern and whose exact description had been problematic because they did not fit into the known typologies of Low Countries or English products, were found to exist in many clay pipe complexes. A comprehensive literature search for pipes with the new technologies has not yet taken place but would be very important, particularly in pinning down the production area and the period of production.

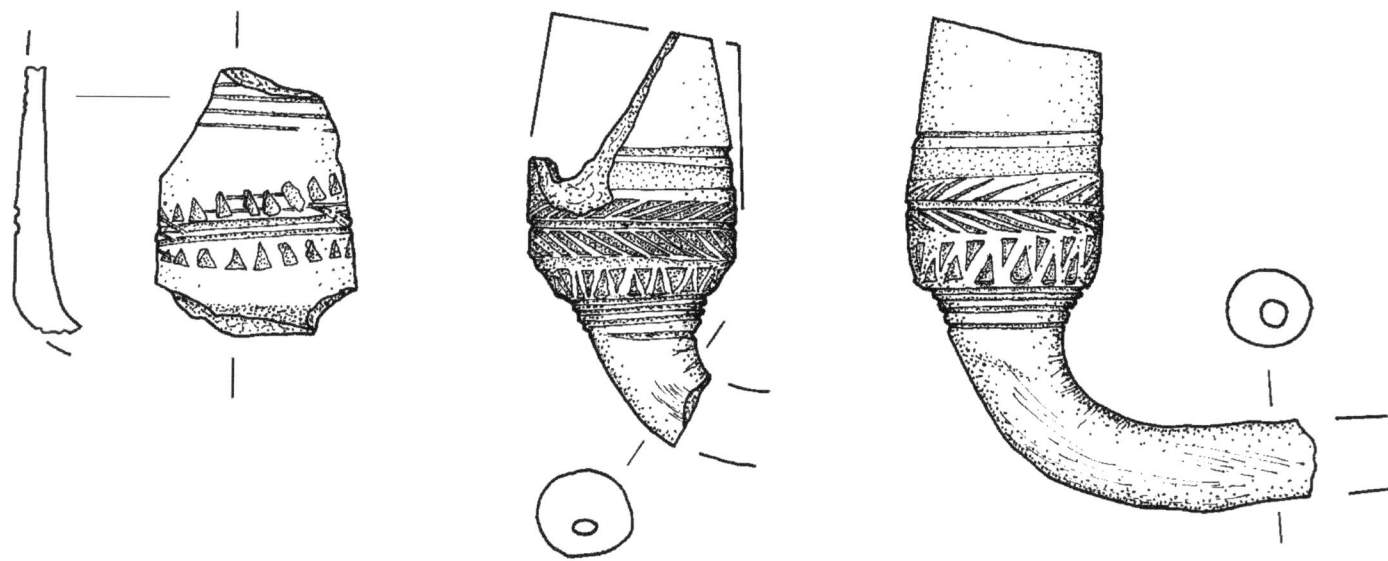

Figure 7.   *Pipes from Görlitz, Schönhof (left, center), and Bernstadt, Folk Museum (right). These are wheel-thrown bowls from long-necked pipes, with roulette decoration and other manually applied ornamentation. Total height of the piece on the right is 5.8 cm (Drawing by author, 2005).*

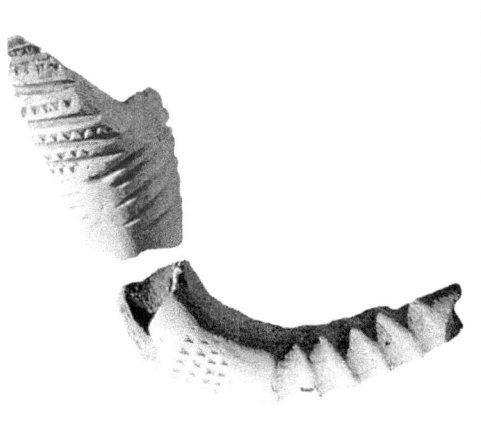

Figure 8. (top, left) Pipe fragments from Zittau, Salzhaus. The bowl and stem pipe fragments are presumably from the same pipe, with a gradual link between bowl and stem (long-necked pipe) and with different manual embellishments. Length of the stem fragment is ca. 4.7 cm (Photo by M. Kügler and R. Kluttig-Altmann, 2004).

Figure 9. (top, right) Three views of a pipe from Kamenz, St. Marien. The handmade pipe, a so-called long-necked pipe, has a gradual link between bowl and stem and manual embellishments (Photo by author, 2005; courtesy of Saxony State Office for Archaeology).

Figure 10. (middle) Two views of a pipe from Pirna, Kirchgasse 2/3. The handmade pipe has a curved stem base (a so-called long-necked pipe) with manual grooves and a large stamped mark (see also Figures 11 and 12). Total height parallel to the axis of the bowl is 7 cm (Photo by author, 2006; courtesy of Saxony State Office for Archaeology).

Figure 11. (bottom) Details of the pipe from Pirna, Kirchgasse 2/3, showing the same impressed mark on the base of the stem (left) and along the stem (right) (see also Figures 10 and 12). (Photo by author, 2006; courtesy of Saxony State Office for Archaeology).

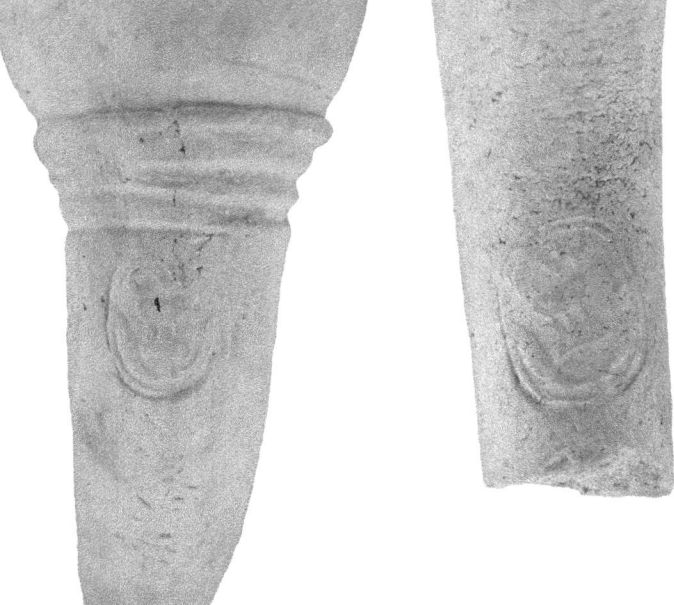

This author nevertheless carried through a substantial, though certainly not complete, examination for this contribution.

In the years following the identification of these new pipe types, our understanding of their distribution rapidly grew to include areas beyond the starting point in Upper Lusatia. Almost identical pipe finds have been made in Prague (Czech Republic) (Vyšohlíd 2007:figures 5, 12, 13; 2009a:82, figures 1, 87; 2009b:971–974, figures 7–10); Amberg (Mehler 2004:figure 1.1) and Bärnau (Mehler 2010:206, figure 86 B 137) (both in Bavaria); Leipzig (Kluttig-Altmann 2000:18, figure 9; Kluttig-Altmann and Mehler 2007:72, figure 2), Dresden (Kluttig-Altmann 2006:221, figures left and center[1]), Pirna (Pirna, Kirchgasse 2/3, Excavation Pl-14, unpublished), and Freiberg (Standke 2004:108, figures 1b, 110) (these four in Saxony); Drebkoin (Lipsdorf 2007:133, figure 4.6) and Kamenz (Kluttig-Altmann 2009:catalog nos. 2, 3, figures 2, 7) (both Lusatia); and Halle (Martin and Petzschmann 2002:390, table 15.4; Standke 2005:figures 1–5) and Wittenberg (Wagschal 2000:295, table 29.2, as well as unpublished material) (both Saxony-Anhalt). Others have been identified in older literature, as in Leipzig (see above) or in Wrocław/Breslau (Poland) (Kluttig-Altmann and Kügler 2004:figure 34; Kluttig-Altmann 2005:figure 16; Witkowska 1998:figures 2-5).

Natascha Mehler produced one of the first summaries of part of the new finds paying particular attention to the situation in northern Bavaria (Mehler 2009:figure 8, table 1). She named a subset of the handmade pipes "Wirfel pipes," on the basis of a related pipe bearing the legend "1672CWIRFE(L)" from Wrocław/Breslau. The finds from the above-mentioned locations are very similar; in some cases exactly the same types are involved. They are therefore likely to originate from the same production sites. Other noteworthy, if differently produced, pipe types from Freiburg im Breisgau (Röber 2002:607, figures 1, 2, 616, table 2.27) and from different locations in northwestern Switzerland, most recently Zug (Roth Heege 2007), have also been published. In this case they are funnel-shaped, hand-rolled pipes produced without molds, the bowls of which are seamlessly connected to the stems. Bowl and stem lay in the same axis before being formed and were subsequently bent. The bowls sometimes sport roulette ornamentation. There are obvious parallels to the eastern Saxon products, particularly the above-mentioned group 3.

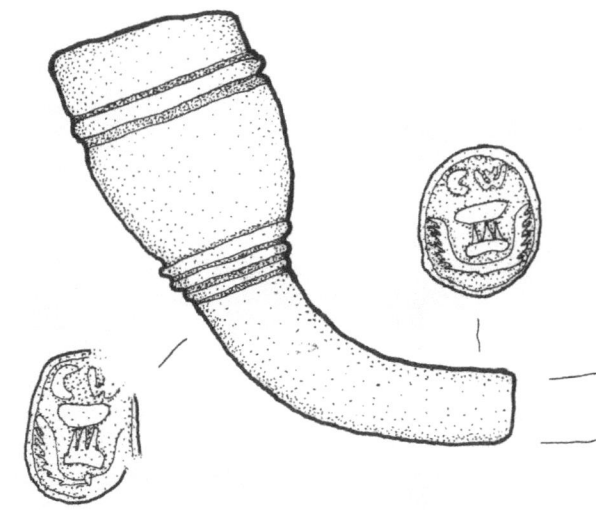

Figure 12. *Drawing of the pipe from Pirna, Kirchgasse 2/3, showing the large twice-stamped mark (see also Figures 10 and 11) (Drawing by Saxony State Office for Archaeology, 2006; courtesy of Saxony State Office for Archaeology).*

A pipe from Pirna, which retains part of the stem, is an exception among the generally "improvised" appearance of most of the finds discussed here. A complicated stamp, consisting of the letters "CW" above a three-legged stool (drum? cup?), which is surrounded by a garland of palm twigs, is to be found on both sides of the area connecting the bowl and the stem. This mark has not yet been found in the Low Countries lists and is likely to be from a local Saxon manufacturer (Figure 12).

A question that has not yet been addressed is the possibility of identifying stem fragments from these pipes. To date, hardly any bowls have been found among the "fitted" pipes with the base of the stem still attached, the result of the particularly weak spot between bowl and stem. Stem fragments exist from several locations, which, because of their crude nature, their curved shape, or ornamentation similar to the bowls, could belong to handmade pipes. There are examples from Prague (Vyšohlíd 2009b:973, figure 9), Halle (Standke 2005:90-91, figures 3–5), Kamenz (Kluttig-Altmann 2009:123, figure 2.3), Leipzig (Kluttig-Altmann 2000:17f., figures 6–9), and Zittau (unpublished).

ORIGINS

Zittau (Lusatia) has seemed to be a likely production site for at least some of these pipes, as a considerable proportion of the Salzhaus finds complex in that town, a complex that was partly responsible for the discovery of the new technologies, consisted of unused pipes. This author's observations are based on a preliminary examination of the material in 2002. A more precise evaluation of the clay pipe finds from the excavation Zi-05 has not yet taken place, which means that the supposition has neither been disproved nor confirmed, but should instead be scrutinized with the help of further research.

A more concrete indication of local production in the Görlitz/Zittau area takes the form of a pipe from Bernstadt. The pipe bears the raised lettering "BERNSTA...," the last part of the name being incomplete. It is nevertheless certain that Bernstadt, where the pipe was found, is meant. It is the first handmade pipe found that carries the name of its place of origin. Clay pipe production in Bernstadt can be confirmed by written sources from around 1720 onwards, but it seems to have existed for some time before (Kluttig-Altmann and Kügler 2003:89). Following the Low Countries pipe bowl typology the Bernstadt pipe can be said to date to around the third quarter of the 17th century. The object was documented by this author in 2002, but was not available at the time of writing, so that further examination was limited to the evaluation of photos. Bernstadt is about halfway between Görlitz and Zittau, ca. 15 km from each place, which means that the unused pipes from Zittau could quite easily have originated in Bernstadt and represent a sales inventory—the complex consists of a conspicuously decorative variety of unglazed and green-glazed, handmade pipes. The finds from Görlitz and Wrocław/Breslau could also have originated in Bernstadt. Of course this first evidence of a production site in Bernstadt does not mean that we can locate Upper Lusatia's entire production there. Several production centers are probable.

Despite the rapid expansion of known finds in recent years and the definite traces of production in Bernstadt, other possible origins of this technological peculiarity are not known. The reasons that led several regions of central Europe to disregard the usual western European technology in the mid – to second half of the 17th century and to an acceptance (at least temporary) of lesser quality are also unclear. Difficulties in acquiring Dutch-style clay pipes and unfamiliarity with the relevant technologies could be reasons as could an attempt by potters to venture into a gap in the market using their own methods (potters' wheel, roulette, the joining of different parts to each other, no mold). Considerable research will be needed to verify the thoughts presented here, above all the evaluation of written sources at the finds locations.

Regional concentrations can thus be demonstrated in eastern Saxony/Silesia and in the western Czech area, but above and beyond this, widely scattered individual pieces show that these pipes were considered worthy of export or that single pipes could travel by various ways to other locations. The relatively recent identification of these pipe types implies that the finds picture is likely to harden in the years to come. At the same time, however, the complicated and, in product quality terms, suboptimal production of the handmade pipes suggests that, given the same amount of time and labor, their production rate was hardly likely to match that of "normal" manufacture with a two-part mold. This is shown in typical finds inventories of the period, which, at a distance from the known production sites, only ever include individual pieces and instead consist largely of pipes in the western European tradition. To put it differently, finds complexes with a high or exclusive stock of the new pipes imply a production site in the near vicinity.

OUTLOOK

The existence of clay pipe production forms outside of the common western European pattern in the 17th century has completely changed our view of technological development in this period. Previously, German smokers were thought to have been almost completely dependent on Dutch products. Now we know that in eastern Germany—and in other central European regions—several independent technologies existed, technologies that differed from the method of clay pipe production generally employed further westwards, before western European technology triumphed in more and more places in Germany during the course of the second half of the 17th century. These older autonomously developed technologies had clearly left the purely experimental stage behind them and traveled further than their own immediate regional boundaries. One could say that the idea of clay pipe smoking spread faster than the Dutch technology of manufacturing pipes. The more detailed study of the origins of the technology discussed in this article, the pipes' regional distribution, and their period of production promise to be interesting themes in the future. The results will form an important part of the larger story of the rise, the blossoming, and the decline of clay tobacco pipe manufacture in Europe.

NOTES

1. The two pipes pictured were the result of a random selection, a deliberate search of the Dresden material would produce a significant proportion of handmade pipes, if only because of Dresden's central position in the known distribution area.

ACKNOWLEDGMENTS

I am grateful to my colleagues Natascha Mehler (Vienna) and Joanna Dabal (Gdansk/Danzig) for their helpful literature tips.

REFERENCES

KLUTTIG-ALTMANN, RALF

2000   Tonpfeifen in Leipzig—zweiter Vorbericht über die Neufunde seit 1990 [Clay Pipes in Leipzig—Second Prelimary Report about New Finds since 1990]. *Knasterkopf—Mitteilungen für Freunde irdener Pfeifen* 13:10–28.

2005   Tonpfeifenfunde im südlichen Ostseeraum und in Schlesien. Erste Ergebnisse einer internationalen Ausstellung im Ostpreußischen Landesmuseum Lüneburg [Clay Pipe Finds in the Southern Baltic Area and in Silesia. First Results of an International Exhibition in the East Prussian Regional Museum at Lüneburg]. *KnasterKOPF—Fachzeitschrift für Tonpfeifen und historischen Tabakgenuss* 18:18–26.

2006   Genuss und Produktpiraterie. Tonpfeifen in Dresden [Consumption and Product Piracy. Clay Pipes in Dresden]. In *Dresden 8000—eine archäologische Zeitreise,* Judith Oexle, editor, pp. 220-221. Druckerei Wagner, Verlag und Werbung GmbH, Dresden, Germany.

2009   Rauchzeichen über Kamenz. Die Tonpfeifen der Türmer zu St. Marien [Smoke Signals above Kamenz. The Clay Pipes of the St. Marien Tower Keeper]. *KnasterKOPF—Fachzeitschrift für Tonpfeifen und historischen Tabakgenuss* 20:121–129.

KLUTTIG-ALTMANN, RALF, AND MARTIN KÜGLER

2003   Bewegung in Sachsen. Ein Beitrag zur Emanzipation der deutschen Tonpfeifenforschung [Change in Saxony. A Contribution to the Emancipation of German Clay Pipe Research]. *KnasterKOPF—Fachzeitschrift für Tonpfeifen und historischen Tabakgenuss* 16:88–98.

2004   *Tabak und Tonpfeifen im südlichen Ostseeraum und in Schlesien* [Tobacco and Clay Pipes in the Southern Baltic Area and in Silesia]. Husum-Verlag, Husum, Germany.

KLUTTIG-ALTMANN, RALF, AND NATASCHA MEHLER

2007   Die Emanzipation der deutschen Tonpfeifenforschung. Frühe deutsche Tonpfeifenproduktion im 17. Jahrhundert [The Emancipation of German Clay Pipe Research. Early German Clay Pipe Production in the 17th Century]. *Mitteilungen der Deutschen Gesellschaft für Archäologie des Mittelalters und der Neuzeit* 18:71–80.

KÜGLER, MARTIN

1995   *Pfeifenbäckerei im Westerwald. Die Geschichte der Pfeifenbäckerei des unteren Westerwaldes von den Anfängen um 1700 bis heute* [Clay Pipe Production in the Westerwald. The History of Clay Pipe Production in the Lower Westerwald from its Beginnings around 1700 to Today]. Werken und Wohnen. Volkskundliche Untersuchungen im Rheinland 22. Rheinland-Verlag GmbH, Cologne/Bonn, Germany.

LIPSDORF, JENS

2007   Raucher in der Lausitz. Funde von Tabakspfeifen bei archäologische Ausgrabungen [Smokers in Lusatia. Clay Pipe Finds from Archaeological Excavations]. *KnasterKOPF—Fachzeitschrift für Tonpfeifen und historischen Tabakgenuss* 19:131–134.

MARTIN, IRIS, AND ULF PETZSCHMANN

2002   Ein Quartier an der Stadtmauer. Vorbericht zur Ausgrabung Leipziger Str. 18 in Halle (Saale) [An Urban Quarter on the Town Wall. Preliminary Report of the Excavation Leipziger Str. 18 in Halle]. *Jahresschrift für mitteldeutsche Vorgeschichte* 85:327–391.

MEHLER, NATASCHA

2004   Tönernes Schuhwerk – Stiefelpfeifen und andere
        Besonderheiten des 17. Jahrhunderts aus Bayern
        und Österreich [Pipes in Boot Form and Other
        17th-Century Curiosities from Bavaria and Austria].
        *KnasterKOPF—Fachzeitschrift für Tonpfeifen und
        historischen Tabakgenuss* 17:88-92.

2009   Clay Pipes in Bavaria and Bohemia: Common
        Ground in the Cultural and Political History of
        Smoking. *Studies in Post-Medieval Archaeology*
        3:317–331.

2010   *Tonpfeifen in Bayern (ca. 1600–1745) [Clay Pipes in
        Bavaria ca. 1600–1745]*. Zeitschrift für Archäologie
        des Mittelalters 22. Habelt-Verlag, Bonn, Germany.

RÖBER, RALPH

2002   Tönerne Tabakspfeifen von der Liegenschaft
        Salzstraße 22 in Freiburg [Clay Tobacco Pipes
        from the Property Salzstraße 22 in Freiburg]. In
        *Das Haus "Zum roten Basler Stab" (Salzstraße
        20) in Freiburg im Breisgau*, Luisa Galioto, Frank
        Löbbecke, Matthias Untermann, editors, pp. 607-
        618. Forschungen und Berichte der Archäologie
        des Mittelalters in Baden-Württemberg 25. Theiss-
        Verlag, Stuttgart, Germany.

ROTH HEEGE, EVA

2007   Tonpfeifen des 17.-19. Jahrhunderts im Kanton
        Zug (Schweiz) [Clay Pipes from the 17th to
        19th Centuries in the Canton Zug, Switzerland].
        *KnasterKOPF—Fachzeitschrift für Tonpfeifen und
        historischen Tabakgenuss* 19:100–115.

STANDKE, BERND

2004   Zu einigen Tonpfeifenfunden in Freiberg und deren
        zeitlicher Einordnung [Some Clay Pipe Finds
        from Freiberg and their Temporal Classification].
        Mitteilungen des Freiberger Altertumsvereins 94/95
        (Neue Folge 23/24):101–114.

2005   Ein Tonpfeifenfund in Halle [A Clay Pipe Find in
        Halle]. *KnasterKOPF—Fachzeitschrift für Tonpfeifen
        und historischen Tabakgenuss* 18:87–96.

VYŠOHLÍD, MARTIN

2007   Finds of Clay Tobacco Pipes from Náměsti
        Republiky in Prague's New Town. *Studies in Post-
        Medieval Archaeology* 2:275–304.

2009a   Keramické a porcelánové dýmky z malé strany
        [Pipes of Clay and Porcelain from the Area of Malá
        Strana]. *Staletá Praha* 25/2:81–87.

2009b   Keramické dýmky v archeologických nálezech
        a jejich vypovídací možnosti [Clay Pipes as
        Archaeological Finds and their Importance].
        Archeologie ve středních Čechách 13:965–1000.

WAGSCHAL, MICHAEL

2000   Kacheln und Tonpfeifen aus einem um 1760
        verfüllten Keller in Lutherstadt Wittenberg, Ldkr.
        Wittenberg [Stove-Tiles and Clay Pipes from
        a Cellar Infill of around 1760 in Wittenberg].
        Jahresschrift für mitteldeutsche Vorgeschichte
        83:245–296.

WITKOWSKA, TERESA

1998   Fajki Badań archeologicznych na placu
        Dominikańskim we Wrocławiu [Pipes from the
        Excavations at Dominican Square in Breslau].
        Silesia Antiqua 39:283–336.

//

Ralf Kluttig-Altmann
Zum Kleingartenpark 41
D-04318 Leipzig
Germany

DETLEF HOPP

Industrial Archaeology in Essen: The Former Friedrich Krupp Cast Steel Works

ABSTRACT

Only scant remains of the once extensive Friedrich Krupp Cast Steel Works are visible above ground today. The factory was founded in 1811 and moved in 1819/1820 to a site west of the Essen city center on Altendorfer Straße, which housed the so-called "smelting" and "core" buildings. New construction projects—most recently the new Thyssen-Krupp Quarter, the Berthold-Beitz-Boulevard and Krupp Park sites, and the so-called "Car Zone"—have further truncated the remaining deposits. In response to these projects, archaeologists and geodesists have done their best in tandem with the construction projects to record the remains of heavy industry over a wide area. Laser scanning, photogrammetry, and aerial photography have all been employed.

INTRODUCTION

Essen City Archaeology recorded industrial remains for the first time in 2001. It rapidly became clear that the archeologists faced massive difficulties in documenting the features involved. Remains of the Siemens-Martin works from the second half of the 19th century were revealed on a large building site in only a few days and it became obvious that conventional documentation of the features would not do justice to them. Since then procedures have been developed with the support of the Rheinland Archaeological Department, the City of Essen, the Thyssen-Krupp company, the Krupp Archive, and the geodesists from Bochum College, which make it possible to record industrial archaeological contexts even when working parallel to the construction works. This report concentrates on the technical aspect of this work. Until now, archaeologists in Germany have hardly dealt with remains of heavy industry.

FROM THE CAST STEEL WORKS TO THE THYSSEN-KRUPP QUARTER

In 1811 Friedrich Krupp (1787-1826) founded the "Friedrich Krupp Company for manufacturing English cast steel and all the products thereof" in Essen-Altenessen. In the winter of 1819/1820 he transferred the factory to Altendorfer Straße not far from downtown Essen (Friz 1990; Stenglein 1998; Tenfelde 2000; Stremmel 2005; Beyer 2007; Krupp 2011). After a difficult beginning under Friedrich Krupp the business took off under his son Alfred (1812-1887), so that a hundred years later the Friedrich Krupp Cast Steel Works had grown to occupy a 500-ha site. Inventions such as the smooth tire (1852/1853), with which railroads in North America were also equipped, and stainless steel ("Nirosta," patent filed in 1912), helped the rapid growth of the company. For a long time the works were regarded as one of the most important armaments factory in the German Empire. This was the seat of the enormously powerful Krupp corporation, where steel was produced by methods discovered or improved on-site and also processed further. Not only steel manufacture, but an entire system of facilities was part of the factory complex. This resembles other industrial companies of the time in Germany. Coke works, coal mines, brickworks, an internal company railroad, workers' housing projects, the Krupp shops, and social facilities were all included in the factory complex. During World War II the factory—like other German companies—also employed forced labor to replace employees enlisted in the Nazi army; the cast steel factory was badly damaged during that time (Figure 1). Afterwards, 825,000 m² worth of buildings was demolished and 270,000 metric tons of machines and systems dismantled in order to pay reparations. The so-called "New Central Administration Building" (Figure 2), an imposing building built between 1908 and 1911, was demolished in 1976. The last to go was the older central administration building, the so-called "Hauptcomptoir," which was built in 1874 (Tenfelde 2000; Beyer 2007). The industrial site on Altendorfer Straße, having been used for many decades, remained abandoned until a few years ago. The site began to change rapidly from 2000 onwards, however, a process culminating in the planned opening

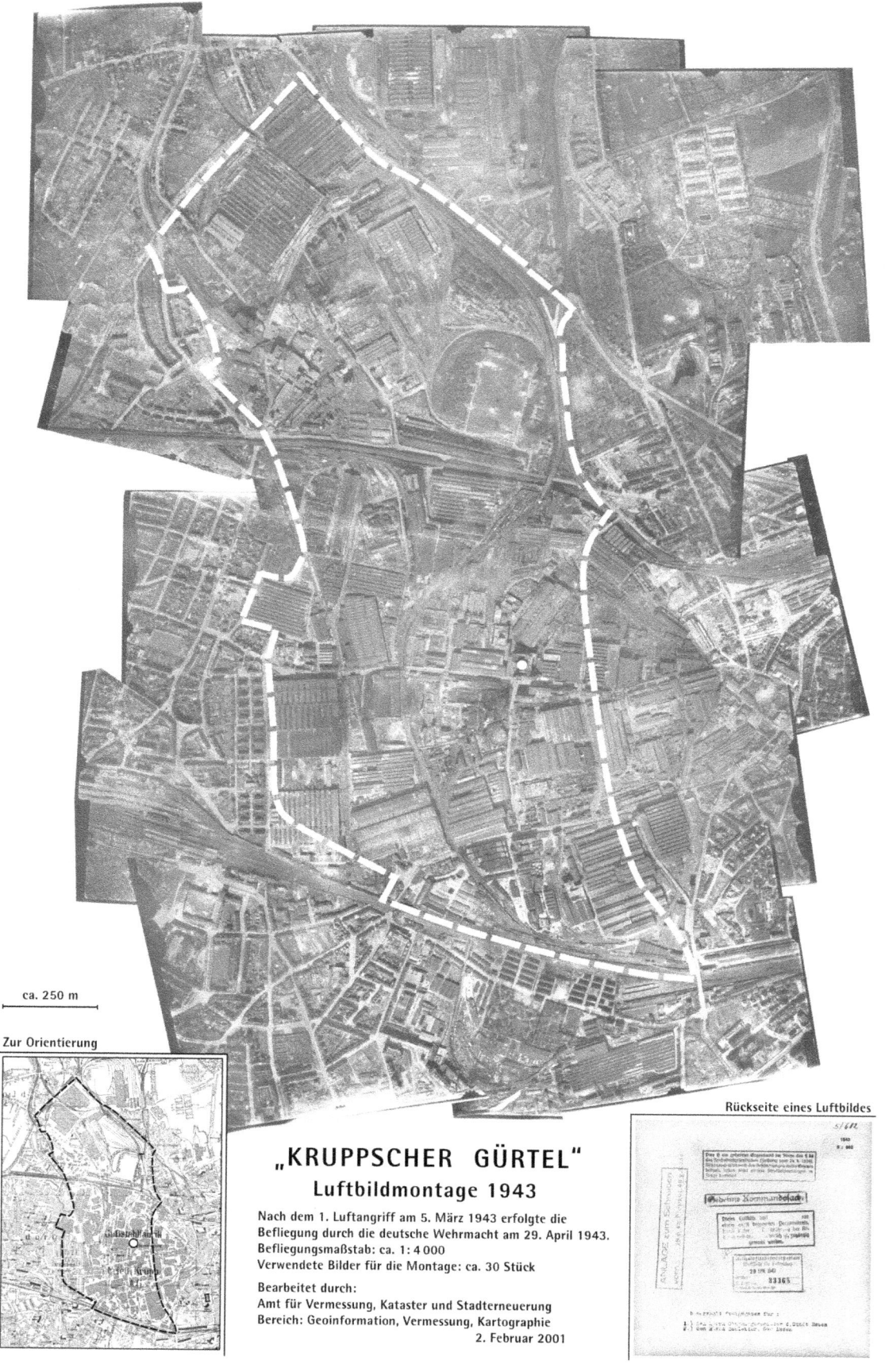

"KRUPPSCHER GÜRTEL"
Luftbildmontage 1943

Nach dem 1. Luftangriff am 5. März 1943 erfolgte die
Befliegung durch die deutsche Wehrmacht am 29. April 1943.
Befliegungsmaßstab: ca. 1:4000
Verwendete Bilder für die Montage: ca. 30 Stück

Bearbeitet durch:
Amt für Vermessung, Kataster und Stadterneuerung
Bereich: Geoinformation, Vermessung, Kartographie
2. Februar 2001

ca. 250 m

Zur Orientierung

Rückseite eines Luftbildes

Figure 1.   Aerial photograph of the Krupp Cast Steel Works, 1943 (Courtesy of Essen City Surveyor's Office).

of the new headquarters of the Thyssen-Krupp corporation, the Thyssen-Krupp Quarter with 2,000 employees, in 2010. This will be the symbolic center of the globally active Thyssen-Krupp corporation, which has 190,000 employees.

DEALING WITH THE REMAINS—THE KRUPP SITE

Only very few factory buildings survive above ground, and subterranean remains from the almost 200-year history of the company can be found only in the central parts of the site—near the so-called "core" (Figure 3) and "smelting" buildings. Almost no traces of pre-industrial structures were found on site, as the entire area has been heavily disturbed by the construction of the Krupp factory.

Archaeological work began on site in 2001 and involved a medieval windmill in the old factory area (Hopp and Khil 2002, 2004a:14-16). Industrial archaeological deposits were also found in 2001—the remains of a Siemens-Martin factory were recorded (Hopp and Khil 2003:191-193, 2004c). The Essen City Archaeology unit subsequently accompanied all construction projects on the former cast steel works' site in which earth was disturbed, either in parts of the complex that were part of the core area and therefore particularly old, or in sectors in which technical processes and procedures had originated or been improved.

At first the industrial archaeological remains were recorded with traditional archaeological methods (Figure 4). It soon became clear, however, that the tools normally available to archaeologists in the recording of archaeological contexts could not cope with the rapid pace of construction on large building sites. Objects such as Test Building H (*Probirhaus H*) (1871) or the Bessemer works, the oldest of their type in continental Europe (1862 onwards), were among the first test objects for new methods (Hopp and Khil 2003:191-193; Hopp et al. 2003). Scientific colloquia in which industrial archaeology was discussed or was the main focus of attention were held in Essen in 2003 and 2008 and

Figure 2.   *The New Central Administration Building (also called the Tower House), ca. 1950s (Courtesy of Essen Photography Department).*

led to an interdisciplinary exchange of ideas (Hopp and Przybilla 2004, 2007; Hopp 2004a, 2004d; Przybilla and Grünkemeier 2009).

FORMER PROCEDURE

During the first recording work on the former Krupp site from 2001 to 2003 it became clear that similar remains in the region, that is, in the Ruhr area, in particular those of the 19th and 20th centuries, had been destroyed with hardly any professional notice taken of them (Hopp 2004c:49-53). Evidence of early industry had only been targeted and excavated in recent years (Obladen-Kauder 2008a:18-19, 2008b:20-21; Przybilla and Grünkemeier 2009).

Industrial archaeology in Germany had previously been regarded as a sort of Industrial Conservation; that is, largely as a question of the preservation of factory complexes. The excavation and documentation of subterranean industrial archaeological remains, particularly from the 19th and 20th centuries, had not been a priority task. Today, industrial archaeology is understood to be an interdisciplinary scientific subject, which, concerned as it is with the registration and documentation of material remains from the history of trade, industry, and transport, is that part of the preservation of monuments and sites concerned with technological and industrial monuments (Albrecht 2009:6; Föhl 1999). In Germany the phrase "industrial culture" (*Industriekultur*) is consequently often used as a synonym for industrial archaeology.

A very good introduction to recent research in industrial archaeology was published in the journal *Archäologie in Deutschland* (vol. 3, 2008), taking as its theme "Industrial Archaeology—Traces of Change."

To sum up, the excavation and recording of subterranean industrial archaeological remains from the 19th and 20th centuries have been exceptions in Germany until now and have mostly taken place around the mining and metal production industries (Obladen-Kauder 2008a:18-19).

Figure 3. (top) The so-called "core building," a reconstruction of the original, which was destroyed in World War II. In the foreground is a test trench to establish its original position (Photo by author, 2007).

Figure 4. (bottom) Example of the drawn record from Siemens-Martin Factory VI (Graphic by author, 2001).

CONSERVATION AT THE KRUPP CAST STEEL WORKS

During the work at the former Krupp site it became apparent that older buildings had only been removed in as far as they had obstructed renovations or new buildings. This is not surprising as the same is true of all archaeological remains. In industrial archaeological terms, this means that while traces of the actual working levels are almost completely absent, the remains of the supply levels below them—steam pipe systems or the foundations of steel hammers and ovens—are often to be found. Post-excavation analysis of the earliest projects has shown that it is often very difficult to reach conclusions about the former working areas based on the supply levels, as the factories grew over the years and the supply levels of different production units are often superimposed upon one another (Hopp and Khil 2007).

ARCHIVES

Systematic archive research should be an important part of preparations for an archaeological intervention whenever possible. In the case of Krupp the relevant archives can be found at the Krupp Archive (Stremmel 2005), the City Library, and the Essen City Archives, but even the Krupp Archive, which is without doubt one of the best factory archives in Germany, does not always have—from the point of view of an archaeologist at least—sufficient material about the early history of the works. Archive investigations into some of the more recent sites at the works, for example the many factory shelters built before and during World War II, also turned up relatively little data (Hopp and Przybilla 2008; Khil 2009). There are many reasons for this, most of them to be found in the history of the company—espionage was a source of concern in wartime for example. There is still considerable research work to be done in this case, including, if possible, investigations in archives outside of Germany.

SELECTED PROJECTS

Test Building H/Siemens-Martin Factory No. 1

Excavations took place in May 2001 and again in Summer 2002 on the site of Test Building H and Siemens-Martin Factory No. 1 south of Altendorfer Straße. These were among the first rescue excavations by the city archaeology department on an industrial site. Subsequently, industrial archaeological remains were not only recorded on the Krupp site, but also at other places in Essen (Hopp 2004b). The fascinating nature of the history of Test Building H first became clear after the archaeological work was finished. The first so-called Siemens-Martin oven began operation at Krupp in mid-1869 after contracts had been negotiated with Wilhelm Siemens (1823-1883) and the Martin brothers. Krupp decided to build an independent building for this project, a long way away from the core area of the factory. For reasons of secrecy the works were given the name "Test Building H." The building was a hall of three aisles, measuring 60 × 40 m and with a casting pit in its central axis. The first oven of the new unit smelted its first batch on 28 September 1871.

During the monitoring surviving fragments of the furnaces with their characteristic loosely set bricks, as well as other features, were found under the forge floor. Remarkably, the bricks from different ovens differed in their composition and color. This may reflect experiments with basoid-lined ovens from 1876 onwards, which aimed to remove the phosphorus, which made steel brittle and useless. The archaeological work was largely limited to photography, supplemented by drawings of selected features (Hopp and Khil 2003).

If this applies to recent structures, then archaeological work is all the more important for factories with origins in the first half of the 19th century or even earlier (Hopp 2004c), in particular when well-organized collections such as those in the Krupp Archive are not available. Archaeology is without doubt the best method of gathering new data.

Sites and monuments legislation in Northern Rheinland-Westphalia, above all regulatory intervention to protect selected sites, makes archaeological research possible when earth-moving measures are planned (Hopp 2008, 2009; Vollmer-König 2009).

Hydraulic Stowing Shaft

Krupp took over the Sälzer & Neuack mine in 1901 and began the renovation of the shaft system. The construction of a hydraulic stowing shaft was a particularly complicated project. Infilling, that is, the filling in of excavated areas in the mine, had become necessary because of increased subsidence in the city center. The material used consisted of slag and ash from the cast steel works, which was ground to a particularly fine consistency by a machine. This material was then mixed with water and flushed through long pipes into the area being filled.

The remains of an only partially infilled stowing shaft were discovered during the construction of a new tax office on Altendorfer Straße in winter 2008/2009 (Figures 5 and 6). The inside dimension of the square shaft, which could be followed for 20 m, was about 10 m. Both the symmetrically arranged bunkers for the infill material and the sides of the shaft were made of concrete. The shaft, having last been used in 1926, was finally filled completely in 2003 as part of the building works.

Photogrammetry was used for recording purposes for the first time during this monitoring effort, in partnership with Bochum College. Essen Photography Department also took aerial photos, and the City Surveyor's Office prepared a 360-degree unwound picture of the site (Hopp and Khil 2004b, 2005:566-567).

New Central Administration Building

The younger of the two central administration buildings was an iconic and substantial building north of Altendorfer Straße. It was built between 1908 and 1911 after extensive preparatory work, which had begun as

Figure 5.   *(top) The immense opening of the hydraulic stowing shaft during building works in 2002 (Photo by author, 2003).*

early as 1905, and opened in the presence of Emperor William II in 1912, as part of the Krupp corporation's 100-year anniversary celebrations. The administration building, 85 × 82 m in size and including a tower 63 m tall, was demolished in 1976 (see Figure 2). The impressive remains of the upper part of the cellars, the perfectly preserved pipe cellar, and also older parts of the building were uncovered in 2005 during the excavation of a construction trench in the tower area. Brick walls from the older industrial buildings had also survived—probably part of Mechanical Workshop No. 1 or of the rolling mill.

Photogrammetry and laser scanning were used by Bochum College on this building site. Aerial photographs (Figure 7) were particularly important in recording the features discovered (Hopp and Khil 2006).

Air-Raid Shelter on Berthold-Beitz Boulevard

In June 2007 a deep air-raid shelter was discovered on the west side of Berthold-Beitz Boulevard, south of Altendorfer Straße. An extensive network of shelters was built over the entire works area during World War II, about which little is known and which is for the most part in bad condition.

The bunker as found appears to have consisted of seven large rooms, a command post, and the connecting passages between. Five rooms were aligned north-south, two east-west. The rooms of the complex, which was built before 1940, were sealed by heavy gas doors, most of which were still in one piece. The bunker could probably have sheltered around 450 employees. Parts of the interior fittings had survived including emergency toilets with spaces for earth and sand, electrical fittings including ceiling lights and switchboxes, and water and

Figure 6. The hydraulic stowing shaft in 360 degrees (Photo by author, 2003; courtesy of Essen City Surveyor's Office / Institute for the Protection and Care of Monuments).

compressed air pipes. In the first room the words *Für russische Arbeiter* ("for Russian workers") had been written on two opposing walls, one of the inscriptions extended over a closed-off entrance. These inscriptions indicate that space was provided in the Krupp company bunkers for forced laborers who were employed at Essen and in many other places.

Terrestrial laser scanning by Bochum College supplemented the archaeological recording work. This procedure allows the rapid and complete three-dimensional documentation of objects. A 3-D photorealistic presentation of the complex was also prepared (Figure 8) (Hopp and Przybilla 2008).

The Thyssen-Krupp Quarter

The focus of industrial archaeological investigation in Essen in 2007 was the 23-ha site of the new Thyssen-Krupp Quarter, parts of which are close to the historic core area. Only five months were scheduled for the excavation of the construction area and the accompanying archaeological monitoring.

Considerable research was carried out by the city archaeological unit in the Krupp Archive, the City Library, and the City Archives before the beginning of the project, financed by the Thyssen-Krupp corporation. This showed that relatively little material about the early years of the Krupp cast steel factory—above all few accurate plans—survive. Research led to the identification of archaeologically key areas. The recording work was planned to take place in tandem with the building work.

Almost all the building features revealed by the construction site were recorded thanks to co-operation between

the Institute for the Protection and Care of Monuments/ Essen City Archaeology and Bochum College, and in consultation with the Rheinland Archaeological Department. The photographic documentation included orthophotos (aerial photography). Laser scans were produced; the Riegl laser scanner used had a reach of up to 1,000 m and could record almost 12,000 points per second. A Zoller & Fröhlich Imager 5006, with a measuring rate of 50,000 pixels per second, but a reach of only 78 m, was also employed (Grünkemeier 2009).

During the fieldwork, which lasted from May to September, it became clear that the problems involved in the documentation of the subterranean features lay not only in the immense size of the area, but also in the rapid and previously unpredictable speed of the construction works: more than 6,500 m^3 were machined away every day (Figures 9 and 10).

Figure 7. Aerial photograph of the New Central Administration Building foundations (Photo by Horst Bühne, 2005; courtesy of Horst Bühne).

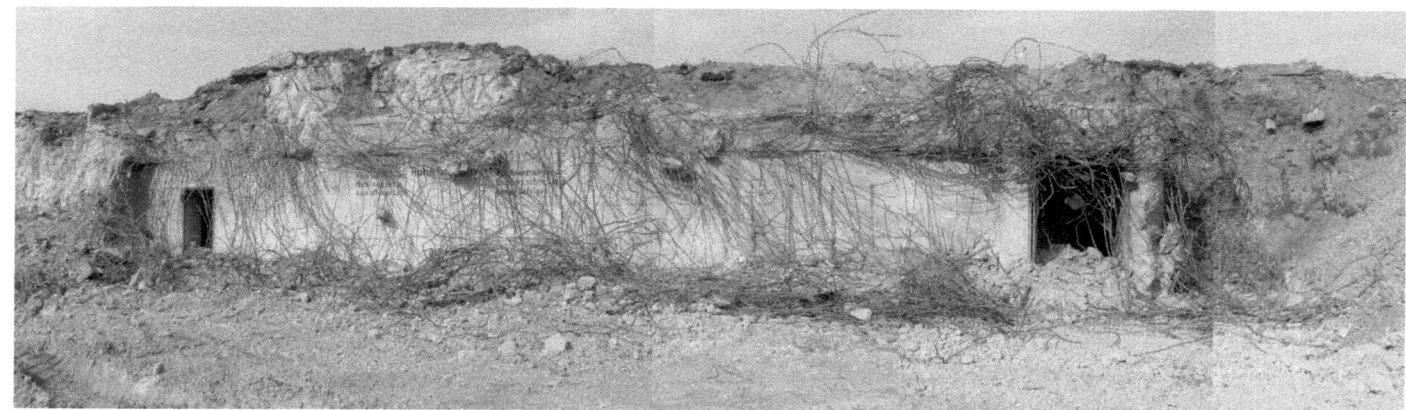

Figure 8.   (top) *Composite photograph of the bunker in 2007 (Photo by author, 2007; courtesy of Essen City Surveyor's Office/Institute for the Protection and Care of Monuments).*

Figure 9.   (bottom) *Work on the site of the new Thyssen-Krupp Quarter. In the picture are drainage shafts and foundations from the 19th and 20th centuries in concrete and stone rubble (Photo by author, 2007).*

Some things did not work out as planned: fewer flyovers of the site took place than intended for example, mostly because of bad weather. The archaeologists were there every day, but the geodesists and their sensitive instruments were not always available when the excavated features demanded it. Also, the weather often prevented their use. The enormous amount of data collected will be analyzed through 2012 in a joint project of Bochum and Mainz colleges (Boochs 2011).

Figure 10.   *Laser scan (point cloud) of contexts of an annealing furnace (Bochum College, 2007).*

FINDS

Countless objects, part of the history of the factory complex, were also salvaged during these projects. These included small finds—tools, personal objects such as nameplates and gloves, and technical objects such as crucible fragments—but also unusually large artifacts. One example of these objects is a 19th-century anvil stand weighing more than 20 metric tons (Figure 11). The salvaging of this object was logistically difficult and would have been impossible without a joint effort by all participants and the support of generous sponsors (Hopp 2009:22).

CONCLUSION

Experience since 2001 has shown that archaeology, when modern recording methods are used, and if necessary in tandem with construction work, can make an important contribution to the history of particular factory areas and to the history of technology through the salvaging of significant industrial archaeological remains.

Findings result not only in a better understanding of the history of technology, but also of other aspects of the company's history. The Krupp bunker, for

Figure 11.   *Salvage of an anvil stand weighing 20 metric tons for a museum (Photo by author, 2003).*

example, provided direct and unexpected insights not only into the past of the company and its role during World War II, but also into the fate of individuals. Test Building H provided insights into the process of technical developments.

In circumstances far removed from a systematically planned excavation, however, it is also clear that a lengthy period of development is necessary before a genuinely interlinked documentation of features by archaeologists and geodesists on large construction sites can be achieved.

The archaeological research at the former Krupp works together with the completed excavations at the St. Antony Forge in nearby Oberhausen and at other locations mark the beginning of a new industrial archaeology in Germany.

REFERENCES

ALBRECHT, HELMUT

2009   Forschung und Lehre im Bereich der Industriearchäologie an der TU Bergakademie Freiberg [Research and Teaching in Industrial Archaeology at Freiberg Geological Academy]. In *Denkmäler3de—Industriearchäologie*, Przybilla Heinz-Jürgen and Antje Grünkemeier, editors, pp. 3-10. Shaker Verlag, Aachen, Germany.

BEYER, BURKHARD

2007   *Vom Tiegelstahl zum Kruppstahl. Technik – und Unternehmensgeschichte der Gussstahlfabrik von Friedrich Krupp in der ersten Hälfte des 19. Jahrhunderts [From Crucible Steel to Krupp Steel. Technical and Company History of Friedrich Krupp's Cast Steel Factory in the First Half of the 19th Century].* Veröffentlichungen des Instituts für soziale Bewegungen. Schriftenreihe A. Klartext Verlag, Essen, Germany.

BOOCHS, FRANK

2011   *Konzeptioneller Ansatz eines räumlichen Informationssystems für die Industriearchäologie [Conceptual Framework of a Spatial Information System for Industrial Archaeology].* Shaker Verlag, Aachen, Germany.

FÖHL, AXEL

1999   *Bauten der Industrie und Technik [Industrial and Technical Buildings].* Schriftenreihe des Deutschen Nationalkomitees für Denkmalschutz 47. Transit Buchverlag, Bonn, Germany.

FRIZ, DIANA M.

1990   *Die Stahlgiganten [The Steel Giants].* Ullstein Taschenbücher, Frankfurt/Main, Germany.

GRÜNKEMEIER, ANTJE

2009   Räumliches Informationssystem zur Erfassung, Dokumentation und Analyse industriearchäologischer Objekte (RIO) Projektteil: Geometrische Objektsdokumentation [A Spatial Information System for the Recording and Analysis of Industrial Archaeological Objects. Project Segment: Geometric Object Recording]. In *Denkmäler3de—Industriearchäologie*, Przybilla Heinz-Jürgen and Antje Grünkemeier, editors, pp. 53-59. Shaker Verlag, Aachen, Germany.

HOPP, DETLEF

2004b   Archäologische Beobachtungen am Holbecks Hof in Steele [Archaeological Observations at Holbeck's Hof in Steele]. In *Archäologie im Rheinland 2004*, Jürgen Kunow, editor, pp. 179-180. Konrad Theiss Verlag GmbH, Stuttgart, Germany.

2004c   Industriearchäologie, eine Herausforderung für Archäologen, Geodäten, Historiker und Denkmalpfleger [Industrial Archaeology. A Challenge for Archaeologists, Geodesists, Historians, and Conservationists]. In *Denkmäler 3D*, Detlef Hopp, editor, pp. 49-53. VDV Schriftenreihe 23. Verlag Chmielorz GmbH, Wiesbaden, Germany.

2008   Krupp: Ein Stahlgigant als Bodenurkunde [Krupp: A Steel Giant as Archaeological Source]. *Archäologie in Deutschland* 3:30-31.

2009   Industriearchäologische Relikte der Krupp'schen Gussstahlfabrik in Essen [Industrial Archaeological Remains of the Krupp Cast Steel Factory in Essen]. *Industrie-Kultur* 2009(1):20.

HOPP, DETLEF (EDITOR)

2004a   *Angeschnitten [Cut].* Klartext Verlag, Essen, Germany.

2004d   *Denkmäler 3D [Monuments in 3D].* VDV Schriftenreihe 23. Verlag Chmielorz GmbH Wiesbaden, Germany.

HOPP, DETLEF, AND BIANCA KHIL

2002   Wind – und Wassermühlen im Kernbereich der Essener Innenstadt [Wind – and Watermills in the Central Part of Downtown Essen]. In *Archäologie im Rheinland 2001*, Harald Koschik, editor, pp. 89-91. Konrad Theiss Verlag GmbH, Stuttgart, Germany.

2003   Stählerne Zeugen der frühen Industriekultur [Steel Witnesses of Early Industrial Culture]. In *Archäologie im Rheinland 2002*, Harald Koschik, editor, pp. 191-193. Konrad Theiss Verlag GmbH, Stuttgart, Germany.

2004a   Es klappern die Mühlen... Wind – und
         Wassermühlen in der Innenstadt [The Clatter of
         the Mills... Wind – and Watermills in the Inner
         City]. In *Angeschnitten*, Detlef Hopp, editor, pp.
         14-16. Klartext Verlag, Essen, Germany.

2004b   Zeche Sälzer und Neuack—archäologisch
         betrachtet [The Sälzer and Neuack Mine Seen
         Archaeologically]. In *Angeschnitten*, Detlef Hopp,
         editor, pp. 91-93. Klartext Verlag, Essen, Germany.

2004c   "Der Martinofen ist wie das Schwein in der
         Landwirtschaft: Er frisst alles" ["The Martin
         Oven is Like a Pig on a Farm. It Eats Everything"].
         In *Angeschnitten*, Detlef Hopp, editor, pp. 96-97.
         Klartext Verlag, Essen, Germany.

2005   ...nicht an einem Tag erbaut.
         Industriearchäologie in Essen [...Not Built in a
         Day. Industrial Archaeology in Essen]. In *Von
         Anfang an. Archäologie in Nordrhein-Westfalen*,
         Heinz Günter Horn, Hansgerd Hellenkemper,
         Gabriele Isenberg, and Jürgen Kunow, editors, pp.
         563-567. Schriften zur Bodendenkmalpflege in
         Nordrhein-Westfalen 8. Cologne, Germany.

2006   Beobachtungen an den alten Hauptverwaltungen
         der ehemaligen Krupp-Gussstahlfabrik
         [Observations at the Older Central
         Administration Building at the Former Krupp
         Cast Steel Factory]. In *Archäologie im Rheinland
         2005*, Jürgen Kunow, editor, pp. 150-152. Konrad
         Theiss Verlag GmbH, Stuttgart, Germany.

2007   In Form gebracht-Überreste der Stahlformerei
         der ehemaligen Krupp'schen Werke [Molded-
         Remains of the Steel Molding Shop at the Former
         Krupp Works]. In *Archäologie im Rheinland 2006*,
         Jürgen Kunow, editor, pp. 218-219. Konrad Theiss
         Verlag GmbH, Stuttgart, Germany.

HOPP, DETLEF, PETER MESENBURG, AND HEINZ-JÜRGEN
PRZYBILLA

2003   *Archäologie und Vermessung [Archaeology and
         Surveying]*. Verlag Fotoforum Schwarzbunt,
         Düsseldorf, Germany.

HOPP, DETLEF, AND HEINZ-JÜRGEN PRZYBILLA

2004   Das Kolloquium Denkmäler 3D in Essen [The
         Monuments in 3D Colloquium at Essen]. In
         Archäologie im Rheinland 2003, Jürgen Kunow,
         editor, pp. 225-226. Konrad Theiss Verlag GmbH,
         Stuttgart, Germany.

2007   Krupp: A Cast Steel Manufactory as
         Archaeological Resource. In *Big Stuff '07, Beyond
         Conservation—Industrial Heritage Management*,
         p. 80. Proceedings of International Conference,
         Bochum and Hattingen, Germany.

2008   Auch "Für russische Arbeiter" ["For Russian
         Workers" Also!]. In *Archäologie im Rheinland
         2007*, Jürgen Kunow, editor, pp. 184-185. Konrad
         Theiss Verlag GmbH, Stuttgart, Germany.

KHIL, BIANCA

2009   Der Beitrag der Archive zur Industriearchäologie
         am Beispiel der Fried. Krupp AG in Essen [The
         Archive Contribution to Industrial Archaeology.
         The Friedrich Krupp Corporation in Essen]. In
         Denkmäler3de—Industriearchäologie, Przybilla
         Heinz-Jürgen and Antje Grünkemeier, editors, pp.
         37-44. Shaker Verlag, Aachen, Germany.

KRUPP

2011   Krupp. Fotografien aus zwei Jahrhunderten
         [Krupp. Photographs of Two Centuries]. Book
         accompanying the exhibition of the Alfried
         Krupp von Bohlen and Halbach Foundation
         in Villa Huegel, Essen. Deutscher Kunstverlag,
         Munich, Germany.

OBLADEN-KAUDER, JULIA

2008a   Geächtet oder geachtet: Industrie vor der
         Haustüre [Ostracized or Respected. Industry on
         the Doorstep]. *Archäologie in Deutschland* 3:18-
         19.

2008b   Wo im Ruhrgebiet alles begann [Where it
         all Began in the Ruhr-Area]. *Archäologie in
         Deutschland* 3:20-21.

PRZYBILLA, HEINZ-JÜRGEN, AND ANTJE GRÜNKEMEIER
(EDITORS)

2009   *Denkmäler3de—Industriearchäologie
         [Monuments in 3D—Industrial Archaeology]*.
         Shaker Verlag, Aachen, Germany.

STENGLEIN, FRANK

1998   *Krupp—Höhen und Tiefen eines
         Industrieunternehmens [Krupp—Ups and Downs
         of an Industrial Company]*. Econ Verlag, Munich,
         Germany.

STREMMEL, RALF

2005   *100 Jahre Historisches Archiv Krupp. Entwicklung,
         Aufgaben, Bestände [One Hundred Years of the
         Krupp Archive. Development, Responsibilities,
         Holdings]*. Deutscher Kunstverlag, Munich,
         Germany.

TENFELDE, KLAUS (EDITOR)

2000   *Bilder von Krupp—Essen im 19. und 20.
        Jahrhundert-Karten und Interpretationen zur
        Entwicklung einer Stadtlandschaft* [*Krupp in
        Pictures—Essen in the 19th and 20th Centuries—
        Maps and Meanings in the Development of
        an Urban Landscape*], 2nd edition. Essener
        Geographische Arbeiten, Sonderband 2. Verlag C.
        H. Beck oHG, Munich, Germany.

VOLLMER-KÖNIG, MARTIN

2009   Frühe Industrieobjekte und andere praemoderne
        Anlagen aus bodendenkmlapflegerischer Sicht
        [Early Industrial Objects and Other Pre-Modern
        Complexes as Archaeological Monuments]. In
        Denkmäler3de—Industriearchäologie, Przybilla
        Heinz-Jürgen and Antje Grünkemeier, editors, pp.
        97-106. Shaker Verlag, Aachen, Germany.

//

Detlef Hopp
Institut für Denkmalschutz und Denkmalpflege
Stadtarchäologie Essen
Rathenaustraße 2
D-45121 Essen
Germany

RAINER SCHREG

Industrial Archaeology and Cultural Ecology: A Case Study at a 19th-Century Glass Factory in Germany

ABSTRACT

Industrial archaeology often follows the narrative of improving technological skills, progress, and success. This article presents a case study that evaluates an alternative point of view based in environmental history as it relates to cultural ecology. Excavations at a 19th-century glass factory in southern Germany initiated by the needs of cultural heritage more than 10 years ago provide an example of the potential of industrial archaeology. Instead of looking for new technologies, research at Schmidsfelden offers a perspective on traditional handicraft and provides insights on environmental and social history. Excavations showed, for example, the failed transformation of the power system from solar to fossil fuel during the mid 19th century.

Industrial archaeology in Germany often follows the narrative of improving technological skills, progress, and success. Most efforts that have been made trace the development of new industrial ways of production. Innovation and invention were at the center of historical and archaeological interest. Effects of industrialization on the daily lives of workers and manufacturers have been studied to a lesser degree. Impacts on the environment have been considered as a conquest of nature rather than as a matter of fundamental changes in the human-environment relationship (Blackbourn 2006).

Processes such as modern industrialization require an understanding that goes deeper than the traditional perspective of focusing on technology and manufacturers. Social history has already enlarged the perspective by looking at workers and daily life, often connected with an approach of micro-history. Fundamental changes

of industrialization such as the transformation of the power system from solar to fossil fuel are, however, at the core of the modern environmental crisis including pollution and climate change. Natural factors and cultural behavior as well as the human world-view are closely connected. Environmental history has been engaged in this research on industrialization for several decades (Sieferle et al. 2006). Within the cultural sciences many concepts have been developed that concern environmental research. Ulrich Beck, for example, introduced the concept of the risk society (*Risikogesellschaft*) (Beck 2007). There are, however, many more possible approaches that could be integrated into archaeological research. Some of them come from cultural ecology, which is based on the idea of culture as an ecological system that overcomes the ties of natural ecosystems by social organization, communication, and technology (Finke 2003).

STAGES OF TRANSFORMATION: THE PANARCHY CONCEPT

Culture as an ecosystem has to be thought of as a complex, self-referenced adaptive system that is characterized by permanent changes. A concise theoretical concept should explain the varying timelines of changes on the one hand; on the other hand it should provide some criteria to characterize different stages of the systemic development avoiding the simple narrative of advance and decline. In recent years resilience theory has been adopted in archaeology (Redman 2005; Schreg 2011). It promises a concept meeting these requirements. As the theory aims to understand changes within complex systems including all possible factors,

the concept is also called "panarchy" theory (Holling 2001; Gunderson and Holling 2002).

Panarchy describes the totality of non-hierarchical organized systems that are determined by a constant interaction within a regime of ecological, social, economic, and cultural forces. It uses the model of an adaptive cycle (Figure 1) characterized by a succession of four stages differing in regard to three dimensions. The stages are (re)organization (α-stage), exploitation (r-stage), conservation (k-stage), and release (Ω-stage). These stages are mainly determined by the three dimensions of the potential, the connectedness, and the resilience of the whole system. The potential refers to the accumulated "capital" of biomass, material, skills/knowledge, or established relationships within a system. Connectedness refers to the complexity of the system: the more elements and interrelationships, the higher the connectedness within the network of forces. Resilience refers to the ability of the system to absorb stress caused by internal interaction as well as by external factors; within the Ω-stage resilience is very low—i.e., the vulnerability of the system is high. Quite small external disturbances—either natural ones or interferences from neighboring systems—can cause stress

and risk during this stage. In consequence they lead to a reorganization or even a collapse of the whole system.

The evaluation and adaptation of these concepts for the needs and challenges of the archaeological record requires detailed case studies within well established contexts. The 19th-century glass factory at Schmidsfelden provides an example that allows some reconsideration of the role of cultural ecology and the usefulness of the panarchy theory within the context of industrial archaeology.

A 19TH-CENTURY GLASS FACTORY AT SCHMIDSFELDEN

The Allgäu, a pre-Alpine landscape northeast of Lake Constance, was a densely urbanized region in the Middle Ages. Free cities such as Ravensburg, Biberach, Kempten, Memmingen, Leutkirch, and Isny and the trade centers of Augsburg and Ulm created a prospering economy based on textile production. Since the 16th century and increasingly in the 18th century the

foundation of new isolated farmsteads (*Vereinödung*) had restructured the settlement landscape from villages to isolated farmsteads. Open field farming on small mixed plots was replaced by separated, closed estates. After the Principal Conclusion of the Extraordinary Imperial Delegation (*Reichsdeputationshauptschluss*) in 1803, the economic and political structures of the landscape changed. The formerly autonomous towns became parts of the territories of Bavaria and Württemberg, shifting the economic centers to the royal residences in the surrounds of Munich and Stuttgart. Even so, production of milk and cheese as well as the production of paper and wood flourished (Grees and Sick 1983).

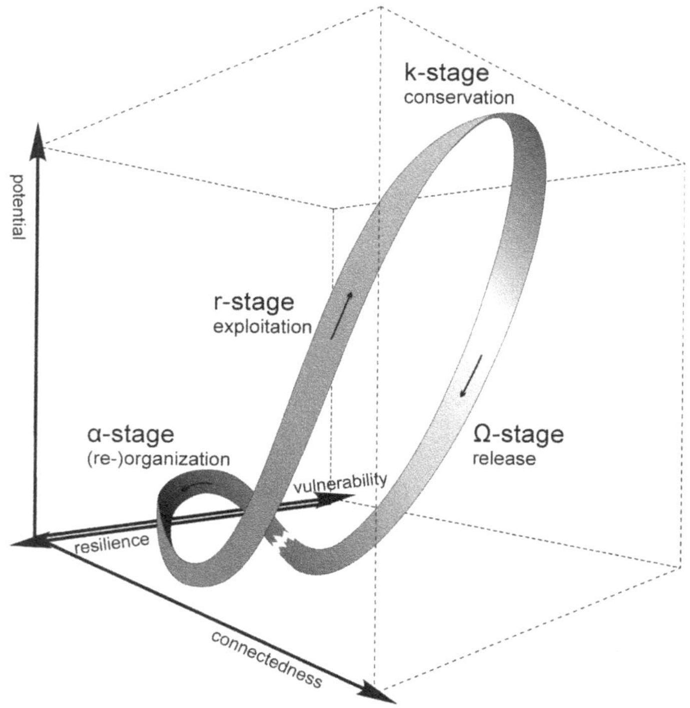

Schmidsfelden is a small village near the borderline between Bavaria and Württemberg (Figure 2) consisting of the glassworks, a storehouse, an administrative

Figure 1. *A single adaptive cycle within panarchy after Gunderson and Holling (2001): an adaptive system develops within the coordinates of potential, connectedness, and resilience/vulnerability and passes different stages. The repeated cycles are never identical but hold specific historical characteristics (Graphic by author, 2011).*

Figure 2. *Schmidsfelden glass factory in a historical photograph prior to 1897 (Courtesy of Heimatpflege Leutkirch).*

318

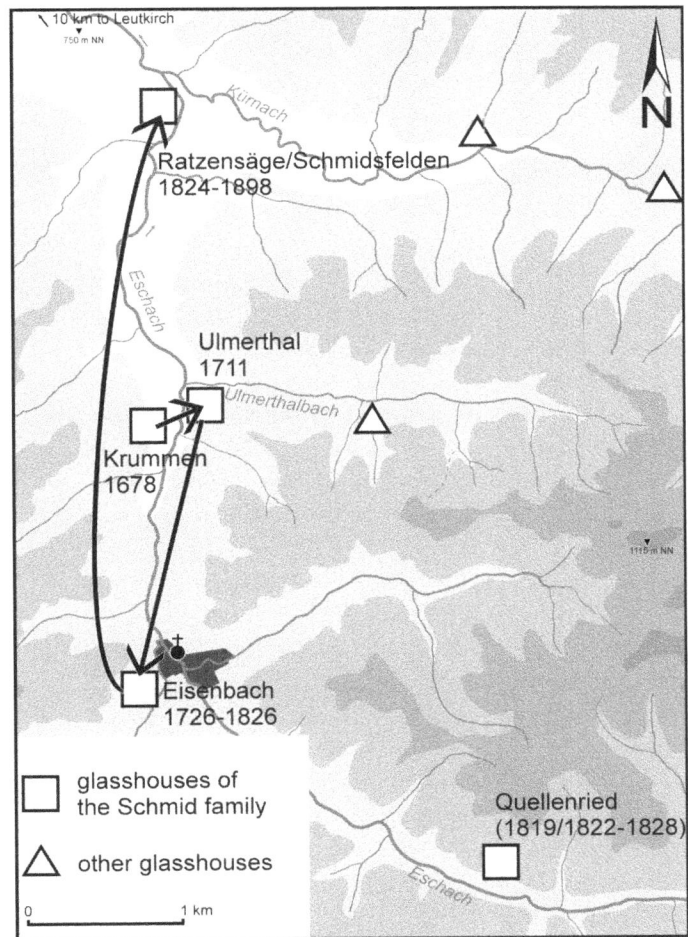

Figure 3. *The situation of 17th- to 19th-century glass facto-ries in the Eschach valley southeast of Leutkirch (Graphic by author, 1999).*

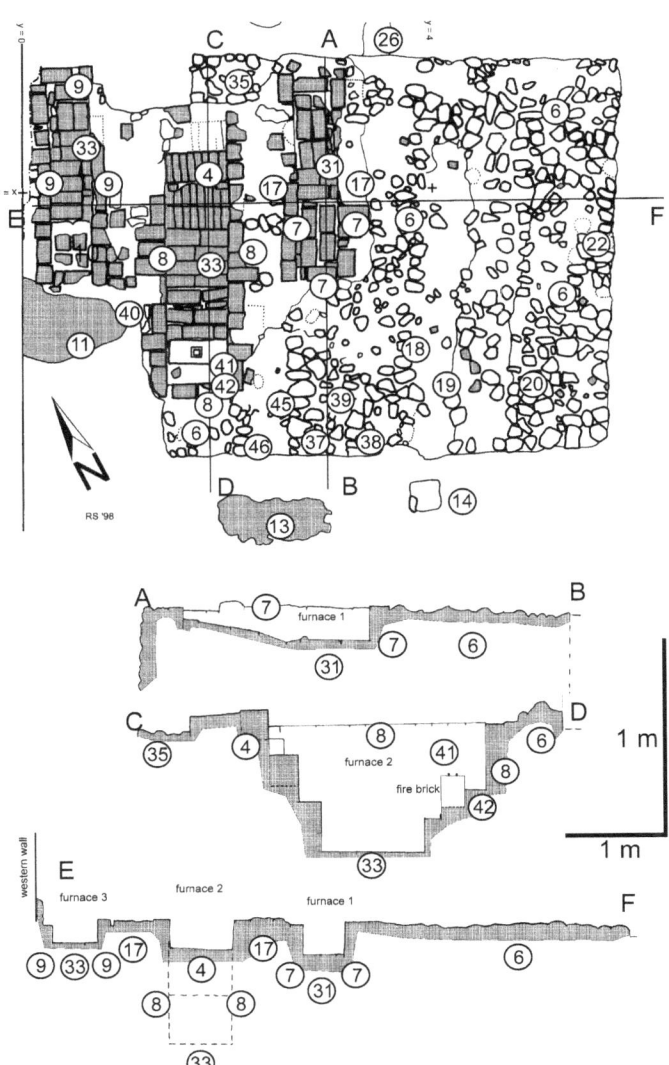

Figure 4. *Excavation plan and profiles showing furnaces at Schmidsfelden. Numbers refer to features as de-scribed in the original field documentation (No 7: furnace 1; No. 4: furnace 2; No. 9: furnace 3; No 6: foundation of the earlier stove) (Graphic by author, 1999).*

building, a manor-house, a chapel, and some workers' houses (Thierer 1988, 1993). Within the storehouse the last carefully wrapped products that had not been sold remained in stock some years ago. It was a broad array of different colorless and some brown vessels, but with a focus on pharmaceutical bottles. The writ-ten record, however, shows the importance of window glass. The glass factory was established 1824-1826 at the location of a mill and was named after its founder Johann Balthasar von Schmidsfeld (1777-1846). He came from a local glassmaker family that was present in the regional written record since the late 17th century. In 1720 the family was ennobled. The glass factory of Schmidsfelden marks the end of the glass-making tra-dition in the Allgäu region. Archaeological finds near Schmidsfelden are not known at this time, but there are indications for glass production in the Allgäu from as early as the 15th century (Kata 1995). There were at least four other glass factories belonging to the Schmid fam-ily since 1678. Actually Schmidsfelden was the last stage of shifting locations along the Eschach valley, a small

river within the Adelegg hills (Figure 3). In contrast to medieval glass factories the Schmid family factories remained in constant use not only for short periods but for several decades.

As the dissertation of Manfred Felle (1977) has shown, there have been important changes in the social orga-nization of glass production. Starting with independent gaffers integrated into a workshop system, wage labor was established during the mid-19th century and changed the social status of the gaffers fundamen-tally. The specialized gaffers came from distant regions, mainly from the Black Forest and Bohemia.

Already before the mid-19th century the Industrial Revolution affected traditional glass production. In 1853 a huge order for the construction of the *Glaspalast* at Munich, an exhibition building made of glass and iron, was an important success for Schmidsfelden, but the production of window glass reduced dramatically in the following years. New production centers near coal mining areas in the Rhineland and Saxony operated with new chemical procedures for the production of soda, for example, using coal as fuel instead of wood and profiting from railway connections. Schmidsfelden suffered from the competition and went into a crisis. Industrial window glass was cheaper. Loyalty to local standards of window glass (groove technology [*Nutenfenster*] instead of glazing with putty [*Kittfenster*]) allowed window glass production in Schmidsfelden to withstand the competing industrial production for some time (Felle 1977:168-169). Finds from Schmidsfelden are similar to materials from late medieval and early modern glass factories in southwestern Germany. In contrast to the known late medieval factories, no bull's-eye panes (*Butzenscheiben)* have been found at Schmidsfelden as they were replaced in early modern times by cylinder glass. In 1859, however, the Schmidsfelden family donated 1,200 pieces of bull's-eye panes for the restoration of the Carthusian church at the Germanic National Museum at Nuremberg (Germanisches Nationalmuseum 1859:179).

After the railway reached Kempten in 1852 and Leutkirch in 1872, Karl Albert Schmid von Schmidsfeld (the son of the founder) along with his son-in-law Julius Christmann (after 1880) endeavored without avail to get a connection on the railway (Felle 1977:159).

In 1897 glass production at Schmidsfelden came to an end, but a hundred years later the last production charge was still stored in the depot and glassmaker tools lay in the glassworks's loft. Of three stoves only one remained, the other two were demolished in order to use the building as a wainwright's workshop. Some years ago a small museum for Allgäu glass history was established, which precipitated a restoration of the glassworks and provided the need and the opportunity for archaeological excavations. In the beginning excavations had two aims (Schreg 1999). The first aim was to document the remains to be affected by the renovation of the building and the installation of the museum. Archaeology was to contribute to site history and the conceptual design for museum didactic exhibits. Portions of the excavation have been preserved. The second aim was grounded in industrial archaeology, with a focus on production processes and the fate of traditional manufacture within the processes of globalization and industrialization in the 19th century.

LATE MEDIEVAL GLASS PRODUCTION IN SOUTHWESTERN GERMANY

Within the last decades there have been several excavations at late medieval and early modern glass factories in southwestern Germany (Kottmann 2001; Lang 2001; Frommer and Kottmann 2004). Glass production began in the medieval era and by the 15th century both potash and natron glass were being produced. The production of window glass was one important field of medieval forest glass production. The main procedure for making window glass in the late Middle Ages was the hand-cylinder technique. A large glass cylinder was blown by the gaffer, which had to be sliced and flattened when it was still hot. For this purpose a special furnace was used. Late medieval glassworks were normally located in forested areas, close to the wood that was necessary not only for fuel, but especially for the production of potash. Quartz was washed from the sand used in glass production in a creek, so forested areas near streams were preferred glass production sites. Another important location factor was access to transportation, which was mainly done by road. In many cases medieval glass houses were at the forefront of rural colonization of mountainous areas. Land clearance as well as the need for manpower in forest operation, potash production, quartz treatment, and transport changed the landscape.

Modern glass production in the Adelegg hills is in many ways still comparable to this medieval craft tradition. The ways of production have changed little, even though furnace technology started to use more permanent tile constructions.

ARCHAEOLOGICAL EXCAVATIONS AT SCHMIDSFELDEN

Excavations realized in 1998 concerned a secondary stove (Figure 4) in the southwestern corner of the preserved glassworks. A square foundation made of cobblestones was found as well as remains of three furnaces made of bricks. The cobblestone remains corresponded well with the original construction plan from 1825: there is a square furnace labeled as *Streckfabrik* (flattening kiln) to smooth large panes made in the hand-cylinder process (Figure 5).

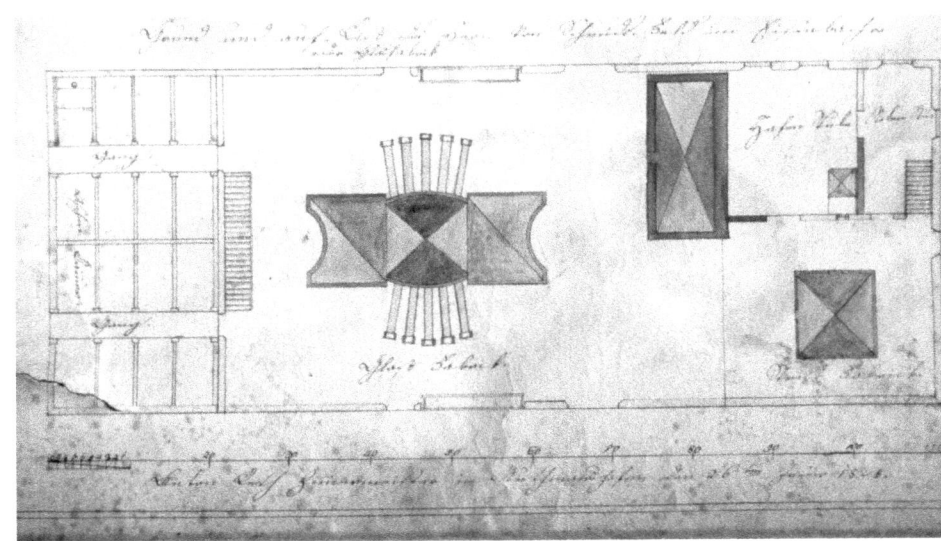

Figure 5.   Original construction plan of Schmidsfelden from 1825. The excavated kiln is shown at the lower right side (Courtesy of Christmann family private archive, Schmidsfelden).

The brick constructions of furnaces 1-3 shown on Figure 4 obviously belong to a later change. As the whole of furnace 3 is close to the western wall of the building, a former annex probably corresponds with it.

The earlier stove had two firing channels at ground level, in the later stage there were three entrenched furnaces made of bricks. The one in the middle (furnace 2) was the deepest (ca. 0.7 m) with steps on the narrow side. Furnace 2 was presumably designed for coal firing. The adjacent firing places were smaller and rather flat. The westernmost furnace (furnace 3) of the later stage was filled by a layer of peat.

Excavations revealed a large number of finds. They mainly came from the infilling of the furnaces and primarily represent the later stage. The largest quantity of finds consisted of production debris of glass panes, suggesting that the stove was still in use as a flattening kiln in the later stage. A comparison of the finds with information from the preserved storehouse (which contained products from the final stage of production), written sources, and archaeological finds from medieval glass factories provides not only insight into the ways of production but also important data necessary for understanding earlier, medieval glass factories. Therefore, historical archaeology in a well-documented 19th-century glass factory has been seen as an opportunity to gain information on typical production debris and to improve archaeological interpretation of earlier sites. Excavations at medieval glass factories often had difficulties in the functional interpretation of the several kilns (Lang 2001; Frommer and Kottmann 2004).

ECOLOGICAL INTERPRETATION

The small village of Schmidsfelden can be regarded as a cultural ecosystem closely connected with its surroundings (Figure 6). In contrast to the most common village ecosystem based on agrarian production, at Schmidsfelden glass manufacture was the main economic basis, associated with small agrarian production. In 1841 only 15 inhabitants were counted, but in the glass factory 26 workers including 14 gaffers were employed. Despite the long tradition of glass production in the Adelegg region, raw materials were sparse and had to be imported or refined: potash and sodium sulphate had to be imported from Bavaria, and quartz had to be collected from river gravel and cracked at a stamp mill (Pauly 1841; Thierer 1993). Wood, however, was the main location factor. In contrast to medieval glassworks, which shifted their locations after some years, however, the Schmidsfelden factory did not follow the wood

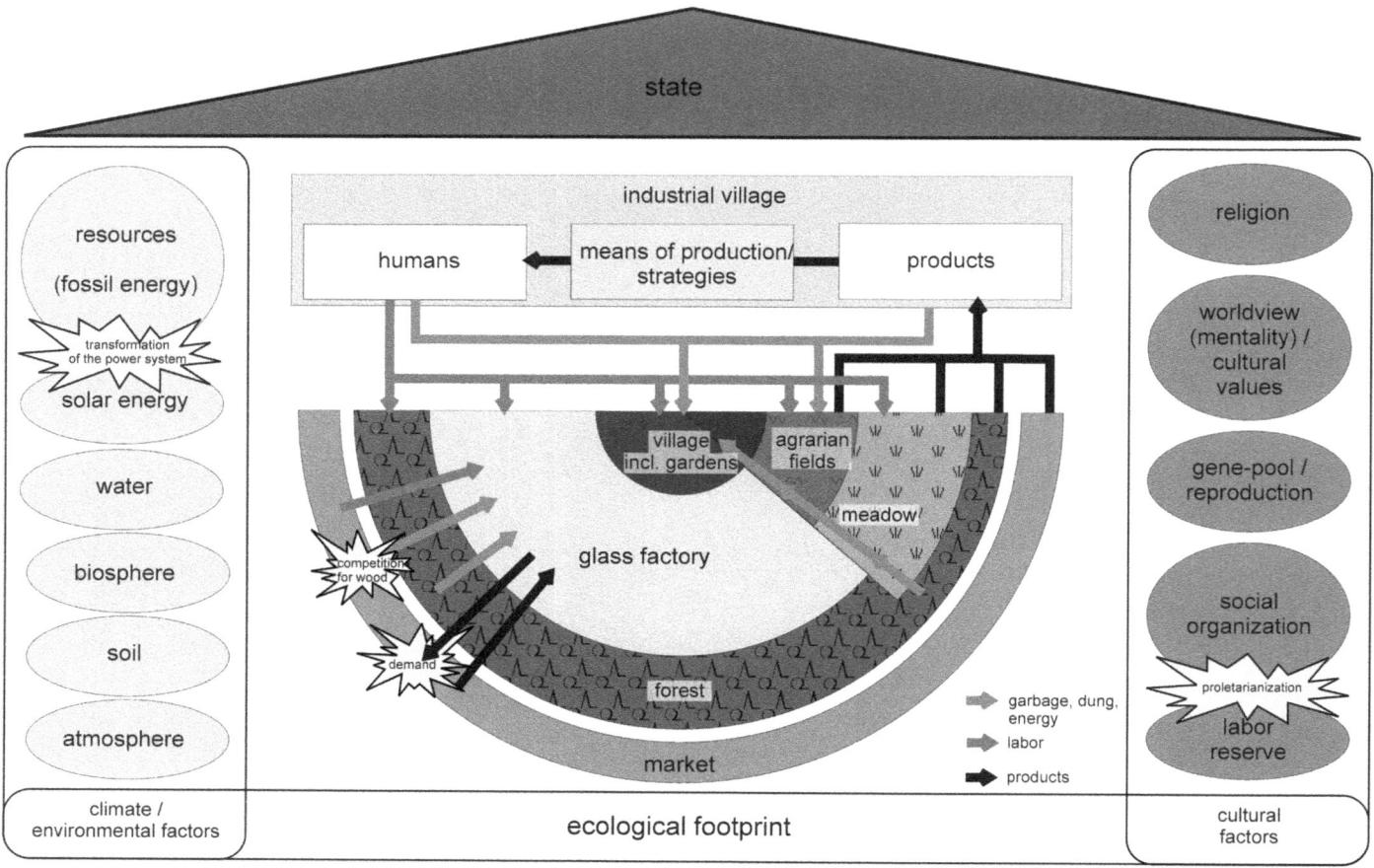

Figure 6.   *The ecosystem of a preindustrial glassmaker's settlement and the stress factors occurring at the time of 19th-century industrialization and globalization (Graphic by author, 2010).*

harvest closely, but stayed in the same place over several decades (see Figure 3).

In the course of the 19th century the system changed slightly. The gaffers, freelancers at the beginning, later became dependent workers. At the same time coal developed into the outstanding energy source of the industry and opened up new technologies. Coal, as well as chemical substitutes of the raw materials needed for glass production, was not available regionally and was too expensive to obtain because a railway connection to Schmidsfelden was never realized. In 1872 a railway station was opened at Leutkirch, but the distance of more than 10 km had to be bridged by road haulage. New modern glass factories developed within industrial areas in Saxony or at the Rhine; these factories were based on coal, were connected to the railway, and were close to chemical industries that provided possibilities for specific new glass products.

The construction of furnaces 1-3 reflects the effort to replace wood with alternative fuels, especially coal. In this light a review of the written record stored in the

private family archive would probably open new perspectives on the environmental and economic history of the factory. The archaeological record showed that the glass factory also tried to use peat. After World War II, when fuel was scarce, Bohemian glassmakers fled to the Allgäu and used peat as fuel for their glass furnaces as well (Thierer 1993:375-376). Peat has only a low energetic efficiency, however, and its usage illustrates the energy problems of glass manufacture.

Taken together these developments caused various stress situations (see Figure 6). New technologies and globalization changed the basic conditions of glass production, caused stress, and brought economic risk to the industrial village. Forest composition changed from a mixed forest to a spruce forest, which is of minor interest as fuel. Despite reforestation firewood became scarce during the 19th century as forestry became more interested in producing for paper factories. At first, the Schmidsfelden factory owners reacted with a short-term coping strategy, trying to change product lines by specializing in specific window glass and pharmaceutical glass as well as by experimenting with alternative fuels such as coal and peat. They could not manage to benefit from new technologies, however, as the import of coal depended on a railway connection. Schmidsfelden therefore has to be regarded as a victim of the transformation of the power system and of early globalization.

The specific glass factory ecosystem collapsed. After reorganization Schmidsfelden became a settlement based on agrarian production and wood processing. The glass factory was used as a workshop or storage, and the small village became a lumber mill. Population declined and many small settlements in the near vicinity were abandoned. The valley of the Ulmerthalbach, for example, was completely deserted.

CONCLUSION

Panarchy theory was used as a general background for an analysis of a 19th-century glassmaker's village. Its usefulness for a detailed analysis is limited because in most cases it will not be possible to create a database that allows for the quantification of potential, connectedness, and resilience in detail. The theory does, however, help to overcome traditional narratives by creating an alternative perspective. For industrial archaeology especially, the analysis of the transformation or decline of the old traditional way of life is probably much more interesting than the reconstruction of new technologies. Regarding Schmidsfelden, which provides an example of the development of traditional technologies during 19th-century industrialization and globalization, previous research focused on competition with the new industrial centers. Felle (1977) identified the main reason for the decline of the glassworks as a failure to adapt. Instead of the narrative of technological progress and entrepreneurial adaptation, however, panarchy theory calls attention to a broad variety of factors, of different stress situations and risks. Furthermore, using the four stages of the panarchy concept, the history of Schmidsfelden is a story of ecological transformation rather than a story of the failure of a handicraft business.

Cultural ecology therefore is neither method nor theory, but an alternative point of view that opens new perspectives and creates new research questions. The ecological point of view can be of special interest for industrial archaeology, which is at the heart of one of the most important cultural changes of human history. Archaeology is situated in a broad interdisciplinary field, where single disciplinary studies can create only fragmentary insights. Historical archaeology proves to be part of historical cultural sciences (Schreg, this volume).

ACKNOWLEDGMENTS

The excavations of 1998, encouraged by Manfred Thierer (Leutkirch) and Walter Lang (Uhingen), were commissioned by the Department of Monuments and Arts of the State Department for Cultural Heritage of Baden-Württemberg. Finds and documentation are stored at the Regierungspräsidium Tübingen. For advice I also thank Stefan Michaelis (Schmidsfelden), who today runs a glass studio within the former factory.

REFERENCES

BECK, ULRICH
2007   *Weltrisikogesellschaft: Auf der Suche nach der verlorenen Sicherheit* [*World Risk Society. In Search of Lost Security*]. Schriftenreihe der Bundeszentrale für politische Bildung, Vol. 644. Bundeszentrale für politische Bildung, Bonn, Germany.

BLACKBOURN, DAVID
2006   *The Conquest of Nature: Water, Landscape, and the Making of Modern Germany*. Norton, New York, New York.

FELLE, MANFRED
1977   *Schmidsfelden: eine Allgäuer Glashütte des 19. Jahrhunderts* [*Schmidsfelden: A 19th-Century Glass Factory in the Allgäu*]. Tuduv-Studien: Reihe Kulturwissenschaften, Vol. 10. Tuduv, Munich, Germany.

FINKE, PETER
2003   Kulturökologie [Cultural Ecology]. In *Konzepte der Kulturwissenschaften: Theoretische Grundlagen—Ansätze—Perspektiven*, Ansgar Nünning and Vera Nünning, editors, pp. 248-277. Metzler, Stuttgart, Germany.

FROMMER, SÖREN, AND ALINE KOTTMANN
2004   *Die Glashütte Glaswasen im Schönbuch: Produktionsprozesse, Infrastruktur und Arbeitsalltag eines spätmittelalterlichen Betriebs* [*The Glass Factory Glaswasen in Schönbuch Forest: Processes of Production, Infrastructure and Daily Life in a Late Medieval Factory*]. Tübinger Forschungen zur historischen Archäologie, Vol. 1. Dr. Faustus, Büchenbach, Germany.

GERMANISCHES NATIONALMUSEUM
1859   Chronik des Germanischen Nationalmuseums [Chronicle of the Germanic National Museum at Nüremberg]. *Anzeiger für Kunde der deutschen Vorzeit* 6:177-186.

GREES, HERMANN, AND WOLF-DIETER SICK
1983   Oberschwaben und Bodenseegebiet [Oberschwaben and the Landscape at Lake Constance]. In *Geographische Landeskunde von Baden-Württemberg*, Christoph Borcherdt, editor, pp. 340-371. Landeszentrale für politische Bildung, Stuttgart, Germany.

GUNDERSON, LANCE H., AND C. S. HOLLING (EDITORS)
2002   *Panarchy: Understanding Transformations in Human and Natural Systems.* Island Press, Washington, D.C.

HOLLING, C. S.
2001   Understanding the Complexity of Economic, Ecological, and Social Systems. *Ecosystems* 4:390-405.

KATA, BIRGIT
1995   Spätmittelalterliche und neuzeitliche Glashütten im Allgäu [Late Medieval and Early Modern Glass Factories in the Allgäu]. In *Kempten und das Allgäu*, Wolfgang Czysz, H. Dietrich, and Gerhard Weber, editors, pp. 95-98. Theiss, Stuttgart, Germany.

KOTTMANN, ALINE
2001   Reconstructing Processes and Facilities of Production: A Late Medieval Glasshouse in the Schönbuch Forest. *Antiquity* 76:35-36.

LANG, WALTER
2001   *Spätmittelalterliche Glasproduktion im Nassachtal, Uhingen, Kreis Göppingen* [*Late Medieval Glass Production in the Nassach Valley, Göppingen District*]. Materialhefte zur Archäologie in Baden-Württemberg, Vol. 59. Theiss, Stuttgart, Germany.

PAULY, AUGUST FRIEDRICH VON
1841   *Beschreibung des Oberamts Wangen* [*Description of the Wangen District*]. J.B. Cotta'sche Buchhandlung, Stuttgart, Germany.

REDMAN, CHARLES L.
2005   Resilience Theory in Archaeology. *American Anthropologist* 107(1):70-77.

SCHREG, RAINER
1999   Industriearchäologie in einer Glashütte des 19. Jahrhunderts: Schmidsfelden (Stadt Leutkirch, Kreis Ravensburg) [Industrial Archaeology at a 19th-Century Glass Factory at Schmidsfelden]. *Denkmalpflege in Baden-Württemberg* 28(2):107-11.

2011   Feeding the Village—Reflections on the Ecology and Resilience of Medieval Rural Economy. In *Processing, Storage, Distribution of Food—Food in Medieval Rural Environment*, J. Klápště, editor, pp. 301-320. Ruralia 8. Brepols, Turnhout, Belgium.

SIEFERLE, ROLF PETER, FRIDOLIN KRAUSMANN, HEINZ SCHANDL, AND VERENA WINIWARTER
2006   *Das Ende der Fläche: Zum gesellschaftlichen Stoffwechsel der Industrialisierung* [*The End of the Surface: Social Metabolism in Industrialization*]. Umwelthistorische Forschungen, Vol. 2. Böhlau, Cologne, Germany.

THIERER, MANFRED
1988   *Die Glashütte Schmidsfelden* [*The Glass Factory at Schmidsfelden*]. Heimatpflege Leutkirch, Leutkirch, Germany.

1993   Glasmacher im Allgäu [Gaffers in the Allgäu]. In *In und um Leutkirch. Bilder aus zwölf Jahrhunderten. Beiträge zum Stadtjubiläum 1993*, Stadtarchiv Leutkirch, pp. 369-380. Leutkirch, Germany.

//

Rainer Schreg
Römisch-Germanisches Zentralmuseum
Forschungsinstitut für Archöologie
Ernst-Ludwig-Platz 2
D-55116 Mainz
Germany

WOLFGANG FALCH

Aviation Archaeology in the Alps

ABSTRACT

For several centuries archaeology dealt mostly with time periods from long ago. Contemporary archaeology was born with the discovery that archaeological methods can be used to research and enlighten events that happened in the more recent past. Aviation archaeology is one segment in the wide field of contemporary archaeology. Aviation is, like contemporary archaeology itself, a young science. Due to its nature and despite its comparably short history, aviation has produced innumerable crash-sites that deserve scientific examination. For more recent incidents, aircraft accident investigation boards are usually in charge of conducting surveys. But when it comes to historic crashes and abandoned aircraft wrecks, historians and museums are now being joined by archaeologists who see the potential benefits of their expertise in conducting professional excavations and evaluating their findings. The following article gives a first insight into aircraft salvage archaeology in central Europe and stresses the importance of developing scientific methods for site assessment and avoiding damage during the recovery.

INTRODUCTION

Aviation archaeology can be considered one of the youngest disciplines in the field of archaeology. It is strongly connected to two other disciplines, contemporary history and aircraft engineering. Though aviation archaeology seems to be comparable to the work performed by aircraft safety boards who investigate accidents, in some respects it is quite different. The approach to crashed aircraft by aviation authorities usually focuses only on the cause of the accident and on the professional removal of the wreck in order to protect people from hazards and to avoid harm to the environment. Aviation archaeology in comparison deals with other aspects. When approaching a wreck, aviation archaeologists have to focus on many more details. Among other reasons, they usually handle crash sites and wrecks of incidents that occurred years previously, sometimes decades ago. The circumstances of crashes or the reasons for abandoning aircraft are often clouded and need to be found. Especially when it comes to pinpointing a wreck location or indentifying the wreck and its history, contemporary history and its many useful tools become a key source. Aircraft engineers play their part by assisting both the archaeologists and the historians and are finally responsible for either restoring the salvaged wrecks or professionally disposing of the hazardous parts and components.

When talking about aviation archaeology we should keep in mind that aviation in terms of "heavier than air" flight is not much older than 100 years. In 1903 the first controlled "heavier then air" motor flight was performed by the Wright brothers in the United States of America. Some 10 years later aircraft made their way into World War I (Murray 1999:16). During World War I the old saying "war is the father of all things" rang true enough and pushed developments in the field of aviation along at a fast pace (Sönnichsen 1942:1). The next four years (1914-1918) saw the appearance of stronger and more reliable engines and airframes all over the world. But the airframes were still mostly made of wood and cotton material. Only during the 1920s and 1930s would aircraft manufacturers, provided with stronger and lighter engines, start to use metal—mainly aluminum—to build more durable, although heavier, airframes. Wood and fabric were still used in abundance, but lost their importance in the field of advanced aviation technology (Gunston 1988:324). The new state of the art airframes were not only stronger in their design, they also resisted deterioration better (Böhne 1937:43).

World War II proved to be the first war in history where air superiority played a major role; it was the first time that aircraft were assembled in unheard of numbers by armament industries all over the planet. The more or less custom-made airframes of the 1920s and 1930s were by then obsolete. Aircraft were being built in large quantities but their life expectancy was limited. Over the small territory of the former Ostmark (today's Austria) the Allied forces saw more than 650 planes crash (Banny and Tuider 1988:408), many vanishing forever. The German Luftwaffe lost large numbers of aircraft as

Figure 1.   Map of the alpine region with places mentioned in the text: (1) Umbalkees glacier, Tyrol, Austria; (2) Bockgrube, Lower Austria, Austria; and (3) Regensburg, Germany (Map provided courtesy of the Department of Prehistory and Medieval Archaeology, University of Vienna, Austria).

well: for example, between September 1939 and May 1945, 1,283 JG77 aircraft were lost (Bekker 1964:382).

After World War II the role of general aviation increased as business aviation and air transportation became more and more important and part of the daily routine of life. At the same time safety improved, though crashes continued to happen. Crashes have usually been managed by different aviation authorities and air transportation boards who would also process the wrecks and remove them from the crash sites. In the early 1990s a strong interest in classic aircraft and military aviation arose, and historic aviation became a feature of cultural heritage.

Despite having scrapped thousands of surplus aircraft and airframes over the decades that followed World War II, governments started to recognize World War II aviation as something worth preserving for generations to come. Public museums featuring fighters and bombers of the World War II era were established all over the world. Already existing aviation museums were provided with World War II airframe left-overs from scrap yards and military depots. Private collectors increased in numbers, and celebrities such as Paul Allen, Peter Jackson, Tom Hanks, Tom Cruise, John Travolta, Harrison Ford, and many others started to build their own collections of classic aircraft or bought and flew so-called warbirds. Since spare parts were limited and old stock soon sold out, teams of hobby historians and archaeologists spread out to search and recover downed aircraft. This niche turned into an important supplier of spare parts for aircraft restoration projects. At the same time this business became increasingly notorious for illegal recoveries, illegal disposal of discovered corpses of crew members, theft, and fraud. Only the profit counted—historic and cultural relics of immeasurable value were destroyed or lost forever.

Though there have been several recoveries of World War II aircraft wrecks performed over the years by enthusiasts, it wasn't until 2002 that a professional group of archaeologists, historians, and aircraft engineers came together to perform the scientific recovery, identification, and partial restoration of a World War II aircraft. I will talk about this recovery and compare the methods used and the results achieved with the recovery of another aircraft undertaken by an enthusiast who had taken the time to collect the parts and pieces of a crashed World War II fighter on a mountain slope in 1984. These two recoveries can be considered good examples, setting high standards for future salvage projects and providing useful reference material for previous recoveries.

Before describing the two aircraft recoveries and their results it is necessary to outline certain parameters that are essential in order to categorize aircraft crashes. Though this paper mainly deals with aircraft recovery in the mountains, several of the parameters remain valid for crashes on flat terrain and in water. The objective is to analyze the chain of events that leads to an aircraft wreck and its recovery.

The focus lies on the aircraft, their constructions, their use, and the possible reasons for crashes. The various interactions between the reasons for a crash and the method of recovery will be outlined. Then I show how terrain and climate play an important role in the preservation of the wreck site and influence recovery strategies. I will discuss the methods of recovery, climate and terrain, as well as the hazards wrecks may contain and the final expected outcome. I will unveil how and when the different disciplines, such as archaeology, history, and aircraft engineering have their part to play and how they interact best. And we must not forget that the approach to the recovery of a wreck can be made from different directions, depending on how the decision was made to start a search and to attempt a recovery.

PARAMETERS FOR AVIATION ARCHAEOLOGY

To begin with, a crash has to happen and somebody has to witness it, or at least files about a missing and/or crashed aircraft have to be recorded and stored. Was it an eyewitness who triggered the interest by talking about what she/he had observed, or was it a piece of the aircraft itself that had surfaced at a certain point? Was it the find in an archive that led to a wreck site or the relatives of a crew member who had started an investigation on their own or commissioned someone to undertake it on their behalf? Regardless of where the project starts and how it continues, the methods that we have developed over the past years usually lead to a successful outcome.

In the following discussion, "landing" is used as a term for the arrival of the aircraft on the ground regardless if the arrival was a controlled landing with no damage to the aircraft or an impact causing the airframe to disintegrate completely.

Reasons for Landing an Aircraft in the Mountains

There are three main reasons that aircraft end up in the mountains. The first is related to the mission; if the aircraft is operating in the mountains, three scenarios are conceivable:

- Mission accomplished and aircraft of no further use, abandoned by the crew though still airworthy, or abandoned by the crew after the aircraft had purposely been made non-airworthy;

- Aircraft damaged during the mission/landing and incapable of taking off/flying again;

- Weather changes made a take-off impossible and forced the crew to leave the aircraft.

The second reason could be that the crew was forced to land the aircraft in a mountainous region, resulting in an unintended emergency landing because of one of the following scenarios:

- The aircraft was in flying conditions, but fuel starvation, unexpected weather conditions (e.g., severe icing, flying below peak level, etc.), or loss of orientation had caused the pilot/crew to opt for an emergency landing;

- The aircraft was damaged in flight while on a mission to an extent that forced the crew to attempt an emergency landing (successfully attacked by enemy fighters, hit by anti-aircraft gunners, friendly fire, mid-air collision with another aircraft, etc.);

- Technical failure such as the loss of avionics, engine failure, structural failure, etc.

The third reason would be an uncontrolled landing (i.e., a crash). In this case we will deal mainly with three scenarios:

- Controlled Flight Into Terrain (CFIT);

- Crashes after the crew lost control;

- Aircraft abandoned in flight; the crew had bailed out.

Different Types of Damage Done to the Wreck

The kinds of damage that might be noted include the following:

- In-flight;

- Landing/impact;

- Caused by the crew (intentional attempts to destroy the aircraft, or during the removal of important items);

- Effects of weather/climate after landing (snow, avalanches, glacier forces, landslide, erosion, corrosion, UV rays, etc.);

- Damage caused by vandalizing hikers, souvenir hunters, local population (collection of scrap metal, removal of usable metals and other parts such as wheels, clocks, etc.), and animals;

- Damage caused during the recovery.

It is important to keep in mind whenever we start a recovery what may have caused the aircraft to land. We may well have knowledge about it before we attempt a recovery. For example if an eyewitness report was the trigger to conduct a search, it is very likely that we may have some intelligence from this source already (e.g., the eyewitness saw a wing breaking off and the plane spinning in, or an in-flight fire setting an engine ablaze, or a fighter downing an enemy aircraft, etc.), though it must be emphasized that the eyewitness report might contain misleading information. This shall always be kept in mind, and every report shall be considered under this possibility. If a file on an aircraft loss surfaces during historical research we might know approximately what had caused the aircraft to terminate its flight. But if we discover a crash site that was reported by locals or tourists without any historic background, it is very likely that the reason for the landing remains unclear at first and has to be found out during the recovery. In this case it is essential to clarify what was responsible for the wreck damage in its current state, and a classic archaeological recovery has to be conducted. An aircraft expert has to oversee the entire operation. This person plays a key role in the entire expedition for she/he might be able to conclude what to expect and, furthermore, what the cause of the incident was initially. This person is also responsible for establishing which aircraft components have been discovered, which components are still missing, and where they should be located.

As an example, a wing might fly off on impact and end up some distance from the plane, still to be found. But if the two engines of the missing wing of a four-engine aircraft are lying at the crash site and only the wing itself is missing, it is very likely that the wing or large sections of it were carried off at some point in the past and are no longer available. Such information will help the archaeologists to extend the search in a certain direction or to quit searching if the evidence indicates that the remains of an aircraft have been properly retrieved (regardless of how damaged they are) and how much is still missing. At this point the historians are taking their turn and join the rest of the team. They will have to start researching the archives for records as soon as a data plate has been found. Data plates were assigned to each airframe under construction and helped to keep records of the aircraft's completion, assignments, and overhauls. They contain such information as manufacturer's name, model, serial number of the airframe, and the date of its completion. If no data plate turns up, an identification of the aircraft is still possible if records in

Figure 2.   *Wreck of Ju 52/3m g6e as recovered in 2002 at Umbalkees glacier, East Tyrol (Photo by Bergrettung Praegraten, Praegraten, 2002; courtesty of Friedl Steiner, Bergrettung Praegraten).*

miscellaneous archives can be located. The presence of historians in the team is essential from the very beginning of an operation. Their assistance can help to cut times short, to end searches early, to identify probable victims, etc. During the recovery the archaeologists along with the aircraft experts will play the primary role while maintaining a constant dialog with the historians.

When the wreck has been completely recovered, the aircraft experts together with the historians have to take over. They will be responsible for fitting the airframe

together and researching its history. In this phase the archaeologists fall back into a consultant role, supplying, for example, information about the recovery locations of aircraft components and identifying damages caused by the recovery team or machines used during the salvage process. Sometimes these kinds of damages are unavoidable, but they have to be recorded and explained. Final documentation of the research, search, and recovery will complete the project. After that, the wreck might find its way to the scrap yard, a collection, a restoration shop, or a museum.

THE JU 52 FROM UMBALKEES, TYROL

In 2001 local authorities were informed by hikers that a "pile of scrap metal" was surfacing at the glacier Umbalkees in East Tyrol in the middle of a nature reserve (Figure 1). A team from a mountain rescue association went to the site and correctly identified the heap of junk as the remains of a long forgotten World War II aircraft. They then informed Harald Stadler, archaeologist at the University of Innsbruck. Harald

Stadler realized the potential of the find and got in touch with Thomas Albrich, historian at the University of Innsbruck, who entrusted the historian Sabine Falch with the historical aspects of the research. Sabine Falch contacted the aircraft expert Wolfgang Falch. The team was complete.

In the following months the members of the mountain rescue association recovered several thousand fragments of the airframe of what turned out to be a German Ju 52/3m g6e *Werk Nummer 6888* along with its three engines and one landing gear (Figure 2). The work was supervised by Harald Stadler and Wolfgang Falch who were present at the site. Since weather and climatic conditions at the glacier allowed the recovery team a time frame of only a few weeks per year to collect parts and bring them down to the valley where they could be identified, cataloged, and stored, the recovery took several years to complete. In the meantime the historian Sabine Falch had started her research. There are still remains of the airframe in the glacier that are expected to surface over the next few years, depending on global warming and the retreat of the glaciers in the Alps.

The Ju 52, also known as the *"Auntie Ju"* or *"Iron Annie,"* was a famous passenger aircraft designed in 1931/1932. After the rise to power by the National Socialists in Germany, the Luftwaffe, the re-established German air force, ordered the Ju 52 from its designer, Hugo Junkers, as a transport aircraft for military use. Among the different versions and a total of 4,845 built (Taylor 1993:539), there was the variant g6e of which only 173 had been manufactured by the end of the war. The Umbalkees find was one of them.

Sabine Falch focused on eyewitness reports from locals who had not seen the aircraft coming down but could remember the crew being rescued. This led her to the archives in Freiburg, Germany, and from there to pilots who had been stationed not far from the site during the course of events. Finally, original pictures were discovered that had been taken by the rescue team. They

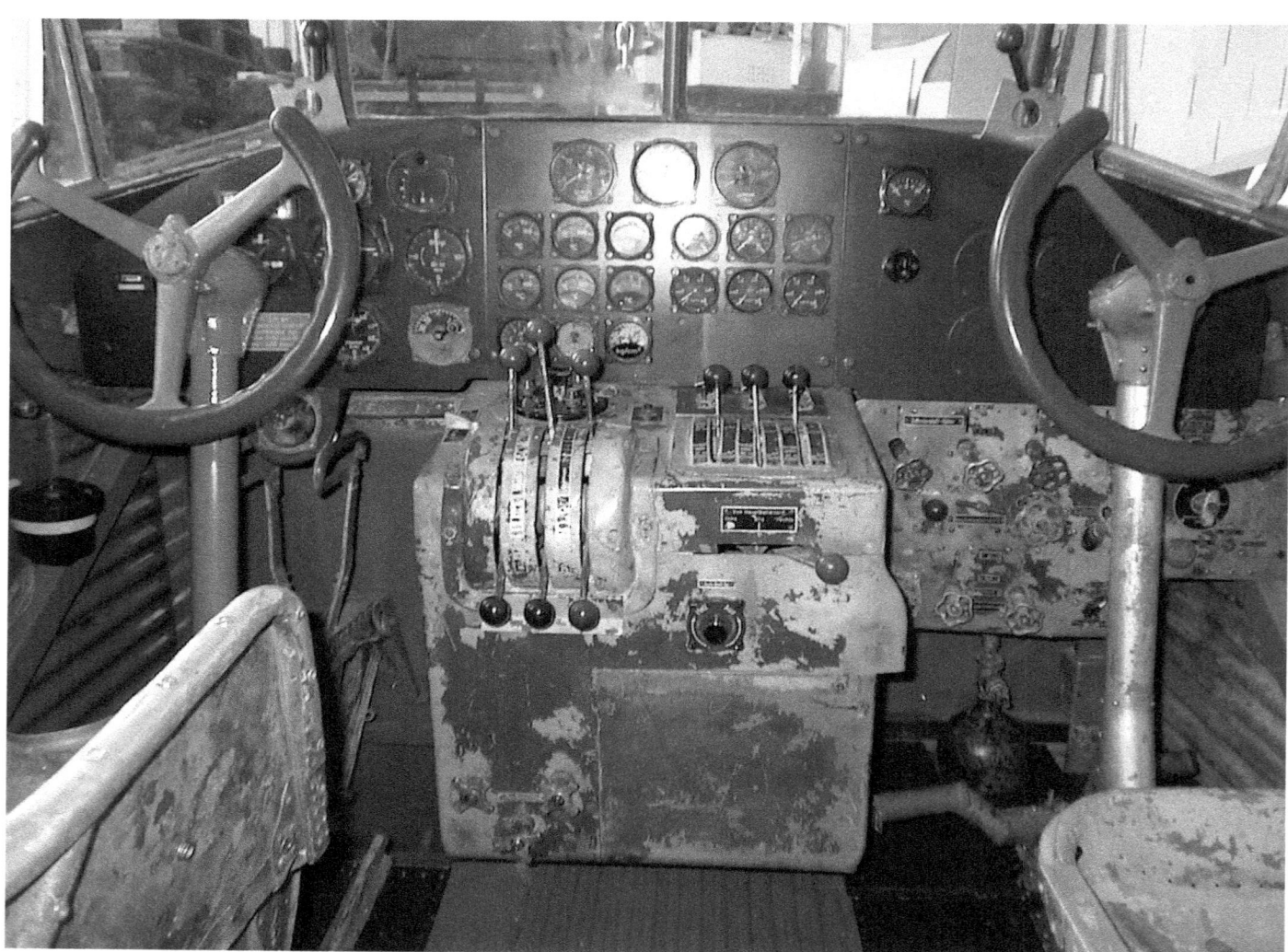

Figure 3.   *Cockpit of the Ju 52 after restoration (Photo by author, 2002).*

Figure 4.   *Restored cockpit section of the Ju 52 (Photo by author, 2007).*

The crew was rescued, and the cargo of the plane removed except for a heavy steel structure (which turned out to be the last existing mount worldwide of the formerly secret Freya radar). Along with the cargo, the instrument boards of the aircraft, the radio equipment, and the still usable tail wheel were removed and taken to a Luftwaffe airfield by the rescue team. In addition to the aircraft wreck, personal belongings of the crew remained on the landing site and were discovered and salvaged during the recovery (Stadler 2006) (Figure 5).

showed an only slightly damaged aircraft sitting on the glacier in 1941. From there, the historical research went along well and uncovered astounding and interesting details about the flight of this Ju 52 and its mission.

At the same time, the recovery team supervised by Harald Stadler was able to fly the severely damaged parts down to the valley where Wolfgang Falch was sorting through the finds until the almost entire cockpit structure was discovered (Figure 3). This led to the authorities of the local community commissioning the restoration of the entire cockpit section along with the static restoration of one of the three radial engines (which were in quite good condition despite having been in glacial ice for decades) (Cohausz 2005) (Figure 4).

Research and restoration lasting several years finally led to the following interpretations. The aircraft was flying overloaded on a secret mission, delivering radar equipment for the Luftwaffe in preparation for the African Campaign of the Wehrmacht. The pilots lost orientation over the Alps in unfavorable weather conditions and decided to attempt an emergency landing, which ended successfully on the glacier. The aircraft was barely damaged during the landing: one landing gear was ripped off and a wing tip bent, and only the radio operator suffered injuries that would finally cause him to perish. The rest of the crew survived several days on the glacier until a team of crew members was able to climb down into the valley and inform the authorities.

The abandoned aircraft was attacked by Allied bombers with incendiary bombs that did not ignite (dud, or *Blindgänger*). The aircraft on the glacier had been mistaken from above for a still functional plane, making it a target. The aircraft was

Figure 5.   *Personal item (a flask) belonging to a crew member of the Ju 52 (Photo by Harald Stadler, Institute of Archaeology, Innsbruck, 2003).*

Figure 6. *The wreck of the Bf 109 E-3 layed out; the parts show the completeness of the airframe (Photo by author, 2010).*

finally absorbed by the glacier ice and resurfaced some 60 years after the emergency landing, wrecked and torn apart by glacial forces.

Some damage occurred during the recovery: a propeller blade got cut off and was carried away by helpers as a souvenir. The pilot's control column was missing, and there were rumors (unproven) that locals had seen a man carrying it off. On the other hand, almost all of the cockpit items were discovered and rescued, suggesting that the pilot's column must have been there but was lost due to theft. Other damages happened when the recovery crew had to hack parts out of the ice of the glacier. In addition, a helicopter pilot dropped the engines on their accessory drives, causing them to crack.

BF 109 E-3 FROM THE BOCKGRUBE, LOWER AUSTRIA

In 2009 the author was offered for purchase the wreckage of a Bf 109 E-3 "L-61" recovered from an Alpine mountain slope called Bockgrube in Lower Austria, along with a detailed file containing information collected on the aircraft, the pilot, the incident, and the salvage operation performed by an amateur in 1984. After a huge pile of aircraft parts had been delivered, the team started to sort them out, identify them, and lay them out on the ground. A day later the results were surprising: the airframe, along with some engine parts, was about 70 percent complete (Figure 6). The private enthusiast who had undertaken the recovery in 1984 had performed an outstanding job.

The Bf 109 counts as one of the most famous fighters of World War II. Built in large numbers, it soon became the leading fighter most of the Luftwaffe aces flew. The early version E-3 was the backbone of the Luftwaffe's failed attempt to secure air superiority over England in the Battle of Britain. Only very few examples of this specific version survive.

Figure 7.   Propeller hub of the Bf 109 E-3; two of the blades were cut off by scrap metal collectors, while the third blade was ripped out on impact (Photo by author, 2010).

The investigation into the crash of "L-61" revealed that this aircraft—built by Messerschmitt Regensburg—had been ordered by the Yugoslavian Air Force in 1939. Due to a change in the policy of the Third Reich, only 73 of the ordered batch of 100 Bf 109s were delivered (Becker 1996:52). "L-61" was not among them. On the wreckage the German symbol *Balkenkreuz* can be found, covering up the Yugoslavian markings on the wings and the tail cone as well as the Yugoslavian registration number "L-61." This indicates that "L-61" had been re-assigned to a Luftwaffe unit.

The research conducted by the former owner of the wreck included evidence that the aircraft had been lost due to a pilot mistake while performing aerobatics during a delivery flight. The pilot, who had died in the crash, was refused military honors for his funeral. He ended up being buried at a quiet civilian ceremony as a *Parteigenosse* (party member).

The aircraft was on a delivery flight over the territory of Lower Austria when it crashed. The impact destroyed the airframe and killed its pilot. The aircraft lay more or less untouched for more than 40 years on the surface of a mountain slope; only the corpse of the pilot had been recovered after the crash. The engine block seems to have been salvaged by locals for scrap metal; the alloy block was missing entirely, though the crankshaft

and the propeller hub were present and barely damaged. Two of the three propeller blades had been cut off before the recovery (Figure 7); the third blade, including the mount, was ripped out on impact and may have been recovered by locals. The airframe showed severe damage to the left wing, slight damage to the right wing, a fractured cockpit section, a damaged but almost complete aft fuselage, a missing tail except for the left horizontal, which was bent severely, and parts of the tail assembly, which indicate that the tail was not salvaged by souvenir hunters but destroyed on impact. The entire airframe leads to the conclusion that either the plane had stalled over its left wing during the maneuver, or the pilot had tried to side slip the aircraft into the ground in order to soften the impact when he realized that he would not make it over the ridge in front of him after coming in too low. This theory seems logical insofar as the historical research has shown that the pilot was a famous glider pilot before the war. The side slip is a common maneuver among glider pilots when they have to make a field landing on the first attempt.

The recovery was done systematically. Except for the difficult terrain it was mostly a matter of collecting visible parts and flying them down to the valley. But it must be emphasized that the recovery crew had searched the site carefully.

CONCLUSION

Comparing the recoveries and the results of the two described case studies provides us with some important insights. Both severely damaged aircraft were discovered in mountainous regions and appeared to be incomplete when discovered. The Ju 52 had landed safely but suffered severe damage mainly from glacial forces and the recovery. The Bf 109 had been destroyed on impact and partially looted. The condition of the airframes upon recovery looked pretty much the same in terms of completeness and sustained damage. In both cases the mountainous terrain made it necessary to have the recoveries carried out by experienced hikers with the assistance of helicopters. The wrecks proved to contain interesting information regarding their destinations, missions, and circumstances of their losses. Professional research had to be carried out in order to gain insight into details of the aircraft and their history.

Archaeological supervision helped to uncover countless important details and facts about the Ju 52 such as

personal items of crew members, small broken-off fragments that were of great value during the restoration phase, etc. In the case of the Bf 109 it is questionable if a second search of the crash site would provide more parts, especially now that the missing sections are so clearly determined. On both excavation sites potential hazards to the public have been removed. It is not common knowledge that besides the dangers of live ammunition and oil leaks, radioactively contaminated paint on dials and in the cockpit area might lead to serious health risks for people involved in a recovery (radiation exposure). Since classical aviation attracts more and more public interest, we can expect aviation archaeology to become an important playground for experts in different areas in the near future.

ACKNOWLEDGMENTS

My special thanks goes to Dr. Ursula Falch, historian, Dr. Sabine Albrich-Falch, historian, and Dr. Thomas Albrich, historian, as well as to Dr. Harald Stadler, archaeologist. They helped to form, and became part of, a qualified team that has undertaken several scientific aircraft recoveries so far.

REFERENCES

BANNY, LEOPOLD, AND OTHMAR TUIDER
  1988   *Dröhnender Himmel, brennendes Land. Der Einsatz der Luftwaffenhelfer in Österreich 1943-1945* [Droning Sky, Burning Land. The Mission of the Airforce Auxiliary Personnel in Austria 1943-1945]. Bundesverlag Wien, Vienna, Austria.

BECKER, HANS-JÜRGEN
  1996   *Flugzeuge die Geschichte machten. Messerschmitt Bf 109* [Aircraft that Made History. Messerschmitt Bf 109]. Motorbuch Verlag, Stuttgart, Germany.

BEKKER, CAJUS
  1964   *Angriffshöhe 4000. Ein Kriegstagebuch der deutschen Luftwaffe* [Attack Altitude 4000. A War Diary of the German Airforce]. Stalling Verlag, Oldenburg, Germany.

BÖHNE, CL.
  1937   *Werkstoffkunde für den Flugzeug – und Motorenbau* [Materials for Aircraft and Engine Construction]. C.J.E. Volckmann Nachf. E. Wette, Berlin-Charlottenburg, Germany.

COHAUSZ, PETER W.
  2005   Junkers aus dem Umbalkees-Gletscher [The Junkers from the Umbalkees-Glacier]. *Flugzeug Classic* 6:24-27.

GUNSTON, BILL
  1988   *The Illustrated Directory of Fighting Aircraft of World War II.* Salamander Books Ltd., London, England.

MURRAY, WILLIAMSON
  1999   *War in the Air 1914-45.* Cassell, London, England.

SÖNNICHSEN, THEO E.
  1942   *Das Flugzeug* [The Aircraft]. Richard Carl Schmidt & Co., Berlin, Germany.

STADLER, HARALD
  2006   Suchschnitte in die Zeitgeschichte. Aktuelle Forschungen zur Neuestneuzeitarchäologie in Tirol [A Survey into Contemporary History. Actual Research into Most-Recent-Modern Archaeology in Tyrol]. In *Beiträge zum Innsbrucker Historikerkongress 2005,* Verband Österreichischer Historiker und Geschichtsvereine, editors, pp. 625-636. Vienna, Austria.

TAYLOR, MICHAEL J.H. (EDITOR)
  1993   *Jane's Encyclopedia of Aviation.* Random House, New York, New York.

Wolfgang Falch
Sandy Air Corp.
Bahnweg 90
A-6405 Pfaffenhofen
Austria

IV. Landscapes and Cities in Change

MICHAEL DONEUS / THOMAS KÜHTREIBER

Landscape, the Individual, and Society: Subjective Expected Utilities in a Monastic Landscape near Mannersdorf am Leithagebirge, Lower Austria

ABSTRACT

This article examines sociology's structural-individualistic approach through questions raised in landscape archaeology. Our starting points are human beings' capacity to act and the duality between the individual and social structure. Social phenomena can be traced back to the action of individuals. Social context and individual action are connected by considering the historical context (Resources and Restrictions) and through assumptions about individual behavior. On this basis we argue that, confronted by several alternative courses of action, humans will make rational decisions, whereby humans as they are considered here can only be incompletely rational (the RREEMM model); they are not wholly informed, they judge their situation and the general conditions according to their social background and maximize their subjective advantage in doing so (theory of Subjective Expected Utilities). Macrophenomena can thus be explained through the aggregation of individual actions. In further course, this system of social explanation is applied to a typical landscape archaeology scenario: an interpretation is offered of a religiously motivated location choice for a Carmelite friary. It is shown that even religiously motivated actions can be explained rationally in their own terms. Rational thinking and action are not necessarily based on the maximization of profit in an economic sense. This illustrates how important knowledge of contextual information is for landscape archaeological analysis. Landscape has meaning for the people who live in it. Its concrete interpretation can only be arrived at through an examination of the contextual background.

INTRODUCTION

In the last two decades landscape archaeology has become established alongside traditional settlement archaeology and environmental archaeology as an independent archaeological field dedicated to space-related cultural phenomena (Gramsch 1996; Gojda 2001; Brather 2006; Meier 2006, 2009). A great variety of different approaches, which exhibit little conceptual demarcation from settlement archaeology in particular, are concealed behind this term, however (Lüning 1997; Schade 2000; Zimmermann 2002; Zimmermann et al. 2004). The authors of this contribution define "landscape" on the basis of two concepts of space taken from the philosophy of nature: "physical space" as physical entity and "cognitive space," which is filtered through human perception or imagination (Hartmann 1980). Landscape has meaning and thus exists both physically (set by nature and, in a historical process and in complex interaction, knowingly and unknowingly shaped by society) and as a concept of its residents (or dwellers).

"Places" play a central role in this model of humans as beings who appropriate space. They are conceptualized through humans' interaction with their environment and in particular with other people as communicative processes. Subjective, but also collective, experiences are usually memorized in spatial terms and thereafter play a leading role in the development and stabilization of individual and collective identity. These experiences constitute social space as "places of memory"—*lieux de memoire* (Löw 2001; Csáky 2004). Thus, places are focal points, which together with their interconnections create cognitive space.

A place as a spatially anchored phenomenon acquires meaning through connotation and is thus acculturated. The point, according to Klaus P. Hansen (2009:17-19), is that culture first emerges through the standardization of individual positions and habitual action; hence, a communicative arrangement is necessary within a collective or parts of a collective, if such positions and actions are to be incorporated into a cultural canon. The methodologically decisive question is, therefore, how can this communicative, interactive process between individual positions and actions and social standardization be grasped archaeologically?

To approach this question, archaeologists need to investigate archaeological phenomena bridging both the levels of individual action (microlevel) and social structure (macrolevel). Similar challenges can be found in sociology. In the following, we will examine sociology's structural-individualistic approach and evaluate its applicability using a case study from landscape archaeology.

FROM MICROSTRUCTURES TO MACROLEVEL: THE STRUCTURAL-INDIVIDUALISTIC APPROACH

Archaeologists attempt to reconstruct previous societies on the basis of their remains. In doing so one is confronted by a problem of scale: when a macrostructure (e.g., a settlement pattern) is examined, different sets of factors appear to be relevant depending on the scale of the investigated area. The scale adopted for research marks a significant difference between functional-processual landscape archaeology and postprocessual approaches. While processualists are chiefly interested in society, widespread and systemic relations, and macrostructures, and they attempt to filter individual phenomena out of their statistical analyses as "deviations," "blips," or "background noise" (Hodder 2000:26), supporters of post-modern approaches criticize the neglect of the individual (Thomas 1993:26; Chadwick 2004).

Modern scientific methods of analysis and the meticulous documentation associated with a careful stratigraphic excavation coax astonishing facts and inferences out of even tiny artifacts. Incorporating results in the macrocontext is often difficult, however. Ian Hodder (2000:21) recently bemoaned the lack of explicit theories connecting the different levels of scale. He suggests a narrative approach instead, in which, while beginning with an individual, a link with the macrolevel is established.

In our opinion such narratives should include both etic and emic aspects, to explain and understand formation and change of social structures in an intersubjective and comprehensible way. That means that an approach must be sought that can help to overcome the dualism between micro – and macrostructures and that will be true to scientific principles. For decades now there have been approaches in sociology that root social phenomena in individual actions, and that are grouped together as "methodological individualism" (or the "structural-individualistic approach")—a term coined by Karl

Popper (2003) and meaning that explanations cannot be exclusively based on macrostructures (Esser 2002:27). According to this approach, explanations of social phenomena can and must be drawn from a multitude of individual actions (Opp 2004:43). This results in "deep" explanations with a high informational content, which can be described as "interpretive explanation."

In his recently published thesis, Knut Petzold (2007) introduced the structural-individualistic approach to archaeology to explain megalithic burial practice in western Europe. We use his ideas as a starting point for this paper. But while Petzold centers his explanation on the reductionist human model of a *homo economicus* excluding restricted knowledge and subjective perception, we build up a different line of argument starting from the more realistic model of a restricted human.

Human Models

The roots of the structural-individualistic approach lie in neoclassical economics (utilitarianism) and in psychology (behaviorism, learning theory) (Treibel 2006:131). The human type taken as a model is the *homo oeconomicus*, who is completely informed and equipped with total foresight, and who acts rationally and in a totally cost-benefit fashion. This objectivized and therefore extremely reductionist version of the approach is not suitable for landscape archaeology, however. Methodological individualism is therefore often—explicitly or implicitly—criticized in archaeology (Clark 2000; Johnson 2000; Hinz 2008).

Newer programs from within the structural-individualistic approach, which distance themselves from the original utilitarian and behaviorist versions (Treibel 2006:134-136), are more interesting and likely to be much more helpful for our purposes. The rendering applied here takes as its starting point the RREEMM model of a human, which Siegwart Lindenberg (1985) opposed to the *homo oeconomicus*. RREEMM stands for *Resourceful - Restricted - Evaluating - Expecting - Maximizing - Man*, meaning a human formed in his or her actions by particular conditions, under which he or she knowingly exploits resources and possibilities, but is also set limits. The individual acts intentionally on the basis of certain expectations and maximizes the benefits of his actions by analyzing his situation and the framework conditions. The model is not harmed by the unrealistic ideas of a *homo oeconomicus*, and for Esser (1999:238) is useful in sociological explanations, not least because it "brings together the most important components of the biological and anthropological foundations of human existence." This model is well suited to the examination of landscape archaeological questions and is used in this paper for that reason.

Combining Interpretation and Explanation

The most important starting point for interpretive explanation is human action. Whether looked at from the viewpoint of sociology, archaeology, or of an activity-orientated geography, an action consists of a certain course of events. The person acting is rooted in a particular situation. This protagonist is the center of his environment, has a certain social position (gender, status, age), is culturally influenced, and has certain technical skills. He or she is set framework conditions in the form of possibilities (resources) and limits (restrictions) based on his or her particular situation. The protagonist is aware of his or her situation and evaluates it on the basis of his or her views, values, and opinions, and develops an idea of the aim of his or her action. He or she has various alternatives and chooses one on the basis of a rule of decision. The action, once it has occurred, results in an effect, which depending on the knowledge and overview of the protagonist can be intentional or unintentional. These effects can reveal themselves in the landscape in the form of artifacts, ecofacts, or structures and thus become empirically measurable consequences of the action. If appreciated, they can be evaluated and become in this way part of the framework of future action (Esser 1999:4-5; Borsdorf 2002:48; Hodder and Hutson 2008:103). This means, put the other way round, that the physical traces of human action can be understood as the remains of past allocations of meaning.

Whether conveniently rational, in accordance with certain values, emotional or traditional (Weber 1972:12), every action has a subjective reason that can be understood by archaeologists, a rule of decision that can be theoretically formulated, and consequences that can be explained through the course of events (Esser 1999:5). A sociological analysis of human actions can therefore understand and explain. One of the founding fathers of sociology, Max Weber (1972), saw this as a fundamental sociological procedure.

Archaeology starts with material remains and attempts to reconstruct past societies on the basis of them. The manifest results of actions can be recognized by prospection or excavation and descriptively recorded (for example through typology, classification, material analysis, etc.). Narratives can be formulated through these descriptions as well as through the spatio-temporal attributes of the remnant concerned. These narratives will be differently structured according to the paradigm employed. In the interpretive (etic) methodologies of cultural-historical and processual archaeology, the artifacts and structures or sites charted are related in space to each other and/or to environmentally oriented variables, and a causal context is constructed. That artifacts and structures are only manifestations of the individual subjects, which stand behind them, is ignored. An intention always lies behind a material remnant, however. It can be seen as a causal relationship between an individual's situation and their decision to act, which can only be understood from the emic standpoint of an insider. Interpretive explanation should be consistently employed in archaeology for this reason.

This confronts archaeology with a dilemma, however. In sociology individuals can be questioned about their intentions, but this is not possible in archaeology. Interpretation and emic observation seem impossible, particularly in eras or areas without remaining written records. There are, however, attractive methods that allow archaeologists to systematize interpretation up to a point. These will now be discussed.

Social Interpretive Explanation in Archaeology

The reconstruction of the accompanying intention and meaning behind every individual object is not a sensible aim, despite the importance of understanding an action when interpreting material remains. Instead one should seek to explain structures on the macrolevel

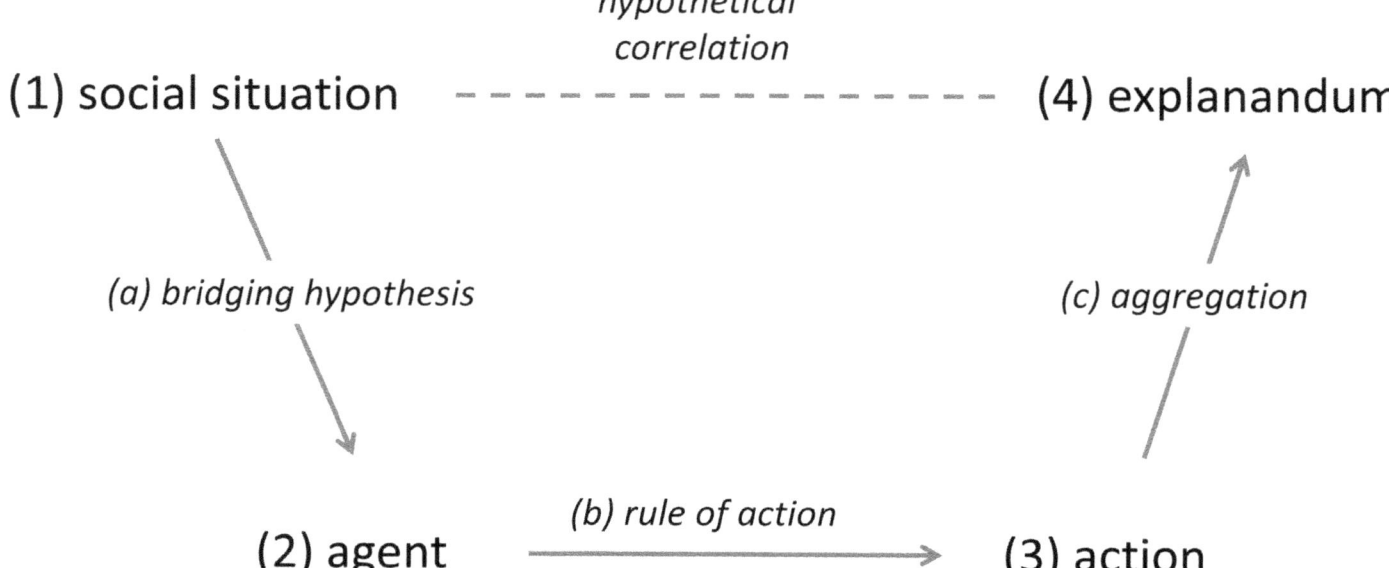

hypothetical
correlation

(1) social situation - - - - - - - - - - - - - - - - - - - (4) explanandum

(a) bridging hypothesis   (c) aggregation

(b) rule of action

(2) agent ————————————————————→ (3) action

Figure 1.   Model of a macro-micro-macro explanation (also known as a "Coleman bathtub") (after Coleman 2010).

(pattern of settlement, roadway network, etc.) through individual action and the spectrum of possible motives within the corresponding spatial-temporal context (Barrett 2000:67).

This is exactly what the explanatory model developed within sociology's structural-individualistic approach offers. It takes as its starting point a phenomenon on the macrolevel, which, as the result of a multitude of individual actions can be explained on the basis of the microlevel. This is therefore known as a macro-micro-macro explanation. The relevant relationships between the macro – and the microlevel in this case are outlined by McClelland (1967) (Figure 1).

In order to explain the *explanandum* in the macrolevel (Figure 1, #4), the model begins with a presumed relationship (Figure 1, dashed line) with the social situation (Figure 1, #1). The preferences of the protagonists on the macrolevel (Figure 1, #2) are based on the social situation, and, presuming there are possible choices, lead to a decision for one of the alternative actions (Figure 1, #3). These actions carried out by many individuals together result at last in the explanandum (Figure 1, #4), which can therefore be traced to individual actions on the microlevel.

This explanatory model is labeled a "deep explanation" (Opp 2004:64) because it connects the macro – and microlevels; the macro-micro-macro model has "interpretive depth" (Esser 1999:417). From an archaeological point of view it has the potential to reconcile

processualism and post-processualism in that on the one hand it takes into account the individual as well as collective phenomena, and on the other it connects etic and emic approaches. In order to function, however, certain assumptions must be made. Essentially, three areas have to be examined and worked on (Petzold 2007:84): (1) the description of the social situation and the formulation of assumptions about likely preferences, as well as about the perception, evaluation, and use of available resources (Figure 1a); (2) the laying down of a rule about the choice of an alternative action (Figure 1b); (3) a rule, which transforms the individual actions on the microlevel to the macrolevel (Figure 1c). This last point corresponds to Hansen's (2009) standardization of individual positions and actions, the cultural process described in the introduction.

Resources and Restrictions: The Importance of Context

The "social situation" of a protagonist is a result of both the resources available and the restrictions that limit behavior. These can be natural phenomena (for example, climate and weather, the surrounding river landscape, etc.), personal characteristics (physique, knowledge, experience, and awareness), societal influences (technology, laws, norms, and values), or the time available. Physical space and cognitive space are thus united in action, as the protagonists are set limits by the physical structure, the socio-cultural superstructure, and their own abilities (Werlen 2010:260-261). The various entries in this list of arbitrary length can be understood both as resources and as restrictions. For example, a river can make the transport of goods possible or easier (river transport), but also more difficult (an overland route, which crosses a river); a wagon drawn by beasts of burden may increase the amount of goods carried, but can also be problematic in hilly or mountainous terrain.

What is important is that the protagonist, in tune with the RREEMM model, is aware of the resources and restrictions involved, and can evaluate and make the most of them. This also means that one must be able to tell the actual physical space environment and the perceived, transformed cognitive space environment apart. However important a resource the environment may be, a protagonist finds his or her bearings on the basis of that part of it known to him – or herself and thus decides whether or not a particular environmental factor plays an important role in his or her actions (Borsdorf 2002:48).

The archaeological context cannot reveal directly which aspects of a given situation actually are or were relevant or to what extent the protagonist's situation dictates his or her interests and motives. A hypothesis is necessary from which, beginning with his or her social situation, it is possible to deduce the protagonist's preferences. The term employed in such cases is "bridging," because the gap between the macrolevel (the protagonist's situation) and the microlevel (individual preferences) is bridged (Petzold 2009:21).

Volker Kunz (2004:107-123) names four different ways of bridging: (1) the testing of different assumptions through simulations ("analytic constructions"); (2) the postulation of "obvious," common-sense preferences (that one usually chooses a quick and easy route when transporting goods, for example); (3) the theory of social production functions (see below); and (4) direct empirical construction through questioning and written documents.

The theory of social production functions (point 3, above) was developed by Siegwart Lindenberg (1996) and takes as its starting point two basic needs, well-being and social esteem (Rössler 1999:76-77), which are said to be the ultimately decisive aims of human action. These fundamental needs can be achieved indirectly through a hierarchically organized string of "instrumental aims"; the ownership of certain goods (e.g., luxury objects or important resources) contributes to status and thus to social esteem. Well-being, for example, is defined by, among other things, contentment, which can be derived from the basic needs of foodstuffs, safety, and comfort (Esser 2002:125-140; Kunz 2004:112-119; Petzold 2009:figure 1).

As social esteem and also well-being can be uniquely defined in different societies, the choice of a bridging measure for any particular question is dependant not least upon the cultural context of a social situation (Cowgill 2000:56).

Subjective Expected Utilities (SEU) as a Rule of Decision

Social situations and bridging for preferred behavior constitute the framework of an action and allow social scientific explanation to address the individual protagonist at the microlevel (Figure 1, #2). The next question concerns the choice of an actual possible action: is there a rule from which we can deduce the possible action a protagonist will take under certain general conditions?

A theory of action is necessary to answer this question. There are a broad range of approaches here. The starting point for the theory preferred in this article is the RREEMM model of a rationally acting person. He or she has a notion of what he/she wants to achieve and can at least partly judge the likely consequences of his actions. He or she can compare the costs (in time, work, financial resources, and so on) of the various alternative actions and subjectively calculate the probable uses of the result. Essentially, one can presume that costs negatively influence the choice of an alternative, while its probability increases with the possible gains to be had. This article therefore assumes that the choice of a possible action is the result of a consideration of costs and benefits involved. The sociologist Karl-Dieter Opp put it simply: "In a given situation, people do, as far as they know, what is best for them" (Opp 2004:45).

This approach is known in general terms as Rational-Choice-Theory. Countless variants are subsumed within this term, ranging from the economic maximization of benefits to minimal regret (Diekmann and Voss 2004:16). The variants of Rational-Choice-Theory are often grouped into "narrow" and "broad" (or sometimes "hard" and "soft") versions (Opp 2004:46, table 1). Boundless self-interest, the exclusive search for material benefit, complete knowledge, and short-sighted (unsustainable) planning are assumed for the narrow version. The perception and evaluation of resources do not play a role in this case. The narrow variant may seem unlikely from these assumptions, but its probability increases with the costs of an activity (Diekmann and Voss 2004:20). Its parameters are also easily measured and modeled, and can be proven false by empirical observation. It is, however, not suitable for a landscape archaeology in which, as defined here, the allocation of meaning plays an important role.

The broad versions of the theory take a "subjective rationality" as their starting point (Opp 2004:51), as does the RREEMM model. A human is seen as a social being. Perception and evaluation are important factors in coming to a decision, and conscience, morality, norms, altruism, or creativity play a role (Treibel 2006:139). Additionally, a person's knowledge (Petzold 2007:81) and his or her ability to process information are limited. A protagonist would be completely unable to cope if forced to consider all possible consequences in all his or her daily activities (Esser 2002:232). Human rationality is therefore limited. This variation is much more realistic, but many of the factors involved are difficult or even impossible to measure or model, and are therefore on occasion unable to be proven false.

In archaeology, Rational-Choice-Theory is usually associated with the narrow version (see for example many articles in Dobres and Robb 2000). In order to avoid misunderstandings this essay will therefore use the term Subjective Expected Utilities (SEU). This a version of the broad Rational-Choice group and the approach most favored in sociology (Kunz 2004:43; Preisendörfer 2004:272). It underlies the arguments presented here.

SEU also begins with a human, who limits costs and maximizes benefits, but it presumes that the protagonist has an idea of what he or she wishes to achieve. This implies that he or she can judge the effects of his or her actions and also evaluate the expected consequences of the action taken, even if this process usually takes place crudely in everyday life (Esser 1999:224). The alternative action is chosen in which "the expected consequences are the highest marked" (Esser 1999:132). The process of assessment takes place with regard to the benefits to be accrued from the expected result and to the probability of that result taking place. This can be calculated scientifically through Bayesian statistics ("sum-product model"), the highest net benefit being decisive for the choice (Preisendörfer 2004:272).

Not only are many critical remarks directed at the narrow versions of Rational-Choice-Theory (Hinz 2008), but the rational human being at the heart of the theory is also often questioned. There are said to be many situations during which "instrumentally irrelevant factors of decision" influence a choice (Kunz 2004:142-143), for example when preceding positive or negative experiences influence actions, even without a direct connection. There are also various types of actions that are not completely rational (for example emotional [re]actions). Hartmut Esser argues, however, that the choice of a type of action must already be understood as a rational decision (Esser 2002:238).

The Rational Landscape: SEU in Landscape Archaeology

SEU is well suited to the definition of landscape as the duality of physical and cognitive space, as outlined at the beginning of this paper. It integrates, as part of a sociological explanation, physical and cultural structure, interpretive approaches to the choice of preferences, and a rule of decision, which is based on a realistic view of humans. Cultural circumstances (for example, the assessment of the environment) and the protagonist's knowledge play an important role. It is generally incomplete knowledge that leads to unintended consequences—a landscape is often affected in this way (erosion, landslides, deforestation, changes in the course of rivers). Many past and present environmental problems can be traced back to the unintended results of human actions. Peter Preisendörfer (2004:275) goes on to argue that environmental problems can be explained from the "logical structure of a prisoner's dilemma." A typical example would be the excessive exploitation of resources. Thus, the use of this theory to answer questions in landscape archaeology is possible and makes sense.

Rational action does not take place in isolation from the given historical, cultural, and physical situation. Protagonists always carry "cultural baggage" and can draw on a body of experience, which triggers characteristic courses of action in specific "typical situations" (Esser 2001:xii). Hartmut Esser calls this state of affairs "framing." People have a frame of reference, which makes it easier to orient themselves in different situations: protagonists "know ... what they have to do and not to do in a particular situation" (Treibel 2006:147).

"Framing" would also appear to be useful in archaeology. Humans "constitute" their own reality through

Figure 2. *Map with places mentioned in the text (all in Austria): (1) St. Anna in der Wüste, Leitha Hills; (2) Vienna; (3) Walpersdorf, Traisen Valley; and (4) Mannersdorf, Leitha Hills (Map provided courtesy of the Department of Prehistory and Medieval Archaeology, University of Vienna, Austria).*

resolute action within a particular perceived framework. This idea is applicable when examining the environmental behavior of (pre-)historic societies, for example when explaining the Norse abandonment of Greenland (Berglund 2010:68). It was not climate change that led to the end of the settlement, but the upholding of a traditional lifestyle in unfavorable ecological conditions. The traditional "framework" of Norse life offset the high "costs" of the exodus through the benefits of the lifestyle thus maintained. Framing defines the environmental behavior of human beings in this way, as has been systematized in "Cultural Theory" (Thompson et al. 1990). People have a particular attitude to nature, which is

derived from their way of life and which is a considerable part of the basis for their actions (Winiwarter and Knoll 2007:122-130).

The modeling of the processes of perception and evaluation is problematic, however. Knut Petzold (2007), in his thesis mentioned above uses the narrow variation in order to explain the erection of megalithic monuments in Western Europe. He rejects the broad variations, to which SEU is to be counted, as unsuitable for archaeological purposes (Petzold 2007:88-89). The perception and evaluation processes are "fundamentally non-measurable," and arguments based on them are ad-hoc explanations.

Nevertheless, there are archaeological methods for modeling perception. Procedures that have already been successfully employed in landscape archaeology are the use of viewsheds (Wheatley 1995; Gillings 1997; van Leusen 1999; Exon et al. 2000; Wheatley and Gillings 2000; Gillings and Wheatley 2001; Ogburn 2006) and topographical prominence (Llobera 2001), and in the integration of these and other models in Cost-Surface-Analysis (Bell and Lock 2000; Wheatley and Gillings 2002; Conolly and Lake 2006:214). These show how the variety of possible human decisions and the available room for maneuver can be meaningfully and comprehensibly limited. Archaeologists cannot tell exactly what is perceived through these methods, but—in the case of cumulative viewsheds, for example—a *potential perception* can be calculated, and thus, on the basis of the distribution of particular structures (for example burial mounds), meaning found. In many regions and periods it is also possible to draw upon written records, which tell the archaeologist about motives and assessments made. The potential residing in the integration of etic and emic approaches in landscape archaeology in periods with written and pictorial sources is examined below through a case study.

Figure 3.   *Aerial photograph of the scanned area from July 2000 (bmlvs [Ministry of Foreign Affairs], used by permission).*

Figure 4.   *Surviving church from the friary complex abandoned in 1783 (Photo by Michael Doneus, 2011).*

Figure 6.   *Foundation of one of the hermitages (Photo by Michael Doneus, 2009).*

CASE STUDY: LOCATIONAL CHOICE OF THE FRIARY "ST. ANNA IN DER WÜSTE" ON BASIS OF SEU

The remains of the friary complex St. Anna in the Wilderness (*St. Anna in der Wüste*) lie in the Leitha Hills (*Leithagebirge*), a hill range on the border between the Austrian federal regions of Lower Austria and Burgenland, which earlier in history was the border between the Holy Roman Empire and the Kingdom of Hungary (Figure 2). The area of this former friary of the Discalced (or Barefoot) Carmelites is wooded and was part of the target area scanned in 2006 and 2007 in high resolution and according to archeological principles as part of the project "LiDAR-supported archaeological prospection in forest areas" (Doneus et al. 2008) (Figure 3). The ruins of the friary are the most prominent surviving above-ground traces of modern landscape formation in the region, alongside old trackways, former quarries, and boundary markers.

The extensive surviving written and pictorial parallel source material makes the friary and its surroundings ideal for a landscape archaeological interpretation that integrates the emic and etic approaches discussed above.

An interpretation will be offered of the siting and, above all, the boundaries of the friary St. Anna in the Wilderness. It is an explanandum at mid-level, of a small social group with rigid and strict behavioral rules and particular,

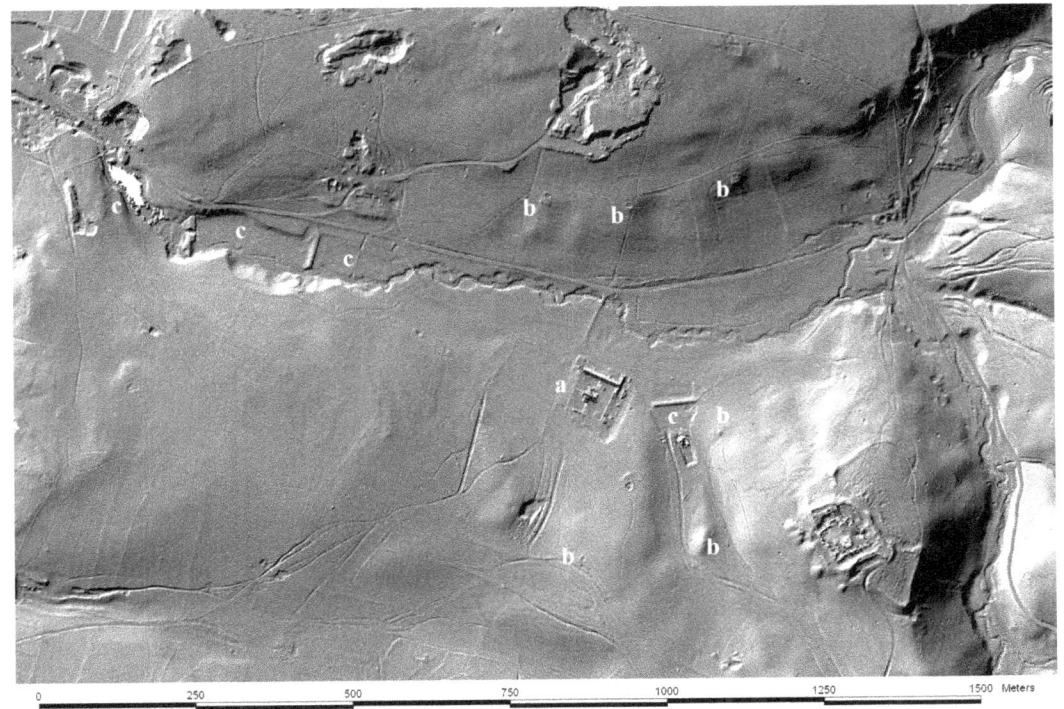

Figure 5.   *Hillshaded digital terrain model of the area around the friary complex: (a) friary, (b) hermitages, and (c) ponds. Light source to the northeast. North is up (Image by Michael Doneus, 2010).*

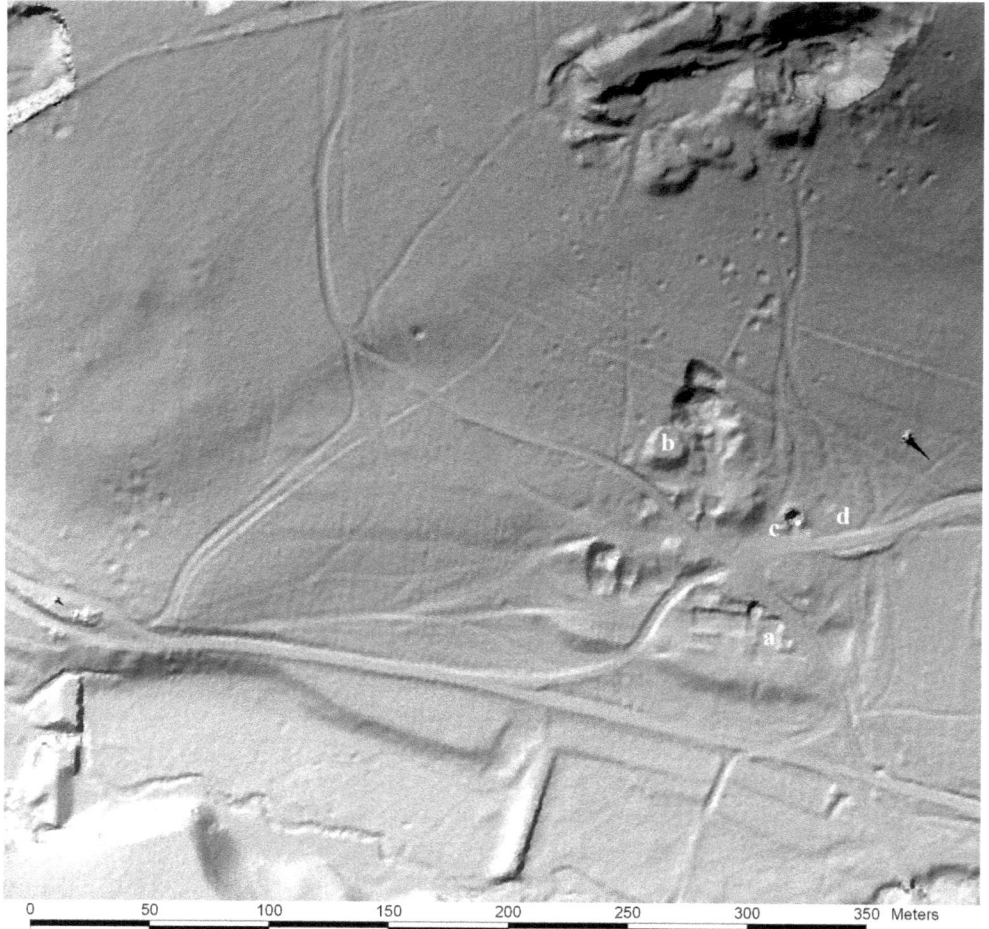

Figure 7. Shaded digital terrain model of the area around the friary farm: (a) farm buildings, (b) quarry, (c) excavated lime kiln, and (d) lime kiln, not excavated. Light source to the northeast. North is up (Image by Michael Doneus, 2011).

cross-section, but around the friary complex the valley widens from east to west along the Arbach Stream. This little valley is flanked by two ridges that rise about 50 m above the Arbach. The little valley basin is today occupied by the remains of the friary complex St. Anna in the Wilderness, abandoned in 1783, which lies at the foot of the so-called Castle Hill (*Schlossberg*). Castle Hill, for its part, was the location of a prehistoric hilltop settlement, repeatedly occupied between the Later Neolithic and the Hallstatt periods (Melzer 1980:77). Within the hillfort, Scharfeneck Castle was erected in the late 14th century. The immediate and more distant vicinity has since the Middle Ages been further shaped by the quarrying of limestone for building stone and the manufacture of mortar. An aerial photograph from June 2003 shows the thickly wooded character of the area. It is mostly mixed woodland of oak and beech, with thick undergrowth in some areas. The immediate vicinity of the friary is largely free of tree cover (Figure 4).

The relatively late foundation of a noble residence—the first appearance of a noble family named for the place dates to 1383, while the castle is mentioned for the first time in 1417—can probably be explained with reference to the castle's location on the border of the Duchy of Austria and the Kingdom of Hungary. The political affiliation of the place changed several times over the course of the centuries (Lampel 1899:49, 51; Mochty 1998). The castle was abandoned in the second half of the 16th century, after lightning had partially destroyed the keep in 1555. In 1683 the ruin served the local population as a place of refuge from Turkish troops, who as part of the expansionary plans of the Ottoman Empire laid siege to Vienna and in doing so laid waste to large parts of eastern Austria.

religiously motivated values known from written sources.

Two questions will stand out in this paper on the basis of this particular combination of circumstances. The first concerns the uses of SEU in the discussion about the choice of location. Can we explain even religiously motivated actions with reference to a theory of rational decision? And on the other hand, and with particular reference to landscape archaeology, the second question is whether or not in this particular case one would reach similar interpretive explanatory conclusions without the benefit of written sources. The answer to the second question will tell us whether or not scientifically based emic interpretation is possible in landscape archaeology.

Our starting point therefore is a description of the physical space in its present condition. Most side valleys in the Leitha Hills take the form of gorges with a V-shaped

Following the desertion of the castle in the 16th century, a friary of the Discalced Carmelites with the name St. Anna in the Wilderness was founded in 1644 on the initiative of the Imperial widow Eleonora (Mayer 1900:85-91; Schatek 1938:1-38; Aguinaga 1993:6-52). The remains of the friary, arranged like a Carthusian complex around the church, are clearly visible in the central part of the valley bottom (Figure 5a). The shaded plan of the terrain model show further details (Figure 5). Individual hermitage buildings, most of which survive only in their foundations (Figure 6), can be seen in the plan clearly (Figure 5b). Some of the surrounding linear features are former tracks, others are probably field boundaries. Ponds beside the Arbach (Figure 5c) and remnants of farm buildings on the left-hand valley slope (Figure 7a) are clearly recognizable remains of the hermitage's economic base, which may have utilized already existing structures from the noble residence. No explanation is possible at the moment of the fact that on the one hand the entire valley basin, including the surrounding slopes, contains intensive traces of medieval and post-medieval use, while on the other hand the evaluation of the documentary sources has to date produced no hint of structures connected with a medieval demesne. Among the known structures are, above all, traces of limestone quarrying and processing, although it is clear from other records that the easily workable Leitha limestone was used for pointed stone and moldings over a wide region from at least the later Middle Ages onwards (Starzer 1900:7.17). Numerous quarries of varying size are scattered over the entire area. A large former quarry can be found north of the ruined friary farm (Figure 7b). Its structure can still be seen more or less clearly in the terrain model, and several later tracks are superimposed on its site. A lime kiln is situated a little north of the farmyard (Figure 7c). This has been partially excavated for presentational purposes and is very clear in the terrain model for this reason. The remains of another kiln can be found not far away, but this has not been prepared for display (Figure 7d).

Physical Space and Cognitive Space in an Idealized Landscape

Landscape can be understood as physical space and cognitive space as discussed at the beginning of this paper. Physical space in our case could be recorded and visualized accurately and in great detail by airborne laser scanning (ALS). Clearly this physical space was highly meaningful for the population settled in it, but the concrete meaning contained in the spatial

organization of human activity is often very difficult to assess, particularly in the prehistoric period.

Nevertheless an attempt will now be made to find out how far the traces of the modern period use of space in the "wilderness" can be interpreted without additional help from the parallel written record.

The Etic Perspective: Archaeological Structures in Physical Space

The most obvious landscape innovation is even today the friary complex in the middle of the Arbach Valley basin. The contained building complex around the central church and including residential and supporting buildings is manifestly the ruins of a former friary. The complex features cells arrayed around a cloisters-type structure, which have primary exits outwards into former gardens and thus has clear parallels with medieval Carthusian architecture (Aniel 1983; Zadnikar 1983; Laurent 1984). The withdrawn location of the friary in the valley basin is also a reminder of the chosen sites of Carthusian, but also of Cistercian monasteries (Evans 2004:78-79). This assessment admittedly uses non-archaeological knowledge. The spatial structure in this case differs, however, from that of the Carthusians and the Cistercians in the presence of seven small buildings in the vicinity of the friary, which for the most part survive in their foundations, but in two cases to a height of two stories. These buildings were apparently equipped with heating units, indicating a residential function. Their small size and two-room structure with a lobby and a living room has parallels in the room structure of Carthusian cells, and is also probable in the central friary building. The friary, the freestanding cells, the remains of a further church building, and a complex arranged around a courtyard at the entrance to the valley basin are surrounded by a lengthy wall, which also encloses the old castle on the hillside.

When summarizing the implications of the architectonic structure of the immediate landscape at this point, it is primarily elements of spatial segregation that stick out and that therefore must be seen as socially constitutive. The complex is close to flowing water, which is often taken to be the most important factor in location choice, but this seems to be of only secondary importance in this case—there are other "more favorable" settlement sites along the further course of the Arbach, which were very apparently not used. The limestone quarries and lime kilns found in the area are either at the edge of the locale or can be shown by stratigraphic superimpositions not to be contemporary with the friary and can thus also be ruled out as a significant factor in the choice of site. The location apart from the settled area in the valley basin, and also the enclosing wall, separate the monastic living space from neighboring communities. Moreover, the buildings within the wall, that is the separately accessed cells in the friary and also the freestanding "cells," also indicate a general division of the space of the members of the monastic community. The spatial distance of the friary to the rural village environs is shared with the old castle. The central difference seems to lie in the visibility of the complexes. For Scharfeneck castle—and therefore presumably also for the Iron Age hill fort on the same site—a height was chosen that is clearly visible from the plain before the valley, but the friary seems to "fade out" through its position in the valley. This impression is admittedly exaggerated by today's forest cover.

Thus, in advance of the written sources, which will form the basis of an emic view, a working hypothesis can be postulated that stresses seclusion, strengthened by non-visibility as the main motive for the choice of site.

The Emic Perspective: Written and Pictorial Sources as a Basis for the Interpretation of the Social Situation

Apart from numerous legal sources, three main sources are available for the emic interpretation of the foundation, endowment, and dissolution of the friary:

- The rules of the order of the Discalced Carmelites, in particular the Eremus instructions from 1689 (Aguinaga 1993:58-63).

- The two-volume friary annals, which today lie in the archive of the surviving Carmelite friary in Vienna (Döbling) (Schatek 1938:3).

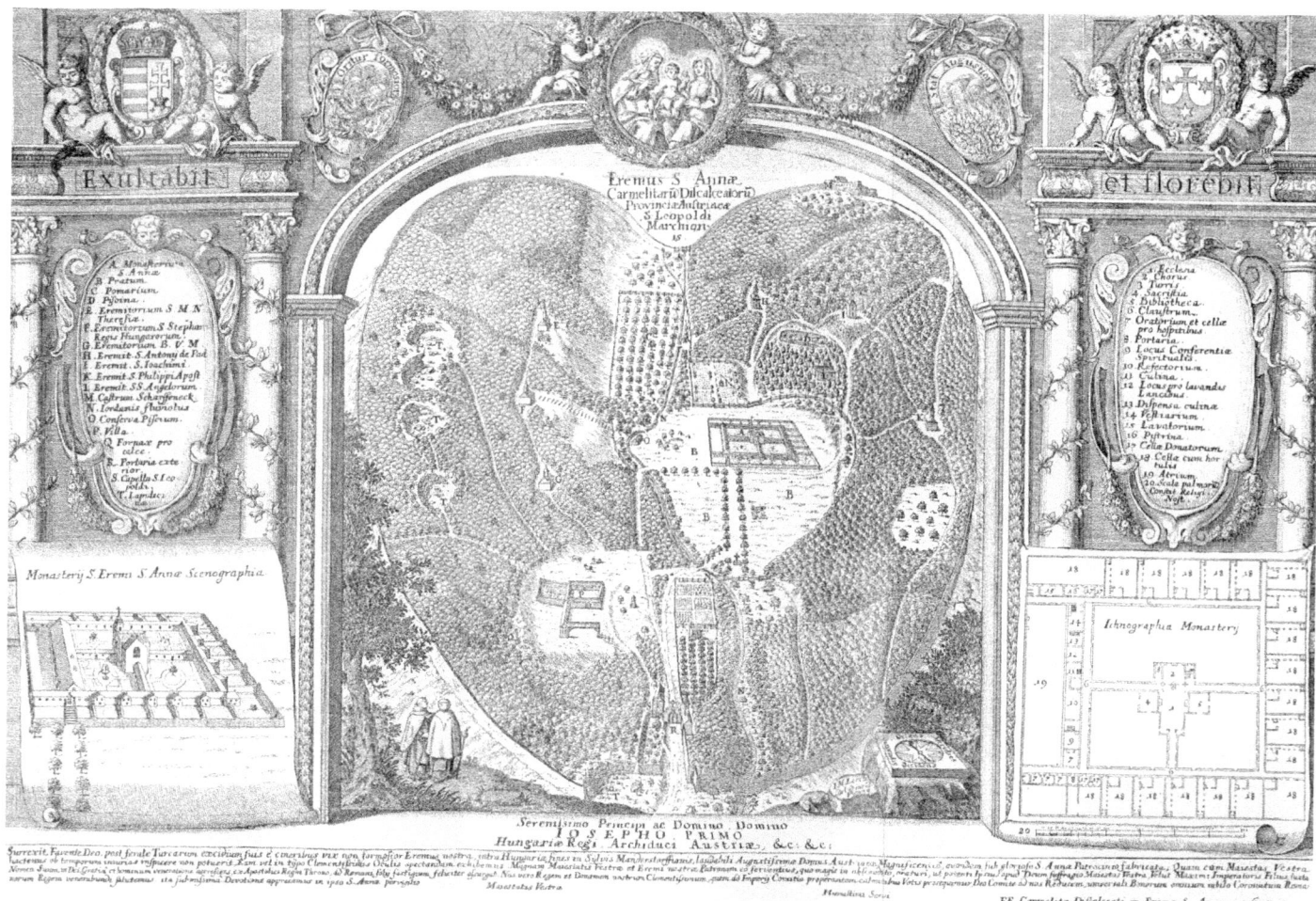

Figure 8.   *Engraving of the friary St. Anna in the Wilderness by J. Martin Lerch, 1689 (Federal Museum of Lower Austria, Topographic Department, Sign. 5337).*

- An engraving by J. Martin Lerch from Vienna in 1689 and a simplified copy from the engraver J. Eberspach from Vienna in 1780 (Schatek 1938:8).

The rules and instructions of the order as normative sources provide us with information about the social situation and therefore about the standardization of this particular monastic culture through the authorities. The annals and the pictorial sources communicate the emic perspective more directly, however, even though admittedly the authors of the friary annals and the engravers are also normatively influenced by their patrons, so that their descriptions are culturally filtered several times over. The religious community of the Carmelites was founded in 1156 through the coming together of hermits at the Elias spring on Mount Carmel in Palestine. The rules of the order, which were authorized in 1171, indicate that the Carmelites—in a fashion similar to the Carthusians, who were founded somewhat later—can be understood as a movement of hermits dedicated to contemplation. Nevertheless, the privileges of the mendicant orders were extended as early as the mid-13th century to the Carmelites, thus explaining the integration of many Carmelite friaries into towns. The "Discalced Carmelites" were founded in 1593 and attempted, as a reform movement, to emphasize the spirituality of the Vita Contemplativa from the foundation period as the central tenet of the order (Schatek 1938:13-15). Every province of the order was expected in the manner of the Carthusians to possess at least one eremus or "wilderness," meaning a hermitage center dedicated to fasting and prayer, a monastic retreat serving the other houses of the order, which were overwhelmingly settled in urban communities. In the 17th century St. Anna in the Wilderness was one of five hermitages belonging to the Italian province of the order, of which the core Habsburg territories formed a part (Schatek 1938:2). The instructions give us detailed information about the practices of the hermitage and its individual parts. These rules tell us that a notice board could be found on every cell door with rules of conduct that described the hermitage as a place of prayer, tranquility, and silence, which would allow God to be heard and seen (Aguinaga 1993:91). Normative statements about seeing are particularly meaningful in this context; the eyes should be directed to heaven in devotion, one should not look out of the cell into the garden. At another point the instructions state that the gaze should "not reach further than the length of

one's own grave" (Aguinaga 1993:150). Visual limitation therefore played a central role in the hermitage's spatial conception.

This is also indicated in that part of the annals that concerns the building of the friary. The importance of distance from mundane things is clearly recognizable in the fact that the territory originally suggested by Eleonora for the construction of the friary was rejected by the head of the province. The Carmelites thought that area, near Walpersdorf on the western slopes of the Traisen Valley, unsuitable, because it was insufficiently remote. A spacious valley surrounded by wooded hills would instead be ideal, as it would both guarantee seclusion and supply the necessary resources for daily use (water, stone, sand, wood, and land for gardens and fish ponds) (Schatek 1938:2.11). These requirements could be satisfied in the lower slopes of the Leitha Hills. The site of the friary and the church was chosen so that all hermitages were visible from it (Schatek 1938:2.19). Seeing and not being seen therefore seem to be important criteria in the choice of a site, and thus appear to be a plausible bridging measure for the preference choice of the friary's founders.

Other important insights about the spatial concept behind the friary complex can be gained from a bird's eye view engraving of the friary St. Anna in the Wilderness by J. Martin Lerch (Schatek 1938:2nd section, 32-38). It is clearly a view of the physical space, but on closer inspection there are unmistakable differences in the form and position of individual structures compared to the ALS-based digital terrain model (DTM). In contrast to modern mapping, the engraving cannot be seen as an exact geometric picture of the physical space, but rather reflects the cognitive space of the artist or his patron.

The central picture of the engraving shows the friary, as restored after the Turkish war of 1683, as part of an idealized landscape encircled by orchards and surrounded by woods, thus visualizing the programmatic term "wilderness" as a place of retreat (Figure 8). The idealized course of the enclosing wall is particularly apparent when compared to the terrain model. The actual course of the wall only bulges out significantly around the prehistoric burial mounds south of the castle, but the engraving shows two symmetric arcs, which together with the hollow of the Arbach valley form the shape of a heart. The heart image is repeated in the middle of the picture in the shape of the meadows surrounding the friary (Schatek 1938:2nd section, 37; Aguinaga 1993:15). It is highly likely that the Sacred Heart motif is in this way being written into the imaginary monastic landscape of the "wilderness." This motif drew on the heart metaphor employed in the New Testament and by Augustine, and was particularly popular during the Counter-Reformation, especially after the introduction of the Sacred Heart holiday in 1672 (Fassbinder 2003:277).

The discrepancy between the "institutional logic" of landscape formation and the actual topography is particularly apparent in the distribution of the hermitages, which in the engraving are distributed relatively evenly around the centrally situated friary, but in the terrain model form a much less regular pattern. These buildings, which included a living space and a chapel, served as individual places of retreat within the wider hermitage, in

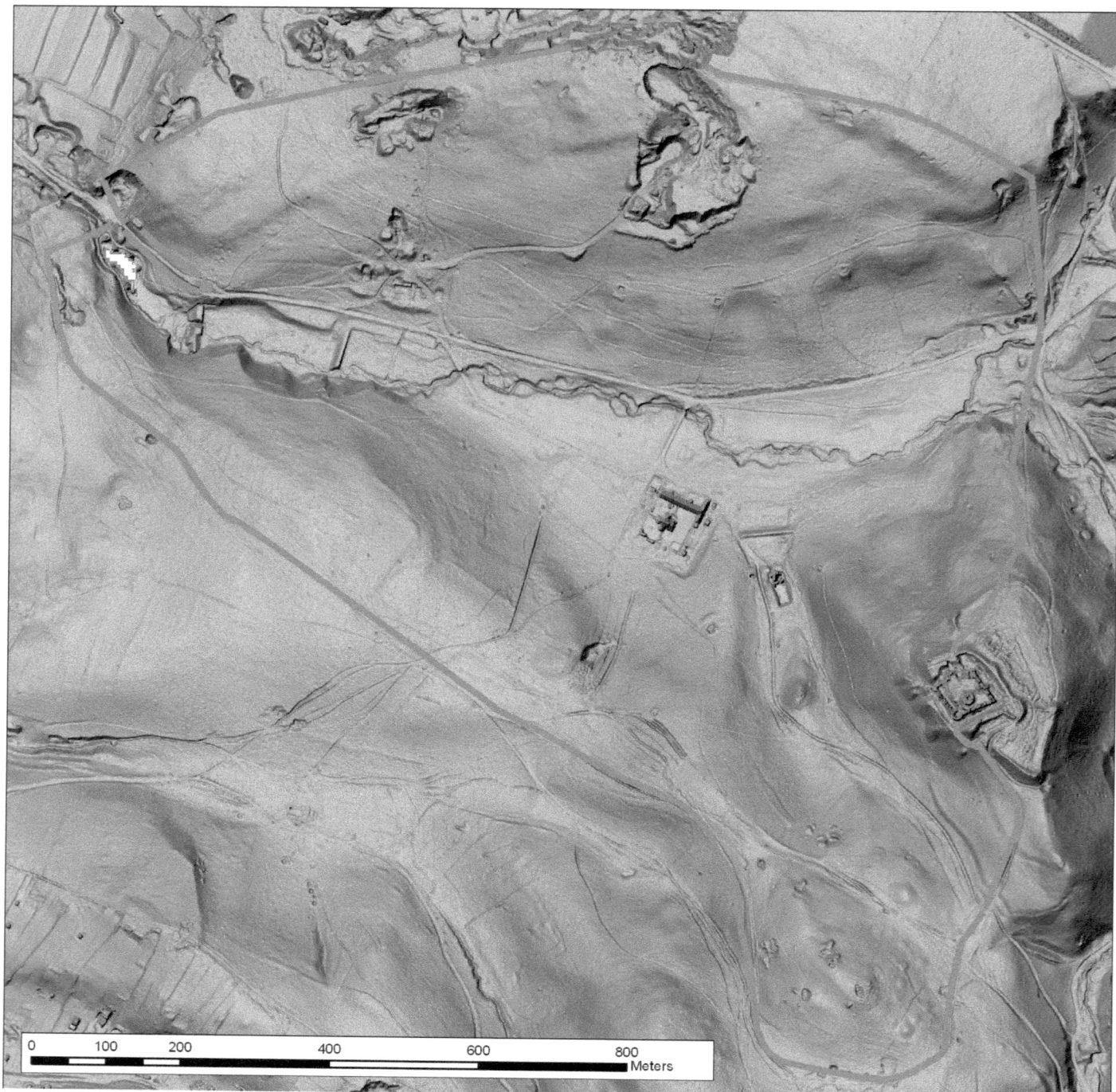

0 100 200 400 600 800
Meters

Figure 9.   *View of the entire friary complex with the course of the wall added. North is up (Image by Michael Doneus, 2011).*

which chosen friars, but also a few highborn laypeople, could pursue meditative acts for a limited period. As in the case of the seven original granges belonging to the Lower Austrian Cistercian monastery at Zwettl, the figure of seven hermitages indicates a further strain of meaning referring to Judeo-Christian number symbolism in the monastic landscape (Weinreb 1978; Meyer and Suntrup 1987:479-566; Predovnik 1998). The comparative analysis of the historic visual source and of a LiDAR-supported terrain model thus makes ideological concepts in the acquisition of space visible and comprehensible.

Interpretation of the Location and of the Course of the Wall

By now it is clear that we are dealing with a landscape that was religiously used and interpreted in the modern period. In this case actions can be seen primarily as value-based, meaning that the decision for a particular action is rational and based on the social situation, but that the most important criterion for a decision is the fulfillment of (religious) values; the consequences of an action are secondary (Esser 2002:226).

This leads us to several pertinent and concrete questions:

- Is a theory of action based upon the Rational-Choice approach applicable in this case, concerning as it does religiously motivated decisions?

- Can we trace the idea of reclusiveness, as transmitted to us by the written sources, with our scientific methods?

- Would we be able to arrive at a similar interpretative explanatory result without written sources?

To answer these questions we have to start with the obvious discrepancy between the actual course of the wall and its portrayal in the engraving by Martin Lerch. Albert Schatek (1938:2.37) pointed out many years ago that the complex's boundary wall was "too much of a heart shape," seeing this as a mistake in the illustration. In fact—as pointed out above—it is

precisely this deviation that reveals the ideological meaning of the course of the wall (the Sacred Heart motif). If this concept really was central, however, then why was the friary complex not actually enclosed by a heart-shaped wall? Figure 9 shows that the wall is only vaguely heart-shaped. The wall does form a point in the west and there is a small indentation on the east side (beside the ruin of Scharfeneck castle), which divides the two "heart chambers," but the indentation does not lie in the middle, but somewhat to the south. The protuberance enclosing the probable Iron Age burial mounds in the southwest corner of the territory is on the other hand very visible. This is a striking deviation from the heart shape, although it would definitely have been avoidable without great difficulty. The presence of this protuberance proves, in fact, that this deviation from a heart shape was deliberate, and that there must instead be another underlying principle behind the course of the wall.

The position of the friary complex and the course of the enclosing wall in its topographical context thus make up the explanandum. The social situation and preference choice can be deduced from the written sources. The friary annals tell us that, after the gift had taken place on the initiative of the Imperial widow Eleonora, the exact boundaries of the area were initially laid out in March 1644 during an inspection by Senior Court Steward (*Obersthofmeister*) Count Friedrich Cavriani,

Figure 10.   *The 4.5-km long enclosing wall still survives to a height of ca. 2 m today (Photo by Michael Doneus, 2011).*

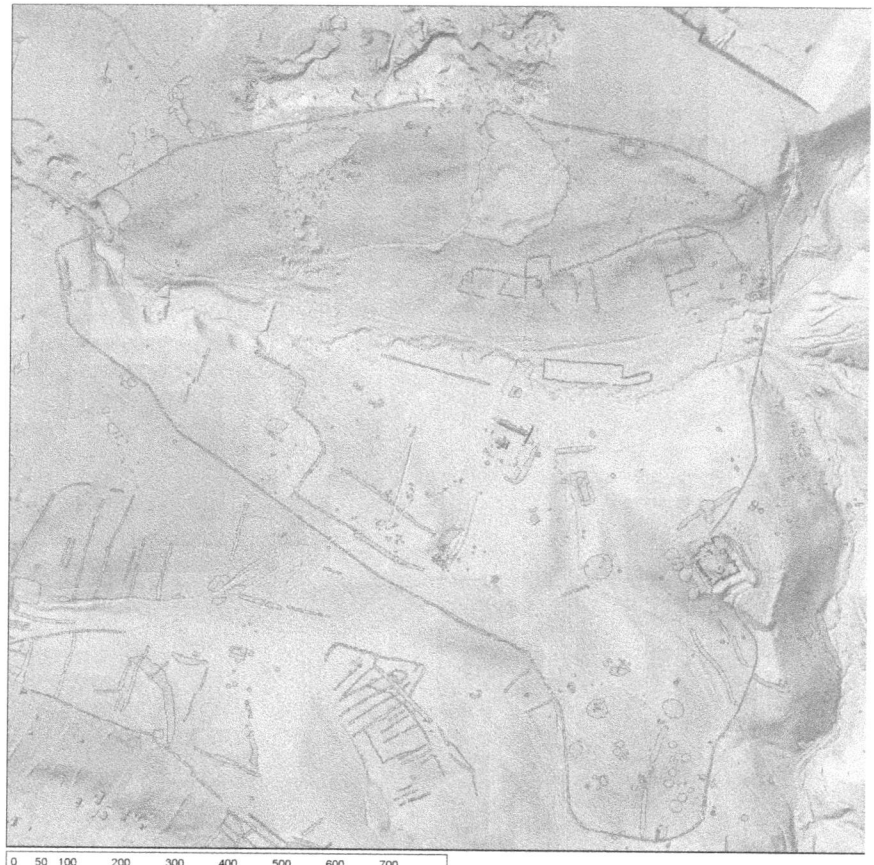

Figure 11. *St. Anna in the Wilderness, cumulative viewshed map (50-m raster width) of the area based on a wide-ranging DTM with raster width of 10 m. North is up (Image by Michael Doneus, 2011).*

Legende

Topo-Prom. 510m

Value

High : 99,988

Low : 0,024

Figure 12. *St. Anna in the Wilderness, topographic prominence map (radius 510 m) based on a wide-ranging DTM with a raster breadth of 10 m. North is up (Image by Michael Doneus, 2011).*

together with the Prior of the Carmelite friary in Vienna and another friar, by means of marks on trees (Schatek 1938:2.16). The erection of the 4.5-km long, ca. 0.5-m wide and typically 2-m high wall (Figure 10) was very expensive and took 118 years.

The sources tell us, therefore, that the course of the wall was fixed during an inspection of the wooded area at a time of year when the vegetation was at a minimum, and that that course was deliberately chosen. The written sources do not reveal which motives were the most decisive on this occasion. One can however refer to the

0 50 100 200 300 400 500 600 700
Meters

Figure 13.   *St. Anna in the Wilderness, cumulative viewshed map, calculated from the seven hermitages with a position height of 1.5 m. Based on an ALS-data-sourced DTM (1-m raster width), target height 1.5 m. North is up (Image by Michael Doneus, 2011).*

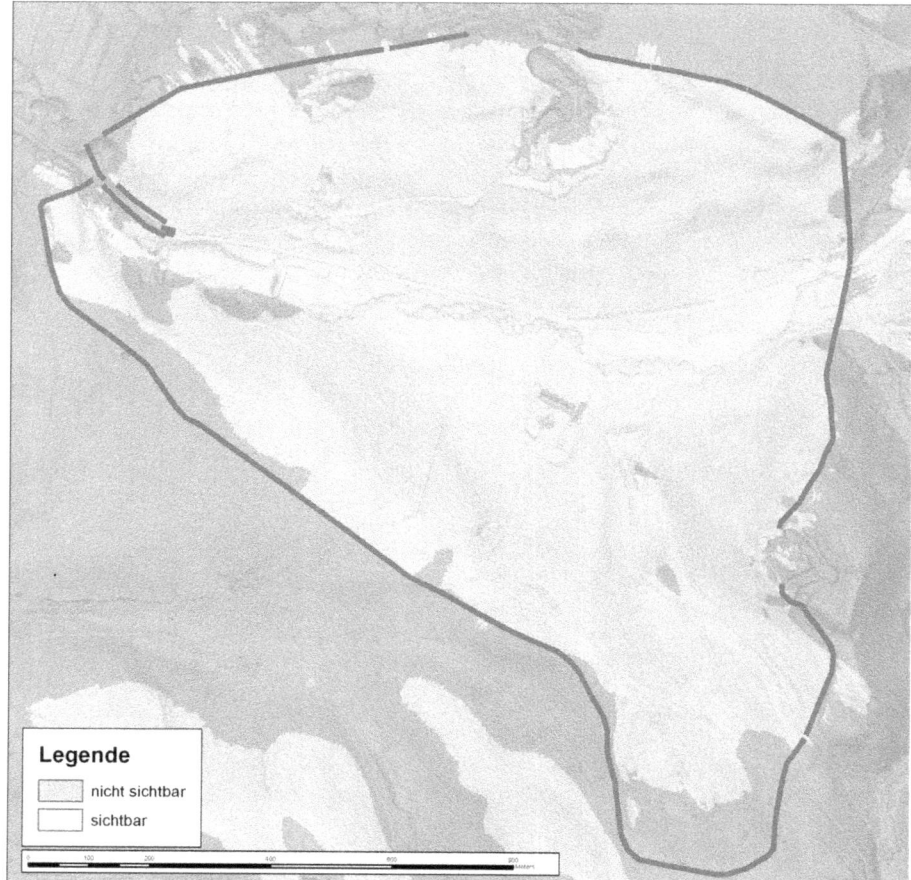

Figure 14.   *St. Anna in the Wilderness, viewshed map calculated from the top of the church tower on the basis of an ALS-data-sourced DTM (2-m raster breadth) and a target height of 1.5 m. The enclosing wall of the friary complex is shown by a red line. North is up (Image by Michael Doneus, 2011).*

(Wheatley and Gillings 2000:11). A total of ca. 10,000 individual viewshed maps were generated in a raster with 50-m intervals, and, not forgetting the earth's curvature, are combined in a total viewshed map. This map shows how many other points of the 50-m raster are visible from every single point of the raster. When a total viewshed map is superimposed on the landscape analyzed (Figure 11), it becomes very clear that the central part of the friary complex possesses very little visibility. The total viewshed of raster elements in the friary area hovers around 100 (that means the friary is visible from around 100 points in the total viewshed map raster). In comparison, the ruined castle is highly visible with values of around 1,600.

Topographic prominence produces similar results. Using the same terrain model employed for the total viewshed map, and on the basis of a 50-m raster, the percentage of the terrain within a 500-m radius below or above every given point was calculated. Deeper lying areas have lower values in this system, while values of more than 80 percent show high and very prominent areas. Scharfeneck castle has high values, for example, with topographic index values of up to 97 percent. The values around the friary are relatively low in comparison (Figure 12).

These two techniques show that the friary complex does indeed lie in a low visibility area. This is not obvious on site because of the heavy forestation. Nevertheless, the idea of seclusion can be modeled and demonstrated in a geographic information system (GIS), thus confirming the historical information. The location of the friary can be judged in this context to be the result of a rational decision within the terms of the expectancy-value theory.

The course of the wall and, in particular, the protuberance around the burial mounds to the southwest have not yet been explained, however. An explanation only emerges when the factor visibility is subjected to further calculations as part of an exploratory data analysis. The

rules of the Carmelite order, which insist on seclusion from worldly things, ideally and in spatial fact. Based on this assumption and on the SEU theory, we can therefore attempt to explain the choice of location from the data available to us. Seclusion can be easily modeled from spatial distance and from the views available. The meaningfulness of visibility to the Carmelites has already been established in the reference to the idea that the seven hermitage units distributed around the friary should be visible from the central complex. The visibility properties of a terrain can be measured through two methods in particular: (1) a total viewshed map (Llobera 2003:33-36), and (2) the calculation of topographic prominence (Llobera 2001).

The total viewshed map was calculated on the basis of a detailed dataset (10-m raster width), which covered the entire Leitha Hills and included a 10-km wide buffer zone. The buffer zone was necessary in order to be able to generate viewshed maps with a maximum radius of 10 km without statistical anomalies at the edges first assertion to be analyzed is that the seven hermitages were located in sight of the friary. This was checked with a cumulative visibility map (Wheatley 1995). The calculations were carried out on the basis of a terrain model derived from ALS-data with a resolution of 2 m. The height of observation and the target height were both fixed at 1.5 m (eye level). Intervisibility can be analyzed in this way: the visibility map shows which areas can be seen from all hermitages. Equally, all hermitages are in their turn visible from those areas. This result would not be applicable in the case of a target height set at ground level (Gillings and Wheatley 2001:32).

The cumulative visibility map can be seen in Figure 13. For reasons of simplicity those areas visible from all seven hermitages are colored dark blue, while the invisible area is grey. The map shows that, alongside a large part of the meadows and of the northern woods, parts of the friary and of the church tower really were visible from all hermitages. Another phenomenon is also apparent; the invisible area matches the course of the wall to a certain extent.

This finding led to further visibility tests. The height of the wall was measured in sections on site and fed into the ALS-data derived terrain model with a 2-m raster width. Ultimately, it was shown that a visibility map with a target height of 1.5 m measured from the top of the friary's church tower reproduced the course of the wall almost exactly (Figure 14). Even the protuberance deviating from the potential heart shape seems explainable, as this section is also part of the area from which the top of the friary's church tower can be seen.

The course of the wall can thus be explained by the desire to be fully isolated from the "surrounding world," a result that fits the written information about the preferences of the Carmelites. How it was possible to demarcate the area visible from the friary so exactly is not entirely understandable from a present-day vantage point. The written sources tell us nothing in this case. The cutting of visibility lanes through the woods around the friary and the staking out of "corners" by which the course of the wall could later be followed is a possibility. Equally possible is a simple rule, which coincides with our observations on site. In this case, the wall would as far as possible not have been built on the hilltops, but instead, as seen from the friary, a certain distance behind them.

Thus it can be shown that a series of decisions preceded the laying-out of the friary and its hermitages, which, in the social context of the Carmelites, must be seen as completely rational. At least two possible locations were available (Walpersdorf in the Traisen Valley and Mannersdorf in the Leitha Hills), whereby the chosen location was evidently the more hidden of the two. Furthermore, the territory of the friary was delineated by a wall, which at the same time enclosed the area from which the friary church would have been visible. Complete visual isolation was guaranteed. The course of the wall thus appears also to have been planned according to rational principles, whereby costs were put up with, which were so high that the erection of the wall took almost one-and-a-half centuries.

The name still attached to the local landscape today, "wilderness," therefore largely concurs with the idea of *eremus*, which lies behind it (Nauroy 2003). The original remoteness from the world, which the "desert fathers" of the 4th and 5th centuries A.D. established, changed with the expansion of the hermitage idea to other parts of the Christianized world. In particular the "wilderness" of wooded areas was employed in adapting the desert concept (Evans 2004:78). This also applies to the countless individual hermitage sites, which emerged in many European regions from the early Middle Ages onwards and which were generally founded in somewhat remote valleys that nevertheless usually had a good water supply and good transport links, and that in many cases became the target of regional and trans-regional pilgrimages (Wand 1993:72-79).

Particularly significant in our case is that, primarily in Great Britain, Carthusian and other monasteries that sought out remote locations were set up by noblemen in areas previously used as hunting parks in the immediate vicinity of their castles (Evans 2004:79). Hunting parks were exclusive places of noble representation and of socially motivated spatial segregation (Creighton 2002:188-193, 2009:122-166; Pluskovski 2002; Beglane 2010) and were therefore highly suitable as a choice of location for orders with an analogous institutional logic. The locations of comparable medieval parks in wet valley meadows beneath a castle can be found in Austria through field names and scattered written sources (Kühtreiber 2004). Such sites are ecologically and topographically comparable with the economic support area of Scharfeneck Castle, which was later altered by the hermitage. Another ideological similarity between the "wilderness" and the (medieval) parks comes to mind, although there is no concrete evidence because of a lack of written sources and archaeological excavations: the taming of the (natural) wilderness through colonization plays a central role in both concepts. The taming of "wild animals" is seen as a task for the nobility, while the re-conversion of the "wilderness" into the "Garden of Eden" is a civilizing achievement of spiritual institutions, both in terms of actual landscape formation and in a figurative sense as "the cultivation of human nature" (Evans 2004:78). For this reason there is a dynamic tension between the aesthetic aims of the order's rules and the structuring of the landscape, which echoes the medieval concept of *locus amoenus*—the idea of a "delightful landscape"—which draws on ideas about paradise (Thoss 1972; Schulze-Belli 2007; Brunner 2000). The wilderness/desert is watered by the Jordan (as the Carmelites called the Arbach), made fruitful by work, and transformed into a new "Garden of Eden" (Evans 2004:79).

In reaching a conclusion a question remains that is particularly relevant to landscape archaeology: in this particular case, would one come to a similar result in terms of interpretive explanation without written sources? The answer is a qualified yes, for even without knowledge of the social context, total viewsheds and topographic prominence would imply that deliberate isolation was involved. The reason for that isolation would however be much more difficult to establish without the information available to us from the written records. Seclusion and not being seen can, to name a few examples, be religiously motivated, result from a need for protection, express a deliberate social distance to the political elites or to subordinates, or be enforced by those in power. The location factor "remoteness" would be recognizable then, but the choice of one of the possible explanations cannot take place on the basis of a topographic GIS analysis itself, but must instead include in the interpretation the available information about the social context.

SUMMARY

Beginning from a critical view of landscape as physical reality and cognitive perception as part of a dynamic relationship between the individual and society, this paper introduces the structural-individualistic approach in sociology. This can help to overcome the significant differences between processual and post-processual landscape archaeology by connecting the macro – and microlevels of social structure and individual people, and, through the technique of interpretive explanation, unite etic and emic interpretation.

The starting point is the ability of humans to act and the duality between the individual and social structure. Social phenomena can thus be traced back to individual actions. The connection between the macro – and the microlevels, that is, between societal conflict and the level on which individuals act, takes place through the description both of resources and of limits, as well as through bridging measures to the individual's preferred behavior. On this basis, it is argued that given the presence of several alternative actions humans make rational decisions, whereby in the method employed here human beings can be understood as rational only in a limited sense. They are not completely informed and evaluate their situation and the framework conditions they encounter according to their social background and maximize their subjective advantage (Subjective Expected Utilities [SEU]). Macrophenomena can be interpretively explained through the aggregation of individual actions in this way.

This system of social explanation was then applied to a typical landscape archaeological situation, the explanation of a religiously motivated location choice. The example showed that Rational-Choice in its SEU-version can be successfully used for questions of landscape archaeology. The choice of location was interpretively explained through the inclusion of bridging measures and perception variables. A combination of etic and emic observation was carried out in a scientific and reproducible way.

In the course of this paper it was shown that even religiously motivated actions can be understood rationally within their own context. Rational thought and action are not necessarily based on the economic maximization of returns. This is shown by the importance that background knowledge has for landscape archaeological analysis. Landscape means something to its inhabitants; how this is to be concretely interpreted can be only deduced from the given context.

ACKNOWLEDGMENTS

This research has been supported by the Austrian Science Fund (FWF) under project no. P18674-G02. The Ludwig Boltzmann Institute for Archaeological Prospection and Virtual Archaeology (archpro. lbg.ac.at) is based on an international cooperation between the Ludwig Boltzmann Gesellschaft, Austria; the University of Vienna, Austria; the Vienna University of Technology, Austria; the Austrian Central Institute for Meteorology and Geodynamic, Austria; the office of the provincial government of Lower Austria; Airborne Technologies, Austria; RGZM-Roman-Germanic Central Museum Mainz, Germany; RAÄ-Swedish National Heritage Board, Sweden; IBM VISTA-University of Birmingham, England; and NIKU-Norwegian Institute for Cultural Heritage Research, Norway.

REFERENCES

AGUINAGA, J.
1993   Die Karmeliteneinsiedelei "St. Anna in der Wüste" zu Mannersdorf am Leithagebirge (1644-1783) [The Carmelite Hermitage "St. Anna in the Wilderness" at Mannersdorf am Leithagebirge (1644-1783)]. Master's thesis, Department for Catholic and Prostestant Theology, University of Vienna, Vienna, Austria

ANIEL, JEAN-PIERRE
1983   *Les maisons des Chartreux. Des origines à la chartreuse de Pavie* [*The Cartusian Houses. From the Origins up to the Charterhouse of Pavia*]. Bibliothèque de la S.F.A. 16, Droz, Geneva, Switzerland.

BARRETT, JOHN C.
2000   A Thesis on Agency. In *Agency in Archaeology*, Marcia-Anne Dobres and John E. Robb, editors, pp. 61-68. Routledge, London, England.

BEGLANE, FIONA
2010   Deer and Identity in Medieval Ireland. In *Bestial Mirrors. Using Animals to Construct Human Identity in Medieval Europe*, Aleksander Pluskowski, Günther K. Kunst, Matthias Kucera, Manfred Bietak, and Irmgard Hein, editors, pp. 77-84. Vienna Institute for Archaeological Science, Vienna, Austria.

BELL, T., AND GARY LOCK
2000   Topographic and Cultural Influences on Walking the Ridgeway in Later Prehistoric Times. In *Beyond the Map*, Gary Lock, editor, pp. 85-100. IOS Press [u.a.], Amsterdam, the Netherlands.

BERGLUND, JOEL
2010   Did the Medieval Norse Society in Greenland Really Fail? In *Questioning Collapse*, Patricia A. McAnany and Norman Yoffee, editors, pp. 45-70. Cambridge University Press, Cambridge, England.

BORSDORF, AXEL
2002   Die Mensch-Umwelt-Beziehung—ein zentrales Forschungsthema der Geographie[The Relationship between Human and Environment—A Central Research Topic of Geography]. In *Historische Humanökologie*, Verena Winiwarter and Harald Wilfing, editors, pp. 27-58. Facultas-Verlag, Vienna, Austria.

BRATHER, SEBASTIAN
2006   Entwicklungen der Siedlungsarchäologie. Auf dem Weg zu einer umfassenden Umwelt – und Landschaftsarchäologie? [Developments in Settlement Archaeology. Towards a Comprehensive Environmental and Landscape Archaeology?]. *Siedlungsforschung. Schwerpunktthema: Historische Kulturlandschaftsforschung* 24:51-97.

BRUNNER, K.
2000   Das Paradies ist ein Baumgarten [Paradise is an Orchard]. In *Kontraste im Alltag des Mittelalters. Forschungen des Instituts für Realienkunde des Mittelalters und der frühen Neuzeit*, Gerhard Jaritz, editor, pp. 25-34. Verlag der Österreichischen Akademie der Wissenschaften, Vienna, Austria.

CHADWICK, ADRIAN M.
2004   "Geographies of Sentience"—An Introduction to Space, Place and Time. In *Stories from the Landscape: Archaeologies of Inhabitation*, Adrian M. Chadwick, editor, pp. 1-31. Archaeopress, Oxford, England.

CLARK, JOHN E.
2000   Towards a Better Explanation of Hereditary Inequality: A Critical Assessment of Natural and Historic Human Agents. In *Agency in Archaeology*, Marcia-Anne Dobres and John E. Robb, editors, pp. 92-112. Routledge, London, England.

COLEMAN, JAMES S.

2010   *Grundlagen der Sozialtheorie. Band 1: Handlungen und Handlungssysteme* [*The Foundations of Social Theory. Volume 1: Action and Systems of Action*]. Scientia nova Vol. 1, Oldenbourg, Munich, Germany.

CONOLLY, JAMES, AND MARK LAKE

2006   *Geographical Information Systems in Archaeology.* Cambridge Manuals in Archaeology, Cambridge University Press, Cambridge, England.

COWGILL, GEORGE L.

2000   "Rationality" and Contexts in Agency. In *Agency in Archaeology*, Marcia-Anne Dobres and John E. Robb, editors, pp. 51-60. Routledge, London, England.

CREIGHTON, OLIVER H.

2002   *Castles and Landscapes.* Continuum, London, England.

2009   *Designs upon the Land. Elite Landscapes of the Middle Ages.* Boydell Press, Woodbridge, England.

CSÁKY, MORITZ

2004   Die Mehrdeutigkeit von Gedächtnis und Erinnerung. Ein kritischer Beitrag zur historischen Gedächtnisforschung [The Ambiguity of Memory and Recollection. A Critical Contribution to Historical Memory Research]. Digitales Handbuch zur Geschichte und Kultur Russlands und Osteuropas. Virtuelle Fachbibliothek Osteuropa <http://epub.ub.uni-muenchen.de/603/1/csaky-gedaechtnis.pdf>. Accessed 22 July 2012.

DIEKMANN, ANDREAS, AND THOMAS VOSS

2004   Die Theorie rationalen Handelns. Stand und Perspektiven [The Theory of Rational Action. The Present Situation and Perspectives]. In *Rational-Choice-Theorie in den Sozialwissenschaften*, Andreas Diekmann and Thomas Voss, editors, pp. 13-29. Oldenbourg, Munich, Germany.

DOBRES, MARCIA-ANNE, AND JOHN E. ROBB (EDITORS)

2000   *Agency in Archaeology.* Routledge, London, England.

DONEUS, MICHAEL, CHRISTIAN BRIESE, AND THOMAS KÜHTREIBER

2008   Flugzeuggetragenes Laserscanning als Werkzeug der archäologischen Kulturlandschaftsforschung. Das Fallbeispiel "Wüste" bei Mannersdorf am Leithagebirge, Niederösterreich [Airborne Laser Scanning as a Tool in the Archeological Research of Cultural Landscapes. The Example "Wilderness" near Mannersdorf am Leithagebirge, Lower Austria]. *Archäologisches Korrespondenzblatt* 38:137-156.

ESSER, HARTMUT

1999   *Soziologie. Allgemeine Grundlagen* [*Sociology. The Basics*]. Campus-Verlag, Frankfurt, Germany.

2001   *Sinn und Kultur* [*Consciousness and Culture*]. Soziologie: Spezielle Grundlagen Vol. 6, Campus-Verlag, Frankfurt, Germany.

2002   *Situationslogik und Handeln* [*Situational Logic and Activity*]. Soziologie: Spezielle Grundlagen Vol. 1, Campus-Verlag, Frankfurt, Germany.

EVANS, HELEN

2004   Who's Afraid of the Big Bad Woods? Forest Wilderness in the Middle Ages. In *Stories from the Landscape: Archaeologies of Inhabitation*, Adrian M. Chadwick, editor, pp. 73-86. Archaeopress, Oxford, England.

EXON, SALLY, VINCENT GAFFNEY, ANN WOODWARD, AND RON YORSTON

2000   *Stonehenge Landscapes. Journeys through Real-and-Imagined Worlds.* Archaeopress, Oxford, England.

FASSBINDER, STEFAN

2003   *Wallfahrt, Andacht und Magie. Religiöse Anhänger und Medaillen; Beiträge zur neuzeitlichen Frömmigkeitsgeschichte Südwestdeutschlands aus archäologischer Sicht* [*Pilgrimage, Devotion, and Magic. Religious Pendants and Medallions; Archaeological Contributions to the Modern Period History of Piety in Southwestern Germany*]. Zeitschrift für Archäologie des Mittelalters, Beiheft 18, Habelt, Bonn, Germany.

GILLINGS, MARK

1997   Not Drowning but Waving? The Tisza Flood-Plain Revisited. In *Archaeological Applications of GIS*, Ian Johnson and MacLaren North, editors (CD-ROM). University of Sydney, Sydney, Australia.

GILLINGS, MARK, AND DAVID WHEATLEY

2001   Seeing is Not Believing. In *On the Good Use of Geographic Information Systems in Archaeological Landscape Studies*, Bozidar Slapsak, editor, pp. 25-36. Office for Official Publications of the European Communities, Luxembourg.

GOJDA, MARTIN

2001   Archaeology and Landscape Studies in Europe: Approaches and Concepts. In *One Land, Many Landscapes*, Timothy Darvill and Martin Gojda, editors, pp. 9-18. Archaeopress, Oxford, England.

GRAMSCH, ALEXANDER

1996   Landscape Archaeology: Of Making and Seeing. *Journal of European Archaeology* 4:19-38.

HANSEN, KLAUS P.
2009   Kultur und Kollektiv: Eine essayistische Heuristik für Archäologen [Culture and the Collective. Essayistic Heuristics for Archaeologists]. In *Kulturraum und Territorialität*, Dirk Krausse and Oliver Nakoinz, editors, pp. 17-26. Leidorf, Rahden/Westf, Germany.

HARTMANN, NICOLAI
1980   *Philosophie der Natur. Abriß der speziellen Kategorienlehre* [Philosophy of Nature. An Outline of Categorialism]. de Gruyter, Berlin, Germany.

HINZ, MARTIN
2008   Rezension. Knut Petzold, Soziologische Theorien in der Archäologie. Konzepte, Probleme, Möglichkeiten (Saarbrücken 2007) [Review. Knut Petzold, Sociological Theories in Archaeology. Concepts, Problems, Possibilities (Saarbrücken 2007)]. *Rundbrief Arbeitsgemeinschaft TheorieArch* 7:33-39.

HODDER, IAN
2000   Agency and Individuals in Long-Term Processes. In *Agency in Archaeology*, Marcia-Anne Dobres and John E. Robb, editors, pp. 21-33. Routledge, London, England.

HODDER, IAN, AND SCOTT HUTSON
2008   *Reading the Past. Current Approaches to Interpretation in Archaeology.* Cambridge University Press, England.

JOHNSON, MATTHEW
2000   Self-Made Men and the Staging of Agency. In *Agency in Archaeology*, Marcia-Anne Dobres and John E. Robb, editors, pp. 213-231. Routledge, London, England.

KÜHTREIBER, THOMAS
2004   Wirtschaft im Schatten der Burg. Zur Bedeutung herrschaftlicher Strukturen im unmittelbaren topographischen Kontext mittelalterlicher Burgen [Economic Activity in the Shadow of the Castle. The Importance of Manorial Structures in the Immediate Topographic Context of Medieval Castles]. *Chateau Gillard* 21:163-177.

KUNZ, VOLKER
2004   *Rational Choice.* Campus-Einführungen, Campus-Verlag, Frankfurt, Germany.

LAMPEL, JOSEF
1899   Erörterungen und Materialien zur Geschichte der Leithagrenze [Questions and Materials in the History of the Leitha Border]. *Blätter des Vereins für Landeskunde von Niederösterreich* 33.

LAURENT, JEAN-PIERRE (EDITOR)
1984   *Les Chartreux, le désert et le monde (1084-1984): neuvième centenaire de la fondation de la Grande Chartreuse* [The Carthusians, the Desert, and the World (1084-1984): 900 Year Anniversary of the Founding of the Grand Chartreuse]. Exposition réalisée au Musée Dauphinois, Musée Dauphinois, Grenoble, France.

LINDENBERG, SIEGWART
1985   An Assessment of the New Political Economy: Its Potential for the Social Sciences and for Sociology in Particular. *Sociological Theory* 3:99-114.

1996   Die Relevanz theoriereicher Brückenannahmen [The Relevance of Theory-Intensive Bridging]. *Kölner Zeitschrift für Soziologie und Sozialpsychologie* 48:126-140.

LLOBERA, MARCOS
2001   Building Past Landscape Perception with GIS: Understanding Topographic Prominence. *Journal of Archaeological Science* 28:1005-1014.

2003   Extending GIS Based Analysis: The Concept of Visualscape. *International Journal of Geographic Information Science* 17:25-49.

LÖW, MARTINA
2001   *Raumsoziologie* [The Sociology of Space]. Suhrkamp, Frankfurt, Germany.

LÜNING, JENS
1997   Landschaftsarchäologie in Deutschland—Ein Programm [Landscape Archaeology in Germany—A Program]. *Archäologisches Nachrichtenblatt* 2:277-285.

MAYER, A.
1900   Die Karmeliter-Eremie St. Anna in der Wüste [The Carmelite Hermitage St. Anna in the Wilderness]. *Blätter des Vereines für Landeskunde von Niederösterreich* XXXIV:120-137.

MCCLELLAND, DAVID C.
1967   *The Achieving Society.* Free Press, New York, NY.

MEIER, THOMAS
2009   Umweltarchäologie—Landschaftsarchäologie [Environmental Archaeology—Landscape Archaeology]. In *Historia archaeologica. Festschrift für Heiko Steuer zum 70.Geburtstag*, S. Brather, D. Geuenich, and C. Huth, editors, pp. 697-734. Reallexikon der Germanischen Altertumskunde-Ergänzungsband 70, Walter de Gruyter, Berlin, Germany.

MEIER, THOMAS (EDITOR)
2006   *Landscape Ideologies.* Archaeolingua—Series Minor 22. Archaeolingua Alapítvány, Budapest, Hungary.

MELZER, GUSTAV
1980   Verzeichnis der archäologischen Fundstellen
        in Au am Leithaberge, Hof am Leithaberge,
        Mannersdorf am Leithagebirge und Sommerein
        [Directory of Archeological Sites in Au am
        Leithaberge, Hof am Leithaberge, Mannersdorf
        am Leithagebirge, and Sommerein]. In *Katalog
        des Museums Mannersdorf*, Kultur – und
        Museumsverein Mannersdorf am Leithagebirge,
        editor, pp. 55-99. Museum Mannersdorf am
        Leithagebirge, Austria.

MEYER, HEINZ, AND RUDOLF SUNTRUP
1987   *Lexikon der mittelalterlichen Zahlenbedeutungen
        [Lexicon of the Symbolism of Medieval Numbers]*.
        Münstersche Mittelalter-Schriften 56, Wihlem
        Fink Verlag, Munich, Germany.

MOCHTY, CHRISTINA
1998   Die Marktgemeinde Hof am Leithagebirge von
        ihren Anfängen bis 1600 [The Township Hof am
        Leithagebirge from its Beginnings until 1600].
        In *Die Marktgemeinde Hof am Leithagebirge
        im Wandel der Zeit*, C. Mochty and E. Bezemek,
        editors, pp. 39-57. Marktgemeinde Hof am
        Leithagebirge, Austria.

NAUROY, GÉRARD
2003   *Le désert, un espace paradoxal. Actes du colloque
        de l'Université de Metz, 13-15 septembre 2001
        [The Desert, a Paradoxical Place. Proceedings of
        the Symposium at the University of Metz, 13-15
        September 2001]*. Recherches en littérature et
        spiritualité vol. 2. Lang, Bern, Switzerland.

OGBURN, DENNIS E.
2006   Assessing the Level of Visibility of Cultural
        Objects in Past Landscapes. *Journal of
        Archaeological Science* 33:405-413.

OPP, KARL-DIETER
2004   Die Theorie rationalen Handelns im Vergleich
        mit alternativen Theorien Soziologie [The Theory
        of Rational Action in Comparison to Other
        Theories]. In *Paradigmen der akteurszentrierten
        Soziologie*, Manfred Gabriel, editor, pp. 43-68.
        VS Verlag für Sozialwissenschaft, Wiesbaden,
        Germany.

PETZOLD, KNUT
2007   *Soziologische Theorien in der Archäologie.
        Konzepte, Probleme, Möglichkeiten [Sociological
        Theories in Archaeology. Concepts, Problems,
        Possibilities]*. Univ., Diplomarbeit—Leipzig, 2005.
        VDM-Verlag Müller, Saarbrücken, Germany.

2009   Rational Choice in der Archäologie: Die "harte"
        Version, die "weiche" Version und das Problem
        der Brückenannahmen. Erwiderung auf eine
        Rezension von Martin Hinz im Rundbrief der
        Arbeitsgemeinschaft Theorie in der Archäologie
        [Rational-Choice in Archaeology: The "Hard"
        Version, the "Soft" Version, and the Problem of
        Bridging. Answer to a Review by Martin Hinz in
        the Newsletter of the Working Group "Theory
        in Archaeology"]. *Rundbrief Arbeitsgemeinschaft
        TheorieArch* 8:21-32.

PLUSKOVSKI, ALEKSANDER G.
2002   Predators in Robes: Materialising and Mystifying
        Hunting, Predation and Seclusion in the
        Northern European Medieval Landscape. In
        *Centre—Region—Periphery. Medieval Europe
        2002*, Guido Helming, Barbara Scholkmann, and
        Matthias Untermann, editors, pp. 236-242. folio-
        Verlag Dr. G. Wesselkamp, Hertingen, Germany.

POPPER, KARL R.
2003   *Die offene Gesellschaft und ihre Feinde. Bd. 2:
        Falsche Propheten. Hegel, Marx und die Folgen
        [The Open Society and its Enemies. Vol. 2: False
        Prophets Hegel, Marx, and the Consequences]*.
        Gesammelte Werke, Mohr Siebeck, Tübingen,
        Germany.

PREDOVNIK, K.
1998   Die Kartause Seitz. Natürliche und ideologische
        Momente in der Genese einer Kulturlandschaft
        [The Charterhouse at Seitz. Natural and
        Ideological Aspects of the Genesis of a
        Cultural Landscape]. In *Mensch und Natur im
        mittelalterlichen Europa*, Konrad Spindler, editor,
        pp. 261-280. Wieser, Klagenfurt, Austria.

PREISENDÖRFER, PETER
2004   Anwendungen der Rational-Choice-Theorie
        in der Umweltforschung [The Uses of
        Rational-Choice-Theory in Environmental
        Research]. In *Rational-Choice-Theorie in den
        Sozialwissenschaften*, Andreas Diekmann and
        Thomas Voss, editors, pp. 271-288. Oldenbourg,
        Munich, Germany.

RÖSSLER, MARTIN
1999   *Wirtschaftsethnologie. Eine Einführung
        [Economic Ethnology. An Introduction]*. Second,
        expanded edition. Dietrich Reimer Verlag, Berlin,
        Germany.

SCHADE, CHRISTOPH C.J.

2000   Landschaftsarchäologie—eine inhaltliche Begriffsbestimmung [Landscape Archaeology—a Textual Definition]. In *Studien zur Siedlungsarchäologie II*, Seminar für Vor – und Frühgeschichte Frankfurt, editor, pp. 135-225. Habelt, Bonn, Germany.

SCHATEK, ALBERT

1938   *Führer durch die Wüste der Karmeliten bei Mannersdorf am Leithagebirge [Guide to the Wilderness of the Carmelites near Mannersdorf am Leithagebirge]*. Vienna, Austria.

SCHULZE-BELLI, P.

2007   From the Garden of Eden to the Locus Amoenus of Medieval Visionaries. In *Fauna and Flora in the Middle Ages*, S. Hartmann, editor, pp. 209-224. Peter Lang Verlag, Frankfurt, Germany.

STARZER, ALBERT

1900   Mannersdorf am Leithagebirge und Umgebung [Mannersdorf am Leithagebirge and its Surroundings]. Offprint from *Blätter für Landeskunde von Niederösterreich* Ser. NF, vol. 34:37-83. Vienna, Austria.

THOMAS, JULIAN

1993   The Politics of Vision and the Archaeologies of Landscape. In *Landscape*, Barbara Bender, editor, pp. 19-48. Berg, Oxford, England.

THOMPSON, MICHAEL, RICHARD J. ELLIS, AND AARON B. WILDAVSKY

1990   *Cultural Theory, Political Cultures*. Westview Press, Boulder, CO.

THOSS, D.

1972   Studien zum locus amoenus im Mittelalter [Studies in the Locus Amoenus in the Medieval Period]. *Wiener Romanistische Arbeiten* 10.

TREIBEL, ANNETTE

2006   *Einführung in soziologische Theorien der Gegenwart [Introduction to Contemporary Sociological Theory]*. VS Verlag für Sozialwissenschaften—GWV Fachverlage GmbH Wiesbaden, Wiesbaden, Germany.

VAN LEUSEN, MARTIJN

1999   Viewshed and Cost Surface Analysis Using GIS (Cartographic Modelling in a Cell-Based GIS II). In *New Techniques for Old Times, CAA 98*, Juan A. Barceló, Ivan Briz, and Assumpció Vila, editors, pp. 215-223. Archaeopress, Oxford, England.

WAND, NORBERT

1993   *Mittelalterliche Einsiedeleien, Quellheiligtümer und Wallfahrtsstätten im Odenwald [Medieval Hermitages, Holy Sites at Springs and Pilgrimages in the Odin Forest]*. Verlag Laurissa, Heppenheim, Germany.

WEBER, MAX

1972   *Wirtschaft und Gesellschaft. Grundriss der verstehenden Soziologie [Economy and Society. An Outline of Interpretive Sociology]*. Hauptwerke der großen Denker, Mohr-Siebeck, Tübingen, Germany.

WEINREB, FRIEDRICH

1978   *Zahl Zeichen Wort. Das symbolische Universum der Bibelsprache [Number, Symbol, Word. The Symbolic Universe of Bible Language]*. Rowohlt, Reinbek, Germany.

WERLEN, BENNO

2010   *Orte der Geographie [The Sites of Geography]*. Gesellschaftliche Räumlichkeit 1. Steiner, Stuttgart, Germany.

WHEATLEY, DAVID

1995   Cumulative Viewshed Analysis: A GIS-Based Method for Investigating Intervisibility, and its Archaeological Application. In *Archaeology and Geographical Information Systems: A European Perspective*, Gary Lock and Zoran Stančič, editors, pp. 171-185. Taylor and Francis, London, England.

WHEATLEY, DAVID, AND MARK GILLINGS

2000   Vision, Perception and GIS: Developing Enriched Approaches to the Study of Archaeological Visibility. In *Beyond the Map*, Gary Lock, editor, pp. 1-27. IOS Press [u.a.], Amsterdam, the Netherlands.

2002   *Spatial Technology and Archaeology. The Archaeological Applications of GIS*. Taylor & Francis, London, England.

WINIWARTER, VERENA, AND MARTIN KNOLL

2007   *Umweltgeschichte. Eine Einführung [Environmental History. An Introduction]*. UTB Geschichte, Naturwissenschaften 2521, Böhlau, Cologne, Germany.

ZADNIKAR, MARIJAN

1983   Die frühe Baukunst der Kartäuser [The Early Architecture of the Carthusians]. In *Die Kartäuser. Orden der schweigenden Mönche*, Marijan Zadnikar, editor, pp. 51-138. Wienand Verlag, Cologne, Germany.

ZIMMERMANN, ANDREAS

2002   Landschaftsarchäologie I. Die Bandkeramik auf
        der Aldenhovener Platte [Landscape Archaeology.
        Linear Ceramics from the Aldenhoven Ledge].
        Berichte der Römisch-Germanischen Kommission
        83:17-38.

ZIMMERMANN, ANDREAS, JÜRGEN RICHTER, THOMAS FRANK,
AND KARL P. WENDT

2004   Landschaftsarchäologie II. Überlegungen
        zu Prinzipien einer Landschaftsarchäologie
        [Landscape Archaeology. Thoughts about the
        Principles of Landscape Archaeology]. *Berichte
        der Römisch-Germanischen Kommission* 85:37-95.

///

Michael Doneus
Institut für Ur- und Frühgeschichte
Universität Wien
Franz Klein Gasse 1
A-1190 Wien
Austria

Thomas Kühtreiber
Institut für Realienkunde des Mittelalters
    und der Frühen Neuzeit
Körnermarkt 13
A-3500 Krems an der Donau
Austria

PAUL MITCHELL

Vienna, The Architecture of Absolutism

ABSTRACT

The architecture and archaeology of the 16th and 17th centuries in Vienna can be understood through four related phenomena connected to the rise of the absolutist system. In the face of the Ottoman threat, fortifications based on the bastion system (parts of which have been excavated in recent years) were built in several phases with the help of Italian specialists. The Royal, later Imperial castle (Hofburg), currently the subject of a significant research project, expanded to become a heterogeneous collection of buildings and open spaces accessed by walkways and imposing entrances. Other residences were constructed in the city's outskirts. The rise of the court meant a migration of nobles to Vienna, leading to the domination of the urban landscape by aristocratic houses. In the 17th century, the Counter-Reformation prompted a wave of new religious buildings. The 1848 revolution marked the beginning of the end of absolutism.

INTRODUCTION

Vienna is one of central Europe's great cities. It lies on the right bank of the river Danube, not far from a small river of the same name. In the Middle Ages the town prospered from a privileged position in the Danube trade and from the wine industry. By 1520 the city had a population of around 30,000. This increased to an estimated 110,000 in 1710 (Weigl 2003:110). At that time city center and suburbs covered an area of more than 30 km² (more than 12 square miles).

Archaeologists in Vienna have by and large only recently begun to treat post-medieval remains with the attention they deserve. There have been large-scale excavations and a range of smaller projects, most of them under the aegis of the Vienna urban archaeology unit, some by the central government. There have also been several dozen surveys of standing buildings (structural archaeology), often to provide information as a basis for decisions by the Department of Monuments.[1] These have analyzed the medieval and post-medieval histories of houses and palaces, churches, and imperial, local government, and industrial buildings. Dendrochronology, which has become fully operational in Austria in the last decade, has played an important role. While most of these projects have been connected to an analysis of the written record as a matter of course, there have been as yet few attempts to discuss themes by drawing on material from across several sites.

Absolutism

Between the 16th and the early 18th centuries Vienna—a significant, but not necessarily very unusual medieval town—was transformed into the center of a multilingual dynastic empire. This was the age of the rise and flowering of "absolutism," taken here as a system of government centering on the supreme rule of the monarch, in which representative institutions were marginalized and other feudal formations—nobility, the church—survived in a dependant role and were accompanied by new forces such as a bureaucracy and a standing army (Anderson 1979; Vocelka 2010:175-180). In historical writing about Austria the term "absolutism" is often used exclusively for the period after the Habsburgs' victory over the Bohemian Protestants (Battle of the White Mountain, 1620), during which the nobility's autonomy in the western part of the empire was broken. There are however important reasons—at least in Vienna—for beginning the story in the 16th century, a period that can be labeled "early absolutism" (Anderson 1979:48; Perger 1983:27); notably the abolition of the city's medieval constitution (1522-1526) and the construction of new fortifications (from 1530 onwards).

The first development began in 1522 as Ferdinand I (1503-1564), recently arrived from the Netherlands to take over the stewardship of Habsburg Austria, summoned the mayor of Vienna and several other city councilors to his castle at Wiener Neustadt, south of Vienna. Together with two nobles, they were put to death after a show trial for trying to assert their rights in Lower Austria following the death of Emperor Maximilian I (Ferdinand I's grandfather) in 1519. The "blood court" (*Blutgericht*) of Wiener Neustadt was followed in March 1526 by the unilateral abolition of Vienna's medieval constitution. In the new constitution the governing "inner council" was no longer allowed to include artisans and was drawn from an oligarchy of 100 men, the mayor became a figurehead of the attorney-general (*Stadtanwalt*), and the emperor selected or approved all office-holders (Pauser 2003). This was a watershed, a clear statement of intent by Ferdinand who thereafter avoided the troubled relations of his predecessors with the town council, which had peaked in 1462 as the Viennese besieged the Imperial residence (the so-called Hofburg).

The second factor, part of what has been called the "military revolution" of the 16th century (Downing 1992),

Figure 1.   *Symbolic reconstruction of the Braun Bastion, Theodor-Herzl-Platz, Vienna (Photo by author, 2009).*

began for Austria with the arrival of the Ottoman army in central Europe. After wiping out a large part of the Hungarian aristocracy at the battle of Mohács in 1526, the Turks besieged Vienna for several weeks in 1529. They retreated for logistical reasons on that occasion, but warfare broke out repeatedly until after 1683, the year in which an Ottoman army besieged Vienna for a second time and was defeated after a bloody battle in the city's suburbs. Vienna was therefore not simply the main Habsburg residence in this period, but also became a crucial and re-fortified stronghold not far from an unruly border. The Habsburg military was enlarged considerably: by the late 16th century the dynasty maintained a network of more than 120 fortresses with a permanent garrison of more than 20,000 men along the Ottoman (Hungarian-Croatian) border (Pálffy 2009). The Turkish wars demanded a bureaucracy and military whose interests could, when necessary, override those of the noble "estates."

Ferdinand became Bohemian, Hungarian, and German King in 1526-1531 and Holy Roman Emperor after the abdication of his brother (Charles V) in 1556. A range of new government institutions based in Vienna, the most important of which was the "court war council" (*Hofkriegsrat*) of 1556, were set up during his reign and formed a crucial element of Habsburg power (Anderson 1979:304).

Architecture

The architecture of absolutism has two meanings in the context of this essay: on the one hand it is the processes and institutions connected with the rise of absolutism in Vienna/Austria and on the other hand it is their monumental and archaeological remains. The absolutist architecture of Vienna can be understood through four related phenomena:

· From 1530 until the 1560s the transformation of the city into a modern and powerful fortress. Among other relevant projects, the Vienna urban archaeology unit has carried out four major excavations of the town defenses in recent years (Krause, Reichhalter, Gaisbauer et al. 2009).

· Throughout the period the increased importance of the court (*Hof*) as the center of political life and the source of privilege as reflected in the expansion of the Hofburg and the construction of other Imperial palaces in the immediate vicinity of Vienna. Recent survey work and/or archaeological excavations have taken place in the Hofburg, at the hunting castle of Kaiserebersdorf, and at the garden palace at Vienna Augarten.

- Prompted by the rise of the court, the increasing importance to the nobility of maintaining a suitable residence in the city, launching a migratory movement that transformed the old burgher town. This development, which began in the Middle Ages, escalated in the 16th century, but was particularly associated with the 17th century, as Habsburg loyalist families arrived from other parts of the empire, and reached a peak around 1700 with many splendid and extensive city and garden palaces. Two of these, the Liechtenstein city palace and the city palace of Prince Eugene, have recently seen substantial work.

- From the early 17th century onwards the victorious Counter-Reformation, which lead not only to the expulsion of the Viennese Protestants in 1627, but also to a wave of monastic reconstruction and new foundations, redrawing the religious and physical map of the city. Archaeological projects have as yet been small at such sites or have tended to concentrate on medieval phases.

Archaeology is not essential to tell the story of the city's history in the earlier part of the absolutist age, but it is playing an important role in recovering the submerged shape of the city in that period. The focus of the research reported here is architectural; portable antiquities, including those artifacts that are the most common archaeological finds, are not dealt with in this article.

THE FORTRESS

The Turkish siege of Vienna in 1529 led to the burning of many buildings in the suburbs and the surrounding villages, as the analysis of standing buildings has repeatedly shown (Buchinger, Legen et al. 2008). The continuing threat afterwards meant that the city's fortifications, which up to that point were still largely of mid-13th-century origin, had to be improved (Krause, Reichhalter, Gaisbauer et al. 2009). As an immediate measure several bastions and artillery platforms were thrown up around the walls. A fragment of one of the early bastions (the Castle Bastion) was recently rediscovered in a cellar near the Hofburg (Mitchell 2010a). The bastion took the form of four sides of a hexagon, open to the northeast, and was without the flankers (recessed artillery emplacements) typical of later structures in Renaissance Vienna.

A more systematic circuit was erected from the 1540s onwards (Krause, Reichhalter, Gaisbauer et al. 2009). Massive arrowhead-shaped bastions and ramparts of several meters width, founded on stone and fronted by a brick scarp, were placed immediately before the medieval walls. As recent archaeology has shown, deep buttresses reached into the interior of the earthen mounds to anchor the outer walls. The mostly dry ditch in front of the walls was up to 80 m (ca. 262 ft.) wide and was preceded by a glacis, an open area several hundred yards wide to allow artillery a clear field of fire. Several armory buildings were also constructed in different parts of town in this period, two of which have been analyzed (Buchinger, Günther, et al. 2005; Mader 2008; Novak 2001). The city council armory was built in the heart of the town from 1562 to 1564. Now the headquarters of the Fire Department, the building's original cellars include a well, the bottom part of which is entirely of curved, pointed stone. Similar wells were apparently included in every bastion, as can be seen in the surviving part of the Braun Bastion today (Figure 1). In 2004 a well dating to 1672/1675 and entirely built of such masonry was rediscovered at the Imperial Stables (Stallburg, see below). In Vienna, wells are typically 15-16 m (ca. 50-52 ft.) deep.

The 16th-century urban fortifications were in no small part the work of Italian engineers/architects, who not only drew up the plans, but often supervised the construction, bringing with them from Northern Italy teams (families) of stone masons, bricklayers, and other artisans. Italian brick makers set up kilns in the new city ditch, mining the blue-gray clays and producing bricks immediately in front of the defenses. The Italian "fortification bricks" were 30-32 cm (ca. 12-13 in.) long, instead of the typical medieval lengths (20-24 cm, ca. 8-9 in.) or the more usual early modern lengths (26-28 cm, 10-11 in.). Fortification bricks became up to 34 cm (more than 13 in.) long in the 17th century and were used for all types of buildings in that period, before the government forced a return to a more easily portable size. Another development in the rapidly expanding brick industry of the 16th century was the

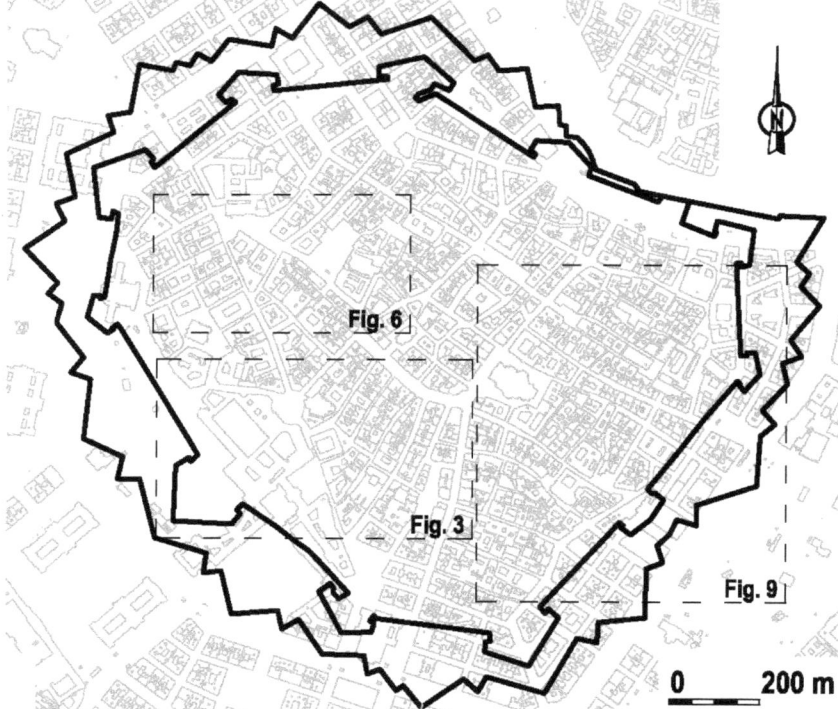

Figure 2. *Maximum extent of the Vienna fortress in the early 18th century, showing ravelins (outer line) and city wall with bastions (inner line), as well as the positions of Figures 3, 6, and 9 (Drawing by author, 2010, based on Eberle [1909] and multipurpose plan of the City of Vienna, MA41).*

a few miles south of the city, known as Schloss Neugebäude. Seasonally migrant Italian brick makers remained part of rural life in Austria until the collapse of the Habsburg Empire in 1918.

Due to further hostilities the fortress was extended again from 1637 to 1673 to include ravelins (advanced earthworks) and a covered road behind a counterscarp (outer wall of the ditch). The river front was re-fortified and the Castle Bastion was also greatly enlarged enabling it to withstand the siege of 1683 (Figure 2). The beginning of the following century saw the construction of countermine tunnels of up to 100 m (ca. 328 ft.) in length, in which explosives could be planted under the feet of an advancing enemy. One of these, a simple brick-vaulted structure technically similar to sewage canals of the same period, was excavated in 2005/2006 (Krause 2011). Between 1704 and 1738 an outer line of defenses (the "Vienna Lines" or *Linienwall*) was built around the city suburbs to head off the so-called *Kuruzzen*, or Hungarian insurgents.

Vienna was one of the most strongly fortified cities in Europe, a symbol of Habsburg power and of Christian defense against Islam. The great fortress also made the medieval defenses of the Hofburg irrelevant, allowing the court to expand within the town far beyond the boundaries of the old castle.

introduction of molds instead of open frames in the production process. This meant that signs, numbers, or initials could be carved into the base of a mold, and from the 18th century onwards the resulting marks are so common that archaeologists can date their phases by them (Mitchell 2009). The Italian architects not only went on to play a major role in the construction of the Habsburg fortress system in Hungary, but also to erect buildings of the Imperial court including a garden palace

THE ROYAL AND IMPERIAL RESIDENCE

Early in his reign Ferdinand set up boards around the perimeter of the Hofburg on which the drawing of a hand signified the terrible penalty that awaited those who dared to violate the security of the complex (Alterthumsverein zu Wien 1896: No. 1361). With the exception of a period in the late 16th and early 17th centuries (ca. 1583-1619), the Hofburg was to be the main residence of the Habsburgs thereafter. The transformation of a medieval castle (founded in the first half of the 13th century beside a gate in the city wall) into an extended residence had begun in the reign of Ferdinand's great-grandfather Emperor Frederick III (ruler in Vienna 1440-1493, with interruptions)

(Figure 3). Recent archaeological work has included the excavation of part of Frederick's never-consecrated New Church (begun ca. 1480), and has resulted in the discovery that it was he who completed the Augustinian Friary church beside the Hofburg more than a hundred years after it was begun in 1327 (Buchinger and Schön 2011a). More importantly, however, it was in Frederick's time that several houses adjoining the Hofburg were purchased and demolished in order to extend the castle gardens and improve the situation of the residence in the city (Buchinger and Schön 2011b). The corner wall of the garden complex is visible in Michaelerplatz (St. Michael's Square) today (Krause, Reichhalter,

Sakl-Oberthaler 2008:88-94; Mitchell 2010b).

Ferdinand for his part not only renovated and extended the Old Castle, but also erected substantial new works in its vicinity, including the Tennis Court (1540), the Hospital (from 1549), the residential Children's Wing (1553-1559), and a large square intended for tournaments and pageants (Holzschuh-Hofer 2007). Recent work has also revealed something of the color scheme of Ferdinand's castle: the main gate (Swiss Gate, 1552/1553), which in recent times has been painted a sturdy red, has been shown to

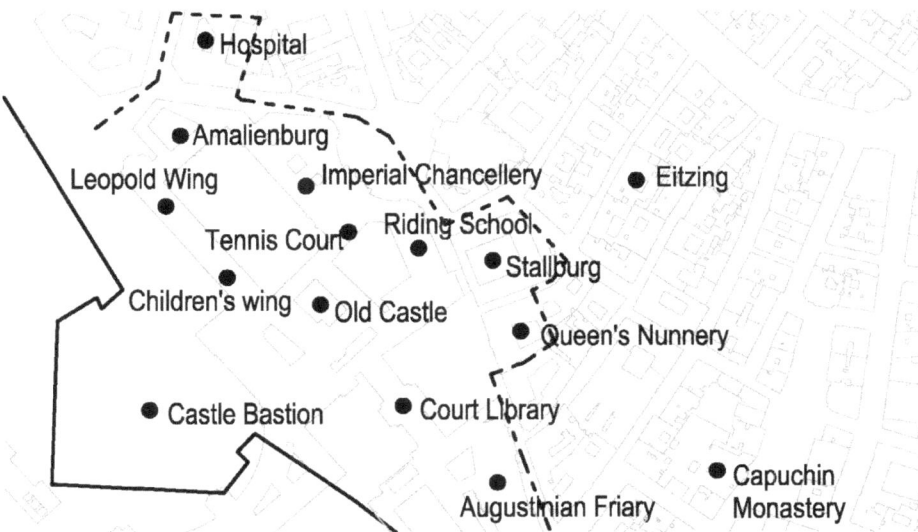

Figure 3.   Southwestern part of Vienna city center with buildings mentioned in the text, showing maximum extent of Hofburg complex. (Drawing by author, 2010, based on multipurpose plan of the City of Vienna, MA41).

have been originally in the gray and gold inherited by the Habsburgs after the Burgundian succession in 1477 (Holzschuh-Hofer and Beseler 2008). The windows of the Old Castle were picked out in a startling dark gray against an off-white background, a color scheme that has recently been reconstructed on one façade (Figure 4). Ferdinand's successors continued to build, the most important projects being the Stallburg (ca. 1558-1566), a typically Renaissance building with a large courtyard and three stories of open arcades, and the residential Amalienburg (in stages from 1575 to 1611). Both buildings appear largely unchanged today.

By the early 17th century most of the area west of the present-day city streets Schauflergasse and Augustinerstrasse and within the town walls, an area measuring 480 × 150 m (ca. 1,574 × 492 ft.), was part of the Hofburg complex. A heterogeneous collection of buildings (the Old Castle, the Children's Wing, the Amalienburg, the Augustinian Friary, etc.) and open areas (among them the extensive gardens and the tournament square) were connected by three of the elevated walkways/arcades typical of the Renaissance period: from the Old Castle through the Children's Wing, along the city wall to the Amalienburg; from the Old Castle to the Tennis Court and the gardens; and from the Old Castle through another part of the gardens to the Augustinian Friary. Ferdinand's notice boards were replaced by a triumphal arch-type structure near the Old Castle (1608) and by high archways on the northern perimeter of the complex—the base of one of these entrances was excavated in 2009 (Mitchell 2010a). Visitors

Figure 4.   Northeast façade of the Old Castle restored in the colors of the early 17th century, Hofburg, Vienna (Photo by author, 2009).

would have recognized they were in an entire Hofburg district, for elevated galleries also reached out from the complex over the Schauflergasse-Augustinerstrasse line to incorporate further Imperial buildings—the Hospital in the north and the Stallburg and the Queen's nunnery (Order of St. Clare, 1582) in the southeast.

Remaining empty spaces were filled in the 17th and 18th centuries. This was done with baroque buildings on a monumental scale, with the Leopold Wing (1660-1681) and—in the reign of Charles VI (1711-1740), arguably the high-water mark of Austrian absolutism—with the Court Library (1722-26), the Imperial Chancellery (1723-1730), and the Winter Riding School (1729-1734), among others. These younger buildings give the Hofburg a more homogenous appearance and are architecturally impressive—the roof of the Winter Riding School rests on wooden beams of 22 m length, for instance—but they rob the complex of the greenness and airiness, the gardens and open spaces that it had in the Renaissance.

Recent research by a team of art historians, historians, archaeologists, and architects organized by the Austrian Academy of Sciences, has found out a great deal more about the Hofburg's development (Österreichische Akademie der Wissenschaften 2010). Dendrochronology (Buchinger and Grabner 2006-2009) has shown which roofs were replaced after the Turkish siege of 1683 (those of the Old Castle and the Amalienburg); has supplied previously unknown construction dates (e.g., 1421 for the Castle Chapel); and has revealed unacknowledged secondary phases (e.g., at the Stallburg ca. 1640, a date supported by the excavation of large rectangular lime-slaking pits in that building's courtyard, which produced corroborating pottery and coin evidence).

Among the various Imperial residences of the early modern period in and around Vienna (e.g, Favorita, Augarten, Schönbrunn), only the hunting castle at Kaiserebersdorf has been more thoroughly examined than the Hofburg. This medieval moated castle was extended considerably in the period between 1550 and 1564, but despite employing Italian stone masons and brick makers it was not fortified in the new fashion (Müller et al. 2008). It was soon surpassed by a structure

Figure 5.   Schloss Neugebäude (first phase 1568-1576), Vienna (Photo by author, 2009).

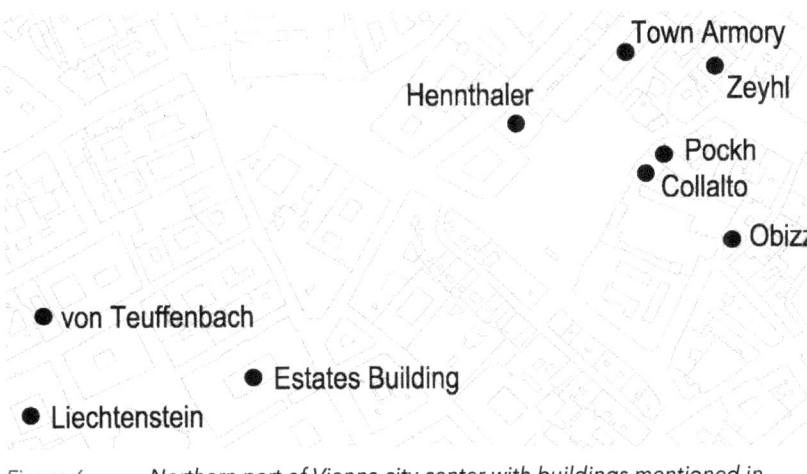

Figure 6. *Northern part of Vienna city center with buildings mentioned in the text (Drawing by author, 2010, based on multipurpose plan of the City of Vienna, MA41).*

for the keeping of exotic animals, and a fine late 16th – or early 17th-century stable building with Tuscan columns supporting groin vaulting. With the unexpected death of its builder, Emperor Maximilian II (1564-1576), in 1576, work shuddered to a halt, and despite periodic attempts to continue it, the palace slowly sank into a state of Romantic hibernation, punctuated by the removal of its sculptures for garden architecture at the baroque palace Schönbrunn. Considerable archaeological and historical work took place at Neugebäude in the late 1980s, which has sadly never been published in full (Wehdorn 2004).

only a few miles away, the so-called Schloss Neugebäude, one of the most important Renaissance structures in Austria and among the most impressive buildings in Vienna today (Figure 5). Begun in 1568 Neugebäude was a courtly leisure facility initially planned as a system of elaborate gardens, but greatly expanded to include three tower-type buildings connected by spacious arcades and surmounted by a gallery at roof level. The complex, which was built almost entirely of "Italian fortification bricks," further included a chapel, a grotto, two artificial lakes, fish ponds, various circuits of crenellated walls, a probable tennis court, facilities

The Hofburg complex not only dominated a large part of Vienna, but became a residence more appropriate to the magnificent lifestyle and absolutist aspirations of its rulers. A great deal of Imperial space—whether flights of rooms or open areas—was devoted to etiquette, ceremony, and procession (and also to horses!), but the complex also housed, in the Imperial Chancellery and the upper floors of the Stallburg for example, part of the growing bureaucracy on which the system depended. The court in its turn became a center that no self-respecting aristocrat could afford to ignore.

THE HOUSES OF THE ARISTOCRACY

Noble families and court functionaries (the chamberlain, various stewards, etc.) had begun to build houses around the castle as early as the late 13th and early 14th centuries. The topography of the late medieval town was bi-polar, with the merchants and aldermen based in the northeast around the main markets and the so-called gentlemen's quarter *(Herrenviertel)* in the southwest, but the expansion of the Hofburg and the court led to the growth of the aristocratic district in the 16th and 17th centuries. Elisabeth Lichtenberger and others have plotted this expansion into the northwestern (former Jewish district, destroyed 1420-1421) and the southeastern sections of the town (Lichtenberger 1977; Pils 2003). The displacement of the previous inhabitants was exacerbated by the enforced billeting of over 100 court functionaries (and their families) in burgher houses. If they extended their buildings the burghers were allowed to postpone these unwelcome guests for a while, but many aristocrats were at all times freed from this burden. Between 1566 and

1779 inner-city property in the hands of the nobility and court officials grew from 21.6 percent to 44.3 percent of the total (Polleroß 2003:480-481).

Despite considerable redevelopment of the city center in the 18th and 19th centuries, which destroyed or overlaid a great deal of Renaissance and early baroque architecture, fragments of buildings from the beginning of this process have been recovered in recent years. The important (and Lutheran) Lower Austrian Eitzing family, for instance, built a large palace not far from the Hofburg in the mid-16th century. Today only the lower story of a large two-story cellar resting on 2-m-wide, squat columns is clearly visible (Buchinger, Günther, et al. 2002b:520-522). Christoph von Teuffenbach, the general who commanded the Vienna garrison from 1584 to 1596 built a town house (Bankgasse 8) after 1568, in what had until then been a low-status area (Figure 6). This was a typical large house of the period with four wings arranged around a central space, but the use of free-standing columns in the ground floor and of oriels in the courtyard gave the house an airy feel. Court office holders were anxious to demonstrate their modernity—around 1630 the Hofkriegsrat official Wolff Hennthaler clad the entrance to his house at Tiefer Graben 4 with thin stone slabs, an elaborate, rusticating decoration copied from the Imperial Amalienburg, which had been finished in this fashion two decades earlier (Buchinger, Günther, et al. 2006).

The most impressive houses surviving today, however, were built after the defeat of the Turks in 1683. The city palaces of the Prince of Liechtenstein (built 1691-1705) and of the great general Prince Eugene of Savoy (built 1695-1724), both of which were being refurbished at the time of writing, are at the very top of the scale. They both replaced several smaller houses, as has been proven by excavation, and were devoted to presentation, centering on grand entrances and spectacular staircases that led to the elegant room sequences of the *belle étage*. Prince Eugene's entrance and staircase included statues, reliefs, and frescoes of Hercules, Neptune, Apollo, and other deities with whom he presumably wanted to be compared. His lack of interest in the less public parts of his house resulted in the preservation of at least one medieval (15th-century) cellar and, on the ground floor, an earlier baroque theater room (Buchinger, Günther, et al. 2002b:522-528). Ongoing excavations, in which this author is playing a central role, are exploring baroque features in the many courtyards of the complex. Several houses of the lesser nobility have also been analyzed, including that of the Collalto family from Lombardy at Am Hof 13 (façade ca. 1730), who were gifted their house after the property of the previous Protestant owner, Count Thurzo, was confiscated in 1620 (Buchinger, Günther, et al. 2002a). The house of the Countess Zeyhl at Judenplatz 8 has been dated to 1694 by a combination of written sources and dendrochronology (Schön 2003). Such houses routinely retain medieval fragments; in the Collato house, for example, are part of a 13th-century tower and an entire late medieval cellar.

The city was surrounded from this time on by the garden palaces of the upper nobility. Crucial to these complexes were the carefully prepared garden landscapes in which they stood. Most visitors to Vienna still stop at Prince Eugene's garden palace of Belvedere (1700-1725), which consists of a terraced hillside separating an upper and a lower complex. The gardens were laid out almost before anything else—the tree-trunk water pipes that supplied the many fountains have produced a dendrochronological date of 1699. Greenhouses also appeared in this period—the last surviving baroque example in Vienna, in the western suburbs, was effectively destroyed in 2000 (Baumgartner 2002).

Figure 7.   *Johann Pockh's house (1716-1718), Am Hof 12, Vienna (Photo by author, 2010).*

These great houses were undertakings on a great scale. They took many years to build and meant a considerable expenditure of resources. The palace of the Esterhazys at Wallnerstrasse 4 (1687-1695) employed more than a million bricks (Mitchell 2009:5). The house at Am Hof 12 (1716-1718), the creation of burgher Johann Pockh, a (presumably very successful) shoemaker, around a 14th-century core has no less than six habitable stories above ground (Buchinger, Maldoner et al. 2008) (Figure 7). Two stories of cellars were implanted under many standing buildings, complexes that were both a product of the conspicuous consumption of aristocratic families and masterpieces of spatial organization: the late 17th-century house of the town guard (police) chief Ferdinand von Obizzi at Schulhof 2 (Figure 8) includes a cellar accessed by a spiral staircase at one end of the property and a ramp at the other. The two cellar stories are linked by circular and square transportation openings and ventilated by shafts in the thickness of the walls. The cellars at Schulhof 2 are now largely abandoned; dozens of Viennese houses include such rooms for which little use can be found today.

Archaeology can demonstrate the many technological advances that made an aristocratic lifestyle possible. Ice cellars, either free-standing or part of larger cellar systems, are recorded regularly (Hölzmann 2007). They are recognizable by an upper opening into which ice was shoveled in winter and another entrance for the delivery and removal of foodstuffs, these being separated from the ice by wooden partitions. Baroque society could thus enjoy iced or rare dishes in June. Toilets are also often impressive: in the aristocratic Obizzi house at Schulhof 2, a 4-5 m (13-16 ft.) deep latrine shaft opens into a chamber of around 20 m³ (more than 700 cubic ft.). Rain water was channeled into the shaft apparently in the hope that the excrement would be flushed into an underground stream connected to the latrine by a

Figure 8.   *Ferdinand von Obizzi's house (late 17th century), Schulhof 2, Vienna (Photo by author, 2010).*

canal 10 m (more than 30 ft.) under street level. In the similarly dated Leopold Wing of the Hofburg, wooden chutes survive that connected the private toilets of the Imperial family in the upper stories to a great vat at ground level.

Servants' quarters—small rooms divided by timber-framed partition walls—have been recorded at the top of some of the houses.

THE COUNTER-REFORMATION

Ferdinand I's pre-emptive strike against potential difficulties from the burghers in the 1520s did not mean a complete lack of opposition in Vienna. This often took a religious form, and by ca. 1580 half the population had become Lutheran (Vocelka 2003:316). The condition of the city's Roman Catholic churches deteriorated and monasteries were threatened with extinction. As a result there was little new religious architecture in 16th-century Vienna. The Lutherans for their part tended to improvise their places of worship

around the houses of noble supporters in and outside the city, for example at the nearby estate of the Jörger family at Hernals (Pils 2003:246-249). The Lower Austrian nobility did install a Protestant chapel in their "Estates" building in the Herrengasse, a great complex that was built in several stages, incorporating both late gothic (from 1513; including elaborate and still visible net vaulting) and Renaissance (repeated activity between 1551 and 1593).

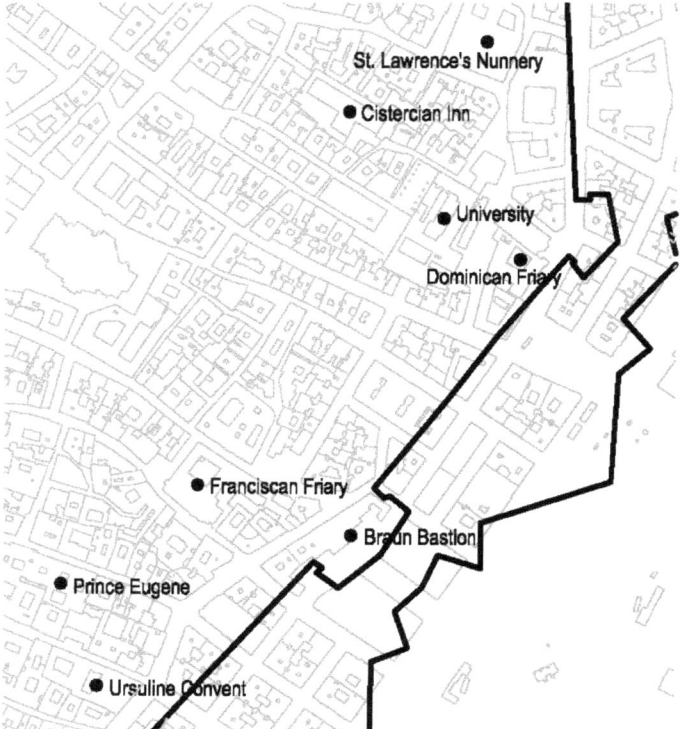

Figure 8. *Eastern part of Vienna city center with buildings mentioned in the text (Drawing by author, 2010, based on multipurpose plan of the City of Vienna, MA41).*

Despite the arrival of the Jesuits ca. 1550-1552, the Counter-Reformation did not really get under way in Vienna until after the death of the relatively tolerant emperor Maximilian II. The screw was tightened repeatedly until the expulsion of 1627, with many of the Protestant nobles losing their property around 1620/1621 (for example the Eitzing, Thurzo, and Jörger families). In terms of architecture, the Counter-Reformation saw a massive wave of religious building, which more than compensated for previous neglect (Figure 9). Existing institutions such as the Dominican Friary were renewed in the mid-17th century (Figure 10). There the old church was replaced completely by a building in a style typical of baroque Rome (Polleroß 2003). Medieval remains of the church have only been found below ground, but a medieval core remains within the friary buildings, in particular around the cloisters and in one façade, in which no less than 24 medieval windows were discovered by this author in 2007. Dynamic orders took over decrepit religious buildings and breathed new life into them, as for example the Franciscans did at a former medieval nunnery (from 1603). There were also many completely new complexes in the town and in the suburbs. The Ursuline Convent in the city center, for example, was one of several institutions that took over and demolished burgher houses, in this case no less

than eight. This wave of new building, including the reconstruction of entire urban quarters and paralleled, for example, in Prague (Staňková et al. 1992:112-116) and the Lower Austrian town of Tulln (Scholz et al. 2007), was no simple result of piety, but served the entrenchment of absolutist power (Öhlinger 1998:76; Vocelka 2010:426).

As had been the case in the medieval period, the Church was an enormous landowner. The inn of the Heiligenkreuz Cistercians, a sales center for the products of their landed estates, was twice expanded in this period, ca. 1584 and after 1658. For structural archaeologists, the complex is a textbook example of the development of construction techniques in the early modern period as medieval stone rubble walls were replaced or extended by walls consisting of stones set in a "net" of smaller stones and bricks and then again by walls of bricks with occasional stone (Kaltenegger and Mitchell 2002). Similar developments have been observed by this author at the St. Rochus church in the former southeastern suburbs, built and re-built three times in the 17th century. Land ownership meant diverse economic interests—among the most common bricks in the baroque period, for example, are those of the St. Lawrence's Nunnery brickworks. These are marked by a sign in the shape of a grill, St. Lawrence having apparently been roasted to death.

The period also brought the foundation of several new religious houses in the vicinity of the Hofburg, the most important of which was the Capuchin Monastery (1617-1632), which became the burial place of the dynasty. The most significant order in the Counter-Reformation movement, however, was that of the Jesuits. They took over the university (founded 1365) in 1623 and not only built a church there, but rebuilt the entire complex in the decades that followed, even changing the surrounding street plan.

There is still a great deal to find out about the archaeology of the Counter-Reformation in Vienna, for while there have been many excavations of post-medieval suburban cemeteries in Vienna in recent years—at Hernals for example, possibly including graves from the Lutheran period (1577-1625) (Krause 2010)—there has yet been little opportunity to analyze religious architecture archaeologically.

Figure 10.   Dominican Friary (mid-17th century), Vienna (Photo by author, 2010).

THE LIMITS OF ABSOLUTISM

The absolutist system re-shaped Vienna. Behind the high walls of the fortress the houses were often grand, but confined space meant that the streets were narrow, an enormous contrast to the openness of the glacis. The aristocracy could find compensation in their garden palaces, and over time great parks and broad avenues emerged around the suburban Imperial residences. The houses and workplaces of the lower and middling orders have survived only rarely, the suburbs to which a large part of that population was displaced having been burnt down twice, in 1529 and in 1683. An exception to this is a water mill in the Vienna River valley, the so-called "Hay Mill," where not only the medieval mill stream, with its sides clad in pointed stone, but also the 16th-century openings connecting the water wheels to the machinery inside the building have been recorded. The nearby bakery has been excavated, proving to have been founded as a timber-framed building in the late medieval period and rebuilt in stone later (Buchinger, Legen et al. 2008).

As the Turkish threat receded new forces began to emerge that could no longer be confined by the old system. The empress Maria Theresa (1717-1780) and her "enlightened" son Joseph II (1741-1790) introduced bureaucratic, social, and liberal reforms after 1740. The first factories—more concentrations of labor than concentrations of machines—appeared in the suburbs and the villages south of the city. A steam engine appeared in Vienna as early as 1722—albeit to power spectacular fountains at the Schwarzenberg garden palace (Horejs and Harl 1999).

Much further on in time Vienna was one of the key centers of the revolutionary upheavals of 1848, and many of the places introduced in this text, part of the urban landscape of absolutism, played host to important events. The uprising began after soldiers shot at demonstrators in front of the newly extended (1837-1848) Lower Austrian Estates building. The outraged crowd went on to storm the town armory and also the Stallburg, in which part of chancellor Metternich's censorship apparatus was based, breaking dozens of windows in the second building. In further course Schloss Neugebäude was fortified by loyalist forces—loopholes replaced windows—in order to defend it against Hungarian revolutionaries. In the dying hours of the revolution the citizens made a desperate attempt to defend the early 18th-century outer defenses (Linienwall), while the Habsburg loyalists were forced to bombard the Hofburg itself, setting alight the roofs of Frederick III's Augustinian Friary and Charles VI's court library. The revolution was defeated and the years afterwards are sometimes referred to as the "neo-absolutist period." It had, however, at least been the beginning of the end.

NOTES

1. When not otherwise stipulated, all dates in this paper are from the Dehio monument inventory series (Bundesdenkmalamt 1993, 1996, 2006).

REFERENCES

ALTERTHUMSVEREIN ZU WIEN
1896   *Quellen zur Geschichte der Stadt Wien* [*Sources for the History of Vienna*], I. Abtheiliung, II. Band. n.p., Vienna, Austria.

ANDERSON, PERRY
1979   *Lineages of the Absolutist State.* Verso, London, England.

BAUMGARTNER, THOMAS
2002   Das letzte barocke Glashaus Wiens [Vienna's Last Baroque Greenhouse]. *Fundort Wien* 5:256-274.

BUCHINGER, GÜNTHER, AND MICHAEL GRABNER
2006-
2009   Dendrochronologische Untersuchung der Dachstühle der Wiener Hofburg [Dendrochronological Examination of the Roofs of the Vienna Hofburg]. Manuscript, Austrian Academy of Sciences, Department of Art History, Vienna, Austria.

BUCHINGER, GÜNTHER, MANUELA LEGEN, BRUNO MALDONER, PAUL MITCHELL, AND DORIS SCHÖN
2008   Baugeschichte und Adaptierung der Heumühle in Wien [Building History and Adaptation of the "Hay Mill" in Vienna]. *Österreichische Zeitschrift für Kunst und Denkmalpflege* 62(2/3):159-169.

BUCHINGER, GÜNTHER, BRUNO MALDONER, PAUL MITCHELL, AND DORIS SCHÖN
2008   Baugeschichte und Adaptierung des Urbanihauses, Wien I, Am Hof 12 [Building History and Adaptation of the "Urbani House," Vienna 1, Am Hof 12]. *Österreichische Zeitschrift für Kunst und Denkmalpflege* 62(2/3):170-178.

BUCHINGER, GÜNTHER, PAUL MITCHELL, AND DORIS SCHÖN
2002a   Das Palais Collalto. Vom Herzogshof und Judenhaus zum Adelspalast [The Collalto Palace. From Ducal Court and Jewish House to Aristocratic Palace]. *Österreichische Zeitschrift für Kunst und Denkmalpflege* 56(4):402-419.

2002b   Katalog des Projektes "Hausforschung in der Wiener Innenstadt" [Catalog of the Project "House Research in Downtown Vienna"]. *Österreichische Zeitschrift für Kunst und Denkmalpflege* 56(4):506-534.

2005   Wien 1—Am Hof 10. Fundchronik: Hoch – und Spätmittelalter [Vienna, 1st District—Am Hof 10. Chronicle of Finds: High and Late Middle Ages]. *Fundberichte aus Österreich* 44:627-630.

2006   Wiener Renaissancepaläste—von der Bauforschung wieder ans Licht gebracht [Vienna's Renaissance Palaces—Brought to Light by Structural Archaeology]. *Kunstgeschichte aktuell. Mitteilungen des Verbandes österreichischer Kunsthistorikerinnen und Kunsthistoriker* 22(2):6-8.

BUCHINGER, GÜNTHER, AND DORIS SCHÖN
2011a   "...jene, die ihre hände hilfreich zum bau erheben..." Zur zeitlichen Konkordanz von Weihe und Bauvollendung am Beispiel der Wiener Augustinerkirche und Georgskapelle ["Those who Raise their Hands to Help us Build." The Relationship between Consecration and Completion—The Case of the Augustinian Church and St. George's Chapel]. *RIHA Journal* 0020 (18 April 2011) <www.riha-journal.org/articles/2011/2011-apr-jun/buchinger-schoen-wiener-augustinerkirche>. Accessed 22 July 2012.

2011b   "...gelegn bei der purgk zu wien..." Zur städtebaulichen Entwicklung des Wiener Burgviertels im Spätmittelalter ["Next to the Castle in Vienna." The Urban Development of the Vienna Castle District in the Later Middle Ages]. *Jahrbuch des Vereins zur Geschichte der Stadt Wien* 2011:[in press].

BUNDESDENKMALAMT (FEDERAL DEPARTMENT OF MONUMENTS)

1993   *Dehio-Handbuch: Wien II. bis IX. und XX. Bezirk [Dehio Handbook: Vienna, 2nd to 9th and 20th Districts]*. Anton Schroll & Co., Vienna, Austria.

1996   *Dehio-Handbuch. Wien X. bis XIX. und XXI. bis XXIII. Bezirk [Dehio Handbook: Vienna, 10th to 19th, 21st to 23rd Districts]*. Anton Schroll & Co., Vienna, Austria.

2003   *Dehio-Handbuch. Wien I. Bezirk—Innere Stadt [Dehio Handbook: Vienna—City Center]*. Anton Schroll & Co., Vienna, Austria.

DOWNING, BRIAN M.

1992   *The Military Revolution and Political Change: Origins of Democracy and Autocracy in Early Modern Europe*, Princeton University Press, Princeton, NJ.

EBERLE, LUDWIG

1909   Wien als Festung [Vienna as Fortress]. In *Geschichte der Stadt Wien*, Vol. 4, pp. 218-282. Vienna, Austria.

HÖLZMANN, HEINZ

2007   Eiskeller in Wien [Ice Cellars in Vienna]. *Höhlenkundliche Mitteilungen des Landesvereins des Höhlenkunde in Wien und Niederösterreich* 63(5):76-77.

HOLZSCHUH-HOFER, RENATE

2007   Die Wiener Hofburg im 16. Jahrhundert. Festungsresidenz Ferdinands I [The Vienna Hofburg in the 16th Century. Fortified Residence of Ferdinand I]. *Österreichische Zeitschrift für Kunst und Denkmalpflege* 61(2/3):307–325.

HOLZSCHUH-HOFER, RENATE, AND SUSANNE BESELER

2008   Nobles Grau-gold. Bauforschung am Schweizertor in der Wiener Hofburg [Noble Gray-Gold. Structural Archaeology at the Swiss Gate in the Vienna Hofburg]. *Österreichische Zeitschrift für Kunst und Denkmalpflege* 62(4):643-670.

HOREJS, BARBARA, AND ORTOLF HARL

1999   Der Urselbrunnen—Wasser für Wiens erste Dampfmaschine [The Ursel Well—Water for Vienna's First Steam Engine]. *Fundort Wien* 2:146-152.

KALTENEGGER, MARINA, AND PAUL MITCHELL

2002   Zur Baugeschichte des Heiligenkreuzerhofes [The Building History of Holy Cross Yard]. *Österreichische Zeitschrift für Kunst und Denkmalpflege* 56(4):377-401.

KRAUSE, HEIKE

2010   Wien 17, St-Bartholomäus-Platz [St. Bartholomew's Square]. *Fundort Wien* 13:231-233.

2011   Der Stadtgraben und das Glacis der Festung Wien. Die Grabung Wien 1, Weihburggasse [The Ditch and the Glacis of the Vienna Fortress. The Excavation at Weihburggasse]. *Fundort Wien* 14, 2011: 32-70.

KRAUSE, HEIKE, GERHARD REICHHALTER, AND SYLVIA SAKL-OBERTHALER

2008   Neuzeitliche Befunde der Grabungen Wien 1, Michaelerplatz (1990/19991) [Post-Medieval Contexts from the Excavations at St. Michael's Square, 1990/1991]. *Fundort Wien* 11:86-131.

KRAUSE, HEIKE, GERHARD REICHHALTER, INGEBORG GAISBAUER, INGRID MADER, SYLVIA SAKL-OBERTHALER, AND CHRISTINE RANSEDER

2009   *Mauern um Wien. Die Stadtbefestigung von 1529 bis 1857 [Walls around Vienna. The Urban Fortifications from 1529 to 1857]*. Wien Archäologisch, 6. Phoibos, Vienna, Austria.

LICHTENBERGER, ELISABETH

1977   *Die Wiener Altstadt. Von der mittelalterlichen Bürgerstadt zur City [The Old City of Vienna. From Medieval Burgher Town to Inner City]*. Franz Deuticke, Vienna, Austria.

MADER, INGRID

2008   Bericht über die archäologischen Untersuchungen in Etablissement Ronacher [Preliminary Report about the Archaeological Research at the Ronacher Theater]. *Fundort Wien* 11:56-73.

MITCHELL, PAUL

2009   Bricks in the Central Part of Austria-Hungary. Key Artefacts in Historical Archaeology. *Historische Archäologie* <http://www.histarch.uni-kiel.de/2009_Mitchell_low.pdf>. Accessed 22 July 2012.

2010a   Die Hofburg als Festung (13.–16. Jh.) [The Hofburg as a Fortification, 13th to 16th Century]. *Österreichische Zeitschrift für Kunst und Denkmalpflege* 64(1/2):35-44.

2010b   Reassessing the Vienna Hofburg in the 15th century. How New Sources are Changing the Picture. *Château Gaillard* 24:203-212.

MÜLLER, MICHAELA, HEIKE KRAUSE, IAN LINDNER, AND MICHAEL SCHULZ
2008   Die archäologischen und bauhistorischen Untersuchungen im Schloss Kaiserebersdorf. Band 1, Text & Band 2, Abbildungen [The Archaeological and Buildings Historical Research in Kaiserebersdorf Castle]. Monografien der Stadtarchäologie Wien, 3. Phoibos, Vienna, Austria.

NOVAK, RUDOLF R.
2001   Das kaiserliche Zeughaus in Wien [The Imperial Armory in Vienna]. Fundort Wien 4:248-255.

ÖHLINGER, WALTER
1998   Wien zwischen den Türkenkriegen [Vienna Between the Turkish Wars]. Geschichte Wiens, 3. Pichler, Vienna, Austria.

ÖSTERREICHISCHE AKADEMIE DER WISSENSCHAFTEN
2010   Die Wiener Hofburg. Forschungen zur Bau – und Funktionsgeschichte [The Vienna Hofburg. Research into Building and Functional History]. Kommission für Kunstgeschichte, Österreichische Akademie der Wissenschaften, Zentrum Kulturforschungen <www.oeaw.ac.at/kunst/projekte/hofburg/hofburg.html>. Accessed 22 July 2012.

PÁLFFY, GÉZA
2009   Die Türkenabwehr der Habsburgermonarchie in Ungarn und Kroatien im 16. Jahrhundert: Verteidigungskonzeption, Grenzfestungssystem, Militärkartographie [The Anti-Turkish Defenses of the Habsburg Monarchy in Hungary and Croatia in the 16th Century. Defense Strategy, Border Fortress System, Military Cartography]. In Türkenangst und Festungsbau. Wirklichkeit und Mythos, Harald Heppner and Zsuzsa Barbarics-Hermanik, editors, pp. 79-108. Peter Lang, Vienna, Austria.

PAUSER, JOSEF
2003   Verfassung und Verwaltung der Stadt Wien [Constitution and Adminstration of Vienna]. In Wien—Geschichte einer Stadt. Band 2: Die frühneuzeitliche Residenz (16. bis 18. Jahrhundert), Karl Vocelka and Anita Traninger, editors, pp. 47-90. Böhlau, Vienna, Austria.

PERGER, RICHARD
1983   Die politische Rolle der Wiener Handwerker im Spätmittelalter [The Political Role of the Viennese Artisans in the Later Middle Ages]. Wiener Geschichtsblätter 38(1):1-36.

PILS, SUSANNE C.
2003   Adel: Zuzug, Adeliges Haushalten, Sozialtopographie [The Aristocracy: Immigration, Aristocratic Housekeeping, Social Topography]. In Wien—Geschichte einer Stadt. Band 2: Die frühneuzeitliche Residenz (16. bis 18. Jahrhundert), Karl Vocelka and Anita Traninger, editors, pp. 241-255. Böhlau, Vienna, Austria.

POLLEROSS, FRIEDRICH
2003   Renaissance and Barock [Renaissance and Baroque]. In Wien—Geschichte einer Stadt. Band 2: Die frühneuzeitliche Residenz (16. bis 18. Jahrhundert), Karl Vocelka and Anita Traninger, editors, pp. 453-500. Böhlau, Vienna, Austria.

SCHOLZ, UTE, ASTRID STEINEGGER, MARIANNE SINGER, AND MARTIN KRENN
2007   Stadtkernarchäologie—Vom antiken Comagenis zum heutigen Tulln [City Center Archaeology—From Ancient Comagenis to Modern Tulln]. Archäologie Österreichs 18(2):4-18.

SCHÖN, DORIS
2003   Von mittelalterlichen Mauern, renaissancezeitlichen Fenstern und barocken Fußböden. Bauforschung im Haus Wien 1, Judenplatz 8 [Medieval Walls, Renaissance Windows, and Baroque Floors. Structural Archaeology at Judenplatz No. 8, Vienna]. Fundort Wien 6:96-139.

STAŇKOVÁ, JAROSLAVA, JIŘÍ ŠTURSA, AND SVATOPLUK VODĚRA
1992   Prague. Eleven Centuries of Architecture. PAV, Prague, Czech Republic.

VOCELKA, KARL
2003   Kirchengeschichte [Church History]. In Wien—Geschichte einer Stadt. Band 2: Die frühneuzeitliche Residenz (16. bis 18. Jahrhundert), Karl Vocelka and Anita Traninger, editors, pp. 311-363. Böhlau, Vienna, Austria.

2010   Geschichte der Neuzeit 1500-1918 [History of the Modern Period 1500-1918]. Böhlau, Vienna, Austria.

WEHDORN, MANFRED
2004   Das Neugebäude. Ein Renaissance-Schloss in Wien [Neugebäude. A Renaissance Palace in Vienna]. Perspektiven (Sondernummer), N.J. Schmid, Vienna, Austria.

WEIGL, ANDREAS
2003   Frühneuzeitliches Bevölkerungswachstum [Population Growth in the Early Modern Period]. In Wien—Geschichte einer Stadt. Band 2: Die frühneuzeitliche Residenz (16. bis 18. Jahrhundert), Karl Vocelka and Anita Traninger, editors, pp. 109-131. Böhlau, Vienna, Austria.

Paul Mitchell
Vogelsanggasse 4/4
A-1050 Vienna
Austria

JERZY PIEKALSKI

The Environment and Living Conditions in Wrocław (Breslau) in the 16th–18th Centuries

ABSTRACT

The aim of this outline is to analyze sanitary status of a post-medieval city of lowland central Europe. This subject is discussed using Wrocław, the main center in Silesia, Poland, as a case study. Special focus is placed on the relationship between man and the natural environment, including the intensity of change caused by man. The boundaries of the city were established during the medieval period, at which time the city was enclosed by a system of fortifications. Their moderniza-tion and adjustment to post-medieval requirements was the main investment realized in the city in the period from the 16th to the late 18th centuries. This hindered territorial expansion of the city and investments in its infrastructure. The enclosed space became too small for the dynami-cally growing number of town dwellers. Houses and other town buildings crowded the confined space and encroached on the backyard of town plots reducing their sanitary function. The system of waste disposal that had been developed during the Middle Ages became inadequate. The town moats and the river became severely polluted causing epidemiological threat. Overpopulation and the critical sanitary situation of the city, as well as new developments in warfare, led to a decision to pull down the fortifications. This opened the way for the city to expand its territory during the 19th and the 20th centuries, the age of growing industrialization, and allowed a further rapid population increase.

INTRODUCTION

Wrocław's form and the way of life of the townspeople result from a combination of several factors of geography, economy, politics, culture, local traditions, and adopted foreign models. The purpose of the present outline is to inves-tigate the dependence of urban living conditions on the natural and man-made features of the environment. This theme is examined using Wrocław as a case study, a town established in a zone of transition between differ-ent cultures and spheres of political influence. During the Middle Ages it alternated between belonging to the Czech and Polish kingdoms, while during the 16th-18th centuries it became the capital of the province of Silesia in the Habsburg monarchy and subsequently in the Kingdom of Prussia. Its name in Czech was Vratislav, while in German, the main language for many of its late medieval and early modern inhabitants, it was known as Breslau (Figure 1).

This outline covers the pre-industrial period—from the beginning of the post-medieval age until the first devel-opments that ushered in the Industrial Revolution of the 19th century. We need to note at this point that both these dividing lines, especially the transition from the medieval to the post-medieval age, are in Wrocław and

Silesia rather arbitrary. The early modern Wrocław was to a great extent a legacy of the Middle Ages, and the changes at work during the 16th century had the nature more of an accelerated evolution than of a revolution-ary breakthrough (Piekalski and Wachowski 2010). The process resulted from changes in the mentality and ideology of the local townspeople brought about by the Reformation according to the Lutheran model, the new developments in methods and strategies of warfare, the growing importance of cities in state politics, and the relative economic prosperity enjoyed by Silesia until the Thirty Years' War. Let us add that there could be no question of a "revival" of models drawn from the culture of classical antiquity for it had never spread to this region of Europe. The term Renaissance, used for describing styles in art and architecture reflects trends that reached the area, by different routes, from Italy and, later, from the Netherlands, introduced in Wrocław by the nobility, the Church elite, and by rich burghers. The end of the processes proper for post-medieval Wrocław and the onset of the industrial development of the city of the most recent age came with the French-Prussian War of 1806-1807, when the decision was made to pull down the town fortifications. Freed from the constraint of the town walls, Wrocław took advantage of legal

Figure 1.   *Map of northern Europe showing the location of Wrocław (Map provided courtesy of the Department of Prehistory and Medieval Archaeology, University of Vienna, Austria).*

changes introduced at this time and responded by territorial expansion, economic growth, demographic increase, and associated changes in the lifestyle of most of its inhabitants.

THE CITY IN THE CONTEXT OF ITS NATURAL ENVIRONMENT, HYDROGRAPHIC NETWORK, FEATURES OF RELIEF, AND THE EXTENT OF ANTHROPOGENIC CHANGE

The selection of a suitable site to set up a city appears to be a decision of key importance for its later development. Paradoxically, in the case of most European cities, this choice was not made consciously. The location of cities tended to be influenced by other factors and decisions that did not apply to the city itself. In the case of Wrocław, its location resulted from a decision made a few centuries before the incorporation of the communal town. This is when the site was selected for a small timber stronghold, raised during the first half of the 10th century on one of the islands of the River Oder, known later as Cathedral Island (*Ostrów Tumski*). The site of this stronghold was dictated by its naturally defensive character and the purpose it was to serve. Apparently, this was to guard the ford on the Oder. The later career of the stronghold and its development into a center of political, military, and ecclesiastic power made the location in its neighborhood attractive as a town site, understood as both a municipal and an economic formation. The presence of the ducal stronghold, whose residents were the main recipients of luxury goods, made the future town an important stopover on an important trade route, the Via Regia, which linked the east with the northwest of Europe. The role of the geographic setting in locating the center was secondary to proximity to the stronghold with its military determinants, while during the 16th-18th centuries the stronghold was a thing of the past (Piekalski 2001:38-42, 114-116).

The Oder is one of the great rivers of east-central Europe. It flows from the Sudety Mountains to the Baltic Sea crossing Silesia from southeast to northwest. Wrocław lies at a special location in its lowland course where the river flows down a broad depression forming numerous channels that have shifted course in a natural manner. In the city the Oder receives its tributary the Oława, and nearby there are four other rivers and numerous minor streams. In its natural form the Oder and its tributaries formed a rich hydrographic network consisting of many viable meandering channels and old river beds and numerous low-lying islands. Most likely the river had six or seven main channels, rather shallow, with an average depth of ca. 50 cm (Badura 2010:16). Without human interference the islands changed their form freely and often, with every flood (Figure 2). Therefore, one of the measures needed to continue occupation was to protect the site against the destructive power of the river. After the proto-urban stage in the 11th-12th centuries, during which Wrocław continued as a center of settlement with a ducal stronghold, bishopric, two abbeys, and a trading settlement, the communal town was established on the southern side (left bank) of the Oder valley. Protecting the river banks, constructing embankments and dykes, regulating the river channels, and digging new canals to straighten its course became the regular concern of the townspeople starting in the Middle Ages until the most recent times (Leonhard 1901; Born 1948). Thus, by the 19th century, the hydrographic network, stabilized by man, had assumed a form considerably altered from its natural state (Figure 3). Some channels had been cut off joining some islands to the mainland, many old river channels had been filled in, and large tracts of marshy ground had been drained. Much of the river water now flowed down a man-made channel that bypassed the town from the north. Nevertheless, water continued to be an important feature in the city's landscape. No location in the town was farther than 300 m from the moat or one of the river channels. Communication in the city was conditioned by a great number of larger and smaller bridges. In the 16th century there were about 30 bridges, and in the 19th century more than 100. During the first half of 20th century there were some 300 or so bridges and footbridges. Nowadays the city has about 100 bridges (Łagiewski 1998:15-42).

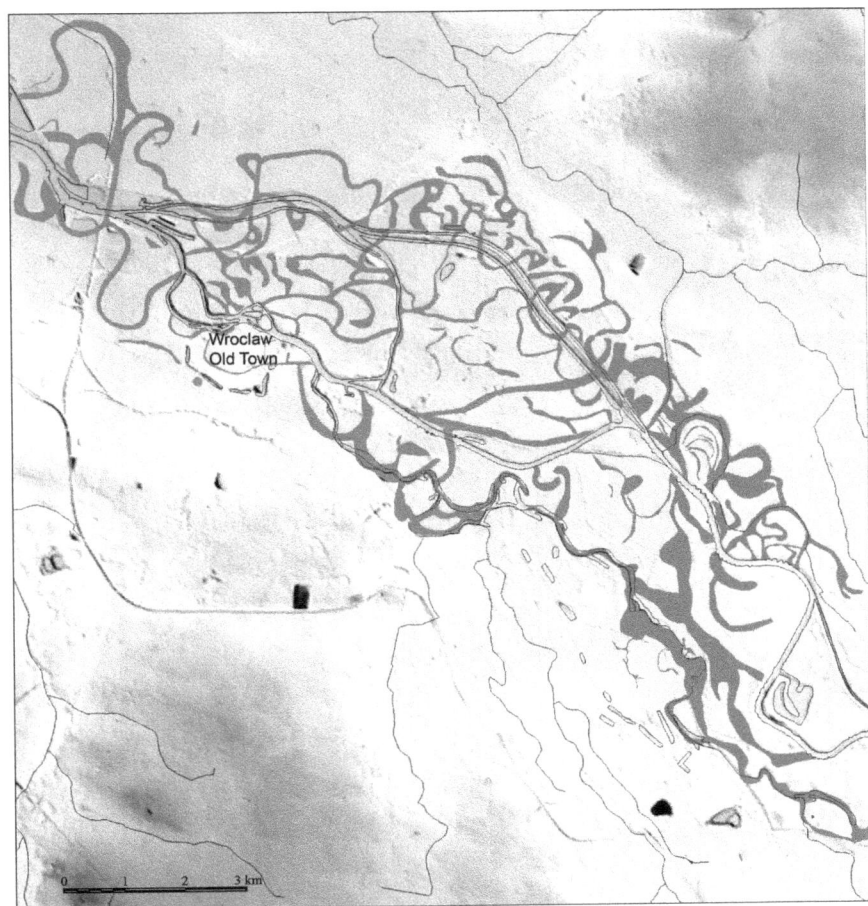

Figure 2.   *The Oder Valley in Wrocław before the rise of the town (Badura 2010:figure 1).*

Differences in the ground level in the town and its surrounding area were negligible. The average water level in the Oder before the rise of the communal town is estimated at about 111 m above sea level. In the occupied river islands it was between 115 m and 116 m. This was also the level of the area on the left bank, which started to be built up during the first half of the 13th century. Its main town square (Market Square) was laid out on a terrace at about 117 m above sea level, or 5-6 m higher than the average water level in the river, to guarantee relative safety from flooding. Going north, the ground level descended to a natural depression that was used for a moat, known as "the outer moat." For all this, great tracts of the town, especially in its northern zone, continued to be marshy. Projects designed to improve

this situation and make the land suitable for settlement started back in the 13th century. Much of the town area was spread with a layer of sand that raised the ground level by approximately 50 cm. A side effect of urban life soon turned out to be an uncontrolled accumulation of a layer of refuse, which while admittedly raising the ground level further, even by as much as 3 m, was a great problem for the sanitary status of the town and for communication. River regulation projects and construction of ponding structures that raised the water level for economic purposes also had an unwelcome effect in the form of a rising groundwater table (Badura 2010:40-44; Konczewski and Piekalski 2010:91-151; Sowina 2009:52-65).

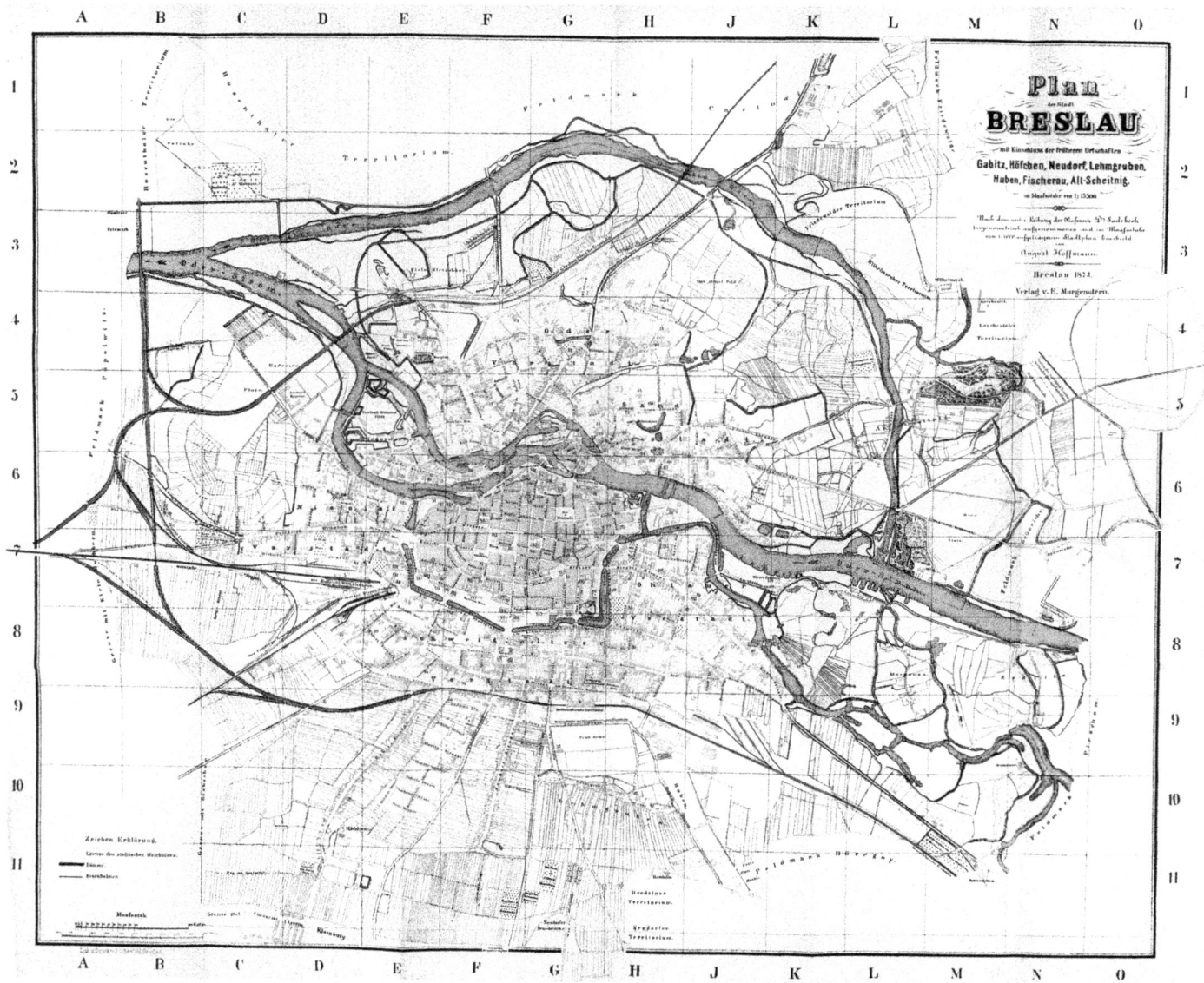

Figure 3. *The river Oder in Wrocław in 1873, map by August Hoffmann (Młynarska and Eysymontt 2001:figure 34).*

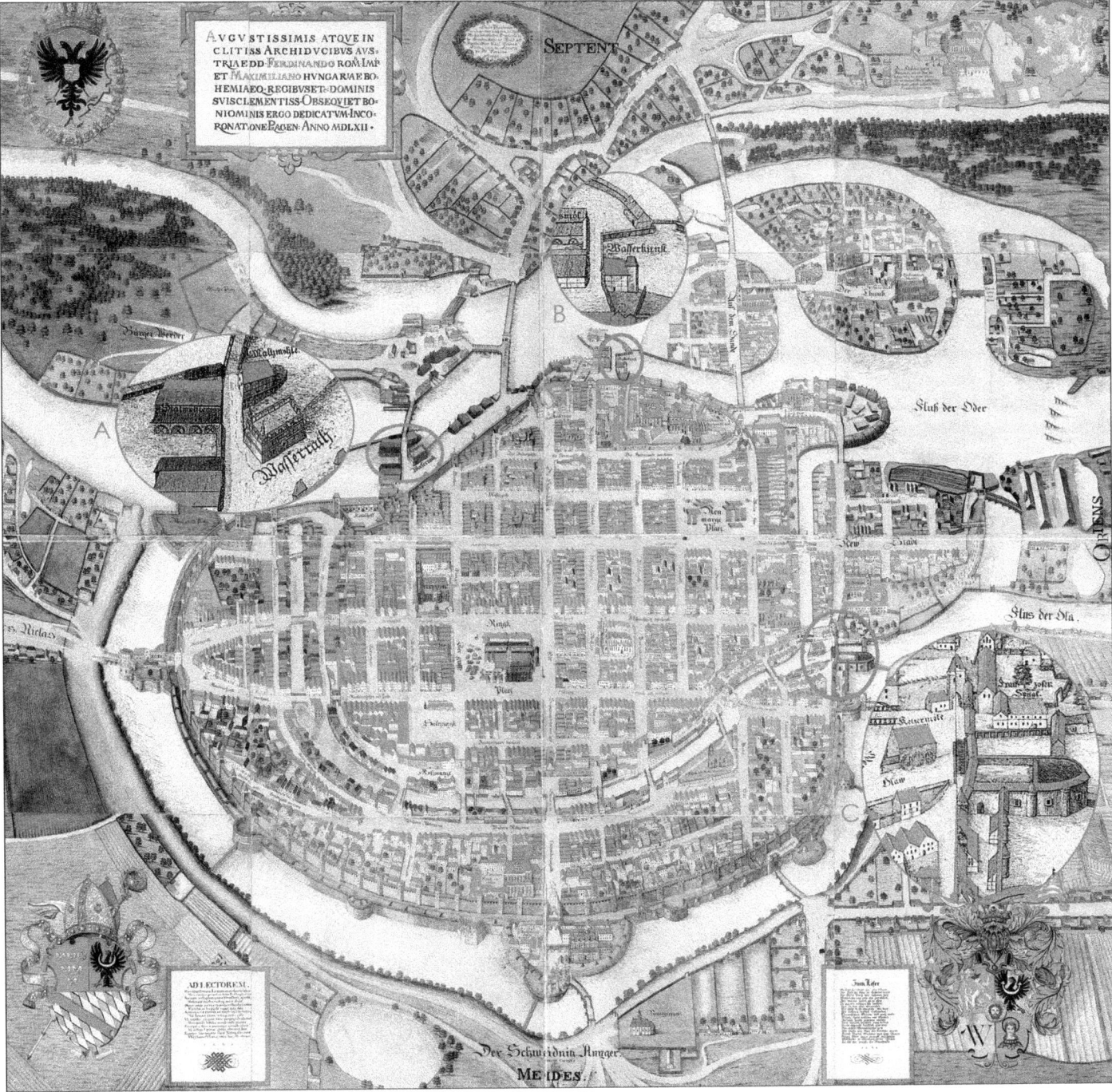

Figure 4.   *Wrocław on Barthel Weyner's panoramic map from 1562: (A) the Wasserrath water house on the Oder by the Lesser Mill Gate; (B) the water house by St. Matthew Island; and (C) Ketzerberg (Młynarska and Eysymontt 2001).*

THE POST-MEDIEVAL TOWN WITHIN MEDIEVAL BOUNDARIES

The topographic make-up of the post-medieval town included several features that had taken form during earlier stages of its development (Piekalski 2008). One of them was the regular plan of its central district (Figure 4) where streets, squares, and blocks of buildings were on a plan of a mostly regular grid, some 60 ha in area. This oldest part of the town, founded in the first half of the 13th century, was surrounded by a line of fortifications—brick walls and a moat watered by the Oława river. To the north the city was hemmed in by the Oder. Access to this part of town was through seven gates and bridges and many lesser gates with footbridges for pedestrians. From the south and the west there was an adjoining zone described as

Outer Town, with an area of approximately 40 ha. Its plan was roughly crescent-shaped. Here the street plan was irregular, adjusted to the line of the fortifications and the location of the town gates. Barthel Stein, in his description of Wrocław made in 1512, noted that this zone had different uses from the central district. In the Outer Town there were malt-houses, granaries, and weavers' workshops large enough to accommodate their looms and wares (Stein 1995:71-72). This role of the Outer Town finds support in archaeological evidence from excavation (Jastrzębski et al. 2001). During the 1260s the older central district was joined from the east by a smaller New Town, some 10 ha in area. The boundaries of the Outer Town and the New Town ran at the foot of the town wall, which was sturdy and modernized regularly. At first this system consisted of a moat and an earthen wall of late 13th-century date, subsequently by a brick wall with towers raised during the first half of the 14th century. Around 1500 the fortifications were adjusted according to the new development in techniques of warfare, making it possible to use artillery (Piekalski 2007). The development of cannons necessitated major investment projects designed to improve the city's walls during the post-medieval period—these eventually turned it into a bastion-like fortress. In keeping with general trends prevailing across Europe of the day, the city, like other larger cities, was developed into a state fortress—at first, in the Austrian Empire of the Habsburgs, and after 1740 in the Kingdom of Prussia. The new political and military situation was at odds with the interests of the town authorities. It reduced the independence of the Town Council and largely prevented its territorial expansion with adverse consequences for its economic growth. The town, with its growing population, was confined within boundaries laid out during the 13th century. By the end of the medieval period areas left without development had all been nearly built over.

During the 14th century the city no longer had zones without buildings. The small number of larger open spaces remained only in the outer districts of the town, next to the fortifications. Early into the 16th century an area of some 140 ha had a population of approximately 20,000. According to the written records relating to town taxes it appears that these people were occupying approximately 2,300 houses, more exactly town plots, which, next to the main building, may have harbored other, smaller buildings. This gives us an average of 8.7 residents per town plot. At the end of the study period, in 1787, the tax records list 3,388 houses, the number of their residents at 50,975 or, statistically, 15 inhabitants per house. Let us add that these were all taxpayers, but the town was also a place of residence for seasonal

Figure 5. Wrocław, Dominikański Square, medieval and early modern development along the inner moat: (1) Dominican church; (2) moat; (3) Zaułek Niski Street; (4) Kacerska Górka Street; (5) Nowa Street; (a) town wall; (b) late medieval development; (c) early modern development (Konczewski 2007:figure 7).

Figure 6.   *Wrocław, Białoskórnicza Street. Inner moat in 1826, drawing by Heinrich Mützel (Łukaszewicz 2008:figure 72).*

laborers, people from the surrounding rural area periodically resident in Wrocław, and finally, the homeless whose number cannot be estimated easily. Between the year 1500 or so and the end of the 18th century the number of the townspeople living in the same urban space grew by more than 150 percent (Ziątkowski 2001:22-23).

The benefits of having a town set up on a river are generally known and discussed in many publications (Maschke and Sydow 1978; Kaniecki 2004; Fejtová et al. 2005; Sowina 2009:41-132). Wrocław is not an exception. We need to stress here the importance of easy access to water needed by the municipal economy, especially for the important weaving, brewing, tanning, and dyeing trades in the city as well as water needed for household uses. In addition, the Oder and the Oława were a source of energy for numerous mills, fulleries, and sawmills situated within the city. They formed a cheap water source and helped defend the city by supplying abundant water to its moats. Fishing was also of some importance although somewhat restricted by legal regulations. That the people of Wrocław were aware of these advantages is documented by a detailed description given by Bartholomäus Stein (1995:31-32) in 1512. This positive importance of the river is especially marked during the Middle Ages. In the post-medieval age, with the great congestion of buildings and pronounced overpopulation, the situation took a turn for the worse. Despite huge expenditures on engineering projects undertaken from the medieval period until the 19th century, the adverse impact of a lowland river and marshy banks on living conditions in Wrocław was hard to remedy. Especially during the autumn and winter seasons—of six months' duration in Silesia (November to April)—dirt piling up in the streets and backyards and the ever present humidity were a major discomfort for the townspeople.

The town moats increasingly became a sanitary problem, especially the so-called Black Oława, which washed the inner districts of the town. Originally it had had a substantial width of some 45 m, reaching as much as 4.5 m in depth (Piekalski 2001:191). After the construction of a second, outer ring of town defenses, its military significance declined and finally came to an end. During the 15th-16th centuries its width was reduced greatly and its banks were stabilized with walls creating a canal inside the city. Houses were built along its banks along with all manner of other structures from a great mill with seven wheels down to small platforms for the washerwomen (Figures 5 and 6). In particular,

with the presence of houses on the river the earlier bans on casting waste into the water cannot have been effective. On each of the town properties cesspits were dug on the banks of the canal into which household sewage was also disposed. The result was a steady deterioration of water purity. During the second half of the 19th century the canal was identified as one of the causes of a cholera epidemic. It was filled in and a street was laid out in its place. The original nature of the waste drain was recalled by cesspits situated on the margins of the town plots (Figure 7).

Permanent action aimed at improving the sanitary situation of the town brought only a short-lived effect, and radical investment in municipal infrastructure projects was not feasible. These problems were apparent not only

Figure 7. Wrocław, Zaułek Niski Street, former inner moat in the early 20th century (Postcard from the collection of Paweł Konczewski).

to the townspeople themselves but also, or perhaps all the more so, to travelers. Johann Wolfgang Goethe contrasted Silesia, which he considered an attractive region, with its capital city. In the summer of 1784 he found it to be "... a crowded, ill-drained, riverside town ..." Neither was he happy with the prospect of returning to the city after an excursion to the Sudety Mountains "... again in the noisy, dirty, stinking Breslau" (Boyle 2000:83-84). John Quincy Adams, ambassador of the United States to the Kingdom of Prussia and subsequently sixth President of the United States of America, had traveled in Silesia in 1800-1801 and noted that

> *Before we left Berlin to come upon this tour, we were advised not to pass through Breslau at all. It was said to be a large old city, resembling all other great cities, and containing nothing that deserved the attention of travelers; we had,*

> *therefore, not put it down upon the original list of our route. But, when we found ourselves in the course of our excursion within a few miles of it, we thought, after making so long a tour of the whole province, it would be showing the capital too great a mark of contempt to neglect it altogether, and concluded to give it a few days of our time upon our return. We have no reason to repent of this final determination; for although the place is, as it had been described to us, nothing more than a large, old, and very dirty city; and although the weather, since we came into it, has been constantly such as to confine us a great part of the time to the house, we have still met with objects of curiosity sufficient to amuse and employ the few days we have devoted to the place [Adams 1804:219-220].*

THE INFRASTRUCTURE OF THE POST-MEDIEVAL CITY

Next to the natural conditions, not too favorable in the case of Wrocław, the sanitary status of the town was influenced significantly by the quality of its water supply and its waste disposal systems. The solutions used in the post-medieval period were to a large extent a continuation of technical projects and systems developed during the Middle Ages (Piekalski 2004; Goliński 2007).

The post-medieval city was supplied with water chiefly from water mains and, to a lesser extent, from traditional wells. The system of water mains relied on three structures to draw water from the rivers. These were known as *Wasserrath*, *Wasserkunst*, or *Wasserhaus*. Water from the Oder was drawn by a structure with a water-wheel installed next to the Lesser Mill Gate (*Mühlpfort*) at the end of Kiełbaśnicza Street. It is known to have been in operation already during the 14th century and had been the subject of numerous repairs and major overhauls. In a town established on a lowland river, water had to be drawn by using a water wheel, a system known already during antiquity, since the less complicated and more efficient system based on gravitation could not be used (Sowina 2009:281-282). Starting from 1538 Wasserrath was installed—a new water wheel with 160 scoops and a diameter of 48 ft., or ca. 14 m. According to calculations made by Klaus Grewe (1991:65) this wheel raised water to the height of 28 ft. and had an output of 500 litres per minute. The new water house built at that time continued to operate until the 19th century (see Figure 4A). The Wasserrath by the Lesser Mill Gate supplied the privileged part of the town, with the Market Square, Salt

Figure 8.   Wrocław, the Ketzerkunst water house in a drawing by Heinrich Mützel from 1826 (Łukaszewicz 2008:figure 78).

Figure 9. *Wrocław, the Ketzerkunst water house, bottom and bank of the moat from the 16th century (Piekalski 2004:figure 7) (Photo by Paweł Konczewski, 1998; courtesy of Paweł Konczewski).*

Market (Solny Square), Kiełbaśnicza Street, and Ofiar Oświęcimskich Street. Another Wasserhaus, also going back to the 14th century, was by Kacerska Górka on the southeast margin of the town; it drew water from the Oława river at its inlet to the inner moat (Goliński 2001). After 1596 it was given a post-medieval form by Hans Schneider von Lindau, master builder active earlier in Gdańsk (Figure 8). At this time the channel of the Oława was faced with stone. A structure described at a later date as *Ketzerkunst* consisted of two brick buildings, one of them with a single story, raised on arches over the narrowed down river channel from which it drew the water. The second waterworks, built on the outer bank of the moat, was fitted with a tank. According to Hermann Markgraf, this structure raised water to the highest level of all the three water systems in the city and supplied the southern area of the town and parts of its eastern districts. The Ketzerkunst was in operation as late as the 1840s and was pulled down in 1857 (Markgraf

Figure 10. *Wrocław, the Ketzerkunst water house, bottom and bank of the moat from the 16th century (Piekalski 2004:figure 7) (Photo by Paweł Konczewski, 1998; courtesy of Paweł Konczewski).*

1896:88). Archaeological investigation revealed some details of its construction. The channel of the river had banks faced with stone masonry and a bottom lined with a durable timber structure. The submerged parts of the brick walls were reinforced with decorative cut sandstone. Elements of wooden structures that drew the water from the river were fixed to the walls (Figures 9 and 10).

A third water house—Wasserkunst—drew water from the Oder at the outlet of Szewska Street, by St. Matthew Island. It was the youngest, built during the 1630s (Grewe 1991:65). The ponding structures were housed in a single story frame building and an only slightly taller tower with a tank (see Figure 4B). Archaeological investigations in the area have revealed relics of the poorly preserved brick foundations of the tower bound to the wall of the embankment of the Oder.

Water from the waterhouses was distributed by pipes installed under the surface of the streets. The pipes supplied public wells in the streets and town squares. The pipelines under the streets were town property as were the water houses and public wells. Pipes that branched off to the town plots were private property. The depth at which the pipes were installed under the streets was not uniform and was, at most, 3.7 m. During the Middle Ages ceramic pipes, thrown on a potter's wheel and laid in 36-60 cm long segments were used. This is in contrast to most medieval towns in central Europe, where wooden pipes where characteristic during the medieval period (Sowina 2009:298-309). From the late 15th century the ceramic pipes began to be replaced successively with wooden pipes. Dendrochronology dates show that Market Square was given new wooden pipes around 1500. They had the form of unhewn tree trunks up to 40 cm in diameter, with a drilled conduit approximately 8-8.5 cm in diameter. A later improvement was to join the wooden segments with iron connecting pieces (Bresch et al. 2002:292-295). Wooden pipes used in later centuries varied in quality. Some were of carefully dressed timber with a square cross-section, up to 3 m, or approximately 10 ft., long. They have turned up in many locations, the youngest are dated dendrochronologically to after 1831 (Limisiewicz 1998:218-219; Janczewski 2005:87). At the same time, we know that even back in the 18th century wooden pipes were being replaced by iron, lead, or ceramic ones (Berger 1926:16).

Medieval timber water wells were replaced during the post-medieval period by wells with a stone or, less often, brick casing. Beginning in the 16th century a standard well consisted of 3-4 segments hewn from sandstone, elliptical or round in cross-section. The lowermost segment had a specially molded bottom. Similar wells have been discovered in the streets as well as in town plots. One such well, discovered in a rich town plot in no. 6 Rynek (Market Square), was connected to an iron pipe. The mark of its manufacturer seen on one of the sandstone segments dates the well to the year 1727 (Figure 11).

It seems that the regularly repaired and improved water systems supplied the post-medieval town with a sufficient volume of water. Water drawn from the lowland rivers was vulnerable to seasonal natural contamination and polluted by urban sewage. The mechanical devices used in those days were able only to pond and transport water, but not to clean it of impurities, as in the days to come. No wonder, therefore, that traditional wells continued in use. Water from wells, drawn from the ground, was not of a high quality but was considered better than water from the water mains (Berger 1926:15; Brzezowski 2005:306).

The problem of the rapid accretion of the layer of refuse had been solved during the 14th century. At that time the Town Council had regulated by law the responsibility of garbage removal and its disposal in the city outskirts (Goliński 2010). Early into the post-medieval period, the streets were laid with stone pavements replacing the earlier timber road surfaces (Konczewski and Piekalski 2010). It seems that the sanitary status of the town at the transition from the medieval to the post-medieval age was relatively good and the Town Council was capable of overcoming various hazards. As time passed, steady population growth in a greatly

a

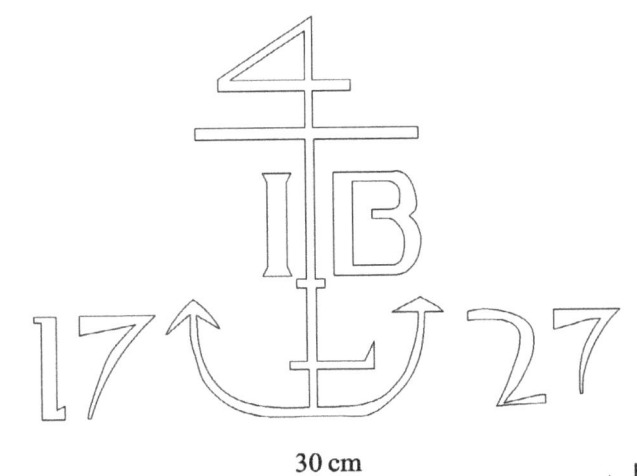

30 cm

b

Figure 11.   Wrocław, no. 6 Rynek (Market Square): (a) well; (b) manufacturer's mark (Photo by Paweł Konczewski, 2010; courtesy of Paweł Konczewski. Drawing by Witold Wierzbicki, 2010; courtesy of Instytut Archeologii Uniwersytetu Wrocławskiego).

restricted space made disposal of urban waste increasingly difficult. The system of removal of impurities from town plots remained nearly the same as during the

Figure 12. Wrocław, block of houses bounded by Szewska, Ofiar Oświęcimskich, and Łaciarska Streets and inner moat: (1) medieval town wall; (2) gothic; (3) Renaissance; (4) baroque; (5) 19th-20th centuries; (6) partly demolished brick wall; (7) abutting walls; (8) toothing; (9) extent of vaulting; (10) probable circuit of the wall; (11) sunken features; (12) dry moat; (13) ceramic water mains, and (14-15) edge of excavations (Konczewski 2007:figure 8).

Middle Ages. Consequently, the function of a sanitary backup area was served by the backyards of the town plots. Impurities were deposited on its surface or in periodically cleaned cesspits. The plots, large enough during the earlier age were by the close of the Middle Ages subdivided into more narrow units, their boundaries made permanent by brick town houses. The results of archaeological investigations show that during the 16th-18th centuries the backyards were largely built over with outbuildings (annexes) and other wooden structures (Figure 12). There was no longer space for any greenery, the only room left was used for the cesspits. The construction technology of the latter was in general the same as during the medieval period. They continued to be pits shored up with timber which allowed the impurities to sink into the ground (Figure 13). The high cost of emptying the cesspits discouraged the majority of the townspeople from doing this more often than once every dozen-odd years, based on archaeological observations and historical research (Brzezowski

2005). Let us add that the contents of the emptied cesspits found their way into the Oder or were disposed of in specified locations on the outskirts of the town (Piekalski 2004:figure 5; Brzezowski 2005:308-310).

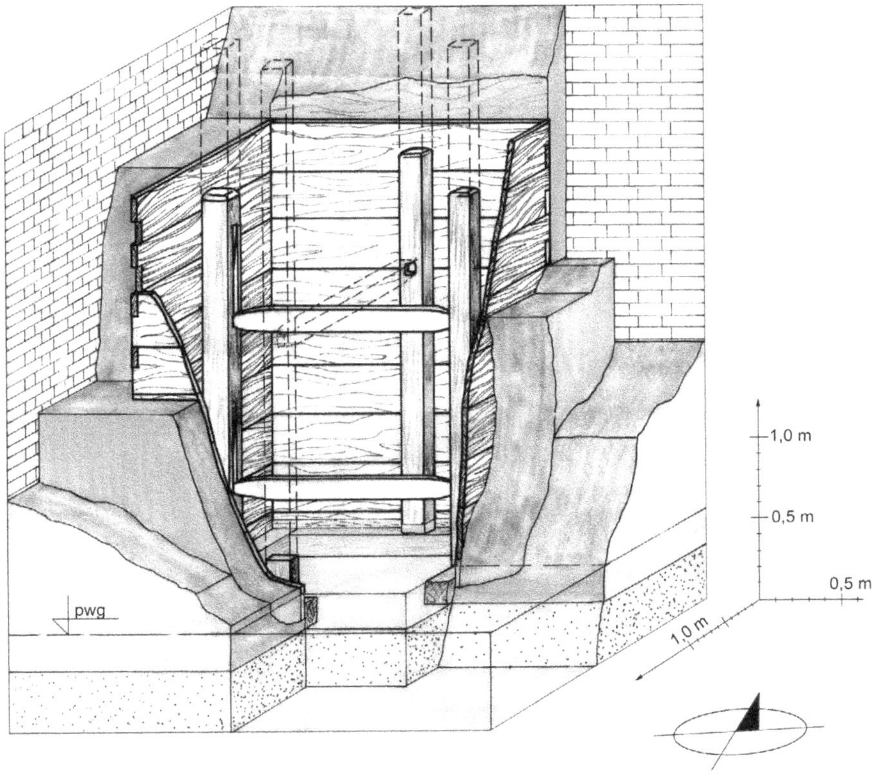

Some of the sewage drained from the town plots directly into street sewers. Their form largely remained the same as during the medieval period—a shallow trough running the length of the street covered over with planks (Piekalski 2004:352-354). With time the "classic sewer" formed by molding the stone pavement became widespread. Sewers operated on the principle of gravity, carrying their contents to the Oder or into the town moats. We have evidence that this system was faulty and bothersome—there were attempts to pass new regulations, conflicts and quarrels between neighbors to be settled in court, and complaints and petitions submitted by the townspeople to the Building Office (Brzezowski 2005:307-312). All of this suggests that the technical measures designed to keep the town clean during the 16th-18th centuries were unsatisfactory.

Figure 13. Wrocław, underground part of an 18th-century cesspit in the back of a town plot at 29/30 Więzienna Street (Drawing by Krzysztof Tomaszewicz, 1991, after Piekalski 2004:figure 5).

The problem of disposal of feces and liquid sewage was solved only around 1900 with the construction of a sewage disposal system.

CONCLUSIONS

In this present outline a discussion and assessment is made of factors that influenced the quality of life in the town imposed by the natural and anthropogenic features of the city's environment.

The town's location on a large meandering river of many channels with its range of benefits for defense and economy is well known. Less attention has been paid in past research to the unfavorable impact of the river on town life—the need for regular investment in projects to protect the town from flooding and make the land suitable for building construction, the water-logging of river bank districts, the poor quality of potable water, problems with removal of impurities, and a damp and an unhealthy micro-climate.

During the medieval stages of the city's development these problems were solved successfully by passing appropriate laws that activated all of the townspeople and by municipal investment in urban infrastructure. The area occupied by the town was large enough to accommodate its population with ample room for tracts of ground empty from urban development to be used for grassland. The town moats were protected from pollution. It is significant that most decisions concerning the town were made by its own government—a council elected from among the townspeople. At the present stage of research we can claim that the medieval town had not caused any drastic disturbance to the natural environment.

In the post-medieval period the situation deteriorated dramatically. The focus placed on the defenses and the function of the town as a fortress in the military system of the country got in the way of the town's territorial expansion, keeping it within its 13th-century boundaries. At the same time, regularly expanded and modernized bastion fortifications were the main investment project undertaken in the city starting from the 16th century until the late 18th century, reducing expenditure on urban infrastructure. The confined space of the city became too small for its rapidly growing population. Houses and outbuildings became congested, and tracts of grassland were swallowed up by urban development. Backyards were also built over, reducing their sanitary function. Substantial accretion of waste and impurities from town plots made the system of waste disposal, still based on medieval models, inefficient. The town moats and the river became drastically polluted and, with time, threatened to cause an epidemic.

Overpopulation and the disastrous sanitary status of the city assisted by new developments in methods of waging war in the times of Napoleon prompted the decision, in 1807, to pull down the city's fortifications. This opened for the town the way to an extensive spatial expansion during the 19th and 20th centuries in an age of advancing industrialization, and further rapid population increase.

REFERENCES

ADAMS, JOHN QUINCY
1804   *Letters on Silesia, Written during a Tour Through that Country in the Years 1800, 1801*. J. Budd, London, England.

BADURA, JANUSZ
2010   *Geomorfologiczne uwarunkowania lokalizacji lewobrzeżnego osadnictwa Wrocławia* [*The Geomorphology and Topography of Wrocław Old Town and Adjacent Areas*]. In *Ulice średniowiecznego Wrocławia*, Jerzy Piekalski and Krzysztof Wachowski, editors, pp. 15-45. Wratislavia Antiqua 11. Institute of Archaeology, University of Wrocław, Poland.

BERGER, OTTO
1926   *Die Bauordnungen der Stadt Breslau von 1605 bis 1925* [*Building Regulations in Wrocław from 1605 to 1925*]. Grass, Barth & Comp., Breslau [Wrocław], Poland.

BORN, ARTUR
1948   *Regulacja Odry i rozbudowa urządzeń technicznych* [*Regulation of the Oder and Development of Technical Devices*]. In *Monografia Odry*, Andrzej Grodek, Maria Kiełczewska-Zaleska, and August Zierhoffer, editors, pp. 419-453. Instytut Zachodni, Poznań, Poland.

BOYLE, NICOLAS
2000   *Goethe. The Poet and the Age, vol. II. Revolution and Renunciation, 1790-1803*. Oxford University Press, England.

BRESCH, JOLANTA, CZESŁAW LASOTA, AND JERZY PIEKALSKI
2002   Północna pierzeja Rynku. Stratygrafia nawarstwień kulturowych [North Side of Market Square and Stratigraphy of the Cultural Deposits]. In *Rynek wrocławski w świetle badań archeologicznych*, part 2, Jerzy Piekalski, editor, pp. 11-69. Wratislavia Antiqua 5. Institute of Archaeology, University of Wrocław, Poland.

BRZEZOWSKI, WOJCIECH
2005   Urządzenia wodno-kanalizacyjne w domach wrocławskich w XVII i XVIII w. [Water and Sanitary Facilities in Houses in Wrocław in the 17th-18th Centuries]. *Kwartalnik Historii Kultury Materialnej* 53(3-4):306-312.

FEJTOVÁ, OLGA, VACLAV LEDVINKA, AND JIRI PEŠEK (EDITORS)
2005   *Město a voda. Praha, město u vody* [*City and Water. Prague, the City on the Water*]. Dokumenta Pragensia 24. Prague City Archives, Czech Republic.

GOLIŃSKI, MATEUSZ
2001   XV-wieczny opis wrocławskiej sieci wodociągowej [Fifteenth-Century Description of the Water Supply System in Wrocław]. In *Studia i materiały z dziejów Śląska i Małopolski*, Rościsław Żerelik, editor, pp. 104-123. Oficyna Wydawnicza Arboretum, Wrocław, Poland.

2007   *Socjototografia późnośredniowiecznego Wrocławia* [*Socio-topography of Late Medieval Wrocław*]. Wydawnictwo Uniwersytetu, Wrocławskiego, Wrocław, Poland.

2010   Ulice średniowiecznego Wrocławia w świetle źródeł pisanych [The Streets of Late Medieval Wrocław in Light of the Written Sources)]. In *Ulice średniowiecznego Wrocławia*, Jerzy Piekalski and Krzysztof Wachowski, editors, pp. 57-66. Wratislavia Antiqua 11. Institute of Archaeology, University of Wrocław, Poland.

GREWE, KLAUS
1991   Wasserversorgung und – entsorgung im Mittelalter [Water Supply and Waste Disposal in the Middle Ages]. In *Die Wasserversorgung im Mittelalter, Geschichte der Wasserversorgung 4*, Klaus Grewe, editor, pp. 11-86. Frontinus Gesellschaft, Mainz am Rhein, Germany.

JANCZEWSKI, PIOTR

2005   Urządzenia wodno-sanitarne we wschodniej części Starego Miasta we Wrocławiu [Water Supply and Sanitary Facilities in the Eastern Part of the Old Town in Wrocław]. In *Wschodnia strefa Starego Miasta we Wrocławiu w XII-XIV wieku. Badania na placu Nowy Targ*, Cezary Buśko, editor, pp 85-96. GAJT Wydawnictwo 1991 s.c., Wrocław, Poland.

JASTRZĘBSKI, ANDRZEJ, JERZY PIEKALSKI, AND IRENA WYSOCKA

2001   Badania dawnych działek mieszczańskich przy ulicach św. Mikołaja 19-25 i Nowy Świat 38-40 we Wrocławiu, Śląskie [Excavations in Former Burgher Plots in 19-25 St. Nikolai Street and Nowy Swiat Street in Wrocław]. *Sprawozdania Archeologiczne* 43:363-374.

KANIECKI, ALFRED

2004   *Poznań. Dzieje miasta wodą pisane [Poznan. History of Water in the City]*. Poznańskie Towarzystwo Przyjaciół Nauk, Redakcja Wydawnictw, Poznań, Poland.

KONCZEWSKI, PAWEŁ

2007   *Działki mieszczańskie w południowo-wschodniej części średniowiecznego i wczesnonowożytnego Wrocławia [Burgher Plots in Southeast Part of Late Medieval and Post-Medieval Wrocław]*. Wratislavia Antiqua 9. Institute of Archaeology, University of Wrocław, Poland.

KONCZEWSKI, PAWEŁ, AND JERZY PIEKALSKI

2010   Stratygrafia nawarstwień i konstrukcje ulic [Stratigraphy of the Cultural Deposits and Methods of Street Construction]. In *Ulice średniowiecznego Wrocławia*, Jerzy Piekalski and Krzysztof Wachowski, editors, pp. 91-157. Wratislavia Antiqua 11. Institute of Archaeology, University of Wrocław, Poland.

ŁAGIEWSKI, MACIEJ

1998   *Mosty Wrocławia [Bridges of Wrocław]*. Ossolineum, Wrocław, Poland.

LEONHARD, RUDOLF

1901   Die Entwicklung der Stromlage der Oder bei Breslau [Development of Odra Channels in Wrocław]. In *Hafen Anlagen zu Breslau*, pp. 1-122. von CT Wiskott, Breslau [Wrocław], Poland.

LIMISIEWICZ, ALEKSANDER

1998   Zaopatrzenie w wodę [Water Supply]. *Silesia Antiqua* 39:215-220.

ŁUKASZEWICZ, PIOTR (EDITOR)

2008   *Ikonografia Wrocławia, vol. II, Rysunek i akwarela, obrazy olejne, dioramy, medalierstwo, rzemiosło artystyczne [Iconography of Wrocław, vol. II. Drawing and Watercolor, Oil Painting, Diorama, Medallic Art, Handicraft]*. Muzeum Narodowe we Wrocławiu, Wrocław, Poland.

MARKGRAF, HERMAN

1896   *Die Straßen Breslaus nach ihrer Geschichte und ihren Namen [The Streets of Wrocław According to its History and Names]*. Verlag von E. Morgenstern, Breslau [Wrocław], Poland.

MASCHKE, ERICH, AND JUERGEN SYDOW (EDITORS)

1978   Die Stadt am Fluss. 14. Arbeitstagung in Kehl, 14.-16. 11. 1975, Stadt in der Geschichte [Town by the River. The 14th Conference in Kehl, 14.-16.11.1975, Town in History]. *Veröffentlichungen des Südwestdeutschen Arbeitskreises für Stadtgeschichtsforschung* 4. Jan Thorbecke, Sigmaringen, Germany.

MŁYNARSKA, MARTA, AND RAFAŁ EYSYMONTT

2001   *Atlas historyczny miast polskich, IV, Śląsk, 1, Wrocław [Historical Atlas of Polish Towns, IV, Silesia, 1. Wrocław]*. Wydawnictwo Via Nova, Wrocław, Poland.

PIEKALSKI, JERZY

2001   *Von Köln nach Krakau. Der topographische Wandel früher Städte [From Cologne to Krakow. Transformation of the Topography of Early Towns]*. Zeitschrift für Archäologie des Mittelalters, Beiheft 13. Dr. Rudolf Habelt GmbH, Bonn, Germany.

2004   Die Infrastruktur der mittelalterlichen und frühneuzeitlichen Stadt Breslau [The Infrastructure of Medieval and Post-Medieval Wrocław]. In *Lübecker Kolloquium zur Stadtarchäologie im Hanseraum, IV. Die Infrastruktur*, Manfred Gläser, editor, pp. 343-358. Verlag Schmidt-Römhild, Lübeck, Germany.

2007   Neubau oder Weiterentwicklung? Frühneuzeitliche Stadtbefestigung in Breslau und Krakau [New Building or Expansion? Post-Medieval Fortification of Wrocław and Krakow]. *Mitteilungen der Deutschen Gesellschaft für Archäologie des Mittelalters und der Neuzeit* 18:131-141.

2008   Entwicklung der urbanen Struktur Breslaus im Mittelalter [Development of Urban Structures in Medieval Wrocław]. In *Das Bild von Wrocław/Breslau im Laufe der Geschichte*, Jan Harasimowicz, editor, pp. 15-28. Wissenschaftliches Zentrum der Polnischen Akademie der Wissenschaften in Wien, Austria.

PIEKALSKI, JERZY AND KRZYSZTOF WACHOWSKI

2010   Wende des 15. und 16. Jahrhunderts in den Städten Schlesiens [Turn of the 15th and 16th Centuries in the Silesian Towns]. In *Zwischen Tradition und Wandel. Archäologie des 15. und 16. Jahrhunderts*, Barbara Scholkmann, Sören Frommer, Christina Vossler, and Marcus Wolf, editors, pp. 409-420. Tübinger Forschungen zur historischen Archäologie, Verlag Dr. Faustus, Tübingen, Germany.

SOWINA, URSZULA

2009   *Woda i ludzie w mieście średniowiecznym i
        wczesnonowożytnym. Ziemie polskie z Europą
        w tle* [*Water and People in a Late Medieval
        and Early Modern Town. Polish Lands on the
        European Background*]. Instytut Archeologii i
        Etnologii PAN, Warsaw, Poland.

STEIN, BARTHOLOMÄUS

1995   *Bartłomieja Steina renesansowe opisanie
        Wrocławia (Die Beschreibung der Stadt Breslau
        der Renaissancezeit durch Bartholomäus Stein)*
        [*Bartholomäus Steins Description of Wrocław*],
        Rościsław Żerelik, editor. Oficyna Wydawnicza
        Arboretum, Wrocław, Poland.

ZIĄTKOWSKI, LESZEK

2001   Die räumliche und architektonische Entwicklung
        Breslaus vom 16. bis zum 18. Jahrhundert [Spatial
        and Architectural Development of Wrocław
        from the 16th until the 18th Century]. In *Atlas
        historyczny miast polskich*, IV, *Śląsk*, 1, *Wrocław*,
        Marta Młynarska and Rafał Eysymontt, editors,
        pp. 21-24.Wydawnictwo Via Nova, Wrocław,
        Poland.

Jerzy Piekalski
Instytut Archeologii Uniwersytetu Wrocławskiego
ul. Szewska 48
PL-50-139 Wrocław
Poland

RALF KLUTTIG-ALTMANN

Archaeology in Pirna: The Systematic Study of Post-Medieval Finds Based on the Example of a Small Town in Saxony

ABSTRACT

Everyday archaeological research in Germany, particularly in recent decades, has triggered a huge increase in medieval and post-medieval finds. Due to intensified building activity since 1990, this has been particularly true of the eastern German states. In 2005/2006 the Saxony State Office for Archaeology in Dresden ran a pilot project that consisted of giving a number of long-term unemployed an opportunity to acquire basic archaeological knowledge and to sort and process the entire body of finds recovered from the small Saxon town of Pirna under the supervision of the author. The actual work consisted mainly of sorting and reconstructing the pottery, which constituted the bulk of the finds. The material was then photographed and drawings were made. The scientific analysis of the finds carried out by the author focused on the ceramic tableware, stove-tiles, mineral water bottles, glass vessels, and clay pipes. The study also took into account the finds from more recent periods, such as porcelain and Bunzlau-type crockery, which do not usually receive much attention from archaeologists. Despite its limited timeframe, the pilot project showed how effective such endeavors can be, even using an untrained but motivated workforce. The inventory of finds created by the project is now available as a basis for further analyses. It is recommended that other archaeological institutions launch similar projects.

PRECONDITIONS AND METHODS

Comprehensive studies of post-medieval finds with the aim of compiling a complete record and analysis of a particular site or region are still a rarity in Germany. This is due to a variety of reasons, the most crucial being the enormous accumulation of finds, particularly in eastern Germany, over the past 20 years, which has overwhelmed all of the archaeological institutions. Prompted by ambitious building projects, which had a profound impact on the town – and cityscapes, and assisted by relatively modern monument conservation legislation that included a costs-by-cause principle, numerous small, large, and very large excavations took place that yielded millions of finds, very quickly inundating the storage facilities that had been simultaneously created. Because some of the excavations were carried out in town and city centers, and due to an increasing acceptance of post-medieval/modern archaeological research, a particularly large proportion of those finds date from post-medieval times.

Usually the majority of these finds are put into storage without any post-excavation work being carried out. The funding and organizational structure of the excavation projects are usually stretched to capacity with the work in the field and very little time is left for the post-excavation analysis. Only short preliminary reports are initially published, if at all. Studies of larger finds assemblages or overviews of particular categories of finds are often assigned to candidates for scientific theses or final papers. Individual outstanding finds are presented in exhibitions. Naturally, this approach to the analysis of the archaeological material can only deal with a fraction of the daily increase in finds. Conventional archaeological services do not have the capacity to undertake an adequate scientific study of the accumulated artifacts. This is an unfortunate development since, besides safe-guarding and protecting the finds from destruction, their recovery is, in fact, inextricably linked with the aim and promise of their scientific analysis.

All the more credit is due to some state archaeological services for their efforts to begin and continue systematic studies of the finds. Worth mentioning besides the project presented here is a study of post-medieval finds from the Lutheran town of Wittenberg, which has rich archaeological and historical sources, launched by the Saxony-Anhalt State Office for the Preservation of Historical Monuments and Archaeology in Halle/Saale

Figure 1.   Map with places mentioned in the text (in Saxony, Germany, unless otherwise noted): (1) Pirna; (2) Dresden; (3) Wermsdorf/ Hubertusburg; (4) Leisnig; (5) Bylany/Püllna, Bohemia, Czech Republic; (6) Eger/Cheb, Bohemia, Czech Republic; and (7) Waldenburg, Thuringia, Germany (Map provided courtesy of the Department of Prehistory and Medieval Archaeology, University of Vienna, Austria).

in 2007. Begun in 2007 by the author and continued as part of other projects, the task has not yet been completed due to the large amount of finds and because of other ongoing excavations. (The author is currently also engaged in the project "Archaeology around Martin Luther" set to run until 2014).

In 2005/2006 the Saxony State Office in Dresden took the opportunity presented by the availability of funding from the Federal Employment Agency to undertake a study of all the information gleaned from excavations in the small Saxon town of Pirna. Besides compiling a general record of the body of information and gaining new knowledge about the finds and features, the scientific aim was to create an easy to understand and richly illustrated archaeological guide to the town that would include the information gathered by archaeological research in Pirna from prehistory to modern times. To achieve this goal, 15 people without any archaeological knowledge were hired and paid no regular salary, but certain social security benefits and an expense allowance of just €1 per hour. The project was therefore geared toward the integration of these mainly long-term unemployed people, to prevent their social isolation and to reintegrate them into the so-called "active labor market." In introducing them to working with finds, the author first had to train them how, for example, to sort and cross-mend pottery, to take photographs, and to create drawings of the finds. Besides this training program, the author also worked on a scientific study of the finds and features. By organizing several supporting events, the workers were introduced to the world of archaeology, which previously had been largely unknown to them, while stimulating an abiding interest in their work, which in turn manifested itself in its high quality.

PIRNA AS AN EXAMPLE

Pirna on the River Elbe, a small town east of Dresden (Figure 1), was chosen for this project because the local archaeological service had produced a considerable, but in comparison to larger cities, manageable amount of finds. It was thus deemed possible to achieve meaningful results within a period of 18 months. While the study incorporated all archaeological finds and features from prehistory to modern times, this paper is focused on early modern times in order to suit the subject matter of this volume. By choosing Pirna, the State Office also wished to elevate the current state of research in a small Saxon town, since extensive

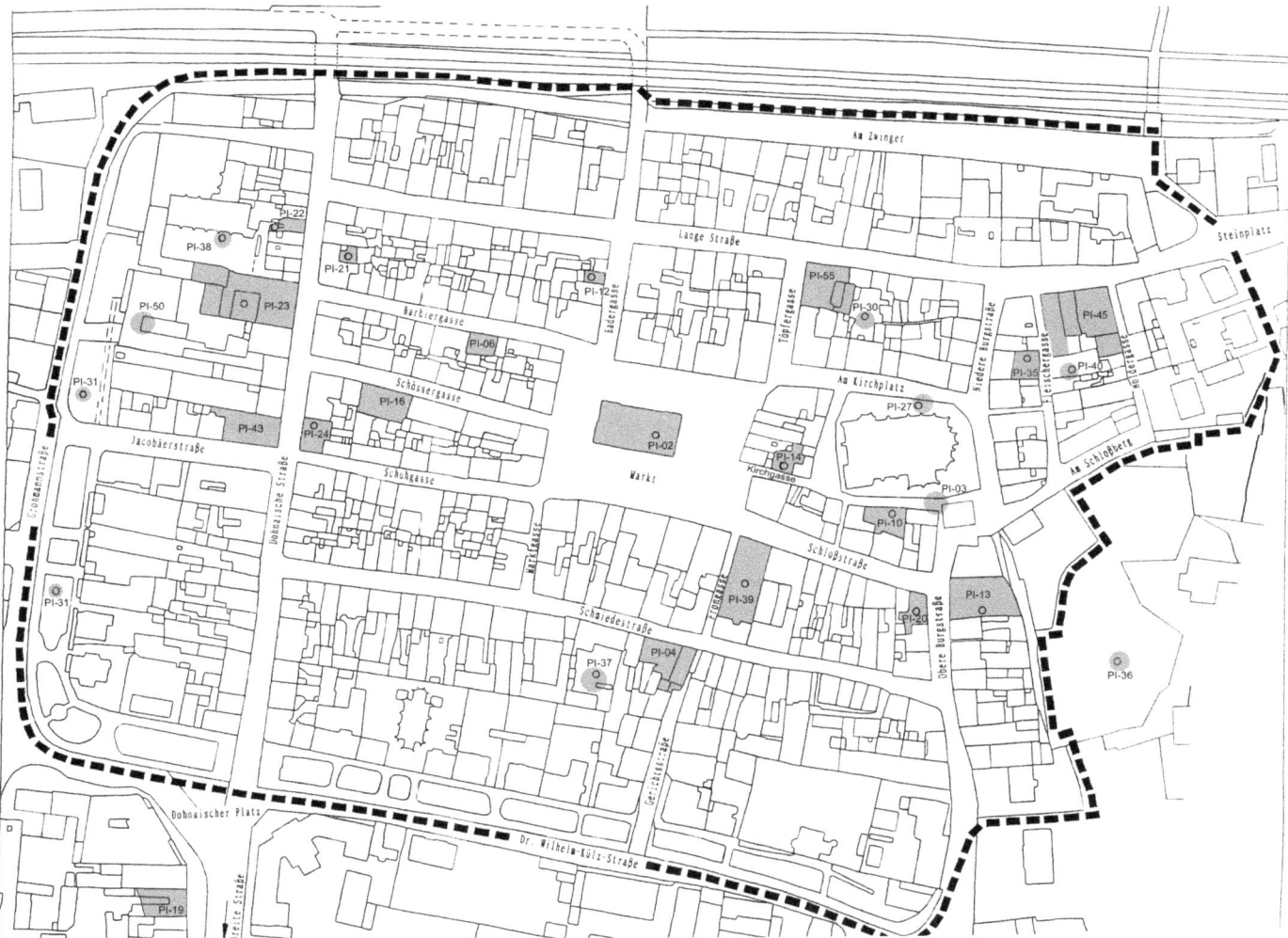

Figure 2. Land register map of the historical center of Pirna (outlined), oriented to north. The excavations carried out between ca. 1992 and 2006 are marked in green and are labeled with their excavation numbers (Courtesy of Saxony State Office for Archaeology).

building projects over the past number of years had resulted in mainly large cities such as Dresden, Leipzig, and Chemnitz being the subject of intensive archaeological research.

Pirna is situated at the entrance to the Elbe Sandstone Mountains. Its location is therefore extremely favorable—not only has the River Elbe long been a convenient transportation route, but ever since prehistoric times Pirna has been a spot where important trade routes converged. In the Middle Ages these included the arterial roads from Meissen to Königstein/Tetschen and from Prague to Bautzen, both running via Dresden. A tranquil small town today, Pirna was granted a town charter in 1239 and over the centuries became a bustling center of trade and commerce; before Dresden became a royal residence, Pirna was significantly larger and more important (Eigenwill 1989:134-135).

The buildings in Pirna had been quite dilapidated during the final years of the German Democratic Republic. Numerous houses, some of great historical value, could not be saved and had to be demolished. A wave of redevelopment and new building projects that gradually began after the reunification of Germany offered an opportunity for the Pirna Town Archaeological Service, which only existed for a limited period, and subsequently for the Dresden State Office for Archaeology, to mount excavations in numerous plots (Figure 2).

DEVELOPMENT OF THE TOWN STRUCTURE FROM THE MIDDLE AGES TO MODERN TIMES

The numerous excavations that were carried out in the area of the old town of Pirna gave archaeologists a large-scale insight into the archaeological and geological strata. An imaginary north-south axis shows quite significant altitude differences mainly in the eastern section of the town. The natural soil declines by almost five percent toward the River Elbe. Obere Burgstraße and Kirchplatz in the northeast of the town are situated on an outcrop of the Sonnenstein hill, on a plateau high above the old part of the town, where several fortifications have existed since no later than the Late Middle Ages (Figure 3). The other areas of the town center are located at a much lower altitude and are thus prone to considerable flooding despite repeated attempts having been made from as far back as the Middle Ages to rectify this situation by introducing large-scale fills. To this day, almost the entire old part of the town is flood-prone, as was clearly shown by flooding in 2002.

The present-day structure of Pirna shows a planned layout typical of the towns planted during the High and late medieval German colonization of the east. Continuity in the design of the plots and orientation of the houses is therefore apparent from as early as the 12th-14th centuries. Some of the timber – and stone-built houses were oriented with eaves facing neighboring plots, a trend that continued until quite recently, thus attesting to a strong, unbroken tradition. The German settlement expanded in the 12th and 13th centuries into the flood-prone areas of the town, which had previously been avoided, between the castle hill promontory and the River Elbe, and in the location where the Dominican Monastery would later be built in the northwest of the town center. The oldest nucleus of the town on the slope of the Sonnenstein hill (Obere Burgstraße 2, PI-13) still showed a completely different structure in the 13th century and was not incorporated into the town's system of plots until the end of the century and therefore quite a while after the founding of the town. When it was integrated into the town, it adopted the usual layout consisting of residential buildings facing the streets and commercial buildings in the back yards.

Figure 3. *The historical center of Pirna as seen from the north. The Sonnenstein hill can be seen on the left side of the image, the former Dominican monastery is on the right side in the middle, and the train line between Dresden and Prague can be seen in the foreground (Courtesy of Saxony State Office for Archaeology).*

In the 14th century the infrastructure of the emergent trading town of Pirna was increasingly built in stone. In the area around the monastery, the final grid of plots appears to have been created at a later stage, in the 14th century, which can be explained by the construction of the monastery and the shifting of the town wall to encompass it.

In post-medieval times the town developed further within the structures that had existed since the late Middle Ages. The suburbs grew, while additional new houses were built in certain locations within the town center. Important historical events occurred during this period, some of which had profound consequences for the development of Pirna. The main event was the Thirty Years' War, during the turmoil of which Pirna suffered severe damage (Eigenwill 1989). After Saxon troops had themselves razed the suburbs outside the Dohnaisches and Elbtor gates in order to create a clear field of fire for their defense, the siege of the town by Swedish troops began on 16 April 1639. Having laid waste to the remaining suburbs and surrounding villages, the Swedes launched a direct attack on Pirna on 23 April and the town was conquered amid scenes of destruction, while the Saxon garrison retreated to the Sonnenstein hill. Despite repeated attempts at fighting a decisive battle outside Pirna, the Swedish troops under Marshal Banèr did not manage to conquer the Sonnenstein hill, and before moving off decided to at least destroy the town completely. This, however, was avoided thanks to the intervention of the brave citizens and eventually "only" the town walls and the salt-house were demolished. The situation after the withdrawal of the Swedes on 25 September 1639 was, all the same, devastating: 70 houses in the town and almost all the houses in the suburbs were destroyed, and 600 Pirna citizens had lost their lives. This pivotal event in the life of the flourishing town resulted in an economically very difficult period and is remembered to this day as *Pirnsches Elend* (Pirna's misery). The event is reflected in the archaeological record in the form of destruction layers and numerous early 17th-century finds.

One of the main aims of the project and the most important part of the actual work was the study of the finds. After this short introduction on the methods and the history of the town, the presentation of some of the finds categories studied will now follow.

SELECTED EARLY POST-MEDIEVAL FINDS (16TH-18TH CENTURIES)

Pottery

Several plots yielded ceramic finds, which were not overly abundant but could be clearly identified as fragments of wasters or at least very poor-quality pottery, showing that pottery was produced on-site from the late Middle Ages onward. Most of the fragments have sunken rims that caved in due to excessive temperatures during firing. It is not possible to ascertain in every case whether the pottery had been "third-class" ware knowingly purchased or whether the area had been used by a potter to discard his waste. Since a large proportion of this pottery was recovered from plots relatively close to the River Elbe, in particular in the area of Lange Straße/Plangasse, the possibility remains that ceramic waste was used for a systematic raising of the ground level. The location of the workshop or workshops has not actually been pinpointed so far.

From the 16th century onwards post-medieval pottery was produced in an ever-increasing variety of wares, particularly glazed wares (Figure 4, nos. 1-3). Unglazed wares continued to be used, some in characteristically unglazed shapes, some as simple cooking vessels (Figure 4, nos. 4-7). Pirna potters made high-quality pottery, and over the course of the study many of the fragments could be joined back together to recreate their original shapes. It was probably thanks to the outstanding quality of the simple earthenware that hardly any slip-trailed ware was produced or brought in and that only small amounts of stoneware were imported. Compared to other Saxon sites, these wares were clearly underrepresented in Pirna. Most of the slip-trailed ware that was present consisted of plates, bowls, or jugs (Figure 4, no. 8). The simple utility stoneware came from Saxon/Thuringian production sites. The most popular vessels were large bowls, small dishes, flower pots, and bottles made of light brown stoneware and jugs and pitchers made of grey stoneware with blue trailing (Figure 4, nos. 9-10). The vessels were quite robust and, unlike lead-glazed earthenware, chemically resistant, even to acidic contents.

Mineral water bottles, used by spas from the 18th century onwards to ship their water, were an obvious indication regarding the health consciousness of our ancestors. The high consumption of mineral water led to a large-scale production of appropriate "jugs" or "bottles," for example in the Waldenburg area. Starting

Figure 4a.   Selected finds.

(1) Unusually large tripod skillet made of green-glazed earthenware with heavy traces of wear, height 19 cm, diameter of the bowl 35 cm, entire width 51 cm. Niedere Burgstraße 5/Fleischergasse (PI-35).

(2) Cup with brown glaze both inside and out, height ca. 6 cm. Schlossstraße 4/Kirchplatz 9a (PI-10).

(3) Green-glazed flower pot with cruciform openings near the bottom so that excess water could escape, height ca. 20 cm. Lange Straße 33/34 (PI-55).

(4) Unglazed red earthenware pot with handles showing traces of lime, height ca. 15 cm. Schlossstraße 4/Kirchplatz 9a (PI-10).

(5) Large storage pot made of unglazed stoneware-like hard earthenware with partial vapor glazing, height ca. 40 cm. Lange Straße 33/34 (PI-55).

(6) Hollow lid made of unglazed yellow earthenware, diameter ca. 12 cm. Significant traces of soot on the underside and parts of the outside suggest that the mouth of the vessel that it covered had a smaller diameter. Lange Straße 33/34 (PI-55).

(7) Unusual bell-shaped lid made of unglazed orange earthenware. The knob is perforated from the inside of the lid, diameter ca. 14 cm. No traces of soot, suggesting that it was used for some kind of fermentation process rather than cooking. Schmiedestraße 16/17 (PI-04).

(8) Pear-shaped slip-trailed jug, height ca. 20 cm. Red earthenware with reddish-brown and in parts dark brown basic slip and yellow trailing, provenance uncertain. Lange Straße 33/34 (PI-55).

9   10   11   12

Figure 4b.   *Selected finds, continued.*

(9) Small grey stoneware pot with blue trailing, height ca. 11 cm. Probably Saxon. Niedere Burgstraße 5/Fleischergasse (PI-35).
(10) Small ochre stoneware jug, height ca. 14 cm. Provenance uncertain, possibly from Waldenburg. Dohnaische Straße 76 (PI-23).
(11, left) Mineral water bottle slightly flattened on all four sides made of salt-glazed stoneware from Püllna near Most (present-day Bylany, Czech Republic), height ca. 22 cm, 1830s. Dohnaische Straße 76 (PI-23). (11, right) Detail of a stamp from an identical bottle showing a circular stamp with "PILLNAER BITTER WASSER*" (Pillna bitter water) around the initials "AU" above an oval stamp that reads "A: ULBRICH," the owner of the spring, Adalbert Ulbrich. Schmiedestraße 16/17 (PI-04).
(12) Salt-glazed stoneware mineral water bottle, height ca. 25 cm. Stamp on the shoulder with the Eger coat of arms and a circumscription that reads "FRANZENSBAD BEI EGER" (Franzensbad near Eger), below the stamp "EGER. S.B," and below "BH." Dohnaische Straße 76 (PI-23).
(All images courtesy of Saxony State Office for Archaeology.)

in the 19th century, mineral water was increasingly sold in glass bottles that could be produced industrially and therefore more cheaply (see below).

Thick-walled ceramic mineral water bottles, or their remains, were almost inevitably found in the waste layers of Pirna from the 18th century onwards. The bottles usually bore two markings: the stamp of the spring where the bottle would be filled, and the potter's signature mark. Based on the marks denoting the springs, it was possible to ascertain where the town of Pirna had generally sourced their mineral water: mainly in the south, from springs in Bohemia. Particularly popular was the "Pillnaer Bitterwasser" (mineral water from Püllna, present-day Bylany, Czech Republic), since most of the bottles bore that mark (Figure 4, no. 11). In the early 19th century this water was apparently successfully used to treat the mentally ill, as is gushingly testified to by positive reports from the Prague Lunatic Asylum in the *Augsburger Anzeiger* (a local newspaper of Augsburg) in May 1835.

Eger-Franzensbad (present-day Cheb and Františkovy Lázně, Czech Republic) was also quite important for Pirna consumers. While it is known that the Eger spring initially used mainly Waldenburg bottles, repeated complaints about their poor quality led Eger in 1723 to open their own bottleworks nearby (Brinkmann 1984:171). Moreover, from 1789 onwards, round bottles began

to replace the square bottles (compare the find from Pillna). The initials "B.H." on a bottle from Eger (EGER SB = Eger Sauerbrunnen) point to the local bottle manufacturer Bartholomäus Hart, a master bottle maker from a large family of bottle potters, who began his production in 1801 (Brinkmann 1984:174, 1997:71-71) (Figure 4, no. 12).

Stove-Tiles

The Pirna finds also included numerous ceramic stove-tiles. Until modern times (that is, ca. 17th/18th centuries) houses and apartments only contained a single tiled stove, which provided a cozy focal point in the house and was a prestigious object, cooking facility, and center of communication. Later, several rooms contained tiled stoves. The tiles were made by specialty potters. Renaissance panel tiles were decorated with a particularly wide range of images. From the late 15th century onwards the tiles bore allegorical scenes, portraits of secular and clerical rulers, heroes from antiquity, etc., framed in almost architectural decorations and portraying a multi-faceted image of the spiritual world of the time. Initially green-glazed, polychrome tiles became popular from the early 16th century onward, and from 1600 the glaze was often blackish-brown.

An important feature uncovered in a plot at Schlossstraße 4/Kirchplatz 9a (PI-10) was likely linked

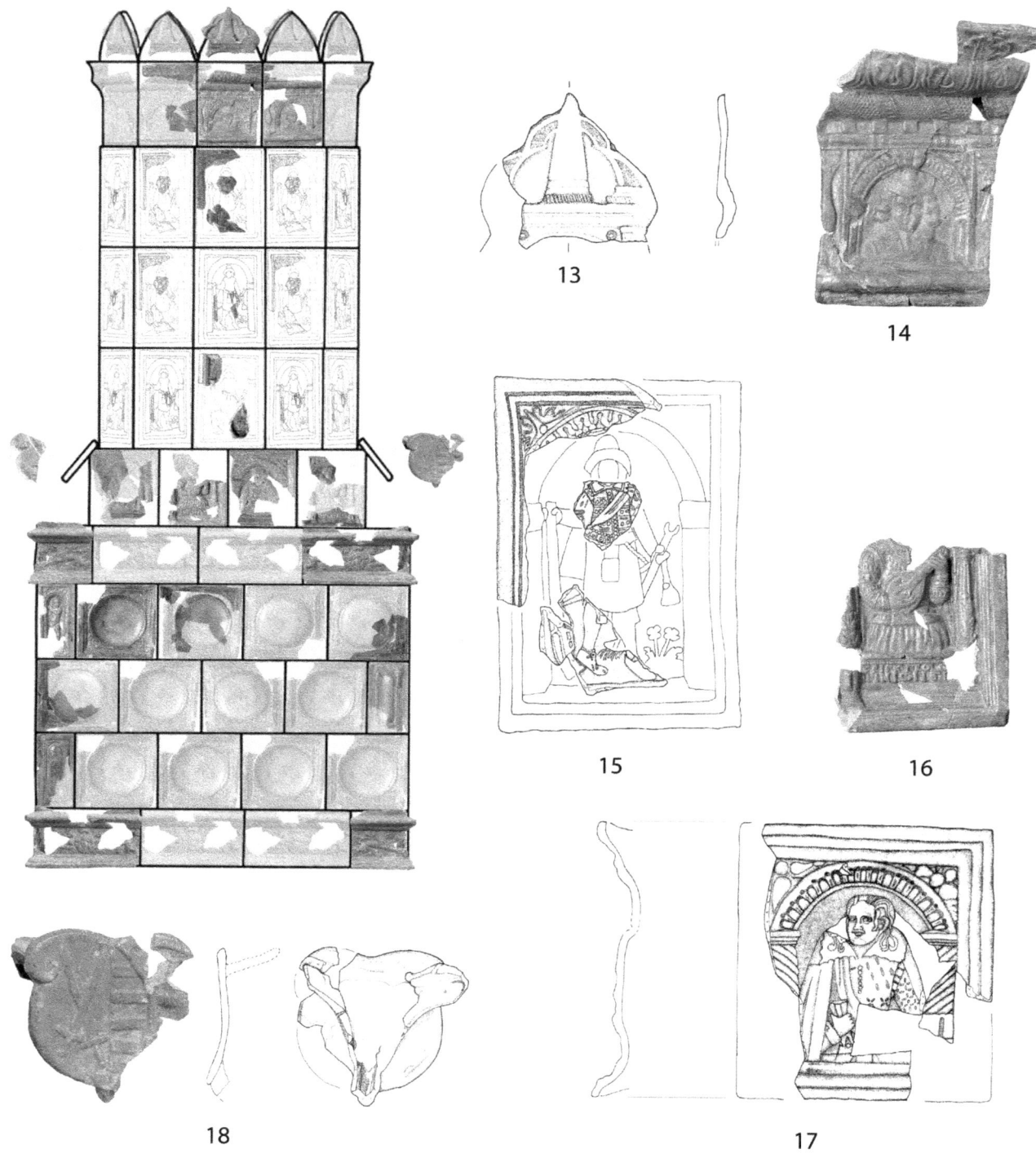

Figure 5a. First attempt at reconstructing a stove with green-glazed tiles (late 16th/early 17th centuries) from the large assemblage of tiles found at Schlossstraße 4/Kirchplatz 9a (Pl-10).

(13) Crown-tile, green-glazed earthenware, height 12.5 cm (fragment).

(14) Cornice-tile with portrait of a lady and protruding upper edge, green-glazed earthenware, height 24 cm.

(15) Fragments of one of three panel-tiles with depiction of a mercenary, green-glazed earthenware, reconstructed height 30.5 cm.

(16) Panel-tile with depiction of a lutist bearing the inscription "FRISK FROLICH BINICH 161..." (happy and cheerful am I 161...), green-glazed earthenware, height 18 cm (fragment).

(17) Panel-tile with depiction of a ruler, green-glazed earthenware, height 22 cm.

(18) Cornice-tile in the shape of an escutcheon from the corners of the squat lower part of the stove bearing the coat of arms of the Elector of Saxony, green-glazed earthenware, height 16 cm.

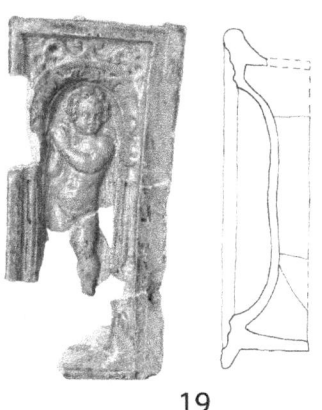  

19   20   21

Figure 5b.   *Continued.*

(19) Corner-tile with depiction of a cupid in a flat-concave panel. Green-glazed earthenware, height 22 cm.

(20) Panel-tile with flat-concave panel and floral motifs in the corners, green-glazed earthenware, height 22 cm.

(21) Cornice-corner-tile with portrait of a lady flanked by a pair of lions on the wider side and a solitary lion on the narrower side, green-glazed earthenware, height 17 cm.

(All images courtesy of Saxony State Office for Archaeology)

to the violent events of the Thirty Years' War. A large number of green-glazed early post-medieval stove-tiles were found there in a rectangular waste pit unevenly set with stones. The tiles had come from at least two different stoves dating from the late 16th century and first quarter of the 17th century, which may well have fallen victim to the devastation of 1639. More than 20 different types of tile were recovered, whose faces bear decorations ranging from abstract geometric patterns to various portraits and figural depictions.

The first stove was reconstructed using the tiles with figural depictions (Figure 5). The reconstruction is described here from the top down. A crown-tile with an obelisk-like motif would have formed the top finial of the stove (Figure 5, no. 13) and would have rested on an upper cornice-tile with projecting upper edge and a portrait of a (perhaps aristocratic) lady (Figure 5, no. 14). A number of fragments from six such tiles were found. A tile bearing a depiction of a mercenary with an arquebus and a forked rest may have formed the remainder of the superstructure. At least three examples of this upright oblong shape were recovered; parallels have been found as far away as Sweden (Figure 5, no. 15) (Strauss 1983:105, plate 83.3). A panel-tile with a depiction of a man holding a lute, at least three examples of which were recovered, may have been part of some kind of middle section between the superstructure and the lower part of the stove (Figure 5, no. 16). The inscription below the image reads "FRISK FROLICH BINICH 161..." (happy and cheerful am I 161...) giving us not only a worthwhile life motto but also an approximate date for the stove. If the mold for the manufacture of this

tile was made between 1611 and 1619, the tiles can date from any time after that period. These tiles may have formed a row alternating with tiles bearing the portrait of a man in aristocratic dress holding a pouch(?) in his right hand (Figure 5, no. 17). This type, of which at least five examples were found, may show the Elector or Emperor (Strauss 1972:136, plate 90.4). The pouch as an attribute displaying wealth is also known from a tile from Lübeck that bears a portrait of Jacob Fugger, a wealthy Augsburg merchant (Arnold and Westphalen 1990:58, figure 49). Special tiles bearing the coat of arms of the Elector of Saxony would have probably sat on the corners of this middle section or on the corners of the squat lower part of the stove. An identical example is known from Wittenberg (Strauss 1972:126, plate 56.1-2) (Figure 5, no. 18). Several corner-tiles bearing a naked boy or cupid standing with his hands held up to his right shoulder were attributed to the lower part of the stove, which probably consisted of panel-tiles with circular flat-concave panels (Figure 5, nos. 19-20) (Hoffmann 2001:149, figures 4.20-4.22). Other corner-tiles just bore blank oval scrolls on their slim panels. The circular panels on the tiles mentioned above were decorated with various types of floral motifs including grapes and blossoms. The lower part of the stove was probably framed by a row of cornice-tiles at its upper and lower edges that show the portrait of a lady set between a pair of lions facing each other (Figure 5, no. 21).

The second stove was reconstructed from tiles with different proportions and decorations consisting of ornamental geometric patterns (Figure 6). This stove may also have had crown-tiles with an obelisk motif.

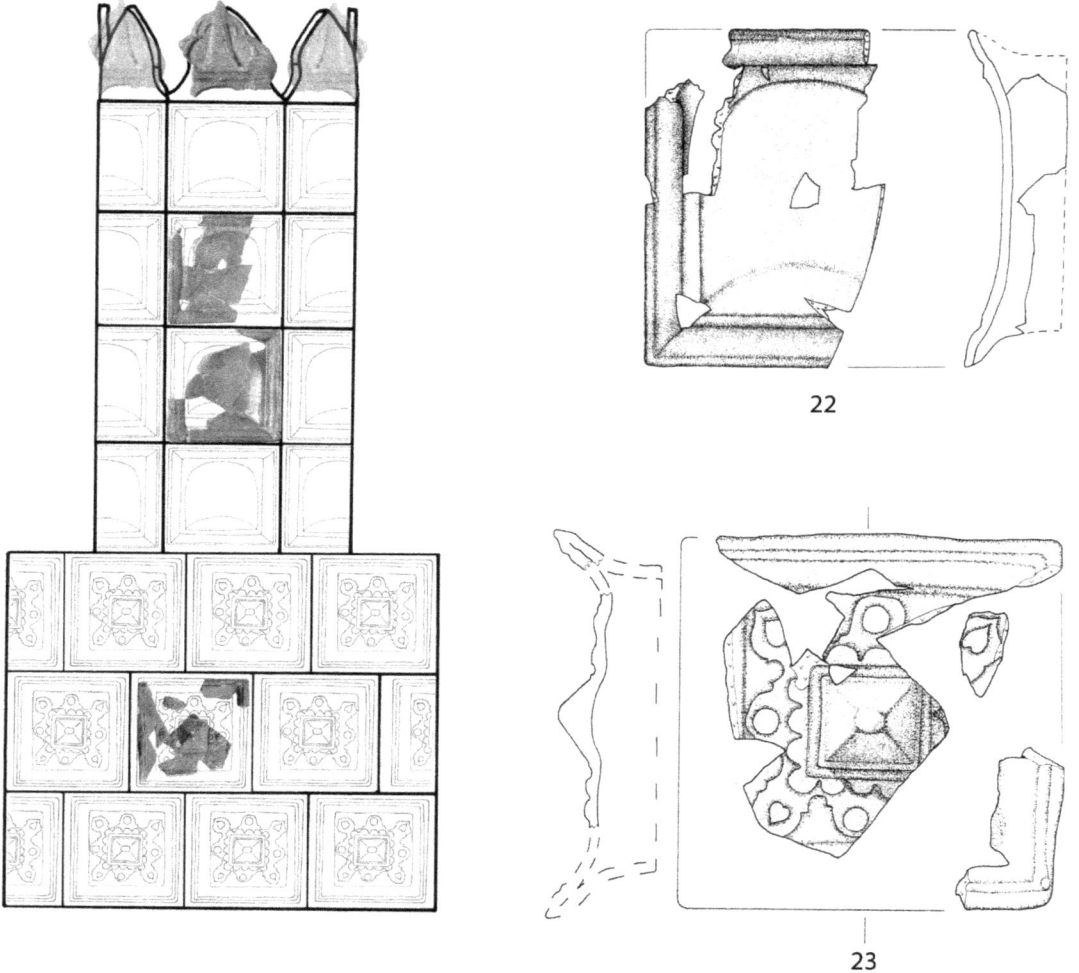

22

23

Figure 6. Second attempt at reconstructing a stove with green-glazed tiles (late 16th/early 17th centuries) from the large assemblage of tiles found at Schlossstraße 4/Kirchplatz 9a (PI-10).
(22) Panel-tiles with sunken window-shaped panels, green-glazed earthenware, height 19.5 cm.
(23) Panel-tile with raised geometrical decoration, green-glazed earthenware, height 21 cm (reconstructed).
(All images courtesy of Saxony State Office for Archaeology)

The superstructure of the stove perhaps consisted of square panel-tiles with window-shaped panels, several examples of which were found (Figure 6, no. 22). The lower part of the stove could have consisted of tiles with geometric relief decorations bearing pyramidal central bosses (Figure 6, no. 23).

A Cloth Seal and Clay Pipes

One of the more unusual finds from Pirna was a cloth seal from Lange Straße 33/34 (PI-55) (Figure 7, no. 24). Its circumscription, stylistically pointing to the 16th/17th centuries, can probably be reconstructed as "LEISNIC" or "LEISNIG." While in early post-medieval times cloth seals were only attached to bales of expensive woolen cloth, they were later also used on linen and blended fabrics. This seal, which besides the name of the town may have also originally indicated the quality of the fabric (density of the weave), is therefore evidence of a delivery of cloth from the Saxon town of Leisnig, approximately 80 km northwest of Pirna.

As was the case at other locations in Saxony, clay pipes and the "drinking of tobacco" in Pirna were probably also introduced mainly by bands of soldiers from the Thirty Years' War. The earliest pipe bowls found in Pirna may actually date from the Swedish siege of 1639. Due to the exorbitant cost of tobacco, which had to be imported from America, pipe bowls, most of which were produced in the Netherlands, were still quite small in the early 17th century. By the 18th century at the latest, however, tobacco was being grown all over Europe and

24   25   26

Figure 7.   Selected finds.

(24) Lead cloth seal, front with "LEISNIC" or "LEISNIG" stamp, length 2.6 cm. Lange Straße 33/34 (PI-55).

(25) Ribbed bowl of a clay pipe with substantial traces of tobacco juice; 19th century, probably produced in Saxony, height 4.5 cm. Niedere Burgstraße 5/Fleischergasse (PI-35).

(26) Bowl of a clay pipe with slight traces of tobacco juice. "Windmill" spur mark, highly polished bowl. Probably from Gouda, around 1730, height 3.3 cm. Töpfergasse/Kirchplatz, private finder.

(All images courtesy of Saxony State Office for Archaeology)

had become much more affordable, leading to the production of pipes with larger bowls. Accordingly, more finds have been recovered in Pirna from the later period (Figure 7, no. 25). Since enough pipe works already existed in Saxony to meet the basic demand, genuine Dutch imports were rare; pipes were made, for example, in Dresden, Kötzschenbroda, Königsbrück, Grimma, and Leisnig (Seeliger 1989). Pipe manufacturers from these places put the names of well-known Gouda pipe makers on their pipes in order to profit from their good reputations. In some cases, they put their own name on the pipes but added Gouda as the location, as seen on a pipe stem from Dresden: "E:VERZYL./C.G.PREVOT/IN GOUDA." Prevot or Prevour was an entrepreneur who ran a pipe works in Dresden from 1777 to no later than 1828 (Seeliger 1989:20).

While two particularly small pipe bowls seemed initially to point to 17th-century types, this does not fit with the fact that their polish is of a remarkably high quality. They bear the spur marks "windmill" or crowned "H" (Figure 7, no. 26), and there was, in fact, a small-scale manufacturer of pipes with particularly small bowls in Gouda in the Netherlands in the 18th century. The pipe shown here bears the "windmill" mark and dates from the period around 1730. These rare finds are clearly at odds with the general typology, which shows a gradual increase in the size of the bowls of clay pipes from the 17th to the 19th centuries.

An unusual find among the clay pipes was a handmade pipe recovered at Kirchgasse 2-3 (PI-14), which bears hand-applied decorations on the bowl and two stamps showing some kind of potter's wheel motif. Based on its shape and the technology applied in its manufacture, it came from an autonomous 17th-century works in Lusatia, which did not employ western European techniques (see Figures 9 and 10 in Klutting-Altmann's other contribution in this volume).

Strictly speaking, no pipe maker is known to date to have worked in Pirna itself. The earthenware manufacturer Leyhn, however, who had for a few years produced clay pipes in Wermsdorf near Hubertusburg (ca. 90 km northwest of Pirna), did in fact turn out high-quality crockery and also pipe bowls for stub-stemmed pipes in Pirna from 1815 onwards (see below) (Morgenroth 1997:53-54). Unfortunately, however, none of the pipe bowls found to date could be associated with the "Leyhn" brand.

SELECTED FINDS FROM THE MODERN PERIOD (19TH/20TH CENTURIES)

Finds from the past 200 years were also studied as part of the excavations in Pirna and their subsequent analysis. The assemblage also included so-called Bunzlau pottery. A typical feature of this type of utility ware is its very solid and well-covering brown slip glaze, hence the name "brownware." Unlike clear

27 **28** **29**

Figure 8. *Selected finds.*

(27) Small brownware pot with handles, ca. second half of the 19th century, height ca. 7 cm. Niedere Burgstraße 5/Fleischergasse (PI-35).

(28) Brownware crucible, ca. second half of the 19th century. Slight traces of soot, height ca. 9 cm. Dohnaische Straße 76 (PI-23).

(29) Brownware milk jug, ca. second half of the 19th century, height ca. 12 cm. Dohnaische Straße 76 (PI-23).

(All images courtesy of Saxony State Office for Archaeology)

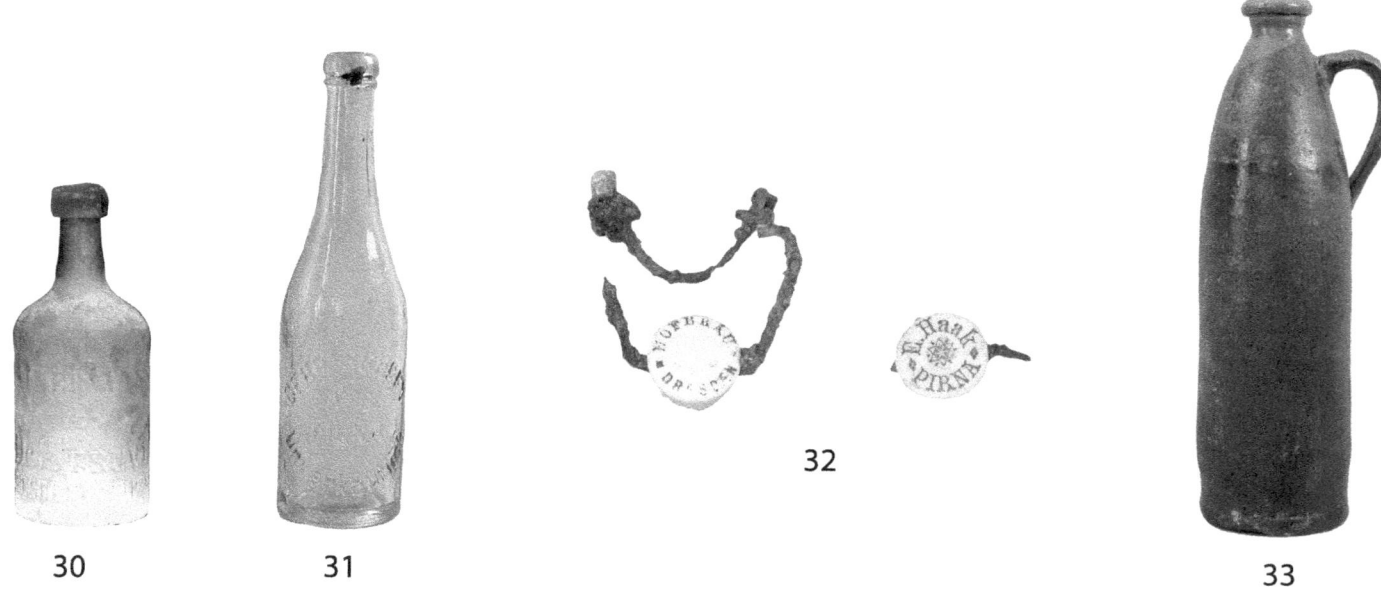

30 **31** **32** **33**

Figure 9. *Selected finds.*

(30) Glass bottle for artificial mineral water, second quarter of the 19th century. Labeled "MINER.WASS: VON Dr.STRUVE IN DRESDEN & LEIPZIG" (miner. wat. by Dr. Struve in Dresden & Leipzig), height ca. 19 cm. Dohnaische Straße 76 (PI-23).

(31) Glass beer bottle with holes for the swing stopper, post 1875. Labeled "GEBR. SCHREY A-G PIRNA Unverkäuflich" (brothers Schrey Ltd. Pirna, not for sale). Label on bottom reads "5.21" (or "S.21"), height ca. 26 cm. Dohnaische Straße 76 (PI-23).

(32) Two swing stoppers for beer bottles, post 1875. Labeled "HOFBRÄU DRESDEN" and "E.Haak PIRNA," with a hexagram. Lange Straße 33/34 (PI-55).

(33) Stoneware bottle with handle, probably beer bottle, pre-1875. Brown stoneware with ochre "apron" on the front, height ca. 30 cm. Dohnaische Straße 76 (PI-23).

(All images courtesy of Saxony State Office for Archaeology)

lead glazes, into which different colors could be mixed but which had a tendency toward hair-line cracks, opaque slip glazes were highly durable. The vessels themselves were also less fragile because from the mid-18th century onwards they were fired at significantly higher temperatures than ordinary earthenware. The fact that modern slip glazes did not require adding lead was another advantage of the Bunzlau-type crockery in the 19th century and led to it sometimes being given the sobriquet *Gesundheits(stein)geschirr* (healthy [stone] wares) (Müller et al. 1986).

Numerous finds from Breite Straße 11/13 (PI-11), Dohnaische Straße 76 (PI-23), Niedere Burgstraße 5/Fleischergasse (PI-35), and Lange Straße 33/34 (PI-55) show that sometimes entire crockery sets consisted of brownware vessels (Figure 8, nos. 27-29). In the 19th century many of the courtyards on Pirna plots were paved with sandstone slabs and this afforded the opportunity to dispose of large amounts of old crockery. Besides brownware pots of various sizes, pitchers and small jugs were also found, whose sharp profiles were clearly reminiscent of enamel vessels. Other finds were tripod skillets, crucibles, small vessels, and lids with various types of handles. Although most of the vessels had been used intensely and had been placed over a fire as attested to by traces of soot, the glaze showed hardly any damage.

By the 19th century the demand for mineral water had increased to such an extent that the natural springs could no longer satisfy it and other avenues had to be explored. The production of artificial mineral water began, with Dr. Struve being one of its main innovators. He started producing mineral water in Dresden in 1820 (Brinkmann 1991:154), and several glass bottles from his manufacture were found in Pirna (Figure 9, no. 30). Most of them bore the inscription "MINER.WASS: VON Dr.STRUVE IN DRESDEN & LEIPZIG" (miner.wat: by Dr.Struve in Dresden & Leipzig) in relief. Beer bottles provided information about well-known Pirna breweries. One such bottle bearing the mark "E.HAAK" was recovered at Lange

Straße 33/34 (PI-55), while another from Dohnaische Straße 76 (PI-23) bore the inscription "GEBR. SCHREY A-G PIRNA Unverkäuflich" (brothers Schrey Ltd PIRNA not for sale) (Figure 9, no. 31). The mark "not for sale" perhaps indicates that it was a returnable bottle similar to the deposit bottles of today. Bottle caps also found in many of the excavations began their success story in 1875 (Haase 1996:106) and also bore the names of beer brands such as the aforementioned "E.HAAK" and the "HOFBRÄU DRESDEN," the six-pointed star being the mark of the beer brewers' guild (Figure 9, no. 32).

Many of the later stoneware bottles, which at that stage rarely bore any proper stamps but rather just painted initials or even no mark at all, were probably intended to hold beer rather than mineral water (Figure 9, no. 33). When the heyday of the small craft breweries slowly came to an end in the 19th century wholesalers began to trade in beer and their marks were then put on the bottles rather than those of the brewers or bottle makers. Prior to the invention of the swing stopper in 1875 these bottles had substantially thickened rims so that the cork could be held in place by wire, similar to present-day champagne bottles (Richter 1996:130-131).

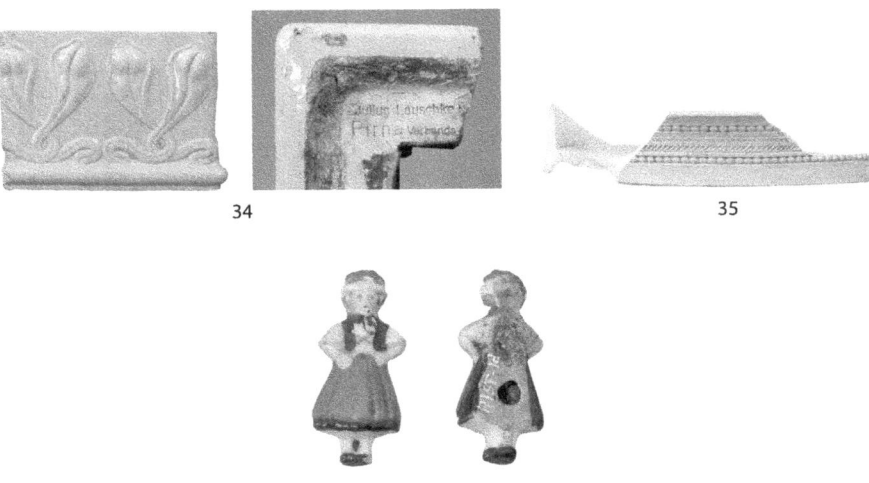

34   35

36

Figure 10.   Seclected finds.

(34) Light turquoise-glazed stove-tile with floral decoration, Art Nouveau, ca. 1910s. Reverse with stamp "Julius Lauschke N... PIRNA Verbands...." Kirchgasse 2-3 (PI-14).

(35) Ironstone bowl, possibly flower pot saucer, diameter ca. 20 cm. Barbiergasse 3 (PI-06).

(36) Porcelain Winter Relief badge, 1940s. Originally glued to a pin, which has not survived, height 3.8 cm. Niedere Burgstraße 5/Fleischergasse (PI-35).

(All images courtesy of Saxony State Office for Archaeology)

Other concrete links between finds and Pirna crafts and industries were also made: an early 20th-century stove-tile bearing the stamp "Julius Lauschke N..." (the "N" standing for *Nachfolger*, successor) (Figure 10, no. 34) points to a company of that name, which at the time was operating from a house at the corner of Breite Straße and Nicolaistraße. The tile was obviously associated with a later phase in the long history of stove-tile production in Pirna.

Another important company from the more recent history of the town was the Leyhn earthenware factory mentioned above, which besides pipe bowls mainly manufactured high-quality crockery in Pirna from 1815 onwards. Leyhn specialized in fine earthenware made of ironstone clay, thus offering a serious alternative to porcelain, particularly in Saxony. The local museum in Pirna has in its possession several vessels, and the excavations also uncovered a number of fragments that can be associated with this company, which was in operation for several decades (Figure 10, no. 35). Overall, however, remarkably few Leyhn objects have survived, which suggests that Leyhn's products may have been intended mainly for export.

A small porcelain doll brings us to the most recent history of Pirna (Figure 10, no. 36). On the back of the figurine, which is painted in the traditional red costume of the Black Forest area, traces of glue show that it was once attached to a pin. This was a badge from the Winter Relief organization—one of many cheaply made pins, usually made of plastic, fabric, or ceramic that were handed out by the Third Reich during the war years as proof of donations to Winter Relief, a fund used by the National Socialist Party to finance social spending and the war effort. These Winter Relief badges generally came in a range of popular motifs (characters from fairy tales, flowers, animals, etc.), which were aimed at encouraging people to collect them.

OUTLOOK

The 18-month-long analysis and study of the archaeological finds from the small Saxon town of Pirna can be seen as a successful example of using positive political circumstances to acquire funding and staff that would usually exceed the possibilities and capacity of the everyday running of a State Office for Archaeology. The Dresden project allowed us to get an overview of the archaeological background of Pirna, which fortunately did not disregard the material evidence from its most recent past. A scientific record of the abundant body of finds recovered between 1992 and 2006 in the small Saxon town, which thanks to its favorable geographical location was an important commercial center for several centuries, is now available and will serve as a basis for further research. One would hope that this project and the circumstances surrounding it will be emulated often so that the opportunities for urgently needed studies and scientific records of finds from the post-medieval and modern periods can be availed of as often as possible.

ACKNOWLEDGMENTS

For useful references on the subject of pipe bowl size and marks, I would like to thank my Dutch colleagues Ruud Stam (Leiden) and Jan van Oostveen (Tiel), who pointed out parallel finds from Zutphen, the Netherlands.

REFERENCES

ARNOLD, VOLKER, AND THOMAS WESTPHALEN

1990   Ofenkacheln des 16. Jahrhunderts aus Lübeck und Heide [Sixteenth-Century Stove-Tiles from Lübeck and Heide]. In *Kachelöfen in Schleswig-Holstein. Irdenware— Gußeisen— Fayence*, Volker Arnold, Thomas Westphalen, and Paul Zubeck, editors, pp. 21-67. Kleine Schleswig-Holstein-Bücher 40. Westholsteinische Verlagsanstalt Boyens & Co., Heide, Germany.

BRINKMANN, BERND

1984   Der Mineralwasserversand in Steinzeugflaschen [Mineral Water Distribution in Stoneware Bottles]. *Der Mineralbrunnen* 34(5):170-180.

1991   Die künstliche Mineralwasser – und Badeanstalt in Köln [The Artificial Mineral Water Works and Public Baths in Cologne]. In *Wasserlust. Mineralquellen und Heilbäder im Rheinland*, pp. 154-161. Rheinland-Verlag, Cologne, Germany.

1997   Töpfer—"Flaschenmacher"—Tonwarenfabrikant. Die Egerländer Flaschenfabrikantenfamilie Hart [Potter—"Bottle Maker"—Pottery Manufacturer. The Hart Family of Bottle Manufacturers in the Egerland]. *Keramos* 157:65-96.

EIGENWILL, REINHARDT

1989   Das "Pirnaische Elend." Die schwedische Belagerung des Sonnensteins im Dreißigjährigen Krieg ["Pirna's Misery." The Swedish Siege of the Sonnenstein Hill during the Thirty Years' War]. In *Mark Meissen. Von Meissens Macht und Sachsens Pracht*, Heinz Weise, editor, pp. 132-144. F.A. Brockhaus Verlag, Leipzig, Germany.

HAASE, GISELA

1996   Flaschen, Trinkgläser, Hofkellereien und Bier in Sachsen [Bottles, Drinking Glasses, Royal Wineries, and Beer in Saxony]. In *Ein bierseliges Land. Aus der Geschichte des Brauwesens von Dresden und Umgebung*, pp. 104-115. Fliegenkopf Verlag, Halle, Germany.

HOFFMANN, CLAUDIA

2001   Auswahl-Katalog der Renaissance-Ofenkacheln im Bestand des Kulturhistorischen Museums der Hansestadt Stralsund [A Selection of Renaissance Stove-Tiles in the Collections of the Kulturhistorisches Museum der Hansestadt Stralsund]. *Stralsunder Beiträge* 3:124-164.

MORGENROTH, WALTER

1997   Ein Pfeifenkopf aus Siderolith [An Ironstone Pipe Bowl]. *Knasterkopf—Mitteilungen für Freunde irdener Pfeifen* 10:51-56.

MÜLLER, HEIDI, EKKEHARD LIPPERT, AND INGE LIPPERT

1986   *Bunzlauer Geschirr. Gebrauchsware zwischen Handwerk und Industrie* [Bunzlau Crockery. Utility Ware between Craft and Industry]. Schriften des Museums für Deutsche Volkskunde Berlin 14. Berlin, Germany.

RICHTER, RAINER

1996   Bierkrüge und Steinzeugflaschen in Sachsen [Beer Jugs and Stoneware Bottles in Saxony]. In *Ein bierseliges Land. Aus der Geschichte des Brauwesens von Dresden und Umgebung*, pp. 116-133. Fliegenkopf Verlag, Halle, Germany.

SEELIGER, MATTHIAS

1989   Pfeifenmacher im Bereich der heutigen DDR [Pipemakers in the Area of the Present-Day GDR]. *Knasterkopf—Mitteilungen für Freunde irdener Pfeifen* 1:17-25.

STRAUSS, KONRAD

1972   *Die Kachelkunst des 15. und 16. Jahrhunderts in Deutschland, Österreich, der Schweiz und Skandinavien II. Teil (neue Folge)* [*The Art of Tile Making in Germany, Austria, Switzerland, and Scandinavia in the 15th and 16th Centuries. Part II*]. P. H. Heitz Verlag, Basel, Switzerland.

1983   *Die Kachelkunst des 15. bis 17. Jahrhunderts in europäischen Ländern III. Teil* [*Fifteenth – to Seventeenth-Century Tile Making in European Countries Part III*]. Konrad Heydenreich Verlag, Munich, Germany.

///

Ralf Kluttig-Altmann
Zum Kleingartenpark 41
D-04318 Leipzig
Germany

RAINER SCHREG / ANNETTE ZEISCHKA-KENZLER

A Case Study on Cultural Contacts and Cultural Adaptation in Colonial Panamá–German Historical Archaeology in the New World

ABSTRACT

Studies by German archaeologists in colonial archaeology are sparse. A research project by the University of Tübingen carried out since the year 2003 in Panamá la Vieja, the oldest Spanish town on the Pacific coast, provides insights into leading research questions. The German Research Foundation financed several campaigns of surveys and excavations that aimed to examine cultural contacts, social structures, and economic aspects within the city. The short existence of Panamá la Vieja from 1519 to 1671, the well-preserved ruins, and the lack of modern buildings—at least in the center of the old town—provide outstanding conditions for archaeological work. Several case studies considered the process of cultural adaptation by focusing on the changes of Spanish/European traditions reflecting the interaction with African and indigenous traditions.

PANAMÁ LA VIEJA

On the 15th of August 1519 the Spanish governor Pedro Arias de Avila relocated his expedition base to Nuestra Señora de la Asunción de Panamá, a small and insignificant indigenous fishing village at the delta of the Río Abajo. Panamá became the first European town on the Pacific coast. Due to its unique geographical situation at the Isthmus of Panamá, the town gained a secure economic basis. When Francisco Pizarro discovered the Inca Empire in 1524 and started its conquest, Panamá developed into an administration center as well as a main trading place.

In 1671 the English pirate Henry Morgan invaded the town of Panamá from its exposed land side. He plundered and burnt the town. Afterwards the city was relocated approximately 10 km to the west, in the area of the present old town Casco Viejo. The old town remained as a ruin and was finally overgrown by tropical vegetation. Its distance from the new city prevented its final destruction through quarrying. Only a few significant architectural elements were transferred to the new city. In 2002 the area became a UNESCO World Heritage Site. Today the entire area is administered by a foundation, the Patronato Panamá Viejo, which oversees the preservation of the historical ruins as well as the archaeological research.

The short existence of Panamá la Vieja from 1519 to 1671, the well-preserved ruins (Figure 1), and the lack of modern buildings—at least in the center of the old town—provide outstanding conditions for archaeological research. At a more sophisticated level Panamá provides interesting possibilities for urban archaeology since it was—from a European point of view—a town of extremes. In the New World, royal authorities dominated the township; society was rather mobile, but there were enormous social differences. The majority of the population in the late 16th and early 17th centuries was made up of slaves of African origin, as well as of indigenous people originating from the Panamanian Isthmus or from other regions of the Americas, such as Costa Rica, Venezuela, or the Caribbean. The local elite was a rather small group of Spaniards of quite different social backgrounds. Political, social, and perhaps also ethnic conflicts were inevitable.

RESEARCH QUESTIONS AND STRATEGIES

In 2003 a team of German archaeologists joined a collaborative project with Panamanian colleagues (Scholkmann et al., in prep.). The Patronato Panamá Viejo had taken the initiative to find European colleagues who could bring to the project their experience in urban archaeology. The German embassy at Panamá arranged the contact with the Department of Medieval Archaeology of the University of Tübingen.

Figure 1.   *The Cathedral at the main plaza, Panamá la Vieja (Photo by Annette Zeischka-Kenzler, 2007; courtesy of the University of Tübingen).*

Under the auspices of Professor Barbara Scholkmann a program was developed, which has been funded for several campaigns by DFG (German Research Foundation) and DAAD (German Academic Exchange Service).

Given the invitation of the Panamanian colleagues it proved necessary for the German project to develop a research program justifying the enormous effort necessary to realize German excavations at Panamá la Vieja. Why would German medieval archaeologists be interested in a Spanish colonial town? From the very beginning we were aware that the aim of German excavations at Panamá could not be to elucidate the local history of the city, despite its function as a global traffic junction. Medieval archaeology, however, has traditionally a rather regional or even local perspective due to its structures being based mainly in cultural heritage management, which is organized on the basis of federal states or even at a communal level. Even prehistoric archaeology in Germany is often missing a comparative approach and a global perspective. Therefore, a German project in Panamá meant something special. We identified three possible fields of contribution: 1) an exchange of field methods and technologies, 2) reflections on methods and interpretations, and 3) a comparative approach regarding cultural changes.

SCIENTIFIC EXCHANGE AND METHODOLOGICAL REFLECTIONS

The German fieldwork focused on geophysical prospections, topographical surveys, and excavations within two areas of the town. Excavations were realized during six campaigns with German-Panamanian crews. Trained in European urban archaeology and accustomed to excavating in stratigraphic

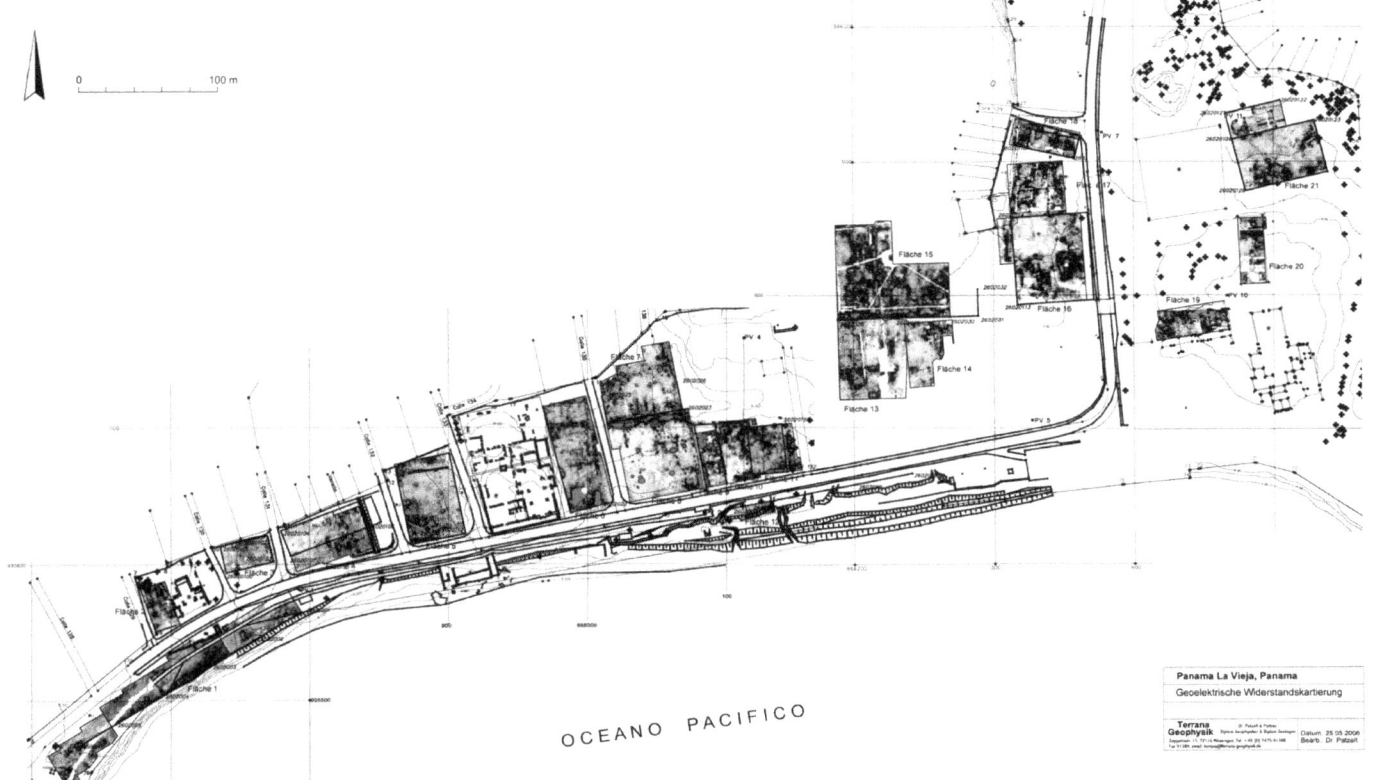

Figure 2.   Map of geophysical prospections, Panamá la Vieja. Red areas indicate highest geoelectric resistivity (Image by A. Patzelt, 2006; courtesy of the University of Tübingen).

layers, we had to learn about the bioturbidity in tropical soils. As there are quite different traditions in excavation strategies and techniques in Germany and Panamá we had interesting discussions, and probably all participants learned to reflect upon their own accustomed archaeological practices. Geophysical prospection—mainly geoelectrical resistivity—covered all free spaces within the old town (Figure 2) and revealed new

information on the dwelling places and houses, which were not built out of stone but out of perishable materials (Patzelt et al. 2007). Surprisingly, at the northern border of the site a large stone building was detected, which was excavated partially within the last campaigns. Furthermore, geophysical prospections facilitated the work of Panamanian colleagues, who are continuing and refining the first results (Mojica et al. 2009).

METHODOLOGICAL STUDIES

At a more abstract level, historical archaeology in Panamá offered possibilities to check different approaches of medieval urban archaeology. Since the 1960s German medieval archaeologists have used material culture to analyze social topography within the urban area. Based on the classifications of Panamanian colleagues and using GIS, a spatial analysis—mainly of ceramics—revealed the problems with this approach: at a micro-scale level of analysis focusing on individual plots, formation processes explain artifact distributions, precluding general social interpretations of the archaeological record (Kottmann 2009). The same is true regarding ethnic interpretations of ceramic wares, which have often been attributed to specific social or ethnic

groups, as for instance the handmade coarse earthenware, the so-called Criollo ware (Figure 3). Presence and absence of Criollo ware in complexes are due to functional aspects rather than to ostensible social reasons (Schreg 2009, 2010). In contrast to urban archaeology in central Europe, which is mostly concentrated on single plots, Panamá la Vieja offers a wide and well preserved topographical framework. This allows an internal comparative approach that brings several excavations in a common context—something that is missing in many urban archaeological projects in Germany.

CULTURAL CONTACT AND CULTURAL ADAPTATION

Several case studies dealing with imported as well as local ceramics or imported Spanish objects (Belecki 2007) considered the process of cultural adaptation by focusing on the changes of Spanish/European traditions that reflect the interaction with African and indigenous traditions.

Since ceramics are the most common archaeological artifacts, sherds have been used for studies on the habits of eating and drinking, social identities, and cultural contacts. Research on ceramics from Panamá la Vieja (Rovira 2001; Martín-Rincón, Zeischka-Kenzler, et al. 2008; Schreg 2009, 2010) is based on the previous work of several colleagues and provides interesting case studies on cultural contacts.

Sherds of stoneware were even imported from the Rhineland to Panamá (Martín-Rincón, Zeischka-Kenzler, et al. 2008). These wares were probably part of the equipage of Spanish ships and do not indicate a direct contact between these two countries.

Figure 3. Criollo ware found in a well filled in approximately 1600 A.D. in Panamá la Vieja, Casas Terrín-Franco (Photo by Rainer Schreg, 2005).

Nevertheless, the cultural contacts become very explicit through the ceramic inventory. In the 16th century, imports from Spain were still crucial. In the course of the 16th century a local ceramic production commenced, which was based on European traditions. Yet new ceramic forms and wares—such as the coarse handmade Panamanian Criollo ware—developed under the increasing influence of African and indigenous traditions. In the ceramic assemblages found in the buildings of the upper class—as for instance in the houses of patricians (Casas Terrín-Franco), the city-hall (cabildo), the building complex excavated in 2007 and 2009, or the bishop's palace (Casa Alarcon)—imported tableware is well represented. As yet, assemblages from lower class buildings are missing. The handmade Criollo ware is dominant in kitchen contexts, however. Pottery is in fact more dependent on function and social status than on ethnic affiliation.

Archaeological features such as burials and material relics of private religion also show the multiple interactions between the official Catholic religion and indigenous and African traditions. The so called higa-amulets, which are made of jet and shaped as a hand with the thumb placed between the index finger and the middle finger (Figure 4), are a specific element that is very common in the Caribbean and probably melds African traditions with Spanish popular belief (Belecki 2007).

Furthermore, the European Catholic standards were not always observed very stringently in Panamá. Churches and burials, as for instance at the Hospital San Juan de Dios, do not follow the traditions of orientation and spatial reference. Adjoining burials could have an opposed orientation, and while in the nun convent the common east-west orientation was followed, the burials in San Juan de Dios and the cathedral were oriented in a north-west direction during the same time period. Obviously the burials were arranged according to the orientation of the churches, which was handled quite individually in Panamá (Martín-Rincón 2002).

ARCHITECTURE AND URBANISM

In recent years colleagues from the Patronato Panamá Viejo were engaged in the reconstruction of the urban road system (Figure 5). The earliest city map drawn by Bautista Antonelli in 1586 showed the right-angled course of the streets.

Archaeological research, however, has uncovered a few divergences from the historic city map. The Antonelli plan, for instance, reproduces a fortification surrounding the city, which, as far as the archaeological data has shown, was never realized. Remarkable about this is the fact that in the Old World a fortification was still an important part of the city's self-concept during the

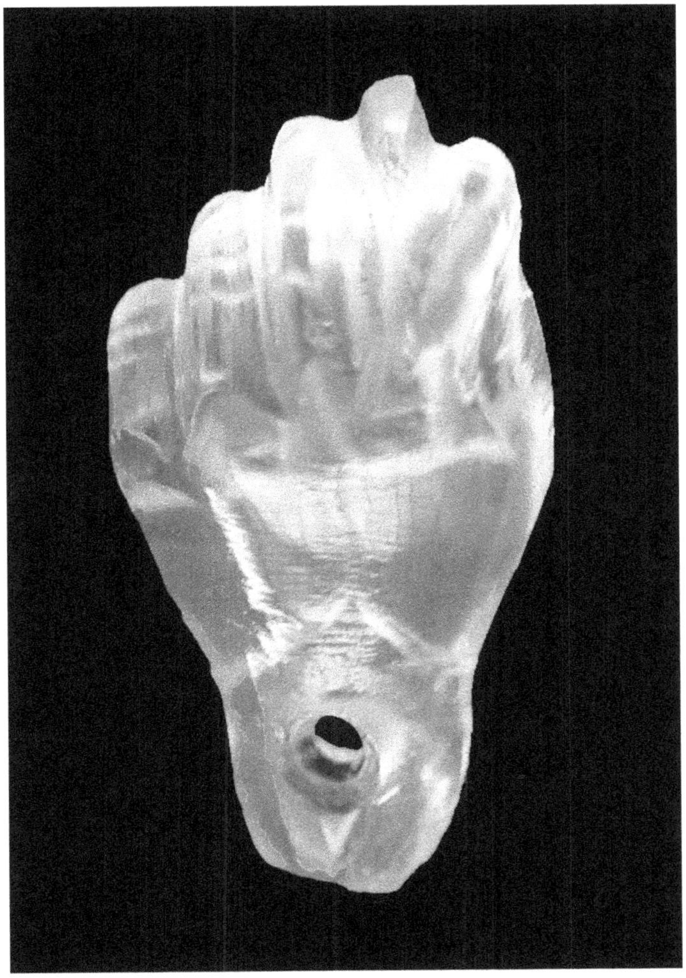

Figure 4.   Higa-amulet from Hospital San Juan de Dios, Panamá la Vieja (1.5 cm in size) (Photo by Rainer Schreg, 2004).

16th century. In general we would expect that under the conditions of the New World, the ideal conceptions of a town would have been reproduced (Schreg 2004).

In order to gain a detailed and authentic plan of the town, topographical and geophysical surveys were carried out. Systematic excavations were conducted between 2003 and 2006 in the Hospital San Juan de Dios and in 2007 and 2009 within a building complex that was probably used as a trading post. Additional monumental research and archaeological test excavations were carried out in order to trace later modifications within the city's outline. Excavations at the Hospital San Juan de Dios as well as a review of the ruins of San Francisco (Löbbecke and Tejeira-Davis 2007) showed minor changes in the outline of the streets, which nevertheless altered the main road axis.

The present-day ruins are dominated by certain monumental buildings, mainly churches and monasteries and some official buildings such as the city-hall or the "house of the Genoese" near the harbor. The archaeological research has shown the importance of timber constructions in the town of Panamá la Vieja. The residential areas, mainly consisting of small lots, were covered with timber houses; only near the central plaza were some houses built as representative stone constructions. The residential areas of the lower classes were probably situated at the periphery of the town and are today covered by the buildings of the modern village.

The topographic location of the city was not chosen very wisely. The city was situated on a narrow coastal strip with just a few sources of fresh water and scant opportunities for digging wells. Some institutions built huge cisterns to assure a supply of fresh water. But in general potable water had to be transported to the city by slaves. The water was carried in ceramic transport vessels, which can be found in huge quantities in every archaeological inventory. After only a few decades the city's harbor silted up and ships had to be anchored in the shelter of some islands in front of the coast. The cargo had to be transshipped by small boats.

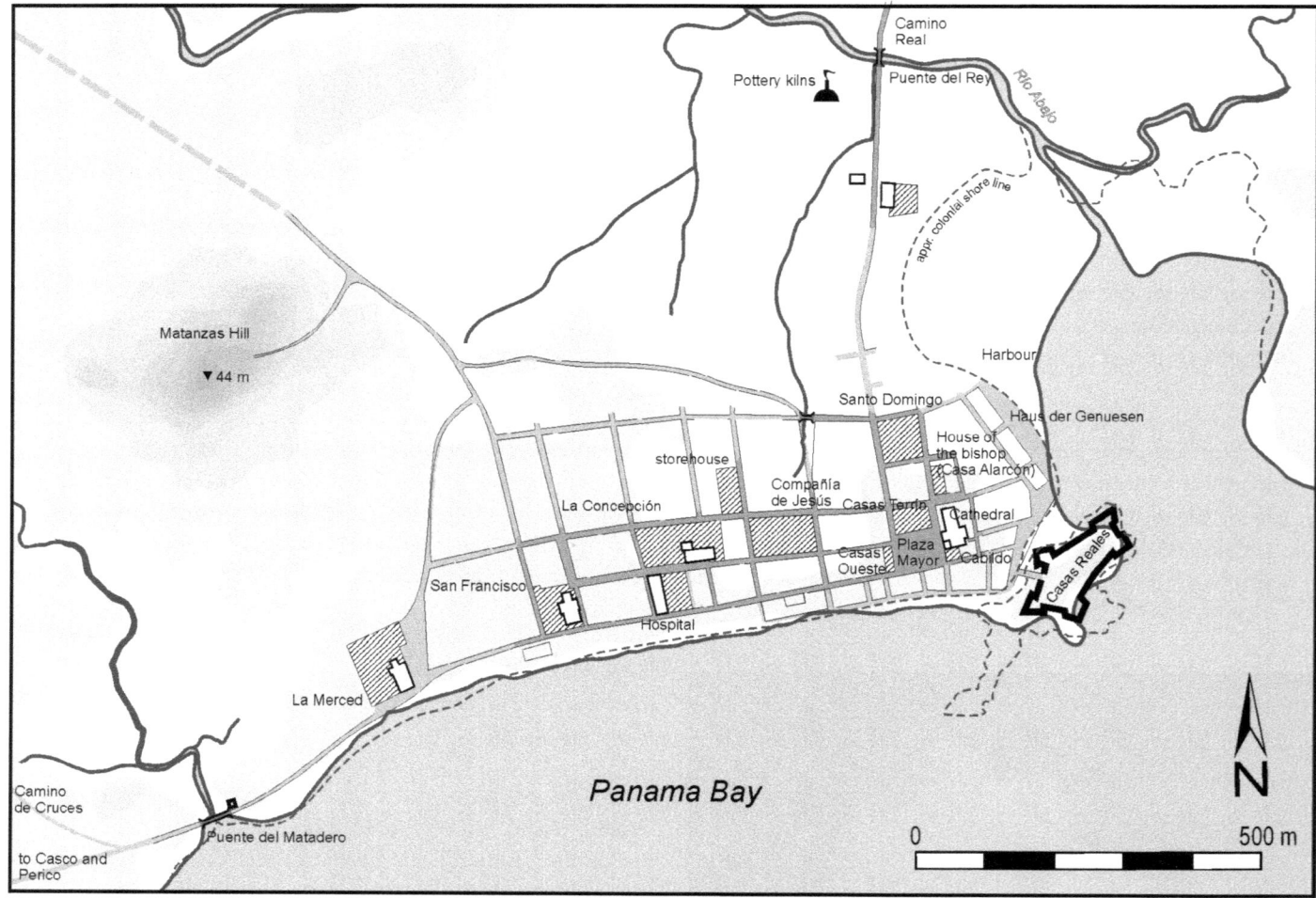

Figure 5.   *Plan of Panamá la Vieja. Hatched areas indicate public buildings (Graphic by Rainer Schreg, 2010).*

ENVIRONMENT

The tropical climate caused thousands of deaths and injuries during the construction of the Panamá Canal in the late-19th and early 20th centuries. It was also one of the most important reasons for the failure of the Scottish colony of New Edinburgh in Darién (eastern Panamá) and a major challenge for the Spaniards as well as for the African slaves. As well, indigenous people were decimated by new diseases brought to the Americas by the newcomers.

By now there has not been intensive research on environmental archaeology in Panamá la Vieja (Hieke 2005; Martín-Rincón, Sandoval, et al. 2009). Zooarchaeological research, however, showed the importance of European livestock and a remarkable impact on the fish population of Panamá Bay (Cooke and Jiménez 2008). Despite the different conditions of soils and climate in Panamá, the Spaniards tried to establish a European form of agriculture based on meadows and large fields for cattle breeding and cereal cultivation.

This caused (and still causes today) important ecological problems such as soil degradation and erosion as well as the need for a shifting cultivation by burning the tropical forest. Efficiency and sustainability of land use was probably lower than in pre-Columbian times, when agriculture was based on garden cultivation in raised fields and on special anthropogenic soils (Schreg, in prep.). At present there are no observations on the ecological changes caused by the *conquista* in the vicinity of Panamá, but there are several pollen diagrams from the Cordilleres Mountains showing an open pre-Columbian landscape and major reforestation in the 16th century (Bush and Colinvaux 1994).

CONCLUSIONS

When the Tübingen project started we were not involved in the long-term research and discussions of colonial archaeology as they have been realized, for example, in the Caribbean Spanish towns (Deagan and Cruxent 2002). As German colonial history ended with World War I, there are few ties encouraging studies in the field of colonial archaeology. German participation in the fieldwork in Panamá la Vieja represents a rare example of a historical archaeological project that looks beyond a regional perspective. As there are neither relevant direct historical relations between Germany and Panamá, nor direct affinities to colonial archaeology, research interest lies rather on more general aspects of cultural sciences than in specific aspects of Panamá's history. Therefore our research at Panamá has to be seen as case studies, with current debates in Old World prehistoric and historical archaeology as an important background. For example, ceramic studies at Panamá provide some interesting lessons within the ongoing debate on cultural change and ethnic identities; an analysis of the colonial town—its infrastructure and its outline as well as its environmental effects—gives important insights into the world view of early modern people. To observe in which fields Panamanian colonial society managed cultural adaptation to new conditions is crucial to judge the meaning of cultural tradition in the transition from the medieval to the early modern world, even in central Europe.

REFERENCES

BELECKI, HANNAH
2007   *Spanish Inheritance and Cultural Adaptation. Small Finds from Panamá la Vieja*. Master's thesis, Tübingen University, Tübingen, Germany.

BUSH, MARK B., AND PAUL A. COLINVAUX
1994   Tropical Forest Disturbance: Paleoecological Records from Darien, Panama. *Ecology* 75(6):1761–1768.

COOKE, RICHARD, AND MÁXIMO JIMÉNEZ
2008   Pre-Columbian Use of Freshwater Fish in the Santa Maria Biogeographical Province, Panama. *Quaternary International* 185(1):46–58.

DEAGAN, KATHLEEN, AND JOSÉ MARÍA CRUXENT
2002   *Columbus's Outpost among the Taínos*. Yale University Press, New Haven, CT.

HIEKE, KATRIN
2005   Ökokulturelle Konsequenzen der spanischen Kolonialisierung Mittelamerikas—Konzeption archäobiologischer Untersuchungen in Panamá la Vieja [Cultural and Ecological Consequences of Spanish Colonization in Central Europe—An Outline of Bio-Archaeological Studies at Panamá la Vieja]. Master's thesis, Tübingen University, Tübingen, Germany.

KOTTMANN, ALINE
2009   Funde als Indikatoren der ehemaligen sozialräumlichen Struktur? Ein Arbeitsmodell der Stadtarchäologie auf dem Prüfstand [Finds as Indicators of Past Social Space. A Concept of Urban Archaeology Reconsidered]. In *Zwischen Tradition und Wandel. Archäologie des 15. und 16. Jahrhunderts. Tübinger Forschungen zur historischen Archäologie 3*, B. Scholkmann, S. Frommer, C. Vossler, and M. Wolf, editors, pp. 331-342. Dr. Faustus, Büchenbach, Germany.

LÖBBECKE, FRANK, AND EDUARDO TEJEIRA-DAVIS
2007   El convento de San Francisco en Panamá Viejo. Investigaciones arqueológicas y arquitectónicas [The San Francisco Convent in Panamá Viejo. Archaeological and Architectural Research]. *Canto Rodado* 2:101–124.

MARTÍN-RINCÓN, JUAN GUILLERMO
2002   Funerales en Panamá la Vieja: ¿existen patrones en la América colonial? [Burials in Panamá la Vieja. The Question of Norms in Colonial America]. In *Arqueología de Panamá la Vieja. Avances de Investigación*, B. Rovirá and J. G. Martín-Rincón, editors, pp. 93–102. Patronato Panamá Viejo, Panama.

MARTÍN-RINCÓN, JUAN GUILLERMO, JAVIER RIVERA SANDOVAL, AND CLAUDIA ROJAS SEPÚLVEDA
2009   Bioarqueología. Su aporte al Proyecto Arqueológico Panamá Viejo [Bioarchaeology. Its Contribution to the Archaeological Research in Panamá Viejo]. *Canto Rodado* 4:117-145.

MARTÍN-RINCÓN, JUAN GUILLERMO, ANNETTE ZEISCHKA-KENZLER, HANS MOMMSEN, AND ALINE KOTTMANN
2008   Gres: la sutil presencia alemana en el Panamá colonial [Stoneware. The Subtle German Presence in Colonial Panama]. *Canto Rodado* 3:65-94.

MOJICA, ALEXIS, ERIC CHICHACO, MELISSA NAVARRO, LOUIS PASTOR, AND RICHARD VANHOESERLANDE
2009   Magnetic Investigation of Cultural Features in the West Zone of the Old Panamá Archaeological Site (Central America). *International Journal of South American Archaeology* 5:55–69.

PATZELT, ARNO, ALINE KOTTMANN, AND MARTIN WALDHÖR
2007   Prospección geoeléctrica en la ciudad colonial
        de Panamá viejo [Geoelectric Prospection in the
        Colonial Town of Panamá Viejo]. *Canto Rodado*
        2:23–43.

ROVIRA, BEATRIZ
2001   Presencia de Mayólicas panameñas en el mundo
        colonial: algunas consideraciones acerca de su
        distribución y cronología [Panamanian Majolica
        in the Colonial World: Some Reflections on its
        Distribution and Chronology]. *Latin American
        Antiquity* 12:291-303.

SCHOLKMANN, BARBARA, ANNETTE ZEISCHKA-KENZLER, AND
RAINER SCHREG (EDITORS)
in prep. *A Step to a Global World. Historical Archaeology
         in Panamá—First Spanish City at the
         Pacific Ocean.*

SCHREG, RAINER
2004   Stadtplanung in der ältesten europäischen
        Stadt an der Pazifikküste: Untersuchungen in
        Panamá la Vieja [Urban Planning in the First
        European City at the Pacific: Research in Panamá
        la Vieja]. *Mitteilungen der Deutsche Gesellschaft
        für Archäologie des Mittelalter und der Neuzeit*
        15:97–104.

2009   Mix der Traditionen—Keramik und
        Kulturadaption in der Neuen Welt.
        Kolonialzeitliche Keramikfunde aus Panamá la
        Vieja, Mittelamerika [A Mixture of Tradition:
        Ceramics and Cultural Adaptation in the
        New World. Colonial Sherds from Panamá la
        Vieja, Central America]. In *Keramik jenseits
        von Chronologie. Theorie-AG auf der Tagung
        des West – und Süddeutschen Verbandes für
        Altertumsforschung in Xanten, 6.-10. Juni 2006.
        Internationale Archäologie. Arbeitsgemeinschaft,
        Symposium, Tagung, Kongress 14,* P.
        Stockhammer, editor, pp. 117-134. VML, Rahden,
        Germany.

2010   Panamánian Coarse Handmade Earthenware as
        Melting Pots of African, American and European
        Traditions? *Post-Medieval Archaeology* 44:135-164.

in prep. A European Town in a Tropical Environment:
        Cultural Adaptation and Environmental Change
        in Colonial Panamá. In *A Step to a Global World.
        Historical Archaeology in Panamá—First Spanish
        City at the Pacific Ocean,* Barbara Scholkmann,
        Annette Zeischka-Kenzler, and Rainer Schreg,
        editors.

Rainer Schreg
Römisch-Germanisches Zentralmuseum
Forschungsinstitut für Archöologie
Ernst-Ludwig-Platz 2
D-5116 Mainz
Germany

Annette Zeischka-Kenzler
Universität Tübingen
Institut für Ur – und Frühgeschichte und
    Archäologie des Mittelalters
Abteilung Archäologie des Mittelalters
Schloss Hohentübingen
D-72070 Tübingen
Germany